Dietary patterns of low overall quality are the single le̲ _____ mortality and chronic morbidity in the modern wor̲ _____ remedy that. Changing dietary patterns so they routinely promote rather than undermine health means changing food choices, meal selection, daily routines, and the skill sets – especially **cooking** – on which they rely. The emergence of "culinary medicine" where once only biochemistry prevailed is testimony to this shift in problem, solution, and the primacy of the actionable and pragmatic. **This textbook** - with a focus on cultivating a discrete set of skills to be practiced, and paid forward through teaching- **takes its place among the important and promising advances in the vanguard of public health nutrition**. If the potential of diet – to add years to lives, life to years and help sustain the vitality of our planet – is to be fulfilled it will owe much to the widespread uptake of the crucial lessons found in the Culinary Medicine Textbook.

David Katz MD, MPH, FACPM, FACP, FACLM

Kuddos to Dr Deb for getting both chefs and nutrition scientists to the table to create a masterpiece. The Culinary Medicine Textbook lists the essential culinary skills that are required to be able to eat and ENJOY a healthy diet. Anyone can learn how to cook; it takes practice and a sense of humor to learn from mistakes. Deliciously eat your way towards health.

Chef Cat Cora

My dad understood that all life begins in the soil and that healthy soil leads to healthy plants, which leads to healthy people and a healthy planet; it is the only way we can literally save ourselves from ourselves! Dr. Deb truly understands this and has put together an incredible work combining nutrition science and the culinary arts by bringing together chefs with nutrition scientists. **Both are pioneers in their own righ**t – helping people to eat healthy plants.

Farmer Lee, author of The Chef's Garden.

The Culinary Medicine Textbook:
A Modular Approach to Culinary Literacy

Part 2
The Food: Dairy, Sodium, Sugar, Beverages, Herbs & Spices

Deborah Kennedy PhD
with Julia Hilbrands MS, MPH, RD

**Content Developed by The Expert Chef Panel
and Nutrition Experts From Around the World**

CONTRIBUTING AUTHORS

FATS & OILS

By Rima Kleiner MS, RDL, LDN,

and Deborah Kennedy PhD,

With the Expert Chef Panel

FRUIT

By Deborah Kennedy PhD

with Natalie Volin MS

With the Expert Chef Panel

GRAINS

By Jody L. Vogelzang PhD,

RDN, FADA, CHES and

Jasna Robinson-Wright, MSc,

RD, CDE, CIEC, Deborah

Kennedy PhD,

With The Expert Chef Panel

HERBS & SPICES

By Chef Natasha MacAller

Jasna Robinson-Wright MSc,

RD, CDE, CIEC

and Deborah Kennedy PhD

PROTEIN

By Deborah Kennedy PhD

Julia Hilbrands MS, MPH, RD

With the Expert Chef Panel

SODIUM

By Karen Byrd PhD, MBA,

RDN,

Deborah Kennedy PhD,

With the Expert Chef Panel

SUGAR

By Dana White MS, RD, ATC,

and Deborah Kennedy PhD,

With the Expert Chef Panel

BEVERAGES

By Joi Lenczowski MD,

Dana Henderson MS RD,

CDCES, Trang Le MD,

Caroline Rosseler MS RD,

Deborah Koehn MD, FACP,

BC-ADM, ABCL,

With Deborah Kennedy PhD

DAIRY

Julia Hilbrands, MS, MPH, RD

and Deborah Kennedy, PhD

with Jasna Wright MSc, RD,

CDE, CIEC,

With the Expert Chef Panel

VEGETABLES

By Betsy Redmond, PhD,

MMSc, RDN, Julia Hilbrands

MS, MPH, RD

and Deborah Kennedy PhD,

With The Expert Chef Panel

THE INCREDIBLE TEAM OF CHEFS

The following are those chefs that participated in The Food Chapters, helping to create culinary competencies and advancing culinary medicine. Some participated in all the chapters, and others in some of them.

Chef Lyndon Virkler (M.Ed., AOS): Senior Core Faculty Member Emeritus and former Dean at New England Culinary Institute. He is co-author of Farm to Table: An Essential Guide to Sustainable Food Systems for Students, Professionals, and Consumers.

Chef Scott Giambastiani: Food at Google Program Manager Video of Chef Scott

Chef Russell Michel (CHC, CWA): Founder of The Culinary Architect LLC

Chef Kate Waters (Dip CNM, mBANT, CNHC): UK chef and nutritional therapist

Chef Cyndie Story (PhD, RDN, SNS, CC): Founder Culinary Solutions Centers LLC

Chef Kelsey Johnson: Previous Owner Café Linnea Edmonton Alberta

Chef Ron Desantis (MBA, CMC): Chief Culinary Officer at the Hungry Planet® and Principle Advisor of CulnaryNXT

Chef Erica Holland-Toll: Culinary Director at The Culinary Edge. Previous Executive Chef at the Stanford Flavor Lab. Executive chef at a university

Chef Dave Barrett : Previous chef at Walt Disney World, owner of Main Street Kitchens in Hanover NH.

Chef Janet Crandall: Head Chef at the Culinary School at the LGBTQ+ Center in Hollywood CA

Chef Natasha MacAller: The Dancing Chef in New Zealand, London and Los Angeles

Chef Deb Kennedy (PhD): Culinary Medicine expert and nutritional biochemist. Owner of Build Healthy Kids, Build Healthy Seniors and Culinary Rehab LLC.

THE STUDENT

Natalie Volin (Tufts University): Sustainability sections in the Food chapters

OTHER CONTRIBUTORS

Joy Hutchinson MSc, RD Reviewed the Grain chapter
Kelly LeBlanc MLA, RD, LDN Reviewed The Grain Chapter
Sustainability: Becky Ramsing MPH, RDN (Sustainability)

5% of the proceeds goes to support the True Health Initiative

https://www.truehealthinitiative.org/

TABLE OF CONTENTS

DAIRY

Julia Hilbrands, MS, MPH, RD
and Deborah Kennedy, PhD
with Jasna Wright
&
The Expert Chef Panel

"I am thankful for laughter, except when milk comes out of my nose."
Quote by Woody Allen

Dairy foods are milk-based foods, most commonly from cow's milk, and include foods such as fluid milk, yogurt, and cheese, among others. Dairy foods are consumed in countries across the globe and are a major source of nutrition in many countries. Milk-producing mammals have been domesticated by humans for thousands of years. Initially, this was done as part of nomadic subsistence farming. Protecting and feeding the animals while moving from area to area was part of a symbiotic relationship between the herders and the animals. Later in history, dairy animals were kept for multiple purposes, including milking as well as working animals, and finally as meat at the end of their lives. Milking by hand turned to machine milking over time with the industrialization of the milk supply. Cows were then bred more specifically for dairy instead of beef. The development of refrigeration and better road transportation in the 1950s allowed milk production to become more centralized in countries such as the United States. In the United States, a dairy cow produced about 5,300 pounds of milk per year in 1950, while in 2019 the average American Holstein cow produced over 23,000 pounds of milk per year (O'Hagan, 2019).

Children are the largest group of milk consumers in the United States, and the nutrients provided in milk are critical for proper growth and bone development (Singh et al., 2015). A recent study by Torres-Gonzalez and colleagues that analyzed data from 2001–2010 found that 80% of children age 2 to 8 years were milk drinkers, and this proportion dropped to 57% among children aged 9 to 18 years, 42% among adults aged 19 to 70 years, and 60% among adults aged 70[+] years (Torres-Gonzalez et al., 2020). Similar findings were reported by Singh et al. (2015) who found that older adults drink more milk than younger adults in every geographic region around the world. This may be a response to the advice given regarding calcium needs and the prevention of osteoporosis.

Global calcium intake is only about half of the recommended 1000 mg to 1300 mg per day suggested by the U.S. National Institutes of Health (NIH), indicating a need for a higher intake of calcium-rich foods such as milk products (National Institutes of Health Office of Dietary Supplements). The study by Singh et al. also found that higher-income countries drink more than twice the amount of milk compared to lower-income countries. Furthermore, countries with high rates of lactose intolerance tend to have lower dairy consumption. Most of the highest dairy-consuming countries in the world are found in Europe, while the lowest dairy-consuming countries are found in Asia and Africa.

SECTION 1: DEFINITION AND CHARACTERISTICS OF DAIRY

TYPES OF DAIRY AND DAIRY PRODUCTS

Milk Source

Most of this chapter will focus on milk and milk products derived from cows unless otherwise noted. However, milk and milk products from other animals have been a staple in many cuisines for years and are becoming more common in the Western world. Table 1 outlines the characteristics of milk from various mammal sources.

Table 1: Milk from Various Mammals and Its Defining Characteristics

Source of Milk	Characteristics
Cow's milk	• 3 % to 4% fat (before processing), 3.5% protein, 5% lactose
Buffalo milk	• About twice the fat content of cow's milk • High casein content that facilitates good cheesemaking
Camel milk	• Similar composition to cow's milk but slightly saltier • Can contain 3 times as much vitamin C as cow's milk. This is important for people living in arid and semi-arid areas who have limited access to fruits and vegetables • Also rich in unsaturated fatty acids and B vitamins
Sheep milk	• Higher fat and protein content than cow's or goat milk, but not as much fat as buffalo or yak milk • Higher lactose content than cow's milk • Good for cheesemaking due to the high solid content
Goat milk	• Similar composition to cow's milk • Often used for cheesemaking
Yak milk	• Slightly sweet taste and smell • High fat and protein content similar to buffalo milk
Equine milk	• Horse and donkey milk is relatively low in fat and protein, similar to human milk • Typically consumed in a fermented form

Source: (Food and Agriculture Organization, 2021)

Liquid Milk

According to the FDA, milk is "the lacteal secretion, practically free from colostrum, obtained by the complete milking of one or more healthy cows" (Code of Federal Regulations Title 21, 2021). Milk is one of the most common beverages consumed worldwide. It comes in several "varieties" if you will, from whole to reduced-fat to skim. The only difference in these types of milk is the fat content — the protein and vitamin/mineral content of all milk varieties are the same. Whole milk contains about 3.5% fat by weight, which is the closest way it comes out of the cow. Fat percentage is reduced from there (see Table 2).

Milk Processing

When processing milk, all fat is removed before the milk is bottled and then re-added (at the various percentages) during bottling. Cream is removed via a cream separator that uses centrifugation to separate the fat/cream from the rest of the milk components. This process is called **standardization**.

Milk often goes through the process of **pasteurization**, where it is quickly heated to kill any potential disease-causing pathogens, which reduces the transmission of diseases such as brucellosis and tuberculosis (Willett & Ludwig, 2020). Typically, raw milk is heated until it reaches 161 °F/72 °C, held at that temperature for at least 15 seconds, and then is quickly cooled back down to 39 °F/4 °C, which is the optimal storage temperature for milk. Pasteurization does not have a significant impact on the nutritional value of milk, though it does destroy the very small amount of vitamin C (<10% of the RDA) that is present in raw milk.

Some milk is ultra-pasteurized and it is often called Ultra High Temperature (UHT) milk, and the U.S. government states "such product shall have been thermally processed at or above 280 °F/ 138 °C for at least two seconds, either before or after packaging, so as to produce a product which has an extended shelf life." UHT milk typically has a shelf life of six to nine months. Once opened, it becomes perishable and must be stored in the refrigerator. The long shelf life of unopened UHT milk is due to the destruction of microbes in the milk and the deactivation of enzymes that can spoil milk. The high temperature processing caramelizes the sugars naturally present in the milk which changes the flavor of the milk slightly.

Since UHT milk can be shipped without refrigeration, it may be slightly better for the environment. UHT milk has slightly less choline than fresh milk, and the quality of the protein in UHT milk may degrade over time, resulting in up to 12% less protein after storage for six months (alKanhal et al., 2001; Manzi et al., 2013). However, UHT milk is the primary type of milk sold in many parts of Europe due to its extended shelf life and ease of transport, and studies have not seen any adverse health outcomes or poor growth trends as a result of UHT milk consumption. UHT milk can be a good source of nutrition for many that is safe, convenient, and reasonably priced.

Once the fat is added back to milk after pasteurization, it must go through a **homogenization** process, otherwise, the fat will continue to separate and rise to the top of the milk. Milk is homogenized by pumping it through very small openings under very high pressure to reduce the size of the fat globules. If the fat globules are small enough, they will stay evenly dispersed throughout the milk and create a uniform, creamy product.

Fortification

Milk is a significant dietary source of **vitamin D,** but this vitamin is not naturally present in dairy products and thus must be added during processing. Vitamin D is crucial for calcium absorption and proper bone mineralization along with many other important functions. Regulations for vitamin D fortification in the United States are set at the federal level and state that when vitamin D is added to milk, it should be at a level not less than 400 International units (IU) per quart (Code of Federal Regulations Title 21, 2021).

Another vitamin that might be added to milk and dairy products is vitamin A. This vitamin is important for eye health, and while it is a fat-soluble vitamin that is naturally present in milk, some of it is lost during the processing of low-fat milks. According to the FDA, vitamin A should be added in an amount not less than 2000 IU per quart (Code of Federal Regulations Title 21, 2021). Interestingly, vitamin fortification of dairy products is not mandatory in the United States whereas it is mandated in Canada and some European countries.

Specialty Milk

Lactose-free Milk

Lactose is a sugar naturally found in milk and many other dairy foods such as yogurt and ice cream. Lactose-free milk is made by taking cow's milk and either enzymatically breaking down the lactose naturally present or filtering it out. Lactose-free milk can be a good option for those with lactase enzyme deficiency. Lactose-free milk is comparable to regular milk in nutritional content in terms of calcium, protein, vitamin D, B vitamins and fat. In the case of lactose-free milk where the lactose has been broken down into its two simple sugars, some people notice that this type of lactose-free milk tastes slightly sweeter, however, the sugar content/carbohydrate content of the milk is the same (National Dairy Council, 2022). Lactose is found in the fluid part of the milk, and so when the fluid is mostly removed to make cheese, for example, much of the lactose is also removed, making hard cheeses naturally low in lactose.

Ultra-filtered Milk
Some companies have a patented process where they take real cow's milk and separate it into its five basic parts: water, vitamins and minerals, lactose, protein and butterfat. They then recombine those parts in different percentages to make beverages that contain more protein and less sugar.

A2 Milk

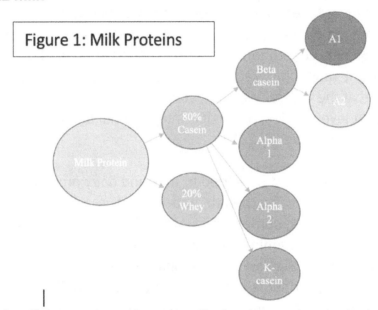

Figure 1: Milk Proteins

A2 milk is a variety of cow's milk that is very low in the beta form of casein proteins (called A1) and has mostly the A2 form of the casein (New Zealand Commerce Commission, 2003). This variety of cow's milk was introduced to the market by the A2 Milk Company and is mostly sold in New Zealand, Australia, China and the United States. Milk from mammals other than cows (humans, sheep, goats, donkeys, yaks, camels, buffalo, etc.) also has the predominant A2 form of casein (Jung et al., 2017). A2 milk is produced by selecting cows who produce milk with the A2 beta-casein using a genetic test developed by the A2 Milk Company (Woodford, 2009). The A2 Milk Company claims that A1 proteins are harmful, however, there has been a lack of scientific evidence that links A1 proteins to any adverse health effects. The European Food Safety Authority reviewed the scientific literature regarding health effects and A1 proteins and found no

relationship between drinking milk containing A1 casein and any disease (De Noni et al., 2009).

Raw Milk

According to the CDC, raw milk can harbor dangerous bacteria. Raw milk has not undergone pasteurization to kill bacteria (which comes from contamination with animal feces, human handling, cow diseases, unsanitary conditions in milk processing, etc.), and so harmful bacteria such as brucella, campylobacter, cryptosporidium, E. coli, listeria, and salmonella can be present. Raw milk does contain enzymes that would be denatured if pasteurized, but there is no evidence that these enzymes are important in human health. Pasteurization does reduce some nutrients available in milk, however those nutrients that are affected, such as vitamin C, are not nutrients of significance in milk. For more information about raw milk, you can visit: https://www.cdc.gov/foodsafety/rawmilk/raw-milk-questions-and-answers.html.

Fermented and Cultured Milks

There are many dairy products that are made by adding certain microorganisms to milk to create a fermented or cultured product. Adding microorganisms increases the acidity of the milk product. Common fermented dairy products that often appear in a Western diet include yogurt, buttermilk, and sour cream. Other fermented dairy products found around the globe include koumiss, dahi, labneh, ergo, tarag, kurut and kefir.

Yogurt

Versions of yogurt have been around for centuries, dating as far back as 10,000 to 5,000 BCE when nomadic people began to domesticate animals. Herdsman in the Middle East would use bags made of animal guts to transport milk and noticed that the intestinal enzymes that were present caused the milk to sour and curdle but also helped to preserve the milk. Fast forward to the 20th century and the first yogurt factory was opened in 1932 in France. Interestingly, yogurt was first sold in pharmacies because its health benefits drew so much interest (What Is Yogurt?). Historically, fermenting milk into yogurt was a good way to preserve milk and prevent further growth of pathogens.

Today, yogurt is made by adding the microorganisms Lactobacillus delbrueckii subsp. bulgaricus and Streptococcus thermophilus to pasteurized and homogenized milk to create a thick, cultured dairy product. These microorganisms convert lactose to lactic acid which gives plain yogurt a tangy or slightly sour taste. After this fermentation process, flavoring agents like fruits, sugar, or other ingredients may be added. Greek yogurt has become common in recent decades — Greek yogurt is yogurt that has been strained multiple times after fermentation to remove some liquid and create a product with a smooth mouthfeel and a higher protein content.

Kefir

Kefir has been consumed for thousands of years and its name in Slavic means well-being. Kefir is produced by kefir grains, that are made up of acetic- and lactic-acid-producing bacteria, and yeast within a polysaccharide and protein mix. Kefir can be a good option for individuals who are lactose intolerant because during the fermentation process, 30% of the lactose is broken down.

Kefir is rich in amino acids, vitamins, minerals, antioxidant compounds and the probiotics present in kefir have probiotic potential. It has both antifungal and antibacterial properties and in animal studies, mostly, has been associated with improved digestion, decreasing cholesterol levels, control of plasma glucose levels, anti-carcinogenic activity, anti-allergenic activity and more (Rosa et al., 2017). More studies are needed in humans as the results in human trials often conflict with results from animal studies, with the exception of kefir improving diabetic markers (Bourrie et al., 2020).

Buttermilk
Traditionally, buttermilk was the liquid that was left behind after making butter, and this liquid included milk protein and a small amount of fat. Prior to pasteurization, this liquid also contained small amounts of bacteria, and when the liquid was left out at room temperature the bacteria would produce a cultured milk product that was thick and had an acidic or sour taste.

Now, buttermilk is made by adding cultures of Lactococcus lactis or Lactobacillus bulgaricus plus Leuconostoc citrovorum to pasteurized and homogenized milk. When these bacteria ferment the lactose present in milk, they produce lactic acid which creates an acidic environment. This acidity lends to a sour taste, but it also creates a thicker liquid as milk proteins precipitate or coagulate in acidic environments. Buttermilk is often used as a raising agent in baked goods.

Sour Cream

Sour cream is made in a similar manner to buttermilk except that lactic acid bacteria are added to pasteurized cream rather than milk. This results in a cultured daily product with a higher fat content of at least 18% milkfat. Commercial sour creams may also contain some thickening or gelling agents such as sodium citrate, guar gum, carrageenan or locust bean gum.

Cheeses

Cheese is produced through the coagulation of casein, one of the proteins in milk. Cheese can be soft, hard, semi-hard, hard ripened, or unripened. There are hundreds of varieties of cheeses worldwide, and the different characteristics are derived from the various types of milk, microorganisms, processes and added ingredients used.

During cheesemaking, coagulation is achieved by either adding an acid or an enzyme called rennet to liquid milk. Common acid cheeses include cream cheese and queso fresco, while most other types of cheese such as cheddar and Swiss make use of rennet. Rennet cheeses also require bacterial cultures for production, making them a fermented food. Lactic acid bacteria are used as the starter culture for cheeses, but there are a wide variety of these cultures available, each of them providing a slightly different flavor and texture to the cheese. For example, Lactobacillus casei and Lactobacillus plantarum are used to make cheddar cheese, while Propionibacterium freudenreichil can be credited for the eye formation in Swiss cheese (Cheese Production).

The wide variety of flavors and textures found in cheeses is not due to different bacterial cultures alone. Differences in temperature, processing time, target pH for each step, the use of salting or brining, and aging time all play a role in the final cheese product. Additionally, cheesemakers may add ingredients like spices, herbs, peppers, or horseradish to create a unique flavor, and the type of milk used (cow, goat, sheep, buffalo, etc.) also contributes to flavor. Additionally, yeasts or molds can be used to provide unique colors and flavors.

Butter and Ghee

Unhomogenized milk and cream contain butterfat in microscopic globules. The globules have phospholipid membranes that keep the fat in milk dispersed rather than clumping together. When cream is agitated, the membranes are damaged and the fats join together and separate from the rest of the cream. Churning creates small butter grains floating in the water-based part of the cream, which is called buttermilk. The buttermilk is drained and rinsed off, and then the fat grains are pressed and kneaded together. Commercially produced butter is about 80% butterfat and 15% water; whereas traditional handmade butter was likely 65% fat and 30% water. Rendering butter removes the water and milk solids, which produces clarified butter, also known as ghee. Ghee is almost entirely butterfat.

Evaporated Milk

This milk product is made by removing about 60% of milk's water. Once the milk is pasteurized, it's piped into an evaporator where it's concentrated. It is a heat-sterilized product with an extended shelf life and is often used in baking.

Condensed Milk

Condensed milk is a type of evaporated milk that has been sweetened with sugar (unsweetened condensed milk is simply evaporated milk). Sugar is added before the milk is canned. Sweetened condensed milk is very thick and sweet — in fact, it contains 45% sugar, so it works well as a dessert ingredient. It has a shelf life of about two years.

Dry Milk or Milk Powder

Dry milk is made by removing water from pasteurized milk using a heat treatment followed by evaporation and spray drying to form a powder. This drying process helps to extend the shelf life considerably. Dry milk can be reconstituted into a liquid product by mixing with water.

Cream

Cream is the higher-fat layer that rises to the top of liquid milk before it is homogenized. Heavy cream contains >36% milkfat, and the fat content can also be lowered to create products like light cream or half and half. Due to its high fat content, cream is also used as the foundation for several dairy desserts.

Ice Cream

This beloved dairy dessert is a mixture of dairy ingredients and ingredients for sweetening and flavoring, such as fruits, nuts, and chocolate. Stabilizers and emulsifiers are often included to promote proper texture and enhance the eating experience. Ice cream must contain at least 10% milkfat before the addition of bulky ingredients and weigh a minimum of 4.5 pounds to the gallon.

Frozen Custard
Similar to ice cream frozen custard must contain a minimum of 10% milkfat but must also contain at least 1.4% egg yolk solids.

Sherbets
As another frozen dairy dessert, sherbets have a milkfat content of between 1% and 2% and a higher sweetener content than ice cream. Sherbets must weigh a minimum of 6 pounds to the gallon.

Gelato
Gelato is characterized by an intense flavor and contains sweeteners, milk, cream, egg yolks and flavoring.

Table 2: A Description of Milk Products and Their Fat Content

Product	Description/Details	Fat Content
Liquid milk	The most widely consumed, processed, and marketed dairy product worldwide.	
○ **Whole milk**		3.5% fat (8 g/cup)
○ **Reduced-fat (2%) milk**		2% fat (5 g/cup)
○ **Low-fat (1%) milk**		1% fat (2.5 g/cup)
○ **Skim milk**		No more than 0.2% fat
Fermented milks		
○ **Yogurts**	Produced by bacterially fermenting milk. Kefir is a fermented drink made from milk.	0.4% to 3.3% fat
Cheeses	Made by coagulating the milk protein casein. Contains the protein and fat of milk but most of the liquid and lactose are removed.	20% to 40% fat (average is 30% fat)
Butter and ghee	Butter is created by agitating cream and	80% for butter, close to 100% for ghee

	allowing the fat portion to separate from the liquid. Ghee is clarified butter, which removes more of the water portion.	
Condensed milk	Milk with part of the water removed; sugar is usually added to sweeten it; often used in baking.	8% fat
Evaporated milk	Fresh milk that has been heated to evaporate about 60% of the water; often used in baking, in soups and in sauces.	No less than 6.5% fat
Dry milk or milk powder	Milk that has been evaporated until all of the liquid is removed; this extends the shelf life considerably and does not require refrigeration.	A variety of milk powder options are available: whole milk powder, skim milk powder etc. The fat percentages are the same as for fluid milk.
Cream		
o **Half and half**	A mixture of whole milk and cream.	10.5% to 18% milkfat
o **Light cream (or coffee cream)**		19% to 30% milkfat (most commonly around 20%)
o **Light whipping cream**	Cream must contain at least 30% milkfat to produce whipped cream. Whipping cream will double in volume when whipped.	30% to 36% milkfat
o **Heavy cream (or heavy whipping cream)**	Can retain its whipped state longer than light whipping cream.	$\geq$ 36% milkfat
Whey products	Whey is a by-product of making cheese; it is often added to foods and used as a protein supplement.	0.3% fat
Ice cream	Made from milk or cream with added sugar and	14% to 25% fat; minimum 10% fat

flavors; served as a frozen
dessert.

Source: (International Dairy Foods Association, 2022)

SECTION 3: RECOMMENDATIONS FOR INTAKE

INFANTS AND TODDLERS

Infants should not consume cow's milk before 12 months of age as the higher protein and mineral content are hard for their young kidneys and digestive system to process. Human milk is the ideal form of nutrition from birth to six months of age, and if human milk is unavailable, an iron-fortified FDA-approved infant formula is recommended. After six months of age, infants can have small amounts of yogurt and cheese as part of their solid food intake.

After 12 months of age, toddlers can be offered plain whole cow's milk as their primary beverage. Whole cow's milk helps to meet their calcium, potassium, vitamin D, protein and fat needs. Flavored milks should be avoided in this age group as they contain unnecessary added sugars. The U.S. Dietary Guidelines recommend that toddlers age 12 to 23 months who are no longer receiving human milk or infant formula consume 1 2/3 to 2 cups of dairy per day (U.S. Department of Agriculture and U.S. Department of Health and Human Services, 2020).

Plant-based milk alternatives should not be used in the first year of life to replace human milk or formula. In the second year of life, unsweetened versions of these beverages may be given in small amounts, but most have significantly less protein than cow's milk and if used as a dairy replacement can impact a child's growth and development. Additionally, some plant-based milk alternatives are not fortified with calcium and/or vitamin D. Fortified soy milk is the only milk alternative that can be considered a dairy equivalent as it has a nutrient content that is similar to cow's milk (Centers for Disease Control and Prevention, 2021).

CHILDREN AND ADOLESCENTS

Dairy products continue to be an important source of nutrition through childhood and adolescence. These life stages are characterized by many transitions and the formation of dietary patterns. Children and adolescents themselves as well as other caregivers and elders exert a great influence on eating habits. Institutions such as schools or daycares may play a large role in what foods and dairy products are available, and other influences such as peer pressure emerge.

As children age, the recommended daily servings of dairy increases to support nutritional needs and higher calcium intake that is needed during these stages of rapid growth. The U.S. Dietary Guidelines recommend that children ages two to eight years consume 2 to 2.3 cups of dairy products each day, and children between the age of nine and 18 years should increase to 3 cups of dairy products each day (U.S. Department of Agriculture and U.S. Department of Health and Human Services, 2020). For children and adolescents who cannot tolerate dairy, fortified soy alternatives can also provide the protein and micronutrients needed during these life stages.

Throughout childhood and adolescence, the types of dairy foods consumed changes. Liquid milk consumption tends to decline, and more dairy is consumed via cheese, often in the form of processed mixed dishes such as sandwiches, pizza, or pasta.

ADULTS

The recommendation to consume 3 cup-equivalents of dairy or dairy products per day continues into adulthood (U.S. Department of Agriculture and U.S. Department of Health and Human Services, 2020). Even though linear growth is finished by early adulthood, the need for adequate calcium and vitamin D to support bone health continues, and milk and dairy products can be a significant source of these nutrients in the diet. Consumption of dairy foods may also lower the risk of CVD and type 2 diabetes in adults, and it's also been shown that overall dairy consumption increases lean body mass and reduces weight gain (Mozaffarian, 2019).

SENIORS

It is recommended that older adults continue to consume 3 cup-equivalents of dairy or dairy products as they age (U.S. Department of Agriculture and U.S. Department of Health and Human Services, 2020). In older adulthood, adequate dairy consumption is important for bone health and retention of lean muscle mass (Hanach et al., 2019; Iuliano et al., 2021).

Table 3: Recommended Dairy Intake Throughout the Lifespan

Age Group	Recommendations
0 to 11 months	Human milk or iron-fortified infant formula only
12 to 23 months	1 2/3 to 2 cup-equivalents
2 to 8 years	2 to 2.3 cup-equivalents
9 to 13 years	3 cup-equivalents
14 to 18 years	3 cup-equivalents
19 to 59 years	3 cup-equivalents

60⁺ years	3 cup-equivalents

Source: (U.S. Department of Agriculture and U.S. Department of Health and Human Services, 2020)

HOW ARE AMERICANS DOING?

According to the Dietary Guidelines for Americans, about **90% of the U.S. population does not meet dairy recommendations** (U.S. Department of Agriculture and U.S. Department of Health and Human Services, 2020). Infants and toddlers typically meet or exceed recommendations, but average daily intake declines from there.

A study by Hess et al. (2020) found that when Americans aged two years and over who met recommendations for dairy intake were compared to those who did not meet dairy recommendations, nutritional intake was generally better among those consuming more dairy (Hess et al., 2020). People meeting the dairy recommendations were more likely to have adequate intakes of calcium, magnesium, phosphorus, riboflavin, vitamin A, vitamin B_{12}, zinc, choline and potassium regardless of age, sex, or ethnicity when compared to those eating less than the recommended number of dairy servings. Those consuming the recommended amount of dairy were also more likely to exceed the recommendations for sodium and saturated fat intake but ate less added sugars.

While very few Americans meet the recommendations for dairy intake, patterns of dairy consumption are changing. In 1975, the average American consumed 539 pounds of dairy in a year, whereas in 2020, the average American consumed 655 pounds of dairy in a year (International Dairy Foods Association, 2021). There was a three-pound increase in dairy consumption per person between 2019 to 2020 alone. This increase in dairy consumption in recent years is due to an increase in ice cream, butter, yogurt and cheese consumption, while intake of liquid milk has been declining. The low-carb/high-fat diet fad, as well as the COVID-19 pandemic, may play a role in these trends in food consumption.

Infants and Toddlers
Children three years old and under tend to be the only age group consuming the recommended number of dairy servings in the U.S. (Dietary Guidelines Advisory Committee, 2020).

Children and Adolescents
Approximately one-quarter of children and adolescents up to age 18 consumed the recommended number of cup equivalents of dairy foods according to NHANES study data from 2013 to 2016 (Hess et al., 2020). Being younger, male, non-Hispanic, white and more physically active was associated with a greater likelihood of consuming the recommended number of dairy servings. Among children, milk allergy was cited as one

of the primary reasons for avoiding dairy foods. Fortified soy beverages and similar plant-based milk alternatives are suitable options for these individuals (Donovan, 2017; Savage et al., 2016).

Adults

Adults aged 20 years and older were found to consume only 1.5 cup equivalents of dairy foods per day — about half of the recommended number of servings (Dietary Guidelines Advisory Committee, 2020). Among adults 19 years and older in the NHANES data 2013–2016, being male, non-Hispanic, white and more physically active were associated with an increased likelihood of consuming the recommended number of cup equivalents of dairy foods. Only about 13% of adults met the recommended number of servings per day of dairy foods (Hess et al., 2020).

Seniors

According to NHANES data from 2013 to 2016, only about 13% of adults and seniors consumed 3 cup equivalents per day of dairy foods. White males who were more active were more likely to consume adequate servings of dairy (Hess et al., 2020). Dairy foods are particularly important in this age group due to their contribution to calcium, potassium, vitamin B_{12} and protein, which are important nutrients for maintenance of bone density, muscle mass, and overall health.

SECTION 4: IMPORTANT NUTRIENTS IN DAIRY PRODUCTS

FAT

Fats (also referred to as lipids) are one of the key constituents of milk and dairy products. Fat provides energy and is also an important carrier for fat-soluble vitamins (vitamins A, D, E, and K). Fat also provides unique sensory characteristics to milk products, such as creaminess, hardness, spreadability and flavor (Alothman et al., 2019; Gómez-Cortés et al., 2018). Fat content is one of the most variable nutrients among milk and other dairy products. Within milk alone, fat content can range from almost 8 g per cup serving in whole milk to only miniscule amounts in skim milk (see Table 2). Among dairy products such as heavy cream, ice cream, and cheese, the fat content can be as high as 86 g, 14 g, and 37 g per cup, respectively.

As shown in Table 4, there are several types of fats in dairy products, and they are all metabolized a bit differently and confer slightly different health benefits. While the American Heart Association recommends limiting saturated fats to 5% to 6% of total caloric intake in order to reduce heart disease risk, it does not appear the consumption of saturated fat from dairy products specifically is atherogenic (Fernandez & Calle, 2010). Short-chain and medium-chain fatty acids (types of PUFAs) are important in the regulation of cell metabolism and have beneficial effects on gut microbiota (Gómez-Cortés et al., 2018; Schönfeld & Wojtczak, 2016). Linoleic acid, another type of PUFA, is capable of inhibiting carcinogenesis (Gómez-Cortés et al., 2018). Milk derived from pasture-fed cows specifically can be a source of a small amount of beneficial PUFAs and omega-3 fatty acids (Gómez-Cortés et al., 2018).

Table 4: Fat Content in One 8oz Serving of Various Types of Cows' Milk

	Total Fat (g)	Saturated Fat (g)	MUFA (g)	PUFA (g)	Trans(g)
Whole Milk	7.97	4.63	1.71	0.27	0.28
2% (Reduced Fat) Milk	4.66	2.72	0.98	0.14	0.17
1% (Low fat) milk	2.34	1.40	0.52	0.08	0.09
Skim milk	0.12	0.12	0.04	0.02	0

Source: (USDA, 2018)

PROTEIN

Milk and dairy products are an excellent source of high-quality protein. One 8 oz serving of milk contains 8 grams of protein, regardless of the fat content, and one 5 oz serving of Greek yogurt can contain up to 16 grams of protein (USDA, 2018). Dairy products are complete proteins, meaning they contain all nine essential amino acids that human beings require in their diets. Protein from milk and dairy products is highly digestible and bioavailable, so the body is able to efficiently absorb close to 100% of the protein consumed from dairy sources (Mathai et al., 2017; Timon et al., 2020). Specifically, dairy is a good source of the branched-chain amino acids leucine, isoleucine, and valine which are especially bioavailable (G. D. Miller et al., 2006; Willett & Ludwig, 2020). In addition, milk protein and several of its post-digestive peptides have been shown to be antimicrobial, antiviral, antifungal, antioxidant, antihypertensive, antimicrobial, antithrombotic, opioid and immunomodulatory (Mills et al., 2011). Milk proteins are also important in the absorption and transport of other nutrients.

The protein found in milk can be classified into two major groups: caseins and whey. Casein is considered an insoluble protein and comprises approximately 80% of the protein in cow's milk while the remaining 20% is whey protein, a soluble protein (Marangoni et al., 2019; Pereira, 2014). There are several different types of whey protein, all of which play important roles in the body (Alothman et al., 2019). Lactoferrin, lactoperoxidase, and lysozyme act as antimicrobial agents, and lactoglobulins and lactalbumin may have tumor-suppressing activity (Jenssen & Hancock, 2009; Parodi, 2007; Pereira, 2014). Lactoglobulin is also a carrier for retinol, a vitamin A derivative, and it has been shown to have antioxidant and fatty acid-binding capabilities (Mills et al., 2011). Lactoferrin is an important component in iron absorption and may also have anticarcinogenic effects (González-Chávez et al., 2009).

Caseins are considered the solid protein in liquid dairy and make up the primary component of cheese. Caseins have a high capacity to bind minerals, especially calcium and phosphorus and are important in the digestion and transport of these minerals (Holt et al., 2013). It's also thought that caseins have an effect on intestinal motility and may play a role in regulating food intake (Pereira, 2014).

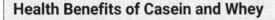

Health Benefits of Casein and Whey

Casein makes up the majority of cow's milk protein, accounting for about 80%, while whey makes up the remaining 20%. The leucine present in cow's milk proteins helps to prevent muscle wasting in conditions where protein breakdown is more prevalent and also helps stimulate muscle protein synthesis. The high content of sulfur-containing amino acids (cysteine and methionine) in whey protein is important for the synthesis of glutathione, a peptide with antioxidant, anticarcinogenic, and immunostimulatory properties. Casein also appears to have anticancer effects, particularly against colon cancer risk. Furthermore, casein appears to have oral health benefits by decreasing plaque-promoting enzymes.

Protein, in general, has a satiating effect, and studies have shown that whey protein specifically helps induce satiety signals, which may help with weight regulation. Casein may also help with cardiovascular health by reducing blood cholesterol. Supplementation studies have found reductions in blood LDL with the addition of casein. For more information on the health benefits of milk and milk proteins, see Section 6 below.

Sources: (Anderson & Moore, 2004; Bendtsen et al., 2013; Chin-Dusting et al., 2006; Hoffman & Falvo, 2004; Johansson & Lif Holgerson, 2011; Luhovyy et al., 2007; MacDonald et al., 1994; Meinertz et al., 1989; G. D. Miller et al., 2006; Onwulata & Huth, 2008; Parodi, 2007; Yalçin, 2006)

CALCIUM

Milk and dairy products are one of the main sources of calcium in a Western diet, and cow's milk contains around 300 mg of calcium per 8 oz serving. However, despite the high calcium content of milk, almost 30% of adult men and 60% of adult women in the United States do not consume enough calcium each day (U.S. Department of Agriculture and U.S. Department of Health and Human Services, 2020). The RDA for calcium is 1,000 mg per day for adults 19–50 years old, as shown in Table 5 below. Most plant-based dairy alternatives are fortified with calcium, but research shows that the calcium in these beverages may not be as bioavailable as the calcium in cow's milk due to oxalic acids and phytic acids in plant-based milk alternatives reducing calcium absorption (Golden et al., 2014). Approximately 66% of the calcium in cow's milk is bound to casein (protein) while the remainder is found in the serum (liquid) portion of milk (Akkerman et al., 2019).

It has been long understood that calcium is important for bone health, and there is research to suggest that calcium from milk products — along with other nutrients like protein and phosphorus — can delay bone loss, prevent osteoporosis, and reduce frailty later in life (Bonjour et al., 2013; R. P. Heaney, 2007; Lana et al., 2015).

In addition to supporting bone health, calcium is important for many other body functions. Calcium is the most abundant mineral in the human body. It is needed for the regulation of blood pH, proper muscle and nerve function, and for the release of several hormones. Hypocalcemia is rare since calcium homeostasis is so tightly regulated in the body. Hypocalcemia usually results from illness, vitamin D or magnesium deficiencies, impaired parathyroid hormones, impaired bone resorption of calcium or medicine use. When signs and symptoms of calcium deficiency do occur, they affect multiple areas of the body since serum calcium is involved in the function of most organs. Low serum calcium can cause neuromuscular irritability, perioral numbness, tingling in hands and feet, muscle spasms, renal calcification, depression, bipolar disorder, cataracts, heart failure and seizures (Fong & Khan, 2012; Pepe et al., 2020). Calcium consumption may also play a role in longer-term health outcomes including risk reduction of cardiovascular disease, preeclampsia, cancer and in weight regulation, as discussed further below in Section 6.

Calcium requirements vary from 200 mg to 1,200 mg per day throughout the life cycle, with increased needs in females ages 51 to 70 years, and in all individuals over 70 years due to decreased absorption. Recommendations for pregnancy and lactation are the same as others in that age group.

Table 5: Recommended Dietary Allowances (RDAs) for Calcium

Age	Male	Female	Pregnant	Lactating
0–6 months*	200 mg	200 mg		
7–12 months*	260 mg	260 mg		
1–3 years	700 mg	700 mg		
4–8 years	1,000 mg	1,000 mg		
9–13 years	1,300 mg	1,300 mg		
14–18 years	1,300 mg	1,300 mg	1,300 mg	1,300 mg
19–50 years	1,000 mg	1,000 mg	1,000 mg	1,000 mg
51–70 years	1,000 mg	1,200 mg		
70+ years	1,200 mg	1,200 mg		

*Adequate Intake (AI)
Source: (Institute of Medicine, 2010)

VITAMIN A

Full-fat cow's milk can be a good source of vitamin A and beta-carotene, but because vitamin A is a fat-soluble vitamin, some of the content is lost when fat is reduced in milk (see Table 6) (Schuster et al., 2018). However, vitamin A is frequently added back to milk during processing at a level of at least 2,000 IU per quart (International Dairy Foods Association, 2022). Vitamin A is important for promoting good eyesight, particularly in low light. Vitamin A is an essential component of rhodopsin, a protein that absorbs light in the retinal receptors. Vitamin A also supports normal differentiation and functioning of the conjunctival membranes and the cornea of the eye (A. Ross, 2006; C. Ross, 2010; Solomons, 2006). In addition, vitamin A is involved in immune function, reproduction and the function of several organs such as the heart, lungs, and kidneys.

VITAMIN D

Vitamin D is not naturally found in many foods including dairy, but much of the dairy in the American diet is fortified with vitamin D (USDA, 2018). This is because vitamin D is necessary for the absorption of calcium and is a nutrient that is low in the American diet. Vitamin D is also important for maintaining calcium and phosphorus concentrations to allow bone mineralization as well as for cell differentiation and growth, regulation of phosphorus, immune health, reduction of inflammation, blood pressure regulation and blood sugar regulation (Institute of Medicine, 2010; Jones, 2014; Norman, 2012).In addition to food sources, vitamin D can also be produced endogenously by the skin through sun exposure, but this process can be limited by many factors such as the time of year, age, and geographic latitude.

Recommendations for vitamin D range from 200 IU to 800 IU throughout the lifespan, with increased needs for those over the age of 70 years (National Institute of Health, Office of Dietary Supplements, 2020b). The active form of vitamin D in the body is 25(OH)D. One 8-oz glass of cow's milk provides approximately 120 International Units of Vitamin D.

PHOSPHOROUS

Phosphorus is an important nutrient for bone health and kidney function, and the phosphorus found in dairy products may help delay sarcopenia and osteoporosis later in life (Bonjour et al., 2013). Cow's milk provides around 250 mg of phosphorus per one-cup serving. Phosphorus is also a component of cell membrane structure and of ATP, the body's main energy source. Additionally, phosphorus plays an important role in regulating gene transcription, activating enzymes, maintaining normal pH in extracellular fluid, and in intracellular energy storage (R. Heaney, 2012).

POTASSIUM

Cow's milk is a significant source of potassium, providing 390 mg per serving. Potassium is a nutrient of public health concern for the general U.S. population as low intakes have been associated with health concerns (U.S. Department of Agriculture and U.S. Department of Health and Human Services, 2020). Potassium is present in all body tissues and is needed for normal cell functioning due to its role in maintaining intracellular fluid volume and transmembrane electrochemical gradients. Sodium is the main regulator of extracellular fluid volume, and as such potassium and sodium have a strong relationship (Institute of Medicine, 2005; Stone et al., 2016). In recent years, higher sodium intakes in Western countries have played a role in high blood pressure, which has impacts on cardiovascular health and risk of stroke. Inadequate potassium intakes equally play a role in hypertension, heart health, and risk of stroke. Consuming a diet with adequate potassium such as the DASH diet and Mediterranean diet have been shown to reduce systolic blood pressure (Champagne, 2006).

VITAMIN B$_{12}$

Vitamin B$_{12}$, also known as cobalamin, is a water-soluble vitamin which is formed from the mineral "cobalt." The main functions include red blood cell production, nerve cell development, central nervous system function, conversion of homocysteine to methionine (which decreases the risk of coronary artery disease, peripheral vascular disease, and stroke) and a co-factor for DNA production and metabolism (Carmel, 2014; Institute of Medicine, 1998; National Institute of Health, Office of Dietary Supplements, 2020a). Vitamin B$_{12}$ is naturally found in all animal source foods such as meat, fish, eggs and milk products.

Milk is an excellent source of vitamin B$_{12}$, with three times higher bioavailability in dairy than in meat, fish, and poultry (Tucker et al., 2000; Vogiatzoglou et al., 2009). Recommendations for this vitamin range from 0.4 µg to 2.4 µg with increased needs being seen during pregnancy and breastfeeding. One 8-oz glass of milk provides 1.29 µg of vitamin B$_{12}$.

RIBOFLAVIN

Riboflavin, also known as vitamin B$_2$, is a water-soluble vitamin found in foods such as milk, eggs, organ meats, lean meats, green vegetables and fortified grains. Riboflavin is an essential component of two important coenzymes, flavin mononucleotide and flavin adenine dinucleotide. These coenzymes are involved in energy production, cellular function, growth, development and metabolism of fats, drugs, and steroids. Riboflavin is also needed to maintain normal homocysteine levels in the blood (Institute of Medicine, 1998; Rivlin, 2010).

NIACIN

Niacin, also known as vitamin B$_3$, is found in a variety of foods and is also added to enriched and fortified foods in the United States and Canada. Milk naturally contains a small amount of niacin, though poultry, fish, brown rice, nuts and enriched cereals contain far more niacin than milk. Niacin is generally well absorbed and highly bioavailable from foods and supplements. Niacin is needed in over 400 enzymes to catalyze reactions in all tissues of the body. Niacin is also needed to create ATP (the body's primary energy form) from carbohydrates, proteins and fats as well as in cholesterol and fatty acid synthesis and in cellular antioxidant functioning (Bourgeois & Moss, 2010; Penberthy & Kirkland, 2012).

PANTOTHENIC ACID

Pantothenic acid, also known as vitamin B$_5$, is found in a wide variety of foods. Almost all plant and animal source foods contain some amount of pantothenic acid, with milk and yogurt being good sources. This water-soluble vitamin is required for the synthesis of coenzyme A (CoA) and acyl carrier protein. CoA is needed for fatty acid synthesis and degradation, transfer of acetyl and acyl groups and many other body processes. Acyl carrier protein is needed in fatty acid synthesis (Institute of Medicine, 1998; J. Miller & Rucker, 2012; Sweetman, 2010).

Table 6: Vitamin and Mineral Content of 8 oz of 2% (Reduced fat) Milk

Nutrient	Per 8oz serving	RDA for adults (% of RDA per 8oz serving)
Calcium	309 mg	1,000 mg (31%)
Vitamin A (RAE)	203 µg	900 µg (23%)
Vitamin D	111 IU	600 IU (19%)
Vitamin B12	1.35 µg	2.4 µg (56%)
Riboflavin	0.336 mg	Women: 1.1 mg (31%) Men: 1.3 mg (26%)
Niacin	0.274 mg	Women: 14 mg (2%) Men: 16 mg (2%)
Phosphorus	252 mg	700 mg (36%)
Pantothenic Acid	0.956 mg	5 mg (19%)
Potassium	390 mg	Women: 2600 mg (15%) Men: 3400 mg (11%)

Source: (USDA, 2018)

SECTION 5: DAIRY AND THE MICROBIOME

The gut microbiome is complex and only beginning to be understood. It impacts many facets of health including gastrointestinal health, weight regulation, mental health and immune function among others. Much of the influence of dairy products on the gut microbiome is by way of probiotics, or beneficial bacteria.

The dairy industry is the largest sector where probiotics are used. A number of dairy products are available with added probiotics including sour/fermented milk, yogurt, cheese, butter/cream, ice cream and infant formula. These probiotics are used as a starter culture or in combination with another traditional starter. Adding probiotics to dairy foods gives both sensory changes to the foods (improved taste, aroma, texture, etc.) as well as health-promoting properties. Yogurt and fermented milk such as kefir are some of the most well-known and widely consumed foods with probiotics. In the past, fermented foods were valued due to their increased shelf life, food safety, and sensory aspects. However, the scientific community is increasingly discovering that the fermentation process enhances nutritional and functional properties in foods by creating bioactive compounds and by adding live microorganisms to the diet (Marco et al., 2017).

Probiotics have four main mechanisms of action: improving the gut barrier, interfering with pathogens, immunomodulation and producing neurotransmitters (Sánchez et al., 2017). Some probiotic strains are effective in treating antibiotic-associated diarrhea (Hempel et al., 2012), while others have been found to be helpful in managing inflammatory bowel disease (Jakubczyk et al., 2020), and due to the gut-brain axis, probiotics have also been found to play a role in mental health. A number of randomized controlled trials have found that probiotic supplementation can help reduce depression and anxiety symptoms (Akkasheh et al., 2016; Kazemi et al., 2019; Slykerman et al., 2017). A systematic review and meta-analysis by Companys et al. found that fermented milk consumption was associated with a 4% reduction in the risk of stroke, ischemic heart disease, and cardiovascular mortality (Companys et al., 2020). Yogurt intake was associated with a 27% reduction in risk of type 2 diabetes and a 20% reduction in risk of metabolic syndrome.

A recent systematic review of the links between dairy food intake and gut microbiota found eight randomized controlled trials of good quality on this subject (Aslam et al., 2020). Seven of the studies examined the effect of type of dairy (milk, yogurt, kefir) and dairy proteins (whey and casein) on the gut microbiota, while one study looked at the effects of quantity of dairy intake on the microbiota. Three studies showed that milk, yogurt, and kefir increases beneficial strains of Lactobacillus and Bifidobacterium in the gut. One study found that yogurt lowered a pathogenic strain of Bacteroides fragilis. The reviewers concluded that milk and fermented milk products such as kefir and yogurt likely help change the gut microbiota in a beneficial manner. Further studies are needed to understand this potential.

SECTION 6: DAIRY INTAKE AND HEALTH OUTCOMES

METABOLIC SYNDROME

Metabolic syndrome (MetS) comprises a constellation of conditions including high blood pressure, high blood sugar, excess body fat around the waist and abnormal blood cholesterol levels. These conditions together increase one's risk of heart disease, stroke, and diabetes. The consumption of dairy products such as milk and yogurt may help to improve these conditions and reduce the risk of chronic disease (Astrup, 2014; Mena-Sánchez et al., 2019). In a recent study of over 15,000 Brazilian adults aged 35 to 74 years, total and full-fat dairy food intakes were inversely associated with MetS (Drehmer et al., 2016). Similarly, a recent meta-analysis of cohort studies found a 15% lower risk of MetS for each one serving per day increment of dairy consumption (Kim & Je, 2016).

Dairy intake may also aid in weight management. Intake of yogurt was found to be inversely associated with weight gain over a four-year time period in both women and men (Mozaffarian et al., 2011), and in 11.2-year cohort study the risk of becoming overweight or obese was lower among women in the highest quintile of dairy intake (Rautiainen et al., 2016).

CARDIOVASCULAR DISEASE

For years, the Dietary Guidelines for Americans and the American Heart Association have recommended the consumption of low-fat and fat-free dairy products so as to minimize saturated fat intake and thus reduce the risk of cardiovascular disease (Arnett Donna K. et al., 2019; U.S. Department of Agriculture and U.S. Department of Health and Human Services, 2020). After all, milk and dairy products can be a major source of saturated fatty acids which have been linked to an increased risk of CVD, CHD, and stroke.

On the contrary, numerous cohort studies and meta-analyses have found that dairy intake is inversely related to cardiovascular disease risk (Astrup et al., 2016; Drouin-Chartier et al., 2016; Fontecha et al., 2019; Gómez-Cortés et al., 2018; Lovegrove & Hobbs, 2016; Siri-Tarino et al., 2015; Soedamah-Muthu et al., 2011).

Data from the PURE study (Prospective Urban Rural Epidemiology) illustrates this relationship well. The PURE study is a large multinational cohort study that includes dietary intakes of over 136,000 individuals between the age of 35 and 70 from 21 different countries in five different contents over a nine-year follow-up period (Dehghan et al., 2018). After nine years of follow-up, researchers observed that those with a higher intake of total dairy (>2 servings/day) had a lower risk of major CVD, CV mortality, and stroke than those with no dairy intake. More specifically, a higher intake of milk and yogurt was associated with lower CVD risk, while cheese intake showed no association. The authors concluded that dairy consumption was associated with a lower risk of mortality and major CVD events.

Fats

Many researchers have been finding that there is no clear evidence that dairy food consumption of any fat level is associated with a higher risk of CVD, and recommendations to reduce dairy food consumption should be made with caution (German et al., 2009).

A review by German and colleagues found that milk fat has been shown to increase plasma HDL-C levels, and most saturated fats in milk have no impact on LDL-C levels (German et al., 2009). A cohort study in Sweden observed that among women, milk fat biomarkers were significantly higher among controls than among those who experienced a myocardial infarction (Warensjö et al., 2010). This relationship was also seen in men, though it did not reach statistical significance. Another finding of this study was that intake of cheese and fermented milk products were inversely related to incidence of myocardial infarction.

Some may question the consumption of cheese in particular as it contains a high amount of saturated fat. In response to this thought, Raziani and colleagues (Raziani et al., 2016) recently conducted a randomized control trial where they had 139 subjects with two or more MetS risk factors, and they divided these subjects into three groups: a regular fat cheese group, a reduced-fat cheese group, and a no cheese group (iso-caloric, higher in carbohydrates). After 12 weeks of follow-up, levels of LDL-C were not significantly different between any of the groups, and HDL-C levels were higher in the cheese groups compared to the no cheese groups. In addition, insulin, blood glucose, blood pressure, and waist circumference did not differ between groups. Their conclusion: a high daily intake of regular cheese does not significantly alter LDL-C levels or other MetS risk factors.

So why is it that saturated fat from dairy products appears to have no or even a beneficial impact on CVD risk, while saturated fat from other sources is harmful? It is thought that when saturated fats are consumed as part of the whole food matrix, like those in milk, cheese, and yogurt, their detrimental effects may be counteracted (Astrup et al., 2019; Gijsbers et al., 2016; Unger et al., 2019). The specific types of fatty acids (15:0 and 17:0) in dairy products may also be beneficial to cardiovascular health, though more research is needed in that area (de Souza et al., 2015; Liang et al., 2018; Yu & Hu, 2018). As reviewed previously, the saturated fat in dairy is also accompanied by numerous other beneficial nutrients including calcium, magnesium, phosphorus, potassium and probiotics (if fermented), and the provision of these nutrients in dairy may ameliorate the impact of saturated fat on CVD risk as well (Astrup, 2014; Soerensen et al., 2014).

TYPE 2 DIABETES

There is also a modest inverse relationship between the consumption of dairy and the risk of type 2 diabetes (Aune et al., 2013; Gijsbers et al., 2016; Gómez-Cortés et al., 2018; Schwingshackl et al., 2017; Tong et al., 2011). It's suggested that the biggest benefit comes with a dairy intake of three servings per day, and this reduces type 2 diabetes risk by 2% to 15% (Mitri et al., 2019). A recent review found that among 12 meta-analyses, most reported an inverse association between the incidence of type 2 diabetes and dairy consumption, and this risk decreases incrementally as consumption of total dairy products and low-fat dairy products increases (Alvarez-Bueno et al., 2019).

This relationship may be strongest when looking at cheese and yogurt specifically. For example, Chen and colleagues conducted a meta-analysis using data from three cohorts: the Health Professionals Follow-Up Study (41,436 men), the Nurses' Health Study (67,138 women), and the Nurses' Health Study II (85,884 women) (M. Chen et al., 2014). While they found that neither low-fat nor high-fat dairy intake was associated with type 2 Diabetes risk, yogurt intake was consistently associated with a reduced risk. Specifically, the pooled data from all three cohorts showed that **each serving of yogurt/day resulted in a 17% decrease in type 2 diabetes risk**. Turning our attention to cheese, a study of almost 27,000 Swedish adults observed a decreased risk of type 2 diabetes among those with higher consumption of cheese, cream, butter and high-fat fermented dairy (Ericson et al., 2015).

The mechanism(s) behind these associations still remains unclear, though it has been observed that a high consumption of dairy products improves insulin sensitivity and reduces circulating insulin levels (Mitri et al., 2019). For example, Stancliffe and colleagues conducted a study where they randomized 48 adults with MetS to receive either an adequate dairy (3.5 daily servings) or low-dairy (0.5 daily servings) diet for 12 weeks (Stancliffe et al., 2011). The adequate dairy group showed a significant reduction in plasma insulin levels after just one week, and these reduced levels were maintained throughout the study. Additionally, despite no change in body weight between groups, fat mass was significantly reduced in the adequate dairy group compared to the low dairy group. This may suggest the possibility of dairy in restricting body-fat accumulation (Wennersberg et al., 2009). Rideout and colleagues produced similar findings of improved insulin resistance and plasma insulin levels when comparing a high intake of low-fat dairy products (four servings/day) with a low intake (one to two servings/day) over a six-month period (Rideout et al., 2013). The specific long-chain fatty acids in dairy products (15:0 and 17:0) may have a role in insulin action as they have been positively associated with lower glucose levels as well as higher systemic and hepatic insulin sensitivity, though more research is needed in this area (Kratz et al., 2014).

CANCER

The relationship between dairy consumption and cancer risk is less clear than it is for cardiovascular disease and type 2 diabetes, but there is some evidence that consuming dairy products decreases the risk of some cancers, particularly colorectal cancer, bladder cancer, and esophageal cancer (Schwingshackl et al., 2018; Zhang et al., 2019). In a recent systematic review, there was consistent evidence of a decrease in colorectal cancer risk with higher consumptions of total dairy products and milk (Barrubés et al., 2019). Interestingly in this study, no significant associations were observed between colorectal cancer risk and intake of low-fat dairy products, whole milk, fermented dairy products or cultured milk. In contrast, other studies have found a significant risk reduction associated with cheese and yogurt intake (Zhang et al., 2019). Yogurt consumption has also been associated with a decreased risk of bladder cancer when comparing those in moderate and high intake categories with non-consumers (Acham et al., 2020; Bermejo et al., 2019). According to the World Cancer Research Fund, the cancer-protecting effects of milk can be attributed to its high calcium content as well as lactic-acid producing bacteria (World Cancer Research Fund/American Institute for Cancer Research, 2018). The other beneficial components of milk such as lactoferrin, vitamin D, and short-chain fatty acids may also have protective benefits.

The influence of dairy on breast cancer risk has also been studied, though this relationship is much less clear. Garcia and colleagues recently conducted a systematic review of the association between breast cancer and dairy product consumption (García et al., 2020). Of the 18 studies that met their inclusion criteria, 11 studies showed that dairy consumption was inversely associated with breast cancer, two studies showed a positive association, and five studies found a non-significant association. A 2019 study by Chen and colleagues found that data does not support a strong association between the consumption of dairy and breast cancer risk, even when comparing low-fat/skim milk, whole milk, and yogurt separately (L. Chen et al., 2019). The World Cancer Research Fund states in their most recent report that there is limited evidence that consuming dairy products may decrease the risk of breast cancer (World Cancer Research Fund/American Institute for Cancer Research, 2018).

BONE HEALTH

Bone, just like muscle tissue, is constantly being remodeled. During early life, adequate intakes of calcium and vitamin D, along with an overall adequate diet, are essential for bone deposition and for adequate growth and development. In later life, decreasing estrogen levels in women during and after menopause leads to increased bone resorption that outpaces bone formation. For this reason, postmenopausal women are at higher risk of osteoporosis due to lower bone mass density and bone quality. Osteoporosis increases the risk of fracture, especially to the hip, vertebrae, and forearms (Institute of Medicine, 2010; Song, 2017). Calcium plays an important role in bone health, however, observational evidence is mixed on the link between calcium intake and measures of bone strength in older adults.

The 2001–2006 NHANES data on adults aged 60 and older (55% women) found an association between higher dietary calcium intakes and higher lumbar spine bone mass density in women only (Yao et al., 2021). In contrast, a randomized controlled trial in Australia in women over 65 years with an average intake of 886 mg per day of dietary calcium found no association between calcium intake and bone mass density (Bristow et al., 2019). A two-year randomized controlled trial in 500 healthy postmenopausal women found that consuming 500 ml (16 oz) per day of enriched skimmed milk (900 mg calcium and 600 IU vitamin D) increased bone mass density at the femoral neck (Reyes-Garcia et al., 2018). The U.S. Preventive Services Task Force (USPSTF) concluded from the body of research on calcium and vitamin D supplementation studies and studies examining effects of dairy consumption that daily doses of less than 1,000 mg calcium and 400 IU vitamin D are insufficient to prevent fractures in postmenopausal women and there is inadequate evidence using higher doses to examine the potential benefits in this population (US Preventive Services Task Force et al., 2018).

While further studies are needed to better understand the role of calcium, vitamin D, and milk products in preventing fractures among older adults, some recent studies may help clarify this relationship. For example, a recent randomized controlled trial found that improving calcium and protein intake by using dairy foods reduced the risk of falls and fractures among over 7,000 institutionalized older adults (Iuliano et al., 2021).

GASTROINTESTINAL HEALTH

Dairy foods have a complex impact on the gastrointestinal (GI) tract. While people with lactose intolerance experience unpleasant and uncomfortable effects from consuming dairy foods that have lactose, milk products can also have beneficial effects on GI health. (For more information on lactose intolerance, see the section below on this topic.) A recent systematic review by Aslam et al. found that consuming milk, yogurt, and kefir increased beneficial bacteria strains and decreased harmful strains, having an overall positive effect on the gut microbiome (Aslam et al., 2020). Fermented milk products such as yogurt and kefir also contain probiotics, which improve the gut barrier and interfere with potential pathogens, thereby improving GI health (Sánchez et al., 2017).

There have been reports that in individuals for whom cow's milk causes GI distress, sheep milk or goats' milk may be better tolerated. There are a few nutritional differences that may account for this. While all animal milk contains casein, cow's milk contains a combination of A1 beta-casein and A2 beta-casein while sheep and goats' milk contains primarily just A2 beta-casein with little to none of the A1 variety (Turkmen, 2017). When A1 beta-casein is digested, it leads to the production of a compound called beta-casomorphine-7 which is associated with intestinal inflammation and various digestive issues in some people (Jianqin et al., 2016). The issues could be avoided by drinking sheep or goats' milk that has very little A1 beta-casein. Another quality of these milks is that they have smaller fat globules and a lower lactose content which may also aid in digestibility. However, research in this area is still in its infancy and there is currently no evidence to support that sheep or goat milk is more healthful or more easily digestible for most individuals.

WEIGHT

Dairy products can aid in weight management due in part to the satiating effect of its protein content. The protein content of milk aids in satiety since protein takes longer to digest than simple carbohydrates. Furthermore, higher-fat dairy products are particularly satiating since fat digests even more slowly than protein. Milk proteins have been found to be more satiating than other protein sources (Anderson & Moore, 2004; McGregor & Poppitt, 2013). Whey protein found in milk induces satiety signals and contributes to short-term and longer-term food intake regulation (Bendtsen et al., 2013; Luhovyy et al., 2007). One study found that 45 g of whey protein resulted in better satiety and more reduced food intake at a subsequent meal when compared to egg albumin and soy protein (Anderson et al., 2004). Another study found that 48 g of whey protein resulted in further reduced food intake at a buffet meal more than a similar intake of casein (Hall et al., 2003). A study examining the impact of whey on the satiety hormone glucagon-like-peptide-1 found that a high-protein breakfast (58% energy from protein) using dairy foods enriched with whey isolate raised glucagon-like-peptide-1 levels over the following three hours more than a breakfast with unenriched yogurt (Blom et al., 2006).

A study by Baer et al. found that 23 weeks of consuming supplemental protein in the form of whey or soy vs the same amount of calories in the form of carbohydrate resulted in lower body weight and body fat in the two protein groups (Baer et al., 2011). Waist circumference was smaller in the whey protein group compared to the other two groups, and fasting ghrelin was also lower in the whey group compared to the soy and carbohydrate groups. In rat studies, similar findings have been shown. Feeding insulin-resistant obese rats whey protein is associated with decreased calorie intake, decrease body fat and improvements in insulin sensitivity compared to feeding them protein from red meat (Belobrajdic et al., 2004).

In general, there have been mixed findings regarding dairy product intake and lower body weight from observational and clinical trials with humans. An observational study found higher intakes of calcium from dairy were associated with less overweight in children in eight European countries (Nappo et al., 2019). In contrast, a Portuguese study found no association between dairy foods and weight among teens and young adults aged 13 to 21 (Marabujo et al., 2018). A systematic review and meta-analysis of 41 randomized controlled trials found that high dairy food intake had no impact on weight or body fat but did see an impact on body fat when high dairy intake was combined with an energy-restricted diet (Booth et al., 2015). In contrast, a recent intervention study among overweight/obese postmenopausal women found a greater degree of weight loss and fat loss among women consuming either low-fat dairy foods (four to five servings/day) or calcium and vitamin D supplements as compared to the placebo group (Ilich et al., 2019).

IMMUNITY

Several animal studies have shown that milk proteins, particularly whey protein, can positively influence immune responses. Mice that were fed with whey protein had higher mucosal antibody responses to ovalbumin and cholera toxin compared to mice on a standard diet (Low et al., 2001). Another study found that mice fed undenatured whey protein had higher T helper cells and a higher ratio of helper to suppressor cells compared to those on a casein diet (Bounous et al., 1993). Mice fed whey have also been observed to have an increase in white blood cells, lymphocyte counts, and IFN-gamma in spleen cells compared to mice fed casein and soy protein (Ford et al., 2001). Several in vitro studies have also found that whey protein improves markers of immunity including cytokine secretion, lymphocytes, and leukocytes (Cross & Gill, 1999; Wang et al., 2000; Zimecki & Kruzel, 2000). Some in vitro and rodent studies have also shown immunomodulatory effects of casein (Hata et al., 1998; Li & Mine, 2004; Otani et al., 2000; Pessi et al., 2001; Requena et al., 2009).

Beyond animal studies, there is also some evidence that points to an immunomodulating effect of cow's milk in humans. There is strong evidence that consumption of cow's milk early in life is associated with a lower prevalence of allergies, respiratory tract infections, and asthma (Perdijk et al., 2018). It has also been shown that children who grow up on a farm have a lower prevalence of these conditions than children who do not (von Mutius & Vercelli, 2010). However, more studies are needed to understand the immune effects of consuming dairy in humans.

INFLAMMATION

There have been an increasing number of studies on the topic of dairy and inflammation in the past few years, indicating a growing interest in this area. A recent systematic review of 16 clinical trials found that consuming milk products did not show a pro-inflammatory effect in healthy subjects or in subjects with metabolic abnormalities such as type 2 diabetes or MetS (Ulven et al., 2019). In fact, the majority of the studies saw a significant anti-inflammatory effect in both groups.

It is well-known that high-fat meals increase the postprandial concentration of proinflammatory cytokines (IL-6 and TNF-alpha) and the acute-phase protein CRP, and it appears that full-fat milk products (cheese and butter) have this same impact on inflammatory responses following their immediate consumption (Emerson et al., 2017; Pacheco et al., 2008; Payette et al., 2009; Poppitt et al., 2008). However, in the longer term, consuming dairy foods high in saturated and total fat as part of an overall balanced eating pattern does not appear to promote inflammation as none of the studies included in the systematic review by Ulven et al. reported an increase in circulating inflammatory markers between the dairy and control groups (Ulven et al., 2019). In other studies, consuming kefir and yogurt actually reduced inflammatory marker TNF-alpha and CRP (O'Brien et al., 2015; Pei et al., 2017).

SECTION 7: WHEN TO LIMIT DAIRY

LACTOSE INTOLERANCE

Lactose is a disaccharide found in milk and dairy foods. The enzyme lactase is needed to break lactose down into galactose and glucose before these sugars can be absorbed in the small intestine. There are two types of lactase deficiency: primary lactase deficiency and secondary lactase deficiency. Primary deficiency is the most common type where a person makes less lactase. It is most common in adults but can also occur in children. Secondary deficiency can be temporary and is a lactase deficiency brought on by a medical condition such as acute illness or diarrhea. Lactose intolerance is not an allergy (see cow's milk protein allergy below for more information). When lactose remains undigested and enters the large intestine, bacteria break the lactose down and cause symptoms such as bloating, gas, cramping, nausea and diarrhea. Lactose intolerance can be diagnosed with a blood test following consumption of a lactose-containing drink. If a person's blood sugar does not rise after the drink, they may be lactose-intolerant. Alternatively, a hydrogen breath test can be done. After consuming a high-lactose drink, high level of hydrogen present in a person's breath can indicate lactose intolerance. A stool acidity test can also indicate lactose intolerance. If someone is not digesting lactose, their stool will contain lactic acid, glucose, and fatty acids. Lactose intolerance can also be diagnosed via biopsies of the small intestine taken during an endoscopy. It's important not to self-diagnose lactose intolerance as symptoms could be indicative of other gastrointestinal conditions, such as irritable bowel disease or Celiac disease.

Lactose intolerance is very common worldwide, though the true prevalence of lactose intolerance is unknown as it is not often tested for and many individuals self-diagnose (Bailey et al., 2013). As shown in Table 7, there are differences in prevalence between ethnic groups, likely due to genetic factors. However, scientific findings indicate that the prevalence of true lactose intolerance may be overestimated as there are many other physiologic conditions that can appear similar to lactose intolerance (McBean & Miller, 1998).

To manage lactose intolerance, lactase pills or drops can be taken when a person eats or drinks foods containing lactose. Alternatively, a person can choose to consume only dairy foods with lower levels of lactose such as hard cheese and small amounts of yogurt. Lactose-free milk is also available in most grocery stores. Having milk products at the same time as other foods may help to lessen symptoms among some people, and data suggests that adults with lactose intolerance may tolerate up to 8 oz of milk with meals (McBean & Miller, 1998). Keeping a food and symptom diary may also help to identify the quantities of lactose-containing foods that can be tolerated. Dairy alternatives such as soy milk and other fortified beverages may also be a good option.

Individuals with lactose intolerance consume less than the recommended levels of dairy foods, and it is known that avoiding dairy may lead to nutrient deficiencies and an increased risk of several chronic diseases (Bailey et al., 2013; Suchy et al., 2010). In most cases, individuals don't need to avoid dairy entirely, and when working with individuals with lactose intolerance it is important to ensure they are still consuming a nutritionally adequate diet.

Table 7: Estimated Prevalence of Lactose Intolerance Among Various Ethnic Groups

Ethnic Group	Prevalence
Northern Europeans	2% to 15%
American Whites	6% to 22%
Central Europeans	9% to 23%
Indians, Northern	20% to 30%
Indians, Southern	60% to 70%
Hispanics	50% to 80%
Ashkenazi Jews	60% to 80%
Blacks	60% to 80%
American Indians/First Nations	80% to 100%
Other Asians	95% to 100%

Source: (Harrington & Mayberry, 2008)

MILK ALLERGY

Cow's milk allergy happens when the body's immune system reacts to proteins found in milk — casein and whey. Milk allergy is most common in young children, though most outgrow the allergy by the age of five. Symptoms of milk allergy can be immediate or delayed. Immediate symptoms may include itchy rash, hives, redness, swelling, itchy eyes, runny nose, coughing, vomiting or in rare cases swallowing and breathing difficulties. Delayed symptoms may include diarrhea, constipation, reflux, vomiting, mucus/blood in stools, nausea, abdominal pain, gas and bloating.

Immediate reactions are usually mediated by Immunoglobulin E (IgE), which triggers histamine to be released and involves symptoms in the skin and gut. This is in contrast to delayed reactions which are usually mediated by non-IgE immune reactions, and may involve IgG or IgA. Non-IgE mediated allergy symptoms typically occur in the gut, but may also occur in the skin. IgE-mediated milk allergy can be diagnosed with a skin prick test, while non-IgE mediated milk allergy can be diagnosed with a blood test. In both cases, milk allergy is managed by avoiding all foods containing milk and milk products. However, as most people do outgrow milk allergy and milk allergy is unusual in adults, reinvestigating tolerance over time (with the help of a health professional such as an allergist or dietitian) may be worthwhile. Some individuals with a milk allergy may be able to tolerate milk baked into products, though this should be discussed with an allergist before attempting.

CONSTIPATION

Randomized controlled trials show that in some children, non-IgE mediated cow's milk protein allergy may be a cause of chronic constipation. In children with chronic constipation, some show improvement in constipation with an oligoantigenic diet (a diet that excludes cow's milk, soy milk, and eggs) (Borrelli et al., 2009; Iacono et al., 2006). Observational studies have shown that among children aged 4 months to 3 years, short duration of breastfeeding and high cow's milk intake increases the risk of constipation (Andiran et al., 2003; Carroccio et al., 2013; Dehghani et al., 2012; Irastorza et al., 2010; Simeone et al., 2008). The body of evidence in this area is small however and further studies may be warranted.

SECTION 8: ENVIRONMENTAL CONSIDERATIONS OF DAIRY

DAIRY AND CLIMATE CHANGE

Agriculture is a significant contributor to greenhouse gas (GHG) emissions worldwide, and recent studies show that the dairy sector's GHG emissions increased by 18% between 2005 and 2015 (FAO & GDP, 2018). Across the globe, all cattle are estimated to produce about 11% of all human-induced GHG emissions. Within the U.S., this figure is a bit lower at 3.4 %, and dairy cattle alone are responsible for about 1.3% of all human-induced GHG emissions (Rotz, 2018). These emissions come from the maintenance of crop and pasture land, manure storage, and the enteric fermentation from the animals themselves. A dairy cow is estimated to produce more than 330 kg of methane annually, a GHG that is 25% more potent than carbon dioxide. However, while total emissions have increased, dairy farming is becoming more efficient, resulting in declining emissions and impact per unit of production (FAO & GDP, 2018).

Water use is another topic of concern in dairy farming. Milk itself is about 87% water, so milking cows need to drink several gallons of water each day in order to sustain production. Additional water is needed to dispose of manure, clean milking equipment, and water pastures, and it's estimated that 30 to 50 gallons of water are needed per dairy cow per day (Brugger, 2007). This water use is especially concerning given that a majority of large dairy farms in the U.S. are in dry states like New Mexico, Texas, and California where water use is a growing concern.

Figure 2: The Amount of CO_2 Equivalents To Create One Kilogram of Product

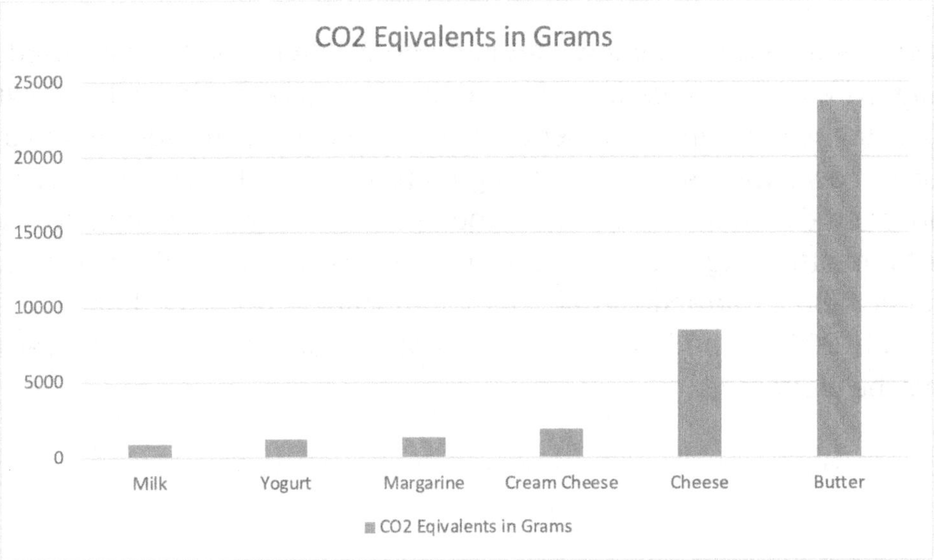

Source: Bundesministerium für Umwelt, Naturschutz und nukleare Sicherheit

It takes 21 pounds of whole milk to make one pound of butter.

DAIRY AND POLLUTION

The majority of milk and dairy products on the market today come from huge dairy farms, or "mega-dairies," that house thousands of cows at a time (Chrisman, 2020). These operations often contribute significantly to land, water, and air pollution. A considerable challenge at these mega-dairies is disposing of manure, as a 2,000-cow farm can generate up to a quarter of a million pounds of manure daily (US Environmental Protection Agency). Manure is high in nitrogen and phosphorus, and while these nutrients are important fertilizers in proper amounts, they are at toxic levels in manure. In these large farms, manure is often scraped or washed into large pits or lagoons which then release large amounts of methane into the air and are prone to leaks into ground or surface water (Flaherty & Cativiela, 2017). On large dry lots, manure may also turn into dust that is inhaled by the cows and the farmworkers and the local community alike. In fact, cities in the San Joaquin Valley which is in the heart of California's dairy country have some of the highest rates of particulate air pollution in the U.S. (Charles, 2016).

However, all dairy farming does not automatically equate to pollution. Smaller herds grazing on pasture deposit much of their waste directly into the land in amounts that break down naturally and are beneficial to the soil. The "wear and tear" of cows on a pasture is also beneficial for the land — the impact of hooves and fertilization helps to build a healthful soil structure and stimulates deeper root growth which in turn help control erosion and make the soil able to retain more water, lessening the effects of droughts and reducing flooding (USDA Natural Resources Conservation Service, Grazing Lands Technology Institute, 1996). While pastured cows still enterically produce methane, well-managed grasslands are able to sequester tons of GHGs and play a vital role in healthful ecosystems (Voth & Gilker, 2017).

DAIRY AND ANIMAL WELFARE

The treatment of animals on large dairy operations is also a growing concern. Many animals on these farms are kept in crowded lots with little vegetation or shade to escape the elements and are given no room to lie down. Cows that are not let out to pasture are fed a diet primarily of grain which can lead to acidosis, a digestive condition that can cause many different health problems for the cow. Cows on mega-dairies also have a shortened life expectancy. While dairy cattle can live to age 15 or 20 in a well-managed herd and can effectively produce milk for 12 to 15 years, cows on mega-dairies often remain in the herd for only about five years until their productivity begins to decline and they are sold to slaughter (Chrisman, 2020).

GROWTH HORMONE AND ANTIBIOTIC USE

Recombinant bovine somatotropin (rBST), previously called bovine growth hormone, is a synthetic hormone sometimes used in dairy cattle to increase milk production. It was approved by the FDA in 1993 and is now found in less than one in five dairy cows (American Cancer Society, 2014; US Food and Drug Administration, 2021). The U.S. does not require companies to label the use of rBST in dairy products, but the use of rBST has been banned in Canada and the European Union. The use of rBST was approved by the FDA because it was not deemed a health risk to humans. It is a large protein that is degraded by digestive enzymes in the stomach and small intestine, and the hormone itself shows no biological activity in humans. Of greater concern is that milk from cows treated with rBST often has higher levels of IGF-1, a hormone that helps cells grow and may influence the development of cancer, especially prostate, breast, and colorectal cancer. However, the exact nature of this association remains unclear, and many studies have found weak or no relationship between the two factors, and the American Cancer Society states they have no formal position regarding rBST (American Cancer Society, 2014).

A related topic is the use of antibiotics in dairy cows. On one hand, the use of antibiotics over the past several decades has resulted in more healthful and more productive animals. However, with the widespread use of antibiotics there is concern about the development of antibiotic-resistant bacteria, both in food-producing animals and strains that could transfer to humans. While there have been isolated reports of antibacterial resistance among food-producing animals, there are not any studies that report the emergence and establishment of antibiotic-resistant microbes among dairy cows or humans (Oliver et al., 2011). Antimicrobial resistance among dairy pathogens, particularly those found in milk, likely poses little risk to humans if milk is pasteurized.

ORGANIC AND GRASS-FED DAIRY

Choosing organic and/or grass-fed dairy products from small, local farms may help to avoid some of the environmental concerns mentioned above. Additionally, grass-fed milk has been found to have nearly twice the amount of beneficial unsaturated fats as conventional milk (Benbrook et al., 2018). However, the total amount of these fats in grass-fed milk is still significantly lower than other good sources such as fatty fish or vegetable oils.

If you are looking for the terms "organic" or "grass-fed" on the labels of dairy products, it's important to know what exactly they refer to. The term "USDA Organic" is regulated by the federal government, and the rules state that cows cannot be given growth hormones or antibiotics, all feed must be certified organic and cannot contain any animal by-products, and the animals cannot be continuously confined (AMS, 2018). Of note, an organic cow can still receive a diet primarily consisting of grain as long as the grain is organic.

The term "grass-fed," on the other hand, is not federally regulated. Some farmers with grass-fed animals keep their cows on pasture all of the time while others supplement the cow's diet with some grain, usually to boost milk production. However, one distinction is that dairy from cows eating nothing but grass (and hay in the winter) can be labeled "100% grass-fed."

SECTION 9: DAIRY AND MEDICATIONS

There are certain medications that should not be taken with dairy products due to the potential for calcium to interfere with the absorption of the medications. This can result in the medication being less effective. It is always best to check with a pharmacist or clinician to make sure which nutrients or foods may interact with any new medication.

Table 8: Medications That Are Affected by Dairy*

Class of Medication	Medication	Time Frame to Avoid Interactions
Antibiotics	Tetracycline – tetracycline, minocycline, and doxycycline	Avoid dairy one hour before and 2 hours after taking this medication
	Fluoroquinolone – ciprofloxacin, levofloxacin, and moxifloxacin	Avoid dairy 2 hours before and 2 hours after taking this medication
Bisphosphonates	Risedronate, alendronate, and ibandronate	Wait one hour after the medication to consume dairy
Iron Supplements	Ferrous sulfate, and ferrous gluconate	Wait at least 2 hours after taking an iron supplement before having any dairy
Thyroid Medications	Levothyroxine, Armor thyroid, and liothyronine	Wait 4 hours after taking medication to consume dairy
Anti-influenza	Xofluza	
Laxative	Bisacodyl (Dulcolax)	Avoid within an hour of dairy consumption

(https://www.goodrx.com/well-being/diet-nutrition/medications-and-dairy-products) and (Christianson & Salling, 2020) *This is not a complete list.

SECTION 10: CLINICAL AND CULINARY RECOMMENDATIONS AND COMPETENCIES

> Messaging from the Menus of Change Annual Report 2020
>
> **REIMAGINE DAIRY IN A SUPPORTING ROLE**

Clinical recommendations and competencies are the foundation from which culinary competencies were created. The goal for the culinary medicine practitioner is to help clients and patients develop the skills necessary to meet the clinical recommendations by teaching skill-based learning outlined in the culinary competencies.

Clinical Recommendations (Knowledge-Based) → Clinical Competencies (Knowledge-Based) → Culinary Competencies (Skill-Based)

CLINICAL RECOMMENDATIONS
1. 3 cup-equivalents of dairy or dairy products per day for adults (U.S. Department of Agriculture and U.S. Department of Health and Human Services, 2020).
2. Consume dairy, "including fat-free and low-fat milk, yogurt, and cheese, and/or lactose-free versions and fortified soy beverages and yogurt as alternatives" (U.S. Department of Agriculture and U.S. Department of Health and Human Services, 2020).

CLINICAL COMPETENCIES
1. List the nutrients for which dairy supplies a "good source"
2. Explain which cohorts are at risk of not meeting their daily dairy requirement of dairy
3. Relate the importance of consuming dairy for overall health
4. Discuss the conditions which require limiting or avoiding dairy in one's diet
5. List medications that react with dairy

CULINARY COMPETENCIES FOR DAIRY

Shopping and Storing Competencies
1. Identify sugar content in a serving of yogurt
   a. Demonstrate how to read the Nutrition Facts panel
   b. Demonstrate how to find the added sugar content in a serving of yogurt
2. Describe the various steps in processing milk
3. Identify protein content in a serving of yogurt
4. Identify low-fat sources of dairy
5. Identify the most healthful milk option
6. Identify the most healthful cheese option
7. Demonstrate proper storage of dairy products

Stocking the Kitchen
1. Stock a variety of milks
2. Stock yogurt
3. Stock a variety of cheeses

Cooking/Preparing Competencies
o Prepare a healthful white sauce
o Prepare a yogurt sauce
o Prepare homemade yogurt (optional)
o Thicken sauces using healthful ingredients
o Prepare a dairy-based breakfast
o Prepare a dairy-based dessert

Flavor Development Competencies
- o   Describe how to use cheese to increase the flavor profile of a dish
- o   Demonstrate how to use dairy products to improve the texture and flavor profile of a dish

Serving Competencies
- o   Model consuming dairy products
- o   Demonstrate proper serving sizes of dairy products
- o   Explain a dairy-equivalent
- o   Serve healthful dairy-based desserts
- o   Serve the appropriate number of dairy servings per day

Safety Competencies
- o   Transport dairy products safely
- o   Identify rancid dairy products
- o   Identify dairy products that can increase the risk of foodborne illness

SECTION 11: AT THE STORE

MILK

There are many milk alternatives available in stores and being able to decode certain terms is necessary. The following are important terms to understand when shopping for milk that was discussed earlier in this chapter — homogenization, standardization, fortification, raw and A2 milk. They also vary in the percentage of fat each contains (Table 9). They are listed here from the lowest to highest fat amount of fat — skim, 1%, 2%, full fat, half and half and whipping cream.

Lactose-free or Minimal Lactose Foods
For some individuals, they cannot digest the sugar — lactose — in milk products. Some manufacturers will add the enzyme that digests lactose (lactase) to the milk to remove the lactose so that individuals can consume it without unwanted side effects. Lactose-free milk has the same nutrient profile (with the exception of the sugar lactose) as regular milk.

Chocolate Milk

48% of Americans have no idea where chocolate milk comes from and 7% think that it comes from brown cows.

Do the benefits of consuming chocolate milk (calcium for example) outweigh the risks of the added sugar that is present in chocolate milk? Let the math answer that question. If a child drinks just one 8-ounce glass of chocolate milk a day, which equals 10 to 15 grams of added sugar, that would equal 890 teaspoons (19 cups) to 1246 teaspoons (26 cups) of added sugar per year.

Organic Milk

For milk to be labeled organic, the cows must (Milk Safety | Dairy Health Benefits):
o Be exclusively given feed grown without the use of pesticides or commercial fertilizers.
o Be given access to a pasture periodically.
o Not be given supplemental hormones to promote growth.
o Not be given certain medications to treat illness. Cows are allowed to be given antibiotics but only in the case of an emergency.

The USDA's Guidelines for Organic Certification of Dairy Livestock lays out the specifics.

Fortified

Fortified milk is more common in the United States than unfortified milk, although there is no law requiring fortification. Many states however require a standard value for certain nutrients present in milk like calcium, iron, and protein. Common nutrients that are added are vitamins A (vitamin A palmitate) and D (vitamin D_3), plus others may also be added like zinc, iron, and folic acid.

Fat Content

Do you choose whole-fat or low-fat dairy at the store? The answer depends on what your total diet looks like and your overall health. The fats present in whole-fat dairy products are a combination of mostly saturated fats and some mono-unsaturated fats. The recommendation for saturated fat intake is to consume no more than 10% of calories, which would equal 20 grams in a 2,000-calorie diet. If your overall diet is relatively low in saturated fat (low in animal products) then there is room for some whole-fat dairy products. Table 9 lists the amount of saturated fat in dairy products. If other saturated fats – animal meat products – are consumed they should be accounted for in the daily consumption of saturated fats.

Table 9: Saturated Fat and Sodium in Whole-Fat Dairy Products

Whole Fat Dairy Product	Saturated Fat* (grams)	Sodium* (mg)
8 ounces: Whole fat milk	4.6	94
Reduced fat (2% milk)	2.7	95
Low fat Milk (1%)	1.4	95

42

Skim milk (fat-free)	0.1	100
Yogurt 1 cup	4.77**	104
Cheese hard		
Cheddar 1 slice (21 grams)	4	135
American 1 slice (20.6 grams)	3.7	342
Swiss 1 ounce (28.35 grams)	4.4	439
Gruyere 1 ounce (28.35 grams)	5.4	202
Parmesan 1 ounce (28.35 grams)	4.2	335
Asiago (30 grams)	6	360
Manchego 1 ounce (28 grams)	8	210
Romano 1 ounce (28.35 grams)	4.9	405
Goat cheese hard 1 ounce (28.35 grams)	7	120
Cheese soft		
Brie 1 ounce (28.35 grams)	5	178
Feta (28.35 grams)	3.8	323
Camembert 1 ounce (28.35 grams)	4.3	239
Queso fresco ¼ cup (30.5 grams)	4	229
Blue cheese 1 ounce (28.35 grams)	5.3	326
Mozzarella 1 ounce (28.35 grams)	3.9	138
Cottage cheese ½ cup (105 grams)	3.6	331
Cream cheese 1 tablespoon (14.5 grams)	2.9	46
Goat cheese soft 1 ounce (28.35 grams)	4	130
Ricotta ½ cup	7.3	125

*U.S. Department of Agriculture, Agricultural Research Service. FoodData Central, 2019. fdc.nal.usda.gov.

** Depending on the brand it can vary widely from 7 to 14 grams for one cup (look at the label).

The Nutrition Source from Harvard summarizes the evidence on whether or not to consume whole-fat or low-fat dairy products. One of the most important factors to consider is what type of food is replacing the calories from fat when one consumes low-fat dairy. If those calories are replaced with whole grains, nuts, and healthful oils, great. If, however, they are replaced with refined grains and sugar, then that is not a more healthful option.

YOGURT

Fermentation is another issue to consider when purchasing and consuming dairy products as that process leads to a product lower in lactose (great for those that are lactose intolerant) and a product that provides healthful bacteria to the gastrointestinal tract, which brings with it a host of health benefits.

Putting it Into Practice: How to Choose a Healthful Yogurt

You are likely bombarded with over 30 different yogurts to choose from when you go to the store. Which one is the most healthful? Let's break it down into simple steps.

> **Type:** Greek yogurt has more protein than regular yogurt. Chobani, Fage, and Skyr are some of the popular high-protein Greek options. If you are going to buy non-Greek yogurt, the lower-fat, plain varieties typically offer the highest protein content.

> **Added sugars:** Find how many grams of added sugar there are per serving? What is the percent daily value? Aim for an unsweetened yogurt or one with minimal added sugar. Be careful, as some yogurts use artificial sweeteners like sucralose (Splenda), acesulfame potassium, and aspartame; of note, stevia and monk fruit are not artificial sweeteners.

> **Fat content:** It depends on the individual situation (see above for more specifics). Choose low-fat or nonfat dairy when fewer calories and saturated fat are desired.

> **Flavor:** Typically, flavored yogurt has a high amount of added sugar. Plain yogurt has 0 grams of added sugar, but some people don't like the taste. If going for a

flavored yogurt, compare the nutrition facts label of different brands to find the one with the least amount of added sugar.

Ingredients list: This is another area where you can compare between two brands. Some brands add in additives, colors, or other unnecessary ingredients. The fewer the ingredients, the better!

For help, check out What's New in The Yogurt Aisle (https://www.cspinet.org/article/whats-new-yogurt-aisle) by The Center for Science in the Public Interest.

CHEESE

A lot of people like cheese and who can blame them. It is savory, creamy, and when melted, who can resist its gooey deliciousness? Since cheese is high in saturated fat it is important to watch the amount consumed. If there was little to no saturated fat consumed that day (little to no animal products) then there is room for cheese. Refer to Table 9 for the amount of saturated fat in a serving of cheese and compare that with the daily allotment (13 grams in a 2,000-calorie diet). It is also important to watch the sodium content in processed cheese.

There are many factors to consider when selecting cheese, the number of calories, lactose content, and the amount of saturated fat and sodium. Depending on what the greatest need is consider the following:

- If lactose intolerance is an issue, select hard cheeses as they are lower in lactose as most of the whey is squeezed out when making it. Cheeses with low lactose levels are — cheddar, parmesan, and Swiss.

- For lower-calorie options, consider cheese made with skim or low-fat milk, be sure to look at the sodium content though as it may be higher to make up for the loss of fat.
- If sodium is an issue, choose lower-sodium cheeses.

Culinary Techniques — shred or grate cheese to get the illusion of a larger portion of cheese. Chooses stronger smelling cheese that boosts the flavor profile so less is needed.

BUTTER VERSUS MARGARINE

Defining Margarine

Figure 3: The Timeline of Margarine

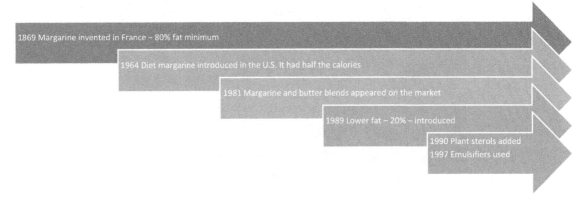

1869 Margarine invented in France – 80% fat minimum
1964 Diet margarine introduced in the U.S. It had half the calories
1981 Margarine and butter blends appeared on the market
1989 Lower fat – 20% – introduced
1990 Plant sterols added
1997 Emulsifiers used

In 1866 Napoleon III offered money for the development of an inexpensive food-fat and three years later a French chemist invented margarine by flavoring beef tallow with milk (McGee, 2004). It certainly was not a healthful product, but it was cheap. It was mass-produced in the United States by 1880 and between the 1970s and mid-1990s, low-fat spreads went from a market share of 5% to more than 74%. Figure 3 lays out the time line for margarine (Dostalova, 2003).

Table 10: Comparing Butter and Margarine

	Butter	Margarine
CO$_2$ emissions (grams per Kg product)	23,794	1,350
Type of fat	High in saturated fat, which increases total and LDL cholesterol.	Some are low in saturated fat and high in unsaturated fat. Some are high in stearic acid.

Hydrogenated oil	Minimal partially hydrogenated trans fat and it is found naturally in butter (0.5g per tablespoon).	No trans fat, but does have fully hydrogenated oils created by force, which leads to stearic acid, a saturated fat.
Percentage of fat	70 to 80%	70 to 80%
Fortified/Enriched	If the milk had vitamin D added, so would the butter.	Some have plant sterols added.

Because both butter and margarine contain saturated fats, neither is really "better" than the other. Both should be used sparingly, and poly and mono-unsaturated oils should replace them as often as they can. The Presidential Advisory from the American Heart Association is very clear that replacing saturated fat with unsaturated fat — especially polyunsaturated fat — will lower the incidence of cardiovascular disease (Sacks et al., 2017).

Oils high in **polyunsaturated fats** include canola, corn, peanut, safflower (high linoleic), sunflower (high linoleic) and soybean oils. Canola, safflower (high oleic), sunflower (high oleic) and olive oils are high in **mono-unsaturated** fat.

From a culinary perspective, many recipes can still achieve good taste and texture with replacing some, if not all, of the butter/margarine with vegetable oil. Other spreads for toast and sandwiches can include heart healthful options such as peanut butter and other nut/seed butters, avocado, and hummus. Low- and reduced-fat margarines do not work well for baking or cooking as they contain stabilizers that can scorch pans. In baking, the increase in water content affects the liquid-solid balance, and the extra starch, gum, and protein prevent melting.

In summary, the choice between butter or margarine will largely be based on an individual's taste preference. Some margarines have functional ingredients added such as plant sterols, and others are dairy/lactose-free and vegan, which allow those with intolerances, allergies, and plant-based diets to use these options. For cardiovascular and overall health, both butter and margarine should be used in smaller quantities, and heart healthful fats such as polyunsaturated and monounsaturated fats should be promoted.

SECTION 12: DAIRY AND SAFETY

Milk is highly perishable and should be kept from direct exposure to oxygen and strong light. Sunlight or fluorescent lights can cause a reaction between riboflavin and methionine, which contains sulfur (McGee, 2004). In addition, even with pasteurization, there are millions of bacteria present.

It is very important to refrigerate milk and limit its exposure to oxygen at room temperature. The odor when milk turns rancid is very distinctive and should be the first clue to discard the milk. Other safety tips for dairy products are listed below.

1. Milk should be kept at or below 40 °F/4 °C. Pasteurized milk has a shelf life of 10 to 21 days and ultra-pasteurized milk (UPM) has a shelf life of 30 to 90 days. Once opened, the UPM can last 7 to 10 days.
2. When shopping, pick up dairy products last (check that they are cold) in order to increase the chance that they remain cool enough until you get them home. If travel time is more than 30 minutes, add frozen items or an ice pack to the bag to keep them cool.
3. Look for the "sell by" date and don't buy products if it is after this date.
4. Don't leave dairy products out at room temperature for more than two hours.
5. Don't return unused milk or cream to their original container.
6. Butter that has been open needs to be kept in the refrigerator where it will last one to two months.
7. Soft cheeses tend to be made with unpasteurized milk, so it is best to avoid in vulnerable populations — those who are immune-compromised, children, and pregnant women, for example.

The Food Keeper App — https://www.foodsafety.gov/keep-food-safe/foodkeeper-app — has a lot more information on food and beverage storage.

SECTION 13: IN THE KITCHEN

ON THE TONGUE

The flavor of milk is subtle and has been described as "milky, acidic, vanilla-like, caramel-like, aldehydic, fruity, beany, buttery, meaty, and vegetative" (Zhu & Xiao, 2017). It has a sweet-like flavor due to the sugar lactose, which is 60% less sweet than sucrose, and a slightly salty taste due to the minerals in milk (Helstad, 2019). Milk also has a pleasant mouthfeel due to fat globules and colloidal protein (Forss, 1969).

The flavor of fresh milk is influenced by the animal's feed. The flavor and color (a yellow hue) of milk from grass-fed cows differs from grain-fed cows due to the higher amount of unsaturated fats and the transfer of carotenoids, phenols, and other molecules in the grass to the milk (Faccia, 2020; Manzocchi et al., 2021).

The flavor of milk can change due to heat with the low temperature of pasteurization adding a slightly sulfur and green-leaf note (McGee, 2004). This is due to breaking down enzymes and bacteria and destroying the more delicate aromas. At high heat — above 170 °F/76 °C — a world of other flavors develops. One can sense notes of almonds, vanilla, and cultured butter in addition to an eggy smell. With prolonged boiling, a butterscotch flavor develops due to the Maillard reaction.

THE ROLE OF DAIRY IN THE KITCHEN

- o Milk has a great ability to foam. Skim milk foams the best due to the higher protein content but has less flavor than higher fat milk.
- o Milk moistens baked goods as well as adds protein, color, flavor and an overall richness.
- o Milk can be a thickened agent along with starch. The salts present in milk promotes protein coagulation.
- o Yogurt's acidity and calcium content act as a natural tenderizer.
- o Yogurt adds moisture and tang to baked goods.
- o Freezing milk will result in the clumping of the fat and protein particles and is not a good idea.

> Culinary Tip: Wet the bottom of a pan before adding milk to prevent scorching when heated.

YOGURT

Making Yogurt

Yogurt has many flavor assets — it is savory, creamy, and acidic. Because of that, yogurt can accompany a variety of dishes from the spicy (to cool it down), to the savory where it is used as a marinade due to its acidity, and to the sweet where it is added on top of desserts. It can add creaminess without saturated fats to meat dishes, dry dishes (grains, waffles, latkes), spread on pitas and flatbreads, mixed into dressings and used as a dip for raw vegetables. The options are almost endless.

Making yogurt is super easy. There are three steps to making your own yogurt — heating, which unwinds the curd proteins and removes unwanted bacteria, cooling the milk to a temperature where healthful bacteria can thrive, and then fermenting the warm milk with bacteria (McGee, 2004).

Milk
- Dairy — full-fat or reduced-fat
- Goat, sheep
- Plant-based — coconut (do not need to heat and cool down)

Heat
- Cook dairy milks at 185 °F/ 85 °C for 10 minutes
- This denatures the whey protein

Bacteria
- Cool the milk to between 86 °F and 104 °F/ 30 °C and 45 °C. At higher tempertures the yogurt will set within 2 hours. At lower temperatures it can take 18 hours.
- Add bacteria (3 tablespoons per quart of milk) from the previous batch or a store bought yogurt with live probiotics, or add *Streptococcus thermophilis* and *Lactobacillus delbrueckii*

Set
- Let rest for 6 to 8 hours in room temperature (in the oven with the light on and no heat works well too)
- For a Greek yogurt, strain the yogurt through a cheesecloth for several hours
- Place in the refrigerator for up to two weeks

Yogurt-Based Sauces

Tzatziki Sauce

Ingredients
- English cucumber 1 small grated without seeds
- Greek yogurt 1 cup
- Lemon juice 1 tablespoon + 1 teaspoon zest
- Garlic 1 clove minced
- Salt ½ teaspoon
- Dill chopped 1 tablespoon
- Mint leaves chopped 1 tablespoon
- Black pepper to taste

Instructions:
1. Prepare the cucumber: Peel the cucumber if it has a thick skin. Remove any seeds and grate. Squeeze any water out by placing the grated cucumber in a clean kitchen towel and wring out the water.

2. Add all ingredients, stir, and enjoy. Allowing the sauce to marinate for at least 2 hours will improve the flavor.

Thickening Sauces
- Yogurt can be used to thicken sauces as long as the heat is only moderate. The sauce will curdle if it reaches boiling. Yogurt adds thickness – as opposed to thickening the liquid – as the casein proteins are already coagulated. Tips to using yogurt as a thickener:
  - Remove the watery whey before adding yogurt as a thickener
  - Add yogurt toward the end of cooking when the dish is cooling, not simmering
  - Beware when using yogurt in an acidic sauce (tomatoes for example) as that will cause it to curdle. To prevent this, lower the heat and use full-fat yogurt (the fat prevents casein proteins from combining)
  - Do not beat the yogurt in sauces vigorously, fold or gently stir instead

Making a White Sauce – Béchamel

A béchamel sauce is a classic French white sauce that is used to make lasagna, creamed chicken, the gravy in a pot pie and much more. There are three basic ingredients plus optional added flavors — salt and nutmeg. Cheese can also be added to make a cheese sauce.

- To make a classic béchamel the ratio of butter: flour: milk is 1 tablespoon: 1 tablespoon: 1 cup.

- To make a béchamel with skim milk, an extra tablespoon of flour is needed for every cup of milk (Lighter Béchamel | Cook's Illustrated)

- For a low-fat version made with olive oil and low-fat milk, The New York Times has a great recipe using 2 tablespoons flour, 2 tablespoons olive oil, and 2 cups 1% (low fat) milk. (Olive Oil Béchamel Recipe).

The key to making this white sauce is to melt the fat (butter or oil) and combine with the flour. Let it cook for several minutes, which will reduce the taste of the flour. Then add the milk slowly, heat on medium (stirring occasionally) until thickened, and add cheese or spices if desired.

Milk and Heat

When cooking with dairy, it is important to not heat the milk too high (do not boil unless directed) as this will lead to curdling. Curdling occurs because the whey protein unfolds (denatures) and binds with the casein creating clumps of protein. To undo this, place in a blender.

Desserts or Breakfast

Yogurt Parfaits

Layer in a glass or bowl yogurt, granola, and fruit. This makes a great breakfast, snack, or dessert item.

Cottage Cheese and Fruit

Add fresh fruit to cottage cheese for a quick and sweet/ savory breakfast, lunch, or a snack. Yum!

Cheese and Fruit Plate

Fresh figs, grapes, pears and apples pair very well with a touch of cheese. Add the ingredients to a plate with nuts for a delicious snack or dessert. For a pop of eye-appeal, drizzle a bit of honey on top.

SECTION 14: SERVING DAIRY

Table 3 lays out the number of dairy or dairy equivalents recommended per day (3 cups a day for those nine years of age and older) and Table 10 defines a dairy equivalent. Refer to previous sections to decide which type of dairy products to serve. Because of the health value of probiotics, it makes sense to have yogurt as one of the dairy servings per day. That leaves one or two cups of milk to consume at mealtime or between meals as part of a snack.

Tale 11: Dairy Equivalents

	Amount That Counts as 1 Cup in the Dairy Group
Milk	1 cup milk
	1 half-pint container milk
	½ cup evaporated milk
	1 cup calcium-fortified soy milk
	1 half-pint container calcium-fortified soy milk
Yogurt	1 cup yogurt (dairy or fortified soy)
Cheese	1 ½ ounces hard cheese (cheddar, mozzarella, Swiss, Parmesan)
	⅓ cup shredded cheese
	1 ounce processed cheese (American)
	½ cup ricotta cheese
	2 cups cottage cheese
	2 ounces Queso fresco
	2 slices Queso blanco

Copied from https://www.myplate.gov/eat-healthy/dairy

The Culinary Institute of America Menus of Change recommends "reimaging dairy in a supporting role" (CIA & Harvard TH Chan, 2020). For example, instead of making a cheesy white sauce for pasta, create an olive oil herb blend and top with grated cheese; replace butter with oil; and use yogurt without added sugar.

SUMMARY

Milk products have been a staple in the diets of many cultures around the world and continue to be an important nutritional source for people today. Dairy foods are high in essential nutrients including protein, fats, calcium, magnesium, potassium, vitamin B_{12} and riboflavin among others. The micronutrients in milk products are highly bioavailable. Milk in the U.S. is also fortified with vitamin D, making it one of the few food sources of this important nutrient. Fermented milk and yogurt also provide additional benefits through their effects on the microbiome.

Despite initial concern over the potential impact of the saturated fat content of dairy foods, studies show that those who consume higher quantities of dairy products tend to have lower rates of cardiovascular disease, type 2 diabetes, and cancer. This may be in part due to the food matrix effect, or the structure of the specific fats found in dairy foods, as well as other beneficial nutrients such as calcium, potassium, magnesium and phosphorus present in milk products. Milk products are an excellent source of highly bioavailable calcium, which is important for bone health and the prevention of osteoporosis. Americans generally consume far less than the recommended number of servings of dairy foods, and more emphasis on the inclusion of dairy as part of a healthy eating pattern may be warranted.

For those who cannot tolerate dairy or for various other reasons prefer plant-based milks, the next section summarizes these beverages and their by-products.

APPENDIX A: USDA Dairy Recommendations Over Time

Date	Recommendation	Food Guide
1930s	2 cups of milk	H.K. Stiebeling
1940s	2 cups or more of milk and milk products	Basic Seven Foundation Diet
1956 to 1970s	Milk group – 2 cups or more	Basic Seven Foundation Diet
1979	Milk-cheese group – 2 (1 cup, 1 ½ oz cheese)	Hassle-Free Foundation Diet
1984	Milk, yogurt, cheese – 2 to 3	Food Guide Pyramid Diet
2005	Consume 3 cups per day of fat-free or low-fat milk or equivalent milk products. Avoid raw (unpasteurized) milk or any products made from unpasteurized milk.	2005 - 2010 DGA
2010	Increase intake of fat-free or low-fat milk and milk products, such as milk, yogurt, cheese, or fortified soy beverages. Choose foods that provide more potassium, dietary fiber, calcium, and vitamin D, which are nutrients of concern in American diets. These foods include vegetables, fruits, whole grains, and milk and milk products.	2010 - 2015 DGA
2015	A healthy eating pattern includes – Fat-free or low-fat dairy, including milk, yogurt, cheese, and/or fortified soy beverages	2015-2020 DGA
2020	Core elements that make up a healthy dietary pattern include – Dairy, including fat-free or low-fat milk, yogurt, and cheese, and/or lactose-free versions and fortified soy beverages and yogurt as alternatives. All fluid, dry, or evaporated milk, including lactose-free and lactose-reduced products and fortified soy beverages (soy milk), buttermilk, yogurt, kefir, frozen yogurt, dairy desserts, and cheeses. Most choices should be fat-free or low-fat. Cream, sour cream, and cream cheese are not included due to their low calcium content.	2020-2025 DGA

https://www.ers.usda.gov/webdocs/publications/42215/5831_aib750b_1_.pdf
https://www.ncbi.nlm.nih.gov/books/NBK469839/

PLANT-BASED MILK ALTERNATIVES

Joi Lenczowski MD, Dana Henderson MS RD CDCES,
Caroline Rosseler MS RD, and Deborah Koehn MD, FACP, BC-ADM, ABCL

Humans have consumed the milk of buffalo, camel, sheep, goats, horses and yaks for thousands of years. While cow's milk remains the most produced and consumed milk beverage worldwide, production and consumption of plant-based milk alternatives are steadily rising. Milk sales in the United States decreased from 55,003 million pounds sold in 2010 to 47,672 million pounds sold in 2018, accounting for a $1.1 billion sales decline in 2018 alone (Dairy Farmers of America). Conversely, plant-based milk alternative sales grew by 9% in 2018, accounting for a growth of $1.6 billion in sales (Singh et al., 2015).

Plant-based milk alternatives are fluids resulting from the size reduction of plant materials extracted in water and homogenized. Although there are numerous types of plant-based milk alternatives, they can be categorized into five main groups, based on their plant origin (Sethi et al., 2016):

1. **Cereal-based**: oat milk, rice milk, corn milk, spelt milk
2. **Legume-based**: soy milk, peanut milk, lupin milk, pea milk
3. **Nut-based**: almond milk, coconut milk, hazelnut milk, pistachio milk, walnut milk
4. **Seed-based**: sesame milk, flax milk, hemp milk, sunflower milk
5. **Pseudo-cereal-based**: quinoa milk, teff milk, amaranth milk

Among these groups, plant-based milk alternatives vary in their production methods, nutritional content, market presence, and sensory qualities. The Food and Drug Administration (FDA) does not have a standard of identity for these beverages, so be sure to read the list of ingredients and nutrition facts panel. For example, soy milk is the oldest plant-based milk alternative on the market and has been touted for its isoflavones' protective effects against cancer, cardiovascular disease, and osteoporosis. However, many consumers were deterred by its beany flavor, resulting in more modern production methods including vacuum treatment at high temperatures to strip the more volatile compounds. Alternatively, newer plant-based milk alternatives, such as quinoa, hemp, and sunflower have limited market presence and research on their nutritional benefits. Production methods of these products continue to evolve with consumer preference, ranging from blending varieties of milk for texture to fortifying products to meet consumers' health needs.

SECTION 1: REASONS CONSUMERS SWITCH TO PLANT-BASED MILK ALTERNATIVES

Specific preferences aside, there are medical — including **allergies and intolerance** — and **ethical reasons** consumers are switching to plant-based beverages. Cow's milk allergy is one of the most common food allergies during the first year of life, with developed countries' prevalence ranging from 0.5% to 3% (Flom & Sicherer, 2019). Lactose intolerance is far more common. Lactose malabsorption, a precondition for lactose intolerance, may be as high as 68% worldwide (Misselwitz et al., 2019). Lactose intolerance varies among populations (see Table 7), with rates ranging as low as 5% in British populations to almost 100% in some Asian countries (Lomer et al., 2008).

As there is tremendous variability in the nutrient profiles among different plant-based milk alternatives, individuals may also choose one of these beverages to better support their **specific dietary concerns**. For example, individuals with diabetes may prefer the lower carbohydrate content of almond milk (4 g) compared to cow's milk (12 g) or oat milk (24 g).

Fat and thus calorie content is also extremely variable among plant-based milk alternatives so those trying to lose weight or reduce their saturated fat consumption may opt for a lower-fat variety while those trying to gain weight may opt for a higher fat variety.

Many popular varieties, such as almond and cashew milk, only contain 1 g of fat and 40 to 60 kilocalories per cup while coconut milk can contain up to 42 g of fat and 424 kilocalories per cup.

Most plant-based milk alternatives are low in protein, ranging between 1 gram to 4 grams of protein per cup compared to the 8 grams in cow's milk. However, those looking for a higher protein variety may opt for a soy (8 grams) or pea milk (8 grams). Micronutrient content varies widely between milks due to manufacturing differences including processing and fortification (see section 2).

Consumers may also switch to plant-based beverages due to ethical reasons regarding animal welfare and environmental impact. Controversial practices of dairying include artificial insemination, removal of calves from their mother hours after birth, and the killing of male calves, and consumers concerned by these practices may shift their shopping habits. Additionally, many plant-  based beverage consumers are attracted to the smaller ecological footprint of nondairy milk; one glass of dairy milks results in almost three times the greenhouse gas emissions, land use, and water use of any nondairy milks (Poore & Nemecek, 2018).

 With the rise of plant-based milk alternatives, consumers are often confused by the labeling of plant-based beverages as "milks," and thus may not understand the nutritional differences between dairy milk and plant-based milk alternatives. A recent Consumer Reports found that more than half of people who buy plant-based milk alternatives believe these beverages are more healthful than cow's milk (Meltzer Warren, 2019). According to the FDA definition, milk is defined as "the lacteal secretion, practically free from colostrum, obtained by the complete milking of one or more healthy cows." The FDA has not set a standard of identity for plant-based milk alternatives, and in the past few years, bills — including the Dairy Pride Act — have been introduced upon the continued insistence of dairy farmers to limit the use of the word "milk" to animal-produced beverage. While this and other bills may protect the interest of dairy farmers and their product(s), it may also

be of benefit to consumers as it will make the nutritional differences between cow's milk and plant-based milk alternatives more explicit and may lead consumers to make a more informed beverage choice.

SECTION 2: COMPARISON OF NUTRIENTS

The focus of this section is on the nutrients present in cow's milk that are also found in alternate sources. This is important to note as when replacing, for example, dairy products in the Mediterranean diet with plant-based milk alternatives, one cannot assume the health benefits are the same due to the specific nutrient profile of dairy milk and food matrix effects. The major nutrients that this section will highlight are calcium, vitamin D, protein, vitamin B_{12} and saturated fat. In Table 12 and Table 13 is a comparison on nutrients in cow's milk versus plant-based milk alternatives.

> With the exception of soy milk, other plant-based milks are not to be considered as part of the dairy group and therefore do not count toward the daily dairy recommendation (U.S. Department of Agriculture and U.S. Department of Health and Human Services, 2020).

Many plant-based milk alternatives are fortified with important nutrients — both macro and micronutrients — that are either lost during processing or not present in adequate amounts in the first place. Note that some fortified nutrients may be more or less bioavailable than their naturally occurring counterparts found in cow's milk, and also that many micronutrients are not measured in plant-based dairy alternatives, so they are unable to be compared (R. P. Heaney et al., 2005). In addition, many retailers are now producing plant-based dairy alternative blends by blending at least two plant-based products together to maximize nutrient offerings.

Table 12: Macronutrient Composition of Cow's Milk and Plant-based Milk Alternatives per 8 oz serving

Type	Product Name	Energy (kcal)	Protein (g)	Fat (g)	Saturated fat (g)	Carbo-hydrate (g)	Fiber (g)	Sugars (g)	Added Sugars (g)
Cow's milk	2% Cow's milk	122	8.2	4.7	2.7	12	0	12	0
Almond	Silk Original	60	1	2.5	0	8	0	7	7
	Almond Breeze Original	60	1	2.5	0	8	<1	7	7

Cashew	Pacific Foods Original	80	1	4.5	0.5	8	N/A	6	5
Coconut	So Delicious Original (diluted beverage)	70	0	4.5	4	9	1	7	7
	Thai Kitchen (canned)	360	0	36	30	3	0	3	N/A
Combination	Silk Original Protein (Pea, Almond and Cashew)	130	10	8	0.5	3	<1	2	2
Flax	Good Karma Original	50	0	2.5	N/A	7	0	7	7
Hemp	Living Harvest/ Tempt Original	101	2	7	0.5	8	0	6	N/A
Oat	Oatly Original	120	3	5	0.5	16	1.9	7	N/A
	Planet Oat Original	90	2	1.5	2	19	2	4	4
Pea	Ripple Un-sweetened Original	80	8	4.5	0.5	<1	<1	0	0
Rice	Rice Dream Original	130	0	2.5	0	27	0	12	12
Soy	Silk Original	110	8	4.5	0.5	9	2	6	5

Sources: (DREAM Plant Based, 2022; Planet Oat, 2022; Ripple Foods, 2022; Silk, 2022; So Delicious Dairy Free, 2022; USDA, 2018)

Table 13: Micronutrient Composition of Cow's Milk and Plant-based Milk Alternatives per 8 oz serving

Type	Product Name	Calcium (mg)	Vit D (IU)	Iron (mg)	Potassium (mg)	Sodium (mg)	Vit B$_{12}$ (mcg)	Vit A (IU)
Cow's Milk	2% Cow's milk	309	111	0	390	95.6	1.4	677
Almond	Silk Original	450	100	0.5	0	150	N/A	500
	Almond Breeze Original	450	200	0.7	170	150	N/A	500
Cashew	Pacific Foods Original	44	N/A	N/A	N/A	95	N/A	N/A
Coconut	So Delicious Original (diluted beverage)	130	100	0.3	40	10	3	140
	Thai Kitchen (canned)	0	N/A	1.1	N/A	N/A	N/A	0
Combination	Silk Original (Pea, Almond and Cashew)	450	100	1.7	80	230	N/A	N/A
Flax	Good Karma Original	N/A	N/A	N/A	N/A	80	N/A	N/A
Hemp	Living Harvest/ Tempt Original	300	101	1	N/A	110	1.5	499
Oat	Oatly Original	350	N/A	0.3	389	101	1.2	N/A
	Planet Oat Original	350	160	0.3	400	120	0.2	600
Pea	Ripple Unsweetened Original	440	240	0	405	125	2.5	367
Rice	Rice Dream Original	20	0	0.5	30	95	N/A	N/A
Soy	Silk Original	450	120	1.3	380	90	3	500

Sources: (DREAM Plant Based, 2022; Planet Oat, 2022; Ripple Foods, 2022; Silk, 2022; So Delicious Dairy Free, 2022; USDA, 2018)

Calcium

As previously discussed, calcium is the most abundant mineral in the body whose functions include supporting bone health, regulating blood pH, and regulating muscle and nerve function. The calcium content in 8 oz cow's milk is about 30% of the daily value, or about 300 mg, but calcium does not naturally occur in adequate amounts in plant-based milk alternatives. Thus, most plant-based milk alternatives are fortified with calcium in the form of calcium carbonate, often to a level even higher than in cow's milk. However, the simple addition of calcium does not mean nutritional equivalence (Singhal et al., 2017). Calcium in cow's milk is highly bioavailable, due in part to the presence of lactose and casein that aid in intestinal absorption. The calcium in plant-based milk alternatives does not have the help of lactose and casein, and additional compounds like phytic acid that are present in many plant-based products may further impede absorption, making the calcium in plant-based milks less bioavailable.

Table 14: Amount of Calcium in Dairy and Plant-Based Milk

Type of "Milk"	Amount*
Cow	300 mg
Almond	22 to 495 mg
Soy	0 to 385 mg
Rice	22 to 330 mg
Coconut	44 to 495 mg

*Higher amounts reflect the amount of calcium being added to the product
Source: (Vanga & Raghavan, 2018a)

Vitamin D

Recall that vitamin D is not found in many foods but is required for the proper absorption and function of calcium as well as for cell differentiation and growth, regulation of phosphorous, immune health, blood pressure regulation and blood sugar regulation.

The FDA ruled in 2016 that plant-based milk beverages may be fortified with up to 205 IU of vitamin D per serving, which could make them better sources of vitamin D than cow's milk. The new nutrition label requires that the amount of vitamin D is to be listed, so consumers will be better able to meet and track their vitamin D intake from plant-based milk alternatives (Harrar, S, 2016).

There are two different forms of vitamin D, though only one is typically used for fortification. The vitamin D in fortified cow's milk is vitamin D_3, the type of vitamin D derived from animals, and is also the type commonly found in plant-based dairy alternatives (Armas et al., 2004; Singhal et al., 2017). The other form, vitamin D_2, is derived from plants and is a good option for supplementation for strict vegetarians or vegans. Additional differences in vitamins D_3 and D_2 are listed in Table 15.

Table 15: Types of Vitamin D

Vitamin D_3	Vitamin D_2
Cholecalciferol	Ergocalciferol
From animal sources	From plant sources
More expensive	Cheaper
Better at raising serum levels of 25(OH)D when a bolus dose (large dose) was given	Raises serum levels of 25(OH)D to the same degree when given as a daily supplement

Source: (Tripkovic et al., 2012)

Protein
Protein is an important macronutrient whose functions include muscle and connective tissue development, enzyme production, and antibody development, among others. Amino acids act as the building block of proteins, and the amino acids present in a protein food can make the food either a complete or an incomplete protein. Complete proteins are those which contain all nine essential amino acids, which must be consumed from the diet, and offer the most bioavailable form of protein from a singular source. Complete proteins are found in animal products, such as cow's milk, as well as the plant-based proteins **soy, amaranth, and quinoa**. Incomplete proteins are proteins that offer some of the essential amino acids, but not all nine. Incomplete proteins are also typically less bioavailable than complete proteins.

In contrast to cow's milk which provides about 8 grams of protein per 8 oz serving, many of the plant-based dairy alternatives on the shelves are low in protein (as low as 1 gram per 8 oz serving) with inadequate information on the types of amino acids present. One exception is soy and pea milk beverages which offer about 8 grams of protein per 8 oz (Parrish, 2018; Singhal et al., 2017). Some plant-based dairy alternatives are fortified with pea protein to increase protein content, however, pea protein is not considered a complete protein.

When thinking about sources of protein, it's also important to consider the quality of protein from those sources. The digestible indispensable amino acids score (DIAAS) is one measure of protein digestibility and degree of absorption. Using this method, dairy proteins can be considered "excellent/high" quality sources of protein with DIAAS $\geq$100, soy protein qualifies as a "good" source of protein with DIAAS between 75 and 100, and pea protein is a lower quality protein with DIASS <75 (Mathai et al., 2017). If an individual is relying on a plant-based milk alternative as a significant source of protein in their diet, it's important to recognize the difference in protein quality and be sure there are other sources of quality protein in the diet if needed.

Vitamin B$_{12}$
Recall that vitamin B$_{12}$ is a water-soluble vitamin that is involved in many processes in the body including red blood cell production, nerve cell development, DNA production and metabolism. It is found naturally only in animal source foods, but milk alternatives may be fortified with B$_{12}$, up to 3.01 µg per 8 oz serving, more than double the amount found in cow's milk however the details regarding the source of fortification and bioavailability are not available in the current research (Parrish, 2018; Singhal et al., 2017). Plant-based milk alternatives can be an important source of vitamin B$_{12}$ for strict vegetarians and vegans who consume little to no natural sources of this vitamin.

Saturated Fat

Saturated fat is a type of fat typically associated with animal products, though it is also found in foods or products containing coconut or palm oil. A diet high in saturated fats is associated with unfavorable health outcomes, such as cardiovascular disease and metabolic syndrome, while research has shown that replacing saturated fats in the diet with unsaturated fats shows more favorable outcomes for health (De Lorgeril et al., 1996; Nordmann et al., 2011).

The USDA recommends less than 10% of calories from saturated fats in the 2020-2025 Dietary Guidelines for Americans (U.S. Department of Agriculture and U.S. Department of Health and Human Services, 2020). Many milk alternatives contain only a small amount of unsaturated fat and are free of saturated fat. One exception to this is coconut milk as it does contain some saturated fat (Parrish, 2018).

Iodine

Iodine is a mineral that is essential for hormone synthesis, and milk is often one of the main dietary sources of iodine. Plant-based milk alternatives tend to have a low iodine concentration and the fortification of iodine in these beverages is inconsistent. Individuals who avoid dairy products and opt instead for milk alternatives may be at risk of iodine deficiency (Eveleigh et al., 2022). In fact, a recent study that examined data from the U.K. National Diet and Nutrition Study found that iodine intake and markers of iodine status were lower in exclusive consumers of plant-based milk alternatives than in cows' milk consumers, and as a group the exclusive consumers of plant-based milk alternatives were classified as iodine deficient by the World Health Organization criterion (Dineva et al., 2021).

SECTION 3: EMULSIFIERS IN PLANT-BASED MILK ALTERNATIVES

Plant-based milk alternatives can have many different types of additives, the most common of which is an emulsifier. Since plant-based beverages are often a mixture of oil and water, a hydrocolloid — a substance that has both a hydrophobic and hydrophilic component — helps to keep the composition smooth and silky.

Interestingly, emulsifiers can originate from animals (gelatin), plants (guar gum, pectin), aquatic plants (seaweeds), microbes (xanthan gum and gellan gum) and/or be synthetically produced such as lecithin. They have a long cultural history, with Asian countries using seaweed, the Americas using fruit pectin, and Mediterranean countries using locust bean gum. In Table 16, emulsifiers that are used within the plant-based beverages are listed. See Appendix A for common plant-based milk alternatives for the type of emulsifier used in each.

Table 16: Safety of Emulsifiers Used in Plant-Based Milk Alternatives

Emulsifier	Source	Safety
Carrageenan	Seaweed	Non-carcinogenic, tumorigenic, genotoxic or reproductively toxic. It is a safe food additive and is released into the feces unchanged [a].
Sodium Alginate	Seaweed	It has been proven to be a safe additive. Caution with infants and young children [b]
Xanthan Gum	Fermented Polysaccharide	Unlikely to be absorbed by the intestinal tract and is partially fermented by the intestinal microbiota in the large intestine. No carcinogenicity effects were seen at the highest doses. Since Xanthan gum is not absorbed by the intestines it can result in abdominal discomfort at higher doses as it acts as a bulk laxative [c].
Gellan Gum	Fermented polysaccharide	At this time, no known genotoxicity, carcinogenic toxicity or reproductive toxicity has been identified in the use of gellan gum [d].
Lecithin	Soybean, egg yolk, sunflower oil, or rape seed oil	At this time, no genotoxicity or carcinogenicity has been identified; however, some animal studies have generated concern about choline's impact on neurodevelopment. Consequently, recommendations at this time include limiting exposure to large doses of lecithin during gestation, lactation, and post-weaning period. In addition, sensitive individuals should avoid this additive as some hypersensitivity can occur to residual soy and egg proteins in the extracted lecithin [e].
Guar Gum	Seed gums	No adverse effects were reported in sub-chronic and carcinogenicity studies at the highest dose tested; no concern with respect to the genotoxicity. No adequate assessment has been done in infants and young children [f.]

a (McKim et al, 2019), b (EFSA Panel, 2017d), c (EFSA Panel, 2017c), d (EFSA Panel, 2018), e (EFSA Panel, 2017b), f (EFSA Panel, 2017a)

In general, most added emulsifiers used in plant-based milk alternatives are safe for adults without any concern for toxicity, though the data is lacking for infants and young children. Lecithin may be harmful for individuals, fetuses and infants who are hypersensitive to egg. Since emulsifiers are complex polysaccharides that pass through the gut without being absorbed or minimally modified by the gut bacteria, they can act as a stool bulking agent. There is potential that these stool bulking emulsifiers can lower cholesterol and blood sugar but at the same time increase stool frequency and flatulence.

SECTION 4: HEALTH BENEFITS OF PLANT-BASED MILK ALTERNATIVES

There is minimal direct research on the health benefits of plant-based milk alternatives. Extrapolation from data derived from health benefits of the basic source of the milk, e.g., soybeans, almonds, or such, may not be justified, as the primary source is modified in commercial production. This modification results in both loss of primary components and addition of supplements. However, there are still some important things to note.

Soy milk and health

Diabetes

Currently, no consensus is available on the impact of soy milk on overall health. Multiple studies have shown a decreased incidence of type 2 diabetes mellitus (T2DM) with ingestion of soy products, primarily tofu. However, studies directly investigating soy milk have reported conflicting results, with both increased risk and decreased risk of T2DM. Nguyen et al noted that a higher dietary intake of soy-foods and isoflavones lowers the risk of T2DM, and this decreased risk was also noted with increased soy milk ingestion (Nguyen et al., 2017). A similar inverse association between soy milk ingestion and T2DM was reported in a sub-analysis of the Shanghai Women's Health Study (Villegas et al., 2008).

However, a study based on data from the Singapore Chinese Health Study (SCHS), a population-based, prospective investigation, found that while consumption of unsweetened non-fried whole soy proteins decreased the risk of T2DM, ingestion of sweetened soymilk beverages was associated with an increased risk of T2DM. In this study, however, 17 grams of added sugar were present per serving of soy milk, complicating the interpretation of the data (Mueller et al., 2012). It is possible that unsweetened soy milk decreases the risk for T2DM, but current research is not conclusive.

Lipid Levels

Research studies are conflicted in their results on the impact of soy milk on lipid profiles. A randomized controlled trial with 31 participants comparing two different commercially available soy milks versus low-fat dairy milk concluded that a 25 g dose of daily soy protein from soy milk led to a modest 5% lowering of LDL-C relative to dairy milk among adults with elevated LDL-C. The effect did not differ by type of soy milk and neither did soy milk significantly affect other lipid variables, insulin, or glucose (Gardner et al., 2007). In contrast, a single-blind randomized trial with 32 postmenopausal women comparing vanilla soymilk and reduced-fat dairy milk showed no significant difference in total, HDL, or LDL cholesterol or triglyceride levels with ingestion of three daily servings of soy milk, (21 g soy protein) (Beavers et al., 2010).

Oat Milk and Health

Oat milk ingestion has been associated with small decreases in total cholesterol and LDL cholesterol when used as a replacement for cow's milk. Two randomized clinical trials of oat milk versus soy milk, rice milk, or cow's milk (<70 participants each) showed a 4% to 9% decrease in total and LDL cholesterol levels with ingestion of oat milk. The high content of beta-glucans in oat milk may be responsible for the decreased plasma cholesterol and LDL cholesterol concentrations, however, the effect could also be due to a replacement of saturated fat by unsaturated fat. Oat milk can be recommended as an alternative to other milk drinks for patients who would benefit from reduced LDL cholesterol values (Onning et al., 1998, 1999).

Almond Milk and Health

Despite the considerable literature on the health benefits of almonds, such as improved glycemic control, there is currently no literature systematically investigating the impact of almond milk on health.

SECTION 5: POTENTIAL RISK OF CONSUMING PLANT-BASED MILK ALTERNATIVES

Arsenic in Rice Milk

Recently there has been concern about arsenic in rice and rice products as one's lifetime exposure to arsenic can increase their risk for bladder and lung cancer. The attributable risk from rice and rice products to bladder and lung cancer remains small at 39 cases per million people (compared to 90,000 total cases of bladder and lung cancer per million people over a lifetime). Risk increases though with increased daily servings of rice and rice products (U.S. Food and Drug Administration, 2016).

Regulations in the European Union and the U.S. state that arsenic levels in drinking water should not exceed 10 micrograms/L (Meharg et al., 2008). However, there have been reports that have found arsenic levels in rice milk that exceed these limits. For example, Meharg and colleagues found a mean arsenic level of 22 micrograms/L among 15 rice milks with a range of 10.2 to 33.3 micrograms/L, and Shannon & Rodriguez found an average arsenic concentration of 7.1 micrograms/L with a range of 2.7 to 17.9 micrograms/L among 15 rice milk samples (Meharg et al., 2008; Shannon & Rodriguez, 2014). The decision whether or not to recommend rice milk in a person's diet should be weighed against the consumption of other rice and rice products in the individual's diet.

Effect of Plant-Based Milk Alternatives on Dentition

Risk of cavity formation due to ingestion of plant-based milk alternatives has been studied in in-vitro models of biofilm formation. Based on these investigations, unsweetened almond milk has the lowest potential to contribute to dental caries, while soy milk has the highest potential. Almond milk sweetened with sucrose does have an increased risk of contributing to dental cavities. Thus, for patients who are lactose-intolerant or suffer from milk allergy, unsweetened almond milk is a better alternative than soy-based products with respect to dental health (Lee et al., 2018).

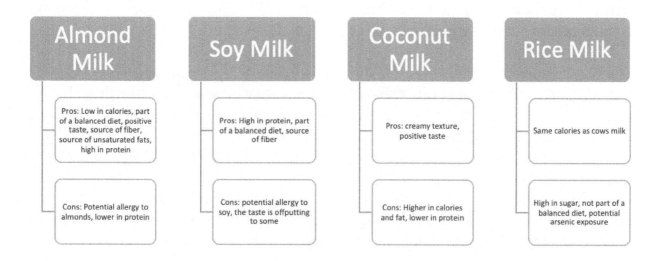

In summary, some plant-based milk alternatives can provide a nutrient profile similar to cow's milk (not identical) as long as the following is met:

- Make sure the plant-based milk has vitamin B_{12} added (1.29 μg), or find an alternate source of B_{12} in the diet, especially for vegetarians
- Calcium is added to provide at least 300 mg — preferably in the form of calcium carbonate
- Vitamin D is added to provide 120 IU — vitamin D_3, which is sourced from animals is better absorbed than D_2 — for vegetarians make sure there are other sources as well
- If protein is a concern, choose soy milk, pea protein milk, or a milk blend with added pea protein that contains at least 5 to 6 grams of protein per 8 oz serving.

SECTION 6: INFANTS, CHILDREN, AND PLANT-BASED MILK ALTERNATIVES

Breast milk or an iron-fortified infant formula should be an infant's sole food source during the first four to six months of life. After one year, the USDA recommends infants over one year of age consume two to three servings of whole cow's milk per day for a nutritionally complete diet. This suggested amount makes up roughly 25% to 30% of total energy needs of those one to three years and provides numerous macro- and micronutrients, including protein, fat, calcium, phosphorus and vitamin B_{12} (Drewnowski, 2011; Fox et al., 2006; Grimes et al., 2017; Groetch & Nowak-Wegrzyn, 2013). Over the past several years, more parents have been opting for plant-based milk alternatives due to allergies, intolerances, cultural traditions or health beliefs. A plant-based milk alternative should provide a similar nutrient profile as cow's milk, or attention is needed to make sure these nutrients are provided elsewhere in the child's diet. Severe nutrient deficiencies have been reported in young infants and children using plant-based milks without proper nutritional guidance (Le Louer et al., 2014).

The North American Society for Pediatric Gastroenterology, Hepatology, and Nutrition (NASPGHAN) claims that **soy milk and soy formula may be a suitable substitute** for the majority of infants and young children. However, parents opting for almond, rice, coconut, hemp, flaxseed and cashew milks should be advised that these products have inadequate nutrient profiles to meet the nutritional needs for protein, calcium, and vitamin D. While these products can be included safely as a component of the diet, families with children where cow's milk is medically contraindicated or not culturally appropriate should receive special counseling from clinicians or registered dietitians to determine alternative dietary sources of protein, calcium, iron, vitamin B_{12} and vitamin D (Merritt et al., 2020).

SECTION 7: THE ELDERLY AND PLANT-BASED MILK ALTERNATIVES

Similar to the way plant-based milk alternatives should be approached with caution for infants and young children, they may also be problematic for the elderly. Older individuals have limited appetites and consume fewer calories, so the foods they do consume must be nutrient-dense in order for their nutrient needs to be met. In this population especially, poor nutrition could induce frailty and speed the progression of chronic disease.

It is well established that adequate calcium and protein intake in the elderly can delay sarcopenia and bone loss (Lana et al., 2015). Dairy products are good sources of these important nutrients, but it's unclear if the same benefits could be gained from fortified plant-based milk alternatives, especially if the bioavailability of the protein, vitamin, and mineral content of these beverages is in question. Some researchers have suggested that increasing plant-based foods, including plant-based milk alternatives, and reducing animal-based products could have unintended consequences on the protein intake of older adults and put them at risk of nutrient deficiencies (Houchins et al., 2017; Scholz-Ahrens et al., 2020). Like with infants and children, if older adults wish to consume a plant-based milk alternative or are required to do so for medical reasons, it is important to be sure that they are consuming sufficient amounts of protein, vitamins, and minerals elsewhere in their diet.

SECTION 8: ENVIRONMENTAL CONSIDERATIONS OF PLANT-BASED MILK ALTERNATIVES

It is well established that the production of dairy products from cow's milk has a significant environmental impact, but plant-based milk alternatives also come with an environmental impact of their own. One thing to keep in mind is that different producers and manufacturers may have different processing methods that impact the beverage's environmental impact, so even plant-based milk alternatives from the same plant source may not be equivalent.

The first environmental issue that comes to mind regarding plant-based milk alternatives is **water usage**. Almond milk especially has a high water footprint, and a recent study calculated that it takes 3.2 gallons of water to grow a single almond (Fulton et al., 2019). This becomes especially problematic considering that about 80% of the world's almonds are grown in California, an area with ongoing concerns regarding their water supply (USDA Foreign Agricultural Service). Of all the plant-based milk alternatives, oats generally use the least water and soy and pea are a close second. Hemp farming requires more water than these three but still less than almond (Mekonnen & Hoekstra, 2010).

Land use is another environmental factor to consider. Soybeans require a lot of land compared to other plants like almonds or rice (Poore & Nemecek, 2018). On the other hand, soybeans and peas are nitrogen-fixing plants, so they naturally add nitrogen back into the soil, eliminating the need for nitrogen-containing fertilizers.

GHG emissions associated with plant-based milk alternatives are certainly lower than cow's milk. Soy and pea protein milks have comparable GHG emissions, and a study by the brand Oatly found that oat milk production results in 80% lower GHG emissions and uses 60% lower energy than cow's milk (Climate Footprint).

While plant-based milk alternatives have a lower impact on the environment overall, the issue is more complex as cow's milk contains several key nutrients that prove to be challenging to replace (Vanga & Raghavan, 2018b). In a recent modeling study by Cifelli and colleagues, a nutritionally optimal diet that eliminates dairy foods requires a greater volume of food and more calories and still falls short of several key nutrients (Cifelli et al., 2020). Additionally, an optimal dietary pattern that incorporates plant-based milk alternatives may cost up to six times as much as a diet that follows the USDA pattern that incorporates dairy. While a diet that removes dairy may lead to lower GHG emissions, careful consideration needs to be given to nutritional adequacy.

SECTION 9: CLINICAL AND CULINARY RECOMMENDATIONS AND COMPETENCIES

1. Identify the plant-based milk alternative for the infant and young child.
2. Compare and contrast "good sources" of nutrients in dairy versus plant-based milk.
3. List the advantages and disadvantages of replacing dairy with various plant-based milks.
4. Choose a plant-based milk based on the nutrient(s) needed.
5. Make a plant-based milk (optional).

SECTION 10: AT THE STORE

Steps to Choosing a Plant-Based Milk Alternative

There is no one-size-fits-all when selecting plant-based milk alternatives at the store as it depends on what purpose the beverage needs to serve. For example, reasons can include that you want it to be:

- **Similar to dairy in its overall nutrient profile**. For various reasons described previously, individuals switch to a plant-based milk alternative and many do so not realizing that dairy comes with its unique nutrient profile. Reasons may include it being:
  - A substitute when following the Mediterranean diet. In this case, data is not sufficient enough to say the benefits of following a Mediterranean diet would be the same if for example soy milk was substituted for dairy.

- A dairy substitute for children after weaning. As described above, NASPGHAN suggests substituting soy milk for dairy for infants and young children.
- Lactose intolerant. These individuals can consume Lactaid and other dairy products with little or no amount of lactose. This is described in the Dairy – In the Store section.
- A dairy allergy.
- An overall substitute for vegetarians or flexitarians.

- **A good source of protein**. In this case, look for an equivalent of 8 grams of protein in an 8-ounce (1 cup) serving on the Nutrition Facts Label. Choose from soy, amaranth, and quinoa, which are complete sources of protein.
- **A good source of calcium, vitamin D, and/or vitamin B$_{12}$**. In this case look for 300 mg calcium, 120 IU of vitamin D, and/or 1.29 µg of vitamin B$_{12}$ per 8-ounce (1 cup) serving on the Nutrition Facts Label. Note 20% DV of vitamin B$_{12}$ = 0.48 µg and in order to get 1.29 µg per serving the DV would need to be 54%.
- **A substitute for dairy in recipes** – see Section 11.

SECTION 11: IN THE KITCHEN

Plant-Based Milk

Making homemade nut milks is quite simple but does require some planning. They will not contain the fortified amounts of calcium, vitamin D, protein or B$_{12}$, so making sure that these nutrients are consumed from somewhere else in the diet is important.

Cashew Milk

- For drinking 2% like-milk:
  - Soak 1 cup raw cashews overnight and then purée in a food processor with 4 cups of water.
  - Add additional flavorings (optional): maple syrup, dates, honey, vanilla, and purée .
  - Place in a nut-bag or cheese cloth and strain the milk from the nut residue. The nut residue can be baked and added to granola or cookie batter.

- For cashew milk that you are going to use in a soup where you need a creamier whole-like milk
  - Soak 1 cup raw cashews overnight and then purée in a food processor with 2 cups of room temperature water.

Consumers may choose plant-based milk alternatives based on their cooking properties. Soy milk is the most common replacement in recipes calling for cow's milk due to its similar protein content. Its protein content adds structure for baking and its stability at high temperatures enables its use in savory dishes. In comparison, sweeter and lower-protein milk varieties such as almond milk are better for desserts and smoothies. For creamier dishes, many opt for coconut milk due to its higher fat content and thus creamy texture.

Plant-Based Yogurt in Three Easy Steps

Step 1: Select a plant-based milk — 14 ounce can of coconut milk or 1 ¾ cup soy or cashew milk. The milk with higher fat content makes a creamy yogurt whereas the milk with lower fat content — almond and rice — makes a thin pourable mixture.

Step 2: Add 4 probiotic capsules (or 1 teaspoon), mix together, add to a clean glass jar (do not use metal), top with cheesecloth and a rubber band. Make sure the probiotics are 'live' and contain L. acidophilus or S. thermophilus.

Step 3: Allow to ferment for 24 to 48 hours in a warm space (oven with light on but no heat).

*Note: to make a Greek yogurt, place the prepared yogurt in a cheesecloth over a bowl and let the liquid seep out. Keep an eye on it as you don't want to turn into cheese (or do you?).

SUMMARY

Plant-based milk alternatives are plentiful, and some can offer a similar nutrient profile as dairy milk. However, only soy fortified beverages can count toward a dairy serving. Specifically, for the nutrients calcium, vitamin D, protein and vitamin B_{12} many plant-based milk alternatives are fortified to help them offer just as much, if not more than dairy milk, though the bioavailability of these nutrients is not yet known (Parrish, 2018). Most plant-based milk alternatives also offer a beverage choice that is lower in saturated fat than full-fat or reduced-fat dairy milk, with the exception of coconut milk (Parrish, 2018). There is a need for further research on the micronutrient composition of these dairy alternatives, as well as the types of nutrients they are being fortified with, and the bioavailability of these nutrients to better determine the impact that they have on a person's health.

Plant-based beverages can not only be incorporated into a healthful eating pattern but also promote a healthful environment. It is important for clients and clinicians alike to understand that the type of plant-based dairy alternative they are choosing will differ in terms of fortification of nutrients and the presence of emulsifiers.

APPENDIX A: Plant-Based Milk Alternatives and Emulsifiers

		Xanthan Gum	Gellan Gum	Guar Gum	Sunflower Lecithin	Locust Bean	Carrageenan	None
Pacific								
	Almond Original	x	x					
	Cashew Original	x	x	x				
	Hemp Original	x	x					
	Coconut Original	x	x	x				
	Oat Original		x					
	Hazelnut	x	x		x	x		
	Soy							x
West Soy								x
Almond Breeze								
	Almond Original		x		x			
Silk								
	Soy		x					
	Almond		x		x	x		
	Cashew		x		x	x		
	Oat		x		x	x		
	Coconut		x		x	x		
Simple Truth								
	Soy						x	
	Almond	x	x		x			
	Oat		x					

	Coconut	x	x	x			x	
Ripple								
	Original		x	x	x			
Whole foods								
	365 soy		x			x		
	365 Almond		x			x		
	365 Coconut		x			x		
	Cosmic Cashew							x
	Oatley							x
Walmart								
	Soy		x					
	Almond				x		x	
	Planet Oat		x					

References

Acham, M., Wesselius, A., van Osch, F. H. M., Yu, E. Y.-W., van den Brandt, P. A., White, E., Adami, H.-O., Weiderpass, E., Brinkman, M., Giles, G. G., Milne, R. L., & Zeegers, M. P. (2020). Intake of milk and other dairy products and the risk of bladder cancer: A pooled analysis of 13 cohort studies. European Journal of Clinical Nutrition, 74(1), 28–35. https://doi.org/10.1038/s41430-019-0453-6

Akkasheh, G., Kashani-Poor, Z., Tajabadi-Ebrahimi, M., Jafari, P., Akbari, H., Taghizadeh, M., Memarzadeh, M. R., Asemi, Z., & Esmaillzadeh, A. (2016). Clinical and metabolic response to probiotic administration in patients with major depressive disorder: A randomized, double-blind, placebo-controlled trial. Nutrition (Burbank, Los Angeles County, Calif.), 32(3), 315–320. https://doi.org/10.1016/j.nut.2015.09.003

Akkerman, M., Larsen, L. B., Sørensen, J., & Poulsen, N. A. (2019). Natural variations of citrate and calcium in milk and their effects on milk processing properties. Journal of Dairy Science, 102(8), 6830–6841. https://doi.org/10.3168/jds.2018-16195

alKanhal, H. A., al-Othman, A. A., & Hewedi, F. M. (2001). Changes in protein nutritional quality in fresh and recombined ultra high temperature treated milk during storage. International Journal of Food Sciences and Nutrition, 52(6), 509–514.

Alothman, M., Hogan, S. A., Hennessy, D., Dillon, P., Kilcawley, K. N., O'Donovan, M., Tobin, J., Fenelon, M. A., & O'Callaghan, T. F. (2019). The "Grass-Fed" Milk Story: Understanding the Impact of Pasture Feeding on the Composition and Quality of Bovine Milk. Foods (Basel, Switzerland), 8(8), E350. https://doi.org/10.3390/foods8080350

Alvarez-Bueno, C., Cavero-Redondo, I., Martinez-Vizcaino, V., Sotos-Prieto, M., Ruiz, J. R., & Gil, A. (2019). Effects of Milk and Dairy Product Consumption on Type 2 Diabetes: Overview of Systematic Reviews and Meta-Analyses. Advances in Nutrition (Bethesda, Md.), 10(suppl_2), S154–S163. https://doi.org/10.1093/advances/nmy107

American Cancer Society. (2014, September 10). Recombinant Bovine Growth Hormone. https://www.cancer.org/cancer/cancer-causes/recombinant-bovine-growth-hormone.html

AMS. (2018). Guidelines for Organic Certification of Dairy Livestock. USDA. https://www.ams.usda.gov/sites/default/files/media/Dairy%20-%20Guidelines.pdf

Anderson, G. H., & Moore, S. E. (2004). Dietary proteins in the regulation of food intake and body weight in humans. The Journal of Nutrition, 134(4), 974S-9S. https://doi.org/10.1093/jn/134.4.974S

Anderson, G. H., Tecimer, S. N., Shah, D., & Zafar, T. A. (2004). Protein source, quantity, and time of consumption determine the effect of proteins on short-term food intake in young men. The Journal of Nutrition, 134(11), 3011–3015. https://doi.org/10.1093/jn/134.11.3011

Andiran, F., Dayi, S., & Mete, E. (2003). Cows milk consumption in constipation and anal fissure in infants and young children. Journal of Paediatrics and Child Health, 39(5), 329–331. https://doi.org/10.1046/j.1440-1754.2003.00152.x

Armas, L. A. G., Hollis, B. W., & Heaney, R. P. (2004). Vitamin D2 is much less effective than vitamin D3 in humans. The Journal of Clinical Endocrinology and Metabolism, 89(11), 5387–5391. https://doi.org/10.1210/jc.2004-0360

Arnett Donna K., Blumenthal Roger S., Albert Michelle A., Buroker Andrew B., Goldberger Zachary D., Hahn Ellen J., Himmelfarb Cheryl Dennison, Khera Amit, Lloyd-Jones Donald, McEvoy J. William, Michos Erin D., Miedema Michael D., Muñoz Daniel, Smith Sidney C., Virani Salim S., Williams Kim A., Yeboah Joseph, & Ziaeian Boback. (2019). 2019 ACC/AHA Guideline on the Primary Prevention of Cardiovascular Disease: A Report of the American College of Cardiology/American Heart Association Task Force on Clinical Practice Guidelines. Circulation, 140(11), e596–e646. https://doi.org/10.1161/CIR.0000000000000678

Aslam, H., Marx, W., Rocks, T., Loughman, A., Chandrasekaran, V., Ruusunen, A., Dawson, S. L., West, M., Mullarkey, E., Pasco, J. A., & Jacka, F. N. (2020). The effects of dairy and dairy derivatives on the gut microbiota: A systematic literature review. Gut Microbes, 12(1), 1799533. https://doi.org/10.1080/19490976.2020.1799533

Astrup, A. (2014). Yogurt and dairy product consumption to prevent cardiometabolic diseases: Epidemiologic and experimental studies. The American Journal of Clinical Nutrition, 99(5 Suppl), 1235S-42S. https://doi.org/10.3945/ajcn.113.073015

Astrup, A., Geiker, N. R. W., & Magkos, F. (2019). Effects of Full-Fat and Fermented Dairy Products on Cardiometabolic Disease: Food Is More Than the Sum of Its Parts. Advances in Nutrition (Bethesda, Md.), 10(5), 924S-930S. https://doi.org/10.1093/advances/nmz069

Astrup, A., Rice Bradley, B. H., Brenna, J. T., Delplanque, B., Ferry, M., & Torres-Gonzalez, M. (2016). Regular-Fat Dairy and Human Health: A Synopsis of Symposia Presented in Europe and North America (2014-2015). Nutrients, 8(8), E463. https://doi.org/10.3390/nu8080463

Aune, D., Norat, T., Romundstad, P., & Vatten, L. J. (2013). Dairy products and the risk of type 2 diabetes: A systematic review and dose-response meta-analysis of cohort studies. The American Journal of Clinical Nutrition, 98(4), 1066–1083. https://doi.org/10.3945/ajcn.113.059030

Baer, D. J., Stote, K. S., Paul, D. R., Harris, G. K., Rumpler, W. V., & Clevidence, B. A. (2011). Whey protein but not soy protein supplementation alters body weight and composition in free-living overweight and obese adults. The Journal of Nutrition, 141(8), 1489–1494. https://doi.org/10.3945/jn.111.139840

Bailey, R. K., Fileti, C. P., Keith, J., Tropez-Sims, S., Price, W., & Allison-Ottey, S. D. (2013). Lactose intolerance and health disparities among African Americans and Hispanic Americans: An updated consensus statement. Journal of the National Medical Association, 105(2), 112–127. https://doi.org/10.1016/s0027-9684(15)30113-9

Barrubés, L., Babio, N., Becerra-Tomás, N., Rosique-Esteban, N., & Salas-Salvadó, J. (2019). Association Between Dairy Product Consumption and Colorectal Cancer Risk in Adults: A Systematic Review and Meta-Analysis of Epidemiologic Studies. Advances in Nutrition (Bethesda, Md.), 10(suppl_2), S190–S211. https://doi.org/10.1093/advances/nmy114

Beavers, K. M., Serra, M. C., Beavers, D. P., Hudson, G. M., & Willoughby, D. S. (2010). The lipid-lowering effects of 4 weeks of daily soymilk or dairy milk ingestion in a postmenopausal female population. Journal of Medicinal Food, 13(3), 650–656. https://doi.org/10.1089/jmf.2009.0171

Belobrajdic, D. P., McIntosh, G. H., & Owens, J. A. (2004). A high-whey-protein diet reduces body weight gain and alters insulin sensitivity relative to red meat in wistar rats. The Journal of Nutrition, 134(6), 1454–1458. https://doi.org/10.1093/jn/134.6.1454

Benbrook, C. M., Davis, D. R., Heins, B. J., Latif, M. A., Leifert, C., Peterman, L., Butler, G., Faergeman, O., Abel-Caines, S., & Baranski, M. (2018). Enhancing the fatty acid profile of milk through forage-based rations, with nutrition modeling of diet outcomes. Food Science & Nutrition, 6(3), 681–700. https://doi.org/10.1002/fsn3.610

Bendtsen, L. Q., Lorenzen, J. K., Bendsen, N. T., Rasmussen, C., & Astrup, A. (2013). Effect of dairy proteins on appetite, energy expenditure, body weight, and composition: A review of the evidence from controlled clinical trials. Advances in Nutrition (Bethesda, Md.), 4(4), 418–438. https://doi.org/10.3945/an.113.003723

Bermejo, L. M., López-Plaza, B., Santurino, C., Cavero-Redondo, I., & Gómez-Candela, C. (2019). Milk and Dairy Product Consumption and Bladder Cancer Risk: A Systematic Review and Meta-Analysis of Observational Studies. Advances in Nutrition (Bethesda, Md.), 10(suppl_2), S224–S238. https://doi.org/10.1093/advances/nmy119

Blom, W. A. M., Lluch, A., Stafleu, A., Vinoy, S., Holst, J. J., Schaafsma, G., & Hendriks, H. F. J. (2006). Effect of a high-protein breakfast on the postprandial ghrelin response. The American Journal of Clinical Nutrition, 83(2), 211–220. https://doi.org/10.1093/ajcn/83.2.211

Bonjour, J.-P., Kraenzlin, M., Levasseur, R., Warren, M., & Whiting, S. (2013). Dairy in adulthood: From foods to nutrient interactions on bone and skeletal muscle

health. Journal of the American College of Nutrition, 32(4), 251–263.
https://doi.org/10.1080/07315724.2013.816604

Booth, A. O., Huggins, C. E., Wattanapenpaiboon, N., & Nowson, C. A. (2015). Effect of increasing dietary calcium through supplements and dairy food on body weight and body composition: A meta-analysis of randomised controlled trials. The British Journal of Nutrition, 114(7), 1013–1025.
https://doi.org/10.1017/S0007114515001518

Borrelli, O., Barbara, G., Di Nardo, G., Cremon, C., Lucarelli, S., Frediani, T., Paganelli, M., De Giorgio, R., Stanghellini, V., & Cucchiara, S. (2009). Neuroimmune interaction and anorectal motility in children with food allergy-related chronic constipation. The American Journal of Gastroenterology, 104(2), 454–463.
https://doi.org/10.1038/ajg.2008.109

Bounous, G., Baruchel, S., Falutz, J., & Gold, P. (1993). Whey proteins as a food supplement in HIV-seropositive individuals. Clinical and Investigative Medicine. Medecine Clinique Et Experimentale, 16(3), 204–209.

Bourgeois, C., & Moss, J. (2010). Niacin. In P. Coates, J. Betz, M. Blackman, G. Cragg, M. Levine, J. Moss, & J. White (Eds.), Encyclopedia of Dietary Supplements (2nd ed., pp. 562–569). Informa Healthcare.

Bourrie, B. C. T., Richard, C., & Willing, B. P. (2020). Kefir in the Prevention and Treatment of Obesity and Metabolic Disorders. Current Nutrition Reports, 9(3), 184–192.
https://doi.org/10.1007/s13668-020-00315-3

Bristow, S. M., Horne, A. M., Gamble, G. D., Mihov, B., Stewart, A., & Reid, I. R. (2019). Dietary Calcium Intake and Bone Loss Over 6 Years in Osteopenic Postmenopausal Women. The Journal of Clinical Endocrinology and Metabolism, 104(8), 3576–3584. https://doi.org/10.1210/jc.2019-00111

Brugger, M. (2007). Fact Sheet: Water Use on Ohio Dairy Farms. Ohio State Univeristy Extension, 3.

Carmel, R. (2014). Cobalamin (vitamin B12). In A. Ross, B. Caballero, R. Cousins, K. Tucker, & T. Ziegler (Eds.), Modern Nutrition in Health and Disease (11th ed., pp. 369–389). Lippincott Williams & Wilkins.

Carroccio, A., Mansueto, P., Morfino, G., D'Alcamo, A., Di Paola, V., Iacono, G., Soresi, M., Scerrino, G., Maresi, E., Gulotta, G., Rini, G., & Bonventre, S. (2013). Oligo-antigenic diet in the treatment of chronic anal fissures. Evidence for a relationship between food hypersensitivity and anal fissures. The American Journal of Gastroenterology, 108(5), 825–832. https://doi.org/10.1038/ajg.2013.58

Centers for Disease Control and Prevention. (2021, July 23). Fortified Cow's Milk and Milk Alternatives. Centers for Disease Control and Prevention.
https://www.cdc.gov/nutrition/infantandtoddlernutrition/foods-and-drinks/cows-milk-and-milk-alternatives.html

Champagne, C. M. (2006). Dietary interventions on blood pressure: The Dietary Approaches to Stop Hypertension (DASH) trials. Nutrition Reviews, 64(2 Pt 2), S53-56. https://doi.org/10.1111/j.1753-4887.2006.tb00234.x

Charles, J. (2016). Menu of State Laws Regarding Odors Produced by Concentrated Animal Feeding Operations. Centers for Disease Control, Office of State, Tribal, Local and Territorial Support, 8.

Cheese Production. (n.d.). Milk Facts. Retrieved January 23, 2022, from http://milkfacts.info/Milk%20Processing/Cheese%20Production.htm

Chen, L., Li, M., & Li, H. (2019). Milk and yogurt intake and breast cancer risk: A meta-analysis. Medicine, 98(12), e14900. https://doi.org/10.1097/MD.0000000000014900

Chen, M., Sun, Q., Giovannucci, E., Mozaffarian, D., Manson, J. E., Willett, W. C., & Hu, F. B. (2014). Dairy consumption and risk of type 2 diabetes: 3 cohorts of US adults and an updated meta-analysis. BMC Medicine, 12, 215. https://doi.org/10.1186/s12916-014-0215-1

Chin-Dusting, J., Shennan, J., Jones, E., Williams, C., Kingwell, B., & Dart, A. (2006). Effect of dietary supplementation with beta-casein A1 or A2 on markers of disease development in individuals at high risk of cardiovascular disease. The British Journal of Nutrition, 95(1), 136–144. https://doi.org/10.1079/bjn20051599

Chrisman, S. (2020). The FoodPrint of Dairy. https://foodprint.org/reports/the-foodprint-of-dairy/

Christianson, E., & Salling, J. (2020). Meded101 Guide to Drug Food Interactions.

CIA, & Harvard TH Chan. (2020). Menus of Change: 2020 Summit & Resources. https://www.ciaprochef.com/MOC/Resources.pdf/

Cifelli, C. J., Auestad, N., & Fulgoni, V. L. (2020). Replacing the nutrients in dairy foods with non-dairy foods will increase cost, energy intake and require large amounts of food: National Health and Nutrition Examination Survey 2011-2014. Public Health Nutrition, 1–12. https://doi.org/10.1017/S1368980020001937

Climate footprint. (n.d.). Oatly. Retrieved February 6, 2022, from https://www.oatly.com/en-us/stuff-we-make/climate-footprint

Code of Federal Regulations Title 21. (2021, October 1). U.S. Food and Drug Administration. https://www.accessdata.fda.gov/scripts/cdrh/cfdocs/cfcfr/CFRSearch.cfm?fr=133.3

Companys, J., Pla-Pagà, L., Calderón-Pérez, L., Llauradó, E., Solà, R., Pedret, A., & Valls, R. M. (2020). Fermented Dairy Products, Probiotic Supplementation, and Cardiometabolic Diseases: A Systematic Review and Meta-analysis. Advances in Nutrition (Bethesda, Md.), 11(4), 834–863. https://doi.org/10.1093/advances/nmaa030

Cross, M. L., & Gill, H. S. (1999). Modulation of immune function by a modified bovine whey protein concentrate. Immunology and Cell Biology, 77(4), 345–350. https://doi.org/10.1046/j.1440-1711.1999.00834.x

Dairy Farmers of America. (n.d.). Retrieved February 6, 2022, from https://www.dfamilk.com/

De Lorgeril, M., Salen, P., Martin, J. L., Mamelle, N., Monjaud, I., Touboul, P., & Delaye, J. (1996). Effect of a mediterranean type of diet on the rate of cardiovascular complications in patients with coronary artery disease. Insights into the cardioprotective effect of certain nutriments. Journal of the American College of Cardiology, 28(5), 1103–1108. https://doi.org/10.1016/S0735-1097(96)00280-X

De Noni, I., FitzGerald, R. J., Korhonen, H. J. T., Le Roux, Y., Livesey, C. T., Thorsdottir, I., Tome, D., & Witkamp, R. (2009). Review of the potential health impact of β-casomorphins and related peptides (pp. 1–107). European Food Safety Authority. https://www.efsa.europa.eu/en/efsajournal/pub/rn-231

de Souza, R. J., Mente, A., Maroleanu, A., Cozma, A. I., Ha, V., Kishibe, T., Uleryk, E., Budylowski, P., Schünemann, H., Beyene, J., & Anand, S. S. (2015). Intake of saturated and trans unsaturated fatty acids and risk of all cause mortality, cardiovascular disease, and type 2 diabetes: Systematic review and meta-analysis of observational studies. BMJ (Clinical Research Ed.), 351, h3978. https://doi.org/10.1136/bmj.h3978

Dehghan, M., Mente, A., Rangarajan, S., Sheridan, P., Mohan, V., Iqbal, R., Gupta, R., Lear, S., Wentzel-Viljoen, E., Avezum, A., Lopez-Jaramillo, P., Mony, P., Varma, R. P., Kumar, R., Chifamba, J., Alhabib, K. F., Mohammadifard, N., Oguz, A., Lanas, F., … Prospective Urban Rural Epidemiology (PURE) study investigators. (2018). Association of dairy intake with cardiovascular disease and mortality in 21 countries from five continents (PURE): A prospective cohort study. Lancet (London, England), 392(10161), 2288–2297. https://doi.org/10.1016/S0140-6736(18)31812-9

Dehghani, S.-M., Ahmadpour, B., Haghighat, M., Kashef, S., Imanieh, M.-H., & Soleimani, M. (2012). The Role of Cow's Milk Allergy in Pediatric Chronic Constipation: A Randomized Clinical Trial. Iranian Journal of Pediatrics, 22(4), 468–474.

Dietary Guidelines Advisory Committee. (2020). Scientific Report of the 2020 Dietary Guidelines Advisory Committee: Advisory Report to the Secretary of Agriculture and the Secretary of Health and Human Services.

Dineva, M., Rayman, M. P., & Bath, S. C. (2021). Iodine status of consumers of milk-alternative drinks v. cows' milk: Data from the UK National Diet and Nutrition Survey. The British Journal of Nutrition, 126(1), 28–36. https://doi.org/10.1017/S0007114520003876

Donovan, S. M. (2017). In V. A. Stallings & M. P. Oria (Eds.), National Academies of Sciences, Engineering, and Medicine. Finding a Path to Safety in Food Allergy. National Academies Press.

Dostalova, J. (2003). Low Fat Foods: Low Fat Spreads. In Encyclopedia of Food Sciences and Nutrition | ScienceDirect. Academic Press. https://www.sciencedirect.com/referencework/9780122270550/encyclopedia-of-food-sciences-and-nutrition

DREAM Plant Based. (2022). Dream Plant Based. https://www.dreamplantbased.com/

Drehmer, M., Pereira, M. A., Schmidt, M. I., Alvim, S., Lotufo, P. A., Luft, V. C., & Duncan, B. B. (2016). Total and Full-Fat, but Not Low-Fat, Dairy Product Intakes are Inversely Associated with Metabolic Syndrome in Adults. The Journal of Nutrition, 146(1), 81–89. https://doi.org/10.3945/jn.115.220699

Drewnowski, A. (2011). The contribution of milk and milk products to micronutrient density and affordability of the U.S. diet. Journal of the American College of Nutrition, 30(5 Suppl 1), 422S-8S. https://doi.org/10.1080/07315724.2011.10719986

Drouin-Chartier, J.-P., Brassard, D., Tessier-Grenier, M., Côté, J. A., Labonté, M.-È., Desroches, S., Couture, P., & Lamarche, B. (2016). Systematic Review of the Association between Dairy Product Consumption and Risk of Cardiovascular-Related Clinical Outcomes. Advances in Nutrition (Bethesda, Md.), 7(6), 1026–1040. https://doi.org/10.3945/an.115.011403

EFSA Panel. (2017a). Re-evaluation of guar gum (E 412) as a food additive. https://efsa.onlinelibrary.wiley.com/doi/10.2903/j.efsa.2017.4669

EFSA Panel. (2017b). Re-evaluation of lecithins (E322) as a food additive.

EFSA Panel. (2017c). Re-evaluation of Xanthan gum (E415) as a food additive.

EFSA Panel. (2017d). Re-evaluation of alginic acid and its sodium, potassium, ammonium, and calcium salts. https://efsa.onlinelibrary.wiley.com/doi/full/10.2903/j.efsa.2017.5049

EFSA Panel. (2018). Re-evaluation of Gellan Gum (E418) as Food Additive.

Emerson, S. R., Kurti, S. P., Harms, C. A., Haub, M. D., Melgarejo, T., Logan, C., & Rosenkranz, S. K. (2017). Magnitude and Timing of the Postprandial Inflammatory Response to a High-Fat Meal in Healthy Adults: A Systematic Review. Advances in Nutrition (Bethesda, Md.), 8(2), 213–225. https://doi.org/10.3945/an.116.014431

Ericson, U., Hellstrand, S., Brunkwall, L., Schulz, C.-A., Sonestedt, E., Wallström, P., Gullberg, B., Wirfält, E., & Orho-Melander, M. (2015). Food sources of fat may clarify the inconsistent role of dietary fat intake for incidence of type 2 diabetes. The American Journal of Clinical Nutrition, 101(5), 1065–1080. https://doi.org/10.3945/ajcn.114.103010

Eveleigh, E., Coneyworth, L., Zhou, M., Burdett, H., Malla, J., Nguyen, V. H., & Welham, S. (2022). Vegans and vegetarians living in Nottingham (UK) continue to be at risk of iodine deficiency. The British Journal of Nutrition, 1–46. https://doi.org/10.1017/S0007114522000113

Faccia, M. (2020). The Flavor of Dairy Products from Grass-Fed Cows. Foods, 9(9), 1188. https://doi.org/10.3390/foods9091188

FAO & GDP. (2018). Climate change and the global dairy cattle sector: The role of the dairy sector in a low-carbon future. (CC BY-NC-SA-3.0 IGO). FAO. http://www.fao.org/3/CA2929EN/ca2929en.pdf

Fernandez, M. L., & Calle, M. (2010). Revisiting dietary cholesterol recommendations: Does the evidence support a limit of 300 mg/d? Current Atherosclerosis Reports, 12(6), 377–383. https://doi.org/10.1007/s11883-010-0130-7

Flaherty, R., & Cativiela, J. (2017, August 21). California Dairy 101: Overview of dairy farming and manure methane reduction opportunities. Dairy and Livestock Working Group. https://ww2.arb.ca.gov/sites/default/files/classic/cc/dairy/documents/08-21-17/dsg1-dairy-101-presentation.pdf

Flom, J. D., & Sicherer, S. H. (2019). Epidemiology of Cow's Milk Allergy. Nutrients, 11(5), 1051. https://doi.org/10.3390/nu11051051

Fong, J., & Khan, A. (2012). Hypocalcemia: Updates in diagnosis and management for primary care. Canadian Family Physician Medecin De Famille Canadien, 58(2), 158–162.

Fontecha, J., Calvo, M. V., Juarez, M., Gil, A., & Martínez-Vizcaino, V. (2019). Milk and Dairy Product Consumption and Cardiovascular Diseases: An Overview of Systematic Reviews and Meta-Analyses. Advances in Nutrition (Bethesda, Md.), 10(suppl_2), S164–S189. https://doi.org/10.1093/advances/nmy099

Food and Agriculture Organization. (2021). Gateway to Dairy and Dairy Products. http://www.fao.org/dairy-production-products/en/

Ford, J. T., Wong, C. W., & Colditz, I. G. (2001). Effects of dietary protein types on immune responses and levels of infection with Eimeria vermiformis in mice. Immunology and Cell Biology, 79(1), 23–28. https://doi.org/10.1046/j.1440-1711.2001.00788.x

Forss, D. (1969). Flavors of Dairy Products: A Review of Recent Advances | Elsevier Enhanced Reader. Journal of Dairy Science, 52(6), 832–840. https://doi.org/10.3168/jds.S0022-0302(69)86659-2

Fox, M. K., Reidy, K., Novak, T., & Ziegler, P. (2006). Sources of energy and nutrients in the diets of infants and toddlers. Journal of the American Dietetic Association, 106(1 Suppl 1), S28-42. https://doi.org/10.1016/j.jada.2005.09.034

Fulton, J., Norton, M., & Shilling, F. (2019). Water-indexed benefits and impacts of California almonds. Ecological Indicators, 96(1), 711–717.

García, E. V., Sala-Serra, M., Continente-Garcia, X., Serral Cano, G., & Puigpinós-Riera, R. (2020). The association between breast cancer and consumption of dairy products: A systematic review. Nutricion Hospitalaria, 34(3), 589–598. https://doi.org/10.20960/nh.02649

Gardner, C. D., Messina, M., Kiazand, A., Morris, J. L., & Franke, A. A. (2007). Effect of two types of soy milk and dairy milk on plasma lipids in hypercholesterolemic adults: A randomized trial. Journal of the American College of Nutrition, 26(6), 669–677. https://doi.org/10.1080/07315724.2007.10719646

German, J. B., Gibson, R. A., Krauss, R. M., Nestel, P., Lamarche, B., van Staveren, W. A., Steijns, J. M., de Groot, L. C. P. G. M., Lock, A. L., & Destaillats, F. (2009). A reappraisal of the impact of dairy foods and milk fat on cardiovascular disease risk. European Journal of Nutrition, 48(4), 191–203. https://doi.org/10.1007/s00394-009-0002-5

Gijsbers, L., Ding, E. L., Malik, V. S., de Goede, J., Geleijnse, J. M., & Soedamah-Muthu, S. S. (2016). Consumption of dairy foods and diabetes incidence: A dose-response meta-analysis of observational studies. The American Journal of Clinical Nutrition, 103(4), 1111–1124. https://doi.org/10.3945/ajcn.115.123216

Golden, N. H., Abrams, S. A., & Committee on Nutrition. (2014). Optimizing bone health in children and adolescents. Pediatrics, 134(4), e1229-1243. https://doi.org/10.1542/peds.2014-2173

Gómez-Cortés, P., Juárez, M., & de la Fuente, M. A. (2018). Milk fatty acids and potential health benefits: An updated vision. Trends in Food Science & Technology, 81, 1–9. https://doi.org/10.1016/j.tifs.2018.08.014

González-Chávez, S. A., Arévalo-Gallegos, S., & Rascón-Cruz, Q. (2009). Lactoferrin: Structure, function and applications. International Journal of Antimicrobial Agents, 33(4), 301.e1-8. https://doi.org/10.1016/j.ijantimicag.2008.07.020

Grimes, C. A., Szymlek-Gay, E. A., & Nicklas, T. A. (2017). Beverage Consumption among U.S. Children Aged 0-24 Months: National Health and Nutrition Examination Survey (NHANES). Nutrients, 9(3), E264. https://doi.org/10.3390/nu9030264

Groetch, M., & Nowak-Wegrzyn, A. (2013). Practical approach to nutrition and dietary intervention in pediatric food allergy. Pediatric Allergy and Immunology: Official Publication of the European Society of Pediatric Allergy and Immunology, 24(3), 212–221. https://doi.org/10.1111/pai.12035

Hall, W. L., Millward, D. J., Long, S. J., & Morgan, L. M. (2003). Casein and whey exert different effects on plasma amino acid profiles, gastrointestinal hormone secretion and appetite. The British Journal of Nutrition, 89(2), 239–248. https://doi.org/10.1079/BJN2002760

Hanach, N. I., McCullough, F., & Avery, A. (2019). The Impact of Dairy Protein Intake on Muscle Mass, Muscle Strength, and Physical Performance in Middle-Aged to Older Adults with or without Existing Sarcopenia: A Systematic Review and Meta-

Analysis. Advances in Nutrition (Bethesda, Md.), 10(1), 59–69. https://doi.org/10.1093/advances/nmy065

Harrar, S. (2016, October 17). Is There Vitamin D in Mil Alternatives? Consumer Reports. https://www.consumerreports.org/vitamins-supplements/vitamin-d-in-milk-alternatives/

Harrington, L. K., & Mayberry, J. F. (2008). A re-appraisal of lactose intolerance. International Journal of Clinical Practice, 62(10), 1541–1546. https://doi.org/10.1111/j.1742-1241.2008.01834.x

Hata, I., Higashiyama, S., & Otani, H. (1998). Identification of a phosphopeptide in bovine alpha s1-casein digest as a factor influencing proliferation and immunoglobulin production in lymphocyte cultures. The Journal of Dairy Research, 65(4), 569–578. https://doi.org/10.1017/s0022029998003136

Heaney, R. (2012). Phosphorus. In J. Erdman, I. MacDonald, & S. Zeisel (Eds.), Present Knowledge in Nutrition (10th ed., pp. 447–458). Wiley-Blackwell.

Heaney, R. P. (2007). Bone health. The American Journal of Clinical Nutrition, 85(1), 300S-303S. https://doi.org/10.1093/ajcn/85.1.300S

Heaney, R. P., Rafferty, K., & Bierman, J. (2005). Not All Calcium-fortified Beverages Are Equal. Nutrition Today, 40(1), 39–44.

Helstad, S. (2019). Corn Sweeteners. In Corn: Chemstry and Technology (3rd ed.). Elsevier. https://www.sciencedirect.com/topics/agricultural-and-biological-sciences/sweetness

Hempel, S., Newberry, S. J., Maher, A. R., Wang, Z., Miles, J. N. V., Shanman, R., Johnsen, B., & Shekelle, P. G. (2012). Probiotics for the prevention and treatment of antibiotic-associated diarrhea: A systematic review and meta-analysis. JAMA, 307(18), 1959–1969. https://doi.org/10.1001/jama.2012.3507

Hess, J. M., Cifelli, C. J., & Fulgoni Iii, V. L. (2020). Energy and Nutrient Intake of Americans according to Meeting Current Dairy Recommendations. Nutrients, 12(10), E3006. https://doi.org/10.3390/nu12103006

Hoffman, J. R., & Falvo, M. J. (2004). Protein—Which is Best? Journal of Sports Science & Medicine, 3(3), 118–130.

Holt, C., Carver, J. A., Ecroyd, H., & Thorn, D. C. (2013). Invited review: Caseins and the casein micelle: their biological functions, structures, and behavior in foods. Journal of Dairy Science, 96(10), 6127–6146. https://doi.org/10.3168/jds.2013-6831

Houchins, J. A., Cifelli, C. J., Demmer, E., & Fulgoni, V. L. (2017). Diet Modeling in Older Americans: The Impact of Increasing Plant-Based Foods or Dairy Products on Protein Intake. The Journal of Nutrition, Health & Aging, 21(6), 673–680. https://doi.org/10.1007/s12603-016-0819-6

Iacono, G., Bonventre, S., Scalici, C., Maresi, E., Di Prima, L., Soresi, M., Di Gesù, G., Noto, D., & Carroccio, A. (2006). Food intolerance and chronic constipation: Manometry and histology study. European Journal of Gastroenterology & Hepatology, 18(2), 143–150. https://doi.org/10.1097/00042737-200602000-00006

Ilich, J. Z., Kelly, O. J., Liu, P.-Y., Shin, H., Kim, Y., Chi, Y., Wickrama, K. K. A. S., & Colic-Baric, I. (2019). Role of Calcium and Low-Fat Dairy Foods in Weight-Loss Outcomes Revisited: Results from the Randomized Trial of Effects on Bone and Body Composition in Overweight/Obese Postmenopausal Women. Nutrients, 11(5), E1157. https://doi.org/10.3390/nu11051157

Institute of Medicine. (1998). Dietary Reference Intakes for Thiamin, Riboflavin, Niacin, Vitamin B6, Folate, Vitamin B12, Pantothenic Acid, Biotin, and Choline. In Dietary Reference Intakes for Thiamin, Riboflavin, Niacin, Vitamin B6, Folate, Vitamin B12, Pantothenic Acid, Biotin, and Choline. National Academies Press (US). https://www.ncbi.nlm.nih.gov/books/NBK114318/

Institute of Medicine. (2005). Dietary Reference Intakes for Water, Potassium, Chloride, and Sulfate. National Academies Press.

Institute of Medicine. (2010). Dietary Reference Intakes for Calcium and Vitamin D. National Academies Press.

International Dairy Foods Association. (2021, September 30). U.S. Dairy Consumption Beats Expectations in 2020 and Continues to Surge Upward Despite Disruption Caused by Pandemic. IDFA. https://www.idfa.org/news/u-s-dairy-consumption-beats-expectations-in-2020-and-continues-to-surge-upward-despite-disruption-caused-by-pandemic

International Dairy Foods Association. (2022). IDFA. https://www.idfa.org/news/international-dairy-foods-association

Irastorza, I., Ibañez, B., Delgado-Sanzonetti, L., Maruri, N., & Vitoria, J. C. (2010). Cow's-milk-free diet as a therapeutic option in childhood chronic constipation. Journal of Pediatric Gastroenterology and Nutrition, 51(2), 171–176. https://doi.org/10.1097/MPG.0b013e3181cd2653

Iuliano, S., Poon, S., Robbins, J., Bui, M., Wang, X., Groot, L. D., Loan, M. V., Zadeh, A. G., Nguyen, T., & Seeman, E. (2021). Effect of dietary sources of calcium and protein on hip fractures and falls in older adults in residential care: Cluster randomised controlled trial. BMJ, 375, n2364. https://doi.org/10.1136/bmj.n2364

Jakubczyk, D., Leszczyńska, K., & Górska, S. (2020). The Effectiveness of Probiotics in the Treatment of Inflammatory Bowel Disease (IBD)-A Critical Review. Nutrients, 12(7), E1973. https://doi.org/10.3390/nu12071973

Jenssen, H., & Hancock, R. E. W. (2009). Antimicrobial properties of lactoferrin. Biochimie, 91(1), 19–29. https://doi.org/10.1016/j.biochi.2008.05.015

Jianqin, S., Leiming, X., Lu, X., Yelland, G. W., Ni, J., & Clarke, A. J. (2016). Effects of milk containing only A2 beta casein versus milk containing both A1 and A2 beta casein proteins on gastrointestinal physiology, symptoms of discomfort, and cognitive behavior of people with self-reported intolerance to traditional cows' milk. Nutrition Journal, 15, 35. https://doi.org/10.1186/s12937-016-0147-z

Johansson, I., & Lif Holgerson, P. (2011). Milk and oral health. Nestle Nutrition Workshop Series. Paediatric Programme, 67, 55–66. https://doi.org/10.1159/000325575

Jones, G. (2014). Vitamin D. In A. Ross, B. Caballero, R. Cousins, K. Tucker, & T. Ziegler (Eds.), Modern Nutrition in Health and Disease (11th ed.). Lippincott Williams & Wilkins.

Jung, T.-H., Hwang, H.-J., Yun, S.-S., Lee, W.-J., Kim, J.-W., Ahn, J.-Y., Jeon, W.-M., & Han, K.-S. (2017). Hypoallergenic and Physicochemical Properties of the A2 β-Casein Fractionof Goat Milk. Korean Journal for Food Science of Animal Resources, 37(6), 940–947. https://doi.org/10.5851/kosfa.2017.37.6.940

Kazemi, A., Noorbala, A. A., Azam, K., Eskandari, M. H., & Djafarian, K. (2019). Effect of probiotic and prebiotic vs placebo on psychological outcomes in patients with major depressive disorder: A randomized clinical trial. Clinical Nutrition (Edinburgh, Scotland), 38(2), 522–528. https://doi.org/10.1016/j.clnu.2018.04.010

Kim, Y., & Je, Y. (2016). Dairy consumption and risk of metabolic syndrome: A meta-analysis. Diabetic Medicine: A Journal of the British Diabetic Association, 33(4), 428–440. https://doi.org/10.1111/dme.12970

Kratz, M., Marcovina, S., Nelson, J. E., Yeh, M. M., Kowdley, K. V., Callahan, H. S., Song, X., Di, C., & Utzschneider, K. M. (2014). Dairy fat intake is associated with glucose tolerance, hepatic and systemic insulin sensitivity, and liver fat but not β-cell function in humans. The American Journal of Clinical Nutrition, 99(6), 1385–1396. https://doi.org/10.3945/ajcn.113.075457

Lana, A., Rodriguez-Artalejo, F., & Lopez-Garcia, E. (2015). Dairy Consumption and Risk of Frailty in Older Adults: A Prospective Cohort Study. Journal of the American Geriatrics Society, 63(9), 1852–1860. https://doi.org/10.1111/jgs.13626

Le Louer, B., Lemale, J., Garcette, K., Orzechowski, C., Chalvon, A., Girardet, J.-P., & Tounian, P. (2014). [Severe nutritional deficiencies in young infants with inappropriate plant milk consumption]. Archives De Pediatrie: Organe Officiel De La Societe Francaise De Pediatrie, 21(5), 483–488. https://doi.org/10.1016/j.arcped.2014.02.027

Lee, J., Fu, Z., Chung, M., Jang, D.-J., & Lee, H.-J. (2018). Role of milk and dairy intake in cognitive function in older adults: A systematic review and meta-analysis. Nutrition Journal, 17(1), 82. https://doi.org/10.1186/s12937-018-0387-1

Li, E. W. Y., & Mine, Y. (2004). Immunoenhancing effects of bovine glycomacropeptide and its derivatives on the proliferative response and phagocytic activities of human macrophagelike cells, U937. Journal of Agricultural and Food Chemistry, 52(9), 2704–2708. https://doi.org/10.1021/jf0355102

Liang, J., Zhou, Q., Kwame Amakye, W., Su, Y., & Zhang, Z. (2018). Biomarkers of dairy fat intake and risk of cardiovascular disease: A systematic review and meta analysis of prospective studies. Critical Reviews in Food Science and Nutrition, 58(7), 1122–1130. https://doi.org/10.1080/10408398.2016.1242114

Lighter Béchamel | Cook's Illustrated. (n.d.). Retrieved February 18, 2022, from http://www.cooksillustrated.com/how_tos/5627-lighter-bechamel

Lomer, M. C. E., Parkes, G. C., & Sanderson, J. D. (2008). Review article: Lactose intolerance in clinical practice--myths and realities. Alimentary Pharmacology & Therapeutics, 27(2), 93–103. https://doi.org/10.1111/j.1365-2036.2007.03557.x

Lovegrove, J. A., & Hobbs, D. A. (2016). New perspectives on dairy and cardiovascular health. The Proceedings of the Nutrition Society, 75(3), 247–258. https://doi.org/10.1017/S002966511600001X

Low, P. P. L., Rutherfurd, K. J., Cross, M. L., & Gill, H. S. (2001). Enhancement of Mucosal Antibody Responses by Dietary Whey Protein Concentrate. Food and Agricultural Immunology, 13(4), 255–264. https://doi.org/10.1080/09540100120094519

Luhovyy, B. L., Akhavan, T., & Anderson, G. H. (2007). Whey proteins in the regulation of food intake and satiety. Journal of the American College of Nutrition, 26(6), 704S-12S. https://doi.org/10.1080/07315724.2007.10719651

MacDonald, R. S., Thornton, W. H., & Marshall, R. T. (1994). A cell culture model to identify biologically active peptides generated by bacterial hydrolysis of casein. Journal of Dairy Science, 77(5), 1167–1175. https://doi.org/10.3168/jds.S0022-0302(94)77054-5

Manzi, P., Di Costanzo, M. G., & Mattera, M. (2013). Updating Nutritional Data and Evaluation of Technological Parameters of Italian Milk. Foods (Basel, Switzerland), 2(2), 254–273. https://doi.org/10.3390/foods2020254

Manzocchi, E., Martin, B., Bord, C., Verdier-Metz, I., Bouchon, M., De Marchi, M., Constant, I., Giller, K., Kreuzer, M., Berard, J., Musci, M., & Coppa, M. (2021). Feeding cows with hay, silage, or fresh herbage on pasture or indoors affects sensory properties and chemical composition of milk and cheese. Journal of Dairy Science, 104(5), 5285–5302. https://doi.org/10.3168/jds.2020-19738

Marabujo, T., Ramos, E., & Lopes, C. (2018). Dairy products and total calcium intake at 13 years of age and its association with obesity at 21 years of age. European Journal of Clinical Nutrition, 72(4), 541–547. https://doi.org/10.1038/s41430-017-0082-x

Marangoni, F., Pellegrino, L., Verduci, E., Ghiselli, A., Bernabei, R., Calvani, R., Cetin, I., Giampietro, M., Perticone, F., Piretta, L., Giacco, R., La Vecchia, C., Brandi, M. L., Ballardini, D., Banderali, G., Bellentani, S., Canzone, G., Cricelli, C., Faggiano, P., … Poli, A. (2019). Cow's Milk Consumption and Health: A Health Professional's Guide. Journal of the American College of Nutrition, 38(3), 197–208. https://doi.org/10.1080/07315724.2018.1491016

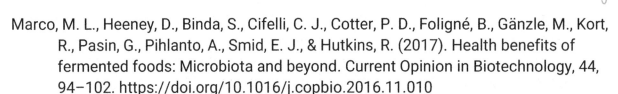

Marco, M. L., Heeney, D., Binda, S., Cifelli, C. J., Cotter, P. D., Foligné, B., Gänzle, M., Kort, R., Pasin, G., Pihlanto, A., Smid, E. J., & Hutkins, R. (2017). Health benefits of fermented foods: Microbiota and beyond. Current Opinion in Biotechnology, 44, 94–102. https://doi.org/10.1016/j.copbio.2016.11.010

Mathai, J. K., Liu, Y., & Stein, H. H. (2017). Values for digestible indispensable amino acid scores (DIAAS) for some dairy and plant proteins may better describe protein quality than values calculated using the concept for protein digestibility-corrected amino acid scores (PDCAAS). The British Journal of Nutrition, 117(4), 490–499. https://doi.org/10.1017/S0007114517000125

McBean, L. D., & Miller, G. D. (1998). Allaying fears and fallacies about lactose intolerance. Journal of the American Dietetic Association, 98(6), 671–676. https://doi.org/10.1016/S0002-8223(98)00152-7

McGee, H. (2004). On Food and Cooking: The Science and Lore of the Kitchen (1st edition). Scribner Books.

McGregor, R. A., & Poppitt, S. D. (2013). Milk protein for improved metabolic health: A review of the evidence. Nutrition & Metabolism, 10(1), 46. https://doi.org/10.1186/1743-7075-10-46

McKim et al. (2019). Clarifying the confusion between poligeenan, degraded carrageenan, and carrageenan: A review of the chemistry, nomenclature, and in vivo toxicology by the oral route. 59(19), 3054–3073.

Meharg, A. A., Deacon, C., Campbell, R. C. J., Carey, A.-M., Williams, P. N., Feldmann, J., & Raab, A. (2008). Inorganic arsenic levels in rice milk exceed EU and US drinking water standards. Journal of Environmental Monitoring: JEM, 10(4), 428–431. https://doi.org/10.1039/b800981c

Meinertz, H., Nilausen, K., & Faergeman, O. (1989). Soy protein and casein in cholesterol-enriched diets: Effects on plasma lipoproteins in normolipidemic subjects. The American Journal of Clinical Nutrition, 50(4), 786–793. https://doi.org/10.1093/ajcn/50.4.786

Mekonnen, M. M., & Hoekstra, A. Y. (2010). The Green, Blue and Grey Water Footprint of Crops and Derived Crop Products, Value of Water Research Report Series No. 47. UNESCO-IHE. https://waterfootprint.org/media/downloads/Report47-WaterFootprintCrops-Vol2.pdf

Meltzer Warren, R. (2019, September 25). Are Plant Milks Good for You? Consumer Reports. https://www.consumerreports.org/plant-milk/are-plant-milks-more-healthful-than-cows-milk/

Mena-Sánchez, G., Becerra-Tomás, N., Babio, N., & Salas-Salvadó, J. (2019). Dairy Product Consumption in the Prevention of Metabolic Syndrome: A Systematic Review and Meta-Analysis of Prospective Cohort Studies. Advances in Nutrition (Bethesda, Md.), 10(suppl_2), S144–S153. https://doi.org/10.1093/advances/nmy083

Merritt, R. J., Fleet, S. E., Fifi, A., Jump, C., Schwartz, S., Sentongo, T., Duro, D., Rudolph, J., Turner, J., & NASPGHAN Committee on Nutrition. (2020). North American Society for Pediatric Gastroenterology, Hepatology, and Nutrition Position Paper: Plant-based Milks. Journal of Pediatric Gastroenterology and Nutrition, 71(2), 276–281. https://doi.org/10.1097/MPG.0000000000002799

Milk Safety | Dairy Health Benefits. (n.d.). The Dairy Alliance. Retrieved April 9, 2022, from https://thedairyalliance.com/dairy-farming/milk-safety/

Miller, G. D., Jarvis, J. K., & McBean, L. D. (2006). Handbook of Dairy Foods and Nutrition (3rd ed.). CRC Press.

Miller, J., & Rucker, R. (2012). Pantothenic acid. In J. Erdman, I. MacDonald, & S. Zeisel (Eds.), Present Knowledge in Nutrition (10th ed., pp. 375–390). Wiley-Blackwell.

Mills, S., Ross, R. P., Hill, C., Fitzgerald, G. F., & Stanton, C. (2011). Milk intelligence: Mining milk for bioactive substances associated with human health. International Dairy Journal, 21(6), 377–401. https://doi.org/10.1016/j.idairyj.2010.12.011

Misselwitz, B., Butter, M., Verbeke, K., & Fox, M. R. (2019). Update on lactose malabsorption and intolerance: Pathogenesis, diagnosis and clinical management. Gut, 68(11), 2080–2091. https://doi.org/10.1136/gutjnl-2019-318404

Mitri, J., Mohd Yusof, B.-N., Maryniuk, M., Schrager, C., Hamdy, O., & Salsberg, V. (2019). Dairy intake and type 2 diabetes risk factors: A narrative review. Diabetes & Metabolic Syndrome, 13(5), 2879–2887. https://doi.org/10.1016/j.dsx.2019.07.064

Mozaffarian, D. (2019). Dairy Foods, Obesity, and Metabolic Health: The Role of the Food Matrix Compared with Single Nutrients. Advances in Nutrition (Bethesda, Md.), 10(5), 917S-923S. https://doi.org/10.1093/advances/nmz053

Mozaffarian, D., Hao, T., Rimm, E. B., Willett, W. C., & Hu, F. B. (2011). Changes in diet and lifestyle and long-term weight gain in women and men. The New England Journal of Medicine, 364(25), 2392–2404. https://doi.org/10.1056/NEJMoa1014296

Mueller, N. T., Odegaard, A. O., Gross, M. D., Koh, W.-P., Yu, M. C., Yuan, J.-M., & Pereira, M. A. (2012). Soy intake and risk of type 2 diabetes in Chinese Singaporeans [corrected]. European Journal of Nutrition, 51(8), 1033–1040. https://doi.org/10.1007/s00394-011-0276-2

Nappo, A., Sparano, S., Intemann, T., Kourides, Y. A., Lissner, L., Molnar, D., Moreno, L. A., Pala, V., Sioen, I., Veidebaum, T., Wolters, M., Siani, A., & Russo, P. (2019). Dietary calcium intake and adiposity in children and adolescents: Cross-sectional and longitudinal results from IDEFICS/I.Family cohort. Nutrition, Metabolism, and Cardiovascular Diseases: NMCD, 29(5), 440–449. https://doi.org/10.1016/j.numecd.2019.01.015

National Dairy Council. (2022). https://www.usdairy.com/about-us/national-dairy-council

National Institute of Health, Office of Dietary Supplements. (2020a, March 20). Vitamin B12 Health Professional Sheet. https://ods.od.nih.gov/factsheets/VitaminB12-HealthProfessional/

National Institute of Health, Office of Dietary Supplements. (2020b, March 24). Vitamin D Health Professional Sheet. https://ods.od.nih.gov/factsheets/VitaminD-HealthProfessional/

National Institutes of Health Office of Dietary Supplements. (n.d.). Vitamin and Mineral Supplement Fact Sheets. Retrieved March 28, 2020, from https://ods.od.nih.gov/factsheets/list-VitaminsMinerals/

New Zealand Commerce Commission. (2003, November 21). Advertising of A2 milk changes following Commerce Commission warning. Commerce Commission. https://comcom.govt.nz/news-and-media/media-releases/archive/advertising-of-a2-milk-changes-following-commerce-commission-warning

Nguyen, C. T., Pham, N. M., Do, V. V., Binns, C. W., Hoang, V. M., Dang, D. A., & Lee, A. H. (2017). Soyfood and isoflavone intake and risk of type 2 diabetes in Vietnamese adults. European Journal of Clinical Nutrition, 71(10), 1186–1192. https://doi.org/10.1038/ejcn.2017.76

Nordmann, A. J., Suter-Zimmermann, K., Bucher, H. C., Shai, I., Tuttle, K. R., Estruch, R., & Briel, M. (2011). Meta-analysis comparing Mediterranean to low-fat diets for modification of cardiovascular risk factors. The American Journal of Medicine, 124(9), 841-851.e2. https://doi.org/10.1016/j.amjmed.2011.04.024

Norman, A. (2012). Vitamin D. In H. Henry, J. Erdman, I. MacDonald, & S. Zeisel (Eds.), Present Knowledge in Nutrition (10th ed.). Wiley-Blackwell.

O'Brien, K. V., Stewart, L. K., Forney, L. A., Aryana, K. J., Prinyawiwatkul, W., & Boeneke, C. A. (2015). The effects of postexercise consumption of a kefir beverage on performance and recovery during intensive endurance training. Journal of Dairy Science, 98(11), 7446–7449. https://doi.org/10.3168/jds.2015-9392

O'Hagan, M. (2019, June 19). From Two Bulls, 9 Million Dairy Cows. Undark Magazine.

Olive Oil Béchamel Recipe. (n.d.). NYT Cooking. Retrieved February 18, 2022, from https://cooking.nytimes.com/recipes/1017372-olive-oil-bechamel

Oliver, S. P., Murinda, S. E., & Jayarao, B. M. (2011). Impact of Antibiotic Use in Adult Dairy Cows on Antimicrobial Resistance of Veterinary and Human Pathogens: A Comprehensive Review. Foodborne Pathogens and Disease, 8(3). https://doi.org/10.1089/fpd.2010.0730

Onning, G., Akesson, B., Oste, R., & Lundquist, I. (1998). Effects of consumption of oat milk, soya milk, or cow's milk on plasma lipids and antioxidative capacity in healthy subjects. Annals of Nutrition & Metabolism, 42(4), 211–220. https://doi.org/10.1159/000012736

Onning, G., Wallmark, A., Persson, M., Akesson, B., Elmståhl, S., & Oste, R. (1999). Consumption of oat milk for 5 weeks lowers serum cholesterol and LDL cholesterol in free-living men with moderate hypercholesterolemia. Annals of Nutrition & Metabolism, 43(5), 301–309. https://doi.org/10.1159/000012798

Onwulata, C. I., & Huth, P. J. (Eds.). (2008). Whey Processing, Functionality and Health Benefits (1st ed.). John Wiley & Sons, Inc.

Otani, H., Kihara, Y., & Park, M. (2000). The Immunoenhancing Property of a Dietary Casein Phosphopeptide Preparation in Mice. Food and Agricultural Immunology, 12(2), 165–173.

Pacheco, Y. M., López, S., Bermúdez, B., Abia, R., Villar, J., & Muriana, F. J. G. (2008). A meal rich in oleic acid beneficially modulates postprandial sICAM-1 and sVCAM-1 in normotensive and hypertensive hypertriglyceridemic subjects. The Journal of Nutritional Biochemistry, 19(3), 200–205. https://doi.org/10.1016/j.jnutbio.2007.03.002

Parodi, P. W. (2007). A role for milk proteins and their peptides in cancer prevention. Current Pharmaceutical Design, 13(8), 813–828. https://doi.org/10.2174/138161207780363059

Parrish, C. R. (2018). Moo-ove Over, Cow's Milk: The Rise of Plant-Based Dairy Alternatives. PRACTICAL GASTROENTEROLOGY, 7.

Payette, C., Blackburn, P., Lamarche, B., Tremblay, A., Bergeron, J., Lemieux, I., Després, J.-P., & Couillard, C. (2009). Sex differences in postprandial plasma tumor necrosis factor-alpha, interleukin-6, and C-reactive protein concentrations. Metabolism: Clinical and Experimental, 58(11), 1593–1601. https://doi.org/10.1016/j.metabol.2009.05.011

Pei, R., DiMarco, D. M., Putt, K. K., Martin, D. A., Gu, Q., Chitchumroonchokchai, C., White, H. M., Scarlett, C. O., Bruno, R. S., & Bolling, B. W. (2017). Low-fat yogurt consumption reduces biomarkers of chronic inflammation and inhibits markers of endotoxin exposure in healthy premenopausal women: A randomised controlled trial. The British Journal of Nutrition, 118(12), 1043–1051. https://doi.org/10.1017/S0007114517003038

Penberthy, W., & Kirkland, J. (2012). Niacin. In J. Erdman, I. MacDonald, & S. Zeisel (Eds.), Present Knowledge in Nutrition (10th ed., pp. 293–306). Wiley-Blackwell.

Pepe, J., Colangelo, L., Biamonte, F., Sonato, C., Danese, V. C., Cecchetti, V., Occhiuto, M., Piazzolla, V., De Martino, V., Ferrone, F., Minisola, S., & Cipriani, C. (2020). Diagnosis and management of hypocalcemia. Endocrine, 69(3), 485–495. https://doi.org/10.1007/s12020-020-02324-2

Perdijk, O., Splunter, M. van, Savelkoul, H. F. J., Brugman, S., & Neerven, R. J. J. van. (2018). Cow's Milk and Immune Function in the Respiratory Tract: Potential Mechanisms. Frontiers in Immunology, 9. https://doi.org/10.3389/fimmu.2018.00143

Pereira, P. C. (2014). Milk nutritional composition and its role in human health. Nutrition (Burbank, Los Angeles County, Calif.), 30(6), 619–627. https://doi.org/10.1016/j.nut.2013.10.011

Pessi, T., Isolauri, E., Sütas, Y., Kankaanranta, H., Moilanen, E., & Hurme, M. (2001). Suppression of T-cell activation by Lactobacillus rhamnosus GG-degraded bovine casein. International Immunopharmacology, 1(2), 211–218. https://doi.org/10.1016/s1567-5769(00)00018-7

Planet Oat. (2022). https://planetoat.com/

Poore, J., & Nemecek, T. (2018). Reducing food's environmental impacts through producers and consumers. Science, 360(6392), 987–992. https://doi.org/10.1126/science.aaq0216

Poppitt, S. D., Keogh, G. F., Lithander, F. E., Wang, Y., Mulvey, T. B., Chan, Y.-K., McArdle, B. H., & Cooper, G. J. S. (2008). Postprandial response of adiponectin, interleukin-6, tumor necrosis factor-alpha, and C-reactive protein to a high-fat dietary load. Nutrition (Burbank, Los Angeles County, Calif.), 24(4), 322–329. https://doi.org/10.1016/j.nut.2007.12.012

Rautiainen, S., Wang, L., Lee, I.-M., Manson, J. E., Buring, J. E., & Sesso, H. D. (2016). Dairy consumption in association with weight change and risk of becoming overweight or obese in middle-aged and older women: A prospective cohort study. The American Journal of Clinical Nutrition, 103(4), 979–988. https://doi.org/10.3945/ajcn.115.118406

Raziani, F., Tholstrup, T., Kristensen, M. D., Svanegaard, M. L., Ritz, C., Astrup, A., & Raben, A. (2016). High intake of regular-fat cheese compared with reduced-fat cheese does not affect LDL cholesterol or risk markers of the metabolic syndrome: A randomized controlled trial. The American Journal of Clinical Nutrition, 104(4), 973–981. https://doi.org/10.3945/ajcn.116.134932

Requena, P., Daddaoua, A., Guadix, E., Zarzuelo, A., Suárez, M. D., Sánchez de Medina, F., & Martínez-Augustin, O. (2009). Bovine glycomacropeptide induces cytokine production in human monocytes through the stimulation of the MAPK and the NF-kappaB signal transduction pathways. British Journal of Pharmacology, 157(7), 1232–1240. https://doi.org/10.1111/j.1476-5381.2009.00195.x

Reyes-Garcia, R., Mendoza, N., Palacios, S., Salas, N., Quesada-Charneco, M., Garcia-Martin, A., Fonolla, J., Lara-Villoslada, F., & Muñoz-Torres, M. (2018). Effects of Daily Intake of Calcium and Vitamin D-Enriched Milk in Healthy Postmenopausal Women: A Randomized, Controlled, Double-Blind Nutritional Study. Journal of Women's Health (2002), 27(5), 561–568. https://doi.org/10.1089/jwh.2017.6655

Rideout, T. C., Marinangeli, C. P. F., Martin, H., Browne, R. W., & Rempel, C. B. (2013). Consumption of low-fat dairy foods for 6 months improves insulin resistance without adversely affecting lipids or bodyweight in healthy adults: A randomized

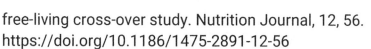
free-living cross-over study. Nutrition Journal, 12, 56. https://doi.org/10.1186/1475-2891-12-56

Ripple Foods. (2022). https://www.ripplefoods.com/

Rivlin, R. (2010). Riboflavin. In P. Coates, J. Betz, & M. Blackman (Eds.), Encyclopedia of Dietary Supplements (2nd ed., pp. 691–699). Informa Healthcare.

Rosa, D. D., Dias, M. M. S., Grześkowiak, Ł. M., Reis, S. A., Conceição, L. L., & Peluzio, M. do C. G. (2017). Milk kefir: Nutritional, microbiological and health benefits. Nutrition Research Reviews, 30(1), 82–96. https://doi.org/10.1017/S0954422416000275

Ross, A. (2006). Vitamin A and Carotenoids. In M. Shils, M. Shike, A. Ross, B. Caballero, & R. Cousins (Eds.), Modern Nutrition in Health and Disease (10th ed., pp. 351–375). Lippincott Williams & Wilkins.

Ross, C. (2010). Vitamin A. In P. Coates, J. Betz, & M. Blackman (Eds.), Encyclopedia of Dietary Supplements (2nd ed., pp. 778–791). Informa Healthcare.

Rotz, C. A. (2018). Modeling greenhouse gas emissions from dairy farms. Journal of Dairy Science, 101(7), 6675–6690. https://doi.org/10.3168/jds.2017-13272

Sacks, F. M., Lichtenstein, A. H., Wu, J. H. Y., Appel, L. J., Creager, M. A., Kris-Etherton, P. M., Miller, M., Rimm, E. B., Rudel, L. L., Robinson, J. G., Stone, N. J., & Van Horn, L. V. (2017). Dietary Fats and Cardiovascular Disease: A Presidential Advisory From the American Heart Association. Circulation, 136(3), e1–e23. https://doi.org/10.1161/CIR.0000000000000510

Sánchez, B., Delgado, S., Blanco-Míguez, A., Lourenço, A., Gueimonde, M., & Margolles, A. (2017). Probiotics, gut microbiota, and their influence on host health and disease. Molecular Nutrition & Food Research, 61(1). https://doi.org/10.1002/mnfr.201600240

Savage, J., Sicherer, S., & Wood, R. (2016). The Natural History of Food Allergy. The Journal of Allergy and Clinical Immunology. In Practice, 4(2), 196–203; quiz 204. https://doi.org/10.1016/j.jaip.2015.11.024

Scholz-Ahrens, K. E., Ahrens, F., & Barth, C. A. (2020). Nutritional and health attributes of milk and milk imitations. European Journal of Nutrition, 59(1), 19–34. https://doi.org/10.1007/s00394-019-01936-3

Schönfeld, P., & Wojtczak, L. (2016). Short- and medium-chain fatty acids in energy metabolism: The cellular perspective. Journal of Lipid Research, 57(6), 943–954. https://doi.org/10.1194/jlr.R067629

Schuster, M., Wang, X., Hawkins, T., & Painter, J. (2018). Comparison of the Nutrient Content of Cow's Milk and Nondairy Milk Alternatives. Nutrition Today, 53(4), 153–159.

Schwingshackl, L., Hoffmann, G., Lampousi, A.-M., Knüppel, S., Iqbal, K., Schwedhelm, C., Bechthold, A., Schlesinger, S., & Boeing, H. (2017). Food groups and risk of type 2 diabetes mellitus: A systematic review and meta-analysis of prospective studies.

European Journal of Epidemiology, 32(5), 363–375. https://doi.org/10.1007/s10654-017-0246-y

Schwingshackl, L., Schwedhelm, C., Hoffmann, G., Knüppel, S., Laure Preterre, A., Iqbal, K., Bechthold, A., De Henauw, S., Michels, N., Devleesschauwer, B., Boeing, H., & Schlesinger, S. (2018). Food groups and risk of colorectal cancer. International Journal of Cancer, 142(9), 1748–1758. https://doi.org/10.1002/ijc.31198

Sebastian, R., Goldman, J., Cecilia Wilkinson Enns, & LaComb, R. (2010). Fluid Milk Consumption in the United States: What We Eat in America, NHANES 2005-2006. Food Surveys Research Group Dietary Data Brief, 3, 8.

Sethi, S., Tyagi, S. K., & Anurag, R. K. (2016). Plant-based milk alternatives an emerging segment of functional beverages: A review. Journal of Food Science and Technology, 53(9), 3408–3423. https://doi.org/10.1007/s13197-016-2328-3

Shannon, R., & Rodriguez, J. M. (2014). Total arsenic in rice milk. Food Additives & Contaminants: Part B, 7(1), 54–56. https://doi.org/10.1080/19393210.2013.842941

Silk. (2022). Silk. https://silk.com/

Simeone, D., Miele, E., Boccia, G., Marino, A., Troncone, R., & Staiano, A. (2008). Prevalence of atopy in children with chronic constipation. Archives of Disease in Childhood, 93(12), 1044–1047. https://doi.org/10.1136/adc.2007.133512

Singh, G. M., Micha, R., Khatibzadeh, S., Shi, P., Lim, S., Andrews, K. G., Engell, R. E., Ezzati, M., Mozaffarian, D., & Group (NutriCoDE), G. B. of D. N. and C. D. E. (2015). Global, Regional, and National Consumption of Sugar-Sweetened Beverages, Fruit Juices, and Milk: A Systematic Assessment of Beverage Intake in 187 Countries. PLOS ONE, 10(8), e0124845. https://doi.org/10.1371/journal.pone.0124845

Singhal, S., Baker, R. D., & Baker, S. S. (2017). A Comparison of the Nutritional Value of Cow's Milk and Nondairy Beverages. Journal of Pediatric Gastroenterology and Nutrition, 64(5), 799–805. https://doi.org/10.1097/MPG.0000000000001380

Siri-Tarino, P. W., Chiu, S., Bergeron, N., & Krauss, R. M. (2015). Saturated Fats Versus Polyunsaturated Fats Versus Carbohydrates for Cardiovascular Disease Prevention and Treatment. Annual Review of Nutrition, 35, 517–543. https://doi.org/10.1146/annurev-nutr-071714-034449

Slykerman, R. F., Hood, F., Wickens, K., Thompson, J. M. D., Barthow, C., Murphy, R., Kang, J., Rowden, J., Stone, P., Crane, J., Stanley, T., Abels, P., Purdie, G., Maude, R., Mitchell, E. A., & Probiotic in Pregnancy Study Group. (2017). Effect of Lactobacillus rhamnosus HN001 in Pregnancy on Postpartum Symptoms of Depression and Anxiety: A Randomised Double-blind Placebo-controlled Trial. EBioMedicine, 24, 159–165. https://doi.org/10.1016/j.ebiom.2017.09.013

So Delicious Dairy Free. (2022). So Delicious Dairy Free. https://sodeliciousdairyfree.com/

Soedamah-Muthu, S. S., Ding, E. L., Al-Delaimy, W. K., Hu, F. B., Engberink, M. F., Willett, W. C., & Geleijnse, J. M. (2011). Milk and dairy consumption and incidence of cardiovascular diseases and all-cause mortality: Dose-response meta-analysis of prospective cohort studies. The American Journal of Clinical Nutrition, 93(1), 158–171. https://doi.org/10.3945/ajcn.2010.29866

Soerensen, K. V., Thorning, T. K., Astrup, A., Kristensen, M., & Lorenzen, J. K. (2014). Effect of dairy calcium from cheese and milk on fecal fat excretion, blood lipids, and appetite in young men. The American Journal of Clinical Nutrition, 99(5), 984–991. https://doi.org/10.3945/ajcn.113.077735

Solomons, N. (2006). Vitamin A. In B. Bowman & R. Russell (Eds.), Present Knowledge in Nutrition (9th ed., pp. 157–183). International Life Sciences Institute.

Song, L. (2017). Calcium and Bone Metabolism Indices. Advances in Clinical Chemistry, 82, 1–46. https://doi.org/10.1016/bs.acc.2017.06.005

Stancliffe, R. A., Thorpe, T., & Zemel, M. B. (2011). Dairy attentuates oxidative and inflammatory stress in metabolic syndrome. The American Journal of Clinical Nutrition, 94(2), 422–430. https://doi.org/10.3945/ajcn.111.013342

Stone, M. S., Martyn, L., & Weaver, C. M. (2016). Potassium Intake, Bioavailability, Hypertension, and Glucose Control. Nutrients, 8(7), E444. https://doi.org/10.3390/nu8070444

Suchy, F. J., Brannon, P. M., Carpenter, T. O., Fernandez, J. R., Gilsanz, V., Gould, J. B., Hall, K., Hui, S. L., Lupton, J., Mennella, J., Miller, N. J., Osganian, S. K., Sellmeyer, D. E., & Wolf, M. A. (2010). NIH consensus development conference statement: Lactose intolerance and health. NIH Consensus and State-of-the-Science Statements, 27(2), 1–27.

Sweetman, L. (2010). Pantothenic acid. In P. Coates, J. Betz, M. Blackman, G. Cragg, M. Levine, J. Moss, & J. White (Eds.), Encyclopedia of Dietary Supplements (2nd ed., pp. 604–611). Informa Healthcare.

Timon, C. M., O'Connor, A., Bhargava, N., Gibney, E. R., & Feeney, E. L. (2020). Dairy Consumption and Metabolic Health. Nutrients, 12(10), E3040. https://doi.org/10.3390/nu12103040

Tong, X., Dong, J.-Y., Wu, Z.-W., Li, W., & Qin, L.-Q. (2011). Dairy consumption and risk of type 2 diabetes mellitus: A meta-analysis of cohort studies. European Journal of Clinical Nutrition, 65(9), 1027–1031. https://doi.org/10.1038/ejcn.2011.62

Torres-Gonzalez, M., Cifelli, C. J., Agarwal, S., Fulgoni, V. L., & III. (2020). Association of Milk Consumption and Vitamin D Status in the US Population by Ethnicity: NHANES 2001–2010 Analysis. Nutrients, 12(12). https://doi.org/10.3390/nu12123720

Tripkovic, L., Lambert, H., Hart, K., Smith, C. P., Bucca, G., Penson, S., Chope, G., Hyppönen, E., Berry, J., Vieth, R., & Lanham-New, S. (2012). Comparison of vitamin D2 and vitamin D3 supplementation in raising serum 25-hydroxyvitamin D status: A systematic review and meta-analysis. The American Journal of Clinical Nutrition, 95(6), 1357–1364. https://doi.org/10.3945/ajcn.111.031070

Tucker, K. L., Rich, S., Rosenberg, I., Jacques, P., Dallal, G., Wilson, P. W., & Selhub, J. (2000). Plasma vitamin B-12 concentrations relate to intake source in the Framingham Offspring study. The American Journal of Clinical Nutrition, 71(2), 514–522. https://doi.org/10.1093/ajcn/71.2.514

Turkmen, N. (2017). Chapter 35—The Nutritional Value and Health Benefits of Goat Milk Components. In R. R. Watson, R. J. Collier, & V. R. Preedy (Eds.), Nutrients in Dairy and their Implications on Health and Disease (pp. 441–449). Academic Press. https://doi.org/10.1016/B978-0-12-809762-5.00035-8

Ulven, S. M., Holven, K. B., Gil, A., & Rangel-Huerta, O. D. (2019). Milk and Dairy Product Consumption and Inflammatory Biomarkers: An Updated Systematic Review of Randomized Clinical Trials. Advances in Nutrition (Bethesda, Md.), 10(suppl_2), S239–S250. https://doi.org/10.1093/advances/nmy072

Unger, A. L., Torres-Gonzalez, M., & Kraft, J. (2019). Dairy Fat Consumption and the Risk of Metabolic Syndrome: An Examination of the Saturated Fatty Acids in Dairy. Nutrients, 11(9), E2200. https://doi.org/10.3390/nu11092200

U.S. Department of Agriculture and U.S. Department of Health and Human Services. (2020). Dietary Guidelines for Americans, 2020-2025 (9th Edition; p. 164).

US Environmental Protection Agency. (n.d.). Ag 101: Dairy Production: Lifecycle production phases. EPA, 424.

U.S. Food and Drug Administration. (2016). Arsenic in Rice and Rice Products Risk Assessment Report. https://www.fda.gov/media/96071/download

US Food and Drug Administration. (2021, April 13). Bovine Somatotropin (bST). FDA; FDA. https://www.fda.gov/animal-veterinary/product-safety-information/bovine-somatotropin-bst

US Preventive Services Task Force, Grossman, D. C., Curry, S. J., Owens, D. K., Barry, M. J., Caughey, A. B., Davidson, K. W., Doubeni, C. A., Epling, J. W., Kemper, A. R., Krist, A. H., Kubik, M., Landefeld, S., Mangione, C. M., Silverstein, M., Simon, M. A., & Tseng, C.-W. (2018). Vitamin D, Calcium, or Combined Supplementation for the Primary Prevention of Fractures in Community-Dwelling Adults: US Preventive Services Task Force Recommendation Statement. JAMA, 319(15), 1592–1599. https://doi.org/10.1001/jama.2018.3185

USDA. (2018). FoodData Central. FoodData Central | U.S. Department of Agriculture, Agricultural Research Service. https://fdc.nal.usda.gov/

USDA Foreign Agricultural Service. (n.d.). Tree Nuts: World Markets and Trade. USDA Foreign Agricultural Service. Retrieved February 6, 2022, from https://www.fas.usda.gov/data/tree-nuts-world-markets-and-trade

USDA Natural Resources Conservation Service, Grazing Lands Technology Institute. (1996). Dairy Farmer Profitability Using Intensive Rotational Stocking: Better grazing management for pastures. USDA. https://www.nrcs.usda.gov/wps/PA_NRCSConsumption/download?cid=STELPR DB1257144&ext=pdf

Vanga, S. K., & Raghavan, V. (2018a). How well do plant based alternatives fare nutritionally compared to cow's milk? Journal of Food Science and Technology, 55(1), 10–20. https://doi.org/10.1007/s13197-017-2915-y

Vanga, S. K., & Raghavan, V. (2018b). How well do plant based alternatives fare nutritionally compared to cow's milk? Journal of Food Science and Technology, 55(1), 10–20. https://doi.org/10.1007/s13197-017-2915-y

Villegas, R., Gao, Y.-T., Yang, G., Li, H.-L., Elasy, T. A., Zheng, W., & Shu, X. O. (2008). Legume and soy food intake and the incidence of type 2 diabetes in the Shanghai Women's Health Study. The American Journal of Clinical Nutrition, 87(1), 162–167. https://doi.org/10.1093/ajcn/87.1.162

Vogiatzoglou, A., Smith, A. D., Nurk, E., Berstad, P., Drevon, C. A., Ueland, P. M., Vollset, S. E., Tell, G. S., & Refsum, H. (2009). Dietary sources of vitamin B-12 and their association with plasma vitamin B-12 concentrations in the general population: The Hordaland Homocysteine Study. The American Journal of Clinical Nutrition, 89(4), 1078–1087. https://doi.org/10.3945/ajcn.2008.26598

von Mutius, E., & Vercelli, D. (2010). Farm living: Effects on childhood asthma and allergy. Nature Reviews. Immunology, 10(12), 861–868. https://doi.org/10.1038/nri2871

Voth, K., & Gilker, R. (2017, November 14). What 30 Years of Study Tell Us About Grazing and Carbon Sequestration. On Pasture. https://onpasture.com/2017/11/13/what-30-years-of-study-tell-us-about-grazing-and-carbon-sequestration/

Wang, W. P., Iigo, M., Sato, J., Sekine, K., Adachi, I., & Tsuda, H. (2000). Activation of intestinal mucosal immunity in tumor-bearing mice by lactoferrin. Japanese Journal of Cancer Research: Gann, 91(10), 1022–1027. https://doi.org/10.1111/j.1349-7006.2000.tb00880.x

Warensjö, E., Jansson, J.-H., Cederholm, T., Boman, K., Eliasson, M., Hallmans, G., Johansson, I., & Sjögren, P. (2010). Biomarkers of milk fat and the risk of myocardial infarction in men and women: A prospective, matched case-control study. The American Journal of Clinical Nutrition, 92(1), 194–202. https://doi.org/10.3945/ajcn.2009.29054

Wennersberg, M. H., Smedman, A., Turpeinen, A. M., Retterstøl, K., Tengblad, S., Lipre, E., Aro, A., Mutanen, P., Seljeflot, I., Basu, S., Pedersen, J. I., Mutanen, M., & Vessby, B. (2009). Dairy products and metabolic effects in overweight men and women: Results from a 6-mo intervention study. The American Journal of Clinical Nutrition, 90(4), 960–968. https://doi.org/10.3945/ajcn.2009.27664

What is Yogurt? (n.d.). The Yogurt in Nutrition Initiative. Retrieved January 23, 2022, from https://www.yogurtinnutrition.com/what-yogurt/

Willett, W. C., & Ludwig, D. S. (2020). Milk and Health. The New England Journal of Medicine, 382(7), 644–654. https://doi.org/10.1056/NEJMra1903547

Woodford, K. (2009). Devil in the Milk—Illness, Health and the Politics of A1 and A2 Milk. Chelsea Green Publishing.

World Cancer Research Fund/American Institute for Cancer Research. (2018). Diet, Nutrition, Physical Activity and Cancer: A Global Perspective. Continuous Update Project Expert Report 2018. dietandcancerreport.org

Yalçin, A. S. (2006). Emerging therapeutic potential of whey proteins and peptides. Current Pharmaceutical Design, 12(13), 1637–1643. https://doi.org/10.2174/138161206776843296

Yao, X., Hu, J., Kong, X., & Zhu, Z. (2021). Association between Dietary Calcium Intake and Bone Mineral Density in Older Adults. Ecology of Food and Nutrition, 60(1), 89–100. https://doi.org/10.1080/03670244.2020.1801432

Yu, E., & Hu, F. B. (2018). Dairy Products, Dairy Fatty Acids, and the Prevention of Cardiometabolic Disease: A Review of Recent Evidence. Current Atherosclerosis Reports, 20(5), 24. https://doi.org/10.1007/s11883-018-0724-z

Zhang, K., Dai, H., Liang, W., Zhang, L., & Deng, Z. (2019). Fermented dairy foods intake and risk of cancer. International Journal of Cancer, 144(9), 2099–2108. https://doi.org/10.1002/ijc.31959

Zhu, G., & Xiao, Z. (2017). Creation and imitation of a milk flavour. Food & Function, 8(3), 1080–1084. https://doi.org/10.1039/c7fo00034k

Zimecki, M., & Kruzel, M. L. (2000). Systemic or local co-administration of lactoferrin with sensitizing dose of antigen enhances delayed type hypersensitivity in mice. Immunology Letters, 74(3), 183–188. https://doi.org/10.1016/s0165-2478(00)00260-1

SODIUM

By Karen Byrd, PhD, MBA, RDN
and Deborah Kennedy PhD
with The Expert Chef Panel

"Food shouldn't be salty; it should be salted."
Quote by Samin Nosrat, author of Salt, Fat, Acid, Heat

INTRODUCTION

In many households in the United States, the saltshaker and its companion, pepper, take center stage in the middle of the dining room table. Salt, however, is much more than a condiment, as it has been influential in the development of human civilization — not only in regard to our food supply but also in the development of cultures, cities, roads, ports and world powers. The earliest recordings of salt harvest date back to 6000 B.C.E. in China, and extensive salt mining and transportation began around 4,000 years ago (Adshead, 1992). Historically, salt was considered so valuable that it led to wars between countries, and it was used as currency to pay for goods and services. In fact, the word "salary" is rooted in the word "salt" (Kurlansky, 2003; Salt Association). Yet what once was highly valued and difficult to access is now ubiquitous in our food supply. Although salt is still vital in the human diet, **excess intake has now been identified as a worldwide public health concern.**

105

High sodium consumption **did not begin in recent times**. In fact, it is believed that the origins of today's high salt consumption began 5,000 to 10,000 years ago when sodium was commonly used for preservation of foods such as animal meats (F. J. He et al., 2014; MacGregor & Wardener, 1998; Man, 2007; Multhauf, 1978). In 300 B.C.E in China, sodium intake was estimated to be 5,000 mg per day for men and 3,000 mg per day for women (Adshead, 1992). Sodium consumption in Britain and France during the 1850s was as high as 4,000 to 5,000 mg per day (Multhauf, 1978). Today, sodium is used extensively by food processors to inhibit bacterial growth, extend shelf life, and enhance the flavor of foods.

Despite this long history of excess sodium consumption, sodium reductions are warranted to improve the health of individuals. It is postulated that a 1,200 mg per day reduction in individual sodium intake would save the lives of 44,000 to 92,000 persons annually by reducing the incidence and prevalence of high blood pressure, heart attacks, and strokes (Bibbins-Domingo et al., 2010), thus saving $18 billion per year in health care costs (Palar & Sturm, 2009). These projections have provided an impetus for food companies and researchers worldwide to actively pursue avenues to reduce or replace sodium in foods without sacrificing safety and quality (Christopher & Wallace, 2014; Raybaudi-Massilia et al., 2019).

SECTION 1: SODIUM CHARACTERISTICS

Chemically, "salt" is a broad term for an ionic compound formed from the reaction between an acid and a base. The most common type of salt humans consume is in the form of sodium chloride (e.g., chemical symbol NaCl), often referred to as "common" or "table" salt. By weight, 40% of the weight of salt comes from sodium and 60% from chloride. The sodium portion of this compound is of great importance from a health, culinary, and food safety perspective.

Figure 1: Sodium Chloride

SODIUM VERSUS SALT

The word sodium is sometimes used interchangeably with the word salt; however, sodium in our food supply is also found in combination with compounds other than chloride, both naturally and as an additive. In the United States, dietary recommendations are presented in terms of "sodium," whereas other countries and the World Health Organization have established recommendations for "salt" consumption. In this textbook, the focus will be on "sodium," and the term "salt" will be used when necessary to discuss sodium chloride (NaCl) specifically.

Research studies and dietary recommendations discuss sodium and salt intake in various units of measure. Conversions for salt and sodium are as follows:

> 1 tsp salt (sodium chloride) = 5,000 mg salt ≈ 2,000 mg sodium = 87 mmol sodium = 87 mEq sodium (*tsp = teaspoon; g = gram; mg = milligram; mmol = millimole; mEq = milliequivalent)
>
> **To convert sodium to salt** — milligrams of sodium x 2/5 = milligrams of salt
> or go to the American Heart Association's Sodium and Salt Converter

Sodium is important physiologically as well as for food safety and quality. **It is essential in the human diet, working alongside potassium to maintain fluid and acid-base balance in the body.** However, too much sodium has been linked to detrimental health outcomes, such as cardiovascular disease and hypertension (HTN). Decreasing dietary sodium intake to prevent these outcomes is challenging as it is abundant in our food supply, playing an important role in the preservation, texture, appearance and palatability of food.

SECTION 2: RECOMMENDATIONS FOR SODIUM INTAKE

In 2019, the National Academies of Science, Engineering, and Medicine (NASEM, formerly known as the Institute of Medicine, IOM) released an updated review of the Dietary Reference Intakes (DRI) for sodium (see Table 1) (NASEM, 2019). As in earlier versions of the sodium DRIs, the committee was unable to establish Estimated Average Requirement (EAR) or Recommended Dietary Allowance (RDA) values due to insufficient evidence. Instead, an Adequate Intake (AI) was reestablished to denote the level of intake where the diet is most likely adequate to prevent deficiency. For adults, this level was set at **1,500 mg per day,** although physiological need has been reported to be as low as 200 to 500 mg per day (Aburto, Ziolkovska, et al., 2013; NASEM, 2019). Consuming sodium from natural sources in our food supply like milk, meat, and shellfish would likely meet the physiological need of most adults, assuming there is dietary diversity. Caloric intake is linked to sodium consumption, which is why the daily recommended limit is less in children younger than 14 years of age as they need fewer calories overall (USDA & HHS, 2020).

Table 1: Sodium Dietary Reference Intake (DRI)

	Recommendations		
	AI (mg/d)	UL	CDRR
Infants			
0 to 6 months	110[a]	ND[b]	ND[c]
7 to 12 months	370	ND[b]	ND[c]
Children			
1 to 3 years	800[a]	ND[b]	Reduce intakes if above 1,200 mg/day[d]
4 to 8 years	1,000[a]	ND[b]	Reduce intakes if above 1,500 mg/day[d]
Adolescent/teen			
9 to 13 years	1,200[a]	ND[b]	Reduce intakes if above 1,800 mg/day[d]
14 to 18 years	1,500	ND[b]	Reduce intakes if above 2,300 mg/day[d]
Adults, 19 to 50 years	1,500	ND[b]	Reduce intakes if above 2,300 mg/day
Adults, 50 to >70 years	1,500[a]	ND[b]	Reduce intakes if above 2,300 mg/day
Pregnant/lactation, 14 to 50 years	1,500	ND[b]	Reduce intakes if above 2,300 mg/day[e]

Adapted from (NASEM, 2019) S-2, pg. S-11.

Abbreviations: AI = Adequate Intake; CDRR = Chronic Disease Risk Reduction Intake; ND = not determined; UL = Tolerable Upper Intake Level.

[a]Updated DRI value, compared to the 2005 DRI

[b]Lack of toxicological indicator specific to excessive sodium intake

[c]Insufficient strength of evidence for causality and intake response

[d]Extrapolated from adult CDRR based on sedentary Estimated Energy Requirements

[e]Extrapolated from adult CDRR based on sedentary Estimated Energy Requirements for ages 14 to 18 years

RISK REDUCTION LEVEL FOR SODIUM

The NASEM did not establish a tolerable upper limit due to a lack of evidence indicating a toxicological risk of high sodium intake; however, a **Chronic Disease Risk Reduction (CDRR) level was established for Americans 14 years of age or older based on evidence of a link between sodium intake greater than 2,300 mg for adults and an increased risk of high blood pressure and cardiovascular disease** (NASEM, 2019). This recommendation lends continued support for the 2020 – 2025 Dietary Guidelines for Americans (DGA) and other national and worldwide dietary sodium guidance at 2,300 mg per day for adults based on a 2,000 daily caloric intake (USDA and HHS, 2020; Arnett et al., 2019; World Health Organization, 2018).

Table 2: Daily Recommended Limit for Sodium on a 2,000 Daily Caloric Intake for Adults

Reference	Recommended Limit for Daily Sodium Intake
2020 – 2025 DGA	< 2,300 mg
2019 AHA/ACC [a]	Consume a diet with reduced amounts of sodium
2019 AHA/ACC for additional blood-pressure-lowering benefits	1,500 mg, or lowering current sodium intake by 1,000 mg/day
WHO[b]	5 grams of salt (e.g., ~2,000 mg of sodium)

[a] American Heart Association/American College of Cardiology (AHA/ACC) (Arnett et al., 2019)

[b] World Health Organization (World Health Organization, 2020)

SODIUM INTAKE AMONG AMERICANS

Despite recommendations to decrease sodium intake first appearing the 1980 Dietary Guidelines for Americans, as well as every iteration since (see Appendix A), sodium intake in the U.S. is considered excessive, with nearly **90% of U.S. adults consuming more than 2,300 mg of sodium** (DiNicolantonio & O'Keefe, 2017; Jackson et al., 2016). Based on the 2013 – 2014 National Health and Nutrition Examination Study (NHANES) 24-hour dietary recalls, average sodium consumption was estimated to be approximately 3,500 mg/day for adults and 3,000 mg/day for persons aged 2 to 19 years (Quader et al., 2017). Persons **20 to 50 years** of age had the highest sodium intake (3,754 mg/day) compared to other age groups. **Men** consumed more sodium than women, probably due to their higher caloric intake. **Non-Hispanic Asian** persons aged 2 years and older had the highest mean sodium intake (3,538 mg/day) compared to other race/ethnic groups.

Figure 2: Average Intake of Sodium in Milligrams Per Day by Age-Sex Groups, Compared to Tolerable Upper Intake Levels (UL)[a]

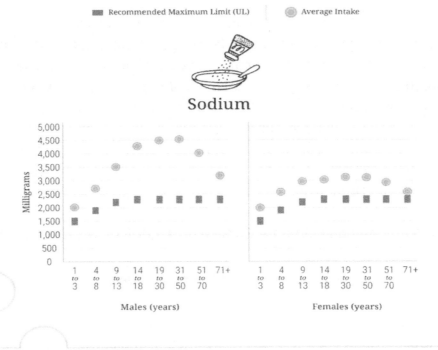

Source:
https://health.gov/our-work/food-nutrition/2015-2020-dietary-guidelines/guidelines/chapter-2/a-closer-look-at-current-intakes-and-recommended-shifts/
Data from What We Eat in America, NHANES 2007-2010 for average intakes by age-sex group. Healthy U.S.-Style Food Patterns, which vary based on age, sex, and activity level, for recommended intake ranges.
[a]With the 2019 Dietary Reference Intakes, the NASEM established a Chronic Disease Risk Reduction (CDRR), and a value for the "upper tolerable limit" was discontinued. The CDRR for sodium is 2,300 mg per day.

Sodium intake based on 24-hour urinary sodium excretion (a valid marker of sodium intake) has been estimated to be even higher than recall data at approximately 4,017 mg/day (Va et al., 2019). Regardless of the methodology used, **adult sodium intake is clearly high in the U.S. and exceeds the Chronic Disease Reduction Risk (CDRR) level by 1,200 to 1,700 mg per day.**

Seventy-one percent of the sodium consumed comes from food prepared outside the home (see Figure 2) and only 11% comes from the saltshaker (5% at the table and 6% in home food preparation). The rest comes from sodium that is innately present in food (Harnack et al., 2017).

SECTION 3: THE BENEFITS OF SODIUM

Salt evaporation ponds from Gran Canaria Salinas de Tenefé

Although excessive sodium ingestion is considered detrimental to health, sodium is essential both physiologically and for our food supply and should not be eliminated from the human diet completely. Physiologically, the majority of total body sodium (60% to 65%) is in body fluids, with the remainder stored in the skeleton (Mahan & Raymond, 2017). Sodium is the principal electrolyte in the extracellular fluid (ECF), which includes blood, interstitial fluid (fluid between cells), and transcellular fluid (such as cerebrospinal and joint fluids) (Ichai & Bichet, 2018a; Mahan & Raymond, 2017).

Because much of the body's sodium is found in body fluids, it plays a crucial role in maintaining blood pressure and blood volume. The renin-angiotensin-aldosterone system (RAAS) is the major regulatory pathway (Ichai, 2018; Ichai & Bichet, 2018; Mahan & Raymond, 2017). Concentrations of sodium, potassium, and water in the ECF and intracellular fluid (ICF) trigger this pathway to reabsorb, excrete, or retain these nutrients to maintain arterial pressure and cardiac output. This process is complex and involves other hormonal factors and organs, predominantly the kidney and brain (Ichai, 2018 Ichai & Bichet, 2018; Mahan & Raymond, 2017).

Potassium (K⁺) is sodium's (Na⁺) nutrient partner and is the principal electrolyte inside cells. These two electrolytes work together to actively maintain fluid balance in the body. The Na⁺/K⁺ ATPase pump in cell membranes pumps sodium out of the cells and moves potassium into the cells to maintain appropriate intra- and extracellular water concentrations. Body processes such as the transport and absorption of nutrients like glucose, amino acids, and water; nerve impulses; muscle contractions; renal function and cardiac output are all dependent on the homeostasis created by the balance of sodium and potassium (Ichai, 2018; Ichai & Bichet, 2018,; Mahan & Raymond, 2017).

> Values for serum sodium (the amount of sodium in the blood) are often included in standard blood test results. **Serum sodium is typically reflective of hydration status, not adequacy of dietary sodium consumption.** Treatment for low (hyponatremia) or high (hypernatremia) sodium levels is complex and depends on the underlying cause (see Braun et al., 2015, for a comprehensive review).

Essential functions of sodium (achieved at intakes of approximately 500 mg/day):
- Regulates intra- and extracellular fluid
- Aids in digestion and metabolism
- Supports the adrenal glands
- Helps maintain and regulate blood pressure
- Helps conduct nerve impulses
- Helps the brain function
- Contraction and relaxation of muscles

SECTION 4: THE RISKS OF TOO MUCH SODIUM

Based on NASEM's extensive review of the literature, sufficient evidence was deemed available to set the CDRR level recommending adults reduce their sodium intake if it is greater than **2,300 mg per day**. This recommendation was based on evidence showing a relationship between **dietary sodium intake above this level and risk of cardiovascular disease, hypertension, and high blood pressure.**

The following paragraphs provide a summary of evidence of the relationship between sodium and the prevention and treatment of chronic diseases, plus other common conditions that typically include recommendations related to sodium. Interestingly, treatment for many chronic medical conditions linked to high dietary sodium intake includes medications that also have implications for sodium intake; therefore, medical management beyond diet is an important consideration.

CARDIOVASCULAR DISEASE (CVD)

Consuming high amounts of sodium causes the body to hold onto fluid, which increases blood pressure — this is especially true in salt-sensitive individuals. At a cellular level, high sodium intake stiffens endothelial cells, blocks nitric oxide, and thickens and narrows resistance arteries (Büssemaker et al., 2010). Data supporting the reduction of sodium in one's diet as a way to prevent cardiovascular events is moderate in strength.

The landmark studies, which looked at the association between sodium intake and cardiovascular disease, are the Trials of Hypertension Prevention (TOPH) I and II (Whelton et al., 1992, 1997). The TOPH studies were randomized clinical trials that included random assignment of pre-hypertensive adults to a sodium intake reduction intervention. TOPH I and II showed a net reduction of approximately 1,000 to 1,170 mg, respectively, from a baseline average sodium intake of roughly 3,500 mg to 4,200 mg, respectively. A longitudinal arm of TOPH was conducted 10 to 15 years after TOPH I and II and found a **reduction in blood pressure and lower incidence of cardiovascular events** in people assigned to a sodium reduction intervention compared to those who were not. The longitudinal study did not include sodium intake measurement; however, participants were asked questions that suggested adherence or not to a reduced-sodium eating pattern.

These studies led the NASEM to conclude **there is moderate strength of evidence supporting sodium reduction as a means to reduce cardiovascular events** (NASEM, 2019). An additional longitudinal follow-up of TOPH (not included in the NASEM literature review) evaluating participants 20-plus years later revealed a linear relationship between sodium intake and cardiovascular mortality, with a higher risk at intakes above 2,300 mg per day at baseline (Cook et al., 2016).

BLOOD PRESSURE AND HYPERTENSION (HTN)

High blood pressure is an independent risk factor for stroke, heart attack, and other cardiovascular conditions. Similar to CVD, HTN etiology is multifactorial with causes ranging from environmental and genetic factors to lifestyle factors, including high dietary sodium intake. Although the pathophysiological connection between HTN and dietary sodium continues to be investigated, current thinking suggests the association is based on an increased blood and extracellular volume and increased arterial stiffness from excess dietary sodium intake (Grillo, 2019).

A low-sodium diet is generally the standard treatment for existing hypertension with recommendations of **an optimal goal of less than 1,500 mg/day or at least a 1,000 mg per day reduction** of sodium for most adults with hypertension (Whelton, 2018). A comparative effectiveness review of dietary sodium and potassium commissioned by the Agency for Healthcare Research and Quality (AHRQ), based on an analysis of 48 RCTs, resulted in moderate-strength evidence of the following (Newberry et al., 2018):

- A reduction in sodium intake most likely results in a decrease in hypertension in adults with hypertension.
    - An approximate 1,000 mg dietary sodium reduction results in a reduction of systolic BP by 3.23 mm Hg (95% confidence interval [CI] 2.38 to 4.07) and diastolic BP by 2.24 mm HG (95% CI 1.61 to 2.96) in adults.
- The blood-pressure-lowering effect was present in both normotensive and hypertensive individuals, but the effect was greater in hypertensive individuals.

A subsequent study by Jackson et al. (2018) showed a greater blood pressure change of 4.58 mm Hg (95% confidence interval [CI] 2.64 to 6.51) and 2.25 mm Hg (95% CI 0.83 to 3.67) difference in systolic and diastolic blood pressure, respectively, for a 1,000 mg difference in sodium consumption, lending additional support to the benefits of lower sodium intake.

Evidence of the relationship between reducing sodium intake and incidence of **developing hypertension,** however, was deemed unclear by both the AHRQ and NAESM due to lack of sufficient studies (NASEM, 2019; Newberry et al., 2018). Yet dietary advice to reduce chronic disease risk, including high blood pressure, includes reducing sodium intake to below 2,300 mg/day (NASEM, 2019).

Salt-Sensitive Individuals
Studies have shown that blood pressure changes after ingesting sodium may be greater in "salt-sensitive" individuals or subgroups (NASEM, 2019). This trait of salt-sensitive blood pressure (SSBP) is an abnormal phenotype that is continuous and normally distributed throughout the population. The SSBP phenotype is a risk factor for cardiovascular morbidity and mortality (Morimoto et al., 1997; Weinberger et al., 2001).

Because there is no biomarker or specific treatment for "salt sensitivity" to date, the same sodium recommendations apply to this cohort as well. However, certain factors are associated with having the SSBP phenotype – a greater age, being a woman, Black ethnicity, obesity and those with certain medical conditions like diabetes, hypertension, and chronic kidney disease (Elijovich et al., 2016; Weinberger, 1996).

Salt Sensitivity of Blood Pressure – A Scientific Statement from the American Heart Association.

Pregnancy

A reduced-sodium diet is generally not recommended for mothers with gestational hypertension and preeclampsia. The current best practice is considered a moderate sodium intake of 2,000 to 3,000 mg/day as further reductions in sodium intake have not been associated with improved outcomes; however, women with a history of hypertension, obesity, or metabolic disorders may need dietary sodium restriction

(Academy of Nutrition and Dietetics) and this should be done only under the guidance of a clinician.

A Word on Potassium

Products containing potassium

A discussion of the association of dietary sodium to CVD, hypertension, and stroke would be incomplete without mentioning potassium. Evidence does suggest that potassium — sodium's partner in maintaining fluid balance in the body — also plays an important role in these cardiovascular conditions. For example, prospective data from NHANES III (1988 – 1994) showed that a high sodium intake was associated with all-cause mortality and an increase in CVD risk and all-cause mortality was related to higher sodium-to-potassium ratio (e.g., consuming more sodium than potassium), when comparing the highest ratio (1.57:1) to the lowest ratio (0.98:1) (Yang et al., 2011). Results also showed that while high sodium and low potassium intakes, respectively, were associated with all-cause mortality, the sodium-to-potassium ratio was more impactful on this outcome measure than either nutrient alone. For stroke, the sodium and potassium story is similar: both a high sodium intake and a high sodium-to-potassium ratio were associated with increased stroke incidence (Jayedi et al., 2019).

For blood pressure, decreased sodium intake, increased potassium intake, and a favorable sodium-to-potassium ratio (e.g., at or close to 1:1) have each demonstrated positive outcomes. For example, Jackson et al. (Jackson Sandra L. et al., 2018) showed linear but opposite relationships of sodium and potassium intake on hypertension. Specifically, the following outcomes were reported based on 24-hour urine samples (e.g., a means of surrogate measurement of dietary intake):
- 1,000 mg difference in sodium intake was associated with 4.58 mm Hg (95% confidence interval [CI] 2.64 to 6.51) and 2.25 mg Hg (95% CI 0.83 to 3.67) difference in systolic and diastolic blood pressure, respectively.
- 1,000 mg difference in potassium intake was associated with a -3.72 mm Hg (95% CI -6.01 to -1.42) difference in systolic blood pressure.

These findings supported results from other studies (Perez & Chang, 2014; Z. Zhang et al., 2013), and demonstrate that all three approaches can lower blood pressure. However, other data has suggested that improving the sodium-to-potassium ratio is only associated with improved blood pressure when the average daily intake is at or exceeds approximately 2,400 mg of sodium (Rodrigues et al., 2014). Furthermore, other epidemiological studies have suggested that high potassium intake may blunt the adverse effects of a high-sodium diet on blood pressure (Aburto, Hanson, et al., 2013; Gay et al., 2016; F. J. He et al., 2013).

Even with the body of evidence suggesting the importance of the sodium-to-potassium ratio, there is no definitive recommendation for what the ratio should be. However, if daily sodium and potassium intake recommendations from the World Health Organization (World Health Organization, 2012) and the U.S. DRI (NASEM, 2019) were met, the ratio would be around 0.5 to 0.9. While research of the relationship of dietary sodium and potassium is ongoing, health professionals are encouraged to advise patients and clients to decrease sodium intake and increase potassium intake to improve cardiovascular health.

STROKE

Dietary sodium reduction is often prescribed to stroke patients as a means to control blood pressure (Mahan & Raymond, 2017). Evidence for decreasing sodium for stroke prevention was demonstrated in a meta-analyses from Aburto et al. (2103) and Strazzullo et al. (2013). Of note, however, the Strazzullo et al. analysis showed the association was not significant in a subset analysis of nine of the 19 cohorts that used 24-hour sodium excretion to evaluate dietary sodium intake. Aburto et al. also noted methodological heterogeneity in determining dietary sodium intake but did not report a subset analysis similar to Strazzullo et al. Both the AHRQ dietary sodium effectiveness review and the NASEM sodium DRI committees **rated the evidence for linking reduced dietary sodium intake and reduced incidence of stroke as low** (NASEM, 2019; Newberry et al., 2018).

MYOCARDIAL INFARCTION (MI)

Both the AHRQ and DRI committees concluded there were few studies and, thus, **insufficient evidence** to link the risk of MI and a reduction in dietary sodium intake (NASEM, 2019; Newberry et al., 2018). Similar to stroke, dietary sodium reduction is often prescribed to post-MI patients as a means to control blood pressure (Mahan & Raymond, 2017).

HEART FAILURE (HF)

Hypertension has been noted to be an etiological factor in HF development. Evidence suggests that the risk of HF can be moderated with effective management of high blood pressure, including interventions such as reducing sodium consumption, although a clear causal relationship between HF incidence and sodium intake has not been established (Oliveros et al., 2018). The Heart Failure Society of America (HFSA) recommends sodium intake of less than or equal to **1,500 mg of sodium per day** for everyone with HTN to decrease the risk of HF development (Lindenfeld et al., 2010).

A reduced-sodium diet has also historically been a standard intervention for individuals diagnosed with heart failure (Mahan & Raymond, 2017). Yet the suggested limit and whether sodium should even be limited has recently been questioned (Aronow & Shamliyan, 2018; Yang et al., 2011). Recommendations from various health organizations across the globe recommend either no sodium restriction or a restriction between 2,000 to 3,000 mg/day (Aronow & Shamliyan, 2018; Mahan & Raymond, 2017). Some guidelines add caveats to base the sodium restriction recommendation on fluid retention (e.g., edema), clinical symptoms, and heart failure classification.

HFSA 2010 guidelines suggest a 2,000 to 3,000 mg sodium restriction per day for individuals with preserved or depressed left ventricular ejection fraction, with consideration of further limitation to less than 2,000 mg per day in the presence of moderate to severe HF (Lindenfeld et al., 2010). The ACC/AHA 2013 guidelines state that 1,500 mg per day is generally appropriate for stages A and B HF (Yancy et al., 2013). However, for stages C and D HF, mixed evidence showing both positive and adverse clinical outcomes led to a vague recommendation stating a degree of sodium restriction, such as <3,000 mg per day, for symptom improvement. Determination of optimal sodium intake for HF patients is the subject of ongoing research.

OBESITY

Calories have been well established as the nutrient of most concern in the development of obesity. Yet observational studies have shown an association between high sodium intake and a greater risk of obesity, independent of energy consumption (Moosavian et al., 2017; Zhao et al., 2019). A cross-sectional study with New York City adults revealed that a difference in intake of 1,000 mg of sodium per day was associated with higher odds of being obese, characterized by higher weight, body mass index (BMI), and waist circumference, with the association being more robust for women than men (Yi & Kansagra, 2014).

Ma et al. (2015) found a significant relationship between higher body fat mass in adults and children and higher sodium intake, after adjusting for co-factors. Etiologically, animal models revealed increases in white adipocyte mass and a concentration of blood leptin with high sodium intake compared to normal sodium intake, despite receiving isocaloric diets between groups. Furthermore, a randomized controlled trial in adults showed higher ghrelin (a peptide produced primarily in the stomach and believed to stimulate appetite and fat accumulation) levels in non-obese, normotensive subjects when they consumed a high-sodium (7,200 mg) compared to a low-sodium diet (1,200 mg) (Y. Zhang et al., 2016). More human research, however, is needed to determine causal relationships and to confirm possible mechanisms.

OSTEOPOROSIS

Osteoporosis is a debilitating metabolic bone disease resulting in an increased risk of fractures. A predictor of osteoporotic fractures is lower bone mineral density (BMD). Low BMD is associated with higher urinary calcium excretion, which has been linked to sodium intake (Mahan & Raymond, 2017). Yet a meta-analysis and a prospective observational cohort study showed no direct association between dietary sodium intake (as measured by 24-hour sodium excretion) and osteoporosis, bone mineral density, or fractures (Carbone et al., 2016; Fatahi et al., 2018).

KIDNEY DISEASE

Chronic Kidney Disease (CKD)
Chronic kidney disease (CKD) is characterized by decreased renal function, evidenced by proteinuria and/or glomerular filtration rate (GFR) reduction. Despite high blood pressure being a known risk factor for CKD, evidence to establish a direct causal relationship between dietary sodium intake and CKD risk has been deemed insufficient (NASEM, 2019; Newberry et al., 2018).

Restriction in dietary sodium, however, is a standard recommendation for CKD patients. High sodium intake has been associated with undesirable trends in markers of renal function in this population (Smyth et al., 2014). Referral to a registered dietitian nutritionist (RDN) is important, especially during advanced CKD stages and when receiving dialysis. Current joint recommendations from the National Kidney Foundation and the Academy of Nutrition and Dietetics suggest an intake of <2,300 mg per day for adult CKD patients 3 to 5, CKD 5D (i.e., dialysis); and post-transplantation (Handu et al., 2021). Recommendations differ for children. Consult a RDN for advice.

Kidney Stones

Afsar et al. (2016) outlined a rationale for reducing sodium intake as a means to decrease the risk of calcium-based kidney stones; however, clear evidence of a reduced risk of stone formation is lacking (Afsar et al., 2016).

GASTRIC CANCER

Gastric cancer ranks third in world deaths caused by cancer (Rawla & Barsouk, 2019). The World Cancer Research Federation/American Institute for Cancer Research reported strong evidence supporting a probable link between gastric cancer incidence and high consumption of salt-preserved food, such as pickled foods (including pickled vegetables), salted fish, processed meat, and other high-salt foods. D'Elia et al. (2014) outlined a possible mechanism of a high salt intake damaging the gastric mucosa, making it susceptible to salt-stimulated colonization of the bacteria Heliobacter pylori, the strongest known risk factor for gastric cancer. Investigations for other possible mechanisms are in progress (D'Elia et al., 2014).

LIVER DISEASE

Non-alcoholic Fatty Liver Disease (NAFLD)

As the name suggests, NAFLD is an accumulation of fat in liver cells, unrelated to alcohol consumption. Researchers in Asia showed a possible link between NAFLD and high sodium intake; however, results should be interpreted cautiously because the gold standard 24-hour urinary sodium excretion method was not used to estimate sodium intake (Huh et al., 2015; Shen et al., 2019). More research is needed to confirm this link.

Ascites Management

A manifestation of chronic liver disease is ascites — an accumulation of fluid in the peritoneal cavity. The American Association for the Study of Liver Diseases recommends sodium restriction of 2,000 mg per day along with diuretics for the treatment of ascites in cirrhotic patients (Runyon & AASLD Practice Guidelines Committee, 2009).

HEADACHE

Headaches are classified as primary or secondary, with a wide variety of reported causes for each type. High blood pressure appears on the list of potential causes for secondary headaches, and therefore, may be linked to dietary sodium consumption. A randomized control trial did provide evidence of a lower rate of headaches in individuals with stage 1 HTN who received a low-sodium diet compared to those on a high-sodium diet, with mean sodium intakes of 1,470 mg/day and 3,240 mg/day, respectively, based on 24-hour urinary sodium excretion (Amer et al., 2014). Additional studies, however, are needed to provide corroborating evidence and pathophysiology.

SECTION 5: CONDITIONS WARRANTING INCREASED SODIUM INTAKE

Although reducing sodium intake is a recommended means of improving population health and treating specific chronic diseases and conditions, certain circumstances may warrant a higher dietary sodium intake.

Postural Orthostatic Tachycardia Syndrome (POTS)

POTS is an orthostatic intolerance disorder afflicting about 1% of the U.S. population (Zadourian et al., 2018). When an individual with POTS stands up, their blood pressure can plummet, causing fainting or feelings of fainting. This condition can be debilitating and reduce quality of life. A uniform treatment approach for this syndrome has yet to be defined; however, sodium intake of 4,000 to 4,800 mg daily is the suggested recommendation for most patients as one of several first-line, non-pharmacologic interventions. The increase in salt intake is to purposely cause a rise in blood pressure, thus preventing its decline upon standing.

High Sweat Production

Physiological sodium needs may increase above the AI in the presence of high sweat production. This increased need can occur in high-intensity exercise of long duration or in individuals working in a high-heat environment who have not acclimated to the temperature. Reported average sodium loss in sweat is 1,012 mg per liter; however, losses are highly variable depending on numerous factors such as overall diet, sodium intake, sweating rate, hydration status, body size, sex, age, heat exposure and stress, heat acclimatization, physical activity intensity and duration, as well as sodium reabsorption by the sweat glands (Baker, 2017; Kaptein et al., 2016; NASEM, 2019). In high-intensity exercise lasting more than two hours, a fluid-replacement solution containing sodium (300 to 425 mg per 20-ounce bottle) is generally warranted to promote thirst, minimize the risk of muscle cramping, and maintain serum sodium homeostasis (Mahan & Raymond, 2017). A RDN should typically be consulted to individualize sodium recommendations for persons with high sweat production.

Acute Diarrhea

Acute diarrhea in infants and children is usually defined as twice the average number of stools per day in infants or three or more loose, watery stools per day in older children. The World Health Organization and the Academy of Pediatrics recommend an oral rehydration solution (such as Pedialyte, Enfalyte, Lytren, Equalyte, Rehydrate) that includes 90 mEq of sodium per liter (among other electrolytes and glucose) to compensate for sodium loss in the stool (Mahan & Raymond, 2017).

SECTION 6: SODIUM AND MEDICATIONS

Several over-the-counter and prescribed medications contain sodium, with reports of intakes of 464 to 4,623 mg of sodium per day for individuals receiving certain drugs with high sodium levels (defined as 391 mg or more per dose) (Perrin et al., 2017). Therefore, medication as an additional source of sodium should be carefully evaluated. Additionally, some medications may alter salt taste, resulting in challenges 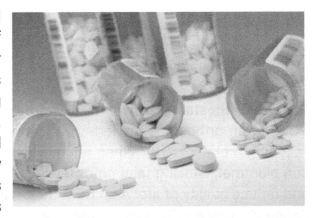 for some individuals to decrease their sodium intake. For example, an observational study of heart failure patients revealed an association between ACE inhibitors and higher sodium intake per calorie (as measured by four-day food diaries) compared to other medicinal management (Smith et al., 2019). Physicians, pharmacists, nurses and RDNs should collaboratively evaluate medications of individuals reporting difficulty decreasing their sodium intake related to food taste. Lastly, some medications may foster (e.g., thiazides) or inhibit (e.g., insulin) sodium excretion; this should be a consideration when determining appropriate dietary sodium interventions and evaluating the effectiveness of a drug.

SECTION 7: THE DASH DIET

The DASH eating pattern was developed over 20 years ago by researchers at NIH's National Heart, Lung, and Blood Institute as a dietary means to lower blood pressure. This dietary pattern is a whole-food approach based on increasing dietary components linked to positive effects on BP and decreasing dietary components associated with adverse BP effects. Two landmark studies were conducted to evaluate the eating plan. The first study focused on increasing foods high in potassium, magnesium, calcium and fiber and decreasing foods high in saturated fat and cholesterol (Appel et al., 1997). This study resulted in **a reduction in BP among participants that was similar to a first-line blood pressure medication,** -5.5 mm Hg for systolic and -3.0 mm Hg for diastolic blood pressures. The second study looked at the added value of reducing sodium along with the DASH eating plan. Results showed that the combination of reducing sodium and following the DASH plan was more effective than either intervention alone (Sacks et al., 2001).

With the DASH diet, reductions in blood pressure occurred **within two weeks** of starting this dietary pattern, which focuses on:

- **Eating more:** Fruits, vegetables, low-fat dairy, whole grains, fish, poultry, and nuts
- **Eating less:** Food high in cholesterol, saturated fat, trans fat, sodium, sweets, sugary drinks and red meat

For more information, go to the chapter on the DASH Diet.

SECTION 8: CLINICAL & CULINARY RECOMMENDATIONS AND COMPETENCIES

Messaging from the Menus of Change Annual Report 2020
CUT THE SALT: RETHINK FLAVOR DEVELOPMENT FROM THE GROUND UP

Clinical recommendations and competencies are the foundation from which culinary competencies were created. The goal for the culinary medicine practitioner is to help clients and patients develop the skills necessary to meet the clinical recommendations by teaching skill-based learning outlined in the culinary competencies.

CLINICAL RECOMMENDATIONS

1. Consume less than 2,300 milligrams (mg) per day of sodium (for individuals ages 14 years and older) (NASEM, 2019; USDA & HHS, 2020).
2. Consume less than 1,500 mg per day of sodium or decrease intake by 1,000 mg per day to prevent and treat high blood pressure, if warranted (Arnett Donna K. et al., 2019).

CLINICAL COMPETENCIES

1. Explain the difference between sodium and salt.
2. List the daily recommendations for sodium intake, including the Adequate Intake and Chronic Disease Risk Reduction recommendations.
3. Outline the function of sodium in the body and the interaction between potassium and sodium.
4. Summarize the typical sodium intake among individuals following a Western diet.
5. Explain the adverse health effects related to high sodium intake.
6. Classify which cohorts are at risk for sodium-related negative health effects.
7. Identify medical conditions that may require increased sodium in the diet.
8. Determine if iodized salt is necessary.
9. Describe how medications can affect sodium recommendations.

CULINARY COMPETENCIES FOR SODIUM

Shopping and Storing Competencies
1. Identify sodium content in a serving of food.
    a. Demonstrate how to read the Nutrition Facts panel.
    b. Demonstrate how to find the sodium content in a serving of food prepared away from home.
2. List the main sources of sodium in a Western diet.
3. Purchase low-sodium food.
    a. Interpret the terms "healthy" and "low sodium" as they relate to food products, meals, or the main dish.
4. Store salt to prevent clumping.
    a. Describe what storage conditions are best for salt.

Stocking the Kitchen
1. Stock a variety of salt with an assortment of flake sizes.
2. Stock a variety of non-salt flavor enhancers.
    a. A variety of herbs and spices
    b. Food-sources of acid (citrus and vinegars)
    c. Umami ingredients like mushrooms, tomatoes, soy sauce and fermented foods
    d. Various onions and capers
    e. Oils and flavored oils
    f. Pungent ingredients like mustard, wasabi and horseradish
3. Stock a variety of salty foods with various flavor profiles.
    a. Anchovies
    b. Parmesan cheese
    c. Low sodium soy sauce
    d. Liquid aminos
    e. Tamari
    f. Fish sauce

Cooking/Preparing Competencies
Flavor Development Competencies (based on the knowledge of the role salt plays in cooking and food preparation)
1. Describe how salt affects flavor and texture
2. Build flavor using umami ingredients.
3. Develop flavor using herbs, spices, and pungent ingredients.
4. Demonstrate how to use acidic ingredients to brighten the flavor of food.
5. Describe cooking techniques that impart new flavor into a dish.

Cooking Competencies

1. Salt food appropriately when needed.
   a. Demonstrate when to add salt during cooking and food preparation.
   b. Summarize the role salt plays in cooking and food preparation.
2. Demonstrate how to dilute the amount of salt per serving when preparing food.
3. Describe the method to reduce the salt content in canned foods.
4. Make use of other ingredients to replace salt in a recipe.

Serving Competencies

1. Remove the salt shaker from the table.
2. Order food low in sodium when dining out.
   a. Request sodium content of meals eaten away from home when there is no nutrient fact label available at point of purchase

Safety Competencies

1. Preserve food
   a. Explain the role of salt in food preservation.

SECTION 9: SALT AT THE STORE AND RESTAURANTS

ON THE LABEL

Even though the saltshaker is a staple in most U.S. homes, it only contributes about 5% to overall sodium consumption from use at the table and 6% from home food preparation. Most of the U.S. sodium intake comes from food prepared outside the home (71%, e.g., commercially processed food, restaurant food preparation, etc.), followed by sodium that is inherent in the food itself (14%) (Harnack et al., 2017).

Packaged foods are required to include sodium on the Nutrition Facts (NF) label to indicate the amount of sodium per serving (Figure 3); however, exemptions exist for low-volume products and some meat and poultry items (CFR, 2012, 2016).

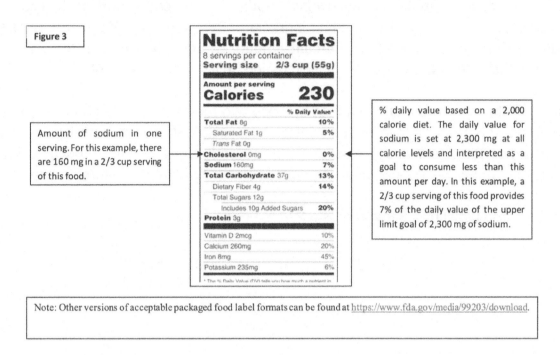

Figure 3

Amount of sodium in one serving. For this example, there are 160 mg in a 2/3 cup serving of this food.

% daily value based on a 2,000 calorie diet. The daily value for sodium is set at 2,300 mg at all calorie levels and interpreted as a goal to consume less than this amount per day. In this example, a 2/3 cup serving of this food provides 7% of the daily value of the upper limit goal of 2,300 mg of sodium.

Note: Other versions of acceptable packaged food label formats can be found at https://www.fda.gov/media/99203/download.

In the United Kingdom, consumers may see sodium on the front-of-the-pack (FOP) labeling on some foods. Below is an example. A similar "Facts Up Front" can be seen on some foods in the U.S. as part of a voluntary, collaborative initiative among food and beverage manufacturers and retailers (About Facts Up Front).

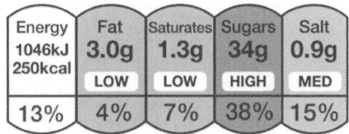

Source: https://www.nutrition.org.uk/putting-it-into-practice/food-labelling/looking-at-labels/#frontofpack

Ingredient List

Most packaged food labels must also include a list of ingredients in descending order of predominance by weight (CFR, 2016). Consumers can look for the word "salt" and "sodium" in the ingredient list to determine if sodium is present. In both of the examples in Figure 4, sodium is listed as the last ingredient. Because **a small amount of salt by weight can deliver a relatively significant amount of sodium**, it is best to look at the Nutrient Facts panel when selecting a food based on its sodium content.

Looking at the label and ingredient lists of these two foods (Figure 4), you would have a hard time distinguishing a typical "salty" food from a typical "sweet" food. The reason is because manufacturers add salt to sweet food and sugar to salty food to enhance palatability, which may make it challenging for some individuals to control intake.

Figure 4: Food Label of a Salty Versus a Sweet Food

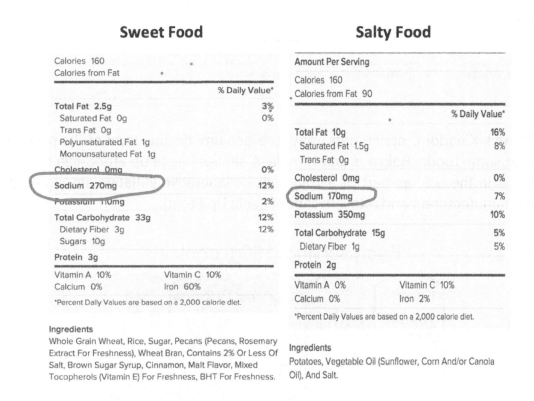

From NPR: How The Food Industry Manipulates Taste Buds With Salt Sugar Fat

Nutrient and Health Claims Regarding Sodium

Food manufacturers can include sodium-related nutrient claims on packaged foods if required criteria are met (Box A) (FDA, 2013). An additional health claim is allowable on foods that meet the criteria to be labeled a "low-sodium" food.

Two specific formats include:

(1) Diets low in sodium may [might] reduce the risk of high blood pressure, a disease associated with many factors.

(2) Development of hypertension or high blood pressure depends on many factors. [This product] can be part of a low-sodium, low-salt diet that might reduce the risk of hypertension or high blood pressure.

Consumers do need to be wary of meat and poultry items labeled as "natural" as these products may contain a flavoring solution that often contains sodium (USDA, 2013). Check the label.

Box A: Nutrient Content Claims (FDA, 2013)

Sodium Nutrient Claims per Reference Amount Customarily Consumed (RACC)

Sodium-free (or salt-free): Less than 5 mg per RACC per labeled serving

Very low sodium: 35 mg or less per RACC or 35 mg per 100 grams for a meal or main dish

Low sodium: 140 mg or less per RACC or 140 mg per 100 grams for a meal or main dish

Reduced/less sodium: At least 25% less sodium per RACC than a standard reference food not reduced in sodium or 25% less sodium per 100 grams for a meal or main dish

Light sodium: Food must meet criteria for "low calorie" and "low fat" and sodium is reduced by at least 50%

Light in sodium: Sodium reduced by 50% per RACC or meet the definition for "low in sodium" for a meal or main dish

No salt added and unsalted: Must declare "This is Not a Sodium Free Food" on information panel if food is not "sodium free"

Lightly salted: 50% less sodium than normally added to a standard reference food not lightly salted; declare "Not Low Sodium" if the "low sodium" criteria is not met

Healthy: Less than or equal to 480 mg per RACC or less than 600 mg for a meal main dish per labeled serving AND meets criteria for total fat, saturated fat, cholesterol and beneficial nutrients

WHERE DOES MOST OF THE SODIUM COME FROM IN THE DIET?

Figure 5: Top Sources of Average Intakes of Sodium: U.S. Population Ages 1 and Older

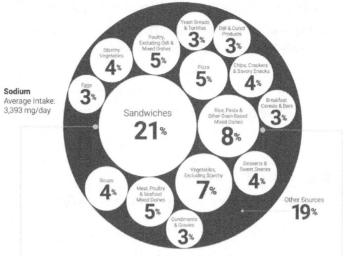

Copied from DGA 2020 – 2025 (Dietary Guidelines for Americans, 2020-2025, n.d.). **Data Source:** Analysis of What We Eat in America, NHANES, 2013-2016, ages 1 and older, two days dietary intake data, weighted.

While the Nutrition Facts label can aid in selecting lower-sodium foods, that is only part of the story. Some of the top sources of sodium in the U.S. diet are not necessarily foods high in sodium — they are just consumed in high quantities. Take bread, for example. One slice (1 ounce) of 100% whole wheat bread has approximately 110 mg of sodium (USDA, 2018). This quantity actually meets the criteria for a "low-sodium" food. However, bread is a frequently consumed food in the U.S. diet. Therefore, shoppers need to not only consider individual foods in their market basket but also how those foods are combined together to make meals and snacks that add up to their total sodium intake for a day.

It doesn't have to taste 'salty' to contain lots of sodium

2 Slices = 300 mg   15 chips = 170 mg

Americans consume 40% of their sodium from the 10 types of food listed below (Quader et al., 2017). Some of these foods may come as a surprise, as many do not consider them to be salty, and a single serving is not always high in sodium (e.g., bread, eggs). Therefore, eliminating these foods is likely not necessary; however, a reduction in the number of servings consumed per day of these items or selecting versions that are less processed (and thus less sodium) may be needed.

- Yeast breads, rolls, buns, bagels, English muffins
- Pizza
- Sandwiches
- Cold cuts and cured meats
- Soups
- Burritos and tacos
- Savory snacks (chips, popcorn, pretzels, snack mixes and crackers)
- Chicken
- Cheese (natural and processed)
- Eggs and omelets

Consumers should focus on selecting items with single or few ingredients in them when shopping. Consumers should be advised to check food labels for products with **140 mg of sodium or less per serving** (e.g., criteria for a low-sodium food), or minimally, compare brands and select the one with the lowest amount of sodium. Swapping out different versions of the same food can substantially reduce the amount of sodium in the shopping cart.

The Centers for Disease Control and Prevention (CDC) offers the following specific shopping tips for consumers (CDC, 2018):

- Buy fresh, frozen, dried or canned vegetables and beans with no salt or sauce added.

- Choose packaged foods labeled "low sodium," "reduced sodium," or "no salt added" when available.
- Read food labels and compare the amount of sodium in different products, then choose the option with the lowest amount of sodium.
- When buying prepared meals, look for those with less than 600 mg of sodium per meal, which is the upper limit set by the Food and Drug Administration for a meal or main dish to be labeled "healthy."
- Check the amount of sodium per serving, and don't forget to check the number of servings per container.
- When possible, purchase fresh poultry, fish, pork and lean meat, rather than cured, salted, smoked and other processed meats. For fresh items, check to see whether saline or salt solution has been added — if so, choose another brand.
- Ask your grocer if they have a low-sodium shopping list available.
- Ask to speak to the registered dietitian nutritionist at your local grocery store to learn more about buying low-sodium products. If your grocer doesn't have an RDN, ask your doctor for a referral. An RDN can provide valuable guidance on reducing your family's sodium intake and managing blood pressure.

Consumers should also be cautioned against purchasing foods with added sauces and seasonings and those labeled "instant." Instead, purchases should include minimally processed foods in their most basic form with home preparation of a sauce or seasoning blend, thereby giving the consumer greater control over the sodium content. For seasonings, the word "salt" (e.g., garlic salt) is an obvious tip that the product contains sodium; however, the ingredient list of all seasoning blends needs to be examined closely as many of them include added salt/sodium. Below is a list of food ingredients that contain sodium.

Ingredients that contain sodium on a label:
- Disodium guanylate (GMP)
- Disodium inosinate (IMP)
- Fleur de sel
- Himalayan pink salt
- Kosher salt
- Monosodium glutamate (MSG)
- Rock salt
- Salt
- Sea salt
- Sodium bicarbonate (baking soda)
- Sodium nitrate
- Sodium citrate

- Sodium chloride
- Sodium diacetate
- Sodium erythorbate
- Sodium glutamate
- Sodium lactate
- Sodium lauryl sulfate
- Sodium metabisulfite
- Sodium phosphate
- Trisodium phosphate

Should I buy iodized salt?

Iodine-fortified table salt has been available in the United States since the 1920s to address iodine deficiency that was primarily occurring in the Great Lakes, Appalachian, and Northwest regions. Iodine fortification is typically only in table salt and not in other specialty salts or salts used in processed foods. Although the U.S. is no longer considered an iodine-deficient population, certain individuals are at risk for deficiency due to increased needs (e.g., pregnant and lactating women) or limited intake of food sources high in iodine (e.g., vegans, individuals who don't consume dairy foods). When selecting table salt, these groups may want to select iodine-fortified salt, as well as discuss the potential need for a multivitamin/mineral supplement that contains iodine with their physician or RDN. Fortified salt, of course, should not be used as a means to correct an iodine deficiency. Iodized salt is considered safe for the general population as toxic iodine levels are unlikely to be reached based on typical U.S. table salt consumption. In clinical practice, symptoms such as goiter, hypothyroidism, and pregnancy-related problems, along with a urinalysis and dietary intake evaluation, can be used to diagnosis an iodine deficiency. Always have the patient/client check with their clinician or RDN to determine their need for iodine in the diet (Mahan & Raymond, 2017; Niwattisaiwong et al., 2017).

Regular canned vegetables, beans, fish, poultry and meat may be the preferred or only realistic choice for some consumers due to cost, longer shelf life, and availability (e.g., socioeconomically challenged consumers may be getting food from food banks where canned is the predominate or only version available). Canned products (except fruit), however, are generally high in sodium. When a low-sodium option is not available, draining, rinsing, and/or soaking canned foods has been shown to decrease sodium content by as much as 40% (IOM, 2010). To remove sodium in canned goods (Mahan & Raymond, 2016):

1. Empty contents of the can into a strainer
2. Drain the liquid
3. Break up chunks of food into flakes or smaller pieces, as needed

4. Rinse the food under running water for at least one minute — until the draining water looks clear
5. Continue to drain the liquid until the liquid is gone

TYPES OF SALT

A variety of salts are available in the grocery store, online, and at specialty stores. Refer to Appendix B — **Description and Sodium Content of Specialty Salts** — for descriptions of commonly consumed salts. Table salt is the most commonly purchased salt and can be purchased with or without iodine. Light salt and salt substitutes are also available in the grocery aisle. Light salt is a blend of salt (sodium chloride) and potassium chloride resulting in 50% less sodium per serving.

Conversely, a salt substitute is typically sodium-free, containing potassium chloride with other additives to reduce bitterness and for anti-caking. While consuming a potassium-containing salt substitute may be a way to increase dietary potassium intake, caution is needed for individuals with kidney disease or on certain medications. These individuals should be advised by a physician or a RDN before using a salt substitute. Alternatively, a variety of salt-free seasonings (e.g., Mrs. Dash, Cavender's) can be used to season foods; however, these seasonings are not suitable in all recipes (e.g., baked goods).

Figure 6: Types of Salt Used in Cooking

Like those pictured In Figure 6, sea and specialty salts have been touted as nutritionally superior; however, the science has yet to support this claim (Drake & Drake, 2011; Vella et al., 2012). All sodium chloride salts have similar amounts of sodium by weight (e.g., per ounce); however, **due to flake size, there is greater variation in the amount of sodium by volume** (e.g., per teaspoon). Some sea and specialty salts (but not all — check the Nutrition Facts label) do have lower sodium content per volume and do contain other minerals not in table salt. Yet there is no evidence at this time that the differences are substantial enough to declare other salts "healthier" than table salt. The mineral content of sea and specialty salts varies widely depending on the location from which it is harvested. The mineral content does provide distinctive flavor for each salt category, as well as differences within a category. Vella et al., however, reported differences in salt taste intensity are marginal (Vella et al., 2012).

The peer-reviewed literature does include reports of possible trace quantities of heavy metals, microplastics, and pollutants in sea salt depending on the water source (Smiechowska et al., 2018). To date, there has not been any evidence reported of detrimental effects from the minute levels of these contaminants in sea salt. The unrefined nature of sea and specialty salts may make them less desirable in some recipes as they may not function the same as table salt (e.g., in baked goods) or may impart an undesirable flavor. The story on table salts and specialty salts is likely to continue to evolve. For now, salt should be selected in reasonable amounts based on its culinary function in a recipe and flavor preferences. Appendix B has a list of commonly used culinary salts, their attributes, and sodium content.

IN A RESTAURANT

Obtaining foods from outside the house is increasingly popular, whether it be prepared meals in a supermarket, dining out, or delivery service. Selecting foods at restaurants or other food-away-from-home locations that are lower in sodium can be challenging because nutrient content is not required at the point of purchase. However, consumers can request nutrition information before placing their order to make an informed choice. The CDC (2018) offers these restaurant food tips (CDC, 2018):

- Ask that no salt be added to your meal
- Order vegetables with no salt added or fruit as a side item
- Split a meal with a friend or family member
- Reserve takeout and eating at a restaurant as an occasional treat

Another word of advice when dining out is to use restraint when it comes to the "free" bread, crackers, or chips brought to the table. Sometimes, consumers mindlessly eat these items while waiting on their meals, and the sodium from these sources can add up quickly. Lastly, for takeout/delivered meals, add more vegetables to "dilute" the sodium content.

Disclosure of Sodium in Restaurant Foods

Restaurant foods from both fast-food and sit-down restaurants alike are often high in sodium, with reports of mean sodium density ranging from 1,336 mg to 2,634 mg of sodium per 1,000 calories (Wu, 2015). This high "dose" of sodium in a single meal is of concern due to evidence that eating a 1,400 mg sodium meal can impair blood flow within 60 minutes post-prandially in healthy, normotensive adults (Dickinson et al., 2011). However, consumer awareness is challenging because sodium information is not generally available at the point of purchase. Restaurants with 20 or more nationwide locations are required to make sodium information available upon request; however, the customer generally must ask for this information (U.S. Congress, 2010). Some local jurisdictions, such as New York City and Philadelphia, do require certain restaurants to print a sodium warning symbol on menus alongside menu items that have 2,300 mg of sodium or more; however, consumer awareness and effectiveness is questionable (Byrd et al., 2018; City of Philadelphia, 2018; NYC Department of Health, 2015).

(For images, go to: https://www1.nyc.gov/site/doh/health/health-topics/national-salt-reduction-initiative.page%20 and http://foodfitphilly.org/sodium-warning-label/)

In addition, for larger chain restaurants or food producers, go online to the brand's website to see what they list for sodium content in the food they prepare.

REDUCING SODIUM IN THE FOOD SUPPLY

In June 2016, the FDA issued draft voluntary sodium reduction goals for commercially processed, packaged, and prepared foods sold in retail stores (e.g., supermarkets, convenience stores, etc.) as well as foods purchased from restaurants (FDA, 2016). Targets for specific food categories were established to encourage manufacturers and restaurateurs to achieve a stepwise reduction in the sodium content in the food supply. With this voluntary initiative, the FDA's goal is to decrease population sodium intake to 2,300 mg within 10 years. The United Kingdom (U.K.) implemented a similar approach in 2006 and attributed a 15% decrease in population sodium intake to the sodium reduction initiative coupled with consumer education (F. He et al., 2014).

Sodium-reducing strategies in the food industry include but are not limited to reducing salt crystal size and using salt alternatives (such as potassium chloride), along with bitter blocking agents, natural flavor enhancers, heterogeneous distribution of salt in foods, use of aroma compounds and technological changes in manufacturing (Allison & Fouladkhah, 2018). Most of these strategies are confined to the food processing industry, while the consumer must be strategic in food selection and preparation to decrease sodium intake.

SECTION 9: SODIUM IN THE KITCHEN

Persian blue salt

Sodium is a multifunctional ingredient in our food supply affecting food safety and spoilage, texture and appearance, and taste and flavor. For food safety and spoilage, sodium is usually not the sole preservation method for most foods; however, it helps create an antimicrobial environment by reducing water activity (Allison & Fouladkhah,

2018; Doyle & Glass, 2010; Taormina, 2010). The reduction in moisture creates less favorable conditions for the growth of various pathogens — bacteria, yeasts, and molds — that can cause foodborne illness and food spoilage. Growth of spoilage microbes can negatively affect odor, taste, texture or appearance of food resulting in food spoilage and, consequently, food waste.

Sodium also contributes to food texture and appearance (Brown, 2018; Taylor et al., 2018). For example, sodium may be needed to retain moisture, enhance color and hue, create desired perceptions of thickness and body, stabilize food texture and structure and prevent undesired chemical reactions amongst ingredients. Therefore, elimination or meaningful reduction in some foods may not be possible as the product would not be considered edible. However, one systematic review did estimate that salt in commercially prepared bread and processed meats could be reduced by up to 40% and 70%, respectively, without significantly affecting food safety and consumer liking (Jaenke et al., 2017). Appendix C — **The Effect of Sodium on Structure and Texture in Home-Prepared and Manufactured Foods** — provides examples of some of sodium's effects on the texture and appearance of foods in home-prepared recipes and manufactured foods.

Salt melts at 800° C and has a neutral pH

CRYSTAL SIZE MATTERS

The amount of sodium per teaspoon can vary based on the size of the salt crystals (see Appendix B). **Use kosher salt because volume-for-volume it contains less sodium than table salt** as the crystals are bigger. The two major types of kosher salt are Morton and Diamond Crystal. "While Diamond Crystal readily adheres to food and crumbles easily, Morton is much denser, and almost twice as salty by volume" (Samin Nosrat, 2017, page 24).

ON THE TONGUE

While food safety and the functional role sodium plays in food are important, flavor and taste are the primary drivers of food selection. Sodium plays a role in overall food palatability beyond just eliciting a salty taste.

Certain sodium concentration levels can decrease the perception of bitterness and augment sweetness of a food (Liem et al., 2011). At high concentrations, salt may reduce sweetness and enhance umami (Mojet, Heidema, & Christ-hazelhof, 2004). Therefore, salt is sometimes used as a flavor enhancer instead of as a means to satisfy a liking for salt. Salt has also been demonstrated to improve the perception of "thickness," "fullness," and "overall flavor strength" in various foods like soup and mask off-putting metallic and chemical flavors (Gillette, 1985). While adding salt to food increases the pleasantness or likeability of the food, too much salt can reduce palatability.

The challenge in recipe development for the home cook and food manufacturers is to decrease sodium while maintaining an acceptable flavor profile based on all taste sensations, not just the taste of salt. In some low-sodium products, potassium chloride is often used, but it can be bitter, making the dish less palatable. There is still work to be done to identify a more healthful "salty" alternative to sodium.

SALT AFFINITY

Salt affinity is multifactorial, including but not limited to the taster's ability to detect and recognize salt on the tongue, genetic characteristics, age, biological need for sodium and behavioral factors such as learned dietary habits (Wessler et al., 2014). Researchers suggest that salt-liking begins around 4 to 6 months of age (Liem, 2017); however, **salt preference in most adults is thought to be primarily driven by salt exposure and learned dietary habits** (Kershaw & Mattes, 2018). As summarized separately by Bobowski (2015) and by Wessler et al. (2014), studies have shown that people with higher compared to lower-sodium diets have a higher threshold sensitivity (e.g., level at which salt is detected and identified) and higher levels of salt preference. In contrast, people on lower-sodium diets have been shown not to need as much sodium in foods to elicit a pleasant response compared to individuals not restricting sodium intake (Bobowski, 2015; Wessler et al., 2014).

Being able to downwardly shift sodium content and maintain taste acceptability is good news in support of worldwide initiatives by food manufacturers to decrease sodium in food products. Making that shift, however, can be challenging, as the sodium content needed in a food for it to be palatable varies greatly from person to person. Some researchers have suggested that certain individuals may have a "salt addiction" possibly resulting in greater sodium reduction challenges for these individuals. Yet most experts agree that a gradual reduction of sodium in the food supply will go unnoticed by consumers (McGuire, 2010). The timeline for a shift in salt hedonics has been reported to **range from two weeks to two months** (Wessler et al., 2014).

A common assumption is that taste sensation declines with age. Researchers postulate that changes that occur with aging — such as decreased amount of saliva, changes in saliva composition, amount and speed of chewing, olfactory changes and cerebral changes in sensory and reward areas — may be contributors (Satin, 2015). However, research results are mixed and varied based on the measured taste sensation (e.g., salt, sour, bitter, sweet, umami). For sodium, some evidence does suggest that older adults may like higher concentrations of salt (Satin, 2015); yet a study by Mojet et al. (2004) showed no difference between younger and older adults on preferred salt concentration in a real food matrix (e.g., tomato soup) (Mojet, Heidema, & Christ-Hazelhof, 2004).

Therefore, there is no clear evidence that seniors need more salt to improve food liking or that decreasing sodium in foods will affect older adults' food intake differently than younger adults.

IS SODIUM/SALT ADDICTING?

The existence of food addiction or an addiction to a nutrient such as sodium in humans has been popularized in the media, but it is hotly debated among scientists. For sodium specifically, the possibility of addiction has been suggested due to associations with salted food intake and stimulation of the opiate and dopamine receptors in the reward and pleasure center in the brain, similar to what is observed in chemical dependencies (Cocores & Gold, 2009). However, "salt addiction" and various "food addiction" hypotheses are primarily based on rodent models with limited human studies (Markus et al., 2017).

Some researchers have suggested that highly processed foods, which are typically high in sodium as well as fat and sugar, may be addictive. Benzerouk et al. (2018) did find an association among obese adults with presumed "food addiction" (based on the behavioral Yale Food Addiction Scale 2.0) and self-reported loss of control of consumption for some, but not all, foods high in salt, carbohydrates, and fat; interestingly, participants classified as "food-addicted" did not differ from those classified as non-"food-addicted" in self-reported loss of consumption control for fruits, vegetables, and grains (Benzerouk et al., 2018). Alternatively, in another study, researchers stated they were unable to conclude that highly processed foods are addictive (Schulte et al., 2017).

While highly palatable foods, such as those high in fat, sugar, and sodium, do appear to trigger behavioral and neurological responses similar to known addictive substances (e.g., alcohol, illicit drugs) and addictive behaviors (e.g., gambling), experts indicate the scientific evidence is not sufficient to classify food addiction as a disease (Markus et al., 2017; Onaolapo & Onaolapo, 2018). More research is needed, especially with humans. Experts do point out a key difference between food addiction and other addictions — food is essential for life.

Since taste is a primary driver of food selection, palatable food is important to humans. The question is whether food manufacturers can decrease these substances and still produce palatable products. The answer is "yes" for decreasing the sodium content in several foods (McGuire, 2010). In 2016, the FDA issued voluntary sodium reduction goals for commercially processed, packaged, and prepared foods (FDA, 2016). The FDA is partnering with researchers to conduct ongoing evaluation of the U.S. food supply to ascertain the effectiveness of the voluntary goals. However, some consumer groups and health professionals are advocating for mandated and not voluntary goals for food manufacturers now.

Bottom line: The evolution of the food addiction science and the need to mandate changes in food manufacturing and processing are topics of ongoing research and scrutiny by consumers and health professionals at this time.

STORING SALT

When storing salt, it is important to prevent contact with moisture and air, or else the salt will clump together. Here are some tips to prevent clumping:
- Add raw rice to a saltshaker to prevent clumping.
- Adding dried white or kidney beans to a container of salt will absorb the moisture so that it doesn't get to the salt.
- If you want to infuse flavor, fill the bottom quarter of a container of salt with dried parsley leaves, coffee beans, or cloves.

IN THE PANTRY

In addition to having various types of salt on hand – finely ground table salt for baking, larger flake sizes for finishing a dish – stock the pantry full of spices and herbs to add flavor to food without adding excessive amounts of sodium. Refer to the chapter on Herbs and Spices for some great ideas. In order to build flavor, also stock the pantry and refrigerator with ingredients that add umami, pungent, and acidic tastes to food.

Salty Alternatives to Salt (Sodium Chloride)

The following is a list of ingredients that can add a salty taste to food, but they should also be used sparingly as a little goes a long way as evidenced by the amount of sodium per teaspoon. As a point of reference, a teaspoon of salt has 2,300 mg of sodium, which is far more than the other alternatives listed in Table 3.

- **Anchovies:** While fresh anchovies are chock-full of healthful ingredients like omega-3 fatty acids, protein, calcium and selenium (without the mercury and other contaminants that other fish can have), canned anchovies are cured in salt and packed in oil. Twenty grams of fresh anchovies have approximately 21 mg of sodium, whereas 20 grams of canned anchovies contain more than 700 mg of sodium.
- **Parmesan cheese** contains 112 mg in 1 tablespoon of dry grated cheese.
- **Soy sauce (shoyu)** was created 2,200 years ago and is made from the fermentation of soy and wheat and the use of a brine (salt) solution. The most prominent taste in soy sauce is saltiness, but there is also a moderate amount of umami and sweet, followed by a smaller amount of bitter. You can purchase a low-sodium variety, which contains about half the amount of sodium — 150 mg/teaspoon.
- **Tamari** is the Japanese version of Chinese soy sauce. It comes in a gluten-free option for those who are intolerant to wheat, have celiac disease, or non-celiac gluten sensitivity. It also has a low-sodium option, which has 163 mg per teaspoon.
- **Fish sauce** was created during the same time period as soy sauce, but instead of fermenting soybeans, fish was fermented with salt. It has the highest sodium content of items listed in the table below — 380 mg per teaspoon.
- **Liquid aminos** are made from either soy or coconut sources. The soy version is a natural soy sauce alternative with an umami flavor containing 16 amino acids, which has comparable levels of sodium to regular soy sauce. Coconut-based liquid aminos, however, are lower in sodium with 130 mg of sodium per teaspoon versus 320 mg in the soy-based aminos.

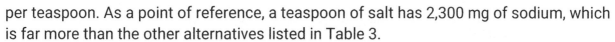

Straight-from-nature soybeans have 34 mg of sodium per

Table 3: Amount of Sodium in Salty Alternatives

Product	Amount of Sodium per Teaspoon
Fish sauce	380 mg
Tamari	327 mg
Soy-based liquid aminos	320 mg
Soy sauce (shoyu)	307 mg
Anchovies	220 mg per piece
Tamari light	163 mg
Light soy sauce	150 mg

Coconut amino acids	130 mg

Values from: USDA National Nutrient Database for Standard Reference Legacy Release, April 2018

Umami Ingredients
- Mushrooms
- Fermented foods
- Tomatoes and tomato paste
- Anchovies

Acidic Ingredients
- Citrus – lemon, lime, orange
- Vinegars

Pungent Ingredients
- Mustard
- Wasabi
- Horseradish

FLAVOR DEVELOPMENT

Because sodium enhances and intensifies other flavors present in food as well as imparts its own salty taste, it is used a lot in cooking and food preparation. Knowing when to add sodium, how much to add, which types to add and how to build flavor using various cooking techniques is important for a delicious and healthful end product. Using less sodium does not mean that the finished dish is any less appealing or flavorful if you know how and when to add flavor in other ways.

Type of Salt and Timing
Cooked foods require more salt than if salt was added throughout the cooking process. Start the salting process (a little bit at a time) as early as possible when cooking. Salting vegetables in a liquid base (not boiled water that is then discarded) earlier leads to the release and drawing out of flavor compounds from within the cells, which produces an incredibly delicious end product.

You can also use less salt by adding flavorful ingredients while cooking and topping with flaked salt at the end to give the illusion of a "salted" dish. The more lavish salts deliver a unique texture to a dish, so it is not necessary to use them in a dish where the crystals dissolve. Instead, add a touch of sea salt, sel gris, Maldon salt or Hawaiian sea salt on the end product — salad, soup, stew or a frittata, for example.

Allow time for meat to absorb salt. Whether you choose to brine — let the meat submerge in a salty liquid solution — or sprinkle salt over chicken, pork, or beef, allow enough time for the salt to absorb fully into the meat before cooking. Salting and letting the meat rest overnight or adding it the morning of is ideal, but any amount of time is better than none. Not only will the flavor change, but salt will also denature protein, which leads to a tender, fall-off-the-bone, juicy piece of meat.

Seafood, on the other hand, is much more delicate than poultry and beef and should be salted no earlier than 15 minutes before cooking to avoid creating a tough piece of fish. The same holds true for eggs — adding a little pinch of salt just before cooking helps the protein in the egg come together more quickly, thus avoiding watery scrambled eggs.

Figure 7: Timing for Adding Salt

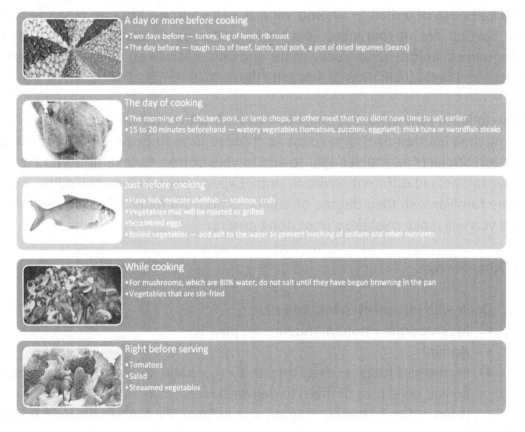

A day or more before cooking
- Two days before — turkey, leg of lamb, rib roast
- The day before — tough cuts of beef, lamb, and pork, a pot of dried legumes (beans)

The day of cooking
- The morning of — chicken, pork, or lamb chops, or other meat that you didnt have time to salt earlier
- 15 to 20 minutes beforehand — watery vegetables (tomatoes, zucchini, eggplant); thick tuna or swordfish steaks

Just before cooking
- Flaky fish, delicate shellfish — scallops, crab
- Vegetables that will be roasted or grilled
- Scrambled eggs
- Boiled vegetables — add salt to the water to prevent leaching of sodium and other nutrients

While cooking
- For mushrooms, which are 80% water, do not salt until they have begun browning in the pan
- Vegetables that are stir-fried

Right before serving
- Tomatoes
- Salad
- Steaamed vegetables

The longer the cooking time, the less salt that is needed. When cooking grains, stewing meat, or cooking potatoes or other vegetables for an extended period of time, less total salt is needed as there is more time for the food to absorb the salt.

Reduction of liquid concentrates flavors, including salt. When reducing sauces, make sure not to add too much salt in the beginning because as water evaporates, what is left is a higher concentrated source of salt.

Wait and adjust. Wait for salt to dissolve before adding more, as some salt crystals dissolve right away while others take time. You risk oversalting if you salt food too fast. It is also **important to taste whatever you are preparing throughout the cooking process.** It is not a one-and-done event, but rather a continuous process of tasting as you add ingredients and finish the dish. Slow and steady will allow you to achieve the perfect level of saltiness, which brings out all the other flavors in a dish without oversalting it. Samin Nosrat's book Salt, Fat, Acid, Heat is a great resource to learn how to bring out the best flavors in food.

Build the saltiness of a dish by adding various salt sources, but don't overdo it. To add complex flavors, look at your ingredient list for salt sources (as mentioned above in the salty alternatives) before adding salt. Taste, and only add more if needed. When preparing soups, reserve the final addition of salt until the last 20 minutes of cooking.

Take time to learn your salts. Learning how to cook with just the right amount of salt and not too much is learned over time. Just as it takes time to develop the perfect taste in different conditions (how much sugar to add to your coffee, for example), it takes time to know how salt acts in different environments. Experiment with various salts — you have to become familiar with their degree of saltiness and/or crunch. You will get better over time, and you will make mistakes. Just don't give up.

Adding Other Flavors

1. **Cook with umami-rich ingredients**
   - Mushrooms — porcini mushroom powder
   - Kombu
   - Fermented foods — even though they contain sodium, they are umami-rich, so you need less of them to deliver flavor
   - Dried or fresh cheese — again, use judiciously due to sodium content
   - Soy sauce or tamari — because it is rich in umami as well as sodium, you need less of it in a recipe
   - Nutritional yeast is both savory and salty. It adds a cheesy edge and can be added to eggs, omelets, and other dishes.
   - Tomatoes and tomato paste

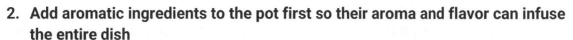

2. **Add aromatic ingredients to the pot first so their aroma and flavor can infuse the entire dish**
   - Onions
   - Garlic
   - Shallots
   - Fresh ginger
   - Scallions

3. **Use herbs and spices generously**
   - Garlic
   - Dried and fresh herbs: Add hardy herbs at the start and finish with soft herbs
   - Anything smoked — e.g., paprika
   - Add flaked salt to the finished dish. You don't need as much compared to what you would have to add to the cooked dish to get the same "salty" taste.

4. **Add an acid source to foods as their tangy, bright flavor can reduce the need for sodium**
   - Citrus juice — lime, lemon
   - Vinegars — red wine, apple cider, balsamic, flavored vinegars and others
   - Fermented or pickling liquids

5. **Add pungent ingredients for bold flavors**
   - Mustard
   - Wasabi
   - Horseradish
   - Tamarind pods

COOKING METHODS THAT DEVELOP FLAVORS

- Roast vegetables like onions, peppers, carrots, celery, potatoes and garlic as the sugars caramelize and bring out a separate flavor. They can then be added to soups, frittatas, pasta dishes, stews, etc.
- Use roasted meats instead of deli meats for added flavor.
- Reduction of liquids intensifies flavor. For example, make your own stock and reduce it for a bold flavor.
- Bloom spices by adding spices to a hot pan with oil to bring out their full flavor profile.
- Use smoked ingredients like jalapeños or meat.
- Grill fruit, vegetables, and meat for a unique flavor.
- Toast seeds, nuts, and some spices to add a depth of flavor.
- Add a bit of fat at the end to the finished dish as it will sit on top. You don't need a lot. For example, olive oil or butter on top of soup or pasta.

OVERSALTING REMEDIES

Before adding any salt or salty ingredient to a food, taste the dish first. It may or may not need additional salt. If you happen to oversalt a dish, try any of the following methods to bring the sodium content and saltiness down:

- Add more food to the dish, which will dilute the sodium content. Unsalted rice and potatoes will draw some saltiness away from the dish. Diluting the original dish with more of anything such as vegetables, grains, or meat will do the trick as well.
- Use the overly salted piece of meat as a new ingredient in a separate dish. For example, shred oversalted beef and make a croquette by adding unsalted mashed potatoes and spices.

RECIPES & HOW-TO

Go to the individual chapters for Vegetables, Fruit, Protein and Grains for individual recipes and how-to guides for each of these foods.

A taco spice mix recipe is depicted in Table 4. Mix all the ingredients together. Store in an airtight container and use on chicken, fish, meat and beans to increase the flavor. See the chapter on Herbs and Spices for many more recipes.

Table 4: Chef Cyndie's Taco Seasoning Ingredients (makes about 2 cups of spice mix)

Oregano, dried, flakes	½ cup + 1 tablespoon
Paprika	½ cup + 1 tablespoon
Parsley, dried, flakes	½ cup + 1 tablespoon
Cumin, ground	1/3 cup + 1 tablespoon
Black pepper	2 tablespoons
Garlic, granulated	2 tablespoons
Salt	2 tablespoons

SECTION 10: SERVING AND MENU PLANNING

When planning a menu, remain below the daily recommendation for sodium (that amount is dependent on the individual – e.g. 2,300 or 1,500 mg/day) and take into account snacks as well as meals. In addition, make sure there is enough potassium in the diet so that there is at least equal amounts of sodium and potassium in one's diet. Good sources of potassium include – fruits, vegetables, nuts and legumes. The Dash Eating Plan is a great resource to learn how to plan a daily or weekly menu with an eye on both sodium and potassium:

https://www.nhlbi.nih.gov/sites/default/files/publications/WeekOnDASH.pdf

Know Your Numbers:
- Low sodium: 140 mg or less per serving
- High sodium: 400 mg or more per serving
- Select meals that have no more than 600 mg of sodium

Tip: Remove the salt shaker from the table, which will require individuals to ask for salt if they need more – there is no need for a salt shaker if food is properly prepared and flavored.

SECTION 11: PRACTICAL TIPS TO DECREASE SODIUM CONSUMPTION

1. Choose fresh meat instead of packaged, processed meats such as cold cuts, bacon, or hot dogs.

2. Minimize use of purchased condiments as they contain a large amount of sodium.

3. Avoid adding salty and high fat sauces to vegetables.

4. Give time for your taste buds to adjust to a lower level of sodium in your diet.

5. Monitor sodium from unexpected places such as breads, cereal, cheese and chicken (e.g., sodium inherent in food).

6. Don't salt food until you have tasted it first, both at the table and when cooking.

7. Always look for the amount of sodium per serving and the number of servings per container when you purchase or consume a packaged product.

8. "Dilute" the sodium content of take-home/delivered meals by adding the same amount of vegetables. You have now decreased the sodium in half. For example, with a typical pint of a Chinese dish, add two cups of steamed vegetables such as broccoli, pea pods, or carrots. Toss and enjoy.

9. Take some time to discover how much sodium is in your favorite restaurant dishes by either going to their website or calling them beforehand.

10. Add lots of other flavors when preparing food by using cooking techniques and other ingredients besides salt.

SUMMARY

Hawaiian red sea salt

With estimates of 90% of U.S. adults averaging dietary sodium intake of more than 2,300 mg of sodium daily, decreasing sodium intake is an appropriate goal for the vast majority of people. Decreasing sodium has been found to prevent cardiovascular disease and hypertension. Lowering one's salt intake can also be a treatment for other diseases such as kidney disease, heart failure, and osteoporosis, for example.

Achieving this goal is challenging due to the function of sodium in food safety and spoilage, texture and appearance, and taste and flavor. Consumers should start with minimizing their intake of processed foods and limiting their dining out frequency. Salt used in home food preparation and salt added at the table are small contributors to overall intake in the U.S. However, these sodium sources should not be discounted or considered a license to have a heavy hand with the saltshaker. Consumers can achieve their sodium goals and decrease their risk for many chronic health conditions by:
- Making incremental changes in salt intake while working toward a low-sodium diet
- Following a healthful eating pattern like the DASH diet
- Increasing preparation of meals and snacks at home using minimally processed ingredients

APPENDIX A

USDA 1980:
- Avoid too much sodium

USDA 1985:
- Avoid too much sodium

USDA 1990:
- Use salt and sodium only in moderation

USDA 1995:
- Choose a diet moderate in salt and sodium

USDA 2000:
- Choose and prepare foods with less salt

USDA 2005:
- Consume less than 2.300 mg (approximately 1 tsp of salt) of sodium per day
- Choose and prepare foods with little salt. At the same time, consume potassium-rich foods, such as fruits and vegetables.

USDA 2010:
- Reduce daily sodium intake to less than 2,300 milligrams (mg) and further reduce intake to 1,500 mg among persons who are 51 and older and those of any age who are African American or have hypertension, diabetes, or chronic kidney disease. The 1,500 mg recommendation applies to about half of the U.S. population, including children, and the majority of adults.

USDA 2015:
- Consume less than 2,300 mg per day of sodium
- Limit calories from added sugars and saturated fats and reduce sodium intake. Consume an eating pattern low in added sugars, saturated fats, and sodium. Cut back on foods and beverages higher in these components to amounts that fit within healthy eating patterns.

USDA 2020:
- Limit foods and beverages higher in added sugars, saturated fat, and sodium, and limit alcoholic beverages.

At every life stage, meeting food group recommendations—even with nutrient-dense choices—requires most of a person's daily calorie needs and sodium limits. A healthy dietary pattern doesn't have much room for extra added sugars, saturated fat, or sodium—or for alcoholic beverages. A small amount of added sugars, saturated fat, or sodium can be added to nutrient-dense foods and beverages to help meet food group recommendations, but foods and beverages high in these components should be limited. Limits are:

- Sodium—Less than 2,300 milligrams per day—and even less for children younger than age 14

APPENDIX B

Description and Sodium Content of Specialty Salts

Type	Amount of sodium per teaspoon (may vary by brand)	Description[a]	Culinary Applications (as compared to table salt)
Table salt + or - iodine	2,360 mg	Harvested from underground salt deposits. Typically, has an anti-caking agent to keep it from clumping.[1]	Not applicable
Himalayan pink	1,520 mg[b,e]	Harvested from a salt mine in the Himalayan mountains. Rich in minerals like iron, potassium, calcium, magnesium and trace elements. Lower in sodium per teaspoon due to large crystal size.	Bolder flavor due to natural elements. Used as a finishing salt.
Fleur de sel	1,532 mg[2]	Hand-harvested by skimming off the top of tidal waves in Brittany, France. It has a blue-gray tint and is packed with minerals. It also retains moisture. Lower in sodium per teaspoon due to large crystal size.	Delicate flavor and texture. Used as a finishing salt.
Sea salt	Fine: 2,240 mg[b,c] Coarse: 2320 mg[b,c]	Harvested from evaporated sea water. Contains trace minerals like calcium, iron, magnesium, potassium, manganese and zinc.	Flakier and coarser; taste varies based on mineral content. Used as a finishing salt.

Type	Amount of sodium per teaspoon (may vary by brand)	Description[a]	Culinary Applications (as compared to table salt)
Kosher	1,920 mg[b,e]	Typically does not have iodine but may have an anti-caking agent. Dissolves quickly. Lower in sodium per teaspoon due to large crystal size; suggested conversion ratio is 1 ¼ teaspoon kosher salt per 1 teaspoon table salt.	Flakier and coarser. Commonly used on margarita glasses and soft pretzels.
Hawaiian salt	2,340 mg[b,f]	Harvested from evaporation of tidal pools, which mixes with the red volcanic clay. Rich in iron and trace elements. Black version contains activated charcoal.	Used as a finishing salt

[a] (Labensky,SR, 2019; Morton Salt, 2020; SaltWorks, 2020.)

[b] (USDA and ARS, 2020)

[c] (Morton Salt, 2020)

[d] (Salt, 2020)

[e] No brand specified

[f] (SaltWorks, 2020)

APPENDIX C

The Effect of Sodium on Structure and Texture in Home-Prepared and Manufactured Foods[a,b]

Food item	Sodium Form	Sodium effect on structure and texture	Comments
Meat, poultry, seafood	Salt (NaCl)	Increase moisture	Often done by brining the meat, poultry, or seafood in saltwater solution; fresh products sold in the supermarket frequently have been injected with a sodium-containing brine
Meat and poultry	Salt (NaCl)	Binder between proteins as well as between meat components and fat	
Meat and poultry	Salt (NaCl)	Gelatinization to improve texture and tenderness	
Meat and poultry	Sodium caseinate	Binder	Used in products such as frankfurters and meat stews
Meat and poultry	Sodium erythorbate	Color stimulator; stabilizer	Used in cured meats and poultry such as ham, bologna, hot dogs and bacon. Added or infused in fresh meats and poultry to extend color stability (and shelf life). Considered an antioxidant.
Meat and poultry	Sodium nitrite	Color stabilization	Used in cured meats and poultry such as ham, bologna, hot dogs and bacon
Cheese[c] (natural and processed)	Salt (NaCl)	Expel whey and moisture from the curd	Affects firmness of cheese

Cheese[c] (natural and processed)	Salt (NaCl)	Meltability, shredding, and stretching	
Cheese[c] (processed)	Sodium phosphate, sodium citrates	Emulsification	
Eggs	Salt (NaCl)	Lower coagulation temperature; speed up coagulation	
Bakery products	Salt (NaCl)	Aid in gluten development; elasticity in the dough; improved volume, texture, and evenness of cell structure in final product	Too much results in low volume, dense cells; too little results in low volume, uneven cell structure, as well as lack of color
Bakery products	Sodium bicarbonate (baking soda, baking powder), sodium acid pyrophosphate, sodium aluminum phosphate, sodium propionate	Leaveners	
Yeast breads	Salt (NaCl)	Control yeast growth	Fermentation is too rapid in the absence of salt, resulting in a sticky dough that is difficult to handle; too much salt inhibits CO_2 production and results in low volume bread

Sauces, gravies, stocks, salad dressings and condiments	Salt (NaCl) and other sodium-containing substances	Stabilize emulsions
Fermented foods (pickled vegetables such as pickles and sauerkraut)	Salt (NaCl)	Crisp texture
Puffed and extruded savory snacks (such as corn puffs, veggie straw snacks, pork rinds cheese puffs)	Salt (NaCl) and other sodium-containing substances	Degree of puffiness, airiness; and color

[a](Brown, 2018; McGuire, 2010; Taylor et al., 2018)

[b]The list is not inclusive of all foods and examples. The list does not include other functions of sodium, such as food preservation and flavor.

[c]Standards of identity for some cheese dictate the inclusion of salt.

REFERENCES

About Facts Up Front. (n.d.) http://www.factsupfront.org/AboutTheIcons.html. Accessed July 1, 2019.

Aburto, N. J., Hanson, S., Gutierrez, H., Hooper, L., Elliott, P., & Cappuccio, F. P. (2013). Effect of increased potassium intake on cardiovascular risk factors and disease: Systematic review and meta-analyses. BMJ, 346, f1378. https://doi.org/10.1136/bmj.f1378

Aburto, N. J., Ziolkovska, A., Hooper, Elliott, Cappuccio, F. P., & Meerpohl, J. J. (2013). Effect of lower sodium intake on health: Systematic review and meta-analyses. BMJ, 346. https://doi.org/10.1136/bmj.f1326

Academy of Nutrition and Deitetics. (n.d.). Nutrition Care Manual. Preexlampsia & Eclampsia. Retrieved July 8, 2019, from https://www.nutritioncaremanual.org/topic.cfm?ncm_category_id=1&lv1=27298 0&lv2=17768&lv3=268290&ncm_toc_id=268290&ncm_heading=Nutrition Care

Adshead, S. A. M. (1992). Salt and Civilization. Palgrave Macmillan UK.

Afsar, B., Kiremit, M. C., Sag, A. A., Tarim, K., Acar, O., Esen, T., Solak, Y., Covic, A., & Kanbay, M. (2016). The role of sodium intake in nephrolithiasis: Epidemiology, pathogenesis, and future directions. European Journal of Internal Medicine, 35, 16–19. https://doi.org/10.1016/j.ejim.2016.07.001

Allison, A., & Fouladkhah, A. (2018a). Adoptable interventions, human health, and food safety considerations for reducing sodium content of processed food products. Foods, 7(16). https://doi.org/10.3390/foods7020016

Allison, A., & Fouladkhah, A. (2018b). Adoptable Interventions, Human Health, and Food Safety Considerations for Reducing Sodium Content of Processed Food Products. Foods, 7(2). https://doi.org/10.3390/foods7020016

Amer, M., Woodward, M., & Appel, L. J. (2014). Effects of dietary sodium and the DASH diet on the occurrence of headaches: Results from randomised multicentre DASH-Sodium clinical trial. BMJ Open, 4(12), 1–7. https://doi.org/10.1136/bmjopen-2014-006671

Appel, L., Moore, T., Obarzanek, E., Vollmer, W., Svetkey, L., Sacks, F., Bray, G., Vogt, T., Cutler, J., Windhauser, M., Lin, P. H., & Karanja, N. (1997). A clinical trial of the effects of dietary patterns on blood pressure. The New England Journal of Medicine, 336(26), 1117–1124.

Arnett Donna K., Blumenthal Roger S., Albert Michelle A., Buroker Andrew B., Goldberger Zachary D., Hahn Ellen J., Himmelfarb Cheryl Dennison, Khera Amit, Lloyd-Jones Donald, McEvoy J. William, Michos Erin D., Miedema Michael D., Muñoz Daniel, Smith Sidney C., Virani Salim S., Williams Kim A., Yeboah Joseph, & Ziaeian Boback. (2019). 2019 ACC/AHA Guideline on the Primary Prevention of Cardiovascular Disease: A Report of the American College of Cardiology/American Heart Association Task Force on Clinical Practice

Guidelines. Circulation, 140(11), e596–e646.
https://doi.org/10.1161/CIR.0000000000000678

Aronow, W. S., & Shamliyan, T. A. (2018). Dietary Sodium Interventions to Prevent Hospitalization and Readmission in Adults with Congestive Heart Failure. The American Journal of Medicine, 131(4), 365-370.e1. https://doi.org/10.1016/j.amjmed.2017.12.014

Baker, L. B. (2017). Sweating Rate and Sweat Sodium Concentration in Athletes: A Review of Methodology and Intra/Interindividual Variability. Sports Medicine (Auckland, N.z.), 47(Suppl 1), 111–128. https://doi.org/10.1007/s40279-017-0691-5

Benzerouk, F., Gierski, F., Ducluzeau, P.-H., Bourbao-Tournois, C., Gaubil-Kaladjian, I., Bertin, É., Kaladjian, A., Ballon, N., & Brunault, P. (2018). Food addiction, in obese patients seeking bariatric surgery, is associated with higher prevalence of current mood and anxiety disorders and past mood disorders. Psychiatry Research, 267, 473–479. https://doi.org/10.1016/j.psychres.2018.05.087

Bibbins-Domingo, K., Chertow, G. M., Coxson, P. G., Moran, A., Lightwood, J. M., Pletcher, M. J., & Goldman, L. (2010). Projected effect of dietary salt reductions on future cardiovascular disease. The New England Journal of Medicine, 362(7), 590–599. https://doi.org/10.1056/NEJMoa0907355

Bobowski, N. (2015). Shifting human salty taste preference: Potential opportunities and challenges in reducing dietary salt intake of Americans. Chemosensory Perception, 8(3), 112–116. https://doi.org/10.1007/s12078-015-9179-6

Brown, A. C. (2018). Understanding Food: Principles and Preparation. Cengage Learning.

Büssemaker, E., Hillebrand, U., Hausberg, M., Pavenstädt, H., & Oberleithner, H. (2010). Pathogenesis of hypertension: Interactions among sodium, potassium, and aldosterone. American Journal of Kidney Diseases: The Official Journal of the National Kidney Foundation, 55(6), 1111–1120. https://doi.org/10.1053/j.ajkd.2009.12.022

Carbone, L., Johnson, K. C., Huang, Y., Pettinger, M., Thomas, F., Cauley, J., Crandall, C., Tinker, L., LeBoff, M. S., Wactawski-Wende, J., Bethel, M., Li, W., & Prentice, R. (2016). Sodium Intake and Osteoporosis. Findings From the Women's Health Initiative. The Journal of Clinical Endocrinology and Metabolism, 101(4), 1414–1421. https://doi.org/10.1210/jc.2015-4017

CDC. (2018). How to Reduce Sodium. https://www.cdc.gov/salt/reduce_sodium_tips.htm

CFR. (2012). Code of Federal Regulations Title 21: Nutrition Labeling (198-253). FDA. https://www.govinfo.gov/content/pkg/CFR-2012-title9-vol2/pdf/CFR-2012-title9-vol2-part317-subpartB.pdf.

CFR. (2016). Code of Federal Regulations Title 21: Food Labeling. FDA. https://www.govinfo.gov/content/pkg/CFR-2011-title21-vol2/pdf/CFR-2011-title21-vol2-part101.pdf.

Christopher, D., & Wallace, C. A. (2014). The food safety impact of salt and sodium reduction initiatives: Perspectives in Public Health. https://doi.org/10.1177/1757913914536701

Cocores, J. A., & Gold, M. S. (2009). The Salted Food Addiction Hypothesis may explain overeating and the obesity epidemic. Medical Hypotheses, 73(6), 892–899. https://doi.org/10.1016/j.mehy.2009.06.049

Cook, N. R., Appel, L. J., & Whelton, P. K. (2016). Sodium Intake and All-Cause Mortality Over 20 Years in the Trials of Hypertension Prevention. Journal of the American College of Cardiology, 68(15), 1609–1617. https://doi.org/10.1016/j.jacc.2016.07.745

D'Elia, L., Galletti, F., & Strazzullo, P. (2014). Dietary salt intake and risk of gastric cancer. Cancer Treatment and Research, 159, 83–95. https://doi.org/10.1007/978-3-642-38007-5_6

Dietary Guidelines for Americans, 2020-2025. (n.d.). 164.

DiNicolantonio, J. J., & O'Keefe, J. H. (2017). The History of the Salt Wars. The American Journal of Medicine, 130(9), 1011–1014. https://doi.org/10.1016/j.amjmed.2017.04.040

Doyle, M. E., & Glass, K. A. (2010). Sodium Reduction and Its Effect on Food Safety, Food Quality, and Human Health. Comprehensive Reviews in Food Science and Food Safety, 9(1), 44–56. https://doi.org/10.1111/j.1541-4337.2009.00096.x

Drake, S. L., & Drake, M. A. (2011). Comparison of salty taste and time intensity of sea and land salts from around the world. Journal of Sensory Studies, 26, 25–34. https://doi.org/10.1111/j.1745-459X.2010.00317.x

Eckel, R. H., Jakicic, J. M., Ard, J. D., de Jesus, J. M., Houston Miller, N., Hubbard, V. S., Lee, I.-M., Lichtenstein, A. H., Loria, C. M., Millen, B. E., Nonas, C. A., Sacks, F. M., Smith, S. C., Svetkey, L. P., Wadden, T. A., Yanovski, S. Z., & American College of Cardiology/American Heart Association Task Force on Practice Guidelines. (2014). 2013 AHA/ACC guideline on lifestyle management to reduce cardiovascular risk: A report of the American College of Cardiology/American Heart Association Task Force on Practice Guidelines. Journal of the American College of Cardiology, 63(25 Pt B), 2960–2984. https://doi.org/10.1016/j.jacc.2013.11.003

Eckel, R. H., Jakicic, J. M., Ard, J. D., de Jesus, J. M., Houston Miller, N., Hubbard, V. S., Lee, I.-M., Lichtenstein, A. H., Loria, C. M., Millen, B. E., Nonas, C. a., Sacks, F. M., Smith, S. C., Svetkey, L. P., Wadden, T. W. a W., Yanovski, S. Z., Miller, N. H., Robert H Eckel, M. D. F., John M Jakicic, P., ... Susan Z Yanovski, M. D. (2013). 2013 AHA/ACC Guideline on Lifestyle Management to Reduce Cardiovascular

Risk: A Report of the American College of Cardiology/American Heart Association Task Force on Practice Guidelines. Journal of the American College of Cardiology, 63(25 Pt B), 2960–2984. https://doi.org/10.1016/j.jacc.2013.11.003

Elijovich, F., Weinberger, M. H., Anderson, C. A. M., Appel, L. J., Bursztyn, M., Cook, N. R., Dart, R. A., Newton-Cheh, C. H., Sacks, F. M., & Laffer, C. L. (2016). Salt Sensitivity of Blood Pressure: A Scientific Statement From the American Heart Association. Hypertension, 68(3). https://doi.org/10.1161/HYP.0000000000000047

Fatahi, S., Namazi, N., Larijani, B., & Azadbakht, L. (2018). The Association of Dietary and Urinary Sodium With Bone Mineral Density and Risk of Osteoporosis: A Systematic Review and Meta-Analysis. Journal of the American College of Nutrition, 37(6), 522–532. https://doi.org/10.1080/07315724.2018.1431161

FDA. (2013). Guidance for Industry: Food Labeling Guide. U.S. Food and Drug Administration; FDA. http://www.fda.gov/regulatory-information/search-fda-guidance-documents/guidance-industry-food-labeling-guide

FDA. (2016). Voluntary sodium reduction goals: Target mean and upper bound concentrations for sodium in commercially processed, packaged, and prepared foods. Regulations.Gov. https://www.regulations.gov/docket?D=FDA-2014-D-0055

Gay, H. C., Rao, S. G., Vaccarino, V., & Ali, M. K. (2016). Effects of Different Dietary Interventions on Blood Pressure: Systematic Review and Meta-Analysis of Randomized Controlled Trials. Hypertension (Dallas, Tex.: 1979), 67(4), 733–739. https://doi.org/10.1161/HYPERTENSIONAHA.115.06853

Gillette, M. (1985). Flavor effects of sodium chloride. Food Technology (USA). http://agris.fao.org/agris-search/search.do?recordID=US8629343

Handu, D., Rozga, M., & Steiber, A. (2021). Executive Summary of the 2020 Academy of Nutrition and Dietetics and National Kidney Foundation Clinical Practice Guideline for Nutrition in CKD. Journal of the Academy of Nutrition and Dietetics, 121(9), 1881–1893. https://doi.org/10.1016/j.jand.2020.08.092

Harnack, L. J., Cogswell, M. E., Shikany, J. M., Gardner, C. D., Gillespie, C., Loria, C. M., Zhou, X., Yuan, K., & Steffen, L. M. (2017). Sources of sodium in US adults from 3 geographic regions. Circulation, 135, 1775–1783. https://doi.org/10.1161/CIRCULATIONAHA.116.024446

He, F., Brinsden, H., & MacGregor, G. (2014). Salt reduction in the United Kingdom: A successful experiment in public health. Journal of Human Hypertension, 28(6), 345–352. https://doi.org/10.1038/jhh.2013.105

He, F. J., Brinsden, H. C., & MacGregor, G. A. (2014). Salt reduction in the United Kingdom: A successful experiment in public health. Journal of Human Hypertension, 28(6), 345–352. https://doi.org/10.1038/jhh.2013.105

He, F. J., Li, J., & MacGregor, G. A. (2013). Effect of longer-term modest salt reduction on blood pressure. Cochrane Database of Systematic Reviews, 4. https://doi.org/10.1002/14651858.CD004937.pub2

Huh, J. H., Lee, K. J., Lim, J. S., Lee, M. Y., Park, H. J., Kim, M. Y., Kim, J. W., Chung, C. H., Shin, J. Y., Kim, H.-S., Kwon, S. O., & Baik, S. K. (2015). High Dietary Sodium Intake Assessed by Estimated 24-h Urinary Sodium Excretion Is Associated with NAFLD and Hepatic Fibrosis. PloS One, 10(11), e0143222. https://doi.org/10.1371/journal.pone.0143222

Ichai, C., & Bichet, D. G. (2018a). Sodium Disorders. In C. Ichai, H. Quintard, & J.-C. Orban (Eds.), Metabolic Disorders and Critically Ill Patients: From Pathophysiology to Treatment (pp. 33–70). Springer International Publishing. https://doi.org/10.1007/978-3-319-64010-5_1

Ichai, C., & Bichet, D. G. (2018b). Water and Sodium Balance. In C. Ichai, H. Quintard, & J.-C. Orban (Eds.), Metabolic Disorders and Critically Ill Patients: From Pathophysiology to Treatment (pp. 3–31). Springer International Publishing. https://doi.org/10.1007/978-3-319-64010-5_1

IOM. (2010). Strategies to Reduce Sodium Intake in the United States (C. S. Henney, Jane E; Taylor, Christine L; Boon, Ed.). The National Academies of Press.

Jackson, S. L., King, S. M. C., Zhao, L., & Cogswell, M. E. (2016). Prevalence of Excess Sodium Intake in the United States—NHANES, 2009-2012. MMWR. Morbidity and Mortality Weekly Report, 64(52), 1393–1397. https://doi.org/10.15585/mmwr.mm6452a1

Jackson Sandra L., Cogswell Mary E., Zhao Lixia, Terry Ana L., Wang Chia-Yih, Wright Jacqueline, Coleman King Sallyann M., Bowman Barbara, Chen Te-Ching, Merritt Robert, & Loria Catherine M. (2018). Association Between Urinary Sodium and Potassium Excretion and Blood Pressure Among Adults in the United States. Circulation, 137(3), 237–246. https://doi.org/10.1161/CIRCULATIONAHA.117.029193

Jaenke, R., Barzi, F., McMahon, E., Webster, J., & Brimblecombe, J. (2017). Consumer acceptance of reformulated food products: A systematic review and meta-analysis of salt-reduced foods. Crit Rev Food Sci Nutr, 57(16), 3357–3372. https://doi.org/10.1080/10408398.2015.1118009

Jayedi, A., Ghomashi, F., Zargar, M. S., & Shab-Bidar, S. (2019). Dietary sodium, sodium-to-potassium ratio, and risk of stroke: A systematic review and nonlinear dose-response meta-analysis. Clinical Nutrition (Edinburgh, Scotland), 38(3), 1092–1100. https://doi.org/10.1016/j.clnu.2018.05.017

Kaptein, E. M., Sreeramoju, D., Kaptein, J. S., & Kaptein, M. J. (2016). A systematic literature search and review of sodium concentrations of body fluids. Clinical Nephrology, 86(10), 203–228. https://doi.org/10.5414/CN108721

Kershaw, J. C., & Mattes, R. D. (2018). Nutrition and taste and smell dysfunction. World Journal of Otorhinolaryngology - Head and Neck Surgery, 4(1), 3–10. https://doi.org/10.1016/j.wjorl.2018.02.006

Kurlansky, M. (2003). Salt. Penguin Books.

Labensky,SR, H., AM. (2019). On Cooking: A Textbook of Culinary Fundamentals (6th ed.). Pearson.

Liem, D. G. (2017). Infants' and Children's Salt Taste Perception and Liking: A Review. Nutrients, 9(9), 1011. https://doi.org/10.3390/nu9091011

Liem, D. G., Miremadi, F., & Keast, R. S. J. (2011). Reducing sodium in foods: The effect on flavor. Nutrients, 3(6), 694–711. https://doi.org/10.3390/nu3060694

Lindenfeld, J., Heart Failure Society of America, Albert, N. M., Boehmer, J. P., Collins, S. P., Ezekowitz, J. A., Givertz, M. M., Katz, S. D., Klapholz, M., Moser, D. K., Rogers, J. G., Starling, R. C., Stevenson, W. G., Tang, W. H. W., Teerlink, J. R., & Walsh, M. N. (2010). HFSA 2010 Comprehensive Heart Failure Practice Guideline. Journal of Cardiac Failure, 16(6), e1-194. https://doi.org/10.1016/j.cardfail.2010.04.004

MacGregor, G. A., & Wardener, H. E. de. (1998). Salt, diet and health. Neptunes poisoned chalice: The origins of high blood pressure. Salt, Diet and Health. Neptunes Poisoned Chalice: The Origins of High Blood Pressure. https://www.cabdirect.org/cabdirect/abstract/19991400998

Mahan, L. K., & Raymond, J. L. (2016). Krause's Food & the Nutrition Care Process—E-Book. Elsevier Health Sciences.

Mahan, L. K., & Raymond, J. L. (Eds.). (2017). Krause's Food and The Nutrition Process (14th ed.). Elsevier.

Man, C. M. D. (2007). Technological functions of salt in food products. In Reducing Salt in Foods: Practical Strategies (pp. 157–173). https://doi.org/10.1533/9781845693046.2.157

Markus, C. R., Rogers, P. J., Brouns, F., & Schepers, R. (2017). Eating dependence and weight gain; no human evidence for a 'sugar-addiction' model of overweight. Appetite, 114, 64–72. https://doi.org/10.1016/j.appet.2017.03.024

McGuire, S. (2010). Institute of Medicine. 2010. Strategies to Reduce Sodium Intake in the United States. Washington, DC: The National Academies Press. Advances in Nutrition: An International Review Journal, 1(1), 49–50. https://doi.org/10.3945/an.110.1002

Mojet, J., Heidema, J., & Christ-hazelhof, E. (2004). Effect of concentration on taste – Taste interactions in foods for elderly and young subjects. Chemical Senses, 29(8), 671–681. https://doi.org/10.1093/chemse/bjh070

Mojet, J., Heidema, J., & Christ-Hazelhof, E. (2004). Effect of concentration on taste-taste interactions in foods for elderly and young subjects. Chemical Senses, 29(8), 671–681. https://doi.org/10.1093/chemse/bjh070

Moosavian, S. P., Haghighatdoost, F., Surkan, P. J., & Azadbakht, L. (2017). Salt and obesity: A systematic review and meta-analysis of observational studies. International Journal of Food Sciences and Nutrition, 68(3), 265–277. https://doi.org/10.1080/09637486.2016.1239700

Morimoto, A., Uzu, T., Fujii, T., Nishimura, M., Kuroda, S., Nakamura, S., Inenaga, T., & Kimura, G. (1997). Sodium sensitivity and cardiovascular events in patients with essential hypertension. The Lancet, 350(9093), 1734–1737. https://doi.org/10.1016/S0140-6736(97)05189-1

Morton Salt. (2020). https://www.mortonsalt.com/article/salt-conversion-chart

Multhauf, R. P. (1978). Neptune's Gift: A History of Common Salt. Johns Hopkins Press.

NASEM. (2019). Dietary Reference Intakes for Sodium and Potassium (National Academies of Sciences, Engineering, and Medicine) (M. Oria, M. Harrison, & V. A. Stallings, Eds.). National Academies Press (US). http://www.ncbi.nlm.nih.gov/books/NBK538102/

National Academies of Science Engineering and Medicine. (2019). Dietary Reference Intakes for Sodium and Potassium. The National Academies Press. https://doi.org/10.17226/25353

Newberry, S. J., Chung, M., Anderson, C. A. M., Chen, C., Fu, Z., Tang, A., Zhao, N., Booth, M., Marks, J., Hollands, S., Motala, A., Larkin, J., Shanman, R., & Hempel, S. (2018). Sodium and Potassium Intake: Effects on Chronic Disease Outcomes and Risks. Agency for Healthcare Research and Quality (US). http://www.ncbi.nlm.nih.gov/books/NBK519328/

NHLBI. (1998). Trials of Hypertension Prevention (TOHP). https://clinicaltrials.gov/ct2/show/NCT00000528

Oliveros, E., Marinescu, K., Suboc, T., & Williams, K. (2018). Hypertension management for the prevention of heart failure: Best strategies. Current Cardiovascular Risk Reports, 12(10). https://doi.org/10.1007/s12170-018-0573-x LK - http://resolver.ebscohost.com/openurl?sid=EMBASE&issn=19329563&id=doi:10.1007%2Fs12170-018-0573-x&atitle=Hypertension+Management+for+the+Prevention+of+Heart+Failure%3A+Best+Strategies&stitle=Curr.+Cardiovasc.+Risk+Rep.&title=Current+Cardiovascular+Risk+Reports&volume=12&issue=4&spage=&epage=&aulast=Oliveros&aufirst=Estefania&auinit=E.&aufull=Oliveros+E.&coden=&isbn=&pages=-&date=2018&auinit1=E&auinitm=

Onaolapo, A. Y., & Onaolapo, O. J. (2018). Food additives, food and the concept of 'food addiction': Is stimulation of the brain reward circuit by food sufficient to trigger addiction? Pathophysiology, 25(4), 263–276. https://doi.org/10.1016/j.pathophys.2018.04.002

Palar, K., & Sturm, R. (2009). Potential societal savings from reduced sodium consumption in the U.S. adult population. American Journal of Health Promotion, 24(1), 49–57. https://doi.org/10.4278/ajhp.080826-QUAN-164

Perez, V., & Chang, E. T. (2014). Sodium-to-Potassium Ratio and Blood Pressure, Hypertension, and Related Factors. Advances in Nutrition, 5(6), 712–741. https://doi.org/10.3945/an.114.006783

Perrin, G., Korb-Savoldelli, V., Karras, A., Danchin, N., Durieux, P., & Sabatier, B. (2017). Cardiovascular risk associated with high sodium-containing drugs: A systematic review. PloS One, 12(7), e0180634. https://doi.org/10.1371/journal.pone.0180634

Quader, Z. S., Zhao, L., Gillespie, C., Cogswell, M. E., Terry, A. L., Moshfegh, A., & Rhodes, D. (2017). Sodium Intake Among Persons Aged ≥2 Years—United States, 2013–2014. MMWR. Morbidity and Mortality Weekly Report, 66(12), 324–238. https://doi.org/10.15585/mmwr.mm6612a3

Rawla, P., & Barsouk, A. (2019). Epidemiology of gastric cancer: Global trends, risk factors and prevention. Przeglad Gastroenterologiczny, 14(1), 26–38. https://doi.org/10.5114/pg.2018.80001

Raybaudi-Massilia, R., Mosqueda-Melgar, J., Rosales-Oballos, Y., Citti de Petricone, R., Frágenas, N. N., Zambrano-Durán, A., Sayago, K., Lara, M., & Urbina, G. (2019). New alternative to reduce sodium chloride in meat products: Sensory and microbiological evaluation. LWT, 108, 253–260. https://doi.org/10.1016/j.lwt.2019.03.057

Rodrigues, S. L., Baldo, M. P., Machado, R. C., Forechi, L., Molina, M. del C. B., & Mill, J. G. (2014). High potassium intake blunts the effect of elevated sodium intake on blood pressure levels. Journal of the American Society of Hypertension: JASH, 8(4), 232–238. https://doi.org/10.1016/j.jash.2014.01.001

Runyon, B. A. & AASLD Practice Guidelines Committee. (2009). Management of adult patients with ascites due to cirrhosis: An update. Hepatology (Baltimore, Md.), 49(6), 2087–2107. https://doi.org/10.1002/hep.22853

Sacks, F. M., Svetkey, L. P., Vollmer, W. M., Appel, L. J., Bray, G. A., Harsha, D., Obarzanek, E., Conlin, P. R., Miller, E. R., Simons-Morton, D. G., Karanja, N., & Lin, P. H. (2001). Effects on blood pressure of reduced dietary sodium and the Dietary Approaches to Stop Hypertension (DASH) diet. DASH-Sodium Collaborative Research Group. The New England Journal of Medicine, 344(1), 3–10. https://doi.org/10.1056/NEJM200101043440101

Salt. (2020). http://www.madehow.com/Volume-2/Salt.html

Salt Association. (n.d.). The History of Salt. Retrieved June 19, 2019, from https://www.saltassociation.co.uk/education/salt-history/

SaltWorks. (2020). https://www.seasalt.com/gourmet-salt.html

Samin Nosrat. (2017). Salt Fat Acid Heat (1st ed.). Simon and Schuster.

Satin, M. (2015). The Salt Debate—Far More Salacious Than Salubrious. Blood Purification, 39(1–3), 11–15. https://doi.org/10.1159/000368971

Schulte, E. M., Smeal, J. K., & Gearhardt, A. N. (2017). Foods are differentially associated with subjective effect report questions of abuse liability. PLoS ONE, 12(8), 1–16. https://doi.org/10.1371/journal.pone.0184220

Shen, X., Jin, C., Wu, Y., Zhang, Y., Wang, X., Huang, W., Li, J., Wu, S., & Gao, X. (2019). Prospective study of perceived dietary salt intake and the risk of non-alcoholic fatty liver disease. Journal of Human Nutrition and Dietetics: The Official Journal of the British Dietetic Association, 32(6), 802–809. https://doi.org/10.1111/jhn.12674

Smiechowska, M., Zapewnienia, P. I., Ci, J. Ś., Morskiej, S., & Bada, P. Ą. D. (2018). Ecological threats for coastal systems in the context of acquiring and providing the quality of sea salt. A review. Journal of Research and Applications in Agricultural Engineering, 63(3), 118–122.

Smith, J. L., Lennie, T. A., Chung, M. L., & Mudd-Martin, G. (2019). Dietary Sodium Intake is Predicted by Antihypertensive Medication Regimen in Patients With Heart Failure. The Journal of Cardiovascular Nursing, 34(4), 313–318. https://doi.org/10.1097/JCN.0000000000000570

Smyth, A., O'Donnell, M. J., Yusuf, S., Clase, C. M., Teo, K. K., Canavan, M., Reddan, D. N., & Mann, J. F. E. (2014). Sodium intake and renal outcomes: A systematic review. American Journal of Hypertension, 27(10), 1277–1284. https://doi.org/10.1093/ajh/hpt294

Taormina, P. J. (2010). Implications of salt and sodium reduction on microbial food safety. Critical Reviews in Food Science and Nutrition, 50(3), 209–227. https://doi.org/10.1080/10408391003626207

Taylor, C., Doyle, M., & Webb, D. (2018). "The safety of sodium reduction in the food supply: A cross-discipline balancing act"-Workshop proceedings. Critical Reviews in Food Science and Nutrition, 58(10), 1650–1659. https://doi.org/10.1080/10408398.2016.1276431

USDA. (2013). Water in Meat and Poultry. https://www.fsis.usda.gov/wps/portal/fsis/topics/food-safety-education/get-answers/food-safety-fact-sheets/meat-preparation/water-in-meat-and-poultry/ct_index

USDA. (2018). FoodData Central. FoodData Central | U.S. Department of Agriculture, Agricultural Research Service. https://fdc.nal.usda.gov/

USDA and ARS. (2020). USDA National Nutrient Database for Standard Reference. FoodData Central. https://fdc.nal.usda.gov/fdc-app.html#/?query=ndbNumber:18075

USDA & HHS. (2020). Dietary Guidelines for Americans, 2020-2025. U.S. Department of Health and Human Services and U.S. Department of Agriculture, 164.

Va, P., Dodd, K. W., Zhao, L., Thompson-Paul, A. M., Mercado, C. I., Terry, A. L., Jackson, S. L., Wang, C.-Y., Loria, C. M., Moshfegh, A. J., Rhodes, D. G., & Cogswell, M. E. (2019). Evaluation of measurement error in 24-hour dietary recall for assessing sodium and potassium intake among US adults—National Health and Nutrition Examination Survey (NHANES), 2014. The American Journal of Clinical Nutrition, 109, 1672–1682. https://doi.org/10.1093/ajcn/nqz044

Vella, D., Marcone, M., & Duizer, L. M. (2012a). Physical and sensory properties of regional sea salts. Food Research International, 45, 415–421. https://doi.org/10.1016/j.foodres.2011.11.013

Vella, D., Marcone, M., & Duizer, L. M. (2012b). Physical and sensory properties of regional sea salts. Food Research International, 45(1), 415–421. https://doi.org/10.1016/j.foodres.2011.11.013

Weinberger, M. H. (1996). Salt sensitivity of blood pressure in humans. Hypertension (Dallas, Tex.: 1979), 27(3 Pt 2), 481–490. https://doi.org/10.1161/01.hyp.27.3.481

Weinberger, M. H., Fineberg Naomi S., Fineberg S. Edwin, & Weinberger Morris. (2001). Salt Sensitivity, Pulse Pressure, and Death in Normal and Hypertensive Humans. Hypertension, 37(2), 429–432. https://doi.org/10.1161/01.HYP.37.2.429

Wessler, J. D., Hummel, S. L., & Maurer, M. S. (2014a). Dietary interventions for heart failure in older adults: Re-emergence of the hedonic shift. Progress in Cardiovascular Diseases, 57(2), 160–167. https://doi.org/10.1016/j.pcad.2014.03.007

Wessler, J. D., Hummel, S. L., & Maurer, M. S. (2014b). Dietary interventions for heart failure in older adults: Re-emergence of the hedonic shift. Progress in Cardiovascular Diseases, 57(2), 160–167. https://doi.org/10.1016/j.pcad.2014.03.007

Whelton, P. K. (2018). Sodium and Potassium Intake in US Adults. Circulation, 137(3), 247–249. https://doi.org/10.1161/CIRCULATIONAHA.117.031371

Whelton, P. K., Appel, L., Espeland, M. A., Applegate, W. B., Ettinger, W. H., Kostis, J. B., Kumanyika, S., Lacy, C. R., Johnson, K. C., Folmar, S., & Cutler, J. A. (1998). Sodium reduction and weight loss in the treatment of hypertension in older persons: A randomized controlled trial of nonpharmacologic interventions in the elderly (TONE). Journal of the American Medical Association, 279(11), 839–846. https://doi.org/10.1001/jama.279.11.839

World Health Organization. (2012). Guideline: Potassium intake for adults and children. https://www.who.int/publications-detail-redirect/9789241504829

World Health Organization. (2018a). Healthy diet. https://www.who.int/news-room/fact-sheets/detail/healthy-diet

World Health Organization. (2018b). Healthy Diet. Fact Sheets. https://www.who.int/news-room/fact-sheets/detail/healthy-diet

Yancy, C. W., Jessup, M., Bozkurt, B., Butler, J., Casey, D. E., Drazner, M. H., Fonarow, G. C., Geraci, S. A., Horwich, T., Januzzi, J. L., Johnson, M. R., Kasper, E. K., Levy, W. C., Masoudi, F. A., McBride, P. E., McMurray, J. J. V., Mitchell, J. E., Peterson, P. N., Riegel, B., … Wilkoff, B. L. (2013). 2013 ACCF/AHA Guideline for the Management of Heart Failure: A Report of the American College of Cardiology Foundation/American Heart Association Task Force on Practice Guidelines. Circulation, 128(16). https://doi.org/10.1161/CIR.0b013e31829e8776

Yang, Q., Liu, T., Kuklina, E. V., Flanders, W. D., Hong, Y., Gillespie, C., Chang, M.-H., Gwinn, M., Dowling, N., Khoury, M. J., & Hu, F. B. (2011). Sodium and potassium intake and mortality among US adults: Prospective data from the Third National Health and Nutrition Examination Survey. Archives of Internal Medicine, 171(13), 1183–1191. https://doi.org/10.1001/archinternmed.2011.257

Yi, S. S., & Kansagra, S. M. (2014). Associations of sodium intake with obesity, body mass index, waist circumference, and weight. American Journal of Preventive Medicine, 46(6). https://doi.org/10.1016/j.amepre.2014.02.005

Zadourian, A., Doherty, T. A., Swiatkiewicz, I., & Taub, P. R. (2018). Postural orthostatic tachycardia syndrome: Prevalence, pathophysiology, and management. Drugs, 78(10), 983–994. https://doi.org/10.1007/s40265-018-0931-5

Zhang, Y., Li, F. X., Liu, F. Q., Chu, C., Wang, Y., Wang, D., Guo, T. S., Wang, J. K., Guan, G. C., Ren, K. Y., & Mu, J. J. (2016). Elevation of fasting ghrelin in healthy human subjects consuming a high-salt diet: A novel mechanism of obesity? Nutrients, 8(6), 1–8. https://doi.org/10.3390/nu8060323

Zhang, Z., Cogswell, M. E., Gillespie, C., Fang, J., Loustalot, F., Dai, S., Carriquiry, A. L., Kuklina, E. V., Hong, Y., Merritt, R., & Yang, Q. (2013). Association between Usual Sodium and Potassium Intake and Blood Pressure and Hypertension among U.S. Adults: NHANES 2005–2010. PLOS ONE, 8(10), e75289. https://doi.org/10.1371/journal.pone.0075289

Zhao, L., Cogswell, M. E., Yang, Q., Zhang, Z., Onufrak, S., Jackson, S. L., Chen, T.-C., Loria, C. M., Wang, C.-Y., Wright, J. D., Terry, A. L., Merritt, R., & Ogden, C. L. (2019). Association of usual 24-h sodium excretion with measures of adiposity among adults in the United States: NHANES, 2014. The American Journal of Clinical Nutrition, 109(1), 139–147. https://doi.org/10.1093/ajcn/nqy285

ADDED SUGAR

By Dana White, MS, RD, ATC and
Deborah Kennedy, PhD
with The Expert Chef Panel

"Neither sugar nor salt tastes particularly good by itself. Each is at its best when used to season other things. Love is the same way. Use it to 'season' people."
Quote by Vera Nazarian

Honey was the first concentrated form of sugar that humans collected 10,000 years ago. It wasn't until Christopher Columbus brought sugarcane stalks from the Spanish Canary Islands to America in 1493 that sugar was available in America, and it took until 1751 for Americans to start growing their own sugarcane (Gritz, 2017; Muhammad, 2019). Today the United States makes 9 million tons of sugar each year and imports more, because that amount is not enough to feed America's appetite for sugar.

Sugar consumption increased as the sugar beet industry grew in the late 1800s when sugar availability increased from the Hawaiian Reciprocity Treaty. What was once consumed as an occasional treat (about two pounds per year), increased in consumption exponentially — to 123 pounds a year in 1970. From 1970 to 2005 alone, "average annual availability of sugars/added sugars increased by 19%, which added 76 calories to Americans' average daily energy intake" (Johnson et al., 2009).

Sugar can be found in food naturally — for example, in fruit and dairy products. Sugar can also be added to food and beverages — added sugar. The difference in terms of their health effects is dramatic. This chapter will review added sugar, the health effects of consuming too much, and how one can consume less added sugar in their diet through shopping and culinary practices.

SECTION 1: SUGAR CHARACTERISTICS

SUGARCANE

SUGAR BEET

Table sugar is sourced from either the tropical plant sugar cane, or sugar beets, which grow in cooler climates. Of the sugar produced domestically, 55% is from the sugar beet. In sugarcane, the sugar is stored in the stalks, as juice and with the sugar beet, the sugar is stored in the root.

At the most basic level, carbohydrates are made up of three molecules — carbon, hydrogen, and oxygen.

SET OF CARBOHYDRATES

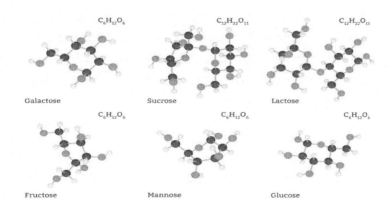

$C_6H_{12}O_6$	$C_{12}H_{22}O_{11}$	$C_{12}H_{22}O_{11}$
Galactose	Sucrose	Lactose
$C_6H_{12}O_6$	$C_6H_{12}O_6$	$C_6H_{12}O_6$
Fructose	Mannose	Glucose

Sugar is one of many types of carbohydrates that can be made up of different lengths of sugar units. The simplest type of carbohydrates are **monosaccharides**, which are made up of one molecule. These include:
- Glucose
- Galactose
- Fructose

All caloric **added sugars** are made up of a combination of these three monosaccharides, mostly glucose and fructose. There are varying amounts of each, as seen in Table 1.

Table 1: Percentage of Glucose and Fructose in Common Sugars

Source	Glucose	Fructose
Sucrose, honey	50%	50%
Agave	30%	70%
HFCS*	45% to 58%	42% to 55%

*High fructose corn syrup (HFCS)

Disaccharides contain two sugar molecules, and include:
- Maltose (glucose + glucose) = starch
- Lactose (galactose + glucose) = the sugar in dairy products
- Sucrose (glucose + fructose) = table sugar

Both monosaccharides and disaccharides can be naturally occurring in food, or they can be added to improve the palatability, texture, and preservation of certain foods. The level of sweetness of each saccharide differs, with fructose being much sweeter than sucrose or glucose, while lactose is the least sweet of them all (Sweetness - an Overview | ScienceDirect Topics).

The body can't decipher whether the sugar that is consumed is naturally occurring in the food or if it was added. The biggest difference however, is how fructose and glucose are metabolized differently. **While glucose can be metabolized by every cell in the body, fructose is primarily metabolized in the liver.** See the section on fructose below for the consequences of this metabolism.

High amounts of sugar, no matter in what form, are harmful to the body.

DIGESTION

Disaccharides begin digestion in the mouth with salivary amylase and digestion is completed by pancreatic amylase breaking down the sugar molecule into its respective monosaccharides. When monosaccharides are digested, the body is able to process them more quickly than disaccharides and longer branched sugar molecules since it doesn't have to break down multiple monomers.

ABSORPTION

Monosaccharides are absorbed at the brush border membrane of the enterocytes of the small intestine. Glucose and galactose first travel through the sodium-dependent carrier, sodium coupled glucose transporters (SGLT) SGLT1, or at times, in larger quantities, through the glucose transporter protein (GLUT) GLUT2, of which it is one of 14 GLUT members (Mahan & Raymond, 2016). Fructose is absorbed by the GLUT5 hexose transporter. All of the sugar molecules then leave the mucosal barrier through diffusion or through the GLUT2 carrier.

METABOLISM

There is not one biochemical reaction in the body that requires fructose, whereas all cells require glucose. After ingestion of glucose, 80% goes to the organs throughout the body and the brain, and 20% goes to the liver where the majority is converted into glycogen. A very small amount goes through denovo-lipogenesis and produces a small number of triglycerides.

Fructose on the other hand, is transported mainly to the liver – about 70% of fructose is metabolized in the liver (Francey 2019). When fructose enters the liver, it is not converted to glycogen. Instead, fructose is converted to triglycerides (TG) where some of it is stored in the liver as lipid droplets (leading to non-alcoholic fatty liver disease when ingested in excess), and some is released into the bloodstream causing a rise in TG.

POST-ABSORPTION

When ingesting sweets with high sugar content, blood glucose levels will naturally rise to a certain degree before the glucose is absorbed. An individual's metabolic health can play a large role in this as well. Glycemic index is a relative measure of glycemic response and assesses how a person's body responds in a given amount of time to consuming 50 grams of carbohydrate (Vega-López et al., 2018).

$$GI = (iAUC_{test\ food}/iAUC_{reference\ food}) \times 100$$

It was originally developed in 1981 with the main purpose of helping people with diabetes control their blood glucose levels (Vega-López et al., 2018). The glycemic load technique was developed 16 years later in 1997 at a lab at Harvard University. It is another way to measure the glycemic response, but it also accounts for the portion size and is more of a predictive measure (Vega-López et al., 2018).

More on Glycemic Index and Glycemic Load
The biggest difference between glycemic index and glycemic load is that glycemic load accounts for the amount of the specific carbohydrate-rich food someone is eating, rather than 50 grams of carbohydrate. It is important to note that **neither glycemic index nor glycemic load can be an indicator of the healthfulness of the food**. For example, watermelon has a high glycemic index, but it is rich in plant compounds and phytonutrients, that have a range of other healthful benefits. Additionally, it has high water content which can contribute to daily fluid intake. **Glycemic load** is a measurement ultimately used more in research, but it **is also a valuable tool for diabetes and weight management.**

For glycemic index, foods are classified as the following (Eleazu, 2016):
- High (> 70)
- Medium (>55 – < 70)
- Low (< 55)

For glycemic load, foods are classified as the following (Eleazu, 2016):
- High (> 20)
- Intermediate (11–19)
- Low (< 10)

Here are some examples of a serving of each food with high, medium/intermediate, and low values (Mahan & Raymond, 2016):

Table 2: The Glycemic Index and Glycemic Load of Various Foods

Food	Glycemic Index	Glycemic Load
Parsnip	97	12
Boiled potato	88	16
Instant rice	87	36
Jelly beans	78	22
Whole-wheat bread	77	9
Bagel	72	25
Watermelon	72	4
Raisins	64	28
Sweet potato	61	17
Sweet corn	60	11
Pineapple	59	7
Pita bread	57	10
Banana	51	13
Brown rice	50	16
Orange	48	5
Green peas	48	3
Carrots	47	3
Spaghetti	38	18
Apple	38	6
Yam	37	13
Yogurt, low-fat	33	10
Lentils	29	5
Chickpeas	28	8
Grapefruit	25	3
Cherries	22	3
Soybeans	18	1

*Adapted from Krause's Food and the Nutrition Care Process (Mahan & Raymond, 2016)

How to Maintain Healthy Blood Glucose Levels

To decrease the rise in blood glucose after ingestion of sugar, it is advised to eat balanced meals that include whole grains, lean proteins, healthful fats, fruits and vegetables. Aiming for a plate that contains half fruits and vegetables, a quarter lean protein (animal or plant sources), and a quarter whole grains, with a side of dairy is the MyPlate recommended target and it will help to maintain healthy blood sugar levels (MyPlate Graphics | MyPlate).

Consuming a balanced meal, including protein and healthful fats, can help blunt the rise in blood sugar (Paterson et al., 2015). Consumption of fat can contribute to gluconeogenesis, impact insulin production, alter hormones involved in glycemic regulation, and delay gastric emptying. Due to these mechanisms, fat creates a slower increase in glucose levels over time, leading to a less drastic blood glucose response overall. Protein can also impact the glycemic response by extending the response over several hours through its impact on hormones and by converting amino acids to glucose (Paterson et al., 2015).

Fiber, which is a carbohydrate in plant-based foods that the body is not able to digest, can also help control the post-absorptive rise in glucose. There are two main types of fiber: insoluble and soluble. Soluble fiber dissolves in water, so it forms a gel-like substance from food and delays gastric emptying. It also delays absorption of nutrients, including glucose, in the small intestine by slowing down motility. Because of this, it can blunt the blood sugar response after a meal. Insoluble fiber does not dissolve in water, and though it increases transit time in the colon, it can decrease the glycemic index of a food by blunting the glucose response.

What does this look like on a plate?
- Instead of having a dish of white pasta with red sauce, the blood glucose response could be improved by choosing whole grain pasta instead, and mixing in steamed vegetables, chicken, and a drizzle of olive oil.
- Instead of a bowl of sweet cereal with milk, choose unsweetened oatmeal and pair it with cinnamon, berries, walnuts and skim milk or almond milk.

FRUCTOSE

High fructose corn syrup (HFCS) is a syrupy substance that contains the monomers glucose and fructose. It is made by enzymatically changing some of the glucose in cornstarch to fructose, and it was introduced to the food industry in the 1970s (White, 2008). This enzymatic modification makes it intensely sweet, easy to transport, and very cost-effective. It is most comparable to sucrose, though HFCS has a slightly sweeter taste. HFCS is energy-dense due to the high amount of sugar in the syrup.

Fructose, besides imparting a sweet taste, also enhances flavor and color, extends shelf life through moisture control, depresses the freezing point of food and provides osmotic stability (Hanover & White, 1993). Because of these traits and the fact that it is very inexpensive, fructose is often used in processed food and beverages. Before sugar was mass-produced, humans had very little exposure to fructose (see Graph 1).

Graph 1: The Increase in Fructose Consumed Over Time

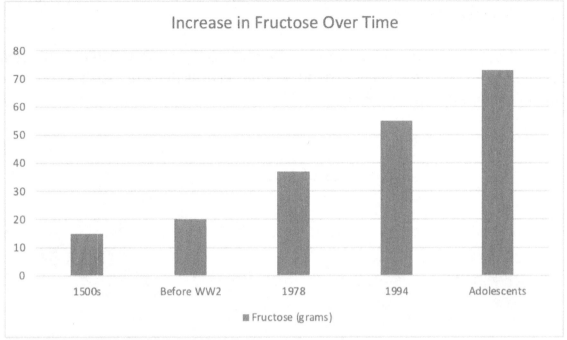

Increase in Fructose Over Time

(Bray, 2007; M. B. Vos et al., 2008)

Most of the fructose found in the American diet comes from sucrose and HFCS found in soft drinks and sweets, not from fruit.

HFCS can have varying amounts of fructose. The one chosen for a product depends on the food type and manufacturer's choice. Contributors to fructose consumption in Americans ages 19 years or older are (M. B. Vos et al., 2008):

- Beverages: 29%
- Whole fruit: 18%
- Sugars/sweets: 11%
- Cakes/pies/snacks: 11%
- Bread/pasta: 8%
- Vegetables: 8%
- Dairy: 5%
- Other: 5%
- Ready-to-eat cereal: 3%
- 100% Fruit juice: 2%

The small intestine has a limited ability to absorb high amounts of fructose, which can lead to intestinal discomfort in some individuals. An overabundance of fructose — from HFCS or sucrose — in the liver can have negative effects on the liver, as well as increase the risk of metabolic syndrome, heart disease, diabetes, obesity and other disease

(Jensen et al., 2018; Mai & Yan, 2019; White, 2008). Research is still examining the full effects of fructose on health.

Sugar: The Bitter Truth is a video by Robert Lustig, MD, from UCSF Pediatric Division of Endocrinology and in it he explains in depth why he believes that fructose is a cornerstone of obesity, along with consuming too little fiber.

Stages of Liver Damage

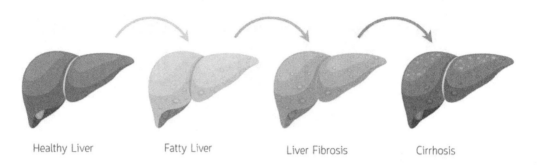

| Healthy Liver | Fatty Liver | Liver Fibrosis | Cirrhosis |

Fructose and Non-Alcoholic Fatty Liver Disease (NAFLD)

Excess consumption of fructose, primarily in the form of added sugars, can lead to fat accumulation in the liver. It is dose dependent; the more fructose that is consumed at one time, the greater the chance it will be turned into triglycerides. This accumulation is due to fructose turning on the switch for lipogenesis while also blocking the oxidation of fatty acids (Jensen et al., 2018). These metabolic changes can induce fatty liver disease.

It is worthwhile to note that these changes can be independent of weight gain, though high consumption of added sugars often coincides with excess caloric consumption which can lead to weight gain (Jensen et al., 2018; Johnson et al., 2009). These mechanisms can also increase the risk of obesity, type 2 diabetes mellitus (T2DM), insulin resistance, hypertension, and dyslipidemia (Johnson et al., 2009).

In general, consuming a balanced diet with the recommended amounts of foods from each food group, while limiting intake of added sugar in the form of sucrose or HFCS, can help prevent excess consumption of fructose.

SECTION 2: RECOMMENDATIONS FOR SUGAR INTAKE

The AHA recommends that children younger than 2 years of age completely avoid added sugars, and children 2 years of age or older limit added sugars to ≤25 grams (100 calories or about six teaspoons) of added sugars per day (M. Vos et al. 2008). Women are advised to limit total calories from added sugars to no more than 100 calories per day (6 teaspoons, 25 grams), and men should limit total daily calories from added sugars to no more than 150 calories (9 teaspoons, 36 grams) (AHA; Johnson et al., 2009).

The 2020 – 2025 Dietary Guidelines for Americans also recommend limiting added sugars to less than 10% of total daily calories. For someone who consumes 2,000 calories per day, this is 50 grams of sugar, or about 12.5 teaspoons of sugar (Dietary Guidelines for Americans, 2020-2025). Similarly, the World Health Organization (WHO) has a strong recommendation for people to limit added sugar consumption to less than 10% of total calorie intake, and a conditional recommendation to further reduce intake to 5% for the potential benefit for dental caries prevention (25 grams, or 6.25 teaspoons) (WHO).

HOW MUCH SUGAR DO AMERICANS ACTUALLY CONSUME?

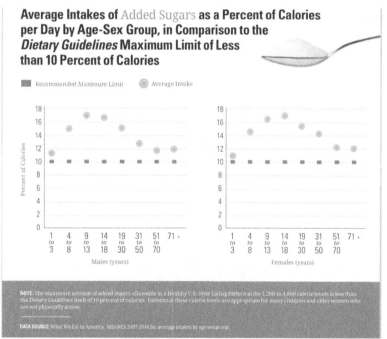

Image Source (2015-2020 Dietary Guidelines | Health.Gov): Taken from USDA DGA 2015-2020
Data from What We Eat in America, NHANES 2007-2010 for average intakes by age-sex group. Healthy U.S.-Style Food Patterns, which vary based on age, sex, and activity level, for recommended intake ranges.

The percent of daily energy from added sugars has declined among U.S. adults from 18% (NHANES 1999 – 2000), to 15% (NHANES 2007 – 2008), to 13% (NHANES 2007 – 2010), but still remains above the national and global targets (Bailey et al., 2018; Bray, 2007; Hanover & White, 1993). Astoundingly, nearly **70% of the population is still at or above the maximum** total daily sugar intake (Current Eating Patterns in the United States - 2015-2020 Dietary Guidelines | Health.Gov). **The average American is consuming close to 17**

teaspoons of sugar a day (270 calories of added sugar) (DGA 2015-2020, 2016). If someone were to consume 17 teaspoons of added sugar daily on top of their caloric requirement, this would equal 6,052 teaspoons (126 cups) of sugar in a year, which translates into an additional 28 pounds of body weight.

Of all the purchased food and beverages in the United States, **68% have added sugar** (Popkin & Hawkes, 2016). In the data collected from 2009 – 2012, the top 10 sources of added sugars for adults (19 years of age or older) in the decile with the highest level of intake were the following in descending order (Bailey et al., 2018):

1. Sweetened beverages
2. Coffee and tea
3. Sweet bakery products
4. Sugars
5. Candy
6. Other desserts
7. Ready-to-eat cereals
8. Fats and oils
9. Breads, rolls, tortillas
10. Quick breads and bread products

In terms of food category sources, **the largest contributor by a wide margin is beverages**, followed by sweets/snacks.

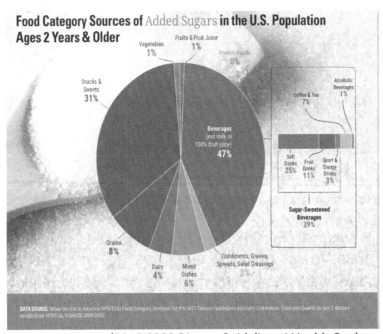

Image Source (2015-2020 Dietary Guidelines | Health.Gov)

SECTION 3: WHAT ARE THE BENEFITS AND RISKS OF ADDED SUGAR?

THE BENEFITS

Glucose is an essential nutrient to consume, as it is one of the body's preferred sources of energy, and the only fuel source for the brain (Sugar and the Brain, 2020). When consumed in adequate and proper amounts, it allows the body to carry on typical processes and can fuel daily activities. The body is able to store glucose as glycogen to help regulate blood glucose levels and to use for energy when needed, e.g., during exercise.

Glucose is naturally present in many foods, and certain foods contain notable amounts of innate sugar. Fruit and dairy products with naturally occurring sugars are part of a healthful, balanced diet and part of a person's carbohydrate recommendations for the day. However, it is possible for someone to have a diet high in carbohydrates. In this case, when glucose is consistently consumed in excess, it can lead to chronically elevated blood glucose levels. This can impact the body's ability to absorb glucose, which can in part be due to decreased insulin production, or a reduced sensitivity to insulin. Over time, if intake of sugar remains high, someone may develop T2DM.

THE RISKS

The risks of overconsumption of sugar apply to all ages, even children. Many people think of diseases starting in adulthood, but cardiovascular disease, obesity, and T2DM are closely related to sugar consumption and can occur in youth as well (M. Vos et al, 2017). The recommendation to limit added sugar consumption to less than 10% of total daily calories, and furthermore to less than 5%, was made to help prevent these negative effects.

Some of the most prominent risks of overconsumption of added sugar include cardiovascular disease, overweight/obesity, T2DM, gestational diabetes, some cancers, cognitive impairment, osteoporosis and dental caries (Malik & Hu, 2019; Pushpanathan et al., 2019; J. M. Rippe & Angelopoulos, 2016). Research is continuously studying these outcomes to provide even more clarity about how the body responds to added sugar — both in the short term and long term.

Obesity/Weight Gain

The intake of sugar and its impact on weight gain, metabolic health, and obesity has been thoroughly studied. Sugar is added to many foods, making them energy-dense and more easily consumed in excess (Prinz, 2019). The WHO identified weight gain as one of the two most prominent health issues related to sugar intake (Breda et al., 2019; WHO).

Both sugar-sweetened beverages and foods with added sugars contribute to this problem. In a recent study, the percentage of daily intake from simple sugars and fat after allowing for ad libitum were associated with weight gain (P = 0.02). It was concluded that greater consumption of these energy-dense foods was a predictor of both overeating and weight gain (Stinson et al., 2018). Additionally, a systematic review by Luger et al. analyzing data from 2013 – 2015 found that out of the prospective cohort studies chosen, 96% had a positive association between consumption of sugar-sweetened beverages (SSB) and weight or BMI in both adults and children. Likewise, the randomized clinical trials with child subjects found a positive association between SSB consumption and BMI, though no significant association was found with adults (Luger et al., 2017).

Children are an important population to target in regard to sugar consumption and weight gain/obesity. Luger et al. also examined SSB consumption data in children ages 2 to 5 years from the Early Childhood Longitudinal Survey – Birth Cohort. They found that 5-year-old children who consumed SSB regularly had a higher odds ratio of being obese than children who were infrequent drinkers or didn't consume SSB at all (1.43, confidence interval 1.10–1.85, P < .01). Regular intake of SSB among 2-year-olds led to greater increases in BMI z scores versus their infrequent/nondrinker counterparts (Luger et al., 2017).

Research is still lacking on whether or not isocaloric diets, despite high sugar consumption, predict weight gain. A thorough systematic review and meta-analysis of randomized controlled trials and prospective cohort studies found that with hypercaloric diets, a reduction in consumption of added sugars was positively associated with a decrease in body weight (0.80 kg, P<0.001), and an increase in sugar consumption was positively associated with an increase in weight (0.75 kg, P=0.001) (Morenga et al., 2013).

Cardiovascular Disease (CVD)

In 2012, NHANES data estimated that **7.4% of cardiometabolic deaths were due to high intake of SSBs** (Micha et al., 2017). The intake of sugar-sweetened beverages has also been linked to CVD risk (Malik & Hu, 2019). However, many studies conducted to date looking at the relation between sugar and CVD have looked at CVD risk factors rather than CVD outcomes such as risk of all-cause or CVD mortality. The data that does exist shows a strong impact of sugar on heart health.

Many studies have consistently seen an association between SSB and cardiometabolic risk factors, weight gain, and T2DM. These associations have contributed to the evidence of a possible direct association between SSB and CVD (Malik & Hu, 2019). The data that exists on sugar and CVD risk factors shows that sugar can have a detrimental effect on several biomarkers related to cardiovascular health. A review by Rippe and Angelopoulos included 14 different studies that identified simple sugars as a cause of **increased triglyceride levels**. Even though sugar intake alone may not increase CVD risk factors, consumption of 20% of daily calories from simple sugars led to notable changes in triglyceride levels (J. Rippe & Angelopoulos, 2015). Elevated triglyceride levels are a risk factor for CVD, among many other health conditions.

Furthermore, a meta-analysis by Narain et al. examining nine prospective cohort studies found an association between SSB intake, stroke, and myocardial infarction (MI). One study showed that an increase in SSB intake by one serving per day was associated with a 13% higher risk of stroke (RR: 1.13, 95% CI: 1.02, 1.24), and two studies showed a 22% higher risk of myocardial infarction (MI) (RR: 1.22, 95% CI: 1.14, 1.30) (Narain et al., 2016). Additionally, a prospective cohort study examining data from the National Health and Nutrition Examination Survey (NHANES) and NHANES III Linked Mortality cohort was used to assess the effect of added sugar on CVD mortality. People who consumed greater than 10% but less than 25% of calories from added sugars had a 30% greater risk of dying from CVD than individuals consuming less than 10% of calories from added sugar per day. This risk more than tripled for those who consumed more than 25%. Additionally, intake of seven or more SSB per week was associated with increased risk of CVD mortality (Yang et al., 2014).

A similar trend was seen in another analysis of data from two prospective cohort studies, the Health Professional's Follow-Up Study and the Nurses' Health Study. Researchers found a dose-dependent relationship between SSB intake and CVD mortality. Risk of death from CVD was 31% higher in individuals who consumed two or more SSB per day, in comparison to people who consumed the beverages less frequently. This was adjusted for lifestyle and diet. It is also worthwhile to note that "SSB consumption was associated with a higher intake of total energy, red and processed meat, and glycemic load and with a lower intake of whole grains and vegetables (Malik et al., 2019)."

In a scientific statement from the American Heart Association, they determined that "strong evidence supports the association of added sugars with increased cardiovascular disease risk in children through increased energy intake, increased adiposity, and dyslipidemia (M. Vos et al. 2017)." Limiting added sugar intake is important for CVD health for both adults and children.

Dental Caries

The CDC has defined dental caries as the most common chronic disease in children ages 6 to 11, and adolescents ages 12 to 19 (Oral Health | CDC, 2018). It is a disease that also impacts 19 out of 20 adults. Dental caries were one of the two critical outcomes the WHO highlighted in its 2015 report related to excess sugar intake (WHO).

DENTAL CARIES

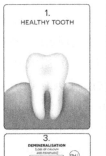
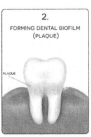
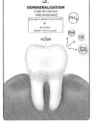
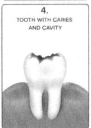

Further examining the applicability of the 10% guideline set by the WHO, a dose-response relationship was examined between total sugar intake and the occurrence of dental caries. A log linear relationship was seen from 0% sugar intake of calories to 10% calories from sugar (Sheiham & James, 2014).

In a systematic review of sugar restriction and caries, moderate-quality evidence was seen with less than 10% calories. Even though a significant relationship was seen with 5%, the evidence was low quality and more research is needed (Moynihan & Kelly, 2013). Given the current evidence, it is advisable to adhere to the WHO guidelines for sugar — to restrict added sugars to 10% of total caloric intake, and furthermore, to 5% for additional health benefits including decreased cariogenic potential.

Type 2 Diabetes Mellitus

According to CDC data, in 2015 9.4% (30.3 million people) of the U.S. population was diagnosed with diabetes (CDC, 2019). Diabetes in youth has also been a growing concern, as 193,000 children and adolescents were diagnosed in 2015 .

Overconsumption of sugar over time can lead to chronically elevated blood sugar levels, and thus development of T2DM. The overload of sugar can make the cells resistant to insulin, and the pancreas may stop producing as much insulin, or both. Insulin resistance is a reduced sensitivity of insulin on the body's tissues, including the muscle tissue, hepatocytes, and adipose tissue. Obesity is one of the largest risk factors for T2DM, highlighting the impact diet and lifestyle can have on an individual's health.

A meta-analysis of 17 prospective cohort studies evaluating SSB consumption and risk of T2DM found that **a one-serving-per-day increment in SSB was associated with an 18% higher risk of T2DM** (not adjusted for adiposity), and 13% (adjusted for adiposity) (Malik & Hu, 2019). Another meta-analysis looking at sugar-sweetened beverages and risk of metabolic syndrome and T2DM found that people in the highest quantile for SSB consumption (typically one to two servings/day) had a 26% greater risk of developing T2DM than individuals in the lowest quantile (none or less than one serving/month) (Malik et al., 2010).

Monitoring sugar intake and consuming a diet of nutrient-dense foods such as fruits and vegetables, whole grains, legumes, nuts and seeds can greatly benefit individuals in terms of diabetes prevention and control. Go to the Diabetes chapter for more information.

Cataracts

Incidence and progression of cataracts is increased in diabetic patients as are potential complications during surgical procedures to correct vision problems. When blood glucose or galactose levels are high, glycation can occur in the lens of the eye leading to cataract formation.
This has been observed in both type 1 and T2DM (Pollreisz & Schmidt-Erfurth, 2010).

Pregnancy/Lactation

Some women are at risk of developing gestational diabetes mellitus during pregnancy, which is impacted by dietary behaviors before and during pregnancy (Shin et al., 2015). In the U.S., about **6% to 9% of women develop gestational diabetes** (GDM) (Diabetes During Pregnancy | Maternal Infant Health | Reproductive Health | CDC, 2019). This form of diabetes only occurs during pregnancy and is a result of hyperglycemia due to inadequate maternal insulin production and insulin-antagonizing placental hormones. It is more common among women with a family history of diabetes mellitus and/or those who are obese. Similar to T2DM, diet and physical activity patterns are key elements for good health and prevention. If uncontrolled, GDM can increase the risk of the child developing T2DM, being obese in childhood, and developing cardiovascular disease in adulthood (Herring & Oken, 2011).

In one study, out of the 249 pregnant women, 14% had GDM. The high consumption of added sugars, refined grains, and fat, combined with the low consumption of fruits and vegetables during pregnancy, directly impacts GDM management (Shin et al., 2015).

Consumption of SSB has also shown to have an impact on birth weight (Grundt et al., 2017).

Athletes

Athletes are a unique population because they require greater amounts of carbohydrates than the majority of individuals. For example, some endurance athletes need to consume 12 grams of carbohydrate per kilogram of body weight per day (Thomas et al., 2016). This may surpass the general recommendation of 45% to 65% of calories coming from carbohydrate per day. For a 170-pound male consuming 12 grams carbohydrates/kg/day, that is nearly 930 grams of carbohydrates in a day. To be able to consume this amount, athletes often need to eat simple carbohydrates that are in sports foods like gels, chews, and sports drinks. These products contain glucose, fructose, and sucrose so that the carbohydrates can quickly be digested and used during exercise.

Additionally, to consume that amount of carbohydrates, athletes have to monitor their fiber intake. A generally healthful diet with whole grains, legumes, fruits and vegetables contains a generous amount of fiber. Fiber can add bulk and also create a satiating effect well before the athlete has reached their nutrition needs. This is where the sugars or simple carbohydrates may provide a benefit to help them reach peak performance. Overall, it is important for any athlete to monitor activity levels and sugar intake over time, as there are different parts of the season where athletes may have a lighter training load and may need to change their eating patterns. More information is available in the Competitive Athlete chapter.

MORE RESEARCH NEEDED

Cancer

According to the American Institute for Cancer Research, excess body weight has been linked to greater risk of 12 cancers: breast (post-menopausal), colorectal, endometrial, esophageal, gall bladder, kidney, liver, mouth/pharynx/larynx, ovarian, pancreatic, prostate (advanced) and stomach (The Sugar and Cancer Connection - American Institute for Cancer Research). As discussed previously, intake of added sugars alone may not lead to weight gain, but the consistent patterns of hypercaloric diets due to energy-dense foods with added sugars is linked to weight gain and other health complications.

Glucose is the main source of energy for cells and the uptake of glucose seems to be pronounced in cancer cells where it has been shown to aid in the generation of new biomass and to regulate cell signaling to progress cancerous cells (Adekola et al., 2012). A recent review by Malik et al. found modest associations between SSB intake and cancer mortality. A positive association was found between intake of SSB and breast cancer mortality. SSB intake and colon cancer was close to a positive association as well (Malik et al., 2019). More research is needed in this area to truly understand the effect of added sugar and excess intake of sugar on the risk of developing cancer and greater mortality rates for different cancers.

Osteoporosis

Overconsumption of sugar has also been linked to an increased risk of developing osteoporosis. Various populations are at risk, particularly adolescents who consume large amounts of sugar during peak times of bone growth. As little as an increase of a half can of sugar-sweetened beverages like soda per day can increase the likelihood of a bone fracture by 1.7 times. High intake of sugar has also been linked to increased excretion of calcium and magnesium in the urine, as well as decreased activation of vitamin D, another nutrient vital to bone mineral density (DiNicolantonio et al., 2018).

Brain Health

Research has shown that sugar can affect the hippocampus, which is the memory center of the brain. Not only does the amount of sugar consumed matter, but the type of sugar consumed does as well. Different types of sugar can impact the brain's regulatory functions differently, including energy homeostasis, reward regions, and hunger hormones (Van Opstal et al., 2021). For example, animal studies have found that sucrose my illicit an increase in calorie consumption aside from the calories provided from the source of sugar itself, while glucose may assist in triggering a feeling of fullness at a meal more efficiently (Murray et al., 2016). This effect on the reward regions of the brain can influence satiety feedback. More research is needed to examine what this means for feeding behaviors and brain health.

A study examining older women (mean age 63.1 years), found cognitive impairment may be impacted by chronically elevated blood glucose, without T2DM or impaired glucose tolerance. It is proposed that these results could be due to changes in the structure of the learning-relevant brain areas (Kerti & A. Veronica Witte, 2022).

In a cross-sectional study with older Malaysian adults, Chong et al. found an association between cognitive function and higher consumption of sugar. Higher consumption of total sugars, free sugars, sucrose, lactose, sugar-sweetened beverages and sugar-sweetened cakes, and desserts led to decreased scores on the cognitive tests performed, as shown in the adjusted OR for risk of cognitive impairment scores for total sugars and free sugar (Chong et al., 2019).

Likewise, in a study examining middle-aged and older Puerto Rican adults without diabetes, excess sugar intake negatively impacted cognitive abilities. There was a significant association between intakes of total sugars, added sugars, and sugar-sweetened beverages and the Word list learning score was negatively impacted (Ye et al., 2011).

Sugar Addiction

The phrases food and sugar addiction are commonly tossed around by individuals, but researchers have examined the terms more closely to properly classify them as a potential clinical diagnosis. Highly processed foods with added sugar and high fat content — known as hyperpalatable foods — are typically in the spotlight for addiction. In 2018, a systematic review examining human studies showed that processed foods with **added sweeteners and fats** have the highest potential to lead to addiction (Gordon et al., 2018). The studies that were examined in the review showed a consistent pattern of brain reward dysfunction and impaired control among the subjects.

Addiction is typically used as a term for substance use disorders. However, this evidence shows that food may travel along the same spectrum. In additional research, the population most likely to exhibit clinical food addiction symptoms was overweight or obese females older than 35 years of age (Pursey et al., 2014).

Dopamine signaling appears to play a role here, as one study found that the appetite suppressant that blocks dopamine was not working properly in adults who tested positive for food addiction with the Yale Food Addiction Scale (Davis et al., 2013). Many studies have also identified a relation of food reward to the opioidergic system, comparable to drug addiction (Daubenmier et al., 2014; Wiss et al., 2018).

Research will continue to evolve in the coming years, but the research to date has identified food addiction in both humans and animals. More information is needed for additional populations, which will ultimately allow for a more tailored approach to preventative and therapeutic methods.

SECTION 4: ARTIFICIAL SWEETENERS

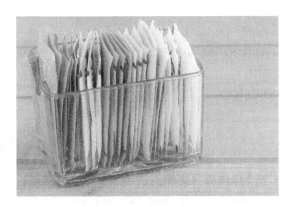

What are artificial sweeteners? In 1975, artificial sweeteners popped into the spotlight and sugar consumption temporarily decreased and their popularity has grown ever since (Gritz, 2017; Muhammad, 2019). They are also commonly referred to as non-nutritive sweeteners, high-intensity sweeteners, low-calorie sweeteners and non-sugar sweeteners (Staff, 2019). In general, they are much sweeter than actual sugar, and can range from 100 times to 20,000 times sweeter than sugar itself (Nutrition, 2020a). Most artificial sweeteners are classified as non-nutritive as they provide zero to no calories.

POTENTIAL BENEFITS AND RISKS

Artificial sweeteners are commonly used to sweeten beverages and food products without the same added caloric value as sugar. The research is still partially inconclusive on whether or not specific forms of non-nutritive sweeteners are either beneficial or harmful to health. However, there are some established benefits and risks to be aware of.

- Potential benefits of artificial sweeteners include decreased risk of dental caries due to a less acidic oral environment (Lohner et al., 2017).

- Many individuals choose artificial sweeteners in an effort to lose weight. Research however, does not support weight loss with the use of artificial sweeteners.

Much of the research around non-nutritive sweeteners is inconclusive and more research is needed. Areas that have shown potential **risks** but warrant further investigation include but are not limited to (2015-2020 Dietary Guidelines | Health.Gov; Azad et al., 2017; Lohner et al., 2017):

- Carcinogenic potential
- Oxidative stress in the brain
- Metabolic effects
- Incidence of T2DM
- Risk of kidney disease
- Impact on weight
- Impact on appetite hormones and gut microbiota
- Impact on birth weight
- Cardiometabolic indicators
- Dementia
- Stroke

Artificial Sweeteners on the Market Today

The sweeteners in the following table are considered Generally Recognized as Safe (GRAS) by the FDA. However, the fact that they are GRAS shouldn't be the sole indication that they are healthful and safe to eat. Many companies are given the role of deciding whether or not the ingredients in their products are GRAS (Food Additive Safety Infographic, 2016). Organizations like the Center for Science in the Public Interest (CSPI) often take a close look at these substances. CSPI rated the safety of common sweeteners and additives, and classified them in the following categories – see Table 3 (Chemical Cuisine, 2016):

- **Safe:** The additive appears to be safe.
- **Caution:** May pose a risk and needs to be better tested. Try to avoid.
- **Cut back:** Not toxic, but large amounts may be unsafe or promote bad nutrition.
- **Certain people should avoid:** May trigger an acute, allergic reaction, intolerance, or other problems.
- **Avoid:** Unsafe in amounts consumed or is very poorly tested and not worth any risk.

Table 3: Artificial Sweeteners, Sources, and Safety

Artificial Sweetener	Source	CSPI Rating of Safety
Stevia	From the leaves of the stevia plant Stevia rebaudiana (Bertoni)	Safe
Aspartame (Nutrasweet, Equal, Sugar Twin)	A laboratory chemical, 1-methyl N- l-[alpha]-aspartyl-l-phenylalanine (C14H18N2O5)	Avoid

Luo han guo fruit extracts	Siraitia grosvenorii (Swingle) (monk fruit)	Caution
Saccharin (Sweet and Low, Sweet Twin, Sweet'N Low, Necta Sweet)	A laboratory – chemical, 1,2-benzisothiazolin-3-one – 1,1 – dioxide (C7H5NO3S)	Avoid
Acesulfame potassium (Ace-K) (Sunett, Sweet One)	A laboratory - potassium salt of 6-methyl-1,2,3-oxathiazine-4(3H) -one-2,2-dioxide.	Avoid
Sucralose (Splenda)	"A mixture of semi- and neutral succinic acid esters of mono- and diglycerides"	Avoid
Neotame (Newtame)	A laboratory - chemical N – [N –(3,3-dimethylbutyl)-L-[alpha]-aspartyl]-L-phenylalanine-1-methyl ester	Safe
Advantame		Safe
Sugar alcohols (xylitol, sorbitol, mannitol, etc.)	Fruits and vegetables	Cut back

Table sources: (CFR, 2012; Chemical Cuisine, 2016; Fitch et al., 2012; Nutrition, 2020b, 2020a)

Cyclamate is a non-nutritive sweetener allowed in some countries, but it is not registered as GRAS by the FDA (Lohner et al., 2017). Alitame, neohesperidine, and thaumatin are also approved in other countries, but not in the U.S. (Fitch et al., 2012).

SECTION 5: A WORD ON CHOCOLATE

Have you ever taken a second to think about where chocolate actually comes from? It originates from the cacao fruit, which has a pulp-like inside, with a seed/bean at the core. These seeds are fermented, then dried. Some are cold pressed to create cacao, and others are roasted to create cocoa. The two are often written about interchangeably, though they do differ slightly in these processing methods and their nutrient composition (Barišić et al., 2019). You will often see the following ingredients listed on products that are byproducts of the cacao fruit (Magrone et al., 2017):

- Cocoa liquor = a paste made from cocoa beans that includes nonfat cocoa solids and cocoa butter
- Cocoa powder = cocoa liquor with some of the cocoa butter removed
- Cocoa butter = the fatty portion from the beans that has both monounsaturated and saturated fat
- Chocolate = a mixture of cocoa liquor with cocoa butter and sugar

> Allow chocolate to slowly melt on the tongue rather than mindlessly biting through it.

Cacao/cocoa powder and cacao nibs are common additions to smoothies, yogurt bowls, and desserts — though, dark chocolate, milk chocolate, and white chocolate are likely what most consumers think of when they hear the word chocolate. Each of these varieties contain a certain percentage of cacao or cocoa. Dark chocolate for example, has the highest cacao content out of the three. This is why you often hear that it is the most healthful. Cacao is rich in polyphenols, a class of phytonutrients that have anti-inflammatory benefits (Barišić et al., 2019; Tiwari et al., 2013; Wollgast & Anklam, 2000).

Even though many of the phytonutrient content is lost during the fermentation and heating process, there is still a substantial amount left, which is why chocolate is known to promote certain health benefits. The higher cacao content in the chocolate, the more of these benefits you will get. Ideally, aiming for **70% cacao** or higher will help you reap the most benefits. Chocolate that has lower cacao content typically has higher milk and sugar content, which increases the total saturated fat and added sugar content.

Cocoa that is rich in flavonols has been shown to have a positive effect on cardiovascular health, with potential mechanisms that aid neurological health too (Garcia et al., 2018; Magrone et al., 2017). It is also believed to have an anti-inflammatory effect via alterations to the microbiota (Magrone et al., 2017). Cocoa contains fiber, which can improve cholesterol markers and decrease risk of T2DM. Other nutrients in cocoa include magnesium, copper, potassium and iron, which can help an individual meet their daily nutrient needs.

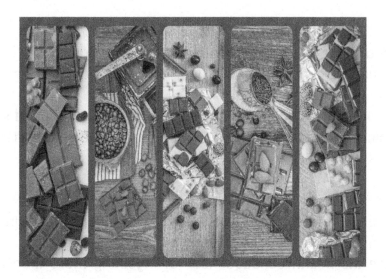

Chocolate is temperamental, but once you know the rules, melting chocolate will be an easy go-to for a delicious recipe — it doesn't get better than dipping fruit in melted chocolate. Learn how to melt dark chocolate . The Chocolate Substitution Chart will describe which types of chocolate can be substituted in recipes.

Melting Chocolate In Two Easy Steps
Step 1: Chop chocolate with a chef's knife, or even easier, slice with a serrated bread knife. Ensure chocolate is uniform in size to melt evenly and not scorch (bad!)
Step 2: Choose one of the melting options below:
- Melt chopped chocolate evenly in a double boiler — or use a small pot of just steaming (not boiling) water with a bowl over the top — and make sure water from the pot does not touch the bowl, add chocolate, stir often until almost melted, and continue to stir until melted.
- Microwave chopped chocolate in a microwave safe shallow bowl for 30 seconds, removing and stirring and repeating until almost melted. Continue to stir until melted.

The trick to melting chocolate is to not overheat the chocolate, which will cause it to lose its shine and become thick and clumpy. Heating past this point can cause the chocolate to scorch and become inedible.

SECTION 6: CLINICAL & CULINARY RECOMMENDATIONS

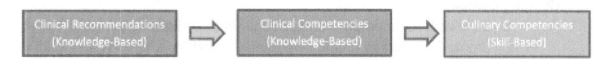

CLINICAL RECOMMENDATIONS

1. Limit added sugar to no more than 10% of daily caloric intake (USDA DGA 2015 – 2020) or no more than half the daily discretionary calories (American Heart Association) (AHA).
2. Examine nutrition facts label to calculate total intake of added sugars compared to daily value of 50 grams (12.5 teaspoons) for a 2,000-calorie diet (Commissioner, 2020).

CLINICAL COMPETENCIES

1. Summarize the nutritional differences between added and natural sugar
2. Discuss which foods blunt the rise in blood sugar levels
3. Summarize the health consequences of ingesting more than the daily limit of added sugar
4. Contrast how glucose and fructose are metabolized and stored in the body and the potential health consequences of each
5. Explain the major sources of added sugar in the diet
6. Calculate the amount of added sugar recommended daily
7. Identify safe artificial sugar products

CULINARY COMPETENCIES FOR SUGAR

Shopping and Storing Competencies

1. Identify added-sugar ingredients in the ingredient list
2. Explain sugar-related nutrient content claims
3. Identify quantity of added sugar in products
4. Store sugar to prevent contact with moisture

Cooking/Preparing Competencies

Flavor Development Competencies

1. Demonstrate the effect of temperature on sweetness
2. Explain how sugar and the other tastes interact with one another
3. Choose spices to amplify the taste of sweetness in recipes
4. Illustrate cooking techniques that increase a food's level of sweetness

Cooking Competencies

1. Bake with reduced amounts of sugar in baked goods
2. Create fruit purées to add sweetness to dishes
3. Describe the roles sugar plays in cooking
4. Roast fruits and vegetables

5. Illustrate the Maillard reaction
6. Macerate fruit
7. Melt chocolate
8. Bake with chocolate
9. Apply the baker's percentage
10. Caramelize fruits and vegetables
11. Reduce vinegar and fruit juices
12. Summarize how artificial sweeteners can be used in cooking

Serving Competencies
1. Serve no more than the recommended limit on sugar per day
2. Serve/prepare a healthful breakfast
3. Serve fruit-based desserts on most nights of the week
4. Create a meal that blunts the rise in sugar levels after a meal or snack

Safety Competencies
1. Explain sugar's role in preserving food
2. Identify artificial sweeteners that cannot be heated at all, or cooked above a certain temperature

SECTION 7: SUGAR AT THE STORE

Each packaged food contains a nutrition label that provides the nutrition composition of that food. On the label, you can find the servings per container, serving size, total calories per serving and more. Sugar is listed under the total carbohydrate category. The new nutrition facts label was introduced in 2016, which **now includes an additional subcategory for added sugars.** You will find the Total Sugars in grams listed under Total Carbohydrate, and the added sugars listed as "Includes ___g of Added Sugars" beneath Total Sugars (Nutrition, 2021).

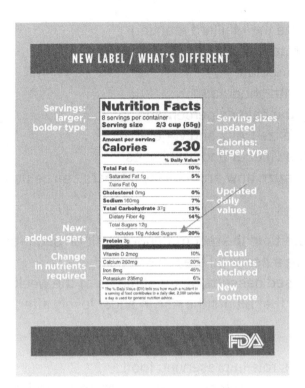

Since many foods have naturally occurring sugars, the Total Sugars value may be higher than the Added Sugars value. The difference in these numbers equals the total of naturally occurring sugars.

Getting in the habit of looking at both the nutrition facts label and the ingredients list can help decrease consumption of added sugars. Common foods with added sugars include (2015-2020 Dietary Guidelines | Health.Gov; More Key Topics | MyPlate):

- Certain beverages (soda, sweetened tea or coffee, fruit juice, sports drinks, energy drinks, alcohol)
- Baked goods (cakes, pies, muffins, brownies, cookies, sweet rolls, pastries, donuts)
- Sauces
- Candy
- Ice cream
- Yogurt
- Jam
- Syrup

There are 56 names for sugar. Common names to look for on the ingredient list are (CDC, 2021; More Key Topics | MyPlate):
- Anhydrous dextrose

- Brown sugar
- Confectioner's powdered sugar
- Corn sweetener
- Corn syrup
- Corn syrup solid
- Dextrose
- Fructose
- High fructose corn syrup (HFCS)
- Honey
- Invert sugar
- Lactose malt syrup
- Maltose
- Maple syrup
- Molasses
- Nectars (e.g., peach or pear nectar)
- Pancake syrup raw sugar
- Raw sugar
- Sucrose
- Sugar
- White granulated sugar

Nutrient Claims

Below are nutrient content claims and health claims that you will see on packaged food and beverages as they relates to sugar.

Sugar free (CFR, 2012):

- **Other common phrases:** no sugar, free of sugar, zero sugar, without sugar, sugarless, trivial source of sugar, negligible source of sugar and insignificant source of sugar

Requirements:

- The food must contain **less than 0.5 grams of sugars**, per labeled serving, or per reference amount customarily consumed (RACC)

- "The food contains no ingredient that is a sugar or that is generally understood by consumers to contain sugars unless the listing of the ingredient in the ingredient statement is followed by an asterisk that refers to the statement below the list of ingredients, which states 'adds a trivial amount of sugar,' 'adds a negligible amount of sugar,' or 'adds a dietarily insignificant amount of sugar'"

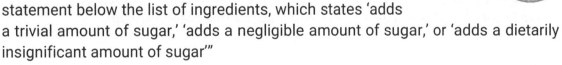

No added sugar:
- **Other common phrases:** without added sugar, no sugar added
- **Requirements:**
  - The product **does not include an ingredient that has added sugars**
  - No amount of sugar is added during processing or packaging

Low in sugar (CFR, 2012):
- **Other common phrases:** reduced sugar, reduced in sugar, sugar reduced, less sugar, lower sugar or lower in sugar
- **Requirements:**
  - The food contains a minimum **of 25% less sugar per RACC** than the reference food

Health or Functional Claims Regarding Sugar

There are health claims related to sugar alcohols and non-nutritive sweeteners for preventing tooth decay. They include:
- The sugar alcohols xylitol, sorbitol, mannitol, maltitol, isomalt, lactitol, hydrogenated starch hydrolysates, hydrogenated glucose syrups and erythritol, or a combination of these
- The sugars D-tagatose and isomaltulose
- Sucralose

The claims can be short — "Does not promote tooth decay" — or long:
"Frequent between-meal consumption of foods high in sugars and starches promotes tooth decay. The sugar alcohols in [name of food] do not promote tooth decay"

Does lactose (found in dairy) and fructose (found in fruit) count as added sugar? Are they as unhealthful for me as table sugar?

No, they do not count as added sugar, and unless you have an allergy to dairy, they are a healthful choice. As covered previously, lactose and fructose are both disaccharides. They are naturally occurring in dairy and fruit, respectively. However, some items like chocolate milk, or certain brands of frozen fruit, dried fruit, or fruit juice, can contain added sugars. The body ultimately processes them the same as table sugar. However, when you consume a dairy product, you are also getting protein, vitamins, and minerals, and some fat depending on the fat content of the product you selected. Likewise, fruit has an abundance of vitamins, minerals and fiber, as well as phytochemicals that can help prevent diseases and promote good health. While the body processes sugar from dairy and fruit the same as table sugar, you receive a long list of benefits from eating the naturally occurring sugars instead.

Is honey or maple syrup better for me than table sugar?

Not really. Honey, maple syrup, and table sugar are all forms of sugar, so they should still be consumed and monitored as added sugars. However, both honey and maple syrup do offer added nutrients over table sugar. Honey contains phytonutrients that have shown to have potential cancer protection mechanisms, as well as anti-inflammatory, anti-bacterial, antioxidant, and immune-stimulating properties (Subramanian et al., 2016). For people with certain medical conditions such as IBS, the high fructose content in honey can trigger symptoms, so maple syrup may be a more favorable option for that population. Similar to honey, maple syrup also contains powerful phytonutrients, as well as many other essential nutrients such as calcium, magnesium, zinc and potassium (FoodData Central). Its phytonutrients have antioxidant properties (Li & Seeram, 2010).

Overall, honey and maple syrup offer some benefits over table sugar, though it is advised to consume any of the three in moderation to stay within recommended amounts of daily added sugar.

Storing Sugar
- Table sugar, confectioner's sugar and superfine sugar can be stored in a cool dry pantry
- Brown sugar must be kept in an airtight container to prevent it from drying out and becoming hard
- Pure honey can be kept indefinitely

SECTION 8: ON THE TONGUE

Out of the five main tastes, the most commonly enjoyed is the taste of sweetness. Each type of sugar has certain characteristics in terms of how quickly the sweetness appears on the tongue and how long it lingers there (see Table 4) (McGee, 2004).

Table 4: The Taste of Sweetness on the Tongue

Sugar	Time to Detect on the Tongue	Lingers on the Tongue
Sucrose	Slow to detect	Lingers
Fructose	Quickly	Fades quickly
Corn Syrup	Slow to detect	Lingers longer than sucrose

The temperature at which a food is served can vastly influence the taste of sweetness, with a low perception at 59°F/15°C or lower and a 100-fold increase at 95°F/35°C

(Talavera et al., 2005). In addition, bitter inhibits the taste of sweetness (Talavera et al., 2008).

Humans evolved to be able to detect the safety of certain foods, with bitter being an indication of potential toxicity or danger. The ratio of sweet to bitter taste can help a human determine the toxicity of a food and whether or not it is safe to eat (Beauchamp, 2016). It is proposed that an innate preference for sweet tastes allowed humans to detect glucose from foods for energy. This responsiveness to sweet occurs right at birth, as seen with nonverbal signals of relaxation and satisfaction, and an increase in sucking, with an addition of a sweet taste in neonates (Mennella et al., 2016). Providing infants and children with a sweet taste has also been shown to attenuate pain.

Even though the body may not detect the difference of various sugars, as a consumer, you may notice a variation in taste, texture, or color. This is due to how refined the sugar is, and the processing methods used. Typically, the darker the sugar, the higher the molasses content, and the more unrefined it is (Staff, 2018).

The culinary goal of this chapter is to teach individuals to cook with less sugar and to know how to amplify the flavor of a dish, including its sweetness, without resorting to sugar and instead using other ingredients and cooking methods.

An Experiment in Sweetness and Flavor

Start with a bunch of carrots. Wash or peel, dry, and cut into a similar shape and size. Next, follow the directions in Table 5. Compare the level of sweetness between each method. Which one has more depth of flavor? Roasting allows for the sugars in the carrot to caramelize, which increases the flavor profile significantly

Table 5: Three Ways to Prepare Carrots

RAW CARROTS	STEAMED CARROTS	ROASTED CARROTS
Serve on a plate and enjoy.	Steam until a fork is able to be inserted with some resistance. Add salt, pepper, dill and a bit of olive oil.	Preheat oven to 400°F/204°C. Place carrots on a cookie sheet. Drizzle with olive oil, salt, pepper and dried thyme. Toss and cook until brown and tender.

To tone down an overly spicy dish, add sugar because:
1. Sugar will compete with the pain signal in the brain caused by the spice (the capsaicin in chiles for example) for the pleasure signal stimulated from sugar.
2. When sugar dissolves in saliva it has a cooling effect in the mouth (The Science of Good Cooking, page 12).

SECTION 8: SUGAR IN THE KITCHEN

One of the most beneficial elements of added sugar is its ability to increase the palatability of food and drinks, which may lead to excessive caloric intake. There are times when sugar is required and other times when it is not, or when reduced amounts can be used.

Sugar is necessary as it provides many essential functions in cooking, but it doesn't have to be overused. Below are some of the many functions that sugar performs in flavor production and in cooking:

- Fills out and balances flavors in dishes
- Sugar is hygroscopic, meaning it holds on to water increasing moisture in recipes
- Enhances the flavor aromas
- Enhances salty and umami tastes, and balances sour, bitter, and spice
- Texture — it interferes with the coagulation of proteins — making bread tender by interfering with gluten, or interacting with egg protein to make a smooth custard
- Provides structure in baked goods
- Gives a fine crumb and texture to cakes
- Aids in Maillard browning
- Caramelization
- Feeds yeast and other fermented products like alcohol and kombucha
- Imparts an appealing color
- Lowers the freezing point of ice-cream and sorbet
- Chemically cooking (e.g., brining meat and fish)
- Preservation — sugar increases the shelf life of foods by binding water, making it less available to micro-organisms

FLAVOR DEVELOPMENT

Words of Culinary Wisdom from Chef Scott

"Flavor development is also about balance and creating what I call craveability. If you leave after one bite of a peach not overly satisfied, what is needed? It could be that the peach is not ripe enough, so by cooking the peach, whether caramelizing or reducing (purée), the flavors get stronger, more pronounced, and sweeter. With that, are you done? Perhaps. If you were to add that now delicious, cooked peach to a salad, what other elements would you add to create craveability? Perhaps crunch of nuts that were also toasted to create an aroma, then cheese for umami, salt, acid etc. Flavor development is crucial to not only make the best out of your ingredients but to ensure balance and craveability ending in deliciousness.

Lastly, when building a profile of flavors and researching traditional flavor combinations, often "what grows together goes together" is a sure-fire way to ensure you are creating harmonious flavors and not just guessing. Using the resources — *Flavor Bible* and *Culinary Artistry* — are proven flavor insights and flavor combinations used by chefs for the last several decades. Highly suggest picking up one of these resources."

Many people are used to overly sweet and salty food. The ultimate goal in culinary medicine is to lead individuals into a world of exquisite tastes and eating experiences that do not require an overload of sugar or salt. In this section, learning how to develop flavor while cooking with less sugar will be reviewed, which will ultimately help to readjust an individual's palate to prefer lower levels of sweetness. Go to the chapter on Sodium to learn how to build flavor without using a lot of salt.

Building a flavor profile with a sense of sweetness involves:

1. Thinking of contrasting tastes to enhance sweetness
Balancing the sweet, salty, sour, and bitter flavors of the palate enhances the taste experience

2. Selecting non-sugar ingredients to add sweetness
Spices — Cinnamon, nutmeg, vanilla bean, all spice and anise, are examples of spices that lend a sense of sweetness to the end product
Salt — A bit of salt will enhance sweetness

3. Choosing a cooking technique if cooking is required/desired
Cooking techniques that bring out sweetness:
- Caramelization is the process of browning sugar in the presence of heat, which leads to a sweet, nutty flavor. The temperature range in which sugar caramelizes is approximately 320° to 360° F/ 160° to 182° C. Many vegetables that are high in sugar can be caramelized — onions, carrots, cabbage, potatoes, beets, peppers, corn, squash — by roasting, baking, grilling, or searing. Pineapples, figs, peaches and bananas are several fruits that caramelize well too.
- **Reduction:** The product that results when a liquid is reduced. For example reducing balsamic vinegar creates a balsamic reduction that is sweeter than the vinegar.
- **Roasting:** To cook in an oven or on a spit over a fire.
- **Purée:** To process food by mashing, straining, or chopping it very finely in order to make it a smooth paste. It is also a product produced using this technique.
  - Tip: Take excess or overripe fruit, remove skin or pits /seeds, and either freeze in Ziploc bags to be puréed later or blend these fruits into purées before freezing. Use the purée to sweeten any recipe calling for sugar. Overripe bananas, apples, persimmons, etc. are loaded with natural sugar that can be substituted for refined sugar in recipes. In smoothies, use a frozen banana or date instead of an added sugar-sweetened yogurt.

Sugar Related Cooking Terms

The Maillard Reaction
SUGAR + AMINO ACIDS + HIGH HEAT (surface heat is ≥ 300°F/ 149°C) = creating new compounds that have a different color, texture and flavor. This happens when toast is made, and when meat is grilled or roasted. Depending on the specific amino acid and the specific sugar, various new flavor compounds are created, which is why toast tastes different than grilled chicken, which tastes vastly different than grilled steak.

Maceration
When sugar is added to fruit, it causes the liquid inside the cell to be released. What was once a firm piece of fruit is left soft and mushy, and the liquid that is released, is full of flavor. This process is called maceration and it is a beginning step in making wine. This process can also be used with other fruits like berries to create a delicious sauce to be used on everything from meat dishes to pancakes. This process is often used when making pies and crumbles so as to prevent a soggy crust or topping.

BAKED GOODS

Depending on what you want to bake, sugar will be more or less important in terms of texture, as a browning agent, and as a structural component to baked goods. There is a scientific formula to work with when reducing the amount of sugar in recipes for certain types of baked goods that is described below. For all, a reduction of sugar is possible, however, how much of a reduction is variable. Go to What's Cooking America for Basic Baking Skills and Tips.

Reducing Sugar in Baking

In order to scientifically reduce the amount of sugar needed in baking it is necessary to understand the term "baker's percentage" and to weigh ingredients (best done in grams), which is often done in Europe but not in the United States.

> The **bakers percentage** (BP) starts with the rule that the weight of flour = 100% and everything else is measured compared to the amount of flour. Below is the BP for sugar:
>
> (BP) = weight of sugar in a recipe divided by the weight of flour in a recipe.
>
> If 1 cup of flour and 1 cup of sugar is called for, the percentage is 100%. If more flour is used than sugar, the percentage will be < 100%, and vice versa — if more sugar is used than flour the percentage is > 100%

Table 6: Reduction in Sugar in Baked Goods

Baked Good	Description
Drop cookie	If the BP is > 100%, reduce sugar by 50% If BP is < 100%, start by reducing just 25% and adjust as necessary Cut down to 25% BP (¼ cup sugar to 1 cup flour) If the BP is >50%, reduce sugar by 50% If the BP is <50%, do not reduce sugar Keep BP of sugar between 80% and 125% for most cakes except foam Sugar is optional
Non-chocolate bars	Needs to be at 100% BP
Brownies	Doesn't do well with reduced sugar as texture gets dry and crumbly. Try reducing sugar by ¼ to ½ the amount in the original recipe
Muffins	Reducing sugar affects texture and volume
Cake	Can reduce total sugar by 10% (and up to 25% for sponge cakes)
Pie crust	Do not need sugar for structure, only for browning the crust
Pie filling	Depending on the filling, can reduce added sugar by 50%
Yeast bread	To maximize flavor, keep sugar at no less than 10% BP

For a less scientific approach follow the advice of *What's Cooking America*:
For every **cup of flour** use the following amount of sugar per item:
Cake and cookies — ½ cup sugar
Muffins and quick breads — 1 Tablespoon sugar
Yeast breads — 1 teaspoon sugar

Cookies

Sugar plays a role when baking cookies. When the amount of sugar is reduced, cookies will not spread as far as they would if the total amount of sugar were used, and they will be drier and crumble more easily.

Cakes

Basically, there are four types of cakes: blended, cream, sponge and foam. When reducing the amount of sugar in cakes, they may not rise as high due to losing some structural support from the sugar left out of the recipe. They can also get tough and take on a rubbery characteristic. Below are the characteristics of the different types of cakes and the role sugar plays:

Blended — All ingredients are put in a bowl and stirred. Sugar does not build volume in this type of recipe.

Creamed — The foundation is a butter and sugar mixture that is beaten until fluffy and light colored. Sugar builds volume and texture in this type of recipe.

Sponge — The foundation is a mixture of eggs and sugar; they have more moisture than creamed cakes.

Foam — The foundation is a well-beaten sugar and egg whites to make a meringue. These cakes are super light, dry, and spongy.

> A 10% reduction in sugar requires removing 5 teaspoons of sugar from 1 cup of sugar.

Pies

Comparatively speaking, pie has much less sugar in it than cake and cookies. In terms of the amount of sugar needed for the pie filling, it will mostly depend on how sweet the filling is to begin with. For example, super sweet strawberries need less sugar added to the recipe than tart apples.

Sugar acts as a sweetener, a thickener and also as a flavor enhancer in pie fillings. When reducing sugar in pie fillings, use more of a thickening agent — cornstarch, flour, xanthan gum — to make up for the loss of sugar. You can also macerate the fruit (add sugar to cut-up fruit to release the liquid within) beforehand to reduce the amount of liquid released when berries cook.

- Apple — Use 25% to 50% less sugar in the filling
- Berry — Decreasing sugar will depend on the tartness of the berries
- Custard pies like pumpkin — Can use up to 50% less sugar in the filling (Note: pies need to bake longer when sugar is reduced)

If serving pie cold it will need more sugar than if serving pie warm, as the sweet taste is dulled at lower temperatures.

Bread

For yeast bread, sugar provides flavor, but it does not provide structure. In fact, bread will rise higher with less sugar, but it will be drier as well. In addition, the more sugar that there is in a dough, the longer it will take for the dough to rise unless you use <u>SAF Gold yeast</u>. If you choose not to use any sugar, the yeast will digest the flour's starch and turn it into sugar.

Using Different Types of Sugar in Baking

Table 7: Different Types of Sugar

Sugar Alternative	Best Used In	Amount Equal to 1 Cup Sugar	Reduction in Liquid in Recipe & Temperature Change
Agave (High in fructose, may want to avoid)	Cakes and breads	2/3 cup	Reduce liquids by 4 tablespoons Reduce oven by 25%
Coconut sugar	Cakes, cookies, quick breads	1 cup	None
Honey*	Moist cakes, quick breads, pudding	¾ cup	Also add baking soda and lower the cooking temperature
Fruit concentrate	Baked goods – adds moistness	2/3 to ¾ cup	Reduce liquids by 3 tablespoons
Maple syrup*	Caramel, candy, ice cream, pudding	¾ cup	Reduce liquids by 3 tablespoons
Molasses	Gingerbread, cookies	1 1/3 cup	Reduce liquids by 5 tablespoons

*Cannot be used to cream together butter and sugar in a recipe

Of note, honey should not be fed to children less than a year of age due to the risk of botulism.

Table 8: Using Fruits and Vegetables Instead of Sugar in Baking

Fruit or Vegetable	Recipe Types	Instruction
Apple and apple sauce (Can also replace up to ½ the fat in the recipe)	Cakes, pancakes, quick breads. Avoid in anything crunchy like cookies	Substitute the same amount of applesauce for sugar but cut back some on the liquid in the recipe (cut back ½ cup liquid for every 1 cup purée).
Bananas (Can replace up to 1 cup sugar)	Quick breads; soft, chewy cookies; muffins; pancakes	Mashed bananas first. Add 1 to 2 tablespoons water.
Date purée	Quick breads; soft, chewy cookies; muffin; pancakes; scones	Soak dates in hot water in a 1:1 ratio until soft. Purée 1 cup pitted dates with ½ to 1 cup hot water until a thick paste. Store in the refrigerator.
Fig purée (Can also replace up to ½ the fat in the recipe)	Quick breads; soft, chewy cookies; muffin; pancakes; scones	Soak 8 oz fresh figs in hot water in a 1:1 ratio until soft. Purée figs with ¼ to 1/3 cup water. Store in the refrigerator.
Carrots	Cakes, pancakes	Mash cooked carrots. This will add density to the end product.
Beets	Cakes, pancakes, brownies	Mash cooked beets. This will add density to the end product.
Sweet potatoes	Cakes, pancakes	Mash cooked sweet potatoes. This will add density to the end product.

Other Tips for Low Sugar Baking

Using the following spices in recipes will give the illusion of sweetness: vanilla bean, cinnamon, nutmeg, star anise, fennel, allspice and almond extract.

- Herbs like tarragon, fennel fronds, various mints (apple mint, pineapple mint), cinnamon and basil are not necessarily sweet but mimic sweetness or draw an association to sweetness when properly combined into dishes
- Salt enhances the sweetness in food. Adding just a touch will amplify the sweet taste.

- For more information and delicious recipes with little to no white sugar, check out Joanne Chang's latest cookbook, <u>Baking With Less Sugar</u>.

As a whole, artificial sweeteners lack the bulk of regular sugar so baked goods come out dense and flat. In addition, regular sugar acts as a liquid in recipes, which adds moisture to the baked good. Replacing sugar with an artificial sweetener (with the exception of sugar alcohols — xylitol and erythritol) will produce a product that is dry and clumpy. Finally, if you are looking for an artificial sugar to produce a brown, caramelized product, that won't happen.

Table 9: Artificial and Alternative Sweeteners Used in Baking (How Sugar Substitutes Stack Up, 2013)

Artificial Sweetener	Baking	Sweetness Compared to Sugar	Notes
Acesulfame Potassium	Yes — can replace some of the sugar	200 times sweeter	It has a strong aftertaste, which is slightly bitter. Keep temperature under 400° F.
Aspartame	No	200 times sweeter	Do not cook with aspartame. It can be added to sweeten drinks.
Erythritol (sugar alcohol)	Yes	150 time sweeter	Can also be used in making jams and jellies.
Monk fruit	Yes	200 times sweeter	

Saccharin	Yes — can replace some of the sugar	200 to 700 times sweeter	It has a strong metallic aftertaste. Creates a lumpy texture.
Stevia	Yes	200 to 300 times sweeter	Does not caramelize, and don't use in meringues. Decrease temperature by 25%.
Sucralose	No — questionable safety data	600 times sweeter	Do not heat to over 250° F as it may produce toxic byproducts, add after cooking.*
Xylitol (sugar alcohol)	Yes — can replace all if using powder. Cut amount in half if using crystals	Not as sweet	Not as sweet but produces a tender, cake-like product.

*(Bundesinstitut Für Risikobewertung, 2019)

Unless it is medically necessary to use artificial sweeteners, try reducing the amount of sugar required in a product, replacing some of the sugar with other healthful ingredients like fruit, or practicing portion control instead.

SUGAR AND PRESERVATION

Sugar helps to preserve the color, texture and flavor of a food. In addition, from a microbial perspective, if enough sugar is added to a food — 68% sugar concentration — it can inhibit microbial activity by acting as a humectant. Basically, sugar attracts water in food by osmosis, making it unavailable for microorganisms to grow.

Both sucrose and fructose are strong humectants whereas glucose alone is not (FAO Corporate Document Repository: General Considerations for Preservation of Fruits and Vegetables). This is important to consider when canning produce, as using lower sugar options can lead to microbial growth. The Colorado State University Extension has a fact sheet on Food Preservation Without Sugar or Salt.

SECTION 9: AT THE TABLE

Of the over 200 food decisions made each day, the option is always there for someone to choose a food or beverage that promotes health or does not promote health (Wansink &

Sobal, 2007). Since most people live in an obesogenic environment — surrounded by highly processed, salty, full-of-sugar options in extremely large portions — it is hard to avoid temptations all day every day.

There is some room for a treat every day for most individuals depending on their health status. The goal is to support individuals in making the majority of their choices, healthful ones. The following are some strategies to help them do just that.

- Unless it is medically necessary, allow room for treats as forbidding can lead them to consuming more.
- Convert grams of sugar allowed per day into actual examples so that your client or patient understands what that actually looks like — two cookies and a sweetened yogurt, for example.
- Teach people to eat the healthful food first in order to ensure that they are receiving all the nutrients they need for maintaining health and preventing disease. "Eat then treat."
- You do not have to use a lot of the often overeaten craveable food — think chocolate here. Adding some shavings of dark chocolate over fruit is appealing to both the eye and taste buds and it gives the illusion of a forbidden treat.
- Often times people use sweets to relieve boredom, anxiety, and other unpleasant emotions. Determine if this is happening to your client or patient and take the necessary steps to both identify the issue and solutions available to resolve their emotional distress in another way, which may require a referral to a mental health practitioner.
- Many dive into dessert or a sweet treat with such fervor that the experience is often over before they have even realized that they ate anything. Eat dessert and treats mindfully, fully savoring the experience.
- To help individuals who consume a significant amount of sugar every day, reduce their sugar intake, follow the five steps laid out in Beat Sugar Addiction Now for Kids — one book in the Beat Sugar Addiction Now series. These steps can also be applied to adults as well.

Steps to Reduce Sugar in Diet

Step 1: Focus on reducing the intake of sugar sweetened beverages first as they are the #1 contributor of added sugar in the diet.

Step 2: Next, focus on breakfast, as the majority of breakfast options are full of sugar — cereal, donuts, waffles, pancakes, pastries, toaster cakes, muffins. Make more healthful choices.

Step 3: When beverages and breakfast have been transformed, look at the intake of unhealthful snacks per day and limit sweet treats to one per day.

Step 4: Make desserts that focus on fruit most days of the week and make an awesome baked good — cake, brownies — occasionally.

Step 5: Finally, look for sources of hidden sugar in the diet and replace with no added sugar options — e.g., no-sugar-added ketchup.

Delicious Desserts

When building a more healthful dessert, think fruit first, followed by scrumptiousness — chocolate, meringue, and cheese. Practice dessert-flips where you offer the indulgence (chocolate torte) in a smaller portion and bulk up the dish with fresh fruit as the foundation of the dish. In addition, plate portions rather than serving dessert family-style, where it is easy to grab a large portion and go back for more.

There is no better dessert than melted chocolate and fresh fruit. You do not even have to add sugar to the melted dark chocolate as the fruit is sweet enough.

For kids, make it a fun experience. You can cut up fruit beforehand and have them build a fruit picture on their plate. Serve with yogurt for a dipping sauce.

Go Mediterranean! Put together a platter of fresh fruit, cheese and nuts at the end of the meal.

Fill a meringue shell with fruit.

Cottage cheese has a salty taste which pairs very well with fruit. Salty + sweet = delicious!

SECTION 10: PRACTICAL TIPS TO DECREASE SUGAR CONSUMPTION

A few other simple ways to reduce total daily added sugar intake include:
- Replace sugar-sweetened beverages with water, flavored sparkling water, unsweetened tea, low-fat milk or 100% fruit juice
- Choose unsweetened or plain versions of foods – you can always add your own fruit or a small amount of honey, maple syrup, or another natural sweetener
- Choose whole foods over processed foods or liquids (e.g., enjoy an apple instead of apple juice for the added fiber)
- Get creative with your own baked goods so you can control the amount of added sugar
- Enjoy fresh fruit, dried fruit (unsweetened), or dark chocolate for dessert and get the added benefit of phytonutrients in each
- Bake fruit in the oven and enjoy with a spoonful of plain Greek yogurt

- Instead of adding an overly sweet dressing or sauce, add pops of sweetness — adding berries to a salad for example

Cookbooks
Beat Sugar Addiction Now! Cookbook
Baking With Less Sugar

SUMMARY

There are various health-related consequences from overconsumption of added sugars — T2DM, cardiovascular disease, stroke, dental caries and risk of weight gain/obesity — whether it be from table sugar, corn syrup, agave or other concentrated sugar. Learning how to identify added sugars and common foods that they are in, in addition to finding healthful alternatives, can help individuals stay within recommended daily limits of added sugar, especially if they eliminate or reserve SSB for special occasions. As with nearly everything, there is a place for small amounts of added sugar in a balanced diet, but moderation is key. For some, moderation is difficult as sugar can be addicting.

There are various culinary techniques that can be used to create craveable dishes that provide a level of sweetness that is thoroughly enjoyed. These techniques don't rely on adding more sugar to a recipe or product; rather, a flavor profile is created by enhancing a food's natural level of sweetness. Focusing primarily on snacks and meals with a variety of fruits, vegetables, whole grains, lean proteins and healthful fats can help promote a healthful lifestyle. Being able to create scrumptious treats with lower amounts of added sugar will provide the joy needed to maintain this eating pattern.

References

2015-2020 Dietary Guidelines | health.gov. (n.d.). Retrieved March 17, 2020, from https://health.gov/our-work/food-nutrition/2015-2020-dietary-guidelines/guidelines/

Adekola, K., Rosen, S., & Shanmugam, M. (2012). Glucose transporters in cancer metabolism: Current Opinion in Oncology. Current Opinion in Oncology, 24(6), 650–654.

AHA. (n.d.). Added Sugars. Www.Heart.Org. Retrieved January 31, 2022, from https://www.heart.org/en/healthy-living/healthy-eating/eat-smart/sugar/added-sugars

Azad, M. B., Abou-Setta, A. M., Chauhan, B. F., Rabbani, R., Lys, J., Copstein, L., Mann, A., Jeyaraman, M. M., Reid, A. E., Fiander, M., MacKay, D. S., McGavock, J., Wicklow, B., & Zarychanski, R. (2017). Nonnutritive sweeteners and cardiometabolic health: A systematic review and meta-analysis of randomized controlled trials and prospective cohort studies. CMAJ, 189(28), E929–E939. https://doi.org/10.1503/cmaj.161390

Bailey, R. L., Fulgoni, V. L., Cowan, A. E., & Gaine, P. C. (2018). Sources of Added Sugars in Young Children, Adolescents, and Adults with Low and High Intakes of Added Sugars. Nutrients, 10(1), 102. https://doi.org/10.3390/nu10010102

Barišić, V., Kopjar, M., Jozinović, A., Flanjak, I., Ačkar, Đ., Miličević, B., Šubarić, D., Jokić, S., & Babić, J. (2019). The Chemistry behind Chocolate Production. Molecules, 24(17), 3163. https://doi.org/10.3390/molecules24173163

Beauchamp, G. K. (2016). Why do we like sweet taste: A bitter tale? Physiology & Behavior, 164(Pt B), 432–437. https://doi.org/10.1016/j.physbeh.2016.05.007

Bray, G. A. (2007). How bad is fructose? The American Journal of Clinical Nutrition, 86(4), 895–896. https://doi.org/10.1093/ajcn/86.4.895

Breda, J., Jewell, J., & Keller, A. (2019). The Importance of the World Health Organization Sugar Guidelines for Dental Health and Obesity Prevention. Caries Research, 53(2), 149–152. https://doi.org/10.1159/000491556

Bundesinstitut Für Risikobewertung. (2019). Harmful compounds might be formed when foods containing the sweetener Sucralose are heated: BfR Opinion No 012/2019 of 9 April 2019. https://doi.org/10.17590/20190409-142644

CDC. (2019). Diabetes Report Card 2019 | CDC. https://www.cdc.gov/diabetes/library/reports/reportcard.html

CDC. (2021, November 28). Know Your Limit for Added Sugars. Centers for Disease Control and Prevention. https://www.cdc.gov/nutrition/data-statistics/added-sugars.html

CFR. (2012). Code of Federal Regulations Title 21: Nutrition Labeling (198-253). FDA. https://www.govinfo.gov/content/pkg/CFR-2012-title9-vol2/pdf/CFR-2012-title9-vol2-part317-subpartB.pdf.

Chemical Cuisine. (2016, February 25). Center for Science in the Public Interest. https://cspinet.org/eating-healthy/chemical-cuisine

Chong, C. P., Shahar, S., Haron, H., & Din, N. C. (2019). Habitual sugar intake and cognitive impairment among multi-ethnic Malaysian older adults. Clinical Interventions in Aging, 14, 1331–1342. https://doi.org/10.2147/CIA.S211534

Commissioner, O. of the. (2020, March 24). Statement on new guidance for the declaration of added sugars on food labels for single-ingredient sugars and syrups and certain cranberry products. FDA; FDA. https://www.fda.gov/news-events/press-announcements/statement-new-guidance-declaration-added-sugars-food-labels-single-ingredient-sugars-and-syrups-and

Current Eating Patterns in the United States—2015-2020 Dietary Guidelines | health.gov. (n.d.). Retrieved June 2, 2020, from https://health.gov/our-work/food-nutrition/2015-2020-dietary-guidelines/guidelines/chapter-2/current-eating-patterns-in-the-united-states/#figure-2-1-desc-toggle

Daubenmier, J., Lustig, R. H., Hecht, F. M., Kristeller, J., Woolley, J., Adam, T., Dallman, M., & Epel, E. (2014). A new biomarker of hedonic eating? A preliminary investigation of cortisol and nausea responses to acute opioid blockade. Appetite, 74, 92–100. https://doi.org/10.1016/j.appet.2013.11.014

Davis, C., Loxton, N. J., Levitan, R. D., Kaplan, A. S., Carter, J. C., & Kennedy, J. L. (2013). "Food addiction" and its association with a dopaminergic multilocus genetic profile. Physiology & Behavior, 118, 63–69. https://doi.org/10.1016/j.physbeh.2013.05.014

DGA 2015-2020. (2016). Cut Down on Added Sugars (p. 2).

Diabetes During Pregnancy | Maternal Infant Health | Reproductive Health | CDC. (2019, January 16). https://www.cdc.gov/reproductivehealth/maternalinfanthealth/diabetes-during-pregnancy.htm

Dietary Guidelines for Americans, 2020-2025. (n.d.). 164.

DiNicolantonio, J. J., Mehta, V., Zaman, S. B., & O'Keefe, J. H. (2018). Not Salt But Sugar As Aetiological In Osteoporosis: A Review. Missouri Medicine, 115(3), 247–252.

Eleazu, C. O. (2016). The concept of low glycemic index and glycemic load foods as panacea for type 2 diabetes mellitus; prospects, challenges and solutions. African Health Sciences, 16(2), 468–479. https://doi.org/10.4314/ahs.v16i2.15

Fitch, C., Keim, K. S., & Academy of Nutrition and Dietetics. (2012). Position of the Academy of Nutrition and Dietetics: Use of nutritive and nonnutritive sweeteners. Journal of the Academy of Nutrition and Dietetics, 112(5), 739–758. https://doi.org/10.1016/j.jand.2012.03.009

Food Additive Safety Infographic. (2016, April 26). Center for Science in the Public Interest. https://cspinet.org/resource/food-additive-safety-infographic

FoodData Central. (n.d.). Retrieved March 28, 2020, from https://fdc.nal.usda.gov/

Francey, C., Cros, J., Rosset, R., Crézé, C., Rey, V., Stefanoni, N., Schneiter, P., Tappy, L., & Seyssel, K. (2019). The extra-splanchnic fructose escape after ingestion of a fructose-glucose drink: An exploratory study in healthy humans using a dual fructose isotope method. Clinical Nutrition ESPEN, 29, 125–132. https://doi.org/10.1016/j.clnesp.2018.11.008

Garcia, J. P., Santana, A., Baruqui, D. L., & Suraci, N. (2018). The Cardiovascular effects of chocolate. Reviews in Cardiovascular Medicine, 19(4), 123–127. https://doi.org/10.31083/j.rcm.2018.04.3187

Gordon, E. L., Ariel-Donges, A. H., Bauman, V., & Merlo, L. J. (2018). What Is the Evidence for "Food Addiction?" A Systematic Review. Nutrients, 10(4), 477. https://doi.org/10.3390/nu10040477

Gritz, J. R. (2017). The Unsavory History of Sugar, the Insatiable American Craving. Smithsonian Magazine. https://www.smithsonianmag.com/history/unsavory-history-sugar-american-craving-180962766/

Grundt, J. H., Eide, G. E., Brantsaeter, A.-L., Haugen, M., & Markestad, T. (2017). Is consumption of sugar-sweetened soft drinks during pregnancy associated with birth weight? Maternal & Child Nutrition, 13(4). https://doi.org/10.1111/mcn.12405

Hanover, L. M., & White, J. S. (1993). Manufacturing, composition, and applications of fructose. The American Journal of Clinical Nutrition, 58(5 Suppl), 724S-732S. https://doi.org/10.1093/ajcn/58.5.724S

Herring, S. J., & Oken, E. (2011). Obesity and diabetes in mothers and their children: Can we stop the intergenerational cycle? Current Diabetes Reports, 11(1), 20–27. https://doi.org/10.1007/s11892-010-0156-9

How Sugar Substitutes Stack Up. (2013, July 17). Science. https://www.nationalgeographic.com/science/article/130717-sugar-substitutes-nutrasweet-splenda-stevia-baking

Jensen, T., Abdelmalek, M. F., Sullivan, S., Nadeau, K. J., Green, M., Roncal, C., Nakagawa, T., Kuwabara, M., Sato, Y., Kang, D.-H., Tolan, D. R., Sanchez-Lozada, L. G., Rosen, H. R., Lanaspa, M. A., Diehl, A. M., & Johnson, R. J. (2018). Fructose and sugar: A major mediator of non-alcoholic fatty liver disease. Journal of Hepatology, 68(5), 1063–1075. https://doi.org/10.1016/j.jhep.2018.01.019

Johnson, R. K., Appel, L. J., Brands, M., Howard, B. V., Lefevre, M., Lustig, R. H., Sacks, F., Steffen, L. M., Wylie-Rosett, J., & American Heart Association Nutrition Committee of the Council on Nutrition, Physical Activity, and Metabolism and the Council on Epidemiology and Prevention. (2009). Dietary sugars intake and cardiovascular health: A scientific statement from the American Heart Association. Circulation, 120(11), 1011–1020. https://doi.org/10.1161/CIRCULATIONAHA.109.192627

Kerti, L., & A. Veronica Witte, B. (2022). Higher glucose levels associated with lower memory and reduced hippocampal microstructure. https://n.neurology.org/content/higher-glucose-levels-associated-lower-memory-and-reduced-hippocampal-microstructure, https://n.neurology.org/content/higher-glucose-levels-associated-lower-memory-and-reduced-hippocampal-microstructure

Li, L., & Seeram, N. P. (2010). Maple Syrup Phytochemicals Include Lignans, Coumarins, a Stilbene, and Other Previously Unreported Antioxidant Phenolic Compounds. Journal of Agricultural and Food Chemistry, 58(22), 11673–11679. https://doi.org/10.1021/jf1033398

Lohner, S., Toews, I., & Meerpohl, J. J. (2017). Health outcomes of non-nutritive sweeteners: Analysis of the research landscape. Nutrition Journal, 16(1), 55. https://doi.org/10.1186/s12937-017-0278-x

Luger, M., Lafontan, M., Bes-Rastrollo, M., Winzer, E., Yumuk, V., & Farpour-Lambert, N. (2017). Sugar-Sweetened Beverages and Weight Gain in Children and Adults: A Systematic Review from 2013 to 2015 and a Comparison with Previous Studies. Obesity Facts, 10(6), 674–693. https://doi.org/10.1159/000484566

Magrone, T., Russo, M. A., & Jirillo, E. (2017). Cocoa and Dark Chocolate Polyphenols: From Biology to Clinical Applications. Frontiers in Immunology, 8, 677. https://doi.org/10.3389/fimmu.2017.00677

Mahan, L. K., & Raymond, J. L. (2016). Krause's Food & the Nutrition Care Process—E-Book. Elsevier Health Sciences.

Mai, B. H., & Yan, L.-J. (2019). The negative and detrimental effects of high fructose on the liver, with special reference to metabolic disorders. Diabetes, Metabolic Syndrome and Obesity: Targets and Therapy, 12, 821–826. https://doi.org/10.2147/DMSO.S198968

Malik, V. S., & Hu, F. B. (2019). Sugar-Sweetened Beverages and Cardiometabolic Health: An Update of the Evidence. Nutrients, 11(8), 1840. https://doi.org/10.3390/nu11081840

Malik, V. S., Li, Y., Pan, A., De Koning, L., Schernhammer, E., Willett, W. C., & Hu, F. B. (2019). Long-Term Consumption of Sugar-Sweetened and Artificially Sweetened Beverages and Risk of Mortality in US Adults. Circulation, 139(18), 2113–2125. https://doi.org/10.1161/CIRCULATIONAHA.118.037401

Malik, V. S., Popkin, B. M., Bray, G. A., Després, J.-P., Willett, W. C., & Hu, F. B. (2010). Sugar-sweetened beverages and risk of metabolic syndrome and type 2 diabetes: A meta-analysis. Diabetes Care, 33(11), 2477–2483. https://doi.org/10.2337/dc10-1079

McGee, H. (2004). On Food and Cooking: The Science and Lore of the Kitchen (1st edition). Scribner Books.

Mennella, J. A., Bobowski, N. K., & Reed, D. R. (2016). The development of sweet taste: From biology to hedonics. Reviews in Endocrine & Metabolic Disorders, 17(2), 171–178. https://doi.org/10.1007/s11154-016-9360-5

Micha, R., Penalvo, J., & Cudhea, F. (2017). Association Between Dietary Factors and Mortality From Heart Disease, Stroke, and Type 2 Diabetes in the United States | Cardiology | JAMA | JAMA Network. JAMA, 317(9), 912–924.

More Key Topics | MyPlate. (n.d.). Retrieved February 1, 2022, from https://www.myplate.gov/eat-healthy/more-key-topics

Morenga, L., Mallard, S., & Mann, J. (2013). Dietary sugars and body weight: Systematic review and meta-analyses of randomised controlled trials and cohort studies | The BMJ. BMJ, 346e(7492). https://www.bmj.com/content/346/bmj.e7492

Moynihan, P., & Kelly, S. (2013). Effect on Caries of Restricting Sugars Intake: Systematic Review to Inform WHO Guidelines—P.J. Moynihan, S.A.M. Kelly, 2014. Journal of Dental Research. https://journals.sagepub.com/doi/abs/10.1177/0022034513508954

Muhammad, K. G. (2019, August 14). The Barbaric History of Sugar in America. The New York Times. https://www.nytimes.com/interactive/2019/08/14/magazine/sugar-slave-trade-slavery.html, https://www.nytimes.com/interactive/2019/08/14/magazine/sugar-slave-trade-slavery.html

Murray, S., Tulloch, A., Criscitelli, K., & Avena, N. M. (2016). Recent studies of the effects of sugars on brain systems involved in energy balance and reward: Relevance to low calorie sweeteners. Physiology & Behavior, 164(Pt B), 504–508. https://doi.org/10.1016/j.physbeh.2016.04.004

MyPlate Graphics | MyPlate. (n.d.). Retrieved February 1, 2022, from https://www.myplate.gov/resources/graphics/myplate-graphics

Narain, A., Kwok, C. S., & Mamas, M. A. (2016). Soft drinks and sweetened beverages and the risk of cardiovascular disease and mortality: A systematic review and meta-analysis. International Journal of Clinical Practice, 70(10), 791–805. https://doi.org/10.1111/ijcp.12841

Nutrition, C. for F. S. and A. (2020a). Additional Information about High-Intensity Sweeteners Permitted for Use in Food in the United States. FDA. https://www.fda.gov/food/food-additives-petitions/additional-information-about-high-intensity-sweeteners-permitted-use-food-united-states

Nutrition, C. for F. S. and A. (2020b). High-Intensity Sweeteners. FDA. https://www.fda.gov/food/food-additives-petitions/high-intensity-sweeteners

Nutrition, C. for F. S. and A. (2021). Changes to the Nutrition Facts Label. FDA. https://www.fda.gov/food/food-labeling-nutrition/changes-nutrition-facts-label

Oral Health | CDC. (2018). https://www.cdc.gov/oralhealth/index.html

Paterson, M., Bell, K. J., O'Connell, S. M., Smart, C. E., Shafat, A., & King, B. (2015). The Role of Dietary Protein and Fat in Glycaemic Control in Type 1 Diabetes: Implications for Intensive Diabetes Management. Current Diabetes Reports, 15(9), 61. https://doi.org/10.1007/s11892-015-0630-5

Pollreisz, A., & Schmidt-Erfurth, U. (2010). Diabetic Cataract—Pathogenesis, Epidemiology and Treatment. Journal of Ophthalmology, 2010, e608751. https://doi.org/10.1155/2010/608751

Popkin, B. M., & Hawkes, C. (2016). Sweetening of the global diet, particularly beverages: Patterns, trends, and policy responses. The Lancet Diabetes & Endocrinology, 4(2), 174–186. https://doi.org/10.1016/S2213-8587(15)00419-2

Prinz, P. (2019). The role of dietary sugars in health: Molecular composition or just calories? European Journal of Clinical Nutrition, 73. https://doi.org/10.1038/s41430-019-0407-z

Pursey, K. M., Stanwell, P., Gearhardt, A. N., Collins, C. E., & Burrows, T. L. (2014). The Prevalence of Food Addiction as Assessed by the Yale Food Addiction Scale: A Systematic Review. Nutrients, 6(10), 4552–4590. https://doi.org/10.3390/nu6104552

Pushpanathan, P., Mathew, G. S., Selvarajan, S., Seshadri, K. G., & Srikanth, P. (2019). Gut Microbiota and Its Mysteries. Indian Journal of Medical Microbiology, 37(2), 268–277. https://doi.org/10.4103/ijmm.IJMM_19_373

Rippe, J., & Angelopoulos, T. (2015). Fructose-containing sugars and cardiovascular disease—PubMed. Adv Nutr, 15(6), 430–439.

Rippe, J. M., & Angelopoulos, T. J. (2016). Relationship between Added Sugars Consumption and Chronic Disease Risk Factors: Current Understanding. Nutrients, 8(11), 697. https://doi.org/10.3390/nu8110697

Sheiham, A., & James, W. P. T. (2014). A reappraisal of the quantitative relationship between sugar intake and dental caries: The need for new criteria for developing goals for sugar intake. BMC Public Health, 14(1), 863. https://doi.org/10.1186/1471-2458-14-863

Shin, D., Lee, K. W., & Song, W. O. (2015). Dietary Patterns during Pregnancy Are Associated with Risk of Gestational Diabetes Mellitus. Nutrients, 7(11), 9369–9382. https://doi.org/10.3390/nu7115472

Staff, E. (2018, December 7). Q. What is the difference between raw sugar and the regular white sugar Im used to? Tufts Health & Nutrition Letter. https://www.nutritionletter.tufts.edu/ask-experts/q-what-is-the-difference-between-raw-sugar-and-the-regular-white-sugar-im-used-to/

Staff, E. (2019, August 9). Sugar Substitutes: Helpful or Harmful? Tufts Health & Nutrition Letter. https://www.nutritionletter.tufts.edu/healthy-eating/sugar-substitutes-helpful-or-harmful/

Stinson, E. J., Piaggi, P., Ibrahim, M., Venti, C., Krakoff, J., & Votruba, S. B. (2018). High Fat and Sugar Consumption During Ad Libitum Intake Predicts Weight Gain. Obesity, 26(4), 689–695. https://doi.org/10.1002/oby.22124

Subramanian, A. P., John, A. A., Vellayappan, M. V., Balaji, A., Jaganathan, S. K., Mandal, M., & Supriyanto, E. (2016). Honey and its Phytochemicals: Plausible Agents in Combating Colon Cancer through its Diversified Actions. Journal of Food Biochemistry, 40(4), 613–629. https://doi.org/10.1111/jfbc.12239

Sugar and the Brain. (2020, March 10). https://neuro.hms.harvard.edu/harvard-mahoney-neuroscience-institute/brain-newsletter/and-brain/sugar-and-brain

Sweetness—An overview | ScienceDirect Topics. (n.d.). Retrieved April 11, 2020, from https://www.sciencedirect.com/topics/agricultural-and-biological-sciences/sweetness

Talavera, K., Yasumatsu, K., Voets, T., Droogmans, G., Shigemura, N., Ninomiya, Y., Margolskee, R. F., & Nilius, B. (2005). Heat activation of TRPM5 underlies thermal sensitivity of sweet taste. Nature, 438(7070), 1022–1025. https://doi.org/10.1038/nature04248

Talavera, K., Yasumatsu, K., Yoshida, R., Margolskee, R. F., Voets, T., Ninomiya, Y., & Nilius, B. (2008). The taste transduction channel TRPM5 is a locus for bitter-sweet taste interactions. The FASEB Journal, 22(5), 1343–1355. https://doi.org/10.1096/fj.07-9591com

The Sugar and Cancer Connection—American Institute for Cancer Research. (n.d.). Retrieved February 1, 2022, from https://www.aicr.org/news/the-sugar-cancer-connection/

Thomas, D. T., Erdman, K. A., & Burke, L. M. (2016). American College of Sports Medicine Joint Position Statement. Nutrition and Athletic Performance. Medicine and Science in Sports and Exercise, 48(3), 543–568. https://doi.org/10.1249/MSS.0000000000000852

Tiwari, B., Brunton, N., & Brennan, C. (2013). Handbook of Plant Food Phytochemicals | Wiley Online Books. Wiley Online. https://onlinelibrary.wiley.com/doi/book/10.1002/9781118464717

Van Opstal, A. M., Hafkemeijer, A., van den Berg-Huysmans, A. A., Hoeksma, M., Mulder, Theo. P. J., Pijl, H., Rombouts, S. A. R. B., & van der Grond, J. (2021). Brain activity and connectivity changes in response to nutritive natural sugars, non-nutritive natural sugar replacements and artificial sweeteners. Nutritional Neuroscience, 24(5), 395–405. https://doi.org/10.1080/1028415X.2019.1639306

Vega-López, S., Venn, B. J., & Slavin, J. L. (2018). Relevance of the Glycemic Index and Glycemic Load for Body Weight, Diabetes, and Cardiovascular Disease. Nutrients, 10(10). https://doi.org/10.3390/nu10101361

Vos, M. B., Kimmons, J. E., Gillespie, C., Welsh, J., & Blanck, H. M. (2008). Dietary fructose consumption among US children and adults: The Third National Health and Nutrition Examination Survey. Medscape Journal of Medicine, 10(7), 160.

Vos, M., Kaar, J., Welsh, J., Van Horn, L., & Feig, D. (n.d.). Added Sugars and Cardiovascular Disease Risk in Children: A Scientific Statement From the American Heart Association | Circulation. Circulation, 135(9), 2017.

Wansink, B., & Sobal, J. (2007). Mindless Eating: The 200 Daily Food Decisions We Overlook. Environment and Behavior, 39(1), 106–123. https://doi.org/10.1177/0013916506295573

White, J. (2008). Straight talk about high-fructose corn syrup: What it is and what it ain't. American Journal of Clinical Nutrition, 88(6), 1716S-1721S.

WHO. (n.d.). Guideline: Sugars intake for adults and children. Retrieved January 31, 2022, from https://www.who.int/publications-detail-redirect/9789241549028

Wiss, D. A., Avena, N., & Rada, P. (2018). Sugar Addiction: From Evolution to Revolution. Frontiers in Psychiatry, 9. https://www.frontiersin.org/article/10.3389/fpsyt.2018.00545

Wollgast, J., & Anklam, E. (2000). Review on polyphenols in Theobroma cacao: Changes in composition during the manufacture of chocolate and methodology for identification and quantification. Food Research International, 33(6), 423–447. https://doi.org/10.1016/S0963-9969(00)00068-5

Yang, Q., Zhang, Z., & Gregg, E. (2014). Added Sugar Intake and Cardiovascular Diseases Mortality Among US Adults | Cardiology | JAMA Internal Medicine | JAMA Network. JAMA, 174(4), 516–524.

Ye, X., Gao, X., Scott, T., & Tucker, K. L. (2011). Habitual sugar intake and cognitive function among middle-aged and older Puerto Ricans without diabetes. The British Journal of Nutrition, 106(9), 1423–1432. https://doi.org/10.1017/S0007114511001760

BEVERAGES

By Joi Lenczowski MD , Dana Henderson MS RD, CDCES, Trang Le MD,
Caroline Rosseler MS RD, and Deborah Koehn MD, FACP, BC-ADM, ABCL
with Deborah Kennedy PhD

"Pure water is the world's first and foremost medicine."
Quote is a Slovakian Proverb

This chapter will cover the many forms of beverages that individuals consume. Although water is the preferred form of hydration, there are many different beverages that individuals choose to drink. These beverages have potential beneficial and detrimental effects on health and it is essential to have an understanding of these effects so as to appropriately guide patients and consumers.

Hydration

Hydration is essential for human life as water accounts for on average over 50% of adult body weight. Every day water is lost through sweating, breathing, defecating and urinating. Hydration — adding or replacing water — is essential for human life as our bodies cannot produce enough to sustain life. Without water, a human would die within several days to a week depending on the circumstances. The majority of water needed to maintain appropriate hydration and fluid balance, comes from liquid beverages in our diet, while **food provides up to 20% to 30%** of the daily fluid requirement.

Water has many roles in the function and health of the human body.

- o It is the main intracellular component of cells and fills the space between cells.
- o It is an excellent solvent for ionic compounds and solutes such as glucose and amino acids (Häussinger, 1996).
- o It is a highly interactive molecule and is involved in all biochemical reactions as a macronutrient, and thus water plays an invaluable role in governing the structure, stability, dynamics and function of biomolecules, such as protein.
- o It is a component of blood, saliva, sweat and tears.
- o It maintains the vascular volume and allows for blood circulation, which is essential for the function of all organs and tissues of the body (Ritz & Berrut, 2005).
- o Is required for digestion, absorption, transportation and dissolving nutrients, plus elimination of waste products.
- o It is a shock absorber and in combination with viscous molecules, it assists in lubricating joints.
- o It is a thermoregulator, performing an essential function for life in the surrounding environment. Water has a large heat capacity, and can buffer changes in body temperature in a warm or cold environment. Through sweat and evaporation of water, one can lose heat from the body even when the ambient temperature is higher than body temperature (Montain et al., 1999).

Since water is vital to human survival, humans have evolved an exquisitely sensitive network of physiological controls to maintain body water, and thirst drives fluid intake to prevent dehydration. While thirst can guide us to increase hydration, there are times when thirst does not function well, as evidenced by the elderly who may have a decreased sense of thirst. A more consistent and accurate method to determine hydration status is the evaluation of urine concentration. In the absence of vitamin supplementation or other medications which can alter urine color, **a well-hydrated individual will excrete clear to light yellow urine with little to no odor**.

It is rare for healthy individuals to develop overhydration, which leads to hyponatremia — low sodium concentration in the blood. Dehydration, on the other hand, is quite common due to decreased water intake, increased exertion, and exposure to high environmental temperatures. Symptoms of dehydration include constipation, delirium and delirium presenting as dementia in the elderly, headaches and changes in physical performance, cognitive performance, kidney function, heart function and hemodynamic status.

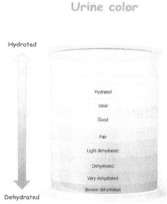

Urine color

Hydrated

Hydrated
Ideal
Good
Fair
Light dehydrated
Dehydrated
Very dehydrated
Severe dehydrated

Dehydrated

Water Storage

In the body, more water is stored in muscle than in adipose tissue — water content in adipose tissue is only 10% — thus body hydration status varies with levels of muscle versus fat. People with a low fat mass and high skeletal muscle have greater hydration status than someone with a high fat mass. Additionally, body water decreases with age: water represents 75% of body weight in newborns and decreases to 56% and 47% in men and women older than 50 years, respectively. Beginning around puberty, females have lower body water content due to a higher fat mass compared to males ("Scientific Opinion on Dietary Reference Values for Water," 2010).

Hydration is Essential for Life.

The rest of the chapter will cover the following types of beverages: water, tea, coffee, alcohol and sugar sweetened beverages like soda, juice, energy drinks and sports drinks (Dairy & Dairy Alternatives will be covered in a separate chapter). Recommendations will be made to increase ingestion of more healthful hydrating beverages and to limit beverages that are detrimental to health. Scientific literature regarding health supporting these recommendations will be cited. Additionally, this chapter will review the history of many beverages and provide practical day to day recommendations.

SECTION 1: WATER

Water is the best source of liquid for the human body as it adequately provides hydration without calories. It is generally readily available and safe in the United States, and it can be obtained for minimal to no cost. Drinking plain water, tap or bottled, instead of caloric beverages, helps to reduce dietary energy density and may contribute to the management of body weight (Dennis et al., 2010; Muckelbauer et al., 2013; Tate et al., 2012). Plain water is the recommended beverage per the Centers for Disease Control as well as many other medical organizations (American Academy of Pediatrics, American College of Physicians, Academy of Nutrition and Dietetics).

The United States has one of the safest water supplies in the world. Two hundred and eighty six million Americans obtain their water from a community water system, which is regulated by the United States Environmental Protection Agency (EPA). Under the Safe Drinking Water Act, the EPA has the authority to set the standards for drinking water quality and oversees states, localities, and water suppliers who implement those standards. Additionally, the public water supply is fluoridated, which effectively prevents tooth decay.

Water has not always been a safe source of hydration. Historically, human settlements were established along waterways for multiple reasons, including the use of the river to provide fresh surface water and the use of the river for removal of raw sewage. Cities grew with time and expanded greatly following the industrial revolution. As populations lived in close proximity, water supplies became contaminated by sewage and people depended on other beverages for hydration. These beverages were safer to ingest due to processing such as the heating of water used in preparation of teas and coffees, or the fermentation of alcoholic beverages such as beer, cider, and wine.

In the 1800s, there were multiple large epidemics of cholera in Europe and America that killed thousands of people. The study of cholera clustering and the presumed transmission hypothesized by John Snow led eventually to better sanitation of public water supplies. Unfortunately, per the World Health Organization, waterborne diseases continue to cause significant disease burden worldwide. Waterborne diarrheal diseases, for example, continue to be a worldwide health concern, responsible for two million deaths each year, with the majority occurring in children under five years of age. Although most of the people in developed nations can rely on public treated water supplies, those in developing areas of the world do not consistently have sources of clean sanitized water.

RECOMMENDED GUIDELINES FOR WATER

There are multiple factors that affect water needs, as it is dependent upon differences in caloric intake, metabolism, environmental conditions, activities and the concentrating/diluting capacity of the kidney. Thus, there is not a single level of water intake that assures adequate hydration and optimum health for half of all apparently healthy persons in all environmental conditions. Therefore, an Adequate Intake (AI) is used instead of an Estimated Average Requirement (EAR) for water.

The recommended guidelines for total water intake include water from drinking water and other beverages (with 85% to 90% water), water from food (ranges from 40% to 80%), and water from substrate oxidation. Water content is high in many fruit and vegetables, with watermelons being 92% water. There is a wide variability in guidelines for drinking water recommendations throughout the world due to differences in diets. For instance, a diet rich in fresh fruit will result in lower recommended beverage amounts. The IOM assumed that the contribution of food to total **dietary water intake is 20%, while 80% is provided by beverages**. This relationship is not fixed and depends on the type of beverage and on the choice of foods.

Food can also be an excellent source of water for hydration. At first blush, we think about fruits as a water source. Besides watermelon, other fruits in this very hydrating class include strawberries, grapefruit, and cantaloupe. Many other fruits are greater than 80% water and this list includes oranges, apples, peaches, plums, nectarines, apricots, Asian pears, mangoes, papayas, pineapples, blackberries, blueberries and raspberries.

Table 1: Recommended Daily Total Water Intake

Age/Gender Group	Adequate Intake*	Intake from Beverages**
Infant 0 to 6 months	3 cups (0.7 L)	2 ½ cups

Infant 7 to 12 months	3 1/3 cups (0.8 L)	2 ¾ cups
Child 1 to 3 years	5 ½ cups (1.3 L)	4 ½ cups
Child 4 to 9 years	7 cups (1.7 L)	5 ½ cups
Female 9 to 13 years	8.9 cups (2.1 L)	7 cups
Female 14 to 18 years	9.7 cups (2.3 L)	7 ¾ cups
Female 19 years and older	11.4 cups (2.7 L)	9 cups
Pregnancy	12.7 cups (3.0 L)	10 cups
Lactation	16 cups (3.8 L)	12 ¾ cups
Male 9 to 13 years	10 cups (2.4 L)	8 cups
Male 14 to 18 years	13.9 cups (3.3 L)	11 cups
Male 19 years and older	15.6 cups (3.7 L)	12 ½ cups

* Total water for Adequate Intake (AI) includes water from drinking water, beverages, and food
1 Liter = 4.23 Cups
** Intake from beverages is calculated based on IOM's assumption that of the total water AI per day, 80% comes from beverages — rounded to nearest ¼ cup (Institute of Medicine (U.S.), 2005).

In addition, many vegetables can also provide significant water in our diet, as well as providing numerous other healthful nutritional benefits of vitamins, polyphenols, and fiber. Quite a few vegetables have a composition that's 89% water or more, according to the USDA. These include lettuce, celery, bok choy, radishes, cucumber, zucchini, watercress, tomatoes, green bell peppers, asparagus, portabella mushrooms, Swiss chard, okra, cabbage, cauliflower and broccoli.

People should be encouraged to drink water when they are thirsty and increase their water intake when exercising or in hot or humid environments. Additionally, water intake may need to be increased with changes in general health such as fever, vomiting, diarrhea, the presence of kidney stones or urinary tract infections. **A good guide is to drink more water when thirsty and to keep urine clear or light yellow.**

> In order to meet the daily requirement for fluids, it is best to consume water, coffee, or tea without any additional additives.

It stands to reason that the more water that is lost from the body, the more water that is needed to replenish it. Water is lost mostly through sweat, defecation, and urination. As a thermo-regulator, water is also needed to cool down the body. Any conditions that increase water loss or body temperature will also increase daily water intake. These can include:

- Nausea and vomiting
- Fever
- Bladder infections

- o Urinary tract stones
- o Hot or humid weather
- o Strenuous exercise or physical labor
- o Certain medications
- o Eating a diet high in dry foods

ARE AMERICANS MEETING THE DAILY RECOMMENDATION FOR WATER?

Americans are not doing very well at consuming plain water. Data, as reported by the CDC, shows water consumption varies by age, race/ethnicity, socioeconomic status and behavioral characteristics.

- o In 2005 - 2010, U.S. youth drank an average of 15 ounces of water and U.S. adults drank an average of 39 ounces of water on a given day (Drewnowski et al., 2013a, 2013b).
- o Among U.S. adults, plain water intake is lower in older adults, lower-income adults, and those with lower education (Drewnowski et al., 2013a; Kant et al., 2009).
- o U.S. adolescents who drink less water tended to drink less milk, eat less fruits and vegetables, drink more sugar-sweetened beverages, eat more fast food and get less physical activity (Park et al., 2012).

Further review of the 2005 - 2010 NHANES data reported on pediatric intake of plain water, revealed that at least **75% of children failed to meet AI reference values for daily water intake** (see Table 2). There was a strong effect of race/ethnicity on total water consumption. Non-Hispanic, white children consumed more plain water on average, as compared to Mexican American and non-Hispanic black children (Drewnowski et al., 2013).

Future guidelines on beverage consumption should take plain drinking water into account. This is particularly important given the size of the shortfall between observed intakes and IOM AI values.

Table 2: Sources of Water By Age and Gender From NHANES 2005-2010 Data (Drewnowski et al., 2013).

Source (in milliliters)	Males (4 to 8 years)	Female (4 to 8 years)	Male (9 to 13 years)	Female (9 to 13 years)
Water	365	365	483	509
Milk	312	279	286	251
Soda	89	94	230	180

Fruit Juice	118	111	110	92
Other*	49	49	117	100
Food Sources	434	429	470	445
TOTAL	1,477	1,415	1,767	1,656

*Other – tea, coffee, sports drink and energy drink

Clinical signs of dehydration (Zheng et al., 2015)(Institute of Medicine, 2006)
- o Impaired mental function
- o Impaired motor control
- o Diminished capacity for aerobic or endurance exercise
- o Enhanced fever response
- o Increased core temperature during exercise
- o Reduced tolerance to heat
- o Heart rate increases when lying down or standing up

BENEFITS OF WATER

Weight and Obesity

Replacing high caloric sweetened beverages with plain drinking water may help control the increased risk of diabetes and metabolic syndrome due to sugar sweetened beverages (SSB). In a six-year cohort study of Danish children, SSB were replaced with either equivalent grams of water or milk, resulting in significant decreases in BMI, waist circumference, and the sum of measurements of four skin folds (Zheng et al., 2015). Another study addressed ease of access to fresh tasting water in school cafeterias in New York city, and showed that the installation of water jets is associated with increased water drinking and decreased likelihood of a student being overweight or obese (Schwartz et al., 2016).

Cardiovascular Disease

Hydration benefits overall cardiovascular health by improving circulatory parameters. Water is essential for adequate circulation and transport of oxygen and nutrients to the organ systems. Observational studies have linked habitual low water intake with increased future risk for adverse cardiovascular events. In addition, arsenic exposure due to tainted water is associated with the development of vascular disease, including stroke, ischemic heart disease and peripheral vascular disease (Palma-Lara et al., 2020).

Evidence suggests hypohydration (a state of low body water), which is rare, impairs vascular function and cardiovascular regulation, impairs cutaneous vascular function, reduces endothelial function, and alters blood pressure regulation at rest, during exercise and during orthostatic stress (Watso & Farquhar, 2019).

Diabetes

Low water intake (less than a half a liter compared to a liter or more of water) is inversely and independently associated with the risk of developing hyperglycemia after only three days (Johnson et al., 2017; Roussel et al., 2011). The theory is that low water intake decreases blood pressure and this stresses the body, which causes a release in cortisol, and cortisol then prompts the release of glucose.

Bowel Health

Water is essential for good bowel health and digestion. Drinking water during or after a meal aids digestion. Water and other liquids help break down food so that the body can absorb nutrients. Water also softens stool, which helps prevent constipation. Adequate hydration has been associated with reduced incidence of constipation (Popkin, 2010).

Water sources may also have an influential impact on the gut microbiome. The mineral and chemical contents may alter the gut environment and interact with components of the food, influencing the gut microbes. The microbiome community in the drinking water may colonize the gut or influence residential microbiome during transit (JHA et al., 2018).

Cancer

Plain, untainted water is not associated with an increased risk of cancer. However, arsenic contamination of water is associated with an increased risk of lung, bladder, skin and possibly kidney cancer (Palma-Lara et al., 2020; Saint-Jacques et al., 2018). Plus, exposure to, and ingestion of water with, elevated nitrate levels, primarily due to runoff from agriculture, is associated with an increased risk of colorectal cancer, even when the nitrate levels are lower than the maximum allowed limits (Schullehner et al., 2018).

A recent review of epidemiological studies suggests there may be a relationship between nitrate ingestion in drinking water and thyroid disease. Nitrate levels in water resources have increased in many areas of the world largely due to applications of inorganic fertilizer and animal manure in agricultural areas (Ward et al., 2018).

Kidney Health

Water intake is associated with decreases in kidney disease. An increased intake of plain water is more often associated with a decreased risk of chronic kidney disease as well as preserving kidney function in those with chronic kidney disease. This is in contrast to the effect of sweetened beverages which increase the risk for chronic kidney disease. Kidney stone formation and stone recurrence is reduced by increasing daily total water intake. Increased plain water intake also retards cyst growth in polycystic kidney disease (Armstrong & Johnson, 2018; Cheungpasitporn et al., 2016; Sontrop et al., 2013; Yuzbashian et al., 2016).

RISKS OF WATER INTAKE

Infection
While the U.S. water supply is well maintained overall, there are potential risks of contamination due to flooding or other natural disasters, which may contain infectious microorganisms. Additionally, some individuals obtain their water from deep well sources, and this water is not monitored for contaminants by the EPA. This water may be contaminated by agricultural chemicals and animal waste products.

Lead Contamination
Lead contamination, as evidenced by recent reports from Flint, Michigan, can be a concern depending on age of piping and maintenance of the water supply. Per the CDC, "the most common sources of lead in drinking water are lead pipes, faucets, and plumbing fixtures. Certain pipes that carry drinking water from the water source to the home may contain lead. Household plumbing fixtures, welding solder, and pipe fittings made prior to 1986 may also contain lead" (Lead in Drinking Water | Sources of Lead | CDC, 2020). There is no safe level of lead for young children, so all sources of lead exposure for children should be controlled or eliminated. Many public water authorities have websites that include data on drinking water quality, including results of lead testing.

Microplastic Exposure
Microplastics can be found in most commercially available bottled waters (Mason et al., 2018). The health impacts of ingested microplastics in humans are undetermined to date, the toxicological outcomes of these exposures are not yet known.

Congestive Heart Failure
Water volumes ingested may present an issue for patients who are on diuretics for other health concerns. Patients with advanced congestive heart failure are recommended to limit total water intake to 1.5 to 2 liters/day.

Food/Drug Interactions
Water is the preferred liquid for taking medications. Other beverages, such as coffee, tea, milks and juices contain active ingredients that may alter absorption or function of certain medications.

CLINICAL COMPETENCIES FOR WATER

Clinical Recommendations
1. Consume the listed amount set by the IOM's AI for total water intake for the specific age and gender group (see Table 1).

Clinical Competencies

1. List conditions where thirst would not be an indicator of hydration status.
2. List situations/conditions that may require more than the daily AI for total water.
3. Evaluate the color and odor of urine for hydration status.

CULINARY COMPETENCIES FOR WATER

Shopping/Storing/Safety Competencies

1. Purchase water without added sodium, sugar and other 'unwanted' ingredients – stimulants for example.
2. Compare and contrast the various types of water.
3. Avoid water that can be contaminated.

Cooking/Preparing/Serving Competencies

1. Prepare flavored water.
2. Drink when thirsty and at mealtime.

Sustainability Competency

1. Drink water from plastic free containers.

AT THE STORE

Plain water is available from many sources – at the tap at home, business, and school. If selecting water to purchase at the store, avoid those with caloric additives, which may negate the previously elaborated health benefits. Many people prefer carbonated water to still water. There are many types of carbonated water available, including club soda, seltzer, sparkling and tonic water, which differ based on mineral content, carbonation — added versus natural — and added sweeteners. Club soda, seltzer, sparkling and tonic water contain very few nutrients and all beverages except tonic water contain zero calories and sugar.

Club Soda

Club soda is carbonated water that has been infused with added minerals, such as potassium sulfate, sodium chloride, disodium phosphate or sodium bicarbonate. The amounts of minerals added to club soda depends on the brand or manufacturer. These minerals help enhance the flavor of club soda by giving it a slightly salty taste.

Seltzer Water

Seltzer water is water that has been carbonated, but without added minerals, which gives it a more "true" water taste.

Mineral Water

Unlike club soda or seltzer, sparkling mineral water is naturally carbonated. Its bubbles come from a spring or well with naturally occurring carbonation. Spring water contains a variety of minerals, such as sodium, magnesium, and calcium. However, the amounts vary based on the source from which they were bottled. According to the FDA: "The name of water containing not less than 250 parts per million (ppm) total dissolved solids (TDS), coming from a source tapped at one or more bore holes or springs, originating from a geologically and physically protected underground water source, may be 'mineral water'." The mineral content of water may change the taste significantly and each mineral water will have its own unique taste. Some producers further carbonate their products by adding carbon dioxide, making them even more bubbly.

  o   If there is less than 500 ppm TDS it has to say on the label "low mineral content"
  o   If there is more than 1,500 ppm TDS it has to say on the label "high mineral content"

Tonic Water

Tonic water has the most unique taste of all four beverages. It is a carbonated water that contains minerals and quinine, which gives tonic water a bitter taste. Today, quinine is only present in small amounts to give tonic water its bitter taste. Tonic water is commonly sweetened with either high-fructose corn syrup or sugar to improve its taste.

Coconut Water

Recently, interest in alternative palatable sources of water include an increase in the commercial sales of coconut water with its claims for health benefits. Coconut water is sourced from the liquid contained inside a green coconut. It contains the nutrients calories listed in Table 3.

Table 3: Comparison of Minerals and Sugar in Gatorade® Versus Coconut Water

Nutrient/Calorie per ounce	Gatorade®	Unflavored/Unsweetened Coconut Water
Calories	6.25 calories	5.45 calories
Sugar	1.75 grams	1.3 grams
Sodium	13.75 mg	5.45 mg
Potassium	3.75 mg	61 mg

The FDA also defines the following:

Artesian Water: "The name of water from a well tapping a confined aquifer in which the water level stands at some height above the top of the aquifer is "artesian water" or "artesian well water."

Ground Water: "The name of water from a subsurface saturated zone that is under a pressure equal to or greater than atmospheric pressure is "ground water."

Purified Water/Distilled Water/ Deionized Water: "The name of water that has been produced by distillation, deionization, reverse osmosis, or other suitable processes and that meets the definition of "purified water" in the United States Pharmacopeia, 23d Revision, January 1, 1995, which is incorporated by reference in accordance with 5 U.S.C. 551(a) and 1 CFR part 51. Alternatively, the water may be called "deionized water" if the water has been processed by deionization, "distilled water" if it is produced by distillation, "reverse osmosis water" if the water has been processed by reverse osmosis..."

Spring Water: The name of water derived from an underground formation from which water flows naturally to the surface of the earth may be "spring water." Spring water shall be collected only at the spring or through a bore hole tapping the underground formation feeding the spring.

Sparkling Water: The name of water that, after treatment and possible replacement of carbon dioxide, contains the same amount of carbon dioxide from the source that it had at emergence from the source may be "sparkling bottled water."

Sustainability and Water

Avoid buying plastic water bottles for many reasons; the top two are that it is contributing to tons of plastic waste per year and microplastic particles are showing up in our environment and in our bodies. By 2017, 8.3 metric tons of virgin plastic was produced and it is estimated that by 2050, 12 billion tons of plastic will end up in the natural environment (Geyer et al., 2017).

Microplastics enter the human body by inhalation, the skin, and ingestion. The health effects are not completely known but it is suggested that they lead to chronic inflammation and an increased risk of cancer (Prata et al., 2020). Microplastics have been found in:

- Placentas (Ragusa et al., 2021)
- Human Organs (American Chemistry Society, 2020)
- Human Stool (Schwabl et al., 2019)
- In the most isolated places in the United States and the world by travelling through the air (Allen et al., 2021). It is estimated that 1,000 tons of microplastics travel through the atmosphere and end up in protected spaces in the United States each year (Brahney et al., 2020)
- The food and water supply
  - Fish (Kim et al., 2018; Smith et al., 2018)
  - Fruits and vegetables (highest in apples and higher in fruits than in vegetables) (Oliveri Conti et al., 2020)
  - Drinking water (Koelmans et al., 2019; Pivokonsky et al., 2018)
  - Plastic tea bags and plastic water bottles are large sources of nano and microplastics (Hernandez et al., 2019; Oßmann et al., 2018; Zuccarello et al., 2019)

Shopping for Water

When shopping for water read the labels carefully, because many commercially available water products contain additives including sugar and sodium, resulting in significant increases in caloric intake. Look at both the ingredient list and the Nutrition Facts Panel for this information. The following three scenarios highlight why it is important to look to see what is in the water that is being purchased.

Scenario One: Are there additional ingredients?

Vitamin Water

The Nutrition Facts Panel lists 32 grams (8 teaspoons!) of sugar and 100% of various B vitamins, which is a clue that the drink is formulated to increase energy. If you didn't also look at the ingredient list for this Vitamin Water, you would not pick up that there is caffeine and another stimulant – guarana seed – in there. In addition, there is no way of telling the amount of 'stimulants', which can be dangerous for some individuals like small children and those with certain types of heart disease.

Depending on the type, it can contain many other ingredients – those underlined contain stimulants. Plus there is 32 grams of sugar in one bottle.

Scenario 2: Are there added ingredients that have zero calories – micronutrients, herbs, artificial sweeteners for example.

Scenario one is a good example of a water with added micronutrients and other ingredients that have zero calories. With the Hint water, looking at the Nutrition Facts Panel does not tell you if this water has artificial sweeteners, colors or flavors. It doesn't, but you have to find the ingredient list and possibly marketing material for that information.

Scenario three: Is sodium or other minerals added or are they there naturally?

The minerals in mineral waters are there naturally – the FDA's rule says that no minerals may be added to drinks labelled as "mineral water." When it comes to sodium added to other types of water, it would be listed in the ingredient list. There is no federal standard for sodium content in water but there is for chloride (250 mg/L).

The Drinking Water Advisory Program sponsored by the Health and Ecological Criteria Division of the Office of Science and Technology (OST), Office of Water (OW), recommends the following levels of sodium in drinking water – between 30 and 60 mg/L based in part on taste (EPA, 2003).

Hint Water

contains no juice

Nutrition Facts
Serving size 1 Bottle (474mL)

Amount per serving

Calories   **0**

% Daily Value

Total Fat 0g   0%

Sodium 0mg   0%

Total Carbohydrate 0g   0%

Total Sugars 0g

Includes 0g Added Sugars   0%

Protein 0g

Not a significant source of saturated fat, trans fat, cholesterol, dietary fiber, vitamin D, calcium, iron, and potassium

Adds "natural flavors" to water. There is no added sugar. To see if there are artificial sweeteners, look at the ingredient list.

IN THE KITCHEN

On The Tongue

Many people claim that water is flavorless. Ever since antiquity, philosophers have claimed that water has no flavor. Aristotle referred to it as "tasteless" around 330 BC. But insects and amphibians have water-sensing nerve cells, and there is evidence of similar cells in mammals, with brain scan studies suggesting that a region of hypothalamus in the brain responds specifically to water (Oka et al., 2015). We may either know we are drinking water by its lack of flavor or because any perceived flavor is just the after effect of whatever we tasted earlier, such as the sweetness of water after we eat salty food.

> **The signal for thirst is oftentimes confused for "hunger." Especially if someone is trying to manage their weight, encourage them to drink water when they first feel hungry.**

Recent scientific information indicates acid-sensing taste receptor cells (TRCs), previously suggested as the sour taste sensors, also mediate taste responses to water (Zocchi et al., 2017). It is theorized that the taste receptors are stimulated by a change in the pH of the cells by water washing out saliva, which is a salty and acidic. Interestingly, while these signals from TRCs in the tongue can trigger drinking, they don't play a role in telling the brain when to stop.

Flavored Water

English lavender and lemon

Berries, mint, and apple slices

Flavored water is the way to go if someone does not like drinking plain water and the options are endless. Make a fresh batch each day for variety using one or a mixture of ingredients. Examples are listed below:

Add citrus: lemon, lime, grapefruit or orange
Add herbs: basil, mint, lavender or rosemary
Add fruit: slice of apple, berries, slice of orange or pomegranate seeds
Add vegetables: slices of cucumber

Lemon juice and mint

Cucumber and carrot tops

Some popular combinations include:
- Lemon, lime, and orange
- Raspberry and lime
- Pineapple and mint
- Lemon and cucumber
- Blackberry and sage
- Strawberry and basil

o Blackberry and ginger
o Peach and vanilla bean
o Peach, lemon, and thyme
o Watermelon and rosemary

Flavored Ice Cubes

Adding flavored ice to a glass of water can be both visually appealing and delicious. Some options for ingredients are berries, citrus slices, and/or herbs.

Invest in a water bottle made out of glass or metal so you can take your flavored water on the go.

SUMMARY

Due to variations in physical activity levels, climate, air conditioning, body size and surface area, there is a wide variation in actual fluid requirements among individuals. As general advice, people should drink before they become thirsty and maintain their urine as a clear or light yellow color, keeping in mind that urine color may be altered by ingestion of certain medications and vitamins.

Government guidelines for adequate fluid intake are based on observations. The often quoted "drink at least eight glasses of water a day" is not based on any scientific evidence. Fluid intake does not have to be only water, but can be achieved by a combination of water and other sources of fluid including tea, coffee, milk and food. Ideally, encourage clients and patients to focus on beverages with no added sugar, salt, or fat.

SECTION 2: COFFEE AND TEA

When prepared plain with no added sugars and fat, coffee and tea are calorie-free beverages brimming with antioxidants, flavonoids, and other biologically active substances that may be good for health. Additionally, water is heated to prepare both coffee and tea in traditional preparations, which decreases the potentially risky pathogen load in the water in areas where clean water is scarce.

Numerous health benefits are associated with the ingestion of both coffee and tea. Some benefits may be due to polyphenols present in these beverages, while other health effects are secondary to the caffeine contained in the beverage. Polyphenols are a category of compounds naturally found in plant foods, and are categorized into four main groups: flavonoids, phenolic acids, polyphenolic amides and other polyphenols. Polyphenols found in coffee and tea are anti-inflammatory and they have antioxidant properties that may promote beneficial gut bacteria.

Studies have been inconsistent in separating the possible contributions of caffeine versus the numerous other plant components of coffee and tea. For more details on the effect of caffeine alone, please see the section on caffeine in Energy Drinks. Coffee and tea ingestion are associated with decreased overall mortality, diabetes mellitus, cardiovascular disease and hypertension, gallstones, depression and neurodegenerative disease.

CAFFEINE

Caffeine   Theophylline   Theobromine

The three xanthines — caffeine, theophylline, and theobromine — occur in plants. They are qualitatively similar but differ markedly in potency:

- o Tea contains caffeine and theophylline.
- o Coffee contains caffeine.
- o Cocoa and chocolate contain caffeine and theobromine.
- o The cola nut ("cola" drinks) contains caffeine.

Regarding mental stimulation, caffeine is more potent than theophylline, but both can stimulate mental activity. There are many reported effects of these stimulants on mentation, including rapidity of thought, decreased reaction time, worsening of performance due to accentuation of anxiety and decreased sensation of fatigue. In general, caffeine induces feelings of alertness and well-being, euphoria, or exhilaration. Onset of boredom, fatigue, inattentiveness and sleepiness is postponed. Theobromine is weak and of no clinical importance — although responsible for the toxicity of chocolate when ingested by dogs.

COFFEE

Coffee is a beverage made from coffee beans, which are the roasted seeds from the fruit of the Coffea flowering plant. Coffea is a member of the taxonomic family Rubiaceae. There are several species of coffee, but two are most commonly grown for coffee drinking: Coffea arabica and Coffea canephora, which is better known as robusta. Coffee is rich in caffeine, vitamin B_2 (riboflavin), magnesium and plant chemicals including polyphenols and diterpenes. One eight-ounce cup of brewed coffee contains about 95 mg of caffeine, however the quantity of caffeine will depend on how it is <u>brewed.</u>

Table 4: Amount of Caffeine in Coffee From Various Brewing Methods

Type of Coffee	Amount of Caffeine in 8 Ounces
Brewed	95 mg
Brewed decaf	2 mg
Cold brew	102 to 159 mg
Instant	62 mg
Espresso	63 mg per 1 ounce

All coffee grown worldwide can be traced back to the ancient coffee forests on the Ethiopian plateau. A legend attributes this worldwide beverage to a goat herder who first noticed his goats eating the berries and becoming energetic and unable to sleep. He shared his story with local monks who made a drink with the berries which kept them awake and alert. In the 13th century, people in Arabia began to roast the coffee beans, starting the process by which we now enjoy coffee. From Arabia, coffee drinking spread to Europe and then due to colonialism, to the rest of the world. In early 17th century Europe, coffee replaced the morning beverage of the time, beer or wine, resulting in alert and energized workers due to caffeine and its stimulatory effect replacing sedating alcohol.

THE BENEFITS OF COFFEE

Overall Mortality
Multiple studies have shown an inverse relationship between coffee or tea ingestion and all-cause as well as cause-specific mortality due to heart disease, respiratory disease, stroke and diabetes. As reported in a 2012 New England Journal of Medicine article, analysis of data from the NIH - AARP Diet and Health Study, with over 400,000 individuals, showed significant inverse associations of coffee consumption with deaths from all

causes and specifically with deaths due to heart disease, respiratory disease, stroke, injuries and accidents, diabetes and infections (Freedman et al., 2012). The inverse association persisted even with over six cups of coffee consumed daily and was similar between caffeinated and noncaffeinated coffee drinkers.

A large cohort study involving over 200,000 individuals followed for up to 30 years, reported an association between drinking moderate amounts of coffee and lower risk of an early death. Compared to nondrinkers, those who drank three to five cups coffee daily were 15% less likely to die early from all causes, including cardiovascular disease, suicide, and Parkinson's. In this study, the association was observed in both caffeinated and the decaffeinated coffee drinkers. This indicates a possible contribution by bioactive compounds in coffee blocking disease through reducing inflammation and insulin resistance (Loftfield et al., 2018).

An observational cohort study of coffee on overall mortality followed more than 500,000 participants in 10 European countries for a mean period of 16 years. During the study, there were approximately 41,700 deaths. The comparison between the highest quarter of coffee consumption, to those with no coffee consumption, revealed a 12% lower risk of all-cause mortality in men and a 7% lower risk in women (Gunter et al., 2017). Additionally, a similar study, but of nonwhite populations, in North America, followed a cohort of over 185,000 participants for a mean duration of 16 years, during which about 58,000 participants died. After adjustment for smoking and other factors, consumption of four or more cups of coffee a day was associated with an 18% lower risk of mortality. Importantly, no harmful associations with coffee intake were identified (S.-Y. Park et al., 2017).

Cardiovascular Disease
Many studies have investigated the impact of drinking coffee and tea on cardiovascular disease. Acute ingestion of caffeinated beverages causes a short-term increase in blood pressure, which does not persist. Coffee consumption is consistently associated with decreased risk of mortality from cardiovascular causes, including following a myocardial infarction, with the **greatest risk reduction noted between three and five cups of brewed coffee a day**.

Multiple observational studies have shown that coffee consumption is consistently associated with a lower risk of mortality from cardiovascular diseases. Compared with nondrinkers, those who drank three cups a day had risks reduced by 19% for mortality from cardiovascular disease, 16% for mortality from coronary heart disease, and 30% for mortality from stroke (Grosso et al., 2016). Increased consumption beyond three cups did not increase risk of disease, but a beneficial effect was less pronounced. In another meta-analysis, coffee consumption was nonlinearly associated with a lower risk of incident cardiovascular disease, coronary heart disease, and stroke with the largest benefits at consumption of three to five cups a day (Ding et al., 2014). Additionally, coffee consumption after myocardial infarction is associated with a lower risk of mortality (Brown et al., 2016). Thus, coffee consumption decreases risk of cardiovascular disease and mortality in a prospective fashion as well as moderates risk of death following cardiovascular insult.

Consumption of coffee, however, is associated with unfavorable changes to the lipid profile. A meta-analysis of studies conducted in western countries showed coffee ingestion aligned with **increases in total and LDL cholesterol and triglycerides and lower HDL**. These lipid changes are more prominent in patients with hyperlipidemia and were **mitigated by drinking filtered coffee** compared to unfiltered coffee. **Decaffeinated coffee is not associated with negative effects on lipid profiles** (Cai et al., 2012).

Early studies into caffeine metabolism and health effects indicated that genetic polymorphisms of the CYP1A2 gene, which account for 95% of the metabolism of caffeine may be responsible for differences in studies regarding risk of hypertension and cardiovascular disease due to ingestion of caffeine (Cornelis et al., 2006; Palatini et al., 2009). However, more recent and large investigations have not shown an association between CYP1A2 genotype, genetic caffeine metabolism and coffee intake and risk of CVD (Zhou & Hyppönen, 2019). Additionally, per data from the very large U.K. Biobank cohort observational study with over 500,000 participants, coffee drinking was associated inversely with all-cause mortality, including in those drinking at least eight cups per day, in both slow and fast metabolizers of caffeine, and in consumers of ground, instant, and decaffeinated coffee (Loftfield et al., 2018).

Diabetes

Coffee and tea consumption is associated with lower risk of diabetes mellitus and metabolic syndrome. Some of this effect is likely due to caffeine, but the benefits persist even with ingestion of noncaffeinated coffee and Camellia sinensis tea. Coffee consumption is consistently associated with lower risk of diabetes mellitus. As reported in a meta-analysis of over 45,000 people, habitual coffee drinkers have a lower risk of developing type 2 diabetes. In this analysis, people with type 2 diabetes were followed for up to 20 years, increasing cups of coffee was associated with a lower risk of developing diabetes, compared to no coffee. The decreased risk ranged from 8% with one cup a day to 33% for six cups a day. While caffeinated coffee showed slightly greater benefit than decaffeinated coffee, there was still a positive impact of drinking decaffeinated coffee (Ding et al., 2014). In another study, a meta-analysis of prospective cohorts, the incidence of diabetes decreased by 12% for every two extra cups of coffee a day and 14% for every 200 mg/ day increase in caffeine — up to 700 mg a day (Jiang et al., 2014).

Coffee and tea may also have a beneficial effect when used as beverages in substitution for drinking sugar sweetened beverages (SSB). Data from EPIC-InterAct revealed that substituting coffee or tea for SSB by 250 g/day was associated with a 21% to 22% lower incidence of type 2 diabetes (Imamura et al., 2019).

As of today, there is mounting evidence of a reduced risk of developing type 2 diabetes by regular coffee drinkers of three to four cups a day. The effects may be due to the presence of chlorogenic acids (R. M. M. Santos & Lima, 2016). Further studies into causality and biologic basis are needed because the mechanisms of this association of coffee and tea and decreased risk of diabetes are unclear. A systematic review and meta-analysis of the effect of coffee and tea on glucose metabolism did not show a reduction in fasting blood glucose with ingestion of caffeinated or decaffeinated coffee or black tea (Kondo et al., 2018).

Metabolic Syndrome

Coffee and tea consumption are associated with a lower likelihood of having metabolic syndrome (MetS), but further research is needed. In a meta-analysis of studies on coffee and MetS, high coffee consumption versus low coffee consumption was associated with a 9% lower risk of MetS (PMID: 26431818). Additionally, pooled analysis of six studies exploring the association between tea consumption and MetS resulted in decreased odds of MetS for individuals consuming more tea (PMID: 27060021).

Cancer

There is some evidence for a beneficial effect of coffee on lowering the risk of specific cancers. However, drinking tea that is very hot may increase the risk of esophageal and stomach cancer, as seen in Asian cohorts. A meta-analysis of 40 cohort studies showed a lower incidence of cancer in high versus low coffee consumers, any versus no consumption, and one extra cup a day (X. Yu et al., 2011). Increased coffee consumption was associated with a lower risk of specific cancers including prostate cancer, endometrial cancer, melanoma, oral cancer, leukemia, non-melanoma skin cancer and liver cancer. For prostate, endometrial, melanoma, and liver cancer the benefit is significant in a linear dose-response. Studies are inconclusive for prevention of colorectal carcinoma, but coffee ingestion is linked to lower mortality in patients with colorectal cancer (Bravi et al., 2017; Caini et al., 2017; Lafranconi et al., 2017; H. Liu et al., 2015; A. Wang et al., 2016; Yew et al., 2016; X. Yu et al., 2011). Coffee consumption and effects on lung cancer have been mixed. Further studies on coffee ingestion and risk of lung cancer in nonsmokers are necessary to identify risk versus benefit.

Gastro-Intestinal and the Microbiome

Patients are frequently advised to eliminate coffee, tea, and soda to reduce symptoms of gastroesophageal reflux (GER) such as heartburn. Data from the prospective Nurses' Health Study II supports this recommendation, as intake of coffee, tea, or soda was associated with an increased risk of GER symptoms, which corresponded to caffeine intake. Drinking water instead of coffee, tea, or soda reduced the risk of GER symptoms (Mehta et al., 2020).

Coffee and tea may promote a well-balanced gut microbiome, with impact on many diseases. The gut microbiome has received considerable scientific attention recently. The gut microbiota works in unison with the host and can promote health or initiate disease depending upon the composition. Dysbiosis is one factor now known to be involved in the etiology of inflammatory diseases and infections. A well-balanced gut microbiota composition is highly relevant to an individual's health status and well-being, helping to prevent and manage chronic diseases.

Nonalcoholic Fatty Liver Disease

Coffee consumption is inversely associated with the risk of nonalcoholic fatty liver disease (NAFLD). Studies in mice have indicated this may be due to coffee reducing hepatic fat deposition possibly through increased fat oxidation in the liver, increasing cholesterol intestinal efflux, reducing lipid digestion and increasing gut barrier function through a restoration of tight junction proteins in the duodenum and colon (Vitaglione et al., 2019). Patients with NAFLD who drink coffee regularly have a decreased risk of liver fibrosis (Chen et al., 2019; Wijarnpreecha et al., 2017). Whether consumption of coffee can be considered a preventative measure against NAFLD and fibrosis needs further investigations.

Neuropsychiatric Disease

Caffeine has prominent effects on the neuropsychiatric system both acutely and chronically and may have a positive effect long term on decreasing depression, suicide, and Parkinson's disease symptomatology (Rodak et al., 2021). Caffeine is a psychostimulant, and its main effects are correlated to actions on the neuroendocrine control systems. Caffeine's psychological effects are responsible for its widespread use, as it provides energy and improves cognitive skills. These effects are a direct result of the caffeine-induced chemical activation of different neuronal pathways through alterations in neurotransmitters' release.

Depression

A reduced risk of depression has been reported in several meta-analyses of observational studies evaluating moderate coffee intake versus minimal to no coffee ingestion (Guo et al., 2014; L. Wang et al., 2016). A decreased risk of suicide has also been associated with increased intake of coffee, with a 45% to 55% reduction, which is not apparent in patients who drink decaffeinated coffee, suggesting this decreased risk is due to caffeine, and not the plant contents (Lucas et al., 2014).

Neurodegenerative Diseases

Multiple epidemiologic studies show a decreased risk of development of Parkinson's disease with drinking caffeinated coffee, especially among men (Ascherio et al., 2001; Costa et al., 2010; Sääksjärvi et al., 2014). This may be due to caffeine effects on the brain by blocking adenosine receptors, in particular the A2A subtype. Blocking these receptors can improve slow movement and rigidity seen in patients with Parkinson's disease.

Initial studies reported a significantly decreased risk of Alzheimer's disease in individuals who drank three to five cups of coffee during midlife; however, three subsequent systematic reviews were inconclusive regarding coffee's effect on Alzheimer's disease (Carman et al., 2014; Eskelinen & Kivipelto, 2010; Panza et al., 2015; C. Santos et al., 2010).

THE RISKS OF CONSUMING COFFEE

The risks associated with ingestion of caffeinated coffee and tea in sensitive individuals include increased jitteriness, anxiety, palpitations and insomnia. An elevation in blood pressure can be seen with ingestion of greater than 400 mg caffeine in a day. The impact of coffee and caffeine on blood pressure is transient — hours post ingestion — and studies on longer term ingestion have not shown an association with chronic consumption and hypertension (Mesas et al., 2011).

Unfiltered coffee, such as French press and Turkish coffees, contains **diterpenes, substances that can elevate LDL cholesterol and triglycerides**. Espresso coffee contains moderate amounts of diterpenes. Filtered coffee — drip-brewed coffee — and instant coffee contains almost no diterpenes as the filtering and processing of these coffee types removes the diterpenes and thus are not associated with these negative lipid alterations.

Caffeine passes across the placenta. Current recommendations limit caffeine intake **to less than 200 mg/day during pregnancy** due to reports of preterm labor and small for gestational age associated with increased daily doses of caffeine (Kobayashi et al., 2019; Okubo et al., 2015; Peacock et al., 2018).

Clinical Recommendations
1. There are no specific recommendations for drinking coffee but rather, risks and benefits of consuming coffee are available.

Clinical Competencies
1. Discuss the benefits of drinking coffee.
2. Discuss the risks of drinking coffee.

Shopping/Storing/Safety Competencies
1. Grind coffee from beans.
2. Identify the amount of sugar, calories, and fat in store bought coffee.

Cooking/Preparing/Serving Competencies
1. Use a coffee filter.
2. Summarize various coffee preparation techniques and the effect each has on caffeine levels and/or flavor.
3. Develop flavor without using — or minimal usage of — sugar and fat.

AT THE STORE

Many times, a cup of coffee contains a heaping spoonful of sugar and milk, and is accompanied by a delicious pastry. Adding sugar and whole milk turns a healthful beverage into one that does not promote health. There is a big difference in a plain cup of coffee and many commercially available options. So, before selecting a coffee, read and review the nutrition information for each beverage, as many have as much sugar as a decadent dessert. For example, a grande Starbucks Caramel Brulée Frappuccino® contains 430 calories with 120 from fat (14 grams total, 9 grams saturated) 72 grams of total carbohydrates, of which 62 are sugars, that is two days' worth of added sugar!

You can find healthy alternatives if you look hard enough. Click on the following to find nutrition information on various coffees:
- Starbucks (https://www.starbucks.com/menu)
- Dunkin Donuts (https://www.dunkindonuts.com/content/dam/dd/pdf/nutrition.pdf)
- Peets (https://www.peets.com/pages/menu)

IN THE KITCHEN

It takes a lot to turn the coffee cherry into your morning cup of salvation. The hearty coffee shrub can survive in a variety of environments, but primarily grows best in the tropics. There are many varieties of coffee and flavor will vary based on the cultivar, where it was grown, how it was processed and how it was dried and roasted. Just as grapes for wines will have different flavor profiles and grow better in different conditions, so do coffee varieties. The plant flowers and fruits three times a year and the cherries are picked, often by hand, once they ripen.

The raw fruit is processed to remove the cherry pulp from the seed, most commonly by either wet processing or dry processing – also known as "natural coffee." Once the bean has been completely separated from the fruit, it is cleaned and sorted according to density, size, and color and then graded. The beans are then roasted, generally into three categories: light roast, medium roast, and dark roast. Light roast coffees tend to yield more acidity or sourness. Medium roast coffees may have roast flavors with a little

bitterness. Dark roast coffees will have almost exclusively generic flavors with little of the coffee bean's own flavor.

Many factors will alter the levels of caffeine, polyphenols, and diterpenes — use a filter to remove these as they raise levels of LDL present in your cup of coffee. The beans you choose play a role in the caffeine level as high altitude beans contain less caffeine and more polyphenols. After that, grind size has a significant impact, as smaller grinds will result in greater extraction and thus higher caffeine content. Different brewing techniques require different grind sizes. Water temperature is also a factor, and higher brew temperatures have higher extractions. Finally, the brewing style also determines how much caffeine you're getting. Immersion techniques and long contact with grounds will increase the extraction of caffeine as well.

Highest to lowest caffeine, assuming same coffee and amounts:

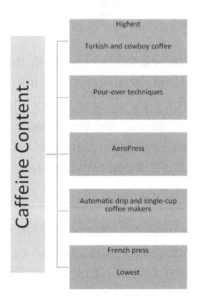

Brew your best cup at home:
- Use freshly roasted coffee beans. Coffee is ideally used within three to four weeks of roasting.
- Grind whole beans just prior to brewing. Whole beans produce a more flavorful coffee as the whole beans hold in the aromatic compounds better than pre-ground coffee, which will become stale with exposure to oxygen and moisture. Grind to a uniform particle size.
- Brew with water at a temperature between 195°F/91°C and 205°F/96°C.

Adding flavor **without** sugar and fat:
- Use skim milk instead of whole milk.
- Use a dairy-free alternative like almond milk or soy milk.
- Add flavors like vanilla extract, ginger powder, nutmeg or pure powdered cinnamon.
- Add 100% unsweetened cocoa powder.

On The Tongue

Caffeine decreases the taste of sweet, so watch the amount of sugar added to coffee. Add other flavors to make up for the reduced perception of sweet – hazelnut or other flavors for example (Choo et al., 2017).

SUMMARY

Consuming moderate (three to five cups) to high amounts (six to 10 cups) of coffee or tea daily may lower the risk of several disease conditions as enumerated previously. Decaffeinated coffee is a good option if one is sensitive to caffeine and it may offer similar health benefits as caffeinated coffee for some health concerns including overall mortality, cardiovascular disease, and diabetes. It is best to keep caffeine levels to no more than 400 mg a day (200 mg a day when pregnant). Use a filter as it will prevent diterpenes from raising levels of LDL cholesterol and triglycerides. While the classic "cup of joe" can be a healthful choice, be cautious when choosing a commercially prepared beverage as you may ingest more calories, fat, and sugar than expected.

TEA

The history of tea dates back to ancient China, almost 5,000 years ago. According to legend, in 2,732 BC Emperor Shen Nung discovered tea when leaves from a wild tree blew into his pot of boiling water. He was immediately interested in the pleasant scent of the resulting brew, and drank some. Legend says the emperor described a warm feeling as he drank the intriguing brew, as if the liquid was invigorating every part of his body.

Up until the 17th century, all Chinese tea was green tea; however, Chinese growers found they could ferment the tea leaves creating black tea and this preservation allowed for long distance transport and economic benefit. Tea spread to China's neighbors, Japan, and Tibet, by the ninth century; but was only exported to Europe by the Portuguese and Dutch in 1610. Through history and the spread of tea into different countries, several special tea cultures have developed. Several notable tea cultures and ceremonies include those of China, Japan, and Great Britain.

Tea is the simple preparation of pouring hot water over the cured leaves of the Camellia sinensis plant. All tea, green, black, white, oolong, puerh and yellow tea, come from the same plant, the **Camellia sinensis**. The flavor of tea varies by where the tea leaves are harvested and how they are grown and processed. Black tea is the most popular worldwide, followed by green, oolong, and white tea. The various types are made possible from the methods used to cultivate and process these leaves. Black tea develops when green tea leaves are oxidized before drying.

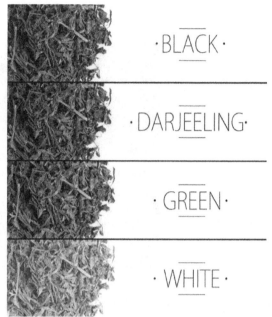

·BLACK·

·DARJEELING·

·GREEN·

·WHITE·

White: White tea is essentially non-oxidized and it is the least processed. The leaves are simply allowed to wither and dry in a carefully controlled environment, which results in the most delicate tasting tea.

Green: In processing, green tea is first steamed to halt the oxidation process and the tea leaves are not allowed to oxidize after rolling, which is why they remain light in color and flavor.

Oolong: Oolong is semi-oxidized, and falls between minimally oxidized green tea and more highly oxidized black tea.

Black: Black tea is fully oxidized, then dried, producing a dark color and rich flavor.

Darjeeling tea is a designated tea, with the name limited to teas grown in the foothills of the Himalayan Mountains in the Darjeeling district of West Bengal, India. The high altitude, soil, and climate of the Darjeeling plantations contribute towards the unique and delicate taste of this tea. Darjeeling is often regarded by connoisseurs as one of the finest teas. It is most commonly processed as a black tea, but it may also be processed into green, white, or oolong tea. When properly brewed, it yields a thin-bodied, light-colored infusion with a floral aroma. The flavor can include a tinge of astringent tannic characteristics and a musky spiciness.

HOW MUCH CAFFEINE?
in a cup of your drink (in mg)

150	135	110	64
brewed coffee	filter coffee	instant coffee	espresso
47	36	24	8
black tea	green tea	white tea	decaf coffee

The Benefits and Risks of Tea (Camellia Sinensis) Consumption

Overall Mortality

Regarding tea, observational research has found that tea consumption of two to three cups daily is associated with a reduced risk of premature death, heart disease, stroke and type 2 diabetes mellitus (Yi et al., 2019).

Cardiovascular Disease

Tea consumption, especially of less processed teas, such as green tea and oolong tea, is associated with lower blood pressure, lower risk of stroke, and decreased mortality from cardiovascular disease. A meta-analyses found an association between regular consumption of black tea and green tea and a decrease in blood pressure. Studies of tea in Japanese men and women have shown associations with green tea and oolong tea consumption and lower risk of death from cardiovascular disease as well as a reduced risk of stroke (Kokubo et al., 2013; Mineharu et al., 2011).

Additionally, tea flavonoids may help to keep the lining of blood vessels smooth and elastic. In a study of green and oolong tea consumption, regular consumption for one year reduced the risk of developing hypertension (Y.-C. Yang et al., 2004). Long-term regular consumption of black tea has been shown to lower blood pressure in some studies, but not in others. Several meta-analyses have attempted to clarify the effect of tea on blood pressure. These reports indicate that regular consumption of black tea and green tea are associated with a decrease in blood pressure, with more prominent effect by green tea (Greyling et al., 2014; G. Liu et al., 2014).

Diabetes

Tea ingestion is associated with decreased risk of diabetes although the data is weak. Tea contains many bioactive components, especially polyphenols, such as catechins, flavonols, theaflavins and thearubigins, which have the potential to decrease the risk of diabetes mellitus and its complications (Ramadan et al., 2009). A large meta-analysis concluded that most epidemiological studies show an inverse relationship between tea ingestion and diabetes incidence; however studies have also shown a lack of association or only an association in patients who also lost weight (Meng et al., 2019). Further studies are needed to enrich related evidence, especially with regard to types of tea. Please refer to the coffee section for studies that focused on the contribution of caffeine in tea to the anti-diabetic effects.

Cancer

There is a possible increased risk of esophageal and stomach cancers from drinking tea that is too hot — 130°F/54°C to 140°F/60°C — as reported in several studies (Loomis et al., 2016; Yi et al., 2019). Interest has been expressed in the potential antineoplastic effect of tea due to catechin antioxidant and antiproliferative effects. However, a meta-analysis of prospective studies summarizing evidence of the association between tea consumption and the risk of breast, colorectal, liver, prostate and stomach cancer did not show a protective role of tea in five major cancers. In fact, subgroup analysis showed that an increase in consumption of three cups of black tea per day was a significant risk factor for breast cancer (RR, 1.18; 95% CI, 1.05-1.32) (F. Yu et al., 2014).

Gastro-Intestinal and the Microbiome

Tea and coffee ingestion have been associated with changes in the gut microbiome. Chlorogenic acid increases diversity of gut microbiota, which may improve overall metabolism in the body (Bhandarkar et al., 2019). Green tea appears to be linked to improved gut microbiota profiles; up to four to five cups of green tea daily is associated with improved colonic bacterial profiles, including increased Bifidobacteria. Teas could benefit gut health, particularly amongst those with dysbiosis triggered by obesity or high-fat diets, mainly by mediating gut microbiota profiles (Y.-C. Liu et al., 2020).

Green Tea

Green tea is one of the most popular drinks in the world and has been studied for its health-promoting properties in various diseases such as cancer, obesity, diabetes, cardiovascular disease and neurodegenerative diseases. Many of the biological effects of green tea are believed to be mediated by its polyphenol catechins and epigallocatechin-3-gallate (EGCG), which represents 10% to 15% of total catechins (Ohishi et al., 2016).

While beneficial effects of green tea have been shown in animal models of cancer, a review of cancer prevention in humans by green tea ingestion was inconclusive, indicating that more rigorous human studies are needed (C. S. Yang et al., 2009). Green tea catechins possess marked inflammation-modulatory activity and in vitro laboratory studies report antioxidant effects and decrease induction of pro-inflammatory cytokines, including TNF-alpha, IL-1beta, and IL-6 (Ohishi et al., 2016). This decrease inflammation is associated with decreased disease severity in animal models of multiple sclerosis and rheumatoid arthritis. Green tea consumption is also reported to reduce the risk of coronary artery disease and cardiac events. Catechins exert vascular protective effects through multiple mechanisms, including antioxidative, anti-hypertensive, anti-inflammatory, anti-proliferative, anti-thrombogenic and lipid lowering effects (Inami et al., 2007; Shenouda & Vita, 2007; Stangl et al., 2006).

Herbal Tea/Tisanes

Herbal teas are not made from the Camellia plant but from dried herbs, spices, flowers, fruit, seeds, roots or leaves of other plants; they do not typically contain caffeine as do traditional teas and should be called tisanes.

There are many popularly reported benefits from the ingestion of herbal teas, but despite a level of global interest in the potential effects of these tisanes, there is a paucity of clinical and observational quality studies. A thorough review, published in 2019, found only 21 research publications that met exclusion criteria for evaluation (Poswal et al., 2019). Despite many claims of anti-infective effects of herbal teas, there is only one clinical study that has investigated herbal teas for the treatment of infection. It was a small placebo controlled study on ingestion of echinacea tea for two weeks in 95 people with early cold and flu symptoms. Ingestion of echinacea tea was associated with decreased symptoms of cold and flu (Lindenmuth & Lindenmuth, 2000).

Chamomile Tea

Chamomile tea, brewed from the flower of the chamomile plant, has been used as a traditional medicine for thousands of years to calm anxiety and settle stomachs. Unfortunately, scientific studies are generally lacking to support these claims.

Chamomile has been shown to have potential positive impact on diabetes mellitus control and premenstrual symptoms. A single-blind randomized controlled clinical trial with three times daily post-prandial consumption of chamomile tea for eight weeks showed positive effect in type 2 diabetics with significant decreased concentration of HgA1c, HOMA-IR, serum insulin and blood glucose (Rafraf et al., 2015). Additionally, a small study from Iran reported chamomile tea as an effective therapy in relieving the pain originated from primary dysmenorrhea within one month of starting intervention (MIAR, 2021). A review article on the effect of chamomile on premenstrual syndrome (PMS) saw a potential effect of chamomile on decreasing symptoms of PMS; however, only one of their included studies used chamomile tea, the majority of studies used an extract or capsule, so this cannot be extrapolated to chamomile tea ingestion (Khalesi et al., 2019).

Mint Tea

Peppermint (Mentha piperita L.) is one of the most widely consumed single ingredient herbal teas, or tisanes. Peppermint tea, brewed from the plant leaves, is used in traditional medicine. Unfortunately, human studies of peppermint leaf are limited. Observational studies have indicated that peppermint oil may be effective as an antispasmodic in irritable bowel syndrome (Ruepert et al., 2011). Additionally, spearmint tea may be helpful for women with polycystic ovary syndrome. In two small studies, ingestion of mint tea two times a day significantly improved hormone levels in patients with polycystic ovary syndrome with decrease in testosterone, elevated FHS and LH (Akdoğan et al., 2007; P. Grant, 2010).

Hibiscus Tea

There are a variety of types of hibiscus used for tea, but the most common is the Hibiscus sabdariffa L. species. These flowers are deep red in color. Some people also use Hibiscus rosa sinensis, which is what many people think of when they hear "hibiscus," a broad-petaled flower that comes in a range of colors. Traditional hibiscus tea is made from dried parts of the hibiscus plant, most often the calyx, or the protective layer around the actual flower part of the plant.

Hibiscus tea is consistently effective in studies on blood pressure, where it has a positive impact on lowering blood pressure in prehypertensive and mildly hypertensive adult as well as in patients with type 2 diabetes (McKay et al., 2010; Mozaffari-Khosravi et al., 2013). There are numerous claims for hibiscus lowering blood pressure, improving cholesterol and triglycerides, antidepressant effects and combating obesity; however none of these claims have been substantiated with studies of hibiscus tea.

Yerba Mate

Yerba mate is an herbal tea made from the leaves and twigs of the Ilex paraguariensis plant. The leaves are typically dried over a fire, then steeped in hot water to make the tea.

Yerba mate contains caffeine and polyphenols. The presence of caffeine, at a level less than a standard cup of coffee, but more than a cup of tea, may contribute to its potential health effects.

A study on the effect of yerba mate tea infusion on lipid profiles revealed improvement in lipid parameters in both normolipidemic and dyslipidemic subjects, and provided an additional LDL-cholesterol reduction in hypercholesterolemic subjects on statin treatment (de Morais et al., 2009).

Risks of Yerba Mate

Studies show that drinking large amounts of yerba mate for a long time may increase the risk of upper respiratory and digestive tract cancers. Mate contains polycyclic aromatic hydrocarbons, which are carcinogens found in tobacco smoke and grilled meat; additionally, mate is often consumed at very hot temperatures, a known risk factor for esophageal and stomach cancer (Dasanayake et al., 2010).

Fennel Tea

The Latin name for fennel is foeniculum vulgare. The ancient Greeks and Romans thought fennel could bring strength and fortitude and lead to longer life. The benefits of fennel tea are very similar to those derived from fennel seeds. Fennel tea is used as a digestive, lactagogue, and diuretic and in treating respiratory and gastrointestinal disorders. Few controlled studies have been done with tea, but a study of infantile colic demonstrated that a tea of Foeniculum vulgare could significantly decrease the crying time when compared with usual care (Arikan et al., 2008), and a systematic review found evidence that fennel was effective in treating children with infantile colic (Anheyer et al., 2017).

Risks of Fennel Tea

Women using fennel as a stimulant for breast milk production should be cautious. Excessive maternal use of an herbal tea containing fennel, anise, and other herbs appeared to cause toxicity in two breastfed newborns that was consistent with toxicity caused by anethole, which is found in fennel and anise. Fennel can cause allergic reactions after oral or topical use affecting the respiratory system or skin, including photosensitivity. Diarrhea and hepatomegaly occurred in a woman taking fennel, fenugreek, and goat's rue as galactagogues. Elevated liver enzymes occurred in another woman taking Mother's Milk Tea, which contains fennel.

Rooibos Tea

Rooibos tea is also known as red tea or red bush tea. It is made using leaves from a shrub called Aspalathus linearis, grown on the western coast of South Africa, where it has been consumed for centuries. Rooibos is associated with health benefits, which is thought to be due to its high levels of antioxidants, which include aspalathin and quercetin. However, studies have shown inconsistent results from rooibos tea ingestion and blood antioxidant levels compared to placebo (Breiter et al., 2011; Villaño et al., 2010). It has been reported to inhibit ACE activity, but no changes in blood pressure were associated with this inhibition (Persson et al., 2010).

Risks of Rooibos Tea

There are risks with ingestion of large quantities of rooibos tea as it may increase liver enzymes and elevate estrogen levels.

Ginger Tea

Ginger is native to Asia and is the flowering plant of the Zingiberaceae family. Ginger is closely related to turmeric. There is a long history of use of ginger in traditional and alternative medicine. Its root, or stem, adds flavor to many types of cuisine, but is also an ancient herbal remedy for a host of ailments. Initially reported to be effective for motion sickness relief, but research has shown that it is ineffective (Brainard & Gresham, 2014). There is a potential role for ginger in weight management based on a small study which found reduced feelings of hunger with ginger beverage consumption (Mansour et al., 2012).

Lemon Balm Tea

Lemon balm (Melissa officinalis) is a lemon-scented herb that comes from the same family as mint. The herb is native to Europe, North Africa, and West Asia, but it's grown around the world. It has been used for centuries to treat anxiety, sleep disorders, indigestion and wounds. Most studies have used an extract of lemon balm, and not investigated the use of a tea. Lemon balm in a beverage or yogurt was associated with improvements in mood and cognitive performance during two cross-over, placebo controlled, double blind studies (A. Scholey et al., 2014).

Risks of Lemon Balm
Lemon balm may interact with thyroid medication and HIV medications.

CLINICAL COMPETENCIES FOR TEA

Clinical Recommendations
1. There are no specific recommendations for drinking tea but rather, risks and benefits of consuming tea are available.

Clinical Competencies
1. Discuss the benefits of drinking various types of tea.
2. Discuss the risks of drinking various types of tea.

CULINARY COMPETENCIES FOR TEA

Shopping/Storing/Safety Competencies
1. Identify the amount of sugar, calories, and fat in store bought tea.
2. Explain the "use by" date.
3. List amounts of caffeine found in various teas.
4. Store tea properly.

Cooking/Preparing/Serving Competencies
1. Brew tea at the correct temperature and for the correct time.
2. Consume tea at a reasonable temperature.
3. Develop flavor without using — or minimal usage of — sugar and fat.

At the Store

There are many options when purchasing teas at the store. Much like coffee, choices are based on personal preference. The easiest approach is purchasing tea in premade tea bags. A tea bag's chief benefits are speed and ease of use: it brews fast with no added equipment. These classic tea bags are filled with tiny tea particles and dust, which can be easily over-steeped and result in a bitter tea, thus you need to be attentive when using these to create a pleasant cup of tea. Manufacturers sell pre-filled tetrahedron bags with "loose leaf" tea bags full of larger leaves and claim these shapes allow for better water circulation and brewing around the leaves, letting more flavor nuances seep into the cup. Tea aficionados will advise you to purchase your tea as loose leaf.

All tea will have expiration dates and these are true "use by" dates. Dried tea leaves that are kept dry will not spoil, and as long as they are stored away from heat, water, light and air, the flavor and phytochemical content can be maintained for up to two years.

Brewed tea has zero calories but at popular chains like Dunkin Donuts and Starbucks, certain types of tea can pack a large amount of sugar. The following are the number of calories and sugar found in tea products sold at popular stores.
   o Dunkin Donuts: Refreshers Peach (medium) – 130 calories and 29 grams of sugar (over 7 teaspoons of sugar); Frozen Chai latte – 520 calories, 83 grams of sugar (21 teaspoons of sugar!)
   o Starbucks: Brewed black tea has zero calories and sugar but a black Tea Latte (tall) has 220 calories and 24 grams of sugar (6 teaspoons).

Go online and find the store where you buy your favorite tea. Look for the nutritional information – you can find healthful options as well as options that can pack several days' worth of added sugar.
Dunkin Donuts https://www.dunkindonuts.com/content/dam/dd/pdf/nutrition.pdf
Starbucks
https://globalassets.starbucks.com/assets/94fbcc2ab1e24359850fa1870fc988bc.pdf

In The Kitchen

Tea Preparation

The classic infusion is probably the simplest — and therefore the most popular — brewing technique that works well for all teas. You can control the temperature and steeping time so the tea will be of the desired strength (see Table 5).

Step 1: Heat water to the desired temperature. Ensure the water isn't boiling as very high temperatures can easily destroy the delicate notes in tea. Place the tea leaves in an infuser.

Step 2: Pour hot water, at the appropriate temperature — see chart below — over the tea leaves until they are submerged.

Step 3: Let it steep for the recommended time. Take care not to over-steep.

Step 4: Remove the tea leaves. Pour the infusion into a cup and enjoy.

Table 5: Preparation Methods for Various Types of Tea

Tea Type	Temperature	Time in minutes
White	160 to 190°F	2 to 5
Green	160 to 180°F	1 to 3
Oolong	185 to 205°F	2 to 6
Black	200 to 212°F	3 to 5
Herbal	200 to 212°F	5 to 7

Depending on the tea, you can choose to add additional flavors, but make sure not to overpower the flavor of the tea. A dash of lemon juice or a sprig of mint are some delicious examples.

Chinese Tea Ceremony

The Chinese tea culture is the oldest tea culture in the world as it was in this very region that tea was first discovered. Traditional Chinese tea ceremonies are often held during formal occasions like Chinese weddings, but they are also done to welcome guests into one's home. As part of the ceremony, tea — traditionally oolong tea — is passed around for participants to examine and admire its appearance, aroma, and quality. It is an elaborate process that involves selection of tea leaves, brewing to perfection, appreciating the tea and consuming it in three sips. Once the tea leaves have been brewed several times, the used tea leaves are placed in a bowl and shown to guests who compliment the tea's quality, which completes the ceremony.

British Tea Culture

The British tea culture is the most prominent feature of the British society. Afternoon tea was introduced in England by Anna, the seventh Duchess of Bedford, in the year 1840. The Duchess would become hungry around four o'clock in the afternoon. The evening meal in her household was served fashionably late at eight o'clock, thus leaving a long period of time between lunch and dinner. The Duchess asked that a tray of tea, bread and butter, and cake be brought to her room during the late afternoon. This became a habit of hers and she began inviting friends to join her. This pause for tea became a fashionable social event. During the 1880s, upper-class and society women would change into long gowns, gloves, and hats for their afternoon tea which was usually served in the drawing room between four and five o'clock. Traditional afternoon tea consists of a selection of dainty sandwiches, including thinly sliced cucumber sandwiches, and scones served with clotted cream and preserves. Cakes and pastries are also served. Tea grown in India or Ceylon is poured from silver tea pots into delicate bone china cups.

Japanese Tea Ceremony

The Japanese tea ceremony, Chanoyu, Sado, or Ocha, is a highly-structured ritual centered on the preparation, service, and consumption of steaming bowls of matcha — a powdered form of green tea — together with traditional sweets to balance the tea's bitter taste. The Japanese tea culture also known as the "Way of Tea" is carried out with an objective to create a relaxed environment of communication between a host and his or her guest(s). It is based, in part, on the etiquette of serving tea, Temae, but also includes intimate connections with architecture, landscape gardening, unique utensils, paintings, flower arrangement, calligraphy, Zen Buddhism and other elements that coexist in harmony with the ceremony.

SUMMARY

Tea, a product from steeping leaves of the Camellia sinensis plant, is the second most common beverage consumed worldwide after water. There are many varieties, with different flavors, polyphenol levels, and caffeine levels. Tea may provide similar health benefits to coffee due to caffeine, or distinct health benefits due to the presence of polyphenols. Separate from true teas are tisanes, otherwise called "herbal teas." These beverages, made from other plants, are by nature caffeine-free, but contain other active compounds that may have nutritional or health impacts — beneficial and potentially toxic. Teas, of all varieties, and tisanes may be enjoyed as a regular beverage providing hydration with minimal contribution to daily calories and macronutrient intake if ingested in their simple infused form.

SECTION 3: SODA

Carbonated beverages were discovered in 1767 in Leeds, England, by chemist Joseph Priestly. He figured out how to infuse water with carbonation by hanging a bowl of water over a tub of fermenting beer. People believed that mineral water held curative properties and the discovery by Priestly allowed for wider distribution of this supposedly healing beverage.

Soda was initially marketed for its medicinal qualities. Pharmacies with the skill set and equipment to carbonate water and add syrups became the birthplace of the soda fountain. As a result, after 1840, soda counters came to be a permanent feature of pharmacies. In the early 1900s, most medications were sold over the counter and so the pharmacist would mix concoctions into the soda water to provide medical treatment, such as cocaine/caffeine for headaches, sarsaparilla for syphilis, and phosphoric acid for hypertension. Initially, the sweetness of a soda was used to help mask the bitterness of the medicinal additive.

In 1789, Jacob Schweppe began selling seltzer in Geneva where the term "soda water" was first coined. 1881 marked the first developed cola. In 1885, Dr. Pepper entered the market and shortly thereafter followed Coca-Cola. The Pure Food and Drug Act of 1906 required labeling of all food and drink products that contained narcotics. Prior to the act, very few regulations were placed on what could be added to soda — caffeine, cocaine, strychnine, cannabis, morphine, opium and heroin. Sodas were touted as a "bracer" or "pick-me-up" to advertise their health benefits associated with physical and mental stimulation. The addictive nature of these additives proved very profitable for the Soda Fountain Industry.

The founder of Coca-Cola, in searching for a cure for morphine-addicted post-Civil War soldiers, stumbled upon the wondrous properties of cocaine. Veteran and pharmacist John Stith Pemberton found that his Coca-Cola concoction — a mixture of the kola nut from Africa and cocaine from South America — greatly soothed his war wounds. The Atlanta Journal in 1886 provided the first advertisement marketing Coca-Cola as a health drink. Even though the Pure Food and Drug Act was initiated in 1906, it took Coca-Cola until 1928 to remove cocaine from all of its products on the market.

In 1942, the American Medical Association (AMA) made its first initial recommendation to limit added sugars in the diet and specifically addressed the use of sodas in the American diet. Afterwards, a transition to diet sodas occurred in 1952: a ginger-ale called No-Cal Beverage was followed by Diet Rite (1958), Tab, Fresca, Diet Pepsi, 7-Up (1970) and lastly Diet Coke (1982). Even though the AMA attempted to address health concerns related to the added sugars in soda-pop, industrialization had already occurred and the wide distribution of sodas and diet sodas was already in effect. The delivery mechanism had already simplified, from consuming a beverage at the local soda fountain, to opening a glass bottle at home, to the current self-service vending machines. The convenience and easy calories of pop-top vending machines have replaced the bottle deposits and soda fountains.

Recommendation for Added Sugar in the Diet

The major source of added sugars, defined as any sugar or syrup added in the processing of food in the American Diet, is **regular soft drinks** (R. K. Johnson et al., 2009). Consuming just one 12-ounce soda a day with eight teaspoons of added sugar, can lead to a weight gain of 12 additional pounds in a year. The current guidelines for added sugar from the American Heart Association (AHA) recommend no more than 100 calories per day or about six teaspoons of sugar for women and no more than 150 calories per day or nine teaspoons of added sugar for men (R. K. Johnson et al., 2009). The World Health Organization (WHO) recommends further reduction in free sugar to less than five teaspoons of sugar per day for an adult (Guideline, 2015). The guidance for minimizing added sugar in the diet stems from trying to decrease obesity and the additional health concerns that arise from excess weight such as diabetes, dyslipidemia, cardiovascular disease, bone health and dental caries. For more information, go to the chapter on Sugar.

Several cross-sectional studies link the use of soft drink consumption to the adverse health outcomes (Vartanian et al., 2007). Energy Intake from beverages has increased from 11.8% in 1965 to 21.0% in 2002 contributing to excess calorie intake (Duffey & Popkin, 2007). In America, the mean intake of added sugars is 22.2 teaspoons per day (R. K. Johnson et al., 2009). Median sugar for the majority of soda brands ranges from 27 to 31 grams. All age and gender groups consume more than the recommended limit of added sugar.

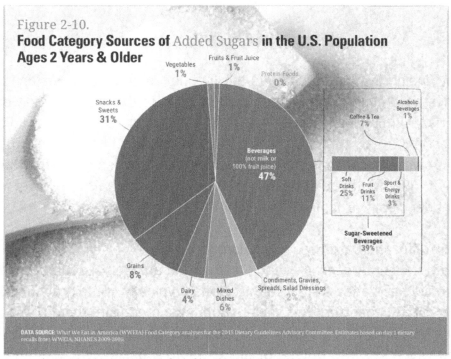

Figure 2-10.
Food Category Sources of Added Sugars **in the U.S. Population Ages 2 Years & Older**

DATA SOURCE: What We Eat in America (WWEIA) Food Category analyses for the 2015 Dietary Guidelines Advisory Committee. Estimates based on day 1 dietary recalls from WWEIA, NHANES 2009-2010.

https://health.gov/sites/default/files/2019-09/2015-2020_Dietary_Guidelines.pdf

In addition, a rise in childhood obesity is being observed. Part of the obesity epidemic is the marketing of sugar-sweetened beverages to children and, in particular, to minority Hispanic and Black populations. Youth are heavily marketed to drink regular sodas through traditional marketing tools such as TV advertisements. Now, in addition, advertisements for SSB are also prominent on social media outlets such as Facebook, Twitter, and YouTube (Popkin & Hawkes, 2016).

HEALTH RISKS OF REGULAR SODA

A consistent finding in many studies is the link between sugar sweetened beverages (SSB) and increased energy compensation, partly due to the fact that individuals do not eat less after consuming liquid calories as they would after consuming solid calories. Go to the chapter on Satiety and Satiation for more information. Further, the SSB distorts the perception of sweetness leading to food choices that are less healthful. Ultimately, the habituation of SSB in the diet leads to food choices that are lower quality and micronutrient deficient (Vartanian et al., 2007).

All-Cause Mortality and Cardiovascular Disease

Dyslipidemia is frequently seen in eating patterns that are high in added sugars, including sugar-sweetened beverages such as soda. Sodas typically contain about 65% fructose and 35% glucose. Glucose and fructose are both absorbed from the gut and transported to the liver via the portal vein. As glucose travels through the portal vein, insulin secretion is stimulated which leads to uptake of glucose into muscle, liver, and adipose tissue. Fructose on the other hand does not signal insulin release to the same degree and instead stimulates de novo lipogenesis in the liver. In obese individuals, this pathway becomes very important and provides 50% of the saturated fatty acids in the very-low-density-lipoproteins (VLDL) released from the liver (Vos et al., 2017). As the triglyceride rich VLDL leave the liver, they are modified by lipoprotein lipase, creating very small LDL particles and contributing to a more atherogenic profile. Thus, an eating pattern high in SSB worsens an individual's dyslipidemia and risk for atherosclerotic disease.

Both European and American studies suggest an increase in both all-cause mortality as well as cardiovascular disease from SSB consumption. EPIC was a population-based cohort study, with 451,743 participants, from 10 countries. Higher all-cause mortality was found in individuals consuming greater than two beverages per day of total soft drinks, sugar sweetened beverages and artificially sweetened beverages. The all-cause mortality was mirrored in death from cardiovascular disease in consumers with a higher intake (>= two beverages/day) of total soft drinks (SSB and Artificially Sweetened Beverages) (Mullee et al., 2019).

A similar study in the U.S. evaluated cause-specific mortality in the Health Professional's Follow- Up Study (HPFUS) and the Nurses' Health Study (NHS) from 1986 to 2014. Once again consumption of SSB increased all-cause mortality. Cardiovascular disease mortality specifically in the group that drank greater than two beverages per day was a health risk of 1.31. A graded dose association was seen between increased consumption and cardiovascular disease mortality. Age-adjusted pooled data between the NHS and HPFUS had an even higher health risk of 1.63 (Malik Vasanti S. et al., 2019).

Obesity

Sugar-sweetened beverages add calories to the diet that are not typically compensated for elsewhere in an individuals' intake. As a result, excessive consumption can lead to an intake of a calorie surplus, potentially leading to weight gain and obesity. Interestingly, research surrounding the influence of soda directly as a causal agent to the onset of obesity has been confounded by several variables including research that consolidates soda with sugar sweetened beverages and/or artificial sweetened beverages, dietary behavior associated with the consumption of soda/SSB, and perhaps the economic affordability of these beverages.

One meta-analysis of eleven studies by Ruanpeng et al was able to show a 1.18 fold increase in overall weight and obesity in those consuming sugar sweetened sodas and a 1.2 fold increased in waist circumference. Surprisingly, only three of the studies were conducted within the United States (Ruanpeng et al., 2017). Further research needs to be conducted to further elucidate a causal relationship between soda and obesity; however, at this time, we do have reasonable epidemiological support to show strong causation.

Diabetes

Extensive meta-analysis shows that the correlation between added sugars from sugar sweetened beverages and type 2 Diabetes (T2DM) is tightly linked (Malik et al., 2010; Popkin & Hawkes, 2016). This information has been known for years and was demonstrated in major cohorts including CARDIA (Hirahatake et al., 2019), MESA8 (Malik et al., 2010), ARIC9 (Malik et al., 2010), and the Framingham Heart Study (Dhingra et al., 2007), which took place in the early 2000s to the present. Simply **drinking one or more sodas per day increases the risk of developing metabolic syndrome, a precursor to diabetes, by 50%** (Dhingra et al., 2007). More recently, analysis of three large cohorts in the U.S. — NHS, the NHS II, and HPFUS — demonstrated that even a smaller amount, less than half serving per day, increased the risk of developing T2DM by 16%. However, if those individuals substituted water, coffee, or tea for SSB, they decreased their risk of T2DM by 10% (Drouin-Chartier et al., 2019).

Nonalcoholic Liver Disease (NAFLD)

A diet high in fructose either from table sugar or from high fructose corn syrup can lead to the development of a fatty liver. SSB has been strongly associated with NAFLD in humans and the severity of hepatic fibrosis demonstrated in a dose-dependent manner (Asgari-Taee et al., 2019). SSB contain a higher amount of fructose than fruit juices and leads to a great degree of de novo lipogenesis. Plus, chronic ingestion of fructose leads to a decreased resting energy expenditure (Jensen et al., 2018).

Dental Caries

Even in the 1500s, Queen Elizabeth proved witness to the havoc that sugar could have on dentition. Increased sugar consumption has been associated with dental caries and periodontal disease for hundreds of years. In general, the mouth contains over 700 species of microorganisms kept within a narrow temperature and close to normal pH in a balanced and diverse community bathed in salvia. The foods we eat provide nutrition to both ourselves and our oral microbiome. Ingestion of sugary foods by bacteria cause them to release acids that attack the tooth enamel as well as their "waste" leaves behind a biofilm caused "plaque." A sugary diet can cause a shift in the oral microbiome and lead to the overproduction of two disease causing microorganisms A. Actinomycetemcomitans and P. Gingivalis (Rother et al., 2018).

Fortunately, during the early 1900s, many communities started to fluoridate their water and reduce caries by 25% (Meyer & Lee, 2015). However, despite brushing and fluorination, dental caries continue to be a problem. The global burden of disease related to dental caries affects close to 2.4 billion people including 621 million children (Kassebaum et al., 2015). Multiple studies have shown decreasing the free sugar intake to less than 10% of daily energy decreases dental caries (Moynihan & Kelly, 2014).

Osteoporosis

The effect of the soda consumption on bone health in post-menopausal women was studied in the Nurses' Health Study. The cohort consisted of 73,572 women. The **risk of hip fracture was noted to increase by 14% for each serving of soda** ingested. The risk was present whether the individual drank traditional sodas or diet sodas. The mechanism of this increased risk has not been identified (Fung et al., 2014). One hypothesis is the ingestion of phosphates found in sodas can complex with the calcium in the bones leading to weakened bone structure and osteoporosis over time.

Menarche

Childhood diet is a modifiable risk factor for a myriad of disease states. The Growing Up Study is a prospective study of 16, 875 children of the Nurses' Health Study II (Carwile et al., 2015). This study looked at premenarchal girls, between the ages of nine and 14 years of age, and associations between onset of menarche and ingestion of SSB. Girls who consumed greater than 1.5 SSB per day were likely to start menarche 2.7 months earlier than the girls consuming less than two SSB weekly. These results were similar if the girls were consuming fruit drinks but not iced tea. Early age of menarche has been associated with increased risk for multiple health issues including breast cancer, uterine cancer, cardiovascular disease and major adverse cardiac events. (Apter & Vihko, 1983; J. J. Lee et al., 2019; Luijken et al., 2017).

SUMMARY

All 12-ounce regular soda beverages exceed the daily recommended amount of added sugar and are difficult to incorporate into a healthful well-rounded dietary pattern. Sodas lack satiety and a diversity of micronutrients found in other food and beverage choices. They have been associated with increased all-cause mortality, cardiovascular disease, fatty liver disease, osteoporosis, early menarche and rotten teeth. As a result of the adverse effects from sodas, it has been recommended that the beverage of choice should be water and unadulterated tea and coffee.

ARTIFICIALLY SWEETENED BEVERAGES (ASB)

As individuals are becoming more concerned about the adverse risks of SSB, many choose to change to an artificially sweetened beverage; however, is this change safer? More Healthful? About 20% of the U.S. population consumes diet drinks on a daily basis. Consumption by age is similar except for a higher consumption by adolescent females between the ages of 12 to 19 years. Typically, consumption of diet drinks is higher in the Caucasian population than black or Hispanic adults and is also higher in individuals of higher income (Fakhouri et al., 2012).

Since the 1980s, we have been aware of a paradoxical relationship between the use of ASB, appetite, and weight (Rother et al., 2018). Randomized controlled trials to **date do not support the use of artificial sweeteners for weight management and observational studies show that artificial sweeteners may be associated with increased BMI and cardiometabolic risk** (Azad et al., 2017).

A person's sense of hunger and appetite are directly related to their eating habits. Artificial sweeteners do not seem to suppress ghrelin, a satiety hormone responsible for signaling to the brain that a person is hungry (Rother et al., 2018). Thus, the use of artificial sweeteners may be associated with increased caloric intake and weight gain.

Other Health Risks

Cardiovascular Disease and Stroke
Several prospective studies have now been conducted that show an increased risk of all-cause mortality and mortality from circulatory disease related to SSB and also to ASB intake in both American and European Cohorts (Mullee et al., 2019). Malik et al evaluated 37,716 men from the Health Professional's Follow-Up Study (HPFS) (1986-2014) and 80, 647 women from the Nurses' Health Study (NHS) (1980-2014) and observed that the relationship between highest consumption of ASB and total/CVD mortality increased

among women but not men (Malik et al., 2019). The reason for this dichotomy was not clear and requires further study.

The Women's Health Initiative-Observational Study (WHI-OS) was a multi-center United Sates study across 24 states and the District of Columbia and was the largest U.S. cohort study of postmenopausal women (Mossavar-Rahmani et al., 2019). It included 81,714 women, ages 50 to 79, enrolled between 1993 and 1998 and followed for a mean of 11.9 years. Individuals consuming the highest levels of ASB, two or more per day, showed the highest risk for fatal and non-fatal stroke, ischemic stroke, CHD and for all-cause mortality. Demographics showed that high consumers of ASB were younger, aged 50 to 59 years, obese, sedentary, with higher energy intake and lower diet quality, more likely to smoke, less likely to drink alcohol and more likely to have diabetes or CVD. Further, the use of ASB was associated with BMI >30 and increased risk of ischemic stroke in black populations.

Even though many of the studies show an association between ASB and worse health outcomes, reverse causation cannot be fully ruled out. For example, an individual who is already overweight or who has health issues may have chosen to switch from SSB to ASB to improve their health. Longer studies with sufficient sample size are needed to help rule in or rule out reverse causation.

It is important to note that there are no studies that show weight loss or improved outcomes from consuming ASB.

Cancer
Mortality from all-cause cancer and cancer specific disease has been less consistent in the literature. Malik et al did not find an association between ASB intake and cancer in his 2019 study looking at data from the NHS and the HPFS, he did however, find an association between ASB and a higher risk of non-Hodgkin's lymphoma and multiple myeloma in men, and leukemia in men and women in an earlier study (Malik et al., 2019; Schernhammer et al., 2012).

Neurodegenerative Disease
The European Prospective Investigation into Cancer and Nutrition study (EPIC) showed an increased risk of Parkinson's disease mortality with consumption of more than one ASB per day, but EPIC did not see an increase in Alzheimer's disease (Mullee et al., 2019).

Gut Microbiome
The microbiome is modified by the foods that we eat. Data about whether ASB increases or decreases the risk of diabetes or weight gain has been inconclusive; however, there

are data that may help to better understand this conundrum (Suez et al., 2014). Perhaps there is a genetic predisposition to the adverse effects of ASB. Suez et al conducted a study that included 11 weeks of exposure to the artificial sweetener saccharin in mice and found functional changes to the microbiome and the development of insulin resistance. Their next step was to transplant the microbiome of mice who developed saccharin-induced insulin resistance into naive mice who then subsequently developed the same insulin-resistant pathology.

Most of the microbiome studies have been conducted in mice and unfortunately there is only one very small interventional study by Suez et al that involved seven human participants for seven days. In this small human intervention study, some individuals developed changes in microbiota in response to ASB and these individuals developed associated insulin resistance (Suez et al., 2015). There are conflicting reports on insulin responses to artificial sweeteners and differences in study design may explain some of this variation (Bonnet et al., 2018; Pepino et al., 2013). Obviously, more human studies need to be conducted; however, the mouse studies suggest possible mechanisms for developing insulin resistance from exposure to the artificial sweeteners.

On the Tongue

Can replacing SSB with ASB decrease one's preference for sweet taste knowing that artificial sweeteners can be up to several hundreds to a thousand times sweeter than sugar, or does consuming ASB set a person up to prefer sweeter tastes? Data points to the latter. Replacing SSB with unsweetened beverages decreased sweet taste preference more than replacing SSB with ASB (Ebbeling et al., 2020). In order to decrease one's baseline preference for sweet, it is best to avoid both naturally and artificially sweetened food and beverages.

At the Store

When shopping for a more healthful soda alternative, look for those that are made with fruit juice or fruit flavors and carbonated water. Compare the following alternatives to soda in Table 6 which has from zero to 21 grams of sugar and zero to 90 calories in a 12-ounce can.

Table 6: A Sample of Soda Alternatives

Product	Sweetener	Amount of Sugar in 1 can	Calories in 1 can
Izze **8.4 oz can**	Fruit juice concentrate	19 to 21 grams depending on the flavor	90 calories
La Croix **12 oz can**	Essential oil of the fruit	0 grams	0 calories
Perrier Carbonated Mineral Water **8.4 oz can**	Fruit flavors	0 grams	0 calories
Perrier and Juice Sparkling Drink **8.4 oz can**	Juice concentrate	9 grams	45 calories
Poland Spring Sparkling Natural Mineral Water **12 oz can**	Fruit flavors	0 grams	0 calories
Sparkling Polar **Seltzer-ade and Seltzers 12 oz**	Natural flavors and fruit essences	0 grams	0 calories
Spindrift **12 oz can**	Fresh fruit juice	0 to 3 grams depending on the flavor	5 to 13 calories

Vintage **Seltzer 12 oz can**	Natural flavors	0 grams	0 calories

In the Kitchen

Make homemade sodas:

Step 1: Start with a carbonated beverage, either regular store-bought seltzer or make some with an at-home soda maker.
Step 2: Add 100% juice — ¾ seltzer to ¼ juice.
Step 3: Add fruit slices or herbs and enjoy!

SUMMARY

Choosing artificial sweetened beverages can be a lifestyle modification to decrease the consumption of SSB in individuals who are trying to better control their blood sugars; however, the ultimate goal would be to limit the intake of artificial sweetened beverages to none considering their potential impact on the microbiome and their potential negative impact on cardiovascular disease. With the added sugar recommendations from the AHA and WHO, it would be most prudent to eliminate all sodas from the diet, or at the least save it for a special occasion.

SECTION 4: JUICE AND JUICING

The United States Food and Drug Administration (FDA) defines juice as "the aqueous liquid expressed or extracted from one or more fruits or vegetables, purées of the edible portions of one or more fruits or vegetables, or any concentrates of such liquid or purée." The amount of juice in a beverage must be labeled as a percentage. Most juice drinks contain between 10% and 99% juice with added sweeteners, flavors, and sometimes fortifiers such as vitamin C or calcium. The FDA mandates that these added ingredients be specified on package labeling.

Fruit juice consists mainly of water. Carbohydrates are the next most prevalent nutrient in juice and include compounds such as sucrose, fructose, glucose and sorbitol. The carbohydrate content between drinks varies based on the type of fruit and the concentration. Juice has little to no fat, and while amino acids may be present in juice, they are found in much lower amounts than carbohydrates.

JUICE INTAKE AND DIET QUALITY

According to an analysis of NHANES (National Health and Nutrition Examination Survey) data, consumption of 100% juice tends to decline significantly from early to later childhood (Drewnowski & Rehm, 2015; Maillot et al., 2019). Among American high school students from 2007 to 2015, daily juice consumption decreased from 37.4% to 21.6% (Miller et al., 2017). In adults worldwide, fruit and vegetable juices are among the least popular beverages after water, coffee, tea and alcohol (Özen et al., 2015).

Higher amounts of whole fruit consumption versus 100% fruit juice is noted in those with higher socioeconomic status, while highest juice consumption is noted among children of racial/ethnic minorities and lower-income groups (Drewnowski & Rehm, 2015). Fruit juice consumption patterns vary worldwide, and is highest among American children, and lower among South American and European children (Özen et al., 2015). The daily contribution of 100% fruit juice to total daily calories in American children increased from 242 kcal/day to 270kcal/day between 1994 and 2004, with the largest increases among children from six to 11 years of age. The greatest increases are concentrated in lower-income families and in at-home, as opposed to in-school consumption patterns (Y. C. Wang et al., 2008).

The relationship between juice consumption patterns and diet quality overall has been studied. Intake of whole fruit is generally associated with better diet quality and overall health and is routinely recommended by many expert-recommended health advisory panels. However, the extrapolation of the benefits of whole fruits to 100% fruit juice is less clear based on the available data and the need to distinguish clearly between fruit juice and whole fruit.

Lower juice consumption per the American Academy of Pediatrics recommendations has been found to be associated with higher consumption of sugar-sweetened beverages (Drewnowski & Rehm, 2015). These findings indicate a potentially concerning unintended side effect of recommending reduced fruit juice consumption in order to combat childhood obesity, as it may result in the substitution of more unhealthful beverages.

Children and adolescents consuming 100% fruit juice **tend to also consume more total fruit and have higher intakes of vitamin D.** In addition, they generally score higher on the Healthy Eating Index 2010, a composite measure of diet quality (Maillot et al., 2018). Almost sixteen percent of adults in the NHANES 2013 to 2016 study, reported being consumers of 100% fruit juice. These adults were reported to have higher diet quality, 10% higher Healthy Eating Index, HEI 2015 score, and higher intakes of energy, calcium, magnesium, potassium, vitamin C and vitamin D than those who did not consume fruit juice, along with a lower risk of being overweight/obesity (-22%), having metabolic syndrome (–27%), and lower consumption of dietary fiber (Agarwal et al., 2019); authors of this study included a representative of the Juice Products Association.

Juice Recommendations

Children

The following is the recommendation for juice intake in children.

Table 7: Juice Recommendations for Children*

Age	Daily Juice Recommendations
0 to 12 months	Juice not recommended
1 to 3 years	No more than 4 ounces of 100% juice
4 to 5 years	No more than 4 to 6 ounces of 100% juice
6 to 18 years	No more than 1 cup

*(Abrams, 2020)

The American Academy of Pediatrics states that "fruit juice offers no nutritional benefits over whole fruit for infants and children and has no essential role in healthy, balanced diets of children" (Heyman 2017).

Adults

One cup of 100% fruit juice is considered as equivalent to a serving of one cup of fruit according to the U.S. Department of Agriculture Choose My Plate guidelines (USDA). Although fruit juice can be part of healthful eating patterns, it is important to consider that fruit juice, due to the nature of the juice extraction process, will contain less dietary fiber than whole fruit, which can lead to delayed satiety, and could contribute to unintended consumption of excess calories. Therefore, **at least half of the recommended amount of fruits should come from whole fruits**. When juices are consumed, they should be **100% juice and without added sugars**. One cup of vegetable juice can count towards one cup of vegetable servings but it is best to make sure the fiber remains in the juicing process and that there is not an excess of added sodium.

There may be a role of fruit juice in achieving the "5-a-Day" recommendation for fruit and vegetables. Although there is strong evidence that consumption of fruit and vegetables is associated with a reduced rate of all-cause mortality, only a minority of the population consumes five servings a day. Reasons given for not consuming whole fruit involve practical concerns like time, cost, and inconvenience. Fruit juice may circumvent some of these barriers to whole fruit consumption and may provide a way to increase fruit intake and the vitamins and minerals it provides (Benton & Young, 2019).

Juicing Defined

From a nutritional standpoint, there are two types of juice and therefore juicers: the first kind separates the fiber from the juice and the other type leaves the fiber in with the juice. Juice without the fiber is produced using many methods: by centrifuge, mastication (cold-press), auger, hydraulic press and manual juicing. Juice that contains the fiber uses blenders in lieu of juicers. Juice which retains the fiber will always be the more nutritious option. The fiber in and of itself has many health benefits, and in addition it helps to increase satiety and lower post prandial blood glucose levels.

Versus

Extracts the juice and leaves the fiber behind   **The fiber and juice remain**

The practice of juicing has been promoted as a way to increase intake of fruit and vegetables. It has been proposed to have wide-ranging benefits such as decreased cancer risk, reduced inflammation, detoxification and weight loss, with little scientific data to support this. However, juicing may provide a way to obtain some of the health benefits of whole fruits and vegetables for those individuals who have difficulty consuming these foods in whole form, and some disease-specific considerations related to juicing are outlined below.

Health Outcomes

Interpretation of human data regarding the relationship between juice intake and health outcomes should be tempered by recognition of the observational, cross-sectional, or retrospective study design. Furthermore, the type of process used to obtain the juice is not consistently described in the literature – whether purchased, juiced at home, or otherwise – which could confound outcomes through unaccounted differences in fiber content. Determination of any potential conflicts of interest related to juice industry ties should be critically assessed in determining the validity and applicability of study findings. Furthermore, due to the complex nature of the various components of fruit juice, which includes not only carbohydrate content but a multitude of biologic compounds, minerals, and vitamins, even in the highly controlled experimental environment of animal models, the interpretation and wider applicability of such studies to humans remains challenging.

Due to the potential relationships between juice consumption and diet quality as outlined above, there is controversy regarding benefits versus harms of juice consumption. There have been calls to eliminate 100% fruit juice from children's recommended dietary intake in favor of whole fruit in an attempt to combat the childhood obesity epidemic (Wojcicki & Heyman, 2012), as the sugar content of certain fruit juices can be comparable to other non-juice sugar-sweetened beverages. Factors that steer individuals and families to choose fruit juice over whole fruit can include: increased convenience, longer shelf-life, more compact storage and lower cost when compared with fresh fruit (Benton & Young, 2019). Of note for patients who may ask, due to insufficient adequately powered large scale randomized controlled trials in humans, there is insufficient data to recommend juice as a treatment for any of the listed conditions below, and specific treatment questions should be addressed to one's health care provider.

Weight, Obesity, and Metabolic Syndrome

In a meta-analysis of pediatric data controlled for total energy intake, each daily serving increase in 100% fruit juice was associated with a 0.003 unit increase in BMI z-score over a one year period in children of all ages (Auerbach et al., 2017). When analysis was restricted to children aged one to six years, for each increment in daily juice servings, there was a 0.087 increase in BMI Z-score, equivalent to a 4% increase in BMI percentile. This effect disappeared in children aged seven to 19 years (Auerbach et al., 2017).

Iowa Adolescents aged 14 to 17 years consuming mainly 100% fruit juice were found to have lower BMI than those who preferred milk, water, sugar-free (diet) beverages and sugar sweetened beverages (Marshall et al., 2017). In an analysis of 14,196 adults participating in NHANES 1999 to 2004, adults who consumed 100% fruit juice were noted to have lower mean BMI, lower waist circumference, and lower insulin resistance when compared to non-consumers (Pereira & Fulgoni, 2010).

In a study of the association between 100% orange juice (OJ) consumption and dietary, lifestyle, and anthropometric characteristics in children and adolescents, analysis of self-reported questionnaires from 26,554 participants indicated that among both boys and girls, OJ intake was positively associated with height, height-for-age z-score (HAZ), intakes of fruits and non-starchy vegetables and physical activity. BMI, BMI z-score, and BMI-for-age percentile did not differ by OJ consumption. After adjustment for cohort, age, race, total energy intake without OJ, physical activity and screen time, prevalence of overweight and obesity was significantly lower with OJ intake in boys compared to non-consumers. This finding was not replicated in girls (Sakaki et al., 2019).

Overall, the decision regarding the benefits and risks of juice consumption with regard to weight is complicated due to the sometimes competing goals of overall calorie reduction versus improved diet quality. Additional studies that more clearly delineate patterns of juice and whole fruit consumption, in addition to overall diet quality, may be difficult to interpret due to the challenges of extracting accurate data from diet-recalls.

Cardiovascular Disease

Flavonones are antioxidant compounds found in high concentrations in citrus fruit and in lower concentration in citrus fruit juices. A meta-analysis of the cardiovascular benefits of citrus flavonones indicates beneficial effects on cerebrovascular and cardiovascular risk in cohorts as diverse as the Nurses' Health Study of 70,000 women in America, Finland, and Japan. Small but significant improvements were also noted in hypertension, dyslipidemia, abdominal obesity and metabolic syndrome (Testai & Calderone, 2017).

Polyphenols, which include the flavonoid family of compounds, are found in dark-colored fruits such as grapes, berries, pomegranates and cranberries, which are discussed in the Fruit chapter. There is concern of differences in bioavailability of these compounds between the whole fruit and the reduction in fiber needed to process whole fruit into 100% fruit juice. Overall, pomegranates, grapes, and red berries have been mildly effective at lowering blood pressure and increasing measure of vascular function, without any significant effects on lipid profiles. There is limited data based on short term – one to two month duration – studies on the benefits of the 100% juice versions of these whole fruits (Ho et al., 2020), and some of the studies had authors affiliated or employed by fruit juice companies.

Unsalted tomato juice has been found to significantly lower blood pressure and LDL cholesterol in a very small study of 94 Japanese subjects with untreated prehypertension or hypertension, regardless of sex or age (Odai et al., 2019).

A meta-analysis of 10 clinical trials indicates that there is potentially some improvement in antioxidant biomarkers and lipid profiles from juice consumption. However, there remains significant heterogeneity in study methods which will require further investigation in larger controlled trials (Crowe-White et al., 2017).

Endocrine Disorders

The main concern regarding juice consumption in patients with diabetes is related to the fructose content of fruit juice. Therefore, it is generally not recommended as part of the routine diet for patients with diabetes.

A meta-analysis of 100% fruit juice consumption, ranging from two to four weeks, in healthy subjects did not note any difference on insulin resistance estimated by HOMA-IR, fasting insulin, or fasting glucose. This analysis included a wide range of fruits and studies of short duration, making interpretation of results difficult to apply clinically (Murphy et al., 2017).

Although whole-fruit consumption is regarded as protective against T2DM, **conventionally manufactured fruit juice is associated with increased T2DM risk**, due to the amount of concentrated fruit sugars found in processed juice. "Nutrient extractor" or "juicer" style blenders have been promoted as an alternative means of juicing fruit, and many patients with diabetes may ask their health care providers about juicing as a way to improve nutrition. Unfortunately, little is known about their effect on postprandial glucose levels.

In a small study of healthy volunteers examining the effect of nutrient extraction on postprandial blood glucose response and glycemic index (GI), compared with a glucose control for both mixed fruit and a high GI fruit (mango), consumption of nutrient-extracted mixed fruit resulted in a significant lowering of the GI (32.7±8.5) compared with whole mixed fruit (66.2±8.2, P<0.05) (Redfern et al., 2017). However, there are no published studies assessing the effects of juicing in patients with diabetes, and without careful attention to the content and portion sizes of fruits or vegetables selected for juicing, specific recommendations for juicing should be individualized to patient-specific goals.

Anti-Inflammatory

Tart cherry juice has been anecdotally described as a treatment or preventive measure for gout. In a very small randomized placebo controlled crossover study (n=26) , it has been shown to reduce serum uric acid concentrations and markers of inflammation (Martin & Coles, 2019).

Gastro-Intestinal and the Microbiome

The gut microbiota is an important contributor to human health. Vegetable and fruit juices provide not only polyphenols, with anti-inflammatory effects as described above, but also oligosaccharides, fiber, and nitrate (beet juice), which may induce a prebiotic-like effect, meaning that they provide food for probiotic organisms and may help beneficial bacteria grow in the GI tract. While juice-based diets are becoming popular, there is a lack of scientific evidence of their health benefits. Some believe that changes in the intestinal microbiota induced by a juice-based diet, possibly by the prebiotic effect described above, may play an important role in their health benefits. In a study of 20 healthy adults consuming only vegetable or fruit juices for three days followed by 14 days of customary diet, there was a significant decrease in weight and body mass index. This change was maintained until day 17 with a shift towards more favorable bacterial species (Henning et al., 2017).

Bone and Teeth

A literature review including prospective cohort and randomized controlled trial (RCT) literature on 100% fruit juice and dental caries or tooth erosion in humans included eight publications representing five independent prospective cohort studies in children or adolescents, and nine publications on nine RCTs in adults (Liska et al., 2019). This review overall found no association in prospective studies of children and adolescents between juice intake and tooth erosion, and the studies assessing incidence of dental caries reported either no relationship or an inverse relationship between 100% fruit juice intake and dental caries incidence. This finding could be potentially related to the relationship between 100% fruit juice consumption and other healthful behaviors, such as increased consumption of whole fruits and other healthful dietary patterns, as outlined above.

The RCTs on tooth erosion in adults, however, showed concerning findings of decreased microhardness, increased surface enamel loss, increased erosion depth and greater enamel softening with 100% fruit juice consumption. Similarly, studies on dental caries showed increased demineralization of enamel with 100% fruit juice. Interpretation of these data were challenging due to the fact that these were small, short-term studies not reflective of real-world consumption patterns (Liska et al., 2019).

Kidney

Severe oxalate nephropathy, leading to acute renal failure, has been reported in the context of juicing oxalate-rich fruit and vegetables – celery, carrots, parsley, beets with greens, spinach, coffee and mixed nuts (Getting et al., 2013). Caution is warranted particularly in individuals with chronic kidney disease, as heavy consumption of oxalate-rich juices is a potential cause of oxalate nephropathy and acute renal failure.

CLINICAL COMPETENCIES FOR JUICE

Clinical Recommendations

1. One serving of 100% juice can count towards a serving of fruit per the USDA MyPlate guidelines and at least one half of the fruit recommendation needs to come from whole fruit (USDA).
2. The American Academy of Pediatrics has recommendations for daily limits of juice (see Table 7) (Abrams, 2020).

Clinical Competencies

1. Consume no more than the recommended amount of 100% juice per day.

CULINARY COMPETENCIES FOR JUICE

Shopping/Storing/Safety Competencies

1. Identify 100% juice
2. Prepare juice properly to avoid bacterial contamination
3. Store juice properly

Cooking/Preparing/Serving Competencies

1. Consume no more than the recommended amount of 100% juice per day
2. Contrast the difference in nutrition quality of juice made from a juice extractor versus a juicer that uses the whole fruit
3. Dilute juice when necessary

The Store

When choosing a juice to buy at the store follow these steps:

Step 1: Make sure it is 100% juice and not "juice cocktail," "juice drink," or "juice-flavored beverage" as these contain added sugar

Step 2: Read the nutrition label carefully, to better understand the nutritional content of manufactured juice — pay attention to fiber content, total sugar, and carbohydrate content and any added sugars

Step 3: If the label says "juice concentrate" make sure it also says "reconstituted" or else it will be higher in sugar than natural 100% juice

Safety

Since juice is made from raw ingredients, there is a potential for bacterial contamination in both the juice and the juicer. The U.S Food & Drug Administration (FDA) What You Need to Know About Juice Safety recommends purchasing pasteurized juice, especially for anyone who may be immune compromised. If a juice is not pasteurized it must by law have the following on the label – "WARNING: This product has not been pasteurized and therefore may contain harmful bacteria that can cause serious illness in children, the elderly, and persons with weakened immune systems." Juice sold by the glass does not need to display this warning.

Safety tips include:
- Store all juice in the refrigerator.
- Wash all fruit before consuming. Bacteria can be on the outside of fruit and when cut, the bacteria can be transferred to the inside of the fruit.
- When making your own juice wash everything: the fruit, juicer, cutting board, glass/jar and utensils.

In the Kitchen

Consider infusing water with fruit in order to enjoy the flavor of fruit without a lot of calories and sugar.

Throughout the chapters, there will be recipes for disease specific smoothies. The basic concept is: three parts vegetable to one part fruit.

1 cup liquid	Fruit fresh/frozen	Vegetables
Low fat milk	Berries	Greens -Kale
Almond or soy milk	Bananas	Collard, mustard…
(with calcium and	Pears	Carrots
vitamin D)	Apples	Broccoli
Water	Oranges etc…	Spinach etc…
Protein	**Fiber**	**Additions**
Tofu or legumes	Flax seeds	Unsweetened cocoa
Nuts or nut butter	Chia seeds	Herbs – turmeric,
Unsweetened yogurt	Wheat germ etc…	ginger
Protein powder		Omega-3 oil

Serving Juice

If someone is consuming too much juice, consider purchasing 100% fruit juice and diluting the juice at home. Most people will not notice a change. Keep diluting until they do and then back up a step. Gradually increasing the dilution of juice may slowly shift taste preferences towards favoring less sweet beverages. Replace the excess juice consumed with water and/or milk.

SUMMARY

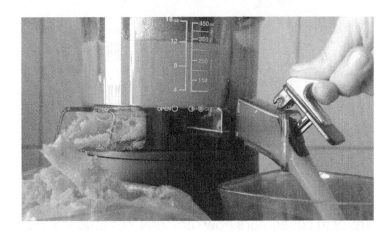

Drinking 100% juice provides essential nutrients and powerful polyphenols. One serving can count as a serving of fruit according to the USDA Choose My Plate guidelines. It is important to make sure there is plenty of fiber in the diet (see the picture above – all that glorious fiber is being thrown away along with some nutrients), be mindful of the accessibility of whole fruit, monitor total calorie intake, and make sure juice does not replace whole fruit in the diet. The reason for this is that the evidence for the healthfulness of eating whole fruit is strong but it cannot be extrapolated to drinking a juiced version of the fruit. When consuming juice make sure it is 100% juice with no added sugars or salt and keep to the daily recommendations.

SECTION 5: SPORTS DRINKS

Sports drinks have risen from humble beginnings on a football field in Florida to becoming a $6.6 billion industry, with consumers now ranging from little league players to NASCAR drivers, in less than 60 years (2019 State of the Beverage Industry: Energy Drinks Maintain Competitive Edge | 2019-07-15 | Beverage Industry, 2020; Gatorade | G Series Sports Drinks for Energy, Hydration and Recovery). Gatorade was the first sports drink and it still is the major market share holder as well as the official drink of the National Football League. It was invented in 1965 after the hospitalization of 25 Florida Gators football players for dehydration and heat exhaustion. A team of physicians at the University of Florida College of Medicine, led by Dr. Robert Cade, created Gatorade to promote optimal fluid balance and prevent dehydration by adding glucose to a salt-water solution to increase the rate at which sodium and water were absorbed by the small intestine (Sports Drinks. Give Up Loving Pop, 2017).

Although sports drinks were originally developed for the athlete, today many consumers are drinking them for other reasons – as an alternative to soda and quenching their thirst for example.

Defining Sports Drinks
Sports drinks are a water based drink, typically **composed of carbohydrates, sugar, electrolytes, and flavors**. Some may contain other nutrients, such as protein and minerals (Sports Drinks. Give Up Loving Pop, 2017). Sports drinks are designed to be consumed before, during, or after exercise to purportedly **prevent dehydration, supply carbohydrates, provide electrolytes, and enhance athletic performance**. Sports drinks have a sweet and slightly tart taste and provide a bold mouthfeel. They typically do not contain caffeine (Coombes & Hamilton, 2000; Sports Drinks. Give Up Loving Pop, 2017).

There are different types of sports drinks, all with different compositions, that are geared towards meeting the needs of different types of athletes.

Types of Sports Drinks

1. **Isotonic drinks** contain similar concentrations of salt and sugar as the human body, which help to replenish fluids and boost carbohydrates. These are appropriate for most athletes, including middle to long distance runners, and those playing team sports. Many popular sports drinks today are isotonic.

2. **Hypertonic drinks** contain a higher concentration of salt and sugar than the human body, which help to supplement carbohydrates and top off muscle glycogen stores after a workout. These drinks typically contain >10% carbohydrates and are appropriate for ultra-endurance runners as they have increased nutrient and carbohydrate needs. They can be used in combination with isotonic fluids to rehydrate if consumed during a workout however there have been more GI complaints associated with hypertonic sports drink use during exercise (Evans et al., 2009).

3. **Hypotonic drinks** contain a lower concentration of salt and sugar as the human body, which help to quickly replace fluids after a workout. These are appropriate for athletes who do not need an extra boost of carbohydrates, such as gymnasts (Coombes & Hamilton, 2000; Sports Drinks. Give Up Loving Pop, 2017).

Components of Sports Drinks

All sports drinks have the similar goal **to optimize hydration via increased rate of gastric emptying, increased intestinal absorption and increased fuel utilization** (Coombes & Hamilton, 2000).

1. **Water** is a crucial liquid to the body as it aids in thermoregulation. During exercise, humans sweat about **one to two liters per hour**, which releases heat and impacts the concentrations of electrolytes within the body ("Scientific Opinion on Dietary Reference Values for Water," 2010). The electrolytes lost in sweat – in order of greatest concentration to least – are **sodium, potassium, calcium, magnesium and chloride** (American College of Sports Medicine et al., 2007).

2. **Carbohydrates** comprise 6% to 8% of commercial sports drinks (Coombes & Hamilton, 2000). Carbohydrates are important during exercise as they can be quickly broken down to produce glucose. Glucose is readily utilized throughout the body; therefore, carbohydrates are usually considered the primary energy source validating their presence in sports drinks. The carbohydrates in sports drinks are typically monosaccharides, or the simple sugars glucose and

fructose; however, the disaccharide sucrose may also be an ingredient. Other types of carbohydrates that may appear in sports drinks include the synthetic sweeteners such as high fructose corn syrup, maltodextrins or glucose polymers.

3. **Electrolytes** enable muscles to contract efficiently, and are also released in sweat during physical activity. Electrolytes found in sports drinks are meant to replace those lost during activity as well as to increase palatability, and most often include sodium and potassium, but may additionally include calcium and/ or chloride (Coombes & Hamilton, 2000; Sports Drinks. Give Up Loving Pop, 2017). Potassium is the major ion of intracellular fluid. **Potassium** imbalances are the primary cause of muscle fatigue, as the body is unable to compensate for potassium deficiencies, whereas sodium, calcium and chloride imbalances can be corrected (Cohen, 2012). The types and amounts of electrolytes in sports drinks greatly varies between brands, with research being unable to determine if any are superior (Coombes & Hamilton, 2000).

   a. **Sodium** is the major ion of the extracellular fluid, and increased concentrations stimulate thirst, which is essential to maintain plasma osmolality. Additionally, **sodium promotes glucose absorption in the small intestine,** contributing to hydration during, and preventing dehydration after exercise (Cairns & Lindinger, 2008; Cohen, 2012). Some researchers propose that to maintain fluid balance, sodium must be ingested. However, others report that sodium supplementation is not necessary, as sodium is secreted by the pancreas into the large intestine, where water is absorbed (Cohen, 2012).

The need for electrolyte replenishment depends upon the intensity of the exercise. During moderate intensity exercise, electrolyte shifts are not large enough to cause fatigue; and at low to moderate intensity exercise, the body corrects for falling levels of sodium and potassium by increasing regional blood flow as needed (Cohen, 2012). The American College of Sports Medicine (ACSM) encourages the consumption of sports drinks during exercise in their 2007 Position Stand on Exercise and Fluid Replacement, stating "During exercise, consuming beverages containing electrolytes and carbohydrates can provide benefits over water alone under certain circumstances" (American College of Sports Medicine et al., 2007). Sports drinks may be warranted for athletes who are **exercising at a moderate- intense exercise lasting longer than 90 minutes, or for those who are exercising at lower intensities but at higher temperatures, or for those exercising in extreme temperatures** (Heneghan et al., 2012).

Research on Sports Drinks

Although almost all of the research on sports drinks has focused exclusively on athletes, they are marketed towards not only athletes but members of the general population, who do not participate in the same degree of intense physical activity. These products are also increasingly marketed to children and adolescents. The American Academy of Pediatrics reports **that the excessive intake of sports drinks substantially increases the risk for overweight or obese children** (Committee on Nutrition and the Council on Sports Medicine and Fitness, 2011). Despite their marketing claims, sports drinks are not necessary to maintain fluid balance and prevent dehydration in the average exerciser.

Additionally, there are concerns regarding the scientific research into sports drinks and hydration status. Research on sports drinks has been primarily funded by the beverage industry, and many of the academic researchers and authors have ties with these same companies, throwing much of the research into question. The studies themselves are also concerning. In a review published in the British Medical Journal in 2012, Heneghan and colleagues evaluated 106 studies, including 101 clinical trials from 1971-2012 (Heneghan et al., 2012). Heneghan and his team did this with minimal support from the beverage manufacturers who funded many of the studies, as only one company complied with their request for the details of the studies. Their review identified several problems associated with the research on sports drinks:

- o Small sample sizes (median sample size = nine), which could mean bias towards the interventions' effectiveness, and the homogeneity of the samples – only athletes, means that the results should only be applied to athletes, and cannot be generalized to the rest of the population.
- o Questionably valid results as some studies did not even measure sports related outcomes and many studies use time to exhaustion as an outcome, and how many elite athletes, or common gym-goers, exercises until exhaustion?

- o Poorly designed research – many studies were considered low quality as they did not define clear protocols or relevant outcomes, lacked blinding and had conflicting outcomes.
- o Data dredging, or the misuse of statistics, which is often used in studies where an outcome is not defined beforehand.
- o Inflated outcomes due to inappropriate use of relative measures – meaning, many studies had athletes completely fast overnight and then perform to exhaustion, which is not realistic for athletes .
- o Many studies (64%) lacked blinding which means that the participants are more likely to be biased and report false outcomes.
  - o Unrealistic pre-workout nutrition – again, having participants fast overnight or eat only low glycemic-index, low carbohydrate foods before the experiment is not the reality for athletes or non-athletes.

For this reason, there is need for more quality research to elucidate the health implications for the general exerciser, and there have not been many studies done on the impact of sports drinks to specific disease states which is another area for future research.

Weight and Obesity

Consumption of sports drinks have been **associated with weight gain and increased levels of BMI in adolescents and young adults,** especially in those who are not as active (Field et al., 2014). A 500 mL bottle of Powerade Ion4 contains 19.6 grams of sugar, Gatorade Perform contains 30 grams of sugar, and when the USDA's sugar recommendations are taken into account, these products quickly propel consumers to exceed the upper limit of 50 grams of added sugars per day. The American Academy of Pediatrics' Clinical report on sports and energy drinks states that pediatric athletes can benefit from using sports drinks, however most children do not need sports drinks, with lead co-author Dr. Holly Benjamin stating **"For most children engaging in routine physical activity, plain water is best**. Sports drinks contain extra calories that children don't need, and could contribute to obesity and tooth decay" (Committee on Nutrition and the Council on Sports Medicine and Fitness, 2011).

Children and Sports Drinks

Children and adolescents in the United States commonly consume sports drinks and not for the reason that they were originally designed – to enhance sports performance. Consumption of sports drinks rose from 2% in 1989 to 12% in 2008 in American children age six to eleven (Lasater et al., 2011). One of the main reasons for this is that sports drink manufacturers are targeting children and teenagers in their marketing campaigns (Harris et al., 2014). They are marketed as a more healthful alternative to soda and sports drink companies are using social media to engage with this age group.

Consuming sugar sweetened sports drinks:
- o Adds excess energy intake in the form of simple sugars, which can increase a child's risk for overweight and obesity (Committee on Nutrition and the Council on Sports Medicine and Fitness, 2011).
- o Can lead to poor dental health (Committee on Nutrition and the Council on Sports Medicine and Fitness, 2011; Noble et al., 2011).
- o Increases the amount of sodium in a child's diet (Committee on Nutrition and the Council on Sports Medicine and Fitness, 2011).
- o Can lead to displacing healthful nutrient consumption with sugar and salt intake (Frary et al., 2004; Keller et al., 2009).

(Boston & Ma 2019)

Per Harvard's Nutrition Source, "For the non-athlete, a sports beverage is just another sugary drink"

Other

While the data on sports drinks is limited in its scope, recommendations regarding impacts on cardiovascular disease, the endocrine system, bone and dental health can be extrapolated from data on other SSB listed earlier in the chapter.

CLINICAL COMPETENCIES FOR SPORTS DRINKS

Clinical Recommendations

1. The American College of Sports Medicine (ACSM) encourages the consumption of sports drinks during exercise under certain circumstances (American College of Sports Medicine et al., 2007)·

2. The American Academy of Pediatrics' Clinical report on sports and energy drinks states that pediatric athletes can benefit from using sports drinks, however most children do not need sports drinks (Schneider et al., 2011).

Clinical Competencies

1. Only consume sports drink if necessary due to prolonged exercise or sweating.

CULINARY COMPETENCIES FOR SPORTS DRINK

Shopping/Storing/Safety Competencies

1. Purchase a sports drink with adequate amounts of water, electrolytes and carbohydrates, and avoid those with added caffeine and other stimulants.

Cooking/Preparing/Serving Competencies

1. Make a homemade version of a sports drink (optional).

At the Store

The most important thing to look at when shopping for sports drinks is the amount of sugar, salt and other ingredients included in this water-based beverage. The Nutrition Facts label will list the amount of carbohydrates and some minerals.

Look for products with the following amounts of nutrients in an 8 oz serving (CHAMP, Uniformed Services University) :

- o Carbohydrates: 12 to 24 grams
- o Sodium: 82 to 163 milligrams
- o Potassium: 18 to 46 milligrams

In addition
- o Avoid products with added caffeine
- o Avoid products with ingredients other than minerals, vitamins and sugar

In the Kitchen

As sports drinks contain excessive amounts of added sugars, athletes should skip the commercial sports drinks, and could consider making their own rehydration drink using water, without excessive added sugars.

Recipe for a Homemade Sports Drink

Sugar and salt are two of the most essential ingredients in any sports drink as they help the body to absorb water more efficiently. To make your own isotonic sports drink, try this recipe from a researcher at the University of California, Berkeley (Make Your Own Sports Drink | Berkeley Wellness):

Combine:
- o 6 ½ cups water
- o ¼ teaspoons sea salt
- o 3 tablespoons sugar
- o The juice from 3 citrus fruits – lemon, lime or orange (one or a variety)

Make sure to stir or shake the mixture well, and keep in the refrigerator until you need to rehydrate!

SUMMARY

For many, choosing a sports drink over a soda may seem like a more healthful choice but they are not, unless of course one is exercising to such a point that they are losing electrolytes through sweat. Athletes who are exercising at a moderate to vigorous intensity for at least 90 minutes, or for a shorter period of time in a hot climate, should consume beverages containing electrolytes and carbohydrates for optimal hydration beyond that provided by water alone. Children and adolescent athletes should only consume sports drinks during periods of prolonged or intense physical activity but for most people, including ordinary exercisers, water is best.

SECTION 6: ENERGY DRINKS

Energy drinks are carbonated beverages that initially have an extremely sweet taste similar to other sugar sweetened beverages like soda or juice, but most have a bitter aftertaste resembling medicine, like cough syrup or pain medicine (Graham, 2001). The extreme sweet taste and instant jolt of energy from these drinks, which can contain a cocktail of stimulants, lure the young and the tired. How safe are they? A quick look at the FDA adverse effect database which includes death and serious health consequences allegedly caused by energy drinks among various brands leads to the conclusion that they are not benign and certainly should not be consumed by children.

A listing of the alleged side effects of RED BULL (https://www.goldbergfinnegan.com/assets/files/adverse_even_reports__red_bull.pdf)

HISTORY OF ENERGY DRINKS

The consumption of beverages to increase energy levels in America dates back to as early as 1050 A.D., when indigenous people in modern day Illinois used to boil toasted holly leaves and bark in water, creating a highly caffeinated tea-like substance, entitled "black drink." They would then ingest it as part of a ritual purification before important events and rites of passage (Crown et al., 2012). Chemical analysis of pottery remains from this time identified the three main ingredients as caffeine, theobromine, and ursolic acid, a biomarker indicating that it came from holly. Though holly is still used in some drinks in both South America and the Southern United States, the ingredients in mainstream energy drinks have evolved as have the drinks themselves.

Energy drinks are caloric beverages that contain caffeine and other presumed energy-enhancing ingredients such as plant based stimulants, amino acids, herbal extracts and vitamins (Heckman et al., 2010). The first energy drink appeared in Europe in 1927 to aid hospital patient's recovery (Lucozade) but it was not until Lipovitan D, recognized as the first real energy drink, was formulated by a pharmaceutical company in Japan in 1962 that energy drinks would start to enjoy mainstream commercialization and success which continues to grow. Dr. Enuf is a soft drink fortified with caffeine and vitamins which was developed in 1949, and distributed out of Johnson City, Tennessee. While it may not be a true energy drink, it was the United States' first hat in the ring, and is still sold in Tennessee, Virginia, and North Carolina (May 13, 2013). The first commercialized energy drink to enjoy success in America, Red Bull, was introduced in 1997 (Reissig et al., 2009).

DEFINING ENERGY DRINKS

Energy drinks fall into the category of functional beverages, which also includes sports drinks and nutraceutical drinks (Heckman et al., 2010). Energy drinks include ready-to-drink products, shots, and powdered forms. The FDA classifies them as dietary supplements or foods/beverages avoiding having to list the amounts or adverse effects of specific ingredients (Higgins & Babu, 2013).

Caffeine is the most common psychoactive ingredient found in energy drinks (Higgins et al., 2018). As previously discussed in Section 2 – Coffee and Tea – when ingested naturally from plant based beverages like tea and coffee, caffeine offers many health benefits, due to antioxidants such as caffeic acid and chlorgenic acid. These components offer metabolic and cardiovascular benefits, and contribute to the potential protective effect of coffee on some cancers (Higgins et al., 2018; Hu et al., 2018; Wolde, 2014). However, **the caffeine in energy drinks is often a synthetic alkaloid, which does not offer the same health benefits and comes with its own risks.**

Naturally occurring caffeine from plants such as guarana and yerba mate may sometimes be found as part of the "energy blends" or "proprietary blends," or herbal extracts in energy drinks. However, the amount of caffeine from these sources is not usually listed on the label and therefore the total amount of caffeine in the product is actually higher than that listed on the label (Higgins et al., 2010, 2018). Caffeine levels in energy drinks may range from 30 to 134 milligrams of caffeine per 100 milliliter. When compared to the FDA-imposed limit of 20 milligrams of caffeine per 100 milliliter of soda, this amount is obviously excessive. Additional ingredients found in energy drinks may include other herbal extracts like ginseng, gingko biloba, and amino acids (Higgins et al., 2018).

Energy drinks commonly contain amino acids, in particular, taurine. Taurine, the most abundant amino acid naturally found in the human body, is most commonly added to energy drinks and can be found in food sources such as meat and fish (Heckman et al., 2010; Timbrell et al., 1995). While taurine was previously considered nonessential, it is now recognized as conditionally essential. Taurine has important roles in the body in aiding with neuromodulation, increasing cellular membrane stability, and modulating intracellular calcium levels. Additionally, new research has shown potential effects of taurine as a hypoglycemic (Brosnan & Brosnan, 2006; Timbrell et al., 1995). Taurine may also aid in the reduction of lactic acid buildup in endurance athletes (Imagawa et al., 2009). Unfortunately, there are significant differences between synthetic and naturally occurring taurine, **and research does not show the same health benefits from consuming synthetic taurine** (Heckman et al., 2010). Synthetic taurine is the type of taurine often found in energy drinks, in very large amounts, averaging about 753 mg per eight ounce beverage (Triebel et al., 2007). Put into perspective, the average human intake of taurine from food sources varies from four to 400 mg/day (Heckman et al., 2010). There is no current research identifying a recommendation for taurine intake.

The B-vitamins are the most common vitamins found in energy drinks, specifically B_3 (niacin), B_6 (pyridoxine) and B_{12} (Heckman et al., 2010). These water soluble vitamins have essential roles in many processes in the body, such as acting as coenzymes in energy metabolism, for other vitamins or macronutrients.

Table 8: B Vitamins in Energy Drinks Compared to the RDA[*]

B Vitamin	RDA for age 9 years+	Average Amount in 250 mL of Energy Drink
B_3	12 to 16 mg/day	120%
B_6	1.0 to 1.7 mg/day	360%
B_{12}	1.8 to 2.4 µg / day[16]	120%

* (Office of Dietary Supplements - Niacin, 2020; Office of Dietary Supplements - Vitamin B6, 2020; Office of Dietary Supplements - Vitamin B12, 2020)

Some drinks, such as 5-hour ENERGY, go as high as 2,000% of the RDA for B_6 and 8,333% the RDA for B_{12} (Heckman et al., 2010). While these are water soluble vitamins, which typically have a lower risk of toxicity due to the excretion of excess amounts in the urine, there are still risks of toxicity as these amounts are well above the tolerable upper intake limit of the vitamins (Heckman et al., 2010). Similar to taurine, the health benefits from the synthetic sources of these vitamins have not been thoroughly researched and studied, and it is entirely possible to meet the needs for B vitamins from eating whole foods as part of a balanced diet.

RECOMMENDATIONS

Most of the literature supports that a moderate intake of caffeine, up to 100 mg for children and adolescents and 400 mg for adults per day, is safe for most of the population (Nawrot et al., 2003; Vercammen et al., 2019). However, energy drinks may exceed this, as there is no regulation on the amount of caffeine that can be added to these drinks (Higgins et al., 2018).

Although athletes were initially the primary consumers of energy drinks, current consumption patterns show that adults ages 18 to 34 years, with less than a high school diploma, a high school diploma, or GED along with middle aged Mexican Americans are the most common consumers (Heckman et al., 2010; Vercammen et al., 2019). Of note, men consumed more energy drinks than women in all categories (Vercammen et al., 2019). These results can guide future efforts for policy and programs towards those with a low socioeconomic status or minorities who are already at an increased risk of negative health outcomes. Additionally, manufacturers are creating more products specifically geared towards women, athletes, and health-conscious consumers as well as populations with dietary restrictions or preferences, such as diabetic, vegetarian-friendly, gluten-free and organic (2019 State of the Beverage Industry: Energy Drinks Maintain Competitive Edge | 2019-07-15 | Beverage Industry, 2020; Heckman et al., 2010).

Energy drinks are reported as being the fastest growing segment of the beverage industry since bottled water (Agriculture and Agri-Food Canada 2008). Top energy drinks brought in more than $11.6 billion in 2018. They are projected to see steady growth in the future. Conversely, energy shots brought in more than $1 billion in 2018 but are not expected to increase as much in the future (2019 State of the Beverage Industry: Energy Drinks Maintain Competitive Edge | 2019-07-15 | Beverage Industry, 2020).

Children and Energy Drinks

While energy drinks are becoming increasingly marketed towards children and adolescents to increase energy, aid in weight loss, and improve sports performance, these beverages pose potential health risks due to their caffeine content, other ingredients, and excessive calorie, carbohydrate, and sugar content (Committee on Nutrition and the Council on Sports Medicine and Fitness, 2011).

Caffeine consumed in excess can harm anyone, adults included but imagine a child with still-developing neurological and cardiovascular systems. The American Academy of Pediatrics discourages children from any caffeine consumption and encourages adolescents 12 years and older to limit caffeine consumption to no more than 100 mg/day, though clearly stating that that caffeine should not come from energy drinks (Energy Drinks | Healthy Schools | CDC, 2019). The additional stimulants and other compounds in combination with excessive caffeine can contribute to harmful health consequences such as – elevated heart rate, elevated blood pressure, reduced blood flow (and therefore oxygen and nutrients) to the heart, increased risk of arrhythmia, seizures, mood or behavioral disorders, inadequate and poor quality sleep as well as potential interaction with medications (Committee on Nutrition and the Council on Sports Medicine and Fitness, 2011; Seifert et al., 2011). The excessive calories, carbohydrate, and sugar content can all increase risk of overweight, obesity, and cardiometabolic syndrome as well as diabetes and nonalcoholic fatty liver disease (Energy Drinks | Healthy Schools | CDC, 2019).

Athletes and Energy Drinks

> The message can be summed up in the clinical report published in 2011 by the Committee on Nutrition and the Council on Sports and Medicine in Fitness titled "Sports drinks and energy drinks for children and adolescents: Are they appropriate?"– NO!

The relationship between athletes and caffeine is a long one. Caffeine has long been used by athletes, both in normal, day-to-day consumption and to benefit their performance, due to the ergogenic impact of caffeine on physical activity. Aside from its abilities to increase energy and improve concentration, caffeine enables the body to use fat for energy, rather than glycogen or stored carbohydrates, which provides more energy while producing less lactate (Spriet, 2014). Lower lactate levels are associated with increased power output and better performance. Caffeine also has been shown to possess analgesic properties, increasing its appeal especially with long distance endurance athletes (Goldstein, 2001). Newer research even identifies that caffeine ingestion of one to 6 mg/ kg can improve performance by up to 3% (Ganio et al., 2009).

Because of caffeine's impact on physical performance, the International Olympic Committee actually banned athletes with greater than 12 µg of caffeine per liter of urine from 1984 to 2004, which is about 1,000 milligrams of caffeine. This ruling was reversed in 2004, and now the World Anti-Doping Agency monitors athletes for patterns of use.

Many studies support the effect of caffeine – including both synthetic and naturally sourced caffeine – on athletic performance in endurance athletics such as running, cycling, rowing and swimming with fewer studies supporting the effect of caffeine on strength power performance (Cox et al., 2002; Doherty & Smith, 2004; Graham, 2001; Kovacs et al., 1998; McNaughton et al., 2008; Pasman et al., 1995). While the dose and timing recommendations differ from sport to sport, a review of the impact of caffeine on endurance exercise shows that as little as 200 milligrams (or < 3 mg/kg of body weight) of caffeine may provide sufficient ergogenic effects and increase athletic performance, while minimizing negative side effects and health consequences associated with higher caffeine intake. Much of the research done has been on the impact of high caffeine intake (5 to 13 mg/kg of body weight) on physical activity.

Excessive caffeine intake can cause side effects such as gastrointestinal distress, diuresis, or tremors and may even have ergolytic (impair performance) effects (Tarnopolsky, 2010)· The ACSM's evidence statement from 2007 reports that, "Caffeine consumption will not markedly alter daily urine output or hydration status" (American College of Sports Medicine et al., 2007). Further research is needed to determine the optimum dosage and timing of caffeine to minimize any unwanted health consequences. It is also important to note that many of these studies associating caffeine with positive athletic performance have small sample sizes, with a majority of the research being done on young and healthy men, measuring exercise to exhaustion which is not a realistic measure, nor does it look at caffeine across a variety of sources. The caffeine source for most research is concentrated caffeine powder, with less studies using other sources like energy drinks, gels, bars and coffee as the source of caffeine (Grgic et al., 2020).

While studies have found evidence of temporary benefits on physical performance and mental stamina from moderate consumption of energy drinks by healthy individuals it is important to remember that the amount of caffeine in energy drinks may actually exceed the amount claimed on the label, and when coupled with physical exertion may result in negative health consequences (A. B. Scholey & Kennedy, 2004; Vercammen et al., 2019). In 2013, the International Society of Sports Nutrition issued a position statement that consuming an energy drink 10 to 60 minutes prior to exercise can improve mental focus, alertness, anaerobic performance and endurance in adults; however, the other ingredients in energy drinks require more research to determine their safety and effectiveness (Campbell et al., 2013). More studies are linking regular consumption of energy drinks to negative health outcomes. Of note, most of the available literature is industry sponsored which clearly shows the need for increased awareness while evaluating information and as a direction for future research.

> Most energy drinks contain a cocktail of stimulants beyond caffeine and as such should not be viewed solely as a source of caffeine when interpreting research on caffeine's effect on exercise performance.

RISKS FROM CONSUMING ENERGY DRINKS

Weight and Obesity

Obesity is associated with energy drink consumption, as a typical can contains 54 to 62 grams of carbohydrates. These carbohydrates are almost always in the form of sucrose, high fructose corn syrup, and/or glucose which supply empty calories. They also lack nutrients found in carbohydrate containing foods like fruits, vegetables, and whole grains, while also providing no satiety like the quality carbohydrates previously listed (Higgins et al., 2010; Ibrahim & Iftikhar, 2014). The carbohydrate content of energy drinks is especially excessive when compared to the general recommendations for healthy individuals, of 30 to 75 grams of carbohydrates per meal.

One energy drink could meet or exceed the carbohydrate equivalent of two meals for a lightly active, or sedentary adult woman with a goal of weight loss. Similar to other SSB, the amount of added sugars in just one serving of some energy drinks far outweighs even the American Heart Association's guidelines of less than six teaspoons a day for women and less than nine teaspoons a day for men. The amount of added sugars in energy drinks may be two to three times the AHA's and WHO's recommendations. Additionally, added sugars in liquid form have been shown to have a positive association with body weight, when compared to added sugars found in foods (Welsh et al., 2018).

Cardiovascular Disease

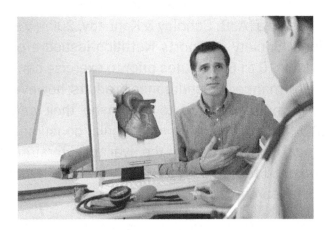

Energy drinks are most commonly responsible for acute cardiovascular adverse effects, with consumption of just one drink a day showing significant increase in blood pressure and the stress hormone norepinephrine (NE). Studied areas of cardiovascular consequences include impaired endothelial function leading to vasoconstriction, poor vascular reactivity, pro-thrombosis, pro-adhesion, pro-inflammation and growth promotion (Higgins et al., 2015; Veerasamy et al., 2015). With chronic use, these acute effects may lead to increased risk for cardiovascular dysfunction resulting in coronary artery disease.

One study noted a 74% increase in NE after energy drink consumption by healthy volunteers (Svatikova et al., 2015). Norepinephrine increases heart rate and initiates the release of stored glucose or glycogen, increasing blood flow to the muscles, as well as increasing blood pressure. About two hours after consumption of energy drinks, healthy individuals demonstrated a six to 10 mm Hg increase in systolic BP, and a three to six mm Hg increase in diastolic BP (Svatikova et al., 2015). Energy drink consumption may also result in atrial fibrillation, and ventricular arrhythmias. Reports of sudden cardiac death have been seen in cases where energy drink use coincides with exercise (Higgins et al., 2015). Studies also show that even as few as two energy drinks, can result in coronary artery spasm as well as aortic dissection and that even just one single energy drink can result in adverse effects on endothelial function (Higgins et al., 2015).

Diabetes
Acute caffeine consumption's impacts on the body include hyperinsulinemia and a 30% decline in insulin sensitivity (Shearer & Graham, 2014). In contrast, as previously discussed, in section two, caffeine consumed in the context of tea and coffee actually show reduced risk for T2DM, due to the presence of other antioxidants such as chlorgenic acid (R. M. M. Santos & Lima, 2016). Additionally, the high glycemic load of energy drinks due to excessive added sugars places an increased strain on blood glucose and insulin

levels and similar to other SSB, may increase risk of the development of T2DM (Brosnan & Brosnan, 2006; Campbell et al., 2013; Higgins et al., 2018).

Dental Erosion

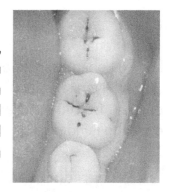

As referenced in the section on Sugar Sweetened Beverages, there is a strong and well researched association between increased sugar consumption and increased dental caries. In addition to the sugar from energy drinks contributing to dental erosion, carbonated beverages are known to cause dental erosion, and energy drinks have an especially high demineralization potential due to their low pH (Li et al., 2012).

Gastrointestinal Health

The emetic effects (causing vomiting) of caffeine are a common concern for many energy drink consumers as it may contribute to gastrointestinal upset like diarrhea (Tarnopolsky, 2010). This is especially a concern when caffeine is consumed in excess and without any other beneficial nutrients. There have been reported cases of elevated transaminases and jaundice, indicative of hepatitis, with heavy energy drink consumption (Wolk et al., 2012). These potential impacts of energy drinks upon gastrointestinal health are in contrast to the impact of an appropriate quantity of natural caffeine consumed in the context of a whole food beverage, where there are many well documented positive health associations.

Mental Health

Psychiatric health consequences associated with energy drinks includes acute psychosis, increased incidence of mind racing, restlessness, jitteriness and trouble sleeping (Higgins et al., 2010). Even an intake of 300 milligrams of caffeine can increase anxiety and tension, especially when paired with a stressful task (A. Smith, 2002). Energy drinks are often combined with alcohol and this leads to consumers indulging in higher risk-taking behaviors. For example, young adults who mix energy drinks with alcohol may consume more alcohol and experience more related harm than other drinkers who do not mix the two (McKetin et al., 2015).

Other

Acute renal failure, elevated creatinine kinase, rhabdomyalsis and metabolic acidosis have all been associated with energy drink consumption (Greene et al., 2014; Wolk et al., 2012). Hypokalemia may also result from energy drink consumption due to increased diuresis from the elevated caffeine content of the drinks, especially when consumed by one who is not accustomed to elevated caffeine intake (Ibrahim & Iftikhar, 2014).

Are energy drinks and sports drinks the same?

They are not, but many teens believe that sports drinks and energy drinks are in the same category. They typically differ in their ingredients and purpose, although combination energy + sports drinks do exist. The purpose of energy drinks is to increase energy levels and promote alertness, while the purpose of sports drinks is to maintain and promote adequate hydration, electrolyte balance, and carbohydrate stores before, during, and after physical activity.

The main ingredient in energy drinks is caffeine, though they typically contain carbohydrates in the form of sugar or sugar alternatives, as well as being fortified with additional nutrients like vitamins and minerals or herbs with stimulatory properties (Heckman et al., 2010). The main ingredients in sports drinks are water, carbohydrates, including sugar or a sugar alternative, electrolytes, including sodium, though they may contain other electrolytes, or additional nutrients like vitamins and minerals and flavors.

While there are some combination energy + sports drink products out on the market, they typically contain less caffeine than a dedicated energy drink, and these would constitute a class all their own. Consuming an energy drink in place of a sports drink during physical activity can contribute to negative health consequences such as increased risk of cardiovascular events, electrolyte imbalance, and dehydration. (*AnnualMeeting_CombinedHandouts.Pdf*, 2007; Cox et al., 2002; Ganio et al., 2009; Goldstein, 2001).

(AnnualMeeting_CombinedHandouts.Pdf, 2007; Cox et al., 2002; Ganio et al., 2009; Goldstein, 2001),

SUMMARY

There is a cocktail of stimulants in many of the energy drinks and little to no research has been done on the interactions of all of these stimulating compounds on the mind and body. After reading about the potential side effects of consuming energy drinks — from cardiovascular events to weight gain and diabetes — the utility of energy drinks should be questioned. Children are especially vulnerable to the adverse effects and they should not consume energy drinks in any amount. For adults who want a jolt of energy from caffeine, choose unsweetened coffee or tea which will offer other health benefits.

As a review of the literature shows, energy drinks have multiple adverse health outcomes associated with their short-term, and long-term consumption. The amount of caffeine found in a standard energy drink, the synthetic nature of the caffeine, as well as additional synthetic additives all contribute to these adverse health outcomes. Further research is needed to determine how these synthetic additives act in the body. For long-term energy, eat a healthful diet and practice healthful sleep habits and stress management.

SECTION 7: ALCOHOLIC BEVERAGES

Humans have enjoyed alcohol for thousands of years. Experts estimate the Chinese were making wine from rice, honey, and fruit as early as 9,000 years ago (McGovern et al., 2004). Some biologists claim humans even evolved to more readily consume alcohol, noting a common ADH_4 gene that exists solely in humans and African apes. This gene helped humans' primate ancestors create an enzyme to digest ethanol up to 40 times faster, allowing them to eat fermented fruits from forest floors (Dudley, 2004). Today, it allows humans to enjoy alcohol in all its varied forms.

Whether from fallen fruit or wine, the common active ingredient in all alcohol is yeast. Yeast is a single-celled organism that consumes sugar to produce carbon dioxide and ethanol. This process of fermentation is common to all beer, wine, and spirits, although each alcoholic beverage varies in the raw materials and processes used to make it. For example, beer involves the fermentation of malt (barley or wheat), wine uses grapes, and spirits are extremely varied, ranging from corn for whiskey to potatoes for vodka.

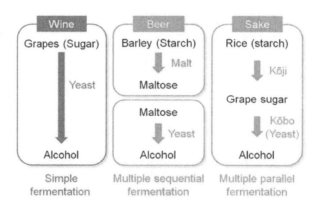

Alcohol played an integral role in early colonial American life. The early colonizers of the 1600s learned to ferment peach juice and apple cider to avoid expensive imported beer.

By 1770, the average colonial American consumed about three and a half gallons of alcohol per year (Rorabaugh, 1991). In the United States today, the 2017 National Survey on Drug Use and Health revealed that 86.3% of people ages 18 or older reported drinking alcohol at some point in their lifetime, 70.1% reported drinking in the past year, and 55.9% reported drinking in the last month (2017 National Survey on Drug Use and Health: Detailed Tables, 2017).

Despite its prevalence in American culture, the United States Dietary Guidelines do not include alcohol as a component of the USDA food patterns. The guidelines do not recommend that individuals start drinking if they do not already, and note that if alcohol is consumed, it should be done so in moderation. **Moderation is considered one drink per day for women and up to two drinks per day for men.** One alcoholic drink equivalent is 12 fluid ounces of regular beer (5% alcohol), five fluid ounces of wine (12% alcohol), or 1.5 fluid ounces of 80 proof distilled spirits (40% alcohol). This recommendation does not include certain populations such as pregnant women or those under the legal drinking age (2015–2020 Dietary Guidelines for Americans - Health.Gov, 2015).

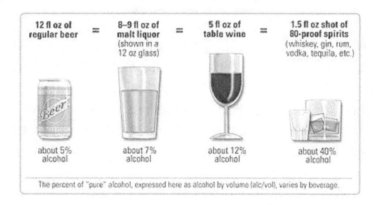

Unfortunately, alcohol consumption beyond the guidelines of moderation is not uncommon in the United States and can lead to adverse health outcomes. Per the National Institute on Alcohol Abuse and Alcoholism, heavy alcohol drinking is defined as having four or more drinks on any day or eight or more drinks per week for women and five or more drinks on any day or 15 or more drinks per week for men. Binge drinking is defined as consuming four or more drinks for women and five or more drinks for men in one sitting, typically in about two hours (Drinking Levels Defined | National Institute on Alcohol Abuse and Alcoholism (NIAAA), 2020).

Alcohol use disorder (AUD), a condition characterized by heavy or binge drinking with a preoccupation with drinking, affects 14.1 million adults ages 18 and older, accounting for 7.5% of men and 4.0% of women in this age group (2017 National Survey on Drug Use and Health Detai.Pdf). AUD also affects 1.8% of youths ages 12 to 17 years and 20% of college students ages 18 to 22 years (Blanco et al., 2008). In 2010, alcohol misuse cost the United States $249.0 billion and was the fifth leading risk factor for premature death and disability (WHO | Global Status Report on Alcohol and Health 2014). Among all liver disease-related deaths in 2015, 47% involved alcohol, and alcohol-related liver disease was the primary cause of almost one in three liver transplants in the United States (2017 National Survey on Drug Use and Health Detai.Pdf; Singal et al., 2013).

RECOMMENDATIONS

It is clear that alcohol has a wide range of impacts on the human body. For adults 21 years and older, including senior citizens 65 years or greater, the United States Dietary Guidelines' advise drinking in moderation — one drink per day for women and up to two drinks per day for men (2015–2020 Dietary Guidelines for Americans - Health.Gov, 2015). However, special populations such as pregnant women, children, and athletes are encouraged to stay completely abstinent.

Under Age 21
Individuals younger than 21 years old are advised not to drink alcohol for a variety of reasons. Firstly, the prefrontal cortex, the part of the brain responsible for decision-making and impulse control, is not fully developed until 21 to 25 years of age (Giedd et al., 1999). Conversely, the brain's reward and sensation centers develop much earlier. Adolescents who start drinking heavily continue to drink heavily into adulthood and are more likely to behave in high-risk behaviors such as sexual and criminal behaviors as a result (Richter et al., 2016). Drinking may also alter brain development, as adolescents who abuse alcohol often have smaller hippocampal volumes and impaired synaptic maturation (Crews et al., 2016; Nagel et al., 2005).

Athletes
The National Strength and Conditioning Association encourages athletes to follow the same guidelines for alcohol consumption as the general public. Athletes may want to abstain altogether as alcohol may reduce athletic performance. It does this by inhibiting

muscle protein synthesis even when adequate protein is consumed, thus reducing the efficacy of exercise as well as prolonging recovery time (Parr et al., 2014). Alcohol may also negatively impact recovery by influencing the hormones responsible for muscle growth, decreasing hydration, and reducing the quality of sleep.

Pregnant Women
The CDC encourages the complete abstinence of alcohol for pregnant women to reduce risk of fetal abnormalities. Fetal alcohol spectrum disorders (FASDS) may greatly reduce a child's quality of life and can include abnormal facial features, speech and language delays, learning disabilities and more. **There is no safe amount of alcohol to drink at any point during pregnancy.**

HEALTH RISKS

Weight and Obesity
At 7 kcals/gram, alcohol intake without compensation elsewhere in the diet can add excessive energy to an individual's daily intake, which can lead to weight gain. Experimental studies evaluating alcohol's impact on adiposity have demonstrated that consuming alcohol before a meal increases appetite and energy intake during the meal despite the preceding additional energy intake, which supports alcohol intake as a source of excess calories (Bendsen et al., 2013; Yeomans, 2010). Alcohol also inhibits fat oxidation, resulting in fat sparing that may lead to higher body fat in the long term (Yeomans et al., 2003). Lastly, individuals who binge drink may also be more likely to binge eat (Fischer & Smith, 2008).

Despite these observations, studies evaluating alcohol's impact on weight gain and obesity have varied in their results. Among most cross-sectional studies, alcohol intake is not associated with increased body mass index (BMI) in men and is either negatively or not associated with BMI in women (Sayon-Orea et al., 2011). Several studies have found that intensity of drinking, that is, drinks per occasion, is more problematic than the frequency of drinking. There is typically a slightly protective effect of frequent light drinking, less than or equal to two drinks per day, compared to binge drinking, greater than or equal to five drinks per day (French et al., 2010). Alternatively, in studies comparing binge drinking to moderation or abstention, individuals who consumed more than five drinks per occasion had greater BMIs, percentage of body fat, and waist circumference (WC) (Coulson et al., 2013). Cumulatively, these results imply a J-shaped curve between consumption and BMI, WC, and waist-to-hip-ratio (WHR) where **light drinking is negatively associated with adiposity and binge drinking is positively associated** (Arif & Rohrer, 2005). Longitudinal studies demonstrate similar results, noting no relationship of light-to-moderate alcohol consumption with weight gain but increasing weight gain with greater alcohol intake (MacInnis et al., 2014).

The discrepancy in the proposed mechanisms for alcohol's impact on adiposity at any consumption pattern and the results of cross-sectional and longitudinal studies may be due to multiple factors.

- Firstly, alcohol intake increases energy expenditure due to its high thermogenic effects, potentially neutralizing the effects of the added energy intake at light-to-moderate intake (Flechtner-Mors et al., 2004).
- Secondly, obesity is a multi-factorial condition in which studies have struggled to truly separate alcohol consumption from other confounding factors. For example:
  - Drinkers who consume beer and liquor tend to have poor dietary habits overall when compared to wine drinkers, resulting in increased adiposity.
  - Men are more likely to drink carbohydrate-rich beer, potentially explaining the link between alcohol consumption and higher BMIs in men but a lack of this relationship in women.
  - Insufficient sleep increases alcohol and overall energy consumption (Chaput et al., 2012) and individuals who engage in light-to-moderate drinking may also enjoy a lifestyle involving exercise and moderate food intake (French et al., 2010).

Cardiovascular Disease

Figure 1: Risk of Cardiovascular Disease and Alcohol Consumption

As seen in Figure 1, the amount of alcohol consumed influences the risk of cardiovascular disease. Light-to-moderate alcohol intake increases high-density lipoprotein cholesterol (HDL-C) and adiponectin. These promote lipid homeostasis, insulin sensitivity, and endothelial function. Light-to-moderate alcohol consumption may also decrease oxidative stress. These factors result in a decreased risk of heart failure (Larsson et al., 2015). Additionally, moderate alcohol consumption decreases the amount of a clot-forming protein fibrinogen, resulting in a reduction of risk for ischemic heart disease and ischemic stroke (Larsson et al., 2016).

Unfortunately, the positive effects of light-to-moderate alcohol consumption do not translate to all cardiovascular disease. For example, there is no evidence of decreased risk of hemorrhagic stroke, as opposed to ischemic stroke, with light-to-moderate drinking (Larsson et al., 2016). In addition, with light-to-moderate drinking there is increased risk for hypertensive disorders in men, although it is protective in women (Briasoulis et al., 2012). Researchers have also found that all alcohol consumption, even at moderate intakes, is a risk factor for atrial fibrillation (Larsson et al., 2014).

In addition, **alcohol consumption above light-to-moderate intake tends to lead to adverse outcomes among all cardiovascular diseases**. Suspected mechanisms include depression of heart function, cardiac conduction abnormalities, morphologic changes, increased oxidative stress, electrolyte imbalances and hypertension (Larsson et al., 2014). Alcohol consumption follows a dose-response model for most classes of cardiovascular diseases, with increasing risk at greater intakes. For example, risk for atrial fibrillation increases by 8% per drink consumed (Larsson et al., 2014). For other cardiovascular disorders, the exact degree of increased risk per drink is less clear. However, chronic heavy drinking, defined as drinking 60 grams or more of pure alcohol (five drinks for men) and 40 grams (~3.3 drinks or more for women) increases the risks of heart failure, ischemic stroke, hemorrhagic stroke and hypertension (Rehm & Roerecke, 2017).

There is an increasing amount of literature examining the cardiovascular benefits of moderate red wine consumption compared to other alcoholic beverages (Ronksley et al., 2011). Red wine, produced from grapes, contains high concentrations of polyphenolic compounds such as flavonoids, resveratrol, and polymeric tannins. These phytonutrients act as antioxidants and anti-inflammatory molecules resulting in beneficial changes in lipid homeostasis, glucose metabolism, and oxidative stress. As a result, **light-to-moderate consumption of red wine has been associated with reduced risk of cardiovascular disease mortality, coronary heart disease incidence and mortality, stroke incidence and mortality and all-cause mortality** (Castaldo et al., 2019). However, as with other alcohols, there is a decreased beneficial impact at light-to-moderate consumption with incidence and mortality of stroke and increased harm with higher intakes for all other cardiovascular outcomes.

Endocrine Disorders

Alcohol consumption affects all the organs of the endocrine system by impacting hormonal release and feedback mechanisms. While some systems benefit from light-to-moderate alcohol consumption, others are negatively impacted at any level of consumption. For example, while light-to-moderate drinking may increase insulin secretion leading to a reduced risk of developing T2DM, all alcohol consumption increases secretion of the stress hormone cortisol (Rachdaoui & Sarkar, 2013a). Long term excessive cortisol exposure can lead to several detrimental long-term effects such as weight gain and elevated blood pressure.

Of all the ways alcohol affects the endocrine system, a few scenarios are worth special consideration. Firstly, alcohol consumption at any level negatively affects bone health by decreasing estrogen in women and increasing cortisol and parathyroid hormones (Rachdaoui & Sarkar, 2013). A reduction in estrogen leads to **reduced bone modeling** while elevated levels of cortisol and parathyroid hormone increase bone breakdown and calcium leaching. Together, these hormonal changes can lead to osteoporosis. In men, heavy alcohol consumption can decrease testosterone, potentially leading to **erectile dysfunction and emotional changes**. Furthermore, while light-to-moderate alcohol consumption is protective against T2DM in some patients through enhanced peripheral insulin sensitivity (Koppes et al., 2005), heavy alcohol consumption is an independent risk factor for the development of T2DM secondary to pancreatic beta-cell dysfunction (Wei et al., 2000).

Liver Health

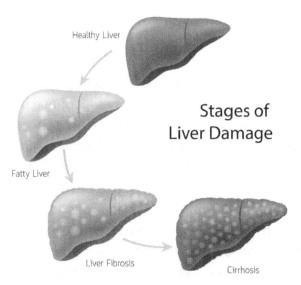

Healthy Liver

Stages of
Liver Damage

Fatty Liver

Liver Fibrosis

Cirrhosis

Alcohol's harmful impacts are most commonly noted as it relates to liver health. Liver diseases contribute markedly to the global burden of mortality and morbidity, making up 2% of all deaths globally (Lozano et al., 2012). Alcohol is a major contributing factor, as alcoholic liver disease (ALD) is a leading cause of cirrhosis, liver cancer, and acute and chronic liver failure. About 15% to 20% of alcohol abusers will develop alcohol hepatitis and/or cirrhosis after consumption of about six to eight drinks daily for several years (Savolainen et al., 1993).

While the complete pathophysiology of how alcohol causes adverse liver outcomes is not fully understood, the most likely explanation is the toxicity of acetaldehyde, the first component of alcohol breakdown in the body. This mutagenic component induces fatty acid synthesis. These fatty acids are then converted to triglycerides, resulting in hepatic steatosis, or fatty liver. Acetaldehyde also contributes to oxidative stress, which may lead to inflammation known as alcoholic hepatitis. Lastly, acetaldehyde can cause alcohol-induced fibrosis by inducing collagen deposition by hepatic stellate cells. With extensive fibrosis, irreversible scarring of the liver tissue, also known as cirrhosis, develops which severely reduces the functionality of the liver (Menon et al., 2001).

Patients with liver disease may develop portal hypertension leading to gastrointestinal bleeding, ascites, hepatic encephalopathy, jaundice, malnutrition, dementia and splenomegaly. While these negative outcomes often occur with increased exposure, symptoms and disease progression are dependent on a variety of additional factors including nutritional status and sex. While abstinence is the best way to slow the progression of liver disease, current treatments range from medicinal management to liver transplantation. Remarkably, alcoholic liver disease is currently the second most common indication for liver transplantation in the United States and patients who undergo the surgery due to ALD have excellent survival rates post transplantation (Menon et al., 2001).

Cancer

Alcohol increases the risk for developing various cancers. Two toxic byproducts of alcohol degradation, **acetaldehyde and reactive oxygen species**, act as carcinogens by causing DNA and protein damage. Different types of alcohols may also include other carcinogens during the fermentation and production process, such as nitrosamines, asbestos fibers, phenols and hydrocarbons. Alcohol reduces the body's ability to break down and absorb nutrients that decrease cancer risk, such as vitamins A, C, D and E.

Due to these negative effects, the national Toxicology Program of the U.S. Department of Health and Human Services' Report on Carcinogens notes alcohol consumption as a known human carcinogen (National Toxicology Program, 2011). In 2009, an estimated 3.5% of cancer deaths were alcohol related with highest risks associated with highest intakes for most cancers (Nelson et al., 2013). However, even light-to-moderate drinkers have increased risk of some cancers.

Alcohol consumption is strongly associated with higher risks of heads and neck cancers. With moderate to heavy alcohol consumption there is a 1.8-fold higher risk of oral cavity and throat cancers and a 1.4-fold higher risk of larynx cancers. These risks increase to five-fold higher risk for oral cavity and throat cancers and 2.6-fold higher risk for larynx cancers at heavy consumption. Similarly, alcohol consumption at any level increases the risk of esophageal cancer. Risk for developing esophageal squamous cell carcinoma is 1.3-fold higher risk with moderate consumption and nearly five-fold higher risk for heavy consumption when compared to nondrinkers (Bagnardi et al., 2015; LoConte et al., 2018). There is also strong evidence demonstrating a two-fold increased risk for liver cancer, a 1.2 to 1.5-fold increased risk for colorectal cancer, and a 1.23 to 1.6-fold increased risk of breast cancer when comparing heavy drinkers to nondrinkers.

Researchers have evaluated the effects of alcohol on other types of cancers as well. There is probable and suggestive evidence supporting increased risk of prostate, stomach, and pancreatic cancers with alcohol consumption (Bagnardi et al., 2015; Zhao et al., 2016). There is currently no consensus or clear association with alcohol consumption and risk for ovary, prostate, uterus, or bladder cancers. Surprisingly, there is probable evidence to support decreased risk of kidney cancers and non-Hodgkin's lymphoma with all levels of alcohol consumption (J. E. Lee et al., 2007; Tramacere et al., 2012). Despite this, studies weighing all the health outcomes data on alcohol concluded the **optimal number of drinks to minimize overall health risk is zero** (GBD 2016 Alcohol Collaborators, 2018).

Gastrointestinal and Dental Erosion
Alcohol is damaging to the human body throughout the entire gastrointestinal tract, leading to medical problems ranging from malnutrition to abdominal pain. Starting at ingestion by mouth, chronic alcohol abuse increases the incidence of tooth decay, gum disease, and loss of teeth (Kranzler et al., 1990). Combined with alcohol's effect on the digestion of certain nutrients and its inflammatory effects, alcohol can induce glossitis (inflammation of the tongue) and stomatitis (inflammation of the mouth) as well.

In the esophagus, alcohol impairs esophageal motility, resulting in a weakening of the lower esophageal sphincter. This allows refluxed gastric acid to seep into the esophagus, causing heartburn and esophagitis. Long-term alcohol abuse can cause Barrett's esophagitis, characterized by changes in the cellular lining of the esophagus that can lead to esophageal cancer. Excessive acute alcohol consumption may also cause repeated retching and vomiting, resulting in upper GI bleeding from tears in the mucosa between the esophagus and stomach. This syndrome, known as Mallory-Weiss syndrome, accounts for 5% to 15% of all upper GI tract bleeding (Bode et al., 1996).

The effects of alcohol on the stomach may vary by alcohol content. In alcohols with a low alcohol content, such as beer and wine, gastric acid secretion increases, while in alcohols with a high alcohol content, such as spirits, gastric acid secretion is unchanged or mildly inhibited (Chari et al., 1993). In chronic alcohol abuse, damage to the gastric mucosa decreases gastric acid secretions, reducing the stomach's ability to destroy bacteria and potentially leading to infection and gastritis. Similarly, beverages with a higher alcohol content appear to reduce gastric motility, delaying gastric emptying. This may lead to feelings of fullness and discomfort (Bode et al., 1996). All alcohol consumption, regardless of alcohol content or frequency, can increase mucosal inflammation and the potential for bleeding gastric lesions.

Alcohol is most detrimental in the small intestine where it is rapidly absorbed, as it reduces the absorption of many vitamins and minerals. Numerous studies have demonstrated decreased absorption of lipids, carbohydrates, and proteins as well as micronutrients such as thiamine, folic acid and vitamin B_{12} (Bode et al., 1996; Pfeiffer et al., 1992). It may also interfere with the activity of many intestinal enzymes, reducing proper metabolism of foods such as lactose as well as some medications.

Similar to how alcohol impacts the mucosa of the stomach, alcohol's damage to the intestinal microvilli can cause lesions and bleeding after a single heavy drinking episode and allow endotoxins and other toxins to more easily enter the bloodstream. These toxins increase the release of cytokine from the Kupffer cells in the liver, which contributes to the development of liver damage and disease. The increased intestinal permeability may also promote bacterial overgrowth, as many chronic alcohol abusers show increased endotoxins in the bloodstream, increases in pathogenic bacteria, and decreases in commensal bacteria (Engen et al., 2015).

Alcohol induces inflammation within the gastrointestinal tract, which promotes leaky gut, bacterial overgrowth and dysbiosis (Bishehsari et al., 2017). Currently, there is little evidence on how alcohol impacts the large intestine. However, some studies have implied that alcohol consumption can reduce the strength of colonic contractions, leading to impaction and constipation (Mezey, 1985). As discussed in the section on cancer, alcohol consumption also increases the risk of colon cancer.

Alcohol impacts more peripheral organs to the digestive system as well, such as the liver (discussed previously) and the pancreas. Although the mechanism is unclear, alcohol consumption has a clear association with acute pancreatitis. With chronic alcohol abuse, repeated episodes of acute pancreatitis can lead to permanent damage of the pancreas, causing chronic pancreatitis. Roughly 70% of chronic pancreatitis cases are due to long-term heavy drinking (Kasicka-Jonderko et al., 2014; Mezey, 1985).

Mental Health

Alcohol abuse can coexist with, contribute to, and be caused by psychiatric disorders. Substance use disorder co-occurs at a high prevalence rate with depression, bipolar disorder, attention deficit hyperactivity disorder, psychotic illness, borderline personality disorder and antisocial personality disorder (Abuse, 2020). In some instances mental illness contributes to alcohol use disorder as a way to self-medicate, and in others it is the opposite – the alcohol use disorder contributes to the development of mental illness (schizophrenia, anxiety, mood, or impulse-control disorders).

The effects of alcohol on mental health varies depending on the frequency and extent of alcohol consumption. For example, small amounts of alcohol can cause euphoric feelings while larger amounts can cause sadness, irritability, and anxiety. Among mood disorders, the prevalence of depression is high (64%) in alcohol dependent individuals (Kuria et al., 2012). Similarly, among patients with bipolar disorder, nearly 50% to 60% abuse or become dependent on alcohol at some point in their illness (Brady & Sonne, 1995). In addition, anxiety disorders and alcohol use disorder co-occurs about two to three times higher than would be expected by chance alone (B. F. Grant et al., 2004; J. P. Smith & Randall, 2012).

Alcohol abuse can also cause many issues with memory and cognition. Alcoholic dementia, also known as Wernicke-Korsakoff syndrome, is permanent brain damage from the atrophy of the brain cells secondary to thiamine deficiency. Alcoholics show both reduced absorption of this vitamin as well as inadequate dietary intake. This damage can result in a variety of both acute and chronic issues ranging from psychosis to reduced problem-solving and learning ability.

CLINICAL COMPETENCIES FOR SPORTS DRINKS

Clinical Recommendations (2015–2020 Dietary Guidelines for Americans - Health.Gov, 2015)
1. For adults 21 years of age and older, choose not to drink, or drink in moderation – one drink per day for women and up to two drinks per day for men.
2. Special populations such as pregnant women, children, and athletes are encouraged to stay completely abstinent.

Clinical Competencies
1. Consume no more than the recommend amount of alcohol if choosing to drink
2. Discuss the proposed health benefits of consuming alcohol
3. Discuss the proposed risks of consuming alcohol

CULINARY COMPETENCIES FOR ALCOHOL

Shopping/Storing/Safety Competencies
1. Store alcohol properly

Cooking/Preparing/Serving Competencies
1. Prepare mocktails
2. Dilute alcohol drinks
3. Prepare mixed drinks with little to no added sugar
4. Pour the appropriate serving size for various types of alcohol

At the Store
Many alcoholic options are available at the store for individuals 21 years of age and older. Each person should drink and shop responsibility. Typically, a bottle of wine contains 25.4 ounces and thus would serve five portions of five ounces. Red wine will last three to five days in a cool dark space whereas white wine will last in the refrigerator for five to seven days if corked.

A standard volume of beer sold at the store is 12 ounces but does not store well after being opened. Beer served in a pint glass at a brewery is slightly larger at 15 ounces. Beers also vary more considerably in the percentage of alcohol, as darker and craft beers are often at a higher alcohol content. Spirits store well after being opened. A bottle of spirits (750 cc) contains 16 individual servings and will store up to 10 years in a cool dark place after being opened.

In the Kitchen

On the Tongue

Alcohol is a very personalized taste and individuals can find a range of sweet to tart to sour beverages. Responsible drinkers should choose what they prefer and be mindful of portion size as well as alcohol content and frequency.

Recipe Tips

Attention should be given to the amount of alcohol consumed as well as the sugar content in mixed drinks. In order to make one-serving (five ounces) of white wine last all night, or to just consume less (or no) alcohol, follow the tips below:

Strategy #1: Dilute white wine with fruit, fruit juice, and/or seltzer water
Strategy #2: Use flavored apple cider vinegar instead of alcohol in a drink
Strategy # 3: Create mocktails that contain no alcohol. They look like the real thing and taste delicious, just watch out for the amount of sugar they contain
Strategy #4: Add a lot of crushed ice to the glass as it will dilute the alcohol as it is melting
Strategy #5: With mixed drinks, avoid SSB and opt for seltzer or other carbonated beverages with no added sugar.

SUMMARY

Alcohol consumption impacts numerous systems within the body at all levels of consumption. Although light-to-moderate consumption is associated with some cardioprotective effects, it results in neutral-to-negative effects in most other systems of the body. Repeated heavy consumption however, defined as four or more drinks on any day, results in increased risk of harm in every part of the body.

Considering the potential for negative health impacts, it is no surprise that a systematic analysis for the Global Burden of Disease Study 2016 report argues "the safest level of drinking is none." However, due to alcohol's role in culture, cuisine, and history this guideline most likely will never be met. In summary, if one desires alcohol, drinking in moderation is the key. Using culinary techniques to reduce or remove the alcohol content per serving is also an option.

REFERENCES

2015–2020 Dietary Guidelines for Americans—Health.gov. (2015). https://health.gov/dietaryguidelines/2015/

2017 National Survey on Drug Use and Health: Detailed Tables. (2017). 2871.

2017 National Survey on Drug Use and Health Detai.pdf. (n.d.). Retrieved December 16, 2020, from https://www.samhsa.gov/data/sites/default/files/cbhsq-reports/NSDUHDetailedTabs2017/NSDUHDetailedTabs2017.pdf

2019 State of the Beverage Industry: Energy drinks maintain competitive edge | 2019-07-15 | Beverage Industry. (2020, Accessed). https://www.bevindustry.com/articles/92242-2019-state-of-the-beverage-industry-energy-drinks-maintain-competitive-edge

Abrams, S. A. (2020). Weighing in on fruit juice: AAP now says no juice before age 1. AAP News. https://www.aappublications.org/news/2017/05/22/FruitJuice052217

Abuse, N. I. on D. (2020). Part 1: The Connection Between Substance Use Disorders and Mental Illness. National Institute on Drug Abuse. https://www.drugabuse.gov/publications/research-reports/common-comorbidities-substance-use-disorders/part-1-connection-between-substance-use-disorders-mental-illness

Agarwal, S., Fulgoni Iii, V. L., & Welland, D. (2019). Intake of 100% Fruit Juice Is Associated with Improved Diet Quality of Adults: NHANES 2013-2016 Analysis. Nutrients, 11(10). https://doi.org/10.3390/nu11102513

Akdoğan, M., Tamer, M. N., Cüre, E., Cüre, M. C., Köroğlu, B. K., & Delibaş, N. (2007). Effect of spearmint (Mentha spicata Labiatae) teas on androgen levels in women with hirsutism. Phytotherapy Research: PTR, 21(5), 444–447. https://doi.org/10.1002/ptr.2074

Allen, S., Allen, D., Baladima, F., Phoenix, V. R., Thomas, J. L., Le Roux, G., & Sonke, J. E. (2021). Evidence of free tropospheric and long-range transport of microplastic at Pic du Midi Observatory. Nature Communications, 12(1), 7242. https://doi.org/10.1038/s41467-021-27454-7

American Chemistry Society. (2020). Methods for microplastics, nanoplastics and plastic monomer detection and reporting in human tissues. https://www.acs.org/content/acs/en/pressroom/newsreleases/2020/august/micro-and-nanoplastics-detectable-in-human-tissues.html

American College of Sports Medicine, Sawka, M. N., Burke, L. M., Eichner, E. R., Maughan, R. J., Montain, S. J., & Stachenfeld, N. S. (2007). American College of Sports Medicine position stand. Exercise and fluid replacement. Medicine and Science in Sports and Exercise, 39(2), 377–390. https://doi.org/10.1249/mss.0b013e31802ca597

Anheyer, D., Frawley, J., Koch, A. K., Lauche, R., Langhorst, J., Dobos, G., & Cramer, H. (2017). Herbal Medicines for Gastrointestinal Disorders in Children and Adolescents: A Systematic Review. Pediatrics, 139(6). https://doi.org/10.1542/peds.2017-0062

AnnualMeeting_CombinedHandouts.pdf. (n.d.). Retrieved May 25, 2020, from https://www.eatrightidaho.org/app/uploads/archive/uploads/AnnualMeeting_Co mbinedHandouts.pdf

Apter, D., & Vihko, R. (1983). Early menarche, a risk factor for breast cancer, indicates early onset of ovulatory cycles. The Journal of Clinical Endocrinology and Metabolism, 57(1), 82–86. https://doi.org/10.1210/jcem-57-1-82

Arif, A. A., & Rohrer, J. E. (2005). Patterns of alcohol drinking and its association with obesity: Data from the Third National Health and Nutrition Examination Survey, 1988-1994. BMC Public Health, 5, 126. https://doi.org/10.1186/1471-2458-5-126

Arikan, D., Alp, H., Gözüm, S., Orbak, Z., & Cifçi, E. K. (2008). Effectiveness of massage, sucrose solution, herbal tea or hydrolysed formula in the treatment of infantile colic. Journal of Clinical Nursing, 17(13), 1754–1761. https://doi.org/10.1111/j.1365-2702.2007.02093.x

Armstrong, L. E., & Johnson, E. C. (2018). Water Intake, Water Balance, and the Elusive Daily Water Requirement. Nutrients, 10(12). https://doi.org/10.3390/nu10121928

Ascherio, A., Zhang, S. M., Hernán, M. A., Kawachi, I., Colditz, G. A., Speizer, F. E., & Willett, W. C. (2001). Prospective study of caffeine consumption and risk of Parkinson's disease in men and women. Annals of Neurology, 50(1), 56–63. https://doi.org/10.1002/ana.1052

Asgari-Taee, F., Zerafati-Shoae, N., Dehghani, M., Sadeghi, M., Baradaran, H. R., & Jazayeri, S. (2019). Association of sugar sweetened beverages consumption with non-alcoholic fatty liver disease: A systematic review and meta-analysis. European Journal of Nutrition, 58(5), 1759–1769. https://doi.org/10.1007/s00394-018-1711-4

Auerbach, B. J., Wolf, F. M., Hikida, A., Vallila-Buchman, P., Littman, A., Thompson, D., Louden, D., Taber, D. R., & Krieger, J. (2017). Fruit Juice and Change in BMI: A Meta-analysis. Pediatrics, 139(4). https://doi.org/10.1542/peds.2016-2454

Azad, M. B., Abou-Setta, A. M., Chauhan, B. F., Rabbani, R., Lys, J., Copstein, L., Mann, A., Jeyaraman, M. M., Reid, A. E., Fiander, M., MacKay, D. S., McGavock, J., Wicklow, B., & Zarychanski, R. (2017). Nonnutritive sweeteners and cardiometabolic health: A systematic review and meta-analysis of randomized controlled trials and prospective cohort studies. CMAJ: Canadian Medical Association Journal = Journal de l'Association Medicale Canadienne, 189(28), E929–E939. https://doi.org/10.1503/cmaj.161390

Bagnardi, V., Rota, M., Botteri, E., Tramacere, I., Islami, F., Fedirko, V., Scotti, L., Jenab, M., Turati, F., Pasquali, E., Pelucchi, C., Galeone, C., Bellocco, R., Negri, E., Corrao,

G., Boffetta, P., & La Vecchia, C. (2015). Alcohol consumption and site-specific cancer risk: A comprehensive dose-response meta-analysis. British Journal of Cancer, 112(3), 580–593. https://doi.org/10.1038/bjc.2014.579

Bendsen, N. T., Christensen, R., Bartels, E. M., Kok, F. J., Sierksma, A., Raben, A., & Astrup, A. (2013). Is beer consumption related to measures of abdominal and general obesity? A systematic review and meta-analysis. Nutrition Reviews, 71(2), 67–87. https://doi.org/10.1111/j.1753-4887.2012.00548.x

Benton, D., & Young, H. A. (2019). Role of fruit juice in achieving the 5-a-day recommendation for fruit and vegetable intake. Nutrition Reviews, 77(11), 829–843. https://doi.org/10.1093/nutrit/nuz031

Bhandarkar, N. S., Brown, L., & Panchal, S. K. (2019). Chlorogenic acid attenuates high-carbohydrate, high-fat diet-induced cardiovascular, liver, and metabolic changes in rats. Nutrition Research (New York, N.Y.), 62, 78–88. https://doi.org/10.1016/j.nutres.2018.11.002

Bishehsari, F., Magno, E., Swanson, G., Desai, V., Voigt, R. M., Forsyth, C. B., & Keshavarzian, A. (2017). Alcohol and Gut-Derived Inflammation. Alcohol Research : Current Reviews, 38(2), 163–171.

Blanco, C., Okuda, M., Wright, C., Hasin, D. S., Grant, B. F., Liu, S.-M., & Olfson, M. (2008). Mental health of college students and their non-college-attending peers: Results from the National Epidemiologic Study on Alcohol and Related Conditions. Archives of General Psychiatry, 65(12), 1429–1437. https://doi.org/10.1001/archpsyc.65.12.1429

Bode, C., Maute, G., & Bode, J. C. (1996). Prostaglandin E2 and prostaglandin F2 alpha biosynthesis in human gastric mucosa: Effect of chronic alcohol misuse. Gut, 39(3), 348–352. https://doi.org/10.1136/gut.39.3.348

Boston, 677 Huntington Avenue, & Ma 02115 +1495-1000. (2019, September 23). Sports Drinks. The Nutrition Source. https://www.hsph.harvard.edu/nutritionsource/sports-drinks/

Brady, K. T., & Sonne, S. C. (1995). The relationship between substance abuse and bipolar disorder. The Journal of Clinical Psychiatry, 56 Suppl 3, 19–24.

Brahney, J., Hallerud, M., Heim, E., Hahnenberger, M., & Sukumaran, S. (2020). Plastic rain in protected areas of the United States. Science, 368(6496). https://www.science.org/doi/10.1126/science.aaz5819

Brainard, A., & Gresham, C. (2014). Prevention and treatment of motion sickness. American Family Physician, 90(1), 41–46.

Bravi, F., Tavani, A., Bosetti, C., Boffetta, P., & La Vecchia, C. (2017). Coffee and the risk of hepatocellular carcinoma and chronic liver disease: A systematic review and meta-analysis of prospective studies. European Journal of Cancer Prevention: The Official Journal of the European Cancer Prevention Organisation (ECP), 26(5), 368–377. https://doi.org/10.1097/CEJ.0000000000000252

Breiter, T., Laue, C., Kressel, G., Gröll, S., Engelhardt, U. H., & Hahn, A. (2011). Bioavailability and antioxidant potential of rooibos flavonoids in humans following the consumption of different rooibos formulations. Food Chemistry, 128(2), 338–347. https://doi.org/10.1016/j.foodchem.2011.03.029

Briasoulis, A., Agarwal, V., & Messerli, F. H. (2012). Alcohol Consumption and the Risk of Hypertension in Men and Women: A Systematic Review and Meta-Analysis. The Journal of Clinical Hypertension, 14(11), 792–798. https://doi.org/10.1111/jch.12008

Brosnan, J. T., & Brosnan, M. E. (2006). The sulfur-containing amino acids: An overview. The Journal of Nutrition, 136(6 Suppl), 1636S-1640S. https://doi.org/10.1093/jn/136.6.1636S

Brown, O. I., Allgar, V., & Wong, K. Y.-K. (2016). Coffee reduces the risk of death after acute myocardial infarction: A meta-analysis. Coronary Artery Disease, 27(7), 566–572. https://doi.org/10.1097/MCA.0000000000000397

Cai, L., Ma, D., Zhang, Y., Liu, Z., & Wang, P. (2012). The effect of coffee consumption on serum lipids: A meta-analysis of randomized controlled trials. European Journal of Clinical Nutrition, 66(8), 872–877. https://doi.org/10.1038/ejcn.2012.68

Caini, S., Cattaruzza, M. S., Bendinelli, B., Tosti, G., Masala, G., Gnagnarella, P., Assedi, M., Stanganelli, I., Palli, D., & Gandini, S. (2017). Coffee, tea and caffeine intake and the risk of non-melanoma skin cancer: A review of the literature and meta-analysis. European Journal of Nutrition, 56(1), 1–12. https://doi.org/10.1007/s00394-016-1253-6

Cairns, S. P., & Lindinger, M. I. (2008). Do multiple ionic interactions contribute to skeletal muscle fatigue? The Journal of Physiology, 586(17), 4039–4054. https://doi.org/10.1113/jphysiol.2008.155424

Campbell, B., Wilborn, C., La Bounty, P., Taylor, L., Nelson, M. T., Greenwood, M., Ziegenfuss, T. N., Lopez, H. L., Hoffman, J. R., Stout, J. R., Schmitz, S., Collins, R., Kalman, D. S., Antonio, J., & Kreider, R. B. (2013). International Society of Sports Nutrition position stand: Energy drinks. Journal of the International Society of Sports Nutrition, 10(1), 1. https://doi.org/10.1186/1550-2783-10-1

Carman, A. J., Dacks, P. A., Lane, R. F., Shineman, D. W., & Fillit, H. M. (2014). Current evidence for the use of coffee and caffeine to prevent age-related cognitive decline and Alzheimer's disease. The Journal of Nutrition, Health & Aging, 18(4), 383–392. https://doi.org/10.1007/s12603-014-0021-7

Carwile, J. L., Willett, W. C., Spiegelman, D., Hertzmark, E., Rich-Edwards, J., Frazier, A. L., & Michels, K. B. (2015). Sugar-sweetened beverage consumption and age at menarche in a prospective study of US girls. Human Reproduction (Oxford, England), 30(3), 675–683. https://doi.org/10.1093/humrep/deu349

Castaldo, L., Narváez, A., Izzo, L., Graziani, G., Gaspari, A., Di Minno, G., & Ritieni, A. (2019). Red Wine Consumption and Cardiovascular Health. Molecules, 24(19), 3626. https://doi.org/10.3390/molecules24193626

Chaput, J.-P., McNeil, J., Després, J.-P., Bouchard, C., & Tremblay, A. (2012). Short sleep duration is associated with greater alcohol consumption in adults. Appetite, 59(3), 650–655. https://doi.org/10.1016/j.appet.2012.07.012

Chari, S., Teyssen, S., & Singer, M. V. (1993). Alcohol and gastric acid secretion in humans. Gut, 34(6), 843–847. https://doi.org/10.1136/gut.34.6.843

Chen, Y.-P., Lu, F.-B., Hu, Y.-B., Xu, L.-M., Zheng, M.-H., & Hu, E.-D. (2019). A systematic review and a dose-response meta-analysis of coffee dose and nonalcoholic fatty liver disease. Clinical Nutrition (Edinburgh, Scotland), 38(6), 2552–2557. https://doi.org/10.1016/j.clnu.2018.11.030

Cheungpasitporn, W., Rossetti, S., Friend, K., Erickson, S. B., & Lieske, J. C. (2016). Treatment effect, adherence, and safety of high fluid intake for the prevention of incident and recurrent kidney stones: A systematic review and meta-analysis. Journal of Nephrology, 29(2), 211–219. https://doi.org/10.1007/s40620-015-0210-4

Choo, E., Picket, B., & Dando, R. (2017). Caffeine May Reduce Perceived Sweet Taste in Humans, Supporting Evidence That Adenosine Receptors Modulate Taste. Journal of Food Science, 82(9), 2177–2182. https://doi.org/10.1111/1750-3841.13836

Cohen, D. (2012). The truth about sports drinks. BMJ, 345, e4737. https://doi.org/10.1136/bmj.e4737

Committee on Nutrition and the Council on Sports Medicine and Fitness. (2011). Sports drinks and energy drinks for children and adolescents: Are they appropriate? Pediatrics, 127(6), 1182–1189. https://doi.org/10.1542/peds.2011-0965

Coombes, J. S., & Hamilton, K. L. (2000). The effectiveness of commercially available sports drinks. Sports Medicine (Auckland, N.Z.), 29(3), 181–209. https://doi.org/10.2165/00007256-200029030-00004

Cornelis, M. C., El-Sohemy, A., Kabagambe, E. K., & Campos, H. (2006). Coffee, CYP1A2 genotype, and risk of myocardial infarction. JAMA, 295(10), 1135–1141. https://doi.org/10.1001/jama.295.10.1135

Costa, J., Lunet, N., Santos, C., Santos, J., & Vaz-Carneiro, A. (2010). Caffeine exposure and the risk of Parkinson's disease: A systematic review and meta-analysis of observational studies. Journal of Alzheimer's Disease: JAD, 20 Suppl 1, S221-238. https://doi.org/10.3233/JAD-2010-091525

Coulson, C. E., Williams, L. J., Brennan, S. L., Berk, M., Kotowicz, M. A., Lubman, D. I., & Pasco, J. A. (2013). Alcohol consumption and body composition in a population-based sample of elderly Australian men. Aging Clinical and Experimental Research, 25(2), 183–192. https://doi.org/10.1007/s40520-013-0026-9

Cox, G. R., Desbrow, B., Montgomery, P. G., Anderson, M. E., Bruce, C. R., Macrides, T. A., Martin, D. T., Moquin, A., Roberts, A., Hawley, J. A., & Burke, L. M. (2002). Effect of different protocols of caffeine intake on metabolism and endurance performance. Journal of Applied Physiology (Bethesda, Md.: 1985), 93(3), 990–999. https://doi.org/10.1152/japplphysiol.00249.2002

Crews, F. T., Vetreno, R. P., Broadwater, M. A., & Robinson, D. L. (2016). Adolescent Alcohol Exposure Persistently Impacts Adult Neurobiology and Behavior. Pharmacological Reviews, 68(4), 1074–1109. https://doi.org/10.1124/pr.115.012138

Crowe-White, K., Parrott, J. S., Stote, K. S., Gutschall, M., Benson-Davies, S., Droke, E., O'Neil, C. E., Wolfram, T., & Ziegler, P. (2017). Metabolic impact of 100% fruit juice consumption on antioxidant/oxidant status and lipid profiles of adults: An Evidence-Based review. Critical Reviews in Food Science and Nutrition, 57(1), 152–162. https://doi.org/10.1080/10408398.2015.1102861

Crown, P. L., Emerson, T. E., Gu, J., Hurst, W. J., Pauketat, T. R., & Ward, T. (2012). Ritual Black Drink consumption at Cahokia. Proceedings of the National Academy of Sciences, 109(35), 13944–13949. https://doi.org/10.1073/pnas.1208404109

Dasanayake, A. P., Silverman, A. J., & Warnakulasuriya, S. (2010). Maté drinking and oral and oro-pharyngeal cancer: A systematic review and meta-analysis. Oral Oncology, 46(2), 82–86. https://doi.org/10.1016/j.oraloncology.2009.07.006

de Morais, E. C., Stefanuto, A., Klein, G. A., Boaventura, B. C. B., de Andrade, F., Wazlawik, E., Di Pietro, P. F., Maraschin, M., & da Silva, E. L. (2009). Consumption of yerba mate (Ilex paraguariensis) improves serum lipid parameters in healthy dyslipidemic subjects and provides an additional LDL-cholesterol reduction in individuals on statin therapy. Journal of Agricultural and Food Chemistry, 57(18), 8316–8324. https://doi.org/10.1021/jf901660g

Dennis, E. A., Dengo, A. L., Comber, D. L., Flack, K. D., Savla, J., Davy, K. P., & Davy, B. M. (2010). Water consumption increases weight loss during a hypocaloric diet intervention in middle-aged and older adults. Obesity (Silver Spring, Md.), 18(2), 300–307. https://doi.org/10.1038/oby.2009.235

Dhingra, R., Sullivan, L., Jacques, P. F., Wang, T. J., Fox, C. S., Meigs, J. B., D'Agostino, R. B., Gaziano, J. M., & Vasan, R. S. (2007). Soft drink consumption and risk of developing cardiometabolic risk factors and the metabolic syndrome in middle-aged adults in the community. Circulation, 116(5), 480–488. https://doi.org/10.1161/CIRCULATIONAHA.107.689935

Ding, M., Bhupathiraju, S. N., Satija, A., van Dam, R. M., & Hu, F. B. (2014). Long-term coffee consumption and risk of cardiovascular disease: A systematic review and a dose-response meta-analysis of prospective cohort studies. Circulation, 129(6), 643–659. https://doi.org/10.1161/CIRCULATIONAHA.113.005925

Doherty, M., & Smith, P. M. (2004). Effects of caffeine ingestion on exercise testing: A meta-analysis. International Journal of Sport Nutrition and Exercise Metabolism, 14(6), 626–646. https://doi.org/10.1123/ijsnem.14.6.626

Drewnowski, A., & Rehm, C. D. (2015). Socioeconomic gradient in consumption of whole fruit and 100% fruit juice among US children and adults. Nutrition Journal, 14, 3. https://doi.org/10.1186/1475-2891-14-3

Drewnowski, A., Rehm, C. D., & Constant, F. (2013a). Water and beverage consumption among children age 4-13y in the United States: Analyses of 2005-2010 NHANES data. Nutrition Journal, 12, 85. https://doi.org/10.1186/1475-2891-12-85

Drewnowski, A., Rehm, C. D., & Constant, F. (2013b). Water and beverage consumption among children age 4-13y in the United States: Analyses of 2005-2010 NHANES data. Nutrition Journal, 12, 85. https://doi.org/10.1186/1475-2891-12-85

Drinking Levels Defined | National Institute on Alcohol Abuse and Alcoholism (NIAAA). (2020, Accesses). https://www.niaaa.nih.gov/alcohol-health/overview-alcohol-consumption/moderate-binge-drinking

Drouin-Chartier, J.-P., Zheng, Y., Li, Y., Malik, V., Pan, A., Bhupathiraju, S. N., Tobias, D. K., Manson, J. E., Willett, W. C., & Hu, F. B. (2019). Changes in Consumption of Sugary Beverages and Artificially Sweetened Beverages and Subsequent Risk of Type 2 Diabetes: Results From Three Large Prospective U.S. Cohorts of Women and Men. Diabetes Care, 42(12), 2181–2189. https://doi.org/10.2337/dc19-0734

Dudley, R. (2004). Ethanol, fruit ripening, and the historical origins of human alcoholism in primate frugivory. Integrative and Comparative Biology, 44(4), 315–323. https://doi.org/10.1093/icb/44.4.315

Duffey, K. J., & Popkin, B. M. (2007). Shifts in patterns and consumption of beverages between 1965 and 2002. Obesity (Silver Spring, Md.), 15(11), 2739–2747. https://doi.org/10.1038/oby.2007.326

Ebbeling, C. B., Feldman, H. A., Steltz, S. K., Quinn, N. L., Robinson, L. M., & Ludwig, D. S. (2020). Effects of Sugar-Sweetened, Artificially Sweetened, and Unsweetened Beverages on Cardiometabolic Risk Factors, Body Composition, and Sweet Taste Preference: A Randomized Controlled Trial. Journal of the American Heart Association: Cardiovascular and Cerebrovascular Disease, 9(15), e015668. https://doi.org/10.1161/JAHA.119.015668

Energy Drinks | Healthy Schools | CDC. (2019, September 6). https://www.cdc.gov/healthyschools/nutrition/energy.htm

Engen, P. A., Green, S. J., Voigt, R. M., Forsyth, C. B., & Keshavarzian, A. (2015). The Gastrointestinal Microbiome: Alcohol Effects on the Composition of Intestinal Microbiota. Alcohol Research: Current Reviews, 37(2), 223–236.

EPA. (2003). Drinking Water Advisory: Consumer Acceptibility Advice and Health Effects Analysis on Sodium. (EPA 822-R-03-006).

Eskelinen, M. H., & Kivipelto, M. (2010). Caffeine as a protective factor in dementia and Alzheimer's disease. Journal of Alzheimer's Disease: JAD, 20 Suppl 1, S167-174. https://doi.org/10.3233/JAD-2010-1404

Evans, G. H., Shirreffs, S. M., & Maughan, R. J. (2009). Postexercise rehydration in man: The effects of carbohydrate content and osmolality of drinks ingested ad libitum. Applied Physiology, Nutrition, and Metabolism = Physiologie Appliquee, Nutrition Et Metabolisme, 34(4), 785–793. https://doi.org/10.1139/H09-065

Fakhouri, T. H. I., Kit, B. K., & Ogden, C. L. (2012). Consumption of diet drinks in the United States, 2009-2010. NCHS Data Brief, 109, 1–8.

Field, A. E., Sonneville, K. R., Falbe, J., Flint, A., Haines, J., Rosner, B., & Camargo, C. A. (2014). Association of sports drinks with weight gain among adolescents and young adults. Obesity (Silver Spring, Md.), 22(10), 2238–2243. https://doi.org/10.1002/oby.20845

Fischer, S., & Smith, G. T. (2008). Binge eating, problem drinking, and pathological gambling: Linking behavior to shared traits and social learning. Personality and Individual Differences, 44(4), 789–800. https://doi.org/10.1016/j.paid.2007.10.008

Flechtner-Mors, M., Biesalski, H. K., Jenkinson, C. P., Adler, G., & Ditschuneit, H. H. (2004). Effects of moderate consumption of white wine on weight loss in overweight and obese subjects. International Journal of Obesity and Related Metabolic Disorders: Journal of the International Association for the Study of Obesity, 28(11), 1420–1426. https://doi.org/10.1038/sj.ijo.0802786

Frary, C. D., Johnson, R. K., & Wang, M. Q. (2004). Children and adolescents' choices of foods and beverages high in added sugars are associated with intakes of key nutrients and food groups. The Journal of Adolescent Health: Official Publication of the Society for Adolescent Medicine, 34(1), 56–63. https://doi.org/10.1016/s1054-139x(03)00248-9

Freedman, N. D., Park, Y., Abnet, C. C., Hollenbeck, A. R., & Sinha, R. (2012). Association of coffee drinking with total and cause-specific mortality. The New England Journal of Medicine, 366(20), 1891–1904. https://doi.org/10.1056/NEJMoa1112010

French, M. T., Norton, E. C., Fang, H., & Maclean, J. C. (2010). Alcohol consumption and body weight. Health Economics, 19(7), 814–832. https://doi.org/10.1002/hec.1521

Fung, T. T., Arasaratnam, M. H., Grodstein, F., Katz, J. N., Rosner, B., Willett, W. C., & Feskanich, D. (2014). Soda consumption and risk of hip fractures in postmenopausal women in the Nurses' Health Study. The American Journal of Clinical Nutrition, 100(3), 953–958. https://doi.org/10.3945/ajcn.114.083352

Ganio, M. S., Klau, J. F., Casa, D. J., Armstrong, L. E., & Maresh, C. M. (2009). Effect of caffeine on sport-specific endurance performance: A systematic review. Journal of Strength and Conditioning Research, 23(1), 315–324. https://doi.org/10.1519/JSC.0b013e31818b979a

Gatorade | G Series Sports Drinks for Energy, Hydration and Recovery. (n.d.). Retrieved December 16, 2020, from http://www.gatorade.com.mx/

GBD 2016 Alcohol Collaborators. (2018). Alcohol use and burden for 195 countries and territories, 1990-2016: A systematic analysis for the Global Burden of Disease Study 2016. Lancet (London, England), 392(10152), 1015–1035. https://doi.org/10.1016/S0140-6736(18)31310-2

Getting, J. E., Gregoire, J. R., Phul, A., & Kasten, M. J. (2013). Oxalate nephropathy due to "juicing": Case report and review. The American Journal of Medicine, 126(9), 768–772. https://doi.org/10.1016/j.amjmed.2013.03.019

Geyer, R., Jambeck, J. R., & Law, K. L. (2017). Production, use, and fate of all plastics ever made. Science Advances, 3(7), e1700782. https://doi.org/10.1126/sciadv.1700782

Giedd, J. N., Blumenthal, J., Jeffries, N. O., Castellanos, F. X., Liu, H., Zijdenbos, A., Paus, T., Evans, A. C., & Rapoport, J. L. (1999). Brain development during childhood and adolescence: A longitudinal MRI study. Nature Neuroscience, 2(10), 861–863. https://doi.org/10.1038/13158

Goldstein, J. (2001). Caffeine as an analgesic adjuvant. InflammoPharmacology, 9(1), 51–61. https://doi.org/10.1163/156856001300248326

Graham, T. E. (2001). Caffeine and exercise: Metabolism, endurance and performance. Sports Medicine (Auckland, N.Z.), 31(11), 785–807. https://doi.org/10.2165/00007256-200131110-00002

Grant, B. F., Stinson, F. S., Dawson, D. A., Chou, S. P., Dufour, M. C., Compton, W., Pickering, R. P., & Kaplan, K. (2004). Prevalence and co-occurrence of substance use disorders and independent mood and anxiety disorders: Results from the National Epidemiologic Survey on Alcohol and Related Conditions. Archives of General Psychiatry, 61(8), 807–816. https://doi.org/10.1001/archpsyc.61.8.807

Grant, P. (2010). Spearmint herbal tea has significant anti-androgen effects in polycystic ovarian syndrome. A randomized controlled trial. Phytotherapy Research: PTR, 24(2), 186–188. https://doi.org/10.1002/ptr.2900

Greene, E., Oman, K., & Lefler, M. (2014). Energy drink-induced acute kidney injury. The Annals of Pharmacotherapy, 48(10), 1366–1370. https://doi.org/10.1177/1060028014541997

Greyling, A., Ras, R. T., Zock, P. L., Lorenz, M., Hopman, M. T., Thijssen, D. H. J., & Draijer, R. (2014). The effect of black tea on blood pressure: A systematic review with meta-analysis of randomized controlled trials. PloS One, 9(7), e103247. https://doi.org/10.1371/journal.pone.0103247

Grgic, J., Grgic, I., Pickering, C., Schoenfeld, B. J., Bishop, D. J., & Pedisic, Z. (2020). Wake up and smell the coffee: Caffeine supplementation and exercise performance-an umbrella review of 21 published meta-analyses. British Journal of Sports Medicine, 54(11), 681–688. https://doi.org/10.1136/bjsports-2018-100278

Grosso, G., Micek, A., Godos, J., Sciacca, S., Pajak, A., Martínez-González, M. A., Giovannucci, E. L., & Galvano, F. (2016). Coffee consumption and risk of all-cause, cardiovascular, and cancer mortality in smokers and non-smokers: A dose-response meta-analysis. European Journal of Epidemiology, 31(12), 1191–1205. https://doi.org/10.1007/s10654-016-0202-2

Guideline: Sugars Intake for Adults and Children. (2015). World Health Organization. http://www.ncbi.nlm.nih.gov/books/NBK285537/

Gunter, M. J., Murphy, N., Cross, A. J., Dossus, L., Dartois, L., Fagherazzi, G., Kaaks, R., Kühn, T., Boeing, H., Aleksandrova, K., Tjønneland, A., Olsen, A., Overvad, K., Larsen, S. C., Redondo Cornejo, M. L., Agudo, A., Sánchez Pérez, M. J., Altzibar, J. M., Navarro, C., … Riboli, E. (2017). Coffee Drinking and Mortality in 10 European Countries: A Multinational Cohort Study. Annals of Internal Medicine, 167(4), 236–247. https://doi.org/10.7326/M16-2945

Guo, X., Park, Y., Freedman, N. D., Sinha, R., Hollenbeck, A. R., Blair, A., & Chen, H. (2014). Sweetened beverages, coffee, and tea and depression risk among older US adults. PloS One, 9(4), e94715. https://doi.org/10.1371/journal.pone.0094715

Harris, J. L., Schwartz, M. B., LoDolce, M., Munsell, C., Fleming-Milici, F., Elsey, J., Liu, S., Hyary, M., Gross, R., Hazen, C., & Dembek, C. (n.d.). Sugary Drink FACTS 2014 Some progress but much room for improvement in marketing to youth. 167.

Häussinger, D. (1996). The role of cellular hydration in the regulation of cell function. The Biochemical Journal, 313 (Pt 3), 697–710. https://doi.org/10.1042/bj3130697

Heckman, M. A., Sherry, K., & Mejia, E. G. D. (2010). Energy Drinks: An Assessment of Their Market Size, Consumer Demographics, Ingredient Profile, Functionality, and Regulations in the United States. Comprehensive Reviews in Food Science and Food Safety, 9(3), 303–317. https://doi.org/10.1111/j.1541-4337.2010.00111.x

Heneghan, C., Perera, R., Nunan, D., Mahtani, K., & Gill, P. (2012). Forty years of sports performance research and little insight gained. BMJ (Clinical Research Ed.), 345, e4797. https://doi.org/10.1136/bmj.e4797

Henning, S. M., Yang, J., Shao, P., Lee, R.-P., Huang, J., Ly, A., Hsu, M., Lu, Q.-Y., Thames, G., Heber, D., & Li, Z. (2017). Health benefit of vegetable/fruit juice-based diet: Role of microbiome. Scientific Reports, 7(1), 2167. https://doi.org/10.1038/s41598-017-02200-6

Hernandez, L. M., Xu, E. G., Larsson, H. C. E., Tahara, R., Maisuria, V. B., & Tufenkji, N. (2019). Plastic Teabags Release Billions of Microparticles and Nanoparticles into Tea. Environmental Science & Technology, 53(21), 12300–12310. https://doi.org/10.1021/acs.est.9b02540

Herreros-Villanueva, M., Hijona, E., Bañales, J. M., Cosme, A., & Bujanda, L. (2013). Alcohol consumption on pancreatic diseases. World Journal of Gastroenterology, 19(5), 638–647. https://doi.org/10.3748/wjg.v19.i5.638

Higgins, J. P., Babu, K., Deuster, P. A., & Shearer, J. (2018). Energy Drinks: A Contemporary Issues Paper. Current Sports Medicine Reports, 17(2), 65–72. https://doi.org/10.1249/JSR.0000000000000454

Higgins, J. P., & Babu, K. M. (2013). Caffeine reduces myocardial blood flow during exercise. The American Journal of Medicine, 126(8), 730.e1-8. https://doi.org/10.1016/j.amjmed.2012.12.023

Higgins, J. P., Tuttle, T. D., & Higgins, C. L. (2010). Energy beverages: Content and safety. Mayo Clinic Proceedings, 85(11), 1033–1041. https://doi.org/10.4065/mcp.2010.0381

Higgins, J. P., Yarlagadda, S., & Yang, B. (2015). Cardiovascular Complications of Energy Drinks. Beverages, 1(2), 104–126. https://doi.org/10.3390/beverages1020104

Hirahatake, K. M., Jacobs, D. R., Shikany, J. M., Jiang, L., Wong, N. D., Steffen, L. M., & Odegaard, A. O. (2019). Cumulative intake of artificially sweetened and sugar-sweetened beverages and risk of incident type 2 diabetes in young adults: The Coronary Artery Risk Development In Young Adults (CARDIA) Study. The American Journal of Clinical Nutrition, 110(3), 733–741. https://doi.org/10.1093/ajcn/nqz154

Ho, K. K. H. Y., Ferruzzi, M. G., & Wightman, J. D. (2020). Potential health benefits of (poly)phenols derived from fruit and 100% fruit juice. Nutrition Reviews, 78(2), 145–174. https://doi.org/10.1093/nutrit/nuz041

Hu, Y., Ding, M., Yuan, C., Wu, K., Smith-Warner, S. A., Hu, F. B., Chan, A. T., Meyerhardt, J. A., Ogino, S., Fuchs, C. S., Giovannucci, E. L., & Song, M. (2018). Association Between Coffee Intake After Diagnosis of Colorectal Cancer and Reduced Mortality. Gastroenterology, 154(4), 916-926.e9. https://doi.org/10.1053/j.gastro.2017.11.010

Ibrahim, N. K., & Iftikhar, R. (2014). Energy drinks: Getting wings but at what health cost? Pakistan Journal of Medical Sciences, 30(6), 1415–1419. https://doi.org/10.12669/pjms.306.5396

Imagawa, T. F., Hirano, I., Utsuki, K., Horie, M., Naka, A., Matsumoto, K., & Imagawa, S. (2009). Caffeine and taurine enhance endurance performance. International Journal of Sports Medicine, 30(7), 485–488. https://doi.org/10.1055/s-0028-1104574

Imamura, F., Schulze, M. B., Sharp, S. J., Guevara, M., Romaguera, D., Bendinelli, B., Salamanca-Fernández, E., Ardanaz, E., Arriola, L., Aune, D., Boeing, H., Dow, C., Fagherazzi, G., Franks, P. W., Freisling, H., Jakszyn, P., Kaaks, R., Khaw, K.-T., Kühn, T., … Wareham, N. J. (2019). Estimated Substitution of Tea or Coffee for Sugar-Sweetened Beverages Was Associated with Lower Type 2 Diabetes

Incidence in Case-Cohort Analysis across 8 European Countries in the EPIC-InterAct Study. The Journal of Nutrition, 149(11), 1985–1993. https://doi.org/10.1093/jn/nxz156

Inami, S., Takano, M., Yamamoto, M., Murakami, D., Tajika, K., Yodogawa, K., Yokoyama, S., Ohno, N., Ohba, T., Sano, J., Ibuki, C., Seino, Y., & Mizuno, K. (2007). Tea catechin consumption reduces circulating oxidized low-density lipoprotein. International Heart Journal, 48(6), 725–732. https://doi.org/10.1536/ihj.48.725

Institute of Medicine (U.S.) (Ed.). (2005). DRI, dietary reference intakes for water, potassium, sodium, chloride, and sulfate. National Academies Press.

Jensen, T., Abdelmalek, M. F., Sullivan, S., Nadeau, K. J., Green, M., Roncal, C., Nakagawa, T., Kuwabara, M., Sato, Y., Kang, D.-H., Tolan, D. R., Sanchez-Lozada, L. G., Rosen, H. R., Lanaspa, M. A., Diehl, A. M., & Johnson, R. J. (2018). Fructose and sugar: A major mediator of non-alcoholic fatty liver disease. Journal of Hepatology, 68(5), 1063–1075. https://doi.org/10.1016/j.jhep.2018.01.019

JHA, R., Davenport, E., Y, G., Bhandari, D., Tandukar, S., Km, N., Gk, F., S, H., Gp, G., J, L., Jb, S., Cd, B., & Jl, S. (2018). Gut microbiome transition across a lifestyle gradient in Himalaya. PLoS Biology, 16(11). https://doi.org/10.1371/journal.pbio.2005396

Jiang, X., Zhang, D., & Jiang, W. (2014). Coffee and caffeine intake and incidence of type 2 diabetes mellitus: A meta-analysis of prospective studies. European Journal of Nutrition, 53(1), 25–38. https://doi.org/10.1007/s00394-013-0603-x

Johnson, E. C., Bardis, C. N., Jansen, L. T., Adams, J. D., Kirkland, T. W., & Kavouras, S. A. (2017). Reduced water intake deteriorates glucose regulation in patients with type 2 diabetes. Nutrition Research, 43, 25–32. https://doi.org/10.1016/j.nutres.2017.05.004

Johnson, R. K., Appel, L. J., Brands, M., Howard, B. V., Lefevre, M., Lustig, R. H., Sacks, F., Steffen, L. M., Wylie-Rosett, J., & American Heart Association Nutrition Committee of the Council on Nutrition, Physical Activity, and Metabolism and the Council on Epidemiology and Prevention. (2009). Dietary sugars intake and cardiovascular health: A scientific statement from the American Heart Association. Circulation, 120(11), 1011–1020. https://doi.org/10.1161/CIRCULATIONAHA.109.192627

Kant, A. K., Graubard, B. I., & Atchison, E. A. (2009). Intakes of plain water, moisture in foods and beverages, and total water in the adult US population--nutritional, meal pattern, and body weight correlates: National Health and Nutrition Examination Surveys 1999-2006. The American Journal of Clinical Nutrition, 90(3), 655–663. https://doi.org/10.3945/ajcn.2009.27749

Kassebaum, N. J., Bernabé, E., Dahiya, M., Bhandari, B., Murray, C. J. L., & Marcenes, W. (2015). Global burden of untreated caries: A systematic review and metaregression. Journal of Dental Research, 94(5), 650–658. https://doi.org/10.1177/0022034515573272

Keller, K. L., Kirzner, J., Pietrobelli, A., St-Onge, M.-P., & Faith, M. S. (2009). Increased sweetened beverage intake is associated with reduced milk and calcium intake in 3–7 y. Old children at multi-item laboratory lunches. Journal of the American Dietetic Association, 109(3), 497–501. https://doi.org/10.1016/j.jada.2008.11.030

Khalesi, Z. B., Beiranvand, S. P., & Bokaie, M. (2019). Efficacy of Chamomile in the Treatment of Premenstrual Syndrome: A Systematic Review. Journal of Pharmacopuncture, 22(4), 204–209. https://doi.org/10.3831/KPI.2019.22.028

Kim, J.-S., Lee, H.-J., Kim, S.-K., & Kim, H.-J. (2018). Global Pattern of Microplastics (MPs) in Commercial Food-Grade Salts: Sea Salt as an Indicator of Seawater MP Pollution. Environmental Science & Technology, 52(21), 12819–12828. https://doi.org/10.1021/acs.est.8b04180

Kobayashi, S., Sata, F., Murata, K., Saijo, Y., Araki, A., Miyashita, C., Itoh, S., Minatoya, M., Yamazaki, K., Ait Bamai, Y., Kishi, R., & Japan Environment and Children's Study Group. (2019). Dose-dependent associations between prenatal caffeine consumption and small for gestational age, preterm birth, and reduced birthweight in the Japan Environment and Children's Study. Paediatric and Perinatal Epidemiology, 33(3), 185–194. https://doi.org/10.1111/ppe.12551

Koelmans, A. A., Mohamed Nor, N. H., Hermsen, E., Kooi, M., Mintenig, S. M., & De France, J. (2019). Microplastics in freshwaters and drinking water: Critical review and assessment of data quality. Water Research, 155, 410–422. https://doi.org/10.1016/j.watres.2019.02.054

Kokubo, Y., Iso, H., Saito, I., Yamagishi, K., Yatsuya, H., Ishihara, J., Inoue, M., & Tsugane, S. (2013). The impact of green tea and coffee consumption on the reduced risk of stroke incidence in Japanese population: The Japan public health center-based study cohort. Stroke, 44(5), 1369–1374. https://doi.org/10.1161/STROKEAHA.111.677500

Kondo, Y., Goto, A., Noma, H., Iso, H., Hayashi, K., & Noda, M. (2018). Effects of Coffee and Tea Consumption on Glucose Metabolism: A Systematic Review and Network Meta-Analysis. Nutrients, 11(1). https://doi.org/10.3390/nu11010048

Koppes, L. L. J., Dekker, J. M., Hendriks, H. F. J., Bouter, L. M., & Heine, R. J. (2005). Moderate alcohol consumption lowers the risk of type 2 diabetes: A meta-analysis of prospective observational studies. Diabetes Care, 28(3), 719–725. https://doi.org/10.2337/diacare.28.3.719

Kovacs, E. M., Stegen JHCH, null, & Brouns, F. (1998). Effect of caffeinated drinks on substrate metabolism, caffeine excretion, and performance. Journal of Applied Physiology (Bethesda, Md.: 1985), 85(2), 709–715. https://doi.org/10.1152/jappl.1998.85.2.709

Kranzler, H. R., Babor, T. F., Goldstein, L., & Gold, J. (1990). Dental pathology and alcohol-related indicators in an outpatient clinic sample. Community Dentistry and Oral Epidemiology, 18(4), 204–207. https://doi.org/10.1111/j.1600-0528.1990.tb00058.x

Kuria, M. W., Ndetei, D. M., Obot, I. S., Khasakhala, L. I., Bagaka, B. M., Mbugua, M. N., & Kamau, J. (2012). The Association between Alcohol Dependence and Depression before and after Treatment for Alcohol Dependence. ISRN Psychiatry, 2012, 482802. https://doi.org/10.5402/2012/482802

Lafranconi, A., Micek, A., Galvano, F., Rossetti, S., Del Pup, L., Berretta, M., & Facchini, G. (2017). Coffee Decreases the Risk of Endometrial Cancer: A Dose-Response Meta-Analysis of Prospective Cohort Studies. Nutrients, 9(11). https://doi.org/10.3390/nu9111223

Larsson, S. C., Drca, N., & Wolk, A. (2014). Alcohol consumption and risk of atrial fibrillation: A prospective study and dose-response meta-analysis. Journal of the American College of Cardiology, 64(3), 281–289. https://doi.org/10.1016/j.jacc.2014.03.048

Larsson, S. C., Orsini, N., & Wolk, A. (2015). Alcohol consumption and risk of heart failure: A dose-response meta-analysis of prospective studies. European Journal of Heart Failure, 17(4), 367–373. https://doi.org/10.1002/ejhf.228

Larsson, S. C., Wallin, A., Wolk, A., & Markus, H. S. (2016). Differing association of alcohol consumption with different stroke types: A systematic review and meta-analysis. BMC Medicine, 14(1), 178. https://doi.org/10.1186/s12916-016-0721-4

Lasater, G., Piernas, C., & Popkin, B. M. (2011). Beverage patterns and trends among school-aged children in the US, 1989-2008. Nutrition Journal, 10, 103. https://doi.org/10.1186/1475-2891-10-103

Lead in Drinking Water | Sources of Lead | CDC. (2020, November 18). https://www.cdc.gov/nceh/lead/prevention/sources/water.htm

Lee, J. E., Hunter, D. J., Spiegelman, D., Adami, H.-O., Albanes, D., Bernstein, L., van den Brandt, P. A., Buring, J. E., Cho, E., Folsom, A. R., Freudenheim, J. L., Giovannucci, E., Graham, S., Horn-Ross, P. L., Leitzmann, M. F., McCullough, M. L., Miller, A. B., Parker, A. S., Rodriguez, C., … Smith-Warner, S. A. (2007). Alcohol intake and renal cell cancer in a pooled analysis of 12 prospective studies. Journal of the National Cancer Institute, 99(10), 801–810. https://doi.org/10.1093/jnci/djk181

Lee, J. J., Cook-Wiens, G., Johnson, B. D., Braunstein, G. D., Berga, S. L., Stanczyk, F. Z., Pepine, C. J., Bairey Merz, C. N., & Shufelt, C. L. (2019). Age at Menarche and Risk of Cardiovascular Disease Outcomes: Findings From the National Heart Lung and Blood Institute-Sponsored Women's Ischemia Syndrome Evaluation. Journal of the American Heart Association, 8(12), e012406. https://doi.org/10.1161/JAHA.119.012406

Li, H., Zou, Y., & Ding, G. (2012). Dietary factors associated with dental erosion: A meta-analysis. PloS One, 7(8), e42626. https://doi.org/10.1371/journal.pone.0042626

Lindenmuth, G. F., & Lindenmuth, E. B. (2000). The efficacy of echinacea compound herbal tea preparation on the severity and duration of upper respiratory and flu symptoms: A randomized, double-blind placebo-controlled study. Journal of Alternative and Complementary Medicine (New York, N.Y.), 6(4), 327–334. https://doi.org/10.1089/10755530050120691

Liska, D., Kelley, M., & Mah, E. (2019). 100% Fruit Juice and Dental Health: A Systematic Review of the Literature. Frontiers in Public Health, 7, 190. https://doi.org/10.3389/fpubh.2019.00190

Liu, G., Mi, X.-N., Zheng, X.-X., Xu, Y.-L., Lu, J., & Huang, X.-H. (2014). Effects of tea intake on blood pressure: A meta-analysis of randomised controlled trials. The British Journal of Nutrition, 112(7), 1043–1054. https://doi.org/10.1017/S0007114514001731

Liu, H., Hu, G.-H., Wang, X.-C., Huang, T.-B., Xu, L., Lai, P., Guo, Z.-F., & Xu, Y.-F. (2015). Coffee consumption and prostate cancer risk: A meta-analysis of cohort studies. Nutrition and Cancer, 67(3), 392–400. https://doi.org/10.1080/01635581.2015.1004727

Liu, Y.-C., Li, X.-Y., & Shen, L. (2020). Modulation effect of tea consumption on gut microbiota. Applied Microbiology and Biotechnology, 104(3), 981–987. https://doi.org/10.1007/s00253-019-10306-2

LoConte, N. K., Brewster, A. M., Kaur, J. S., Merrill, J. K., & Alberg, A. J. (2018). Alcohol and Cancer: A Statement of the American Society of Clinical Oncology. Journal of Clinical Oncology: Official Journal of the American Society of Clinical Oncology, 36(1), 83–93. https://doi.org/10.1200/JCO.2017.76.1155

Loftfield, E., Cornelis, M. C., Caporaso, N., Yu, K., Sinha, R., & Freedman, N. (2018). Association of Coffee Drinking With Mortality by Genetic Variation in Caffeine Metabolism: Findings From the UK Biobank. JAMA Internal Medicine, 178(8), 1086–1097. https://doi.org/10.1001/jamainternmed.2018.2425

Loomis, D., Guyton, K. Z., Grosse, Y., Lauby-Secretan, B., El Ghissassi, F., Bouvard, V., Benbrahim-Tallaa, L., Guha, N., Mattock, H., Straif, K., & International Agency for Research on Cancer Monograph Working Group. (2016). Carcinogenicity of drinking coffee, mate, and very hot beverages. The Lancet. Oncology, 17(7), 877–878. https://doi.org/10.1016/S1470-2045(16)30239-X

Lozano, R., Naghavi, M., Foreman, K., Lim, S., Shibuya, K., Aboyans, V., Abraham, J., Adair, T., Aggarwal, R., Ahn, S. Y., Alvarado, M., Anderson, H. R., Anderson, L. M., Andrews, K. G., Atkinson, C., Baddour, L. M., Barker-Collo, S., Bartels, D. H., Bell, M. L., … Memish, Z. A. (2012). Global and regional mortality from 235 causes of death for 20 age groups in 1990 and 2010: A systematic analysis for the Global Burden of Disease Study 2010. Lancet (London, England), 380(9859), 2095–2128. https://doi.org/10.1016/S0140-6736(12)61728-0

Lucas, M., O'Reilly, E. J., Pan, A., Mirzaei, F., Willett, W. C., Okereke, O. I., & Ascherio, A. (2014). Coffee, caffeine, and risk of completed suicide: Results from three prospective cohorts of American adults. The World Journal of Biological Psychiatry: The Official Journal of the World Federation of Societies of Biological Psychiatry, 15(5), 377–386. https://doi.org/10.3109/15622975.2013.795243

Luijken, J., van der Schouw, Y. T., Mensink, D., & Onland-Moret, N. C. (2017). Association between age at menarche and cardiovascular disease: A systematic review on risk and potential mechanisms. Maturitas, 104, 96–116. https://doi.org/10.1016/j.maturitas.2017.07.009

MacInnis, R. J., Hodge, A. M., Dixon, H. G., Peeters, A., Johnson, L. E., English, D. R., & Giles, G. G. (2014). Predictors of increased body weight and waist circumference for middle-aged adults. Public Health Nutrition, 17(5), 1087–1097. https://doi.org/10.1017/S1368980013001031

Maillot, M., Rehm, C. D., Vieux, F., Rose, C. M., & Drewnowski, A. (2018). Beverage consumption patterns among 4-19 y old children in 2009-14 NHANES show that the milk and 100% juice pattern is associated with better diets. Nutrition Journal, 17(1), 54. https://doi.org/10.1186/s12937-018-0363-9

Maillot, M., Vieux, F., Rehm, C. D., Rose, C. M., & Drewnowski, A. (2019). Consumption Patterns of Milk and 100% Juice in Relation to Diet Quality and Body Weight Among United States Children: Analyses of NHANES 2011-16 Data. Frontiers in Nutrition, 6, 117. https://doi.org/10.3389/fnut.2019.00117

Make Your Own Sports Drink | Berkeley Wellness. (n.d.). Retrieved December 16, 2020, from https://www.berkeleywellness.com/healthy-eating/nutrition/article/make-your-own-sports-drink

Malik, V. S., Li, Y., Pan, A., De Koning, L., Schernhammer, E., Willett, W. C., & Hu, F. B. (2019). Long-Term Consumption of Sugar-Sweetened and Artificially Sweetened Beverages and Risk of Mortality in US Adults. Circulation, 139(18), 2113–2125. https://doi.org/10.1161/CIRCULATIONAHA.118.037401

Malik, V. S., Popkin, B. M., Bray, G. A., Després, J.-P., Willett, W. C., & Hu, F. B. (2010). Sugar-sweetened beverages and risk of metabolic syndrome and type 2 diabetes: A meta-analysis. Diabetes Care, 33(11), 2477–2483. https://doi.org/10.2337/dc10-1079

Malik Vasanti S., Li Yanping, Pan An, De Koning Lawrence, Schernhammer Eva, Willett Walter C., & Hu Frank B. (2019). Long-Term Consumption of Sugar-Sweetened and Artificially Sweetened Beverages and Risk of Mortality in US Adults. Circulation, 139(18), 2113–2125. https://doi.org/10.1161/CIRCULATIONAHA.118.037401

Mansour, M. S., Ni, Y.-M., Roberts, A. L., Kelleman, M., Roychoudhury, A., & St-Onge, M.-P. (2012). Ginger consumption enhances the thermic effect of food and promotes feelings of satiety without affecting metabolic and hormonal parameters in overweight men: A pilot study. Metabolism: Clinical and Experimental, 61(10), 1347–1352. https://doi.org/10.1016/j.metabol.2012.03.016

Marshall, T. A., Van Buren, J. M., Warren, J. J., Cavanaugh, J. E., & Levy, S. M. (2017). Beverage Consumption Patterns at Age 13 to 17 Years Are Associated with Weight, Height, and Body Mass Index at Age 17 Years. Journal of the Academy of Nutrition and Dietetics, 117(5), 698–706. https://doi.org/10.1016/j.jand.2017.01.010

Martin, K. R., & Coles, K. M. (2019). Consumption of 100% Tart Cherry Juice Reduces Serum Urate in Overweight and Obese Adults. Current Developments in Nutrition, 3(5), nzz011. https://doi.org/10.1093/cdn/nzz011

Mason, S. A., Welch, V. G., & Neratko, J. (2018). Synthetic Polymer Contamination in Bottled Water. Frontiers in Chemistry, 6, 407. https://doi.org/10.3389/fchem.2018.00407

May 13, S. L. P. in B. 6. (2013, May 6). The History Of Energy Drinks: A Look Back. Wall Street Insanity. https://wallstreetinsanity.com/the-history-of-energy-drinks-a-look-back/

McGovern, P. E., Zhang, J., Tang, J., Zhang, Z., Hall, G. R., Moreau, R. A., Nuñez, A., Butrym, E. D., Richards, M. P., Wang, C.-S., Cheng, G., Zhao, Z., & Wang, C. (2004). Fermented beverages of pre- and proto-historic China. Proceedings of the National Academy of Sciences of the United States of America, 101(51), 17593–17598. https://doi.org/10.1073/pnas.0407921102

McKay, D. L., Chen, C.-Y. O., Saltzman, E., & Blumberg, J. B. (2010). Hibiscus sabdariffa L. tea (tisane) lowers blood pressure in prehypertensive and mildly hypertensive adults. The Journal of Nutrition, 140(2), 298–303. https://doi.org/10.3945/jn.109.115097

McKetin, R., Coen, A., & Kaye, S. (2015). A comprehensive review of the effects of mixing caffeinated energy drinks with alcohol. Drug and Alcohol Dependence, 151, 15–30. https://doi.org/10.1016/j.drugalcdep.2015.01.047

McNaughton, L. R., Lovell, R. J., Siegler, J., Midgley, A. W., Moore, L., & Bentley, D. J. (2008). The effects of caffeine ingestion on time trial cycling performance. International Journal of Sports Physiology and Performance, 3(2), 157–163. https://doi.org/10.1123/ijspp.3.2.157

Mehta, R. S., Song, M., Staller, K., & Chan, A. T. (2020). Association Between Beverage Intake and Incidence of Gastroesophageal Reflux Symptoms. Clinical Gastroenterology and Hepatology: The Official Clinical Practice Journal of the American Gastroenterological Association, 18(10), 2226-2233.e4. https://doi.org/10.1016/j.cgh.2019.11.040

Meng, J.-M., Cao, S.-Y., Wei, X.-L., Gan, R.-Y., Wang, Y.-F., Cai, S.-X., Xu, X.-Y., Zhang, P.-Z., & Li, H.-B. (2019). Effects and Mechanisms of Tea for the Prevention and Management of Diabetes Mellitus and Diabetic Complications: An Updated

Review. Antioxidants (Basel, Switzerland), 8(6). https://doi.org/10.3390/antiox8060170

Menon, K. V., Gores, G. J., & Shah, V. H. (2001). Pathogenesis, diagnosis, and treatment of alcoholic liver disease. Mayo Clinic Proceedings, 76(10), 1021–1029. https://doi.org/10.4065/76.10.1021

Mesas, A. E., Leon-Muñoz, L. M., Rodriguez-Artalejo, F., & Lopez-Garcia, E. (2011). The effect of coffee on blood pressure and cardiovascular disease in hypertensive individuals: A systematic review and meta-analysis. The American Journal of Clinical Nutrition, 94(4), 1113–1126. https://doi.org/10.3945/ajcn.111.016667

Meyer, B. D., & Lee, J. Y. (2015). The Confluence of Sugar, Dental Caries, and Health Policy. Journal of Dental Research, 94(10), 1338–1340. https://doi.org/10.1177/0022034515598958

Mezey, E. (1985). Effect of Ethanol on Intestinal Morphology, Metabolism, and Function. In H. K. Seitz & B. Kommerell (Eds.), Alcohol Related Diseases in Gastroenterology (pp. 342–360). Springer. https://doi.org/10.1007/978-3-642-70048-4_19

MIAR. (2021). Iranian Jornal of Obstetrics, Gynecology, and Infertility 1680-2993. Iranian Jornal of Obstetrics, Gynecology, and Infertility. http://miar.ub.edu/issn/1680-2993

Miller, G., Merlo, C., Demissie, Z., Sliwa, S., & Park, S. (2017). Trends in Beverage Consumption Among High School Students—United States, 2007-2015. MMWR. Morbidity and Mortality Weekly Report, 66(4), 112–116. https://doi.org/10.15585/mmwr.mm6604a5

Mineharu, Y., Koizumi, A., Wada, Y., Iso, H., Watanabe, Y., Date, C., Yamamoto, A., Kikuchi, S., Inaba, Y., Toyoshima, H., Kondo, T., Tamakoshi, A., & JACC study Group. (2011). Coffee, green tea, black tea and oolong tea consumption and risk of mortality from cardiovascular disease in Japanese men and women. Journal of Epidemiology and Community Health, 65(3), 230–240. https://doi.org/10.1136/jech.2009.097311

Montain, S. J., Latzka, W. A., & Sawka, M. N. (1999). Fluid replacement recommendations for training in hot weather. Military Medicine, 164(7), 502–508.

Mossavar-Rahmani, Y., Kamensky, V., Manson, J. E., Silver, B., Rapp, S. R., Haring, B., Beresford, S. A. A., Snetselaar, L., & Wassertheil-Smoller, S. (2019). Artificially Sweetened Beverages and Stroke, Coronary Heart Disease, and All-Cause Mortality in the Women's Health Initiative. Stroke, 50(3), 555–562. https://doi.org/10.1161/STROKEAHA.118.023100

Moynihan, P. J., & Kelly, S. a. M. (2014). Effect on caries of restricting sugars intake: Systematic review to inform WHO guidelines. Journal of Dental Research, 93(1), 8–18. https://doi.org/10.1177/0022034513508954

Mozaffari-Khosravi, H., Ahadi, Z., & Barzegar, K. (2013). The effect of green tea and sour tea on blood pressure of patients with type 2 diabetes: A randomized clinical trial. Journal of Dietary Supplements, 10(2), 105–115. https://doi.org/10.3109/19390211.2013.790333

Muckelbauer, R., Sarganas, G., Grüneis, A., & Müller-Nordhorn, J. (2013). Association between water consumption and body weight outcomes: A systematic review. The American Journal of Clinical Nutrition, 98(2), 282–299. https://doi.org/10.3945/ajcn.112.055061

Mullee, A., Romaguera, D., Pearson-Stuttard, J., Viallon, V., Stepien, M., Freisling, H., Fagherazzi, G., Mancini, F. R., Boutron-Ruault, M.-C., Kühn, T., Kaaks, R., Boeing, H., Aleksandrova, K., Tjønneland, A., Halkjær, J., Overvad, K., Weiderpass, E., Skeie, G., Parr, C. L., … Murphy, N. (2019). Association Between Soft Drink Consumption and Mortality in 10 European Countries. JAMA Internal Medicine, 179(11), 1479. https://doi.org/10.1001/jamainternmed.2019.2478

Murphy, M. M., Barrett, E. C., Bresnahan, K. A., & Barraj, L. M. (2017). 100 % Fruit juice and measures of glucose control and insulin sensitivity: A systematic review and meta-analysis of randomised controlled trials. Journal of Nutritional Science, 6, e59. https://doi.org/10.1017/jns.2017.63

Nagel, B. J., Schweinsburg, A. D., Phan, V., & Tapert, S. F. (2005). Reduced hippocampal volume among adolescents with alcohol use disorders without psychiatric comorbidity. Psychiatry Research, 139(3), 181–190. https://doi.org/10.1016/j.pscychresns.2005.05.008

National Toxicology Program. (2011). NTP 12th Report on Carcinogens. Report on Carcinogens: Carcinogen Profiles, 12, iii–499.

Nawrot, P., Jordan, S., Eastwood, J., Rotstein, J., Hugenholtz, A., & Feeley, M. (2003). Effects of caffeine on human health. Food Additives & Contaminants, 20(1), 1–30. https://doi.org/10.1080/0265203021000007840

Nelson, D. E., Jarman, D. W., Rehm, J., Greenfield, T. K., Rey, G., Kerr, W. C., Miller, P., Shield, K. D., Ye, Y., & Naimi, T. S. (2013). Alcohol-attributable cancer deaths and years of potential life lost in the United States. American Journal of Public Health, 103(4), 641–648. https://doi.org/10.2105/AJPH.2012.301199

Noble, W. H., Donovan, T. E., & Geissberger, M. (2011). Sports drinks and dental erosion. Journal of the California Dental Association, 39(4), 233–238.

Odai, T., Terauchi, M., Okamoto, D., Hirose, A., & Miyasaka, N. (2019). Unsalted tomato juice intake improves blood pressure and serum low-density lipoprotein cholesterol level in local Japanese residents at risk of cardiovascular disease. Food Science & Nutrition, 7(7), 2271–2279. https://doi.org/10.1002/fsn3.1066

Office of Dietary Supplements—Niacin. (2020, Accessed). https://ods.od.nih.gov/factsheets/Niacin-HealthProfessional/

Office of Dietary Supplements—Vitamin B6. (2020, Accessed). https://ods.od.nih.gov/factsheets/VitaminB6-HealthProfessional/

Office of Dietary Supplements—Vitamin B12. (2020, Accessed). https://ods.od.nih.gov/factsheets/VitaminB12-HealthProfessional/

Ohishi, T., Goto, S., Monira, P., Isemura, M., & Nakamura, Y. (2016). Anti-inflammatory Action of Green Tea. Anti-Inflammatory & Anti-Allergy Agents in Medicinal Chemistry, 15(2), 74–90. https://doi.org/10.2174/1871523015666160915154443

Oka, Y., Ye, M., & Zuker, C. S. (2015). Thirst driving and suppressing signals encoded by distinct neural populations in the brain. Nature, 520(7547), 349–352. https://doi.org/10.1038/nature14108

Okubo, H., Miyake, Y., Tanaka, K., Sasaki, S., & Hirota, Y. (2015). Maternal total caffeine intake, mainly from Japanese and Chinese tea, during pregnancy was associated with risk of preterm birth: The Osaka Maternal and Child Health Study. Nutrition Research (New York, N.Y.), 35(4), 309–316. https://doi.org/10.1016/j.nutres.2015.02.009

Oliveri Conti, G., Ferrante, M., Banni, M., Favara, C., Nicolosi, I., Cristaldi, A., Fiore, M., & Zuccarello, P. (2020). Micro- and nano-plastics in edible fruit and vegetables. The first diet risks assessment for the general population. Environmental Research, 187, 109677. https://doi.org/10.1016/j.envres.2020.109677

Oßmann, B. E., Sarau, G., Holtmannspötter, H., Pischetsrieder, M., Christiansen, S. H., & Dicke, W. (2018). Small-sized microplastics and pigmented particles in bottled mineral water. Water Research, 141, 307–316. https://doi.org/10.1016/j.watres.2018.05.027

Özen, A. E., Bibiloni, M. D. M., Pons, A., & Tur, J. A. (2015). Fluid intake from beverages across age groups: A systematic review. Journal of Human Nutrition and Dietetics: The Official Journal of the British Dietetic Association, 28(5), 417–442. https://doi.org/10.1111/jhn.12250

Palatini, P., Ceolotto, G., Ragazzo, F., Dorigatti, F., Saladini, F., Papparella, I., Mos, L., Zanata, G., & Santonastaso, M. (2009). CYP1A2 genotype modifies the association between coffee intake and the risk of hypertension. Journal of Hypertension, 27(8), 1594–1601. https://doi.org/10.1097/HJH.0b013e32832ba850

Palma-Lara, I., Martínez-Castillo, M., Quintana-Pérez, J. C., Arellano-Mendoza, M. G., Tamay-Cach, F., Valenzuela-Limón, O. L., García-Montalvo, E. A., & Hernández-Zavala, A. (2020). Arsenic exposure: A public health problem leading to several cancers. Regulatory Toxicology and Pharmacology: RTP, 110, 104539. https://doi.org/10.1016/j.yrtph.2019.104539

Panza, F., Solfrizzi, V., Barulli, M. R., Bonfiglio, C., Guerra, V., Osella, A., Seripa, D., Sabbà, C., Pilotto, A., & Logroscino, G. (2015). Coffee, tea, and caffeine consumption and prevention of late-life cognitive decline and dementia: A systematic review. The Journal of Nutrition, Health & Aging, 19(3), 313–328. https://doi.org/10.1007/s12603-014-0563-8

Park, S., Blanck, H. M., Sherry, B., Brener, N., & O'Toole, T. (2012). Factors associated with low water intake among US high school students—National Youth Physical Activity and Nutrition Study, 2010. Journal of the Academy of Nutrition and Dietetics, 112(9), 1421–1427. https://doi.org/10.1016/j.jand.2012.04.014

Park, S.-Y., Freedman, N. D., Haiman, C. A., Le Marchand, L., Wilkens, L. R., & Setiawan, V. W. (2017). Association of Coffee Consumption With Total and Cause-Specific Mortality Among Nonwhite Populations. Annals of Internal Medicine, 167(4), 228–235. https://doi.org/10.7326/M16-2472

Parr, E. B., Camera, D. M., Areta, J. L., Burke, L. M., Phillips, S. M., Hawley, J. A., & Coffey, V. G. (2014). Alcohol ingestion impairs maximal post-exercise rates of myofibrillar protein synthesis following a single bout of concurrent training. PloS One, 9(2), e88384. https://doi.org/10.1371/journal.pone.0088384

Pasman, W. J., van Baak, M. A., Jeukendrup, A. E., & de Haan, A. (1995). The effect of different dosages of caffeine on endurance performance time. International Journal of Sports Medicine, 16(4), 225–230. https://doi.org/10.1055/s-2007-972996

Peacock, A., Hutchinson, D., Wilson, J., McCormack, C., Bruno, R., Olsson, C. A., Allsop, S., Elliott, E., Burns, L., & Mattick, R. P. (2018). Adherence to the Caffeine Intake Guideline during Pregnancy and Birth Outcomes: A Prospective Cohort Study. Nutrients, 10(3). https://doi.org/10.3390/nu10030319

Pereira, M. A., & Fulgoni, V. L. (2010). Consumption of 100% fruit juice and risk of obesity and metabolic syndrome: Findings from the national health and nutrition examination survey 1999-2004. Journal of the American College of Nutrition, 29(6), 625–629. https://doi.org/10.1080/07315724.2010.10719901

Persson, I. A.-L., Persson, K., Hägg, S., & Andersson, R. G. G. (2010). Effects of green tea, black tea and Rooibos tea on angiotensin-converting enzyme and nitric oxide in healthy volunteers. Public Health Nutrition, 13(5), 730–737. https://doi.org/10.1017/S1368980010000170

Pfeiffer, A., Schmidt, T., Vidon, N., Pehl, C., & Kaess, H. (1992). Absorption of a nutrient solution in chronic alcoholics without nutrient deficiencies and liver cirrhosis. Scandinavian Journal of Gastroenterology, 27(12), 1023–1030. https://doi.org/10.3109/00365529209028133

Pivokonsky, M., Cermakova, L., Novotna, K., Peer, P., Cajthaml, T., & Janda, V. (2018). Occurrence of microplastics in raw and treated drinking water. The Science of the Total Environment, 643, 1644–1651. https://doi.org/10.1016/j.scitotenv.2018.08.102

Popkin, B. M. (2010). Patterns of beverage use across the lifecycle. Physiology & Behavior, 100(1), 4–9. https://doi.org/10.1016/j.physbeh.2009.12.022

Popkin, B. M., & Hawkes, C. (2016). Sweetening of the global diet, particularly beverages: Patterns, trends, and policy responses. The Lancet. Diabetes & Endocrinology, 4(2), 174–186. https://doi.org/10.1016/S2213-8587(15)00419-2

Poswal, F. S., Russell, G., Mackonochie, M., MacLennan, E., Adukwu, E. C., & Rolfe, V. (2019). Herbal Teas and their Health Benefits: A Scoping Review. Plant Foods for Human Nutrition (Dordrecht, Netherlands), 74(3), 266–276. https://doi.org/10.1007/s11130-019-00750-w

Prata, J. C., da Costa, J. P., Lopes, I., Duarte, A. C., & Rocha-Santos, T. (2020). Environmental exposure to microplastics: An overview on possible human health effects. The Science of the Total Environment, 702, 134455. https://doi.org/10.1016/j.scitotenv.2019.134455

Rachdaoui, N., & Sarkar, D. K. (2013a). Effects of alcohol on the endocrine system. Endocrinology and Metabolism Clinics of North America, 42(3), 593–615. https://doi.org/10.1016/j.ecl.2013.05.008

Rachdaoui, N., & Sarkar, D. K. (2013b). Effects of alcohol on the endocrine system. Endocrinology and Metabolism Clinics of North America, 42(3), 593–615. https://doi.org/10.1016/j.ecl.2013.05.008

Rafraf, M., Zemestani, M., & Asghari-Jafarabadi, M. (2015). Effectiveness of chamomile tea on glycemic control and serum lipid profile in patients with type 2 diabetes. Journal of Endocrinological Investigation, 38(2), 163–170. https://doi.org/10.1007/s40618-014-0170-x

Ragusa, A., Svelato, A., Santacroce, C., Catalano, P., Notarstefano, V., Carnevali, O., Papa, F., Rongioletti, M. C. A., Baiocco, F., Draghi, S., D'Amore, E., Rinaldo, D., Matta, M., & Giorgini, E. (2021). Plasticenta: First evidence of microplastics in human placenta. Environment International, 146, 106274. https://doi.org/10.1016/j.envint.2020.106274

Ramadan, G., El-Beih, N. M., & Abd El-Ghffar, E. A. (2009). Modulatory effects of black v. Green tea aqueous extract on hyperglycaemia, hyperlipidaemia and liver dysfunction in diabetic and obese rat models. The British Journal of Nutrition, 102(11), 1611–1619. https://doi.org/10.1017/S000711450999208X

Redfern, K. M., Cammack, V. L., Sweet, N., Preston, L. A., SoBHCS Student Team, Jarvis, M. A., & Rees, G. A. (2017). Nutrient-extraction blender preparation reduces postprandial glucose responses from fruit juice consumption. Nutrition & Diabetes, 7(10), e288. https://doi.org/10.1038/nutd.2017.36

Rehm, J., & Roerecke, M. (2017). Cardiovascular effects of alcohol consumption. Trends in Cardiovascular Medicine, 27(8), 534–538. https://doi.org/10.1016/j.tcm.2017.06.002

Reissig, C. J., Strain, E. C., & Griffiths, R. R. (2009). Caffeinated energy drinks—A growing problem. Drug and Alcohol Dependence, 99(1–3), 1–10. https://doi.org/10.1016/j.drugalcdep.2008.08.001

Richter, L., Pugh, B. S., Peters, E. A., Vaughan, R. D., & Foster, S. E. (2016). Underage drinking: Prevalence and correlates of risky drinking measures among youth aged 12-20. The American Journal of Drug and Alcohol Abuse, 42(4), 385–394. https://doi.org/10.3109/00952990.2015.1102923

Ritz, P., & Berrut, G. (2005). The importance of good hydration for day-to-day health. Nutrition Reviews, 63(6 Pt 2), S6-13. https://doi.org/10.1111/j.1753-4887.2005.tb00155.x

Rodak, K., Kokot, I., & Kratz, E. M. (2021). Caffeine as a Factor Influencing the Functioning of the Human Body—Friend or Foe? Nutrients, 13(9), 3088. https://doi.org/10.3390/nu13093088

Ronksley, P. E., Brien, S. E., Turner, B. J., Mukamal, K. J., & Ghali, W. A. (2011). Association of alcohol consumption with selected cardiovascular disease outcomes: A systematic review and meta-analysis. BMJ (Clinical Research Ed.), 342, d671. https://doi.org/10.1136/bmj.d671

Rorabaugh, W. J. (1991). Alcohol in America. OAH Magazine of History, 6(2), 17–19. https://doi.org/10.1093/maghis/6.2.17

Rother, K. I., Conway, E. M., & Sylvetsky, A. C. (2018). How Non-nutritive Sweeteners Influence Hormones and Health. Trends in Endocrinology and Metabolism: TEM, 29(7), 455–467. https://doi.org/10.1016/j.tem.2018.04.010

Roussel, R., Fezeu, L., Bouby, N., Balkau, B., Lantieri, O., Alhenc-Gelas, F., Marre, M., Bankir, L., & D.E.S.I.R. Study Group. (2011). Low water intake and risk for new-onset hyperglycemia. Diabetes Care, 34(12), 2551–2554. https://doi.org/10.2337/dc11-0652

Ruanpeng, D., Thongprayoon, C., Cheungpasitporn, W., & Harindhanavudhi, T. (2017). Sugar and artificially sweetened beverages linked to obesity: A systematic review and meta-analysis. QJM: Monthly Journal of the Association of Physicians, 110(8), 513–520. https://doi.org/10.1093/qjmed/hcx068

Ruepert, L., Quartero, A. O., de Wit, N. J., van der Heijden, G. J., Rubin, G., & Muris, J. W. (2011). Bulking agents, antispasmodics and antidepressants for the treatment of irritable bowel syndrome. The Cochrane Database of Systematic Reviews, 8, CD003460. https://doi.org/10.1002/14651858.CD003460.pub3

Sääksjärvi, K., Knekt, P., Männistö, S., Lyytinen, J., Jääskeläinen, T., Kanerva, N., & Heliövaara, M. (2014). Reduced risk of Parkinson's disease associated with lower body mass index and heavy leisure-time physical activity. European Journal of Epidemiology, 29(4), 285–292. https://doi.org/10.1007/s10654-014-9887-2

Saint-Jacques, N., Brown, P., Nauta, L., Boxall, J., Parker, L., & Dummer, T. (2018). Estimating the risk of bladder and kidney cancer from exposure to low-levels of arsenic in drinking water, Nova Scotia, Canada. Environment International, 110. https://doi.org/10.1016/j.envint.2017.10.014

Sakaki, J. R., Melough, M. M., Li, J., Tamimi, R. M., Chavarro, J. E., Chen, M.-H., & Chun, O. K. (2019). Associations between 100% Orange Juice Consumption and Dietary, Lifestyle and Anthropometric Characteristics in a Cross-Sectional Study of U.S. Children and Adolescents. Nutrients, 11(11). https://doi.org/10.3390/nu11112687

Santos, C., Costa, J., Santos, J., Vaz-Carneiro, A., & Lunet, N. (2010). Caffeine intake and dementia: Systematic review and meta-analysis. Journal of Alzheimer's Disease: JAD, 20 Suppl 1, S187-204. https://doi.org/10.3233/JAD-2010-091387

Santos, R. M. M., & Lima, D. R. A. (2016). Coffee consumption, obesity and type 2 diabetes: A mini-review. European Journal of Nutrition, 55(4), 1345–1358. https://doi.org/10.1007/s00394-016-1206-0

Savolainen, V. T., Liesto, K., Männikkö, A., Penttilä, A., & Karhunen, P. J. (1993). Alcohol consumption and alcoholic liver disease: Evidence of a threshold level of effects of ethanol. Alcoholism, Clinical and Experimental Research, 17(5), 1112–1117. https://doi.org/10.1111/j.1530-0277.1993.tb05673.x

Sayon-Orea, C., Martinez-Gonzalez, M. A., & Bes-Rastrollo, M. (2011). Alcohol consumption and body weight: A systematic review. Nutrition Reviews, 69(8), 419–431. https://doi.org/10.1111/j.1753-4887.2011.00403.x

Schernhammer, E. S., Bertrand, K. A., Birmann, B. M., Sampson, L., Willett, W. C., & Feskanich, D. (2012). Consumption of artificial sweetener- and sugar-containing soda and risk of lymphoma and leukemia in men and women. The American Journal of Clinical Nutrition, 96(6), 1419–1428. https://doi.org/10.3945/ajcn.111.030833

Schneider, M. B., Benjamin, H. J., & Committee on Nutrition and the Council on Sports Medicine and Fitness. (2011). Sports Drinks and Energy Drinks for Children and Adolescents: Are They Appropriate? Pediatrics, 127(6), 1182–1189. https://doi.org/10.1542/peds.2011-0965

Scholey, A. B., & Kennedy, D. O. (2004). Cognitive and physiological effects of an "energy drink": An evaluation of the whole drink and of glucose, caffeine and herbal flavouring fractions. Psychopharmacology, 176(3–4), 320–330. https://doi.org/10.1007/s00213-004-1935-2

Scholey, A., Gibbs, A., Neale, C., Perry, N., Ossoukhova, A., Bilog, V., Kras, M., Scholz, C., Sass, M., & Buchwald-Werner, S. (2014). Anti-stress effects of lemon balm-containing foods. Nutrients, 6(11), 4805–4821. https://doi.org/10.3390/nu6114805

Schullehner, J., Hansen, B., Thygesen, M., Pedersen, C., & Sigsgaard, T. (2018). Nitrate in drinking water and colorectal cancer risk: A nationwide population-based cohort study. 143(1). https://doi.org/10.1002/ijc.31306

Schwabl, P., Köppel, S., Königshofer, P., Bucsics, T., Trauner, M., Reiberger, T., & Liebmann, B. (2019). Detection of Various Microplastics in Human Stool: A Prospective Case Series. Annals of Internal Medicine, 171(7), 453–457. https://doi.org/10.7326/M19-0618

Schwartz, A. E., Leardo, M., Aneja, S., & Elbel, B. (2016). Effect of a School-Based Water Intervention on Child Body Mass Index and Obesity. JAMA Pediatrics, 170(3), 220–226. https://doi.org/10.1001/jamapediatrics.2015.3778

Scientific Opinion on Dietary Reference Values for water. (2010). EFSA Journal, 8(3), 1459. https://doi.org/10.2903/j.efsa.2010.1459

Seifert, S. M., Schaechter, J. L., Hershorin, E. R., & Lipshultz, S. E. (2011). Health Effects of Energy Drinks on Children, Adolescents, and Young Adults. Pediatrics, 127(3), 511–528. https://doi.org/10.1542/peds.2009-3592

Shearer, J., & Graham, T. E. (2014). Performance effects and metabolic consequences of caffeine and caffeinated energy drink consumption on glucose disposal. Nutrition Reviews, 72 Suppl 1, 121–136. https://doi.org/10.1111/nure.12124

Shenouda, S. M., & Vita, J. A. (2007). Effects of flavonoid-containing beverages and EGCG on endothelial function. Journal of the American College of Nutrition, 26(4), 366S-372S. https://doi.org/10.1080/07315724.2007.10719625

Singal, A. K., Guturu, P., Hmoud, B., Kuo, Y.-F., Salameh, H., & Wiesner, R. H. (2013). Evolving frequency and outcomes of liver transplantation based on etiology of liver disease. Transplantation, 95(5), 755–760. https://doi.org/10.1097/TP.0b013e31827afb3a

Smith, A. (2002). Effects of caffeine on human behavior. Food and Chemical Toxicology: An International Journal Published for the British Industrial Biological Research Association, 40(9), 1243–1255. https://doi.org/10.1016/s0278-6915(02)00096-0

Smith, J. P., & Randall, C. L. (2012). Anxiety and Alcohol Use Disorders. Alcohol Research : Current Reviews, 34(4), 414–431.

Smith, M., Love, D. C., Rochman, C. M., & Neff, R. A. (2018). Microplastics in Seafood and the Implications for Human Health. Current Environmental Health Reports, 5(3), 375–386. https://doi.org/10.1007/s40572-018-0206-z

Sontrop, J., Dixon, S., Garg, A., Buendia-Jimenez, I., Dohein, O., Huang, S., & Clark, W. (2013). Association between water intake, chronic kidney disease, and cardiovascular disease: A cross-sectional analysis of NHANES data. American Journal of Nephrology, 37(5). https://doi.org/10.1159/000350377

Sports Drinks. Give Up Loving Pop. (n.d.). Retrieved December 16, 2020, from https://www.foodactive.org.uk/wp-content/uploads/2016/07/GULP-4-Sports-Drinks-v2.pdf

Spriet, L. L. (2014). Exercise and sport performance with low doses of caffeine. Sports Medicine (Auckland, N.Z.), 44 Suppl 2, S175-184. https://doi.org/10.1007/s40279-014-0257-8

Stangl, V., Lorenz, M., & Stangl, K. (2006). The role of tea and tea flavonoids in cardiovascular health. Molecular Nutrition & Food Research, 50(2), 218–228. https://doi.org/10.1002/mnfr.200500118

Suez, J., Korem, T., Zeevi, D., Zilberman-Schapira, G., Thaiss, C. A., Maza, O., Israeli, D., Zmora, N., Gilad, S., Weinberger, A., Kuperman, Y., Harmelin, A., Kolodkin-Gal, I., Shapiro, H., Halpern, Z., Segal, E., & Elinav, E. (2014). Artificial sweeteners induce glucose intolerance by altering the gut microbiota. Nature, 514(7521), 181–186. https://doi.org/10.1038/nature13793

Suez, J., Korem, T., Zilberman-Schapira, G., Segal, E., & Elinav, E. (2015). Non-caloric artificial sweeteners and the microbiome: Findings and challenges. Gut Microbes, 6(2), 149–155. https://doi.org/10.1080/19490976.2015.1017700

Svatikova, A., Covassin, N., Somers, K. R., Somers, K. V., Soucek, F., Kara, T., & Bukartyk, J. (2015). A Randomized Trial of Cardiovascular Responses to Energy Drink Consumption in Healthy Adults. JAMA, 314(19), 2079–2082. https://doi.org/10.1001/jama.2015.13744

Tarnopolsky, M. A. (2010). Caffeine and creatine use in sport. Annals of Nutrition & Metabolism, 57 Suppl 2, 1–8. https://doi.org/10.1159/000322696

Tate, D. F., Turner-McGrievy, G., Lyons, E., Stevens, J., Erickson, K., Polzien, K., Diamond, M., Wang, X., & Popkin, B. (2012). Replacing caloric beverages with water or diet beverages for weight loss in adults: Main results of the Choose Healthy Options Consciously Everyday (CHOICE) randomized clinical trial. The American Journal of Clinical Nutrition, 95(3), 555–563. https://doi.org/10.3945/ajcn.111.026278

Testai, L., & Calderone, V. (2017). Nutraceutical Value of Citrus Flavanones and Their Implications in Cardiovascular Disease. Nutrients, 9(5). https://doi.org/10.3390/nu9050502

Timbrell, J. A., Seabra, V., & Waterfield, C. J. (1995). The in vivo and in vitro protective properties of taurine. General Pharmacology, 26(3), 453–462. https://doi.org/10.1016/0306-3623(94)00203-y

Tramacere, I., Pelucchi, C., Bonifazi, M., Bagnardi, V., Rota, M., Bellocco, R., Scotti, L., Islami, F., Corrao, G., Boffetta, P., La Vecchia, C., & Negri, E. (2012). Alcohol drinking and non-Hodgkin lymphoma risk: A systematic review and a meta-analysis. Annals of Oncology: Official Journal of the European Society for Medical Oncology, 23(11), 2791–2798. https://doi.org/10.1093/annonc/mds013

Triebel, S., Sproll, C., Reusch, H., Godelmann, R., & Lachenmeier, D. W. (2007). Rapid analysis of taurine in energy drinks using amino acid analyzer and Fourier transform infrared (FTIR) spectroscopy as basis for toxicological evaluation. Amino Acids, 33(3), 451–457. https://doi.org/10.1007/s00726-006-0449-0

USDA. (n.d.). Fruits | MyPlate. Retrieved February 13, 2022, from
https://www.myplate.gov/eat-healthy/fruits

Vartanian, L. R., Schwartz, M. B., & Brownell, K. D. (2007). Effects of soft drink
consumption on nutrition and health: A systematic review and meta-analysis.
American Journal of Public Health, 97(4), 667–675.
https://doi.org/10.2105/AJPH.2005.083782

Veerasamy, M., Bagnall, A., Neely, D., Allen, J., Sinclair, H., & Kunadian, V. (2015).
Endothelial dysfunction and coronary artery disease: A state of the art review.
Cardiology in Review, 23(3), 119–129.
https://doi.org/10.1097/CRD.0000000000000047

Vercammen, K. A., Koma, J. W., & Bleich, S. N. (2019). Trends in Energy Drink
Consumption Among U.S. Adolescents and Adults, 2003–2016. American
Journal of Preventive Medicine, 56(6), 827–833.
https://doi.org/10.1016/j.amepre.2018.12.007

Villaño, D., Pecorari, M., Testa, M. F., Raguzzini, A., Stalmach, A., Crozier, A., Tubili, C., &
Serafini, M. (2010). Unfermented and fermented rooibos teas (Aspalathus
linearis) increase plasma total antioxidant capacity in healthy humans. Food
Chemistry. https://agris.fao.org/agris-
search/search.do?recordID=US201301869861

Vitaglione, P., Mazzone, G., Lembo, V., D'Argenio, G., Rossi, A., Guido, M., Savoia, M.,
Salomone, F., Mennella, I., De Filippis, F., Ercolini, D., Caporaso, N., & Morisco, F.
(2019). Coffee prevents fatty liver disease induced by a high-fat diet by
modulating pathways of the gut-liver axis. Journal of Nutritional Science, 8, e15.
https://doi.org/10.1017/jns.2019.10

Vos, M. B., Kaar, J. L., Welsh, J. A., Van Horn, L. V., Feig, D. I., Anderson, C. A. M., Patel,
M. J., Cruz Munos, J., Krebs, N. F., Xanthakos, S. A., Johnson, R. K., & American
Heart Association Nutrition Committee of the Council on Lifestyle and
Cardiometabolic Health; Council on Clinical Cardiology; Council on
Cardiovascular Disease in the Young; Council on Cardiovascular and Stroke
Nursing; Council on Epidemiology and Prevention; Council on Functional
Genomics and Translational Biology; and Council on Hypertension. (2017).
Added Sugars and Cardiovascular Disease Risk in Children: A Scientific
Statement From the American Heart Association. Circulation, 135(19), e1017–
e1034. https://doi.org/10.1161/CIR.0000000000000439

Wang, A., Wang, S., Zhu, C., Huang, H., Wu, L., Wan, X., Yang, X., Zhang, H., Miao, R., He,
L., Sang, X., & Zhao, H. (2016). Coffee and cancer risk: A meta-analysis of
prospective observational studies. Scientific Reports, 6, 33711.
https://doi.org/10.1038/srep33711

Wang, L., Shen, X., Wu, Y., & Zhang, D. (2016). Coffee and caffeine consumption and
depression: A meta-analysis of observational studies. The Australian and New

Zealand Journal of Psychiatry, 50(3), 228–242.
https://doi.org/10.1177/0004867415603131

Wang, Y. C., Bleich, S. N., & Gortmaker, S. L. (2008). Increasing caloric contribution from sugar-sweetened beverages and 100% fruit juices among US children and adolescents, 1988-2004. Pediatrics, 121(6), e1604-1614. https://doi.org/10.1542/peds.2007-2834

Ward, M., Jones, R., Brender, J., de Kok, T., Weyer, W., Bt, N., Cm, V., & Sg, van B. (2018). Drinking Water Nitrate and Human Health: An Updated Review. International Journal of Environmental Research and Public Health, 15(7). https://doi.org/10.3390/ijerph15071557

Watso, J. C., & Farquhar, W. B. (2019). Hydration Status and Cardiovascular Function. Nutrients, 11(8). https://doi.org/10.3390/nu11081866

Wei, M., Gibbons, L. W., Mitchell, T. L., Kampert, J. B., & Blair, S. N. (2000). Alcohol intake and incidence of type 2 diabetes in men. Diabetes Care, 23(1), 18–22. https://doi.org/10.2337/diacare.23.1.18

Welsh, J. A., Wang, Y., Figueroa, J., & Brumme, C. (2018). Sugar intake by type (added vs. Naturally occurring) and physical form (liquid vs. Solid) and its varying association with children's body weight, NHANES 2009-2014. Pediatric Obesity, 13(4), 213–221. https://doi.org/10.1111/ijpo.12264

WHO | Global Status Report on Alcohol and Health 2014. (n.d.). WHO; World Health Organization. Retrieved December 16, 2020, from http://www.who.int/substance_abuse/publications/alcohol_2014/en/

Wijarnpreecha, K., Thongprayoon, C., & Ungprasert, P. (2017). Coffee consumption and risk of nonalcoholic fatty liver disease: A systematic review and meta-analysis. European Journal of Gastroenterology & Hepatology, 29(2), e8–e12. https://doi.org/10.1097/MEG.0000000000000776

Wojcicki, J. M., & Heyman, M. B. (2012). Reducing childhood obesity by eliminating 100% fruit juice. American Journal of Public Health, 102(9), 1630–1633. https://doi.org/10.2105/AJPH.2012.300719

Wolde, T. (2014). Effects of caffeine on health and nutrition: A Review. Food Science and Quality Management, 30(0), 59.

Wolk, B. J., Ganetsky, M., & Babu, K. M. (2012). Toxicity of energy drinks. Current Opinion in Pediatrics, 24(2), 243–251. https://doi.org/10.1097/MOP.0b013e3283506827

Yang, C. S., Wang, X., Lu, G., & Picinich, S. C. (2009). Cancer prevention by tea: Animal studies, molecular mechanisms and human relevance. Nature Reviews. Cancer, 9(6), 429–439. https://doi.org/10.1038/nrc2641

Yang, Y.-C., Lu, F.-H., Wu, J.-S., Wu, C.-H., & Chang, C.-J. (2004). The protective effect of habitual tea consumption on hypertension. Archives of Internal Medicine, 164(14), 1534–1540. https://doi.org/10.1001/archinte.164.14.1534

Yeomans, M. R. (2010). Alcohol, appetite and energy balance: Is alcohol intake a risk factor for obesity? Physiology & Behavior, 100(1), 82–89. https://doi.org/10.1016/j.physbeh.2010.01.012

Yeomans, M. R., Caton, S., & Hetherington, M. M. (2003). Alcohol and food intake. Current Opinion in Clinical Nutrition and Metabolic Care, 6(6), 639–644. https://doi.org/10.1097/00075197-200311000-00006

Yew, Y. W., Lai, Y. C., & Schwartz, R. A. (2016). Coffee Consumption and Melanoma: A Systematic Review and Meta-Analysis of Observational Studies. American Journal of Clinical Dermatology, 17(2), 113–123. https://doi.org/10.1007/s40257-015-0165-1

Yi, M., Wu, X., Zhuang, W., Xia, L., Chen, Y., Zhao, R., Wan, Q., Du, L., & Zhou, Y. (2019). Tea Consumption and Health Outcomes: Umbrella Review of Meta-Analyses of Observational Studies in Humans. Molecular Nutrition & Food Research, 63(16), e1900389. https://doi.org/10.1002/mnfr.201900389

Yu, F., Jin, Z., Jiang, H., Xiang, C., Tang, J., Li, T., & He, J. (2014). Tea consumption and the risk of five major cancers: A dose-response meta-analysis of prospective studies. BMC Cancer, 14, 197. https://doi.org/10.1186/1471-2407-14-197

Yu, X., Bao, Z., Zou, J., & Dong, J. (2011). Coffee consumption and risk of cancers: A meta-analysis of cohort studies. BMC Cancer, 11, 96. https://doi.org/10.1186/1471-2407-11-96

Yuzbashian, E., Asghari, G., Mirmiran, P., Zadeh-Vakili, A., & Azizi, F. (2016). Sugar-sweetened beverage consumption and risk of incident chronic kidney disease: Tehran lipid and glucose study. Nephrology (Carlton, Vic.), 21(7). https://doi.org/10.1111/nep.12646

Zhao, J., Stockwell, T., Roemer, A., & Chikritzhs, T. (2016). Is alcohol consumption a risk factor for prostate cancer? A systematic review and meta-analysis. BMC Cancer, 16(1), 845. https://doi.org/10.1186/s12885-016-2891-z

Zheng, M., Rangan, A., Olsen, N., Anderson, L., Wedderkopp, D, P., K., A, G., M, R.-L., Sm, L., M, A.-F., & Bl, H. (2015). Substituting sugar-sweetened beverages with water or milk is inversely associated with body fatness development from childhood to adolescence. Nutrition (Burbank, Los Angeles County, Calif.), 31(1). https://doi.org/10.1016/j.nut.2014.04.017

Zhou, A., & Hyppönen, E. (2019). Long-term coffee consumption, caffeine metabolism genetics, and risk of cardiovascular disease: A prospective analysis of up to 347,077 individuals and 8368 cases. The American Journal of Clinical Nutrition, 109(3), 509–516. https://doi.org/10.1093/ajcn/nqy297

Zocchi, D., Wennemuth, G., & Oka, Y. (2017). The cellular mechanism for water detection in the mammalian taste system. Nature Neuroscience, 20(7), 927–933. https://doi.org/10.1038/nn.4575

Zuccarello, P., Ferrante, M., Cristaldi, A., Copat, C., Grasso, A., Sangregorio, D., Fiore, M., & Oliveri Conti, G. (2019). Exposure to microplastics (<10 μm) associated to plastic bottles mineral water consumption: The first quantitative study. Water Research, 157, 365–371. https://doi.org/10.1016/j.watres.2019.03.091

HERBS & SPICES

By Chef Natasha MacAller
Jasna Robinson-Wright, MSc, RD, CDE, CIEC
and Deborah Kennedy PhD

"Spices and herbs are the flavors of life and may be the source of well-being for life too"
Quote by Natasha MacAller

Herbs and spices have been used not only for flavor, but also for the health and longevity of human civilizations and cultures for thousands of years. Ancient records show again and again their use as a nutritious and flavorful addition to food. Since the cumin-consuming pharaohs of Egypt and garlic-gluttonous rulers of ancient Greece, spices and herbs have been consumed not only as a flavoring ingredient but as medicine. In present times, herbs and spices continue to be used for medicinal purposes. Ginger is a good example of a modern-day solution for the nausea of seasickness and pregnancy-related morning sickness (O'Donnell et al., 2016; Matthews et al., 2015).

In particular, a diet rich in spices has been shown to help lower the risk of heart disease, neurodegenerative diseases, diabetes and some types of cancer (Tapsell et al., 2006; Kunnumakkara et al., 2018; Balasubramanian et al., 2016; Kaefer and Milner, 2008; Raghavendra and Naidu, 2009; Jungbauer and Medjakovic, 2012). There is also emerging evidence that some herbs and spices may improve cognitive function and mental health (Tapsell et al., 2006; Iriti et al., 2010; Fleenor et al., 2013).

While there is a general belief in the scientific community — as well as long-standing belief among many cultures — that herbs and spices provide health benefits, there continues to be a need for further high-quality studies to help understand the exact mechanisms and full extent of their actions in the body (Tapsell et al., 2006; Opara and Chohan, 2014). One avenue to examine this is by looking at the bioactive compounds in herbs and spices at the quantities that are consumed in a normal diet. **Polyphenols** are the bioactive phytochemicals that are predominate among herbs and spices (Zheng and Wang, 2014; Neveu et al., 2010; Perez-Jimenez et al., 2010; Perez-Jimenez et al., 2010). The health effects of polyphenols at the typical levels consumed through herbs and spices used in foods are of utmost interest.

Polyphenols in other foods such as fruits, vegetables, and green tea have been shown to have **antioxidant** properties, and also provide other health benefits such as being **anti-inflammatory, anti-cancer, and neuroprotective** (Pandey and Risvi, 2009; Singh et al., 2008; Scalbert et al., 2005; Tsai et al., 2007; Romier et al., 2008; Romier-Crouzet et al.,

2009; Hollman et al., 2014; Link et al., 2010; Vauzour et al., 2010; Ebrahimi and Schluesner, 2012; Thomas et al., 2014). Several studies have shown that the polyphenols found in many herbs and spices provide these same health benefits (Tapsell et al., 2006; Kaefer and Milner, 2008; Iriti et al., 2010; Jungbauer and Medjakovic, 2012; Zheng and Wang, 2014; Akhondzadeh et al., 2003; Dragland et al., 2003; Halvorsen et al., 2006; Cheung and Tai, 2014; Moreno et al., 2006; Shan et al., 2007; Shukla and Singh, 2007; Carlsen et al., 2010; Kwon et al., 2010; Mueller et al., 2010; Van Breemen et al., 2011; Keshavarz et al., 2011; Karna et al., 2012; Baker et al., 2013). Polyphenols and their biological actions are further discussed below in Section 1: Polyphenols and Bioactive Properties.

In culinary medicine, herbs and spices are an essential element for turning recipes from bland to exotic. They might be just the right ingredient needed to transform the often-thought-of bitter vegetable to a craveable side dish, or even the main meal. Additionally, herbs and spices can be used in recipes to help replace or reduce the amount of salt, sugar, and/or saturated fat used in marinades, dressings, stir-fries, casseroles, soups, stews and in baking. Preparing meals with herbs and spices can help to make nutritious foods — such as vegetables, fish, and tofu — incredibly delicious.

DEFINING HERBS AND SPICES

The word **spice** is derived from the Latin "species", defined as "merchandise, wares or goods from the Far East." Spices were traded for goods, services, or money as many spices such as cloves, nutmeg, and peppercorn were worth their weight in gold. This is where the phrase "peppercorn rent" tumbled into the spice lexicon. **Herb** is derived from the Latin "herbāceus" meaning "grassy" but generally refers to a much larger plant family of soft leaves, grasses, petals and soft stems.

The definition of what constitutes a spice versus an herb is rather fluid and opinions differ from expert to expert. For example, the allium – garlic – is generally considered a spice as the garlic clove is a flower bud. However, it is often listed as a culinary and medicinal herb. Soft fresh plant leaves such as basil and bay leaf are herbs, but when dried are considered a spice. For the purposes of this book, spices are defined as seeds, berries, bark, sticks (branches), dried stems and leaves, roots, rhizomes, arils (a seed enrobed in a fleshy coating such as pomegranate) and sap. Herbs are defined as fresh leaves, soft stems, flower petals, grasses and edible weeds.

SECTION 1: POLYPHENOLS AND BIOACTIVE PROPERTIES

Polyphenols are the predominating bioactive compounds found in herbs and spices that most likely give these food ingredients the ability to improve health (Tapsell et al., 2006; Kaefer and Milner, 2008; Iriti et al., 2010; Jungbauer and Medjakovic, 2012; Zheng and Wang, 2014; Akhondzadeh et al., 2003; Dragland et al., 2003; Halvorsen et al., 2006; Cheung and Tai, 2014; Moreno et al., 2006; Shan et al., 2007; Shukla and Singh, 2007; Carlsen et al., 2010; Kwon et al., 2010; Mueller et al., 2010; Van Breemen et al., 2011; Keshavarz et al., 2011; Karna et al., 2012; Baker et al., 2013). Polyphenols are found in many plant foods such as broccoli, dark chocolate, brightly colored berries, onions, tea, coffee, as well as herbs and spices (Scalbert et al., 2000; Neveu et al., 2010; Perez-Jimenez et al., 2010; Pandey and Risvi, 2009; Chohan et al., 2008). See Table 1 for the phenolic content of common herbs, spices, and other foods.

Polyphenols are a family of structurally diverse chemical compounds that are classified based on their number of phenol rings and what is bound to those rings (Kondratyuk and Pezzuto, 2004; Scalbert and Williamson, 2000; Pandey and Risvi, 2009). Flavonoids, stilbene, lignans, coumarins and tannins are all common classes of polyphenols found in foods. **Flavonoids** are the most common type of polyphenols found in herbs and spices (Neveu et al., 2010; Perez-Jimenez et al., 2010). Factors in the environment and in the body, affect the bioavailability of the polyphenols we eat. For example, heating spices and herbs can affect the absorption of polyphenols, as can a person's microbiota (Manach et al., 2004). Factors that affect the bioavailability of spices and herbs are discussed further in the section below entitled Section 2: Cooking Methods, Bioavailability, and Toxins.

Foods such as fruits, vegetables, and green tea are well known to contain antioxidant properties, largely due to their polyphenol content. These foods have also been shown to provide other important health benefits such as anti-inflammatory, anti-cancer, and neuroprotective effects (Pandey and Risvi, 2009; Singh et al., 2008; Scalbert et al., 2005; Tsai et al., 2007; Romier et al., 2008; Romier-Crouzet et al., 2009; Hollman et al., 2014; Link et al., 2010; Vauzour et al., 2010; Ebrahimi and Schluesner, 2012; Thomas et al., 2014). There is growing evidence that foods high in polyphenols improve the health of the gut microbiota, which is important for not only gut health but also immune function, risk of chronic diseases, and mental health (Queipo-Ortuno et al., 2012; Tuohy et al., 2012; Etxeberria et al., 2013; He et al., 2013; Belkaid and Segre, 2014; Kelly et al., 2016; Burokas et al., 2015; Morrison and Preston, 2016).

Several studies have demonstrated that herbs and spices also produce these same health benefits, primarily through the action of their polyphenols (Tapsell et al., 2006; Kaefer and Milner, 2008; Iriti et al., 2010; Jungbauer and Medjakovic, 2012; Zheng and Wang, 2014; Akhondzadeh et al., 2003; Dragland et al., 2003; Halvorsen et al., 2006; Cheung and Tai, 2014; Moreno et al., 2006; Shan et al., 2007; Shukla and Singh, 2007; Carlsen et al., 2010; Kwon et al., 2010; Mueller et al., 2010; Van Breemen et al., 2011; Keshavarz et al., 2011; Karna et al., 2012; Baker et al., 2013). While herbs and spices are very concentrated in polyphenols, most people only consume a very small amount of these seasoning ingredients on a daily basis. Depending on the region and dietary pattern, people consume only a few grams (on average less than 4 grams per day per person) of herbs and spices (Opara and Chohan, 2014). Therefore, while herbs and spices are some of the richest sources of polyphenols, most people derive a smaller percentage of their polyphenol intake from these plants. Nevertheless, the phenolic content of herbs and spices in the small quantities in which they are generally consumed has been shown to provide measurable health benefits in clinical trials (Akhondzadeh, et al., 2003; Deyno et al., 2019; HAdi et al., 2020; Hamdan et al., 2019; Hou et al., 2015; Jamali et al., 2020; Maierean et al., 2017; Perry et al., 2018).

TABLE 1: Total Phenolic Content of Common Culinary Herbs, Spices, and Other Foods

Category	Food item	Total phenolic content (mg/100 g FW)
	Coriander (Coriandrum sativum L.)	Dried: 2260 Fresh: 158.90

Herbs	Dill (Anethum graveolens L.)	Dried: 1250 Fresh: 208.18
	Oregano (Wild Marjoram) (Origanum vulgare L.)	Dried: 6367 Fresh: 935.34
	Parsley (Petroselinum crispum (P. Mill.))	Dried: 1584 Fresh: 89.27
	Rosemary (Rosmarinus officinalis L.)	Dried: 2518 Fresh: 1082.43
	Sage (Common) (Salvia officinalis L.)	Dried: 2919 Fresh: 185.20
	Thyme (Common) (Thymus vulgaris L.)	Dried: 1815 Fresh: 1173.28
Spices	Cinnamon (Ceylan) (Cinnamomum verum J. Presl)	9700
	Cloves (Syzygium aromaticum)	16,047.25
	Coriander seed (Coriandrum sativum L.)	357.36
	Ginger (Zingiber officinale Roscoe)	Dried: 473.50 Fresh: 204.66
	Nutmeg (Myristica fragrans Houtt.)	1905
	Turmeric (Curcuma longa L.)	2117
Other foods	Dark Chocolate	1859.80
	Broccoli (Brassica oleracea var. italica Plenck)	198.55
	Blackcurrant (raw) (Ribes nigrum L.)	820.64
	Red raspberry (raw) (Rubus idaeus L.)	148.10
	Strawberry (raw) (Fragaria L.)	289.20
	Red Onion (raw) (Allium cepa var. cepa L.)	102.83

*Adapted from Opara and Chohan, 2014

SECTION 2: COOKING METHODS, BIOAVAILABILITY, AND TOXINS

Most herbs and spices that are used in food preparation are cooked into dishes rather than consumed raw (Opara and Chohan, 2014). A study examining the effect of heat on the **antioxidants** of several herbs and spices — cinnamon, cloves, fennel, ginger, parsley, rosemary, sage and thyme — found that cooking methods using wet heat, such as microwaving, stewing, and simmering increased the antioxidant capacity, whereas dry heat methods, such as grilling and frying decreased their antioxidant capacity (Chohan et al., 2008). Studies looking at the antioxidant abilities and polyphenolic compounds in other foods, such as grapes and mushrooms, have had similar findings (Choi et al., 2006; Kim et al., 2006). A possible reason is that wet heat methods that generally utilize lower cooking temperatures liberate the antioxidant compounds, whereas dry heat methods cause browning which may mean that the byproducts of the Maillard reaction are interfering with the antioxidant capacity of the polyphenols (Kim et al., 2006; Nicoli et al., 1997; Morales and Jimenez-Perez, 2001).

The Maillard reaction is a chemical reaction between amino acids and reducing sugars that gives browned food its distinct flavor (Maillard, 1912; Chichester, 1986). Cooking foods that are high in carbohydrates and/or protein at high temperatures can cause sugars and amino acids to react with each other and form **acrylamide**. Consuming acrylamide has potential negative health consequences, as it has been found to be a carcinogen in both human and animal studies (Tareke et al., 2002; Kahkeshani et al., 2015; Simmone and Archer, 2014). Cooking with antioxidant compounds such as foods that contain polyphenols may help mitigate the formation of acrylamide, however, there has been conflicting evidence that ingredients containing phenolic compounds either increase or decrease the formation of acrylamide. For example, studies on the effect of curcumin (found in turmeric) on acrylamide formation during cooking at high temperatures have found a variety of results, with either a reduction or an increase in acrylamide formation (Hamzalıoğlu et al., 2013; Zhu et al., 2011). The sulfur groups in garlic have been found to inhibit acrylamide formation (Casado et al., 2010; Jin et al., 2013; Yuan et al., 2011), and piperine (found in white, green, and black pepper), being a nitrogenous compound, has been found to weakly reduce the formation of acrylamide (Zhu et al., 2009). Also, rosemary, the barbeque herb, is beneficial in negating the carcinogenic damage from grilling meats and vegetables.

Furthermore, cooking certain herbs and spices can impact their **total phenolic content** and their antioxidant capacity. For example, cooking herbs from the Lamiaceae family (parsley, rosemary, sage and thyme) can increase their phenolic content and directly increase their antioxidant capacity (Chohan, 2011; Miglio et al., 2008; Mulinacci et al., 2009; Pellegrini et al., 2010). Digesting foods containing herbs and spices also plays a role in their phenolic content and antioxidant capacity. The phenolic content of herbs such as rosemary, sage, and thyme was significantly increased after both cooking and digestion, compared to cooked and uneaten and to uncooked controls (Chohan, 2011; Chohan et al., 2012). Whereas the phenolic content and antioxidant capacity of spices (such as cinnamon, cloves, and nutmeg) are affected less consistently by cooking and digestion, largely due to synergistic and antagonistic effects from other phytochemicals present (Baker et al., 2013; Opara and Chohan, 2014). For more information on synergistic and antagonistic combinations of herbs and spices, see the below section entitled "Combinations that enhance and inhibit bioavailability and actions."

The **anti-inflammatory** properties of herbs and spices appear to be intact after cooking and digesting. The amounts of spices and herbs consumed in normal diets also appear to provide a strong anti-inflammatory effect (Baker et al., 2013; Chohan et al., 2012; Cocchiara et al., 2005; Oskabe et al., 2004; Dhandapani et al., 2007). For example, rosmarinic acid (in rosemary) and curcumin (in turmeric) have been found to inhibit pro-inflammatory pathways (Oskabe et al., 2004). Similarly, eugenol (in cloves) and apigenin (in parsley) have been found to down-regulate pro-inflammatory enzymes (Kim et al., 2003; Pan et al., 2010). Finally, lemongrass, rosemary, thyme and sage enhance the activity of antioxidant enzymes, which helps to reduce chronic inflammation (Yoo et al., 2008; Yasui and Baba, 2006; Chohan et al., 2014).

Unfortunately, the literature suggests that absorption of the polyphenols from herbs and spices is generally poor. Polyphenols are largely metabolized by the gut microbiota and by the liver and are often eliminated by the body quite quickly after consumption (Scalbert et al., 2000; Manach et al., 2004; D'Archivio et al., 2010). One study found that about 8% to 10% of the original total phenolic content of thyme, sage, and rosemary was left after cooking and digestion. Nevertheless, **as the total phenolic content of herbs and spices is high prior to cooking and digestion, these flavor-enhancing ingredients still have the potential to contribute health benefits** (Opara and Chohan, 2014).

The effect of polyphenols in herbs and spices may be due to actions in the gut itself, however, the exact mechanism is unclear (D'Archivio et al., 2010; Manach et al., 2004). Phenolic interactions in the gut are likely as there is increasing evidence that polyphenols are helpful in preventing and treating colorectal cancer (Cilla et al., 2009; Wang et al., 2000; Aggarwal et al., 2006; Ramos, 2008; Xavier et al., 2014; Araujo et al., 2011; Carroll et al., 2011; Aggarwal et al., 2012; Macdonald and Wagner, 2012; Garcia-Perez et al., 2013; Haraguchi et al., 2014; Dempe et al., 2013). There are many factors that affect the bioavailability of the active compounds in herbs and spices, such as the **microflora** makeup of the individual, the other food constituents in the meal, and the effects of habitual intake of herbs and spices (versus single-dose amounts of herbs and spices), and these require further investigation (D'Archivio et al., 2010; Bermudez-Soto et al., 2007).

COMBINATIONS THAT ENHANCE AND INHIBIT BIOAVAILABILITY AND ACTIONS

There is an increasing number of studies looking at how the polyphenols found in foods such as herbs and spices interact with other components in foods. Since herbs and spices are generally eaten as part of meals, rather than alone, the other ingredients that they are consumed with are important to consider, as some act synergistically to enhance bioavailability and health-promoting actions, while others act antagonistically to reduce absorption or resulting health benefits (Blasa et al., 2011; Khanum et al., 2011; Yi and Wetzstein, 2011; Epps et al., 2013). Furthermore, the concentrations of the combinations of polyphenols used and the type of assay used in in vitro studies also affects whether polyphenol effects appear synergistic or antagonistic (Opara and Chohan, 2014; Blasa et al., 2011; Khanum et al., 2011; Yi and Wetzstein, 2011; Epps et al., 2013). For a summary of polyphenol combinations and their effects, see Table 2.

Table 2: Synergistic and Antagonistic Combinations of Polyphenols and Polyphenol-Rich Foods

Polyphenol combination	Effect	Synergistic	Antagonistic	Citation
Epigallocatechin gallate (found in tea) and curcumin (found in turmeric)	Enhanced inhibition of tumor growth for breast cancer cells	✓		Somers-Edgar et al., 2008
Curcumin (found in turmeric) and resveratrol (found in grapes)	Enhanced inhibition of colorectal cancer	✓		Majumdar et al., 2009; Kunnumakkara et al., 2017

Curcumin (found in turmeric) and piperine (found in pepper)	Enhanced anti-inflammatory, antioxidant and anticarcinogenic activity	✓		Kunnumakkara et al., 2017; Prasad et al., 2004
Curcumin (found in turmeric) and catechins	Enhanced anti-inflammatory, antioxidant and anticarcinogenic activity	✓		Kunnumakkara et al., 2017
Curcumin (found in turmeric) and quercetin	Enhanced anti-inflammatory, antioxidant and anticarcinogenic activity	✓		Kunnumakkara et al., 2017; Prasad et al., 2004
Curcumin (found in turmeric) and genistein	Enhanced anti-inflammatory, antioxidant and anticarcinogenic activity	✓		Kunnumakkara et al., 2017
Carnosic acid (found in rosemary and sage) and curcumin (found in turmeric)	Inhibited growth and induced apoptosis of leukemia cells	✓		Pesakhov et al., 2010

Chicken and herb/spice based marinating sauces	Marinated and cooking decreased the antioxidant capacity of the herbs and spices		✓	Thomas et al., 2010
Antioxidant-rich spice mix (black pepper, cloves, cinnamon, garlic powder, ginger, oregano, paprika and rosemary) and hamburger meat	Reduction in oxidative stress biomarkers in burgers with spice mix compared to those without spices	✓		Li et al., 2010
Aspalathus linearis (rooibos tea) and Malus domestica (apples)	Increased antioxidant capacity	✓		Blasa et al., 2011
Aspalathus linearis (rooibos tea) and Vaccinium (berries)	Increased antioxidant capacity	✓		Blasa et al., 2011
Myrtillus (berries), Punica granatum (pomegranate), and Malus domestica (apples)	Increased antioxidant capacity	✓		Blasa et al., 2011

Polyphenol-rich herbs (oregano), ajowan (Trachyspermum ammi) and Indian borage (Plectranthus amboinicus)	Adding oregano increased the radical scavenging ability of the other two extracts	✓			Khanum et al., 2011
Peppermint, rosemary, sage, spearmint, thyme	Inhibited colorectal cancer cell growth, but combinations had varying results (synergistic, additive or antagonistic) depending on the concentrations and specific combinations used	✓		✓	Yi and Wetzstein, 2011

Blueberries, grapes, chocolate-covered strawberries, and polyphenol-rich fruit smoothies	Enhanced antioxidant capacity in combinations of chocolate-covered strawberries. Other combinations were either synergistic or antagonistic depending on the combinations used and the assay.	✓	✓	Epps et al., 2013
Cloves and cinnamon	Enhanced antimicrobial effects and reduced meat spoilage when used together on chicken	✓		Sivarajan et al., 2017

Coriander and cumin	Enhanced antibacterial and antioxidant activity resulting in reduced food-borne bacteria growth	✓		Bag and Chattopadhyay, 2015
Thymus vulgaris (mint), Coriandrum sativum (coriander), and Apium graveolens (celery)	Enhanced antioxidant activity	✓		Crespo et al., 2019
Curcumin and its structural analog (Monoacetylcurcumin)	Enhanced inhibition of influenza virus infection	✓		Richart et al., 2018

SECTION 3: 10 ESSENTIAL HERBS AND SPICES

The encyclopedia Britannica lists over 65 different herbs and spices. In this chapter, 10 common spices will be highlighted for their culinary and medicinal benefits.

TURMERIC — THE POWERHOUSE PLANT

Everyone seems to know something about turmeric these days, and the variety of new products flooding the market containing turmeric makes one's head spin. From traditional Asian/Indian curries to the popular turmeric, orange, and chili pepper juice shots, plus a grocery aisle full of energy balls and biscuits, tisanes, and tablets, turmeric is everywhere. India grows a tremendous amount of this incredible rhizome and consumes 80% of the world's turmeric. The finest quality turmeric with the highest concentration of curcumin (the primary polyphenol found in turmeric) is found in Alleppey in the state of Kerala, India.

Bioactive Compounds in Turmeric

Curcuminoids are the main bioactive compounds found in turmeric. These include curcumin, demethoxycurcumin, and bis-demethoxycurcumin (Sharma et al., 2017). The curcuminoids or curcumin in turmeric are the main contributors to the health benefits associated with turmeric (Funk et al., 2006). One study has also proposed that curcuminoid metabolites, including degradative or reduced products, may be the bioactive compounds truly responsible for mediating curcumin effects (Liang and Ji, 2012).

Health Benefits of Turmeric

Turmeric has been used as a medicine and as a food for centuries. It is one of the most talked-about spices in the world today and over a hundred clinical trials have examined its anti-inflammatory, antioxidant, and antimicrobial properties (Prasad et al., 2014). This bright yellow colored finger-staining spice is packed full of culinary and medicinal benefits due to the active compound curcumin (no relation to cumin). Curcumin has been found to be a powerful antioxidant that has the potential to play a role in the prevention and management of several health conditions (Aggarwal and Hrikuma, 2009; Gupta et al., 2013). Furthermore, curcumin has also been shown to be synergistic with other nutraceuticals such as resveratrol, piperine, catechins, quercetin and genistein (Kunnumakkara et al., 2017). Many clinical trials using curcumin as a therapeutic agent have also combined curcumin with other synergistic agents (Gupta et al., 2013). For more information regarding bioavailability, as well as synergistic and antagonistic combinations of spices and herbs, see the section above-entitled Section 2: Cooking Methods, Bioavailability, and Toxins.

Cancer

Several studies have examined the anti-cancer effects of curcumin. Studies using less than 1 gram up to 4 grams per day of curcumin for periods of one to six months have shown reduction in biomarkers for colorectal cancer and reduction in the number and size of polyps (Sharma et al., 2001; Sharma et al., 2004; Garcea et al., 2005; Cruz-Correa et al., 2006; Carrol et al., 2011; He et al., 2011). Studies on the use of curcumin (up to 8 grams per day for up to six weeks) in patients with pancreatic cancer have shown that it is generally safe and well-tolerated with anti-cancerous activity in some, but not all, patients (Kanai et al., 2011; Dhillon et al., 2008; Durgaprasad et al.,2005; Epelbaum et al., 2010). There is also limited evidence that curcumin is safe, well-tolerated, and effective as part of the treatment for breast cancer, prostate cancer, lung cancer, head and neck cancers and multiple myeloma (Bayet-Robert et al., 2010; Ide et al., 2010; Golombick et al., 2009; Vadhan-Raj et al., 2007; Polasa et al., 1992; Kim et al., 2011).

Inflammatory Diseases and Bowel Conditions

Studies using 0.5 to 2 grams per day of curcumin for two to 10 months have found that relapse prevention and/or clinical disease remission can be achieved in people with ulcerative colitis (Hanai et al., 2006; Lahiff et al., 2011). One trial has shown that 1 to 2 grams per day of curcumin for one to two months helps to significantly reduce inflammation biomarkers in people with Crohn's disease and ulcerative proctitis (Holt et al., 2005). Studies using less than or equal to 0.5 grams per day of curcumin found that symptoms of irritable bowel syndrome were also significantly improved (Bindy et al., 2004; Shimouchi et al., 2009). Gastrointestinal ulcers and infections have also been found to be reduced in people taking less than 1 gram up to 3 grams per day of curcumin (Kositchaiwat et al., 1993; Prcksunand et al., 2001; Di Mario et al., 2007).

Aside from bowel conditions, other inflammatory diseases have also been found to be improved with curcumin. Using approximately 1.2 grams of curcumin for 12 weeks up to 18 months has been found to reduce symptoms of certain inflammatory eye diseases and prevent reoccurrence (Lal et al., 1999; Allegri et al., 2010). Rheumatoid arthritis (Deodhar et al., 1980; Chandran ad Goel, 2012) and osteoarthritis (Belcaro et al., 2010; Belcaro et al., 2010) symptoms have also been shown to be improved with the use of curcumin in doses of 0.2 to 1.2 grams per day for two weeks to eight months.

Cardiovascular Health

Studies have shown that less than or equal to 0.5 grams of curcumin per day can lower total cholesterol (11%) and LDL cholesterol and increase HDL cholesterol (29%) (Alwi et al., 2008; Soni and Kuttan, 1992). The studies found that lower doses of curcumin were associated with improvements in lipid profiles. Additionally, curcumin intake significantly decreased serum lipid peroxides (33%), which may suggest that curcumin could play a chemo-preventive role in lowering the risk of arterial disease (Soni and Kuttan, 1992). Further studies are needed to understand the role of curcumin in cardiovascular health.

Diabetes Mellitus

Studies on the use of curcumin to improve diabetes management indicators and reduce complications of diabetes have found that curcumin showed improvements in biomarkers of inflammation, improved fasting glucose, and decreased postprandial circulating insulin (Srinivasan, 1972; Usharani et al., 2008; Wickenberg et al., 2010; Chuengsamarn et al., 2012). An older study on the effects of curcumin on diabetes management found that using 5 grams of curcumin per day for three months resulted in a decrease in fasting blood glucose from 140 mg/dL to 70 mg/dL (Srinivasan, 1972). Studies using 1 to 1.5 grams of curcumin per day have also found that symptoms of diabetic nephropathy and diabetic microangiopathy also improved (Khajehdehi et al., 2011; Appendino et al., 2011).

Other Health Conditions

There is limited evidence that curcumin is also mildly helpful in improving skin conditions such as psoriasis (Heng et al., 2000; Kurd et al., 2008). It may also be helpful in neurodegenerative diseases such as Alzheimer's and Dejerine-Sottas disease (Ringman et al., 2005; Burns et al., 2009; Baum et al., 2008). Another study found that curcumin use helped reduce the reoccurrence of respiratory infections and improved immune function (Zuccotti et al., 2009). Further research is required on the role of curcumin in these conditions.

At the Store

When purchasing turmeric, look for roots from a reputable source that are large, smooth-skinned, and free of mold. Crisp, well-dried turmeric root is easily grated using a fine-toothed grater such as a microplane and its slightly bitter, peppery "earthy" flavor will be noticeable. The easiest and most readily available form is turmeric powder. As with all rhizomes, it is recommended to buy organic as the growing root can absorb toxic chemicals from the soil (such as cadmium) (Daran et al., 2017). Turmeric can be grown indoors in a pot of well-drained rich organic soil in dappled sunlight.

In the Kitchen

Turmeric is fat-soluble and needs heat and some sort of fat – dairy, oil, nut, seed, fatty fish or meat – to activate the bio-compounds. Adding just a little black, white, or green pepper to the mix increases its medicinal benefits since curcumin and piperine (found in peppers) have synergistic properties (Pasad et al., 2014). One study found that in humans, a dose of 2 grams of curcumin alone resulted in very low or even undetectable serum concentrations of curcumin. However, when curcumin was administered together with 20 mg of piperine, bioavailability was increased up to 2,000% (Shoba et al., 1998). A pinch of pepper added to turmeric goes a long way in not only enhancing the flavor of foods, but also in enormously increasing the ability to reap curcumin's health benefits!

The results of this study speaks to the importance of overall dietary patterns and meal composition versus single doses of herbs and spices.

RECIPE: <u>Turmeric Melted Onions</u> (Recipe by ©Chef Natasha MacAller 2019)
Video https://vimeo.com/679500179

Makes 2 cups

Ingredients:

- Grapeseed or vegetable oil: 60 ml/ 1 ¾ fluid ounces/ ¼ fluid cup
- Unsalted butter, ghee, or solid coconut oil: 50 g/ 1¾ ounces/ ½ stick
- 1 teaspoon turmeric
- 4 medium brown onions, peeled, halved, and thinly sliced (about 500 g / 1 pound / 3 cups)
- Fresh ground black pepper to taste
- Optional – 1 teaspoon coriander and/or ½ teaspoon dried oregano or thyme

Method:
- Over medium-high heat, add butter and oil to a pot, stir in turmeric and cook for one minute to bloom (adding turmeric to the sizzling oil for a minute helps to intensify the flavor and nutritional benefits).
- Add in the onions.

o When onions begin to let off steam, turn heat to medium-low and cook for 20 to 30 minutes stirring occasionally until translucent and melted (a light-yellow brown).
o Add pepper, stirring for a few minutes.
o Remove from heat; cool then cover and chill until needed.

A video presentation on how to use the turmeric onions to make a spectacular Country Mushroom Soup.

These onions can be used in many ways including the following (**Introduction Video**):
o As a great base for a twist on French onion soup
o As a base for stews, sauces, and soups
o As a topping over baked chicken — oven bake chicken breast or thighs topped with a layer of melted onions at 160°C for 30 to 40 minutes until juices run clear. Finish with a handful of fresh soft herbs and a few grinds of pepper.
o As a spread or dip — purée the onions with peeled cloves of roasted garlic, a handful of chopped fresh herbs such as parsley, basil, or cilantro (plus a pinch of chili flakes or fresh minced jalapeno and a squeeze of lime juice and a pinch of salt flakes for a bit of spicy heat) into a spreadable topping or thin with vegetable stock into a dip for crudities and super seeded crackers (found on www.dancingchef.net) or add to:
  • Any sandwich like a tomato, avocado, and lettuce sandwich.
  • A piping hot bowl of just-cooked baby new potatoes for a little added beneficial zing and pow to the traditional western side dish.
  • Store any leftover spread tightly sealed in the refrigerator for 2 weeks or freeze up to a month.

CUMIN — THE NILE SPICE PLANT

This humble, hearty, dried, seedlike spice, grows well in drought or flood and thrives in Mexico, India, China, Japan, Africa, Spain and Italy. Cumin was discovered in the pyramids and tombs of the ancient Pharaohs. It has been around for so long that no one seems to know its precise geographic origin. However, it has been speculated that cumin most likely originated from the upper Nile. Ancient records indicate that cumin was a vital spice in early Roman and Levantine cuisine.

Cumin is related to parsley, dill, and its lookalike cousin, the caraway seed — also known as Persian cumin. Technically known as Cuminum cyminum, it is a hot climate-loving petite annual plant with a delicate, feather-like stem, and it is easy to grow indoors with good light and warmth or in a vegetable bed with well-drained soil.

Bioactive Compounds in Cumin

The active compounds in cumin include **terpenes, phenols, and flavonoids.** Cuminaldehyde cymene and terpenoids are the primary compounds in cumin that provide health benefits (Bettaieb et al., 2011). The cuminaldehyde and cuminic alcohol in cumin are what give its distinctive aroma. (Li and Jiang, 2004).

The main active compound in black cumin is thymoquinone (30% to 48%). Black cumin also contains thymohydroquinone, dithymoquinone (nigellone), p- carvacrol, 4-terpineol, t-anethole, sesquiterpene longifolene, α-pinene, and thymol. (Boskabady and Shirmohammadi, 2002; Ali and Blunden, 2003).

Health Benefits of Cumin

Traditionally, cumin was used medicinally for a number of complaints and diseases, including to neutralize the bacteria that causes food poisoning, as a poultice for swollen throats and digestive organs, as an aid to reduce stress, and to lower blood sugar. Modern research has shown that the active constituents of cumin — terpenes, phenols, and flavonoids — have many biomedical and pharmacological uses (Mnif and Aifa, 2015). The predominant bioactive component of cumin seed oil is cuminaldehyde, and it accounts for the majority of the health benefits associated with cumin (Morovati et al., 2019; Muszyńska et al., 2015; Allahghadri et al., 2010; Sowbhagya et al., 2010).

Cardiovascular Health

A meta-analysis of randomized controlled trials showed that cumin is effective at improving blood lipids, specifically lowering low-density lipoprotein (LDL or "bad" cholesterol) and increasing high-density lipoprotein (HDL or "good" cholesterol) (Hadi et al., 2018). A study examining the combined effects of taking 75 mg of cumin for eight weeks resulted in reduced triglycerides, LDL cholesterol, and total cholesterol (Taghizadeh et al., 2016). A study examining the effects of cumin on blood pressure found that using a high dose (200 mg per kg of body weight) administered to rats with hypertension significantly reduced systolic blood pressure (Kalaivani et al., 2013). Further studies are needed to investigate the blood pressure lowering effects of cumin in humans.

Diabetes and Metabolic Conditions

A study examining the combined effects of taking 75 mg of cumin for eight weeks resulted in reduced fasting plasma glucose and was also associated with weight loss among higher-weight participants (Taghizadeh et al., 2016). Further studies are needed to investigate whether smaller amounts of cumin (such as the amounts used in cooking) are sufficient to produce significant blood glucose-lowering effects in humans with diabetes.

Mental Health

A review examining components of the Mediterranean diet and their effects on the risk of Alzheimer's disease found that cumin and its active component cuminaldehyde were strong antioxidants and strongly protective against Alzheimer's disease and cerebral inflammation (Iranshahy M, Javadi, 2019). Cumin has also been found to be helpful in improving mood and is used in many cultures for mental health promotion (Muszyńska et al., 2015; Hamedi et al., 2017).

Inflammation

A randomized, triple-blind, placebo-controlled study found that taking 75 mg of cumin seed oil for eight weeks was significantly associated with a decrease in inflammatory markers and oxidative stress among people with metabolic syndrome (Morovati et al., 2019). Reduction in inflammation has also been seen in other studies examining the effects of cumin (Iranshahy M, Javadi, 2019; Moubarz et al., 2016; Kang et al., 2019).

Black cumin is not biologically related to brown cumin. It is pricier than ordinary cumin and has been studied for its traditional healing properties, primarily for its effect on the immune system. The oil of black cumin is the most potent in active compounds, primarily thymoquinone. Thymoquinone and the other active components of black cumin are concentrated in the essential oils of the cumin seed (Amin and Hosseinzadeh, 2016; Al-Saleh et al., 2006; Muhammad, 2009).

Thymoquinone has been found to have anti-inflammatory properties that prevent the synthesis of several mediators involved in the inflammatory process. It also increases immune function by reducing oxidative stress, increasing chemokinesis, chemotaxis, phagocytic activity, antibody levels and the hemagglutination of immunoglobulins (Shaterzadeh-Yazdi et al., 2018; Majdalawieh and Fayyad, 2015). The literature cites multiple health benefits of black cumin, including anti-inflammatory, antinociceptive, antibacterial, hypotensive, hypolipidemic, cytotoxic, antidiabetic and hepatoprotective effects (Amin and Hosseinzadeh, 2016, Oskouei et al., 2018; Hamdan et al., 2019; Kooti et al., 2016). A summary of the research on thymoquinone is presented below.

Anti-inflammatory and Antioxidant
Use of black cumin oil has been found to have anti-inflammatory effects. A human study looking at inflammation among people with multiple sclerosis found that thymoquinone had anti-inflammatory effects (Mohamed et al., 2003). Antioxidant effects of thymoquinone have been seen in in vitro studies as well (Singh et al., 2014, Marsik et al., 2005; El-Mahmoudy et al., 2005; Vaillancourt et al., 2011).

Health Benefits of Black Cumin

Antinociceptive (Pain Management)
Black cumin has been shown to have pain management properties (Marks, et al., 2009; Lee and Chen, 2010). Oral administration of 50 to 500 mg per kg of body weight was shown to act in a dose-dependent fashion to reduce the nociceptive responses in various animal studies (Abdel-Fattah et al., 2001; Al-Ghamdi, 2001; De Sousa et al., 2012; Bashir and Qureshi, 2010). Human trials have also found that thymoquinone reduces neuropathic pain (Qi et al., 2011; Amin et al., 2014).

Ulcerative Colitis
In a study of black cumin use in ulcerative colitis, thymoquinone (10 and 20 mg per kg) decreased gastric acid secretion and acid output. Biomarkers for inflammation and the ulcer index were also reduced to the level usually achieved by omeprazole, a reference medication (Magdy et al., 2012). Similar effects were seen in a study by Lei et al., 2012. A study using 10 mg per kg body weight found that after three

days of use, colitis symptoms were improved beyond the level usually achieved by standard medications (Mahgoub, 2003).

Diabetes
A study on the effects of black cumin found that thymoquinone lowers serum glucose (Zaoui et al., 2002). Furthermore, a study published in the Canadian Journal of Diabetes acknowledges that black cumin has antidiabetic effects, primarily due to activation of insulin and 5' AMP-activated protein kinase (AMPK) pathways, as well as mitochondrial uncoupling (Benhaddouandaloussi et al., 2008). Further research on the effects of black cumin in diabetes management is needed to examine whether it could play a role as part of dietary modifications to manage hyperglycemia.

Other Health Effects
Thymoquinone has also been found to protect again liver injury (Michel et al., 2011; Nehar and Kumari, 2013). A study using 0.1 mL of black cumin seed oil per kg of body weight for four weeks found that it had an antidepressant effect in participants (Perveen, 2014). Further studies are needed to examine these other health benefits of thymoquinone and black cumin seed oil.

At the Store
This humble, dusty-looking, nutty, slightly peppery spice is included in spice blends of multiple cuisines throughout the world and is an essential component of curries, tacos, tamales, hummus and shawarmas. The best way to use cumin is to purchase whole seeds, lightly toast (this brings out the flavorful and beneficial oils), cool, then grind them before use. Keep any leftovers in a tightly closed container in a cool to room temperature cupboard and use within a few weeks as the volatile and beneficial oils will evaporate and degrade over time.

In the Kitchen
Toast cumin first in a small dry pan over medium-low heat, shaking pan occasionally then cool to room temperature. Once cooled, grind with a mortar and pestle or electric spice (coffee) grinder. Cumin is alluringly aromatic and immediately activates the salivary glands. As with most spices, blooming (heating in oil) ground, toasted cumin helps to amplify its flavor and aroma. Toasting or browning the seeds first using heat also changes the flavor.

Cumin's intense oregano-like scent and slightly bitter flavor pairs best with spicy curries, slow-cooked vegetables, stews and sauces. These powerhouse little black seeds are often sprinkled on crisp, lavash and chewy flatbreads and can be enjoyed lightly toasted and added to salads, soups, and dips to add a little healthy crunch! The addition of cumin is used frequently in international cuisines especially in Mexican, Middle Eastern, and South American dishes and surprisingly found in chocolate espresso and tahini brownies!

RECIPE: <u>Oven Roasted Spice & Herb Vegetables</u> (©Chef Natasha MacAller 2019)

These flavor-packed vegetables can be served as a main or side dish, added to pasta, stir fry tofu rice noodles or a veggie chef's salad.

Serves 4 (estimate about 7 ounces/200 grams per person uncooked)

Ingredients:
- 1 ¾ pounds (800 grams) washed trimmed vegetables*
- ¾ teaspoon fresh cracked pepper
- 2 teaspoons cumin seeds
- 6 thyme sprigs
- ½ teaspoon chipotle or Spanish pimenton chili powder (or to taste)
- 2 teaspoons of either Za'tar or Taco Guaco Mix
- 2 teaspoon of Pizza Pasta Zoodle Herb blend
- 2 tablespoons grapeseed or vegetable oil, divided

Method:
- Preheat the oven to 200°C/400°F or fan bake at 185°C/370°F, and while the oven is heating prepare the spice blend

o   Wash, drain well, trim, and cut vegetables. Cut dense vegetables into smaller pieces and the less dense vegetables into larger pieces so they all finish roasting together

o   Place vegetables in a large mixing bowl and set aside

o   Set up a large baking tray or roasting pan lined with foil or a Silpat (a reusable nonstick surface used for baking) and set aside

o   Heat a small saucepan, then add the pepper and cumin and swirl and toast until you can smell the spices. Add a tablespoon of oil to bloom the spices, letting them sizzle just for a minute. Add the thyme sprigs. Take off the heat and add the chili powder, Za'tar mix, herb blend and remaining oil, combining well.

o   Scrape the herb mix into the prepared vegetables and combine, adding additional oil to coat if needed

o   Transfer to the baking tray or roasting pan and arrange into an even layer. Sprinkle with salt flakes then roast in the oven for 35 to 45 minutes until veggies are just fork-tender, shaking the pan occasionally during cooking.

*The key to this recipe is cutting the well-washed, raw vegetables into similar-sized pieces. However, firm vegetables take longer to cook, so they need to be cut into smaller pieces than the softer vegetables. Firm vegetables include: carrots, parsnips, turnips, beets, sweet potatoes, broccoli stems, brussels sprouts and Hubbard, acorn and butternut squashes. The softer vegetables can be cut into larger pieces and these include: cauliflower florets, zucchini (courgette), aubergine (eggplant) and halved/quartered bell peppers (capsicum).

** While arranging your baking tray you could add in a lightly oiled foil-wrapped head or two of garlic — your kitchen will smell incredible! Squeeze the caramelized garlic cloves and spread onto fresh sourdough bread, drizzle with a little olive oil, grind of pepper and you've got an instant craveable side dish!

CINNAMON — THE SWEET SPICE PLANT

Cinnamon is a spice that comes from the inner bark of several tree species from the genus Cinnamomum. Only a few Cinnamomum species are grown commercially for the purpose of harvesting the spice. Cinnamomum verum is often called the "true cinnamon," however, most of the commercially available cinnamon in the world comes from Cinnamomum cassia (Iqbal,1993; Bell, 2009).

Cinnamon is an evergreen tree with oval-shaped leaves, thick bark, and a berry fruit. Cinnamon plants can grow into trees reaching 20 feet in height. At three years old, cinnamon can be harvested without killing the tree by snipping off the "whips" — the tender offshoot branches. Peeling away the outer bark reveals the cinnamon inside. New shoots will replace those that were cut about a year later. The bark and leaves are the primary part of the plant harvested to make the cinnamon spice (Burlando et al., 2010). All parts including flowers, bark, and leaves contain **cinnamaldehyde**. The aroma, flavor, and health benefits of cinnamon come mainly from the essential oil. This is where the main active component cinnamaldehyde is found, as well as other active components such as eugenol.

Cinnamon Bark

Bioactive Compounds in Cinnamon
Cinnamaldehyde is the principal compound in cinnamon that is responsible for its health effects (Marongui et al., 2007; Chou et al., 2013). Cinnamon bark also contains procyanidins and catechins, which possess antioxidant activities (Nonaka et al., 1983; Peng et al., 2008; Maata-Riihine et al., 2005). Cinnamon also contains other active compounds such as cinnamate, cinnamic acid, and several essential oils such as trans-cinnamaldehyde, cinamul acetate, eugenol, L-borneo, caryophyllene oxide, b-caryophyllene, L-bornyl acetate, E-nerolidol, α-cubebene, α-terpineol, terpinolene, and α-thujene (Senanayake et al., 1978, Tung et al., 2008; Tung et al., 2010). These active compounds contribute to the antioxidant capacity of cinnamon (Mancini-Filho et al., 1998).

Health Benefits of Cinnamon

Diabetes

Cinnamon continues to be studied for its potential benefit in lowering blood glucose in people with diabetes. A meta-analysis showed that cinnamon can help lower fasting blood glucose in people with prediabetes and type 2 diabetes (Deyno et al., 2019). Several other review studies have similarly shown that cinnamon can help lower fasting plasma glucose and/or hemoglobin A1c in people with diabetes (Costello et al., 2016; Allen et al., 2013; Akilen et al., 2012; Leach and Kumar, 2912; Namazi et al., 2019). The quantity found to be needed for reduction in blood glucose was found to be 1 to 6 grams of cinnamon per day for significant blood glucose-lowering (Khan et al., 2003). One study has also found that consuming cinnamon can also help attenuate the rise in postprandial blood glucose following a meal (Bernardo et al., 2015). However, since the studies examining the benefits of cinnamon on blood glucose management have only been conducted for shorter durations (four to 16 weeks), further studies are needed to examine the possible benefits of longer-term use of cinnamon in this population.

Cardiovascular Health

Cinnamon has also been shown to improve cardiovascular health by improving blood lipids. A systematic review has found that cinnamon is effective at reducing blood triglycerides and total blood cholesterol without negatively impacting HDL cholesterol (Maierean et al., 2017). A randomized controlled study found that using 1 to 6 grams per day of cinnamon lowered triglycerides, total cholesterol, and LDL cholesterol among people with diabetes (Khan et al., 2003). A randomized controlled trial using 3 grams of cinnamon per day found that this dose effectively lowered blood cholesterol levels among people with diabetes (Azimi et al., 2014). Furthermore, there is good evidence that cinnamon helps lower blood pressure (Jamali et al., 2020; Hadi et al., 2020). A study using 2 grams per day of cinnamon for eight weeks found that this dose reduced diastolic blood pressure among women with rheumatoid arthritis (Shishehbor et al., 2018).

Neuroprotection

There is also limited evidence that bioactive components in cinnamon can help reduce oxidative stress and have neuroprotective properties which may be helpful in preventing and managing conditions such as Parkinson's disease and Alzheimer's disease (Maiolo et al., 2018; Momtaz et al., 2018). A review article examining the link between cinnamon (particularly cinnamaldehyde) and Alzheimer's disease found that both in vitro and in vivo studies suggest that

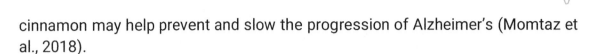

cinnamon may help prevent and slow the progression of Alzheimer's (Momtaz et al., 2018).

Inflammatory Conditions

A study on women with rheumatoid arthritis found that using 2 grams per day of cinnamon for eight weeks reduced inflammation in joints as well as associated pain (Shishehbor et al., 2018). There is also some limited evidence that essential oils from cinnamon may be helpful as an anti-inflammatory and anti-bacterial agent for certain skin disorders (Han et al., 2017; Julianti et al., 2017). Several studies have also shown that consuming cinnamon helps reduce oxidative stress and inflammatory biomarkers (Tuzcu et al., 2017; Kim and Kim, 2019; Schink et al., 2018). A study examining the effect of cinnamon on intestinal health found that cinnamon enhanced tight junctions in the intestines and inhibited inflammation of the intestines (Kim and Kim, 2019).

At the Store

There are two types of cinnamon: **Cassia**, with its strong, sweet, and familiar aroma, is brownish red and has quite a thick bark and the quills can be many feet in length, so it is generally precut to conveniently fit in a spice jar. **Ceylon** (true) cinnamon is lighter brown and is made up of delicate multiple paper-like layers. Its scent is mild and sweet. Cinnamon sticks will keep for about three years.

Ground cinnamon loses fragrance easily in a few months due to its concentration of volatile oils, so grind fresh or buy only what you need. Before grinding, toast cinnamon sticks in a pan over medium-low heat, swirling the pan and moving the pan back and forth to roll the cinnamon sticks until the fragrance is released; it will take about three to five minutes. Once toasted and cooled, they can be left whole and used in slow-cooked recipes or can be ground using a spice or coffee grinder.

In the Kitchen
Cinnamon is found in an international array of dishes: in the U.S. and Northern Europe, it is usually added to baked fruit desserts, cakes, bread, cookies and pastries. In Spain and Mexico, cinnamon is added to chocolate dishes, whereas Middle Eastern cinnamon is a common addition to dishes such as meat-based tagines and traditional chicken and brick-pastry Bastilla. In India, China, and Vietnam, it is laced through a multitude of spice mixes and dishes.

Cinnamon of both culinary varieties is best when purchased as sticks (or quills). When cooking with cinnamon, note that ground cinnamon absorbs liquid very quickly, so when you want to add more cinnamon to a dish than is called for, add a little cinnamon oil rather than more ground cinnamon. This is especially important in baking as it can either clump into a paste or make your finished creation very dry.

Charring Cinnamon Sticks

Turn on the gas flame of the stove and using kitchen tongs, grab the end of a cinnamon stick. Hold the cinnamon stick over the flame and turn slowly back and forth until it is dark brown and charred — you will smell the delicious scent coming from the smoke. It is similar to roasting marshmallows but not as messy.

RECIPE: Charred Cinnamon Cranberry Compote
(©Chef Natasha MacAller 2019)

Ingredients:
- 12 ounces/340 g fresh or frozen whole unsweetened cranberries (1 bag)
- 1 cinnamon stick, flame toasted (see recipe above)
- 1 ½ cups 300 g rapadura or raw sugar
- 1/8 teaspoon ground/or 4 allspice berries
- 2 tangerines or one orange sliced in circles
- ¼ teaspoon ground white pepper
- ¼ teaspoon salt
- 2 cups water

Method:
- Place all ingredients in a pot and bring to a gentle simmer. Cook for about 8 minutes. Gently stir fruit now and again until thickened, leaving some cranberries whole.
- Remove from heat, let cool, and strain out the whole spices, citrus, and the cinnamon stick.
- Spoon into a container with a tightly fitting lid and chill. It will keep two weeks covered and chilled.

High in vitamin C, fiber, and anthocyanins, the taste of cranberries is not only for Thanksgiving feasts. This delectable charred tangy cranberry compote is divine atop your morning oatmeal or multigrain cereal; stirred into yogurt; used as a glaze for slow-cooked pork or a condiment for poultry, butternut squash, and grilled tofu; or spooned into a high-fiber quick bread or muffin recipe. If making the compote into a glaze, strain out the citrus and whole spices first, then purée to make the glaze/coating easier to spread. When adding to muffins or quick breads, make sure you strain out the spices and citrus first before adding the compote.

RECIPE: Coconut Lime Spiced Pudding with Blueberry Coulis
(©Chef Natasha MacAller 2019)

This light, quick, make-ahead dessert uses fresh or frozen blueberries and chia seeds, which are high in fiber and the berries are high in anthocyanins. It can easily be made vegan by substituting honey for coconut sugar or agave. Have fun with plating this colorful, flavorful, and nutrient-filled dessert!

Serves 4

For the Pudding:

Ingredients:
- 240 mL/1 cup coconut cream*
- 1 key lime or ½ regular lime, juice, and zest
- 40 mL/4 teaspoons runny honey, agave, or coconut syrup
- ¼ teaspoon ground cardamom
- ¼ teaspoon ground cinnamon
- pinch salt flakes
- 1 teaspoon pure vanilla extract
- 3 heaped tablespoons/40 g chia seeds

Method:
- Set aside six 6 ounce/175 mL clean glasses, jam jars, martini glasses or whatever you have available.
- In a medium-sized measuring jug (½ qt/liter), measure/weigh out the cream.
- In a small bowl, mix together the citrus juice, sweetener, spices, salt and vanilla.
- Add to the coconut cream mixture, combining well.
- Sprinkle in the chia and quickly whisk to combine so they don't congeal together.
- Divide the pudding evenly into the glasses. Cover and keep chilled.
- While the pudding sets and chills, make the coulis topping.

*You can also use almond, oat, or other milk or cream. These milks will result in a less luxurious panna cotta but delicious nevertheless! You can also use a combination of the two as long as the total liquid weight/volume is 700 mL/24 ounces.

RECIPE: Blueberry-Lime Coulis
(©Chef Natasha MacAller 2019)

Ingredients:
- 170 g/6 ounces blueberries, fresh or frozen
- 3 tablespoons fresh lime juice
- 1 lime, zested
- 1 tablespoon brown or maple sugar
- 3 teaspoons tapioca flour or 2 teaspoons cornstarch
- ½ teaspoon ground cinnamon
- 1 pinch salt

Method:
o Place the blueberries and lime juice and zest in a small pot.
o Mix the sugar, tapioca flour or cornstarch, cinnamon and salt together then fold into fruit.
o Turn heat on medium-low and bring to a low simmer stirring fruit with a wooden or spoon, crushing the blueberries and cooking until the coulis is no longer cloudy but clear and thickened.
o Taste and add a few drops more lemon juice if needed.
o Cover and refrigerate until ready to serve.

To serve – take the chia coconut pudding from the fridge and spoon a generous 2 to 3 tablespoons of the blueberry coulis on the top. Sprinkle a few orange or yellow edible flower petals and some shredded basil leaves or mint springs to garnish – enjoy!

PEPPERCORN – THE BLACK GOLD PLANT

The unassuming pepper plant (Piper nigrum) is a climbing vine and grows almost exclusively in the threatened equatorial tropical rainforests, primarily in the jungles of India and Southeast Asia. Slow to mature, these tiny peppercorn clusters take years to appear. It is the most used culinary spice, second only to salt, and it has been fought over for centuries on land and sea as the world's demand for this spice increased.

Peppercorns are actually a tiny fruit of the drupe variety – a fruit with a single seed in the middle that grows in tiny grapelike bunches on a flowering vine. This unimpressive tough woody vine and the clusters of tiny green peppercorns have no distinctive aroma (similar to the scentless fresh green vanilla pod) until dried, cured, and processed when at last they reveal their recognizable pungent rich scent.

Types of Peppercorn

Green peppercorns are simply unripe black peppercorns with a milder, fresher taste and are most often purchased in little glass jars, preserved in brine or pickled. Firm but easily crushed or chopped, green peppercorns are added to salad dressings, stews, and cocktails and give a pungent pickled finish to the French classic Sauce au Poivre.

White peppercorns are one of the ingredients in the classic quatre épices spice mix. The peppercorns are allowed to ripen on the vine and picked when the skin of the berries turns red. (At this stage only a small amount of red peppercorns are set aside to be sold fresh locally as they have a short shelf life.) The red berries are soaked in water, then the tough outer shell is peeled away, revealing the tiny grayish-white pepper "corn" which is then dried. Aromatic white pepper is generally sold as a finely ground powder and used in numerous classic dishes from white sauce to mashed potatoes and omelets, as well as in sweet and savory Chinese and Scandinavian dishes. Make sure you purchase the smallest amount possible as ground white pepper loses its potency quickly.

Pink peppercorns are not true peppercorns, but the ripe berries of a Brazilian peppertree and a member of the cashew family. Pink peppercorn has a softer pepper taste and is encased in a bright-pink paper-like shell that is easily crushed between finger and thumb to release its seed-like center and delicate peppery aroma. A recipe that calls for red peppercorns usually means pink peppercorns.

Growing peppercorn plants is a bit like growing vanilla as both can be challenging if you don't live in a hot humid environment similar to the climate at 20 degrees north to 20 degrees south of the equator. The slow-growing pepper plant needs partial to full sun and rich, loamy, and moist soil. The most exclusive black pepper grown on the Malabar Coast of India contains the highest amount of piperine; the magic curative compound that many traditional folk healers, (Indian) Ayurvedic masters, and modern-day Western medical professionals laud for its numerous healing properties. This active compound in pepper is the reason why we sneeze and cough when breathing that pepper aroma!

Bioactive Compounds in Pepper

Pepper plants contain a family of bioactive alkaloids called piperamides. The piperine content of peppercorns ranges from 0.3 mg/g piperine equivalents for ground white pepper to 1.4 mg/g piperine equivalents for black peppercorns. Overall, the total piperamide content of peppers consists of 84% piperines and 16% other piperamides (Friedman et al., 2008). Generally, whole peppercorns contain higher amounts of the bioactive piperamides than ground pepper. Piperamides have been found to possess antioxidant, anti-inflammatory, and antibacterial properties (Prashanth et al., 2012; Takooree et al., 2019; Butt et al., 2013; Derosa et al., 2016). Most studies examining the potential health effects of pepper have focused on piperine, as this is the most prevalent bioactive component in pepper. Most of the studies done on pepper and piperamides have been in vitro, and more in vivo studies are needed to examine the true extent of the health benefits of pepper (Takooree et al., 2019).

Health Benefits of Peppercorn

Appetite Regulation and Metabolism

Many cultures have revered pepper for its ability to assist in healing diseases, and it has historically been considered an energy booster and possible metabolism booster. There is some preliminary evidence that pepper has potential to aid in tissue remodeling and metabolism (Han et al., 2018) and that pepper may aid in appetite regulation (Zanzer et al., 2018). However, the evidence on the role of pepper in appetite regulation is conflicting, as another study examining effects on weight, appetite, and ad libitum intake found that dosing with black pepper had no impact (Gregersen et al., 2013). Further studies are needed to ascertain whether longer-term use of pepper in the quantities consumed in a normal diet impacts metabolism, appetite, and intake.

Cardiovascular Health

A review study found that piperamides in pepper decrease total cholesterol, triglycerides, and low-density lipoprotein and increase high-density lipoprotein (Takooree et al., 2019). Further studies are needed to understand the mechanism and extent of lipid-lowering and blood pressure-lowering properties of pepper in a clinical setting (Zhao and Chen, 2018).

Cancer

There is also some evidence that the piperine found in pepper may help lower the risk of some cancers (Zheng et al., 2016). A systematic review found that piperamides in pepper can be helpful in breast, colon, cervical and prostate cancer, primarily through cytotoxicity, apoptosis, autophagy and interfering with signaling pathways (Takooree et al., 2019).

Neuroprotection and Mood

Another study found that the antidepressant-like effects of piperine are likely due to the involvement of the serotonergic system (Mao et al., 2011). A systematic review has also cited the antidepressant effects of black pepper (Butt et al., 2013). Further studies are needed in humans to ascertain the clinical effects of pepper on mood and cognitive function, using quantities of pepper consumed in normal diets.

However, pepper's most astonishing quality that draws the most attention and analysis is its ability to act as a bio-enabler or **bio-enhancer**: a substance when paired with nutrients or even medicine can maximize absorption and longevity of the nutrients or medicine in the bloodstream. For example, piperine acts synergistically with other nutraceuticals such as curcumin in turmeric, enhancing its health benefits (Kunnumakkara et al., 2017). See the above sections entitled Turmeric, and Section 2 for more information on synergistic and antagonist polyphenols.

At the Store

As with most spices, it is best to purchase peppercorns whole. This is especially true for white pepper, which is most commonly used in classic dishes such as bechamel (white cream sauce) based recipes, cooked fruit, vegetable sauces, spiced cookies and any time you don't want black flecks showing in your food.

Use your nose to purchase pepper. If you can smell pungent pepper, that is the one to choose. If buying in a sealed container, purchase the bottle that has the longest sell-by date. Whole pepper will keep three to four years, pre-ground is considerably less; lasting about one year as long as it is stored in a dark cool cupboard.

In the Kitchen

Cooking with Pepper: Considering that black peppercorns at one time were worth their weight in gold, it is astonishing that the humble but nutrient-packed little black tiny fruit is so readily and inexpensively available today. To bring out pepper's magnificent toasty spicy aroma, toast peppercorns before grinding them. Heating releases the oils found within, and pepper is far easier to grind after being toasted.

Toasting Peppercorns

- o Sprinkle peppercorns in a small dry pan over medium-low heat, slowly swirling the pan to evenly toast.
- o When the pepper releases its aroma, remove from the heat and let cool
- o Either grind pepper in a grinder or mortar and pestle or add whole peppercorns to slow-cooked soups, stocks, stews. You can also finish your dish with a few grinds of pepper. A surprising way to use ground pepper is on fresh strawberries that have been sprinkled with a pinch of sugar, which also releases the succulent berry liquid.

RECIPE: A Simple Salad with Roasted Garlic-Shallot Double Pepper Vinaigrette
(©Chef Natasha MacAller 2019)

A Simple Salad of freshly chopped butter lettuce leaves, cubes of avocado, halved cherry tomatoes, crumbled bleu cheese and thinly sliced red onion, garnished with pea shoot microgreens and a drizzle of dressing. Substitute the tomatoes for orange segments, add a sprinkle of poppy seeds, a few grates of orange zest and freshly chopped mint leaves for a sublime citrus salad; the variations are endless with this vinaigrette!

This flavor-packed dressing is naturally thickened by puréed alliums — garlic and shallots — and Dijon mustard spiced up with black and white pepper. It can be used on a green leaf salad, as a dip for asparagus or broccolini, drizzled over an avocado, or brushed on chicken thighs to barbeque or roast.

Serves 4 (Makes 1 ⅓ cups)

Ingredients:

- 2 to 3 shallots (about 75 g), roasted and peeled
- 6 large garlic cloves (about 25 g), roasted and peeled
- 1 tablespoon Dijon mustard
- 60 g/2 ounces/¼ cup white wine vinegar
- 1 tablespoon balsamic vinegar
- zest of ½ a lemon plus 1 tablespoons lemon juice
- ½ teaspoon fresh grated ginger
- ½ teaspoon freshly ground pepper
- ¼ teaspoon ground white pepper
- ¾ cup/6 ounces/175 mL extra virgin olive oil
- Sea salt flakes to taste

Method:

- To roast the shallots: This is a similar method to oven roasting garlic. Turn oven heat to 350°F – 375°F (177°C to 190°C). Place whole unskinned shallots in a lightly oiled baking or roasting tray and bake until shallots are tender, about 35 to 40 minutes. If shallots are large like the banana shallot variety, slice lengthwise in half and cook cut side down until tender and caramelized. Separate the soft flesh and using a spoon mash into a paste.
- In a food processor or blender, mix together the shallots, garlic, and mustard.
- Add remaining ingredients except for the oil and salt and mix well.
- While the motor is running, drizzle in the olive oil to emulsify the ingredients.

- o If making by hand, in a small bowl smash the garlic and shallots to make a smooth paste, add remaining ingredients except for the oil, then whisk and drizzle in the oil at the end to emulsify.
- o Season to taste with sea salt flakes.
- o Store chilled and covered (ideally for 24 hours) or until ready to use. Let come to room temperature before using. Will keep for two to three weeks chilled.

GARLIC – THE SUPERHERO PLANT

The millennia of history, myths, and medical science that mention garlic are astonishing. Chinese records dating from 2700 B.C. indicate that garlic was used as a remedy for its heating and stimulating effects; Egyptian slaves building the great pyramids were fed garlic for strength; ancient Greeks handed garlic cloves to their soldiers and Olympic athletes and prescribed garlic tonics or simply chewed garlic as a remedy for the common cold, deadly viruses, and contagious diseases. Garlic was so revered that it was offered up at temples to the Greek gods. In the Middle Ages, Arabic physicians lauded garlic for its magical curative power, while in Western Europe it was believed that the "stink rose" smell of garlic would repel vampires! During World War II, garlic was known as "Russian penicillin" because, after running out of penicillin, the Russian government issued its soldiers with cloves of garlic to keep them strong and healthy.

Bioactive Compounds in Garlic
Garlic (Allium sativum) contains active organosulfur compounds, which are responsible for its health-giving properties. Garlic contains diverse bioactive compounds such as allicin, alliin, diallyl sulfide, diallyl disulfide, diallyl trisulfide, ajoene, and S-allyl-cysteine. These bioactive compounds have been found in the literature to possess antioxidant and anti-inflammatory properties (Shang A et al., 2019; Bose et al., 2014; Diretto et al., 2017; Szychowski et al., 2018). The main bioactive components in garlic that account for the majority of the health benefits attributed to garlic are the organosulfur compounds such

as diallyl thiosulfonate (**allicin**), diallyl sulfide, diallyl disulfide, diallyl trisulfide, E/Z-ajoene, S-allyl-cysteine, and S-allyl-cysteine sulfoxide (**alliin**) (Yoo et al., 2014; Kodera et al., 2017; Yoo et al., 2014).

Organosulfurs in raw garlic are generally more digestible than in cooked garlic (Torres-Palazzolo et al., 2018). Stir-fried garlic has been found to have stronger antioxidant capacities (Locatelli et al., 2017). In another study, the antioxidant properties of aged garlic were found to be higher than fresh garlic (Jang et al., 2018). Garlic contains more than 20 types of phenolic compounds, with higher content of phenols than many vegetables (Liu et al., 2018). The main phenolic compounds in garlic are β-resorcylic acid, followed by pyrogallol, gallic acid, rutin, protocatechuic acid, and quercetin (Nagella et al., 2014).

Health Effects of Garlic

Antimicrobial
A number of studies have shown that garlic has antibacterial and antifungal properties (Liu et al., 2018; Liu et al., 2017; Guo, 2014). Garlic oil has been found to inhibit the growth of several bacteria such as Staphylococcus aureus, Escherichia coli, and Bacillus subtilis (Guo, 2014). Another study found that garlic oil inhibited the growth of the fungus Penicillium funiculosum (Li et al., 2014). A clinical trial has also shown that garlic inhibited Heliobacter pylori in the stomach of patients with H. pylori infections (Zardast et al., 2016).

Immune Function
The polysaccharides in garlic affect immune function and regulate the expressions of several interleukins, tumor necrosis factors, and macrophages involved in the immune response. Fresh garlic is more potent in terms of immunomodulation effects compared to fermented or "black" garlic (Li et al., 2017). A study in humans found that consuming aged garlic extract reduced the occurrence and severity of cold and flu symptoms (Percival, 2016). In each of these studies, the polysaccharide content of garlic appeared to be the main contributing factor to immune benefits.

Cardiovascular Health
The scientific literature shows that there is good evidence that garlic can help in the prevention of cardiovascular disease by reducing atherosclerosis, hypertension, clotting and hyperlipidemia (Alali et al., 2017; Tapsell et al., 2006; Sun et al., 2018). A review of studies found that half to one whole clove of garlic daily can help lower cholesterol by 9%, and about 7 grams of aged garlic extract

daily can lower systolic blood pressure by over 5% (Tapsell et al., 2006). Consuming garlic powder has been shown to reduce blood pressure, total cholesterol, low-density lipoprotein cholesterol and other risk factors related to cardiovascular diseases (Kwak et al., 2014; Sohn et al., 2012; Ha et al., 2015; Siddiqui et al., 2016). Several studies have found that garlic consumption can help lower blood pressure, namely by reducing oxidative stress, increasing the production of nitric oxide and hydrogen sulfide, and inhibiting the angiotensin-converting enzyme (Cruz et al., 2007; Fasolino et al., 2015; Takachima et al., 2017; Asdaq and Inamdar, 2010; Sausbier et al., 2000; Li et al., 2010).

Garlic has also been shown to have other cardioprotective properties such as inhibiting platelet aggregation (Bradley et al., 2016, Perez-Torres et al., 2016). The polyphenols in aged black garlic extract have a relaxing effect on coronary arteries before and after ischemia-reperfusion (Garcia-Villalon et al., 2016). Aged garlic extract has also been shown to prevent atherosclerosis by reducing serum C-reactive protein and several other factors involved (Morihara et al., 2017), and has also been shown to prevent the development of coronary artery calcification in humans (Morihara et al., 2016).

Diabetes

A meta-analysis found that garlic consumption can also help lower fasting blood sugar, however, more studies are needed to examine whether garlic can also help lower other indicators of diabetes such as postprandial blood sugar (Hou et al., 2015). A meta-analysis of randomized controlled trials of people with type 2 diabetes found that garlic supplementation significantly reduced hemoglobin A1c (Wang et al., 2017). Garlic supplementation and promotion of garlic use may be helpful in people with diabetes to manage and treat symptoms and complications of diabetes (Shang et al., 2019).

Cancer

Several studies have also shown that garlic can protect against certain types of cancer, such as colorectal, lung, gastric and bladder cancers (Wu et al., 2015; Myneni et al., 2016; Kim et al., 2017; Cao et al., 2014; Kodali et al., 2015; Bom et al., 2014). A study showed that the organosulfurs in garlic reduced the activation of carcinogens, thus reducing the risk of cancer (Nicastro et al., 2015). Several studies have shown that the active compounds in garlic suppress cell growth and proliferation of cancer cells (Bagul et al., 2015; Shin et al., 2017; Jiang et al., 2017; Xu et al., 2014; Wang et al., 2015; Xiao et al., 2018; Zhang et al., 2014; Jung et al., 2014; Kaschula et al., 2016). A study also demonstrated that raw and crushed garlic upregulates apoptotic-related genes, which influences the expression of genes related to immunity and cancer in humans (Charron et al., 2015). Other studies have similarly shown that garlic influences apoptosis, contributing to its anti-cancer effects (Jiang et al., 2017; Xu et al., 2014; Wang et al., 2015).

At the Store

One will find garlic in all its guises in kitchens all around the world: it is a vital component of the classic dishes of Italy, France, Greece, Mexico, China and India, to name but a few. Garlic heads vary in size and can contain up to two dozen cloves; choose heads that are firm with no soft cloves, and store in an open container in a cool dry place. Do not store in the refrigerator, as the garlic may grow mold and imprint its odor to the other fridge contents! Properly stored, garlic will keep for up to three months. If it begins sprouting, simply cut away the green growth, as this will be bitter.

Garlic also comes in granulated or powdered form, which will keep for about a year. If it begins to clump, this indicates it has absorbed too much moisture and you'll need to discard it in the compost bin or the rubbish. Of note: Large mild-tasting cloves of elephant garlic are not true garlic, but rather a type of onion related to leeks, so it contains different beneficial active compounds, not those of traditional garlic.

In the Kitchen

Video: <u>Remove Skin From Garlic</u>
Video: <u>Slicing Garlic</u>

When preparing and cooking with garlic, use fresh bulbs or preservative-free frozen crushed garlic cubes. Peel and slice, chop, or **mince your fresh garlic and allow it to rest on the cutting board for at least 10 minutes**. The garlic will become oozy and sticky as the beneficial enzyme alliinase activates its anti-cancer and anti-inflammatory properties (Garlic, 2006; Nicastro et al., 2015).

When cooking with garlic, be mindful that if it is cooked at too high a temperature it will burn very quickly, becoming acrid and inedible; low and slow is the way to go! It is always best when cooking, say, a pasta sauce or sautéed vegetables, start with oil, then the onions and other vegetables such as carrots, celery, and tomatoes. Once the pan is simmering away then add the garlic to the rest of the ingredients. If you simply want to sauté fresh garlic, add oil to the pan and over low-medium heat, quickly cook until the garlic begins to simmer and turn light golden brown, then remove from the pan and drain and cool on paper towels or add to additional ingredients.

RECIPE: Raw Shaved Beetroot, Carrot, Fennel and Apple Crunch Energy Salad
(©Chef Natasha MacAller 2019)

This super nutrient-packed, grab-and-go salad is full of flavor and crunch. Sprinkled with toasted spices, fresh herbs and quinoa, this crunch salad will keep you going through the afternoon energy dips.

Serves 4 to 6 as a side dish.

Step 1: Marinate the fennel (Step 1 and step 2 can be made ahead of time)

Marinated Fennel
- 4 ounces/115 g fennel – thinly sliced

- 1 tablespoon/15 mL apple cider vinegar
- 1 tablespoon/15 mL grassy extra virgin olive oil
- ½ to 1 small garlic clove, minced
- ½ teaspoon salt
- 1 teaspoon ground coriander seed
- 1 tablespoon quinoa
- 1 tablespoon sesame seeds

METHOD:

o   In a small bowl add the sliced fennel with the liquid ingredients and salt, marinating until softened, at least 30 minutes to overnight.

o   Toast the quinoa and sesame in a dry pan until golden brown, then remove from heat and set aside.

Step 2: Make the salad spice paste

The Salad Spice Paste:

Ingredients
- 1 tablespoon grapeseed or vegetable oil
- ½ teaspoon ground fennel seed
- 1/3 teaspoon ground coriander seed
- 1 teaspoon ground cumin seed
- ½ teaspoon cracked black pepper, or more to taste
- ½ teaspoon smoked paprika

Method:

o   In a medium-sized saucepan over medium-high heat, add the oil, then the whole spices letting them sizzle for 1 minute allowing the flavors to temper and bloom.

o   Remove from the heat, mix in the cracked pepper and paprika and let cool.

o   Scrape into a mortar and pestle or a small bullet smoothie maker or grinder and grind to a paste. (If you use pre-ground spices, lightly toast them in a dry pan over low heat swirling the pan to refresh — the cardamom will be much more pronounced if using the seeds and blooming and grinding).

Step 3: Assemble the salad

Ingredients
- 4 ounces/ 120 g raw beetroot (½ medium) – peeled and finely grated
- 2 ounces/ 60 g finely shredded or grated carrot
- Marinated fennel as above

- 0.3 ounces/ 10 g chives cut into ½ inch pieces
- 2.3 ounces/65 g/ approx. half a small granny smith apple – cored, diced with skin on
- 0.2 ounces/5 g mint – torn or chopped
- 0.2 ounces/5 g parsley – torn or chopped
- Zest and juice of ½ lime
- Zest of ½ orange, juice of 1 small orange
- 2 tablespoons/30 mL grassy EVOO
- ¼ teaspoon salt
- ½ teaspoon pomegranate molasses
- 0.7 ounce/20 g toasted walnuts (15 g in salad, 5 g reserved for garnish)

Method:
- In a small bowl, whisk together the zest and juice of the lime and orange, olive oil, salt and molasses. Whisk in the spice paste.
- Drain the fennel from the quick pickling liquid (set aside the liquid for another use)
- Add fennel and the rest of the ingredients (reserve 1 tablespoon walnuts and a pinch of fresh herbs to top the dish) to a medium-sized bowl. Toss to mix.
- Add the dressing and toss again.
- Top with reserved walnuts and mint and a drizzle of extra virgin olive oil
- Serve immediately. It will keep chilled and covered for up to three days.

CHILI PEPPER – THE SPICE UP YOUR LIFE PLANT

Known and grown around the world, chili peppers are native to the Americas where records indicate chilies have been consumed since 6000 B.C. Christopher Columbus is credited for having "discovered" capsicums – the family members include the heatless green bell and sweet banana peppers, to the scorchingly hot ghost chili, Carolina reaper, scotch bonnet and some 3,000 other relatives – while searching unsuccessfully for black pepper. Many believe Columbus found something much better and returned home with a cache of chili peppers. Soon thereafter, chili seeds traveled aboard Spanish and Portuguese galleons and were soon scattered in the far reaches of India, China, Indonesia, Africa and Europe.

It turns out that around the globe, chili-consuming countries have lower rates of cardiovascular disease than populations that eat a bland diet. Multiple studies have demonstrated the antioxidant properties of chili and its ability to scavenge free radicals, reduce oxidative stress, and promote cellular integrity (Muangkote et al., 2018; Lavorgna et al., 2019; Sarpras et al., 2020).

Bioactive Compounds in Chili

Chili is one of the most commonly used spices in the world (Rozin P., Schiller, 1980), especially in Asia (Astrup et al., 2010). In some regions, chili is not only used as a spice but also as a vegetable. Capsaicin is the main active component that has been examined in the literature with regard to health benefits. The highest levels of capsaicin are found in the chili seeds and inner "rib" membrane, and it accounts for the hot spicy tingling sensation one experiences and that "chili heads" crave to distraction. Why, you ask? When you eat a capsaicin-laden chili, your body's pain receptors react immediately: Wow! That's hot! Quickly, the body releases endorphins, a naturally occurring morphine-like compound that floods the body in immediate response to pain. Endorphins are thought to be one of the strongest drugs produced by the body. There may be an instant welling of tears and runny nose, but soon after, you get an exultant whoosh, a pole vaulter's high, a chili rush of pain, then chili pleasure. Incidentally, chili is considered an aphrodisiac for that very reason.

Health Effects of Chili

In clinical trials, capsaicin has been shown to be effective at improving pain issues as well as many other conditions such as cardiovascular conditions, cancer, diabetes, airway diseases, itch, and gastric and urological disorders (Fattori et al., 2016; Ahuja et al., 2006). Chili consumption has been found to be related to mortality (Lv et al., 2015). An epidemiological study with Mediterranean adults found that those who ate more chili (less than four times per week compared to those who ate none or rarely consumed chili) had a lower incidence of all cause death over a five-year period (Bonaccio et al., 2019).

Cardiovascular Health

A five-year study found that a more frequent intake of chili — more than four times per week compared to those who ate none or rarely consumed chili — was associated with a lower incidence of ischemic heart disease and cerebrovascular death risk. The effects of chili were strongest in people without hypertension

(Bonaccio et al., 2019). A number of studies have found that chili pepper intake increases lipid catabolism in different organs and tissues, which may account for its beneficial effects on heart health and mortality risk (Li et al., 2012; Lee et al., 2011; Zhu et al., 2010).

Data from the NHANES III U.S. study (1988 to 1994) found a reduction in mortality from vascular causes among people who consume chili regularly. Total mortality for participants who consumed hot red chili peppers was 21.6% compared to 33.6% for those who did not (Chopan and, Littenberg, 2017). Possible mechanisms include that capsaicin may defend against heart disease via a TRP-mediated modulation of coronary blood flow (Guarini et al., 2012). Capsaicin's antimicrobial properties may indirectly affect the host by altering the gut microbiota and thus reduce the risk of several chronic diseases such as cardiovascular disease (Tang et al., 2013) and diabetes (Qin et al., 2014). Further studies are needed to better understand the mechanism of action of chili and capsaicin on heart disease and other metabolic and chronic illnesses.

Weight Regulation

People who consume chili more frequently are more likely to have lower body weights (Shi et al., 2017) and are less likely to gain weight (Tremblay et al., 2016). Chili intake — in either single doses or ongoing doses over several months — directly affects energy expenditure by activating brown adipose tissue. Improved insulin use in the body also contributes to chili's impact on the body's weight regulation (Varghese et al., 2017). Adding capsaicin to the diet has also been shown to increase the sensation of fullness and reduce total energy intake (Janssens et al., 2014). The effect of chili on improving the body's ability to regulate weight and energy use may contribute to the other health effects of chili such as cardiovascular benefits.

Blood Pressure

Higher intakes of chili are associated with lower rates of hypertension (Shi et al., 2017). When capsaicin binds to its receptor, vascular oxidative stress is inhibited (Sun et al., 2016). Furthermore, chili intake is associated with reduced energy intake, increased energy expenditure, and enhanced fat oxidation (Tremblay et al., 2016; Janssens et al., 2013; Whiting et al., 2013; Ludy et al., 2012; Yoshioka et al., 1999). These effects of capsaicin may be responsible for the beneficial effects of chili on body weight and blood pressure. Li et al. showed that enjoyment of spicy taste enhanced the sensitivity to salty taste and lowered the daily salt intake and blood pressure of participants (Li et al., 2017).

Gastrointestinal Effects

While spicy foods tend to aggravate some gastrointestinal conditions such as gastroesophageal reflux, chili may aid in other gastrointestinal conditions. Chili may have a therapeutic role in functional gastrointestinal disorders through desensitization of the transient receptor potential vanilloid-1 receptor (Patcharatrakul and Gonlachanvit, 2016). Furthermore, while it is commonly believed that chili intake causes hemorrhoids, a prospective randomized placebo-controlled crossover study found that chili intake was not associated with hemorrhoid formation or exacerbation of symptoms (Altomare et al., 2006). There has been debate in the scientific community on whether chili consumption increases the risk of colorectal cancer. A study over two years comparing 400 cases with colorectal cancer and 400 controls found that chili consumption was not associated with an increase or decrease in risk of colorectal cancer (Yang et al., 2019).

Cognitive Function

There is inconsistent evidence regarding whether chili intake is helpful or harmful for preventing cognitive decline in older adults. A cohort study of 4,582 adults over 15 years found that higher chili intake (more than 50 grams per day, which is uncommon in Western cultures) was positively associated with cognitive decline, particularly in older adults with lower body weights. In this study, the effect of chili on cognitive function appeared to be stronger among those with normal body weight. The authors speculated that those with normal body weight may be more sensitive to chili intake and noted that adiposity has been shown to be beneficial for cognitive function among middle-aged and older people, while chili intake is associated with lower weight generally (Qizilbash et al., 2015; Kim et al., 2016).

High doses of capsaicin have been used for denervation of sensory nerves (Pal et al., 2009), which is why it is used for neuropathic pain. Potentially high chili intake could impact neuron viability and thus cognitive function. Conversely, another study examining the effect of chili intake on cognitive function found the opposite effect, where higher chili intake was associated with less cognitive decline (Liu et al., 2016). The link between chili intake and cognitive decline is unclear and needs to be further investigated.

Renal Health

Data from 8,429 Chinese adults between 1991 and 2009 found that higher intakes of chili were associated with a lower risk of renal disease. The prevalence of chronic kidney disease (CKD) was 13.1% in non-consumers of chili and 7.4% among those with chili intake above 50 g/day. The study found that chili consumption is inversely associated with CKD, independent of lifestyle, hypertension, weight, and overall dietary patterns (Shi et al., 2019). Further research is needed to fully understand the mechanisms linking chili intake to renal function.

At the Store

When buying fresh chilies, feel for firmness, a heaviness for their size, and look for shiny, dry skin. If the skin is soft and wrinkly choose another. Refrigerate and store loosely on a plate lined with a dry cloth or paper toweling. It is important to keep chilies dry. They will keep for about two weeks in the refrigerator or three months in the freezer when tightly wrapped.

Dried chilies keep for three to five years threaded on a string in a darkened pantry (hanging in the kitchen or as a wreath is stunning to look at but the dust it attracts makes them not good for eating). Once they age past the three-year mark, they begin to lose their pungent spicy scent and flavor. Jars of chili flakes will last up to two years, and as with all dried jarred spices, if you can't smell them and the color is faded, it is time to go into the composter! In addition, pickled or tinned chilies are a quick flavorful addition but don't contain as much of the health benefits as fresh or dried.

In the Kitchen

If you don't mind the heat, chilies can make food taste better. Imagine the flavor of Louisiana hot-sauced cauliflower, South African Piri Piri potatoes, Mexican chili sans carne, Chinese Kung Pao veggies and India's vegetarian vindaloo curries. In Mexican culture, there are two names for nearly every one of its country's 150 varieties of chili: a fresh green jalapeño, for instance, becomes a rich dark red chipotle when dried. Dried chilies have concentrated, complex, and sweeter flavors lasting an indeterminate amount of time as long as kept covered and dry. Fresh chilies come in shades of green, yellow, orange, red, purple and black and have a freshness and hydrating bite of heat, perfect for fresh salsas, sauces, gazpacho and even chocolate.

Cooking with Chilies

The capsaicin in chilies is found at higher levels in the seeds and rib membrane — the white pith-like substance inside the pepper. Removing the seeds and ribs lowers the spiciness, but do remember to wear gloves on both hands and whatever you do, don't try to remove contact lenses with post chili fondled fingers even if hands have been washed repeatedly as the capsaicin laden oils remain on the skin for several hours ... ouch!

RECIPE: Chilly Chili and Herb Gazpacho with Toasty Chickpeas
(©Chef Natasha MacAller 2019)

This traditional Spanish late summer chilled tomato soup gets an international twist with protein-rich spicy harissa crusted chickpeas in place of toasted and fried bread croutons. The Harissa spice blend makes more than you need, so save it for future use: add oil to the blend, and brush all over vegetables, prawns, or a whole chicken before roasting.

Serves 4 to 6

Ingredients:
- 1.3 kg (3 pounds) fresh soft medium- to large-sized "well-loved" whole fresh tomatoes
- 7 celery sticks, strings peeled

- 550 g (1 pound, 4 ounces) cucumber, peeled and seeded
- 1 large onion, peeled
- 10 g (¼ ounce) soft fresh herbs, e.g. basil, fennel, parsley, and/or cilantro
- 1 tablespoon Gazpacho Harissa Blend in 1 tablespoon oil (see recipe below)
- juice of 3 lemons
- 1 liter (4¼ cups) low-sodium vegetable juice, like V8 chilled
- 3 tablespoons olive oil, plus extra for drizzling
- 2 teaspoons sea salt flakes, or to taste

Method:

Step 1: How to Concasse: Removing the Skin from the Tomatoes

- Bring about 10cm (4in.) of water to a boil in a large pot.
- While water is heating, turn each tomato upside down and make a small 'X' at the base just to pierce the skin. Have a large bowl half-filled with ice and water and a slotted spoon at the ready.
- Add the tomatoes to the boiling water, leave for 30 seconds to one minute, then using a slotted spoon, lift tomatoes from the pot and quickly plunge them into the iced water. This allows the skin to peel away easily without cooking the fresh tomatoes.
- Peel the skins off and discard the skin and core. Pour out the iced water and use the bowl to build your gazpacho. Keep the tomatoes chilled until ready to make the gazpacho.

Step 2: Make the Gazpacho Harissa Blend

Ingredients
- 1 teaspoon fennel seeds
- 2 teaspoons coriander seeds
- 1 teaspoon cumin seeds
- 1 teaspoon black peppercorns
- 1 ½ teaspoons garlic powder (or to taste)
- ¼ teaspoon chili flakes
- 2 teaspoons ground chipotle powder or ground smoked paprika (or Spanish piementon)
- 2 teaspoons ground sweet paprika
- zest of 1 medium-sized lemon
- ¼ teaspoon salt flakes
- 1 teaspoon olive oil

Method:
- o   Toast, then finely grind the fennel, coriander, cumin seeds and peppercorns.
- o   Mix in the garlic powder, chili flakes, the two paprikas, lemon zest and salt.
- o   In a small bowl mix the oil and spice blend together into a paste. This will make more Harissa than you need so save the rest tightly sealed in the pantry.

Step 3: Bake the Crispy Chickpeas (if using dried chickpeas, prepare them the day before you make the gazpacho)

Ingredients:
- •   200 g (7 ounces/1 cup) dried chickpeas, (or 3 cups canned*, rinsed and drained — about two 15-ounce cans)
- •   1 teaspoon baking soda
- •   1 teaspoon grapeseed or olive oil
- •   1 tablespoon Harissa blend

Method:
- o   Put the chickpeas and baking soda in a 1-liter (1-quart) pan and pour over enough water to cover. Cover the pan and leave to soak for 8 hours.
- o   (*Or, if using canned chickpeas, drain and save the liquid –called aquafaba. This thick liquid can be whipped and used as a vegan egg white substitute. Rinse the canned chickpeas well, drain and place on a paper or linen layered tray to dry completely. Follow the directions below to cook them.)
- o   Strain and rinse both chickpeas and the pan of baking soda water. Return rinsed chickpeas to rinsed pan.
- o   Cover with water and bring to a boil, then reduce to a simmer and cook for 2 hours, or until fork-tender.

- o Drain, then cool on a large tray lined with a dry dish towel or paper towels until chickpeas are completely dry.
- o Heat the oven to 375°F/180°C.
- o Scatter chickpeas in a single layer on a large baking pan.
- o Roast chickpeas in oven until crispy and crunchy: about 45 to 60 minutes. Turn and shake the tray every 10 to 15 minutes or so and test them for crunchiness – when the skins begin to turn white and the chickpeas feel light they are properly dried. If insides are still soft, roast for a bit longer.
- o Place chickpeas in a bowl and toss with 1 tablespoon of the Harissa blend spice paste. Sprinkle with a few pinches of salt flakes.

Step 4: Put it all together

- o Roughly chop the tomatoes, celery, cucumber and onion and add to bowl.
- o Chop and add the herbs, along with the harissa paste, lemon juice, vegetable juice and olive oil.
- o Use a stick (or bar) blender to blitz the soup, leaving some small chunks. Season with sea salt flakes to taste and additional harissa to your liking. Chill until icy cold!

To serve, ladle the gazpacho into chilled soup bowls, center a spoonful of avocado pieces on top of the soup. Drizzle with a little olive oil and scatter over the crispy chickpeas.

Ingredients:
- o 1 avocado/about 6 ounces pitted, peeled and cubed
- o Crispy Chickpeas

BASIL – THE ROYAL HERB

Basil belongs to the mint family, and there are over a hundred varieties. The name basil is derived from Medieval Latin and early French languages from the Greek word basilikos, meaning royal, possibly because the plant was historically used in the making of perfumes for royalty. The most common varieties of basil include Genovese, Large Leaf, Thai, lemon, sweet, purple (or opal) and holy basil (tulsi). Holy basil (Ocimum tenuiflorum) is sometimes referred to as hot basil as it is quite spicy, while Thai basil is sweet with a strong anise (licorice) flavor. Genovese and sweet basil are the varieties most commonly consumed in the United States.

Native to, primarily grown in, and revered in India, holy basil, or tulsi, is a comforting but powerful tea blend available worldwide. Holy basil got its name from its use in Indian ceremonial religious gatherings, and its clove-like aroma is due to its higher eugenol oil content, which is the active phytonutrient compound in clove and allspice. It is also available in dried form and as a nutritional supplement.

Bioactive Compounds in Basil

Tulsi basil (Holy basil) contains **eugenol** as the primary active compound, and it's this compound that is attributed to health-promoting effects such as antimicrobial, cardioprotective, antihyperglycemic and similar effects (Pattanayak et al., 2010). Tulsi basil also contains antioxidants such as vitamin C and a variety of phytonutrients. In addition to eugenol, tulsi basil contains eugenol (eugenic acid), ursolic acid, linalool, caryophyllene, methyl carvico (estragole), and sitosterol, as well as saponins, flavonoids, triterpenoids, and tannins (Shishodia et al., 2003; Pattanayak et al., 2010; Jaggi et al., 2003). Other phenolic compounds that have been found to possess anti-inflammatory properties in tulsi basil include rosmarinic acid, propanoic acid, apigenin, cirsimaritin and isothymonin (Pattanayak et al., 2010). Two water-soluble flavonoids, orientin and vicenin, have been found to provide protection against radiation-induced chromosomal damage (Pattanayak et al., 2010).

Thai basil contains similar polyphenolic compounds, but in somewhat different quantities. The primary active constituent in Thai basil is **estragole** and **methyl eugenol**,

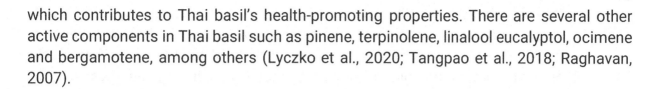

which contributes to Thai basil's health-promoting properties. There are several other active components in Thai basil such as pinene, terpinolene, linalool eucalyptol, ocimene and bergamotene, among others (Lyczko et al., 2020; Tangpao et al., 2018; Raghavan, 2007).

Health Effects of Basil

Basil has been used for centuries for its antimicrobial properties and has been found in research to help reduce bacterial, fungal, and parasitic infections (Sakkas et al., 2017). Thai basil has been shown to have anti-inflammatory and antimicrobial properties (Tuntipopipat S et al., 2009; Wannissorn et al., 2005). However, the majority of research on the link between basil and health improvement through antioxidant and anti-inflammatory effects has been conducted on tulsi or holy basil (Kelm et al., 2000; Singh, 1998; Godhwani et al., 1987). Therefore, tulsi basil is the focus of the following section on the health effects of basil.

Diabetes

Several pre-clinical studies have shown beneficial effects of tulsi basil on diabetes indicators. Rats with diabetes had improved blood glucose, hemoglobin A1c, insulin and glucose tolerance (Narendhirakannan et al., 2006). Tulsi basil was also found to stimulate insulin secretion (Hannan et al., 2006) and lower blood glucose (Grover et al., 2005; Rai et al., 1997; Chattopadhyay, 1993). A study by Ghosap et al. found that the glucose-lowering effect of basil is likely due to the lowering of cortisol and to antiperoxidative effects (Gholap and Kar, 2004). Another study found that tulsi basil has an effect on enzymes involved in carbohydrate metabolism (Vats et al., 2004).

Cognitive Function and Mental Health

Tulsi basil has been shown to help improve cognitive function among older adults, reduce symptoms of depression, and improve oxidative stress (Sampath et al., 2015). An animal study similarly found that tulsi basil consumption helped improve age-induced memory loss in mice, and the authors hypothesized that tulsi basil could potentially be beneficial in treating dementia and Alzheimer's disease (Joshi and Parle, 2006). Another study with mice found that using 400 mg per kg of body weight of tulsi basil provided central nervous system stimulation and anti-stress effects (Maity et al., 2000). Two other animal studies have found similar results in terms of anti-stress effects of tulsi basil (Jggi et al., 2003; Sakina et al., 1990).

Cardiovascular Health

Feeding rats with tulsi basil has been shown to reduce myocardial infarction and other cardiac stress (Sood et al., 2006; Sood et al., 2005; Sharm et al., 2001). A study with rabbits found that giving 0.8 grams of tulsi basil per kg body weight significantly decreased their total cholesterol, LDL, and VLDL levels (Trevisan et al., 2006). Another study found that 1 to 2 grams of tulsi basil for four weeks significantly improved blood lipids in rabbits, including decreasing total cholesterol, triglycerides, and LDL and increasing HDL (Sarkar et al., 1994). Tulsi basil has also been shown to inhibit hypercholesterolemia-induced erythrocyte lipid peroxidation in a dose-dependent fashion (Gupta et al., 2006).

Gastrointestinal Conditions

Another relative of the prosperous mint family, basil has been shown to have a protective effect against gastric ulcers and may also be helpful at reducing inflammation (Abd et al., 2018). Doses of tulsi basil raging from 50 to 200 mg per kg of body weight showed a dose-dependent protective effect against gastric ulcers (Goel et al., 2005). A similar study found that 100 mg of basil per kg of body weight was effective at protecting against peptic ulcers in rats and guinea pigs (Dharmani et al., 2004). One study hypothesized that tulsi basil's ability to protect against ulcers is due to its ability to reduce acid secretion and increase mucus secretion (Mandal et al., 1993).

Cancer

Three animal studies have shown that tulsi basil inhibits the metabolic activation of carcinogens. The oil from the seed of tulsi basil has been found to enhance survival and reduce tumor incidence in animals (Karthikeyan et al., 1999; Prashar et al., 1998; Prakash and Gupta, 2000). Further research is needed to examine the possible role of basil use in preventing cancer in humans.

At the Store

Purchase fresh basil that is perky, not droopy, wilted or with blackened leaves. Many shops offer basil in a pot. If you bring a pot of basil home, make sure to keep the soil moist — it is best to water from the bottom — and don't let it dry out. Pinch leaves from the top as basil likes to be picked frequently; this encourages it to grow.

When purchasing fresh cut basil, only buy what you will need for a few days, as the leaves will blacken and bruise easily once picked especially with traditional common sweet or Genovese varieties. Basil is the singular herb that cannot be refrigerated. Simply and gently wrap this easily bruised herb in a tea or paper towel and place in a plastic box or bag out of the sun in a cool part of the kitchen.

Thai basil is best used fresh or preserved in oil, as when it is dried, it loses the aroma of the fresh leaf. Although it still contains all the active health benefits in a concentrated form, dried basil leaf loses its distinctive fresh flavor so if using dried basil in a recipe the best choice is to season long-cooking dishes.

Holy basil (tulsi) on the other hand is used in teas in dried form. The longer it is cooked, the spicier and stronger it becomes.

In the Kitchen

All types of basil work readily in numerous cuisines and recipes. Nothing could be simpler than the three-ingredient Italian salad of buffalo mozzarella, tomato and basil drizzled with olive oil and balsamic vinegar; or handfuls of basil, garlic, pine nuts and olive oil whizzed together to make a heavenly pesto ready to fold into fresh-cooked pasta! Thai basil is the perfect finish to stir-fries, seafood dishes, and salads. Thai and holy (tulsi) basil leaves are smaller but heartier, so they stand up to curries and slow-cooked dishes and are used primarily to season Malaysian, Indian, and Indonesian cuisine.

A quick tip: If you happen to have a bounty of basil on hand, pick leaves off stems, then blanch leaves for 30 seconds in boiling water – this sets the lush green color. Drain immediately and transfer to a bowl of iced water. Squeeze-dry small handfuls of basil leaves and pat dry with paper towels. Blitz to a purée in a blender with a good glug of olive oil, a pinch each of salt and sugar, adding more oil if needed, until you get a smooth paste. Spoon into ice cube trays and freeze. You now have a supply of basil all winter long!

RECIPE: Sweet Potato Agrodolce
(©Chef Natasha MacAller 2019)

Serves 4

Agrodolce is a flavorful Italian sweet-sour sauce. This version, served with fiber-rich sweet potatoes, is packed with anthocyanin-loaded dried cherries and a bounty of spices and herbs, finished with a generous handful of tender, fragrant, fresh sweet basil leaves!

This can be served hot or at room temperature. Feel free to mix and match the spices and herbs available, but do make sure you have lots of fresh basil on hand!

Ingredients:

- 3 tablespoons/1 ¼ ounces/45 g unsweetened dried sour cherries*, rough chopped
- ½ orange zested, reserve 2 tablespoons juice for later
- 12 ounces (or 1 1/3 cup) red sweet potatoes or yams
- 2 tablespoons/30 mL/1/4 fluid ounce extra virgin olive oil
- 2 teaspoons/10 g/¼ ounce cumin seed, toasted and ground
- 3 tablespoons/60 mL/1 ½ fluid ounce extra virgin olive oil
- 1 pound/450 g/2 medium-size red onion, peeled and thinly sliced
- 2 cloves garlic, peeled and thinly sliced
- 2 jalapeños, seeded, thinly sliced
- ½ teaspoon turmeric powder
- ¼ teaspoon ground allspice
- 3 tablespoons/45 mL/1 ½ fluid ounces balsamic vinegar
- 2 tablespoons orange juice
- 2 tablespoons/30 mL/1 fluid ounce honey
- Kosher salt, to taste
- Fresh thyme and rosemary sprigs, 2 of each
- ½ ounce/¾ cup tightly packed/180 g fresh sweet or Genovese basil leaves, plus extra basil to garnish

*Montmorency sour dried cherries from Trader Joe's are my absolute favorite.

Method:

Step 1: Prepare Cherries

- Put the dried cherries into a small bowl; cover with hot water and let soften for 10 minutes. Drain.
- In a small saucepan mix the drained cherries with the vinegar, jalapeños, turmeric, allspice, balsamic, honey, a pinch of salt and the orange juice.
- Cook over medium heat, stirring until the sauce reduces to a thin syrup, about 5 minutes.
- Remove from heat and set aside.

Step 2: Cook Potatoes

- Preheat oven to 390°F/200°C.
- Peel, skin, and cut sweet potato or yam into 1 g dice/1 cm pieces.

- o Add to a bowl and toss with 2 tablespoons of the oil, salt, and cumin.
- o Spread potatoes evenly on a baking tray.
- o Roast, tossing occasionally, until golden brown and fork-tender, 17 to 20 minutes.
- o Remove from oven, leave on the tray, and set aside to cool.

Step 3: Add all ingredients together

- o In a large saucepan, heat the remaining 1 tablespoon of oil over medium-high heat.
- o Add onions, thyme sprigs, and rosemary and sauté till caramelized.
- o Add garlic, stir and cook for approximately 3 mins, then add cherry mix and reduce.
- o Gently fold in the sweet potatoes (yams). Toss to mix.
- o Add torn fresh basil then gently toss again.
- o Spoon onto a platter or individual plates. Top with extra basil and serve immediately.

ROSEMARY — THE REMEMBER ME PLANT

"There's rosemary, that's for remembrance; pray you, love, remember." This ageless phrase spoken by Ophelia in Shakespeare's *Hamlet* rings true even today as this stalwart plant remains much written about and discussed by both the complementary and clinical medical communities. Rosemary is a member of the mint family and indigenous to the Mediterranean region, but it grows over much of the world in moderately temperate climates.

Strong and prolific with delicate flower blossoms of blue, pink, or purple, rosemary takes hold easily, from containers to vast hedges, and is drought tolerant and frost resistant. It is one of the most important herbs medicinally over the years, dating back to antiquity. Records of rosemary abound in ancient Greek and Roman legends and in past centuries where these bountifully aromatic rosemary branches were touted for their importance medically far in excess of their use as a flavoring ingredient.

Bioactive Compounds in Rosemary

Rosemary leaves contain a wide variety of phenolic compounds, including flavonoids, phenolic diterpenes, and abirtan-type triterpenoids. A study looking at the composition of rosemary found that rosemary grown in different regions has differing amounts of flavonoids. Some of the most prevalent flavonoids and other active compounds in rosemary include carnosol, rosmarinic acid, and carnosic acid (Borrás-Linares et al., 2014; Bai et al., 2010; Del Bano et al., 2004; Vallverdu-Queralt et al., 2014; Genena et a, 2008).

Health Effects of Rosemary

Medicine men of the past who adhered to "the four humours," a holistic Hippocratic medical discipline, believed, as many do today, that rosemary fortifies brain function, especially memory. The active compound in rosemary, cineole, releases a piney-floral-eucalyptus aroma, which may be the key to memory performance while another component, carnosic acid, is believed to be beneficial in fighting free radical damage and slow aging in the brain.

Rosemary has been found in the scientific literature to possess antioxidant (Perez-Fons et al., 2010; Satoh et al., 2008), anti-inflammatory (Altinier et al., 2007; Poeckel et al., 2008; Colica et al., 2018), and antimicrobial (Del Campo et al., 2000; Bozin et al., 2007) properties.

Cognitive Function and Mental Health

In randomized controlled trials, rosemary has been shown to be effective in improving not only memory and cognitive function but also depression, anxiety, and sleep quality (Perry et al., 2018; Nematolahi et al., 2018; Ferlemi et al., 2015). One study has even shown that consuming rosemary in the form of a water infusion has immediate and acute effects on increased cognitive function (Moss et al., 2018). The diterpenes in rosemary have been found to be neuroprotective (Kim et al., 2006).

Cardiovascular Health

A human study has found that rosemary given in doses of 2 to 10 grams per day decreased triglycerides and increased HDL (Sinkovic et al., 2011). More studies are needed to confirm these findings.

Diabetes

Studies have shown that rosemary may help improve diabetes management (Bakirel et al., 2008; Naimi et al., 2007). A number of animal studies have found that rosemary improved indicators of diabetes management such as fasting blood glucose and hemoglobin A1c (Erenmemisoglu et al., 1997; Khalil et al., 2012; Al-Jamal et al., 2011; Alnahdi et al., 2012; Soliman et al., 2013; Vanithadevi et al., 2008). Other animal studies have found that using 100 to 500 mg per kg body weight of rosemary has improved diabetes indicators in animals (Bakirel et al., 2008; Alhader et al., 1994; Kensara et al., 2010). Three human studies have found that rosemary given at 2 to 10 grams per day improved diabetes indicators such as fasting blood glucose (Labban et al., 2014; Sinkovic et al., 2011; Lukaczer et al., 2005).

Cancer

Several studies have shown that rosemary possesses anti-cancer properties, largely due to the actions of the polyphenols carnosic acid and rosmarinic acid and their effects on key signaling molecules (Lo et al., 2002; Dorrie et al., 2001; Huang et al., 2005; Visanji et al., 2006; Moore et al., 2016). Rosemary has been found to have inhibitory effects on the growth of breast, liver, prostate, lung and leukemia cancer cells (Yesil-Celiktas et al., 2010; Johnson, 2011). The carnosic acid and carnosol in rosemary are antioxidant compounds that have been found to have anti-cancer properties in studies of prostate, breast, and leukemia cancers (Visanji et al., 200; Yesil-Celiktas et al., 2010; Johnson et al., 2010).

At the Store

When purchasing fresh rosemary, think of it as a Christmas tree — stroke the needles and if they are bright green with no brown dry bits, soft and flexible, and exude a fresh scent, that is what you want to add to the shopping cart. When purchasing dried rosemary leaves again look for green needles/leaves and upon opening the container, the pungent scent of rosemary should be prominent. If your market or vegetable stand sells rosemary in a pot, keep the soil damp but not wet and place it on the windowsill — it loves sun!

In the Kitchen

Rosemary's needlelike leaves sprouting from strong solid stems make great skewers for barbecue or stovetop grilling of lamb, chicken, veggies and even pineapple wedges. Rosemary is used in both sweet and savory dishes, pairing alongside familiar flavors of roasted lamb, chicken, goat cheese, preserved and fresh lemon peel, olives, garlic and tomatoes. In sweet dishes, it is wonderful in rosemary-infused olive oil polenta cake, rosemary-orange chocolate sorbet, and rosemary-crusted apple galette.

As a brain-clearing treatment during pre-exam cramming, mix 1½ teaspoons of dried rosemary or 1 tablespoon of freshly chopped leaves with 2 teaspoons of cocoa powder in a cup. Stir in 1 cup of boiling water, cover, and let steep for five to seven minutes. Add a squeeze of orange juice and a little zest and/or sweeten as you like, then sip and study! The rosemary will help with clarity and the cocoa with energy.

RECIPE: Heirloom Organic Apple and Walnut Galette (©Chef Natasha MacAller 2019)

Photo by @Manja Wachsmuth

A galette is simple in its shape — a forgiving free-form tart. In this recipe, it is spread with a quickly made homemade apple butter with walnuts, rosemary, and layers of freshly sliced and stacked apples that can all be formed and kept chilled ahead of time ready to bake when you wish! Rosemary is a surprising but delicious pairing with this cinnamon-spiced tart, adding its distinctive pine citrus aroma in addition to its antioxidant and memory-strengthening benefit. Enjoy!

Serves 6

Ingredients

Dough:
- 1 ¾ cups/7 ounces /200 g all-purpose flour
- 1 teaspoon sugar
- 1 tablespoon fresh rosemary leaves, finely minced
- 2 teaspoons ground cinnamon
- 1 stick/115 g/4 ounces cold butter, cut into small pieces
- 2 tablespoons ice cold water

Heirloom apple butter:
- 2 tablespoons /30 g/1 ounce salted butter
- 8 ounces/225 g apples, peeled, cored and chopped
- ½ charred cinnamon stick (as described in the cinnamon section)

- ½ teaspoon lemon juice
- leaves of 1 small rosemary sprig or ¼ teaspoon dried crumbled rosemary
- 1 tablespoon sugar, agave, or maple syrup

Apple stacks:
- 500 g/1 pound 2 ounces mixed crisp eating apples such as granny smith, Gala, Jazz, Canadien du Reinette, (preferably unwaxed and organic)
- ¼ cup/1 ounce/30 g walnuts, roughly chopped (preferably organic)
- 60 g/2 ounce/1/2 stick butter, melted and browned mixed with ¼ teaspoon cinnamon
- 3 tablespoons dark chunky brown or date sugar
- 1 egg, beaten for glazing
- 1 tablespoon cinnamon sugar (1 tablespoon grainy sugar of choice, ½ teaspoon cinnamon, and a big pinch of salt)

Method:

Step 1: Make the dough
- Whisk together flour and spices along with a big pinch of salt.
- Blend butter in with fingertips or pastry cutter until pea-sized.
- Drizzle in ice water, tossing gently with a fork or fingers to combine into a shaggy pile. If needed, add a few more drops of iced water but don't overwork the dough or it will become tough.
- Turn onto a lightly flour-dusted board and gather into a ball. Pat out and fold over twice. Wrap tightly in plastic wrap or beeswax paper and chill for an hour to rest the dough.

Step 2: Make the apple butter
- In a medium pot, melt butter with cinnamon and rosemary over medium heat.
- Simmer until you can smell the spices, about 3 to 4 minutes.
- Add apples, lemon juice, sugar and 1 tablespoon water, give a stir, cover and cook until apples are mushy, about 10 to 15 minutes.
- Remove lid and cook down to a thick paste, stirring occasionally.
- Discard cinnamon stick, then push apples through a sieve until smooth.
- Cool the apple butter, setting aside until ready to assemble the tart.

Step 3: Make the apple stacks
- Cut apples into fourths around the core then slice each chunk into thin slices stacking together on a platter.
- Cover and set aside.

Step 4: Assemble and bake

o   Heat the oven to 375°F/190°C.

o   Unwrap and turn the dough out onto a piece of parchment/baking paper.

o   Roll or pat out the dough into a free-form tart about ¼ in thick.

o   Lift to a baking tray, letting paper edges hang over.

o   Spread ⅓ to ½ cup apple butter onto the chilled dough, then add stacks of apples as shown in photo.

o   Scatter with the walnuts, then drizzle the brown cinnamon butter over all. Crumble the brown sugar on top.

o   Glaze crust with egg wash then sprinkle cinnamon sugar on tart edges for extra crunch.

o   Bake for 25 to 30 minutes until the crust is golden brown. Let cool (if you can wait that long), then cut into pieces and serve.

OREGANO — THE PIZZA PLANT

Oregano, the pizza spice, is indigenous to the Mediterranean but is so hardy it will grow easily in many temperate climates. This strongly scented beauty of the mint family has small oval-shaped green leaves, thrives in full sun and slightly acidic soil, and has been used in food and medicine since ancient times.

Oregano's pungent, aromatic, and slightly bitter flavor is available fresh, and oregano grows easily in most kitchen gardens. However, it is best known and most commonly used in its concentrated dry form. The American craze for Italian-style food — pizza, spaghetti, and garlic bread — began when World War II soldiers returning from Europe could not get enough of this pizza mix.

Oregano is often mistaken for marjoram, which is understandably confusing given that oregano is also known as wild marjoram, but the presence of a thyme aroma in the smaller leaves of true Greek or Italian oregano gives it a stronger flavor than the more delicate marjoram. It is also not to be confused with Mexican oregano, which is related to the lemon verbena family and has a stronger flavor with hints of citrus and is often used in Mexican cuisine.

Bioactive Compounds in Oregano

Oregano's primary essential oils, contained in its fuzzy leaves and stems, are thymol and carvacrol. Oregano also contains the active compounds β-fenchyl alcohol and γ-terpinene. Hot water extracts of oregano have been found to have the strongest antioxidant properties and the highest phenolic content. Essential oils from oregano have been found to inhibit the growth of several bacteria related to foodborne illness (Teixeira et al., 2013; Veenstra et al., 2019). Studies have found that the bioactive compounds in oregano essential oil make up approximately 92% of the oil (Mueller et al., 2013; Bozin et al., 2006; Mancini et al., 2014). Other active compounds in oregano essential oil include 4-hydroxy-4-methyl-2-pentanone, rosmarinic acid, luteolin 7-O-glucoside, and caffeic acid (Kozlowska et al., 2015).

Health Effects of Oregano

Oregano and its oil were used as health remedies not only by Hippocrates but also in numerous European, Asian, and South American cultures and continue to yield many promising health features. Oregano has been shown to have antimicrobial properties (Sakkas et al., 2017; De Martino et al., 2009; Oniga et al., 2018; Dutra et al., 2019) as well as antioxidant (Olmedo et al., 2014; Oniga et al., 2018; Zhang et al., 2014) and anti-inflammatory properties (Oniga et al., 2018; Chuang et al., 2018; Cheng et al., 2018), which is why oregano oil is so commonly used among those trying to prevent and treat colds. Oregano has also been shown to have antispasmodic (Gonceariuc et al., 2015) and neuroprotective effects as well (Gird et al., 2016).

The flavonoids and phenolic acids in oregano also have antioxidant properties with the potential to help lower the risk of cardiovascular disease, cancers, and other chronic diseases (Gutiérrez-Grijalva et al., 2017; Leyva-López et al., 2017). These and other health benefits of oregano are described in further detail below.

Antimicrobial

Several studies have found that oregano has antibacterial and antifungal properties (Sakkas et al., 2017; De Martino et al., 2009; Oniga et al., 2018; Dutra et al., 2019). In a study examining the effect of oregano on pathogens that are relevant in both the food industry and a clinical setting, undistilled essential oil of oregano was found to be effective against Gram-positive bacteria (L. monocytogenes and Staphylococcus aureus), Gram-negative bacteria (Salmonella typhi), and a fungal species (Candida albicans) (de J. Rostro-Alanis et al., 2019). Similar studies have found that carvacrol accounts for the main antimicrobial

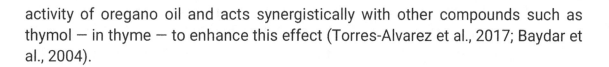

activity of oregano oil and acts synergistically with other compounds such as thymol — in thyme — to enhance this effect (Torres-Alvarez et al., 2017; Baydar et al., 2004).

Gastrointestinal Health

Oregano has been found to have anti-inflammatory effects because of its ability to suppress TNF-α expression (Grondona et al., 2014; Chuang et al., 2018). Mice treated with oregano oil had fewer pro-inflammatory macrophages in their peritoneum and other indicators of gastrointestinal inflammation (Vujicic et al., 2016). A study using a combination of oregano and thyme oils found that the combination of these two oils acted synergistically to improve colonic damage in mice (Bukovska et al., 2007). These studies suggest that oregano oil may reduce gastrointestinal inflammation and improve gastrointestinal health. Further studies are needed to examine this effect in humans.

Cardiovascular Disease

Carvacrol in oregano has also been investigated as beneficial for its anti-inflammatory effects and cardiovascular benefits. Carvacrol has been found to be a potent endothelium-dependent dilator of cerebral arteries (Earley et al., 2010). Carvacrol composes up to 65% of the mass of the essential oil of oregano (Sarer et al., 1982). Therefore, less than 10 mg is enough to provide a vasodilatory response. Earley et al. (2010) suggest that consuming oregano as part of a normal diet could improve vascular health by promoting endothelium-dependent arterial relaxation and reduction of vascular resistance and systemic blood pressure. The authors of this study also suggest that carvacrol could potentially be used to treat cardiovascular diseases involving endothelial dysfunction.

Another study found that oregano possesses antithrombic activity which is beneficial in cardiovascular health (Bojić et al., 2019). A study of participants using 25 mL of aqueous distillate of Greek oregano three times per day for three months found that this resulted in significantly lower LDL, Apolipoprotein B, lipoprotein (a) and C reactive protein and as well as increased HDL. This suggests that Greek oregano could be part of an effective treatment in hyperlipidemia (Ozdemir et al., 2008). Further studies are needed to examine the cardiovascular effects of oregano.

Cancer

Studies have shown that carnosol in oregano possesses anti-cancer properties (De Martino et al., 2009; Elshafie et al., 2017; Johnson, 2011). Carnosol has been shown to inhibit tumor growth in prostate cancer (Johnson, 2011). Carnosol also showed cytotoxic activity against breast cancer cells (Hussein et al., 2007). Similar studies have shown that carnosol inhibits breast cancer (Johnson et al., 2010; Singletary et al., 1996; Singletary and Rokusek, 1997; Zhu et al., 1998). Mouse studies have also shown that carnosol from herbs is protective in skin cancer (Huang et al., 2005; Huang et al., 1994). Carnosol was shown to induce apoptosis in leukemia (Dorrie et al., 2001; Zunino et al., 2009), and it was also found to suppress tumors in colon cancer (Moran et al., 2005; Sharma et al., 2004). Further studies are needed to examine these effects in humans.

At the Store

When shopping for fresh oregano, choose rich green leafy stems free of black bruising. Rub a leaf between your fingers to release the rich pungent scent. If you can't smell it, don't buy it and choose another that is fresher. Again, look at farmer's markets or green-grocers for oregano in pots. It is a hardy grower and will last years in the garden or on the windowsill. When purchasing dried oregano, check the use-by date and notice if the crumbled leaves are green. If they are becoming a bit brown, the volatile oils have dissipated, and it's best to look for another jar. Keep dried oregano tightly sealed in a dark cool pantry.

If drying your own oregano, air or sun-dry it, as the low heat of an oven will reduce the strength of its active oils. Dried oregano leaves will keep tightly sealed in a darkened pantry for about a year.

In the Kitchen

Oregano is much more than simply a pizza spice. Fresh and dried oregano's fragrant pungent leaves are a must-add to minestrone soup, chicken stew, ratatouille, filo crusted spanakopita, Greek salad dressing or my Cal-Greek version of tzatziki, South American chimichurri sauce, Turkish lamb marinades, traditional tomato sauces and of course scattered atop pizzas!

Orange Oregano Tea

Make an orange oregano tea infusion by pouring a cup of boiling water over 1 tablespoon of chopped fresh oregano or 2 teaspoons dried, a piece of orange peel and a clove for sweetness plus a few cracked cardamom pods for spiciness (optional). Cover and let steep for five to eight minutes, then curl up, sip and enjoy.

RECIPE: <u>Toasted Buckwheat Artichoke and Olive Pilaf</u> (©Chef Natasha MacAller 2019)
Video: <u>https://vimeo.com/679500005</u>

This vegan, gluten-free, nutrient-packed bake is a quick and simple supper or side dish filled with flavors of the Mediterranean. Buckwheat is naturally gluten-free and is not part of the wheat family but related to rhubarb and sorrel. Feel free to change up the grain and use freekah, brown rice, or barley groats in place of buckwheat. Check cooking times as grains have different densities and therefore will require different cooking times. Buckwheat cooks particularly quickly, so keep an eye out close to the finishing time. Serve with a side salad of sliced tomatoes drizzled with olive oil, lemon, seasonings and fresh herbs.

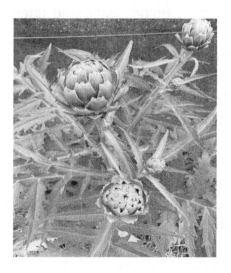

Serves 4 as a main or 6 as a side dish

Ingredients:
- 1 cup/180 g buckwheat groats
- 50 g pine nuts, about 4 tablespoons
- 2 tablespoon olive oil or butter
- 1 large onion (about 250 g), peeled and chopped
- 6 /20 g cloves garlic, sliced
- 4 fresh globe artichoke hearts, cooked, leaves and choke removed, cut into quarters or sixths (or a can of artichoke hearts in water or 2 cups frozen artichoke hearts, thawed)
- 100 g green or black olives, whole or pitted and crushed
- 1 ½ teaspoons oregano, dried
- 3 ½ cups/28 fluid ounces/825 mL vegetable stock
- large pinch to ¼ teaspoon chili flakes or to taste
- medium lemon (about 150 g), juice and zest
- 2 bay leaves
- preserved lemon, thinly sliced to garnish
- fresh oregano leaves to garnish
- 100 g crumbled feta, vegan cheese, or nutritional yeast to sprinkle on top (Optional)

Method:
- Preheat oven to 375°F/185C°
- Spread buckwheat in a dry skillet over medium heat, shaking pan and stirring occasionally, and dry toast 3 minutes until golden.
- Stir in pine nuts and toast another 3 minutes. Once golden brown, transfer to a bowl or tray and set aside.
- In the same pan, stir in the oil, onion, garlic and dried oregano, cooking for 5 to 7 minutes, until the onion is soft and translucent.
- Add grain mixture back to pan, stirring to combine.
- Transfer to a baking dish, spreading the grains to level. Tuck in the artichokes and olives, sprinkle over 1 tablespoon lemon juice and zest then season with chili flakes, salt, and pepper to taste tucking the bay leaves on top.
- Slowly pour in vegetable stock and bake uncovered 20 to 25 minutes until liquid is absorbed and buckwheat is tender. Let rest for 10 to 15 minutes then fluff with a fork. Squeeze remaining lemon juice over all. Garnish with preserved lemon peel, extra olives, fresh oregano leaves, crumbled feta cheese and serve with a wedge of lemon. Can be served hot or room temperature.

CACAO — THE FOOD OF THE GODS

Ahhh, lovely luxurious cocoa. It's all about the flavonols — naturally occurring antioxidants found in various types of plants. Cacao beans — the raw unrefined stage of cocoa — contain a significant amount of flavanols (Grassi et al., 2016). They are good for the heart and good for the soul. Don't confuse cacao (choose chocolate that contains a minimum of 72% cocoa solids) with cocoa made from sugary milk chocolate or white chocolate bars. The higher the percentage of cocoa solids — up to nearly black in color in 99% unsweetened chocolate — the higher the flavanols. The 18th-century biologist and chocolate aficionado, Carl Linnaeus, named his favored spice Theobroma cacao, the "Food of the Gods."

There are 22 species of cacao trees, all indigenous to South and Central America and now grown in the latitudinal region 20% north to 20% south of the equator. The pods are picked and processed, and a growing percentage are being sold as single-origin chocolate. Only a handful — well actually a large bucketful, as the ripe colorful cacao pods are the size of large oval footballs — grow on a single tree trunk per season. The 20 to 40 feet tall cacao tree must be grown in shade to thrive and is also vulnerable to fungi and pests, though new crossbred resistant varieties are now being grown to satisfy the world's hunger for chocolate.

Bioactive Compounds in Cacao

The main compounds in cacao that contribute to its health effects are **flavonoids, theobromine, and magnesium** (Scapagnini et al., 2014). A review of epidemiologic studies found an association between cacao and chocolate consumption and a lower risk of chronic disease, which is attributable to the antioxidant and anti-inflammatory properties of cacao (Ellam and Williamson, 2013; Sola et al., 2012). The phenolic and flavonoid contents and total antioxidant capacities of cacao are higher than that of any other phytochemical-rich food, and these compounds downregulate pro-inflammatory cytokines and their pathways (Corti et al., 2009; Lee et al., 2003; Katz et al., 2011). Catechins in cacao are also responsible for much of the antioxidant activity of this food ingredient (Ellam and Williamson, 2013; Ramiro-Puig et al., 2009). The flavonols in cacao cause the bitterness of cacao and are also responsible for many of the healing properties (Jalil and Ismail, 2008; Heinrich et al., 2006; Neukam et al., 2007).

Health Effects of Cacao

Mental Health

Rich, decadent, and packed full of phenolic antioxidants, cacao also contains the feel-good amino acid tryptophan (Chocolate, 2006), utilized by the brain to make serotonin, which produces feelings of happiness (Strasser et al., 2016). The flavonoids and theobromine in cacao have been found to have a positive impact on cognitive function and may help reduce the risk of Parkinson's disease (Costa et al., 2010; Camandola et al., 2019) and Alzheimer's disease (Grassi et al., 2016; Maia and de Mendonca, 2002; Eskelinen et al., 2009; Camandola et al., 2019). Theobromine in cacao is a potent antioxidant that can be used to improve depressive symptoms (Scapagnini et al., 2012). Theobromine has also been found to have neurocognitive effects (Judelson et al., 2013; Scholey and Owen, 2013).

Cardiovascular Health

Studies have also found that consuming small amounts of dark chocolate can help reduce the risk of cardiovascular disease (Kerimi et al., 2015; Gammone et al., 2018; Higginbotham and Taub, 2015), however, the exact mechanisms are still under debate. The flavonols in cacao possess antioxidant and anti-inflammatory properties and have been found to promote cardiovascular health (Garcia et al., 2018). The polyphenols in cacao cause vasodilation and modulate inflammatory markers, however, overconsumption of chocolate can also cause problems such as tachycardia due to the caffeine content in dark chocolate (Gammone et al., 2018).

One study found that consuming 50 to 500 grams of chocolate was sufficient to cause vasodilation and cardiovascular protective effects (Vlachojannis et al., 2016). A randomized controlled trial found that consuming cacao reduced blood lipids and inflammation markers in patients with hypertension (Sola et al., 2012). Theobromine in cacao has been found to increase HDL and decrease LDL (Neufingerl et al., 2013; Santos and Macedo, 2018; Khan et al., 2012). Another study found that the flavonols in cacao improve lipid peroxidation in mice fed high-fat diets (Gu et al., 2013).

Gut Health

Cacao intake has also been associated with improvements in beneficial gut bacteria such as Lactobacilli and the decrease of less helpful bacteria such as Clostridia (Redovniković et al., 2009; Tzounis et al., 2011). One study found that cacao consumption improves the gut microbiota in a similar way to prebiotics and probiotics (Hayek, 2013). The interactions between the gut microbiota and the body's metabolism may account for many of cacao's beneficial health effects (Tremaroli and Backhed, 2012).

Diabetes

Cacao consumption increases insulin sensitivity (Martin et a, 2016) and improves glucose homeostasis by slowing digestion and absorption of carbohydrates in the gut (Martin et al., 2016; Ramos et al., 2017). Cacao and chocolate consumption have been found to help lower the risk of type 2 diabetes in some populations, with the peak in positive effects at **two servings per week** (Matsumoto et al., 2015; Maskarinec et al., 2019; Yuan et al., 2017). A prospective study of pregnant women found the lowest rates of gestational diabetes among the women with the highest quartile of chocolate intake (Dong et al., 2019). The polyphenol content of the chocolate seems to affect glucose homeostasis. Positive effects on blood glucose have been seen in people consuming high polyphenol chocolate but not in people consuming low-polyphenol chocolate (Almoosawi et al., 2012).

At the Store

Cacao is the raw form of chocolate that comes straight from the cacao beans that grow directly on the branches of the Theobroma cacao tree. Cocoa powder is made from the raw cacao after it is roasted. Raw chocolate and raw cacao powder generally have a stronger and more astringent flavor and contain more of the active flavanol compounds than traditional chocolate, however, there is still an enormous health benefit in adding cocoa powder and chocolate containing 72% or higher cocoa solids to your day. Choosing dark chocolate is recommended for increasing health benefits (Petyaev and Bashmakov, 2017).

Cacao trees grow in Panama to Peru, Ecuador, Costa Rica to Mexico, Madagascar, even the Maldives and the Big Island in Hawaii. Many places now have bean-to-bar single-origin chocolate, which capture the unique flavor and nuances of their particular chocolate growing territory, similar to the regionality notes of wine tasting. Some of my favorite ethical chocolate manufacturers include Guittard International, Pump St. London, Tony Chocoloney worldwide, Compartes Chocolates Los Angeles, TCHO chocolates, Valhrona and my newly discovered favorite is Fire Tree Chocolate: a rich volcanic vegan-based chocolate. The higher the percentage of cocoa, the higher the healthful benefit of chocolate.

When purchasing chocolate follow these tips:
- Look for **70% or higher** cacao solids — the higher the better. To note, with an increase in cacao, caffeine increases as well.
- Look for the words **chocolate, cocoa, or cacao as the first ingredient**. If sugar is the first ingredient, choose a lower sugar option.
- In the United States, a bar cannot be labeled chocolate unless it has cocoa butter in it. Be on the lookout for other fats — vegetable oils, hydrogenated fats — added to it, which is unnecessary.
- **Avoid "alkalized" cocoa** — also known as Dutch processing or Dutching — as this process decreases the flavanol content and antioxidant capacity (Miller et al., 2008). Dutch products are less bitter as much of the flavonols have been removed. See Table 3.

Table 3: The pH of Natural and Alkalized Cocoa Powder

Type of Cocoa Powder	pH
Natural	5.3 to 5.8
Lightly treated	6.5 to 7.2
Medium treated	7.2 to 7.6
Heavily treated	7.61 and higher

- **Avoid fillers, additives, artificial flavors and colors.** The basic recipe for making chocolate is cocoa beans, cocoa butter, sugar and sometimes vanilla (not vanillin as it is an imitation). There is no need for emulsifiers (carboxymethylcellulose,

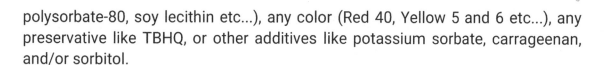

polysorbate-80, soy lecithin etc...), any color (Red 40, Yellow 5 and 6 etc...), any preservative like TBHQ, or other additives like potassium sorbate, carrageenan, and/or sorbitol.

Cadmium and Lead in Chocolate Products

Both cadmium and lead have been found in chocolate products. A study, which measured the amounts of these toxic minerals in chocolate products sold in the United States, found that indeed both cadmium and lead were found in products (Abt et al., 2018). More cadmium was found than lead and the highest concentration of cadmium was found in chocolate that came from cacao sourced from Latin America and not Africa. A recent article provides a critical review of the state of chocolate and cadmium toxicity, which may threaten the livelihood of chocolatiers (Maddela et al., 2020).

Check out a video on How to Find the Best Dark Chocolates and Cocoas and Avoid Cadmium Contamination by the Consumer Lab in January 2020.

In the Kitchen

In the ancient Mayan culture, hot chocolate was never sweetened; instead, this sacred and ceremonial drink was made by roasting the bitter cacao beans over the open fire, then boiling them in water, and finally spicing them up with vanilla, cinnamon sticks, and hot chilies!

Since the 1930s, the British Royal Navy has been known for its traditional hot cocoa beverage Kye or Kai, supposedly made from a massive block of unsweetened chocolate, with the addition of boiling water from a below-deck steam pipe and either sweetened condensed milk or custard powder. It was rigorously stirred and then sipped during the late-night watches (with the occasional addition of Pussers Rum) .

The terms cocoa and cacao are interchangeable in today's chocolate market. Traditional cocoa is the powder left after the cocoa butter has been extracted from the cocoa mass. Raw beans are roasted (in a similar process to that of roasting coffee beans) after the fermentation process. Raw chocolate is also made from fermented beans but left unroasted and is known as cacao.

Culinary Take Away
To preserve flavanol content in cocoa, do not use baking soda – use baking powder instead. Replace baking powder for half the amount of baking soda to retain the benefits.

RECIPE: Peruvian Chocolate Mousse (©Chef Natasha MacAller 2019)

Peru is surprisingly the world's largest organic cacao producer and cultivates primarily three types of cacao: Criollo, Trinitario and Forastero. Peruvian grown chocolate flavor notes, especially the highly regarded Criollo variety, include hints of orange, molasses, and very mild coffee. Lime juice and zest (limón) in the recipe are commonly used in South American and Mexican cuisines, whereas the Northern hemisphere generally uses lemon. This super creamy luxurious chocolatey dessert takes only moments to make and can be kept chilled until it's ready to serve. You won't believe it's good for you!

Serves 6 to 8

Ingredients:
- 3 medium to large avocados (pitted and peeled, yield about one pound/500 g)
- 150 g 72% chocolate, chopped
- 60 g cocoa powder (preferably raw), sifted
- pinch sea salt
- 2 teaspoon vanilla paste or pure vanilla extract
- 130 g agave syrup
- 6 tablespoon/3 ounces cashew nut milk
- 2 teaspoon lime juice

Method:
- Peel, pit, and mash avocadoes until creamy. Push through a fine-mesh chinois until smooth.

- o In a medium-sized metal or glass bowl, melt the chocolate over gently steaming water, gently stirring until smooth and shiny. Remove from heat.
- o Combine cocoa powder, agave, salt, vanilla paste, nut milk and lime juice until smooth, then fold into melted chocolate.
- o Fold in avocado purée until well-combined and silky smooth.
- o Spoon or pipe into glasses or little pots and chill. Let mousse come to temperature for extra creaminess.
- o Serve with a dollop of vanilla-scented whipped cream or coconut cream (and a sprinkle of toasted cocoa nibs on top).

SECTION 4: CULINARY COMPETENCIES

1. Identify fresh and expired herbs and spices
2. Explain the difference in herb/spice frying techniques
    a. Dry
    b. In oil
3. Demonstrate how to improve the flavor of spices by
    a. Toasting
    b. Grinding
    c. Blooming
    d. Tempering
4. Distinguish when you would use a slow or fast blooming technique
5. Demonstrate how to make
    a. An herbal infusion
    b. A pesto
    c. A spice blend
6. Demonstrate the timing of adding herbs to a dish
7. Store herbs and spices appropriately

SECTION 5: AT THE STORE

STORING AND USING SPICES AND HERBS

Spices: Do you open your spice cupboard to a collection of dusty tins, dog-eared paper boxes, and no-longer-see-through small glass jars of reddish or brownish powders of … what? Is there any smell to them? No? Then sprinkle, shake, or pour them into the compost or the rubbish.

The flavor in spices is carried by the essential oil and as such, air, heat and light can break it down. Keeping spices in tightly sealed glass jars will prevent the volatile oils from becoming humid and oxidizing. Stored in a cool dark cupboard, whole spices, including dried leaves and flowers, will keep for one to two years, seeds and roots for two to three years, and ground spices for six to 12 months. Don't keep spices you want to use on a rack above the stovetop: they will look pretty but will perish within weeks.

If you choose to purchase ground spices, the single most important tip is only to buy what you need for a few months. For the best value in terms of both money and quality, purchase spices whole, then toast and grind as you need them. The aroma of freshly ground spice will fill the kitchen with its intoxicating fragrance. Toast and swirl whole spices over low heat in a small dry pan until they release their scent, then allow to cool before grinding with a mortar and pestle or electric spice grinder.

Herbs: The majority of fresh herbs are at their best when freshly picked and used immediately. The easiest way to keep cut fresh soft tender herbs (such as parsley, tarragon, chervil, dill and basil) from the farmer's market or the supermarket looking and tasting great for up to a week is to wrap in a barely damp towel and then into a plastic bag or beeswax wrap and chill in the fresh veggie section of your fridge. Do not wash until you use them as the additional moisture will hasten slime and mold. When they become slimy, blackened, or moldy, it is time to toss them into the composter.

The exception is basil — wrap as noted above but do not refrigerate. Keep in a cool part of the kitchen and turn it over once a day, this allows the leaves to breathe and not turn black. Hard herbs with stems such as rosemary, oregano, and the like can be set in water like a bunch of flowers and will last a week. Just snip off what you need and change the water every day. When the leaves droop or begin to fall off the stems, it is time to get a fresh batch.

> **To Replace Fresh Herbs with Dried Herbs in a Recipe:**
>
> **1 teaspoon of dried = 1 tablespoon of chopped fresh**
>
> Exceptions: In the case of dried sage, use only ½ teaspoon and using dried basil is not worth the effort or cost as the flavor dissipates when dried.

SECTION 6: IN THE KITCHEN

BRINGING OUT THE FLAVOR IN HERBS AND SPICES

The incredible flavor of herbs and spices lies within their cells, and it is the cook's job to extract those flavors into the food being prepared. This can be done quickly with dishes that are cooked for only a brief period of time, or over a long period of time. The flavor of herbs and spices are influenced by the preparation method, the timing of adding herbs to dishes, the matrix surrounding them, and various cooking techniques.

Preparing Herbs
Preparing herbs is accomplished using various methods described below. The pros and cons of each are listed in Table 4. Methods that generate heat or introduce oxygen can cause the odor molecules to be released, which causes a decrease in and/or a change in the flavor profile. Chilling herbs and the grinder before processing is one method to preserve the flavor.

Manual
Chopper

Electric
Food Processor

Manual
Mortar and Pestle

Electric or Manual
Grinder

Table 4: The Effect on Flavor With Various Preparation Methods

Method	Generate Heat	Adds Air	Other
Grinder	Yes	No	
Mortar	Yes	No	
Chopper	Yes	No	
Food processor	No	Yes	
Cut with sharp knife	No	No	Preserves the structural integrity of the herb
Cut with dull knife	No	No	Crushes the herb, causes bruising and discoloration

Timing

Timing is very important in order to make sure a dish isn't over or under flavored (McGee, 2004).

- Longer cooking time: **Hardy herbs can stand up to prolonged cooking times** — oregano, thyme, rosemary, sage, and marjoram for example. They can be added in batches, at the beginning, towards the end of cooking, and/or a dash at the end.
- Shorter cooking time: The more delicate herbs can be added:
  - At the end as a garnish — basil, mint, parsley, cilantro, chives, tarragon, where the odor (and thus the flavor) is released when chewed.
  - Added to a dish briefly before serving — adding basil to olive oil before adding to pasta for example.

Techniques used to incorporate flavor into a dish are:
- Time: The longer an herb/spice is cooked or added to a dish, the more flavor will be released into the surrounding food.
- The cut: Cutting, crumbling, chopping, and/or grinding herbs increases the surface area and thus more flavor can be released quickly.
- Liquid: Adding liquid allows for the transfer of flavors from the herb/spice into the surrounding liquid especially if it is fat based as the essential oils in herbs and spices are fat soluble.

The Matrix

Depending of what is surrounding the herbs and spices, flavor can be extracted easily or without success. It is the odor molecules in the herbs and spices that are responsible for the majority of the flavor profile and these are not readily soluble in water. They dissolve easily in oil, fat and alcohol, but alcohol also releases the flavor quickly (McGee, 2004). For a longer lasting flavor impression, **oils and fats both dissolve the odor molecules with ease and allow for them to stay on the tongue** (taste buds) longer.

COOKING METHODS

There are several ways to intensify the depth of flavors when using dried or fresh herbs and spices– they are **grinding**, **toasting (dry heat), infusing, and blooming in oil (moist heat)**. Just adding herbs and spices to stews, casseroles and other dishes will not bring out the depth of flavor that direct heat will – either dry or with oil. The reason for this is that the essential oils in the herbs and spices will be drawn out using direct heat and/or oil.

Dry Toasting (or Dry Roasting) – for reviving spices and drying them out before grinding

Dry toasting is simply done by adding whole spices to a dry pan over medium-high heat and swirling the spices until you can smell the toasty fragrance. The flavor is changed by the Maillard reaction which browns the spices. This method crisps and dries out the spices further making them easier to grind. It is best to toast spices by size and density; peppercorns take quite a while to toast while cloves, cumin, and mustard seeds only take minutes. This is a great method to revive spices that may have been sitting in the cupboard for a while as well as impart a different flavor profile.

BASIC TECHNIQUE #1 Reviving Spices (https://vimeo.com/661750778)

When the toasted spices are cooled, transfer them to a grinder, mortar and pestle, or smoothie bullet and grind into a powder. Use immediately or store in an airtight container in the pantry. Do not store above the stove!

A genius hot tip: Toast whole black peppercorns using the dry toast method; cool, then load into your pepper grinder. The scent of pepper now takes on a spicy, smoky and intense almost sweet fragrance and taste, plus it is so much easier to grind.

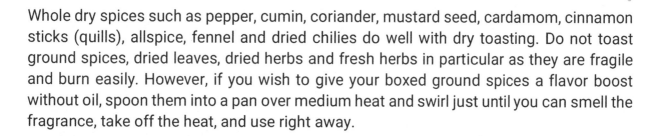

Whole dry spices such as pepper, cumin, coriander, mustard seed, cardamom, cinnamon sticks (quills), allspice, fennel and dried chilies do well with dry toasting. Do not toast ground spices, dried leaves, dried herbs and fresh herbs in particular as they are fragile and burn easily. However, if you wish to give your boxed ground spices a flavor boost without oil, spoon them into a pan over medium heat and swirl just until you can smell the fragrance, take off the heat, and use right away.

Infusing Spices and Herbs – for adding a boost of flavor in a liquid base

There are several methods for infusing liquids with herbs and spices and it all depends on whether the flavor molecules are attracted to/dissolve in fat, water, or alcohol. In addition, heat will coax fat soluble flavors out into a water-based liquid.

Fat Based
- Basil, black pepper, caraway, dried chilies, garlic, ginger, vanilla bean
- Lemon, orange, citrus peel, peppermint, rosemary, tarragon, thyme

Water Based/ Sugar Syrups
- Mint, basil, citrus peels
- Syrup – ginger, pepermint, rosemary, vanilla bean

Vinegar
- Berries, citrus zest, apples
- Basil, ginger, peppermint, rosemary, tarragon, vanilla bean and more

The infusion of spices and herbs can be activated with heat and/or liquid, be it water-based (such as vegetable and chicken stocks, fruit and vegetable juices); alcohol-based liquids; fat-based (milk, nut milks, cream, oil, butter), or a combination. **Many spices are fat-soluble** and require a bit of fat such as oils, butter, or nuts not only to intensify the flavor, but it is crucial for activating the beneficial nutritive compounds within.

Infusion extraction is the ideal method for soft fresh herbs, spices, leaves and flowers, such as basil, tarragon, lemon verbena, parsley, rosemary and thyme, citrus peel, wheat grass, no-spray rose petals, bay and cinnamon leaves and the beloved vanilla pods and cacao beans.

Infusing herbs and spices in water or fat-based liquids is an ideal method for glazes, sauces, soups, stews, gastriques, custards, sorbets, dressings, plus herb and spice flavored oils. An infusion is generally a liquid brought to a simmer for a time (depending on the recipe and the density of the infusing ingredient) with the addition of spices, herbs, and/or botanicals, then the infusion liquid is removed from the heat source and allowed to cool for several hours. To complete the process, the liquid is usually strained of the infused ingredients and either reduced further or used as-is.

Water Infusions allows for herbs and spices that prefer an oil base to dissolve in water to a certain degree. It will require simmering, as heat will help to coax the flavor compounds out into the water base. The base can either be plain water (tea infusions) or a sugar and water solution (flavored simple syrups).

Method:
- Place 1 cup sugar and 1 cup water in a medium saucepan
- Heat until sugar is dissolved
- Add hardier herbs and spices (cinnamon, cardamom, and ginger, for example) in the beginning before heating, and save the more delicate herbs after the syrup is taken off the heat.
- Remove from heat and let it rest for an hour
- Strain and store in a clean jar or bottle.

Vinegar Infusions

It is easy to make a vinegar infusion, just choose the vinegar that you like and add fresh herbs – either one or a combination (see Table 5 for examples).

Directions: In a glass container add herbs that have been washed and dried between paper towels and then lightly crushed to release their flavor and aroma. Add room temperature vinegar, cover with plastic wrap and a metal lid (do not let the vinegar come into contact with the metal). Store in a dark place for two weeks at room temperature. Strain the herbs and place the vinegar in a clean jar.

Table 5: Vinegar and Herb Pairings

Type of Vinegar	Herbs & Spices
Apple Cider	Lavender, dill, lemon balm, garlic, mustard seeds, sage
White Wine	Chevril, chive blossoms, basil, dill, lemon balm, tarragon
Red Wine	Bay leaves, rosemary, parsley, sage, tarragon, thyme
Champagne	Dandelion, lavender
Rice	Delicate herbs and spices, fennel, chive blossoms, garlic, lemon thyme,
Balsamic	Rosemary, thyme

You can also add fruit – 1 cup fruit in 2 cups vinegar – like citrus zest, berries, and apples

Blooming, Tempering, and Frying Spices – to increase the flavor of the spice

Dried whole spices sprinkled into a scant teaspoonful of hot oil for a matter of seconds until lightly browned is all that is needed to increase flavors by tenfold. Blooming, tempering, and frying are similar but use slightly different techniques to intensify the flavors. Use dried whole spices, dried and fresh hearty leaves, and botanicals — ideally ones that are fat-soluble such as, turmeric, coriander, cumin, fenugreek, bay, sage and cinnamon. The blooming technique regenerates old ground spices. It is a simple and satisfying way to intensify the depth of flavor, giving an earthier fresher taste to the ingredient rather than that spoonful of spice measured straight from the jar.

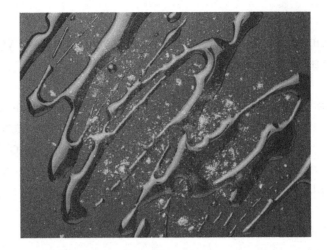

To bloom spices, make sure the pan is no hotter than medium heat. Just as the oil shimmers add the ground spices and stir or swirl just until you can detect a toasty aroma. Take immediately off the heat. The spice is now activated and ready to party!

BASIC TECHNIQUE #2 Blooming Spices (https://vimeo.com/661750707)

There are three classic methods when using fat to increase the flavor of herbs and spices and they are frying, blooming, and tempering:

Fry + Grind: Over medium-high heat, warm a cast iron or sauté pan. When very hot, add a small amount of vegetable oil to coat the pan, then add the whole spices. Remember to add larger denser spices first such as cinnamon sticks and peppercorns, finishing with spice seeds such as mustard, cumin, and cardamom. Fry for about a minute until fragrant and golden brown, stirring continually as spices can burn very quickly. Remove from heat and grind to a paste in a spice grinder. Use immediately as a base for your dish.

Slow Bloom (Bhunooing): This technique uses more fat (oil or ghee), which is heated to just the smoke point, then the heat is turned down low. Whole spices are added such as cinnamon, pepper, cardamom, allspice, coriander plus hearty leaves such as curry, cinnamon, thyme, rosemary and bay. The ingredients are simmered slowly to concentrate and amplify the flavor, followed by the addition of chopped onions, shallots, leeks and/or garlic, plus additional ground spices to finish the dish such as piementon, turmeric, and fenugreek, and dried or fresh herbs such as cilantro (coriander), basil, oregano or chives. This slow-simmering combination of scents and flavors make for creamy, intensely fragrant rich sauces, stews, and soups.

Tempering (Tadka):
This is the lighting speed and most entertaining method for sizzled spices as well as a method to make and jar your aromatic creations. Use as a garnish for a main course dish, or a flavor bomb crunch to starters like salads, dips, and soups. Using this classic technique, spices are quickly fried in smoking oil for mere seconds until they sputter and pop, then additional ingredients are added such as ginger, garlic, turmeric, etc., as a traditional base for Tadka Dal, a delicious lentil-based dish.

When using ground spices such as cinnamon, turmeric, cumin and coriander for example, **low and slow is the best method to perk up ground spices** before adding to a liquid. **Fast blooming on the other hand is used to intensify the flavor of whole spices and seeds** to create a base for sauces, glazes, stews and soups. There is an order that the spices should be added – from the heartiest to the most delicate.

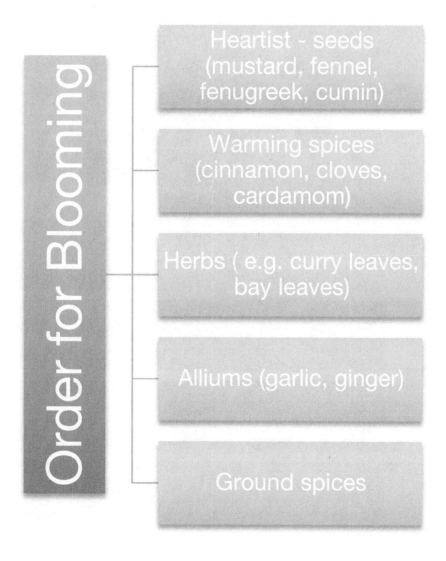

BUILD A PESTO

TIPS FOR AN EASY FLAVOR BOOST
Once a week, purée an herbal blend in a food processor and use throughout the week on sandwiches, stir fry, soup — just about anything that can use a flavor boost.

BASIL BURST
(This can also be made with cilantro, parsley, other herbs, or a blend of several herbs)
Place 2 garlic cloves, ½ teaspoon salt, ¼ teaspoon pepper, 1/3 cup pine nuts and a bunch of freshly washed herbs in a blender. Purée and add extra virgin olive oil until it is a spreadable paste consistency. Place in an airtight container and use throughout the week.

Oil
• Extra virgin olive oil

Herbs
• Basil, mint, cilantro, parsley, etc...

Nuts
• Pine, almond or walnuts

Other
• Salt and pepper, lemon juice to prevent browning
• Garlic

Directions:

Step 1: In a food processor add garlic, salt, pepper and nuts. Process into small particles.

Step 2: Add the herbs and pulse until fine.

Step 3: Drizzle in the oil as the processor is running until a liquid paste is formed

*Optional: To avoid oxidation (browning) add a splash of lemon juice at the end and blend together.

The pesto must be kept refrigerated (up to 5 days) or put in the freezer. A great way to prepare small blasts of flavor is to put the pesto into an ice cube tray and freeze, then wrap each in plastic wrap and keep in the freezer until ready to use. These can be added to soups, stews, etc.

If you are in a hurry or there are leftover herbs, add them to an ice cube tray, add oil and freeze.

HERB AND SPICE MIXES

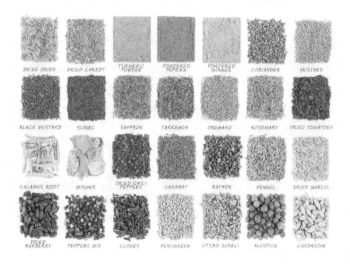

There are so many spices to choose from! They are the number one tool in the culinary arsenal to build flavor into any recipe to make the dish cravable and delicious. Appendix A has recipes for six common blends. Feel free to create your own.

BUILD YOUR OWN SPICE BLEND

The basics when creating a spice blend include:

Step 1: Decide what types of flavors you want to combine. Smell the various individual herbs and spices and look at the various colors and textures. You are looking for spices and herbs that balance and complement each other. You can get inspired by looking at various recipes, selecting traditional spice blends from various regions around the world, or choosing the ones you love.

Step 2: Combine the spices and keep in mind that some spices are much stronger than others – rosemary and chilies for example – so you want to add less of those.

Step 3: Store the spice and herb blend (whole or ground) in the dark in a well sealed, airtight container. Use within three to six months – whole spice blends will last longer than ground spice blends.

See Appendix A for spice mix recipes.

SECTION 7: RECIPES

Below are scrumptious recipes that demonstrate how you can make a cravable dish without resorting to an excess of sugar, salt, and fat.

Super Seeds N' Grains Humble Granola
(©Chef Natasha MacAller 2019)

Makes 2 large canning jars, or about 1.4 kg/2.75 pounds
A super simple dish for breakfast topped with a dollop of plain Greek yogurt and a large spoonful of Lemon Blueberry Compote or pack a small bag of this super seeded snack in your lunchbox. Feel free to mix, match, or substitute the seeds, grains, and dried fruit to what's on hand or what you enjoy.

Step 1: Toast the grains or germ

Ingredient:
- 125 g/¾ cup mixed flaked grains or 125 g/1 cup wheat germ

Method:
- Preheat oven to 300°F/150°C.
- Spread flaked grains or wheat germ on a baking tray and bake for 10 minutes. Set aside to cool.

Step 2: Prepare and assemble all ingredients

Ingredients
- 200 g/2 cups rolled oats
- 1 ½ teaspoons ground cinnamon
- ¾ teaspoon ground cardamom
- ¼ teaspoon white ground pepper
- 35 g/½ cup pumpkin seeds
- ¼ cup chia seeds
- 2 tablespoons sesame seeds
- 2 tablespoons cracked hemp seeds
- 2 tablespoons cracked flax seeds
- ½ cup/45 g sliced almonds
- 160 g/1 cup dried sliced apricots
- 45 g/¼ cup thinly sliced or chopped candied ginger
- 160 g/½ cup chopped pecans, walnuts, or peanuts
- ½ cup millet
- 2 teaspoons poppy seeds (optional)
- ½ to ¾ teaspoon sea salt flakes (optional)

Wet Ingredients
- ¼ cup honey
- ¼ cup maple syrup (or any combo of honey, maple, date syrups)
- ¼ cup vegetable oil

- 2 tablespoons ghee, or coconut oil
- 2 teaspoons pure vanilla extract

Method:
- o Preheat oven to 325°F/165°C fan (350°F/175°C no fan).
- o Prepare 2 baking trays/cookie sheets covering each with Silpats or cut to fit lightly oiled parchment paper.
- o In a large bowl, combine the flaked grains or wheat germ with remaining dry ingredients together.
- o In a separate bowl, stir together all wet ingredients.
- o Add wet ingredients to dry, using a spatula or clean hands to combine (add more honey, maple syrup, or oil if needed).
- o Bake your Humble Granola for 20 minutes, stirring occasionally.
- o Cool completely and store in airtight containers.

So Cal Guacamole
(©Chef Natasha MacAller 2019)

Growing up in Southern California, fresh-made guacamole was often served as an after-school treat alongside a bowl of tortilla chips. I have updated this childhood favorite depending on where I lived and worked but I like this spicy medium-hot version the best. If you like more spice, you can add a few dashes of your favorite hot sauce to make the taste buds dance!

Serves 6 to 8

Ingredients

- 4 medium to large firm but ripe avocadoes
- 2 tablespoons diced pickled jalapenos
- 2 tablespoons diced fresh jalapenos
- 1 small fresh brown onion, peeled and chopped, or to taste
- 3 ounces/85 mL juice of 3 Mexican limes and zest of half a lime
- 2 teaspoons or to taste Guaco spice mix
- ½ to 1 teaspoon salt flakes, or to taste
- 1/2 teaspoon agave

To finish:

- A good handful of fresh cilantro (coriander), parsley, or basil leaves
- 8 to 12 red cherry tomatoes
- 1 lime in 6 wedges

Method:

- Cut the avocados in half, remove and discard the pits (but for one) and set aside.
- Scoop out the flesh from the shell into a medium-sized bowl.
- Add remaining ingredients and mix and mash together making, sure you leave several bite-sized chunks.
- Push remaining avocado pit into the center of the guacamole, cover wrap the bowl tightly and refrigerate until ready to use.
- Just before serving, fold in a good handful of rinsed, dried, and chopped cilantro/coriander, parsley, or fresh basil or a mixture of all 3.
- Add a handful of washed, dried, and quartered fresh red cherry tomatoes into the guacamole.
- Sprinkle over the top a ½ teaspoon of the guaco spice mix and garnish with a few wedges from a fresh lime.

Serving suggestions: Eat with tortilla chips, add as a topping to a big green salad, garnish the top of a smoked salmon omelet, a bowl of gazpacho or add to a cheese or veggie sandwich or wrap.

Clean the Fridge Oven-Roasted Spice and Herb Vegetables
(©Chef Natasha MacAller 2019)

Roasted Vegetables

Serves 4

A no-recipe recipe. This dish can be prepared in a snap and truly allows the spices and herbs to sing! The key is cutting the well-washed raw vegetables into similar-sized pieces. However, the firmer the vegetable the longer cooking time so, for veggies such as carrots, parsnips, turnips, beets, sweet potatoes, broccoli stems (aka tree trunks), Hubbard, acorn and butternut squashes, cut into slightly smaller chunks than the less dense veggies such as cauliflower florets, zucchini (courgette), aubergine (eggplant) or halved/quartered bell peppers (capsicum). You can add a head of garlic doused with oil and wrapped in foil to the baking tray, a halved large beefsteak tomato, whatever is in that produce drawer (except for avocados that is ...)

Step 1: Prepare the vegetables

Ingredients
- 800 g/1 ¾ pounds washed trimmed vegetables
(Estimate about 7 ounces/200 g per person uncooked as the vegetables will shrink as they roast.)

Method:
- o Wash, drain well, trim, then cut dense vegetables into random similar-sized pieces and the less dense vegetables in larger pieces so they all finish roasting together.
- o Place vegetables in a large mixing bowl and set aside.
- o Set up a large baking tray or roasting pan lined with foil or a Silpat and set aside.
- o Preheat the oven to 400°F/200°C.

Step 2: Prepare the spice blend

While the oven is heating, prepare the spice blend.

- ¾ teaspoon fresh cracked pepper
- 2 teaspoon cumin seeds
- 6 thyme sprigs
- ½ teaspoon chipotle or Spanish piementon chili powder (or to taste)
- 2 teaspoons of either Za'tar or Taco Guaco Mix
- 2 teaspoons of Pizza Pasta Zoodle Herb blend
- 2 tablespoons grapeseed or vegetable oil, divided

Method:

- o In a small saucepan, swirl and toast the pepper and cumin until you can smell the spices.
- o Add a tablespoon of oil to bloom the spices, letting them sizzle just for a minute.
- o Add the thyme sprigs. Take off the heat and add the chili powder, Za'tar mix, herb blend and remaining oil, combining well.

Step 3: Cook the vegetables with the spices

- o Scrape the spice blend into the prepared vegetables and combine, adding additional oil to coat if needed.
- o Transfer to the baking tray or roasting pan and spread into an even layer.
- o Roast in the oven for 35 to 45 minutes until veggies are fork-tender, shaking the pan occasionally during cooking.

Serving suggestions: Serve as a main or side dish, add to pasta, stir fry tofu rice noodles or a veggie chef's salad.

Toasted Pita with Spinach and Tadka Seeds
(©Chef Natasha MacAller 2019)

For an afternoon snack or pre-dinner appetizer, make hummus-topped toasted pita wedges with shredded spinach and a good sprinkle of Tadka Seeds. It is so simple and delicious! Substitute the seeds to your liking.

Serves 4

Step 1: Make Tash's Tadka Simple Seed Mix

Ingredients:

- 2 tablespoons oil

- 2 teaspoons yellow mustard seeds (or can do 1 teaspoon each yellow and black)
- 1 teaspoon onion seeds
- 2 teaspoons cumin seeds
- 6 tablespoons sesame seeds
- ½ teaspoon smoked chili powder or paprika

Method:
- Heat the oil in a frying pan until it is smoking hot! Add the mustard, onion, and cumin seeds until they sputter and pop — about 30 to 60 seconds.
- Then add the sesame seeds and stir quickly until they are golden brown.
- Take off heat, sprinkle in the chili powder and transfer to a heat resistant container to cool.
- Store covered in the pantry to use as desired.

Step 2: Arrange the Pita with Spinach

Ingredients:
- 2 plain or whole-wheat pitas
- 1/2 cup/120 g/4¼ ounces prepared hummus
- 2 teaspoons olive oil to drizzle
- ½ a lemon
- 1 ounce/handful fresh spinach leaves, chopped or chiffonade
- 2 teaspoons Tadka seeds

Method:
- In a dry pan, or on the grill, toast the pitas until warmed.
- Transfer to a cutting board and add the hummus on top of the pitas in a swirl.
- Drizzle each with a little olive oil if preferred, and a squeeze of lemon juice.
- Top with greens, Tadka Seed Mix, and a pinch of salt flakes and grinds of pepper (optional).
- Cut into pizza-sized wedges and serve right on the cutting board or transfer to serving plates.

SECTION 8: RESOURCES:

There are many resources for learning how to use herbs and spices, some favorites are listed below.

Books
- Spice Health Heroes by Natasha MacAller

- o Vanilla Table, the essence of cooking from the world's best chefs by Natasha MacAller
- o Cumin, Camels and Caravans by Gary Paul Nabhan
- o Culinary Spices & Herbs of the World by Ben-Erik Van Wyk
- o The Flavor Thesaurus by Niki Segnit
- o Healing Spices by Dr Bharat B Aggarwal
- o Pepper by Marjorie Schaffer
- o Food in History by Reay Tannahill
- o World Spice at Home by Amanda Bevill and Carolyn Cadlicott
- o The Spice Routes by Chris and Carolyn Caldicott
- o The Oxford Companion to Food by Alan Davidson and Tom Jane
- o On Food and Cooking by Harold McGee
- o The Modern Preserver by Kylee Newton
- o Herbarium by Caz Hildebrand
- o Everyday by Chef Peter Gordon
- o The Science of Spice by Stuart Farrimond
- o Essential Spices and Herbs by Christina Nichol
- o Herbs & Spices: Over 200 Herbs and Spices With Recipes For Marinades, Spice Rubs, Oils and More by Jill Norman
- o Ottolenghi Flavor: A Cookbook by Yotam Ottolenghi

Websites and Social Media Tags:
- o www.dancingchef.net
- o https://www.drjohnlapuma.com/
- o https://drgeetamakerclark.com/
- o www.healthbeing.co.uk
- o @christinemanfieldchef
- o @dancingchefnatasha
- o **@chefpetergordon**
- o **@johnlapuma**
- o **@johngs**
- o **@kitchenbee**
- o **@cyrustodi**
- o **@spiceboxtravels**
- o **@kitchenbee**

SUMMARY

Herbs and spices are the number one tool in a cook's arsenal when preparing cravable dishes. Along with their various flavors, textures, and heating or cooling elements come healthful benefits due to the phytonutrients and other components in herbs and spices. The trick is knowing when to add these ingredients to get the most from their flavor and nutrients.

Throw out old spices and reinvigorate your spice cabinet and taste buds with fresh spices. Make a fresh herb pesto once a week to improve the flavor of so many dishes. Like all things in the kitchen, it is important to play around with various combinations and mixes. This is where the art form of the culinary sciences comes into play.

APPENDIX A : SPICE MIXES

Pizza, Pasta, Zoodle Tomato Sauce Spice Mix
(©Chef Natasha MacAller 2019)

This Italian-inspired spice mix can be added to farmer's market finds such as seasonal squashes, eggplant, a plain tomato sauce or a tray of vegetables ready to be roasted, not to mention homemade pizzas, pastas, soups and salads. Be creative with your spice mixtures and let your tastebuds be your guide!

Makes approximately 2/3 cup.

Ingredients:
- 2 tablespoons dried basil, crumbled
- 2 tablespoons dried Marjoram crumbled
- 2 tablespoons dried Oregano, crumbled
- 4 ½ teaspoons dried Rosemary needles, ground
- 1 tablespoon dried Thyme Leaves, crumbled or ground
- 1 ½ teaspoon dried Mint, crumbled
- 2 teaspoons Red Pepper flakes
- 1 ½ teaspoon garlic powder
- 1 ½ teaspoon onion powder
- 1 teaspoon lemon zest

Method:
- Combine all spices together and mix thoroughly.
- Store in an airtight container. Will keep for 12 months in a cool cupboard.

Za'tar Lebanese Spice Mix
(©Chef Natasha MacAller 2019)

Think pita, falafel, hummus or even a crisp green salad of greens, tomatoes, garbanzos or cannellini beans, topped with a quick whisked dressing of olive oil, lemon juice, a spoonful of tahini and a big sprinkle of Za'tar spice mix — it's divine!

Makes approximately 2/3 cup.

Ingredients:
- 1 tablespoon dried thyme, crumbled
- 1 tablespoon dried oregano, crumbled
- 2 tablespoons ground coriander seed
- 2 tablespoons toasted sesame seeds
- 2 tablespoons sumac
- 1 teaspoon salt
- ½ teaspoon Aleppo chili flakes*
- ½ teaspoon lime zest

Method:
- Combine all spices together and mix thoroughly.
- Store in an airtight container. Will keep for 12 months in a cool cupboard.

* Korean gochugaru pepper flakes are a good substitute for the moderately hot Aleppo chili also known as Halaby pepper. Native to war-torn northern Syria and southern Turkey, Aleppo pepper is currently in short supply.

The Sweet Nice Spice Mix
(©Chef Natasha MacAller 2019)

This little mix will calm those sugar cravings as this blend is full of sugary goodness without any sweeteners! Substitute sugar with a sprinkle of Sweet Nice Spice in your morning coffee or tea, add a good dash to your morning bowl of oatmeal or sprinkle on squash or pumpkin with a bit of salt and pepper before roasting. Make a bespoke blend of Sweet Nice Spice mix, a few spoonfuls of raw cacao powder, and a spoonful of your favorite milk into a paste in a teacup. Stir in additional hot milk or water to make a comforting cup of sweet-spiced cocoa.

Makes approximately ¼ cup

Ingredients:

- 3 tablespoons ground cinnamon
- 1 tablespoon ground ginger
- 1 teaspoon ground cloves
- 1 teaspoon ground allspice
- ¼ teaspoon ground cardamom
- ¼ teaspoon ground white pepper

Method:

- Combine all spices together and mix thoroughly.
- Store in an airtight container. Will keep for 12 months if tightly sealed and kept in a cool cupboard.

Taco and Guaco Spice Mix
(©Chef Natasha MacAller 2019)

This spice mix gives a whole new healthy life to classic Mexican flavors. Sprinkle into salads, guacamole dip, mixed bean and fresh tomato salsa salad, and of course tacos, enchiladas, and other Mexican delights!

Ingredients:
- 1 teaspoon (chipotle) pepper flakes
- 1 tablespoon garlic chopped (or 2 teaspoons garlic powder)
- 1 tablespoon onion powder
- 4 teaspoons cumin seed, toasted and ground
- 2 teaspoons dried oregano crumbled
- 2 tablespoons fresh sage chopped (or 1 tablespoon dried)
- 2 tablespoons chili powder
- 1 teaspoon cinnamon
- 1 teaspoon black peppercorns
- 1 teaspoon salt flakes (optional)
- 1 teaspoons ground cayenne pepper
- 1 teaspoon ground hibiscus or 3 calyx petals (optional)

Method:
- Combine all spices together and mix thoroughly.
- Store in an airtight container. Will keep for six months if tightly sealed and kept in a cool cupboard.

Herbs de Provence
(©Chef Natasha MacAller 2019)

Fragrant and colorful, this versatile dried spice blend is great for salads, soups, dressings, sauces, sautéed vegetables, fish and shellfish, chicken and meat dishes, breads and classic French dishes. My version has a gentle colorful heat from pink peppercorns!

Ingredients:
- 1 tablespoon dried rosemary
- 2 teaspoon pink peppercorns
- 1 tablespoon dried fennel seeds
- 1 tablespoon dried chervil
- 1 tablespoon dried marjoram
- 2 tablespoon dried parsley flakes
- 4 teaspoon dried oregano leaves
- 1 tablespoon dried thyme leaves
- 2 teaspoon dried tarragon leaves
- 1 teaspoon bay leaf powder
- 1 to 2 tablespoon dried culinary lavender flowers (depending on how present you like lavender: but is THE ingredient that makes it a Provence herb blend!)

Method:
- Grind rosemary, fennel seed, and pink peppercorns in a spice grinder.
- Transfer to a small bowl and add remaining ingredients.
- Combine well, then store in an airtight container on the pantry shelf where it will last up to six months.

Fresh Herb Chimichurri
(©Chef Natasha MacAller 2019)

This South American pesto herb sauce packed full of parsley, garlic, and oregano is a fresh, quick-to-make spicy pungent blend traditionally served with beef. It also pairs well with other proteins such as grilled chicken, salmon, or prawns. It can be spread on sandwiches, added to soup at the end, or put into a stir fry as a finishing touch. This recipe can be made a day ahead.

Ingredients:
- 66 g /2 bunches fresh parsley, washed and drained
- 22 g/1 bunch fresh oregano, washed and drained
- 4 to 5 cloves garlic, peeled
- ½ c/4 fluid ounces apple cider
- ½ apple, peeled, seeded, chopped
- 1 tablespoon apple cider vinegar or lemon juice
- 1 whole fresh red jalapeno or chili pepper seeded and chopped
- ½ cup/120 mL grassy extra virgin olive oil
- Salt to taste

Method:
- In a food processor or small blender, add all ingredients except oil.
- Pulse until coarsely chopped.
- Slowly drizzle in oil until combined.
- Add salt to taste.
- Spoon into serving bowl, cover, and chill until needed. This will last one week if chilled.

Chef Natasha MacAller @dancingchefnatasha

References

Abd El-Ghffar EA, Al-Sayed E, Shehata SM, Eldahshan OA, Efferth T . The protective role of Ocimum basilicum L. (Basil) against aspirin-induced gastric ulcer in mice: Impact on oxidative stress, inflammation, motor deficits and anxiety-like behavior. Food Funct. 2018;9(8):4457-4468. doi:10.1039/c8fo00538a

Abdel-Fattah AM, Matsumoto K, Watanabe H. Antinociceptive effects of Nigella sativa oil and its major component, thymoquinone, in mice. Eur J Pharmacol 2000; 400: 89-97

Aggarwal BB, Harikumar KB. Potential therapeutic effects of curcumin, the anti-inflammatory agent, against neurodegenerative, cardiovascular, pulmonary, metabolic, autoimmune and neoplastic diseases. Int J Biochem Cell Biol. 2009;41(1):40–59. doi: 10.1016/j.biocel.2008.06.010

Aggarwal, B.B.; Prasad, S.; Yadav, V.R.; Park, B.; Kim, J.I.; Gupta, S.C.; Yoon, S.W.; Lavasanifar, A.; Sung, B. Targeting inflammatory pathways by dietary agents for prevention and therapy of cancer. J. Food Drug Anal. 2012, 20, 213–236.

Aggarwal, B.B.; Shishodia, S.; Sandur, S.K.; Pandey, M.K.; Sethi, G. Inflammation and cancer: How hot is the link? Biochem. Pharmacol. 2006, 72, 1605–1621.

Ahuja KD, Robertson IK, Geraghty DP, Ball MJ. Effects of chili consumption on postprandial glucose, insulin, and energy metabolism. Am J Clin Nutr. 2006;84(1):63-69. doi:10.1093/ajcn/84.1.63

Akhondzadeh, S.; Noroozian, M.; Mohammadi, M.; Ohadinia. S.; Jamshidi, A.H.; Khani, M. Salvia officinalis extract in the treatment of patients with mild to moderate Alzheimer's disease: A double blind randomized and placebo controlled trial. J. Clin. Pharm. Ther.2003, 28, 53–59.

Akilen R, Tsiami A, Devendra D, Robinson N (2012). "Cinnamon in glycaemic control: Systematic review and meta analysis". Clin Nutr. 31 (5): 609–615. doi:10.1016/j.clnu.2012.04.003. PMID 22579946.

Alali FQ, El-Elimat T, Khalid L, Hudaib R, Al-Shehabi TS, Eid AH. Garlic for Cardiovascular Disease: Prevention or Treatment?. Curr Pharm Des. 2017;23(7):1028-1041. doi:10.2174/1381612822666161010124530

Al-brakati A.Y. Protective effect of garlic against diabetic retinopathy in adult albino rats. Res. J. Pharm. Biol. Chem. Sci. 2016;7:2748–2759.

Al-Ghamdi MS. The anti-inflammatory, analgesic and antipyretic activity of Nigella sativa . J Ethnopharmacol 2001; 76: 45-48

Alhader A., Hasan Z., Aqel M. Hyperglycemic and insulin release inhibitory effects of Rosmarinus Officinalis. J. Ethnopharmacol. 1994;43:217–221. doi: 10.1016/0378-8741(94)90046-9.

Ali B. H, Blunden G. (2003). Pharmacological and toxicological properties of Nigella sativa. Phytotherapy Research: PTR, 17: 299–305.

Al-Jamal A.-R., Alqadi T. Effects of rosemary (Rosmarinus officinalis) on lipid profile of diabetic rats. Jordan J. Biol. Sci. 2011;4:199–203.

Allahghadri T, Rasooli I, Owlia P, et al. Antimicrobial property, antioxidant capacity, and cytotoxicity of essential oil from cumin produced in Iran. J Food Sci. 2010;75(2):H54-H61. doi:10.1111/j.1750-3841.2009.01467.x

Allegri P, Mastromarino A, Neri P. Management of chronic anterior uveitis relapses: efficacy of oral phospholipidic curcumin treatment. Long-term follow-up. Clin Ophthalmol. 2010;4:1201–1206.

Allen RW, Schwartzman E, Baker WL, Coleman CI, Phung OJ (2013). "Cinnamon use in type 2 diabetes: an updated systematic review and meta-analysis". Ann Fam Med. 11 (5): 452–459. doi:10.1370/afm.1517. PMC 3767714. PMID 24019277.

Almoosawi S., Tsang C., Ostertag L.M., Fyfe L., Al-Dujaili E.A. Differential effect of polyphenol-rich dark chocolate on biomarkers of glucose metabolism and cardiovascular risk factors in healthy, overweight and obese subjects: A randomized clinical trial. Food Func. 2012;3:1035–1043. doi: 10.1039/c2fo30060e.

Alnahdi H.S. Effect of Rosmarinus officinalis extract on some cardiac enzymes of streptozotocin-induced diabetic rats. J. Health Sci. 2012;2:33–37. doi: 10.5923/j.health.20120204.03.

Al-Okbi SY, Hussein AMS, Elbakry HFH, Fouda KA, Mahmoud KF, Hassan ME. Health Benefits of Fennel, Rosemary Volatile Oils and their Nano-Forms in Dyslipidemic Rat Model. Pak J Biol Sci. 2018;21(7):348-358. doi:10.3923/pjbs.2018.348.358

Al-Saleh IA, Billedo G, El-Doush II. Levels of selenium, dl-α-tocopherol, dl-γ-tocopherol, all-trans-retinol, thymoquinone and thymol in different brands of Nigella sativa seeds. J Food Compost Anal 2006; 19: 167-175

Al Sheyab F.M., Abuharfeil N., Salloum L., Hani R.B., Awad D.S. The effect of rosemary (Rosmarinus officinalis. L) plant extracts on the immune response and lipid profile in mice. J. Biol. Life Sci. 2011;3 doi: 10.5296/jbls.v3i1.906.

Altinier G., Sosa S., Aquino R.P., Mencherini T., Loggia R.D., Tubaro A. Characterization of topical antiinflammatory compounds in Rosmarinus officinalis L. J. Agric. Food Chem. 2007;55:1718–1723.

Altomare DF, Rinaldi M, La Torre F, et al. Red hot chili pepper and hemorrhoids: the explosion of a myth: results of a prospective, randomized, placebo-controlled, crossover trial. Dis Colon Rectum. 2006;49(7):1018-1023. doi:10.1007/s10350-006-0532-3

Al Wafai RJ. Nigella sativa and thymoquinone suppress cyclooxygenase-2 and oxidative stress in pancreatic tissue of streptozotocin-induced diabetic rats. Pancreas 2013; 42: 841-849

Alwi I, Santoso T, Suyono S, Sutrisna B, Suyatna FD, Kresno SB, et al. The effect of curcumin on lipid level in patients with acute coronary syndrome. Acta Med Indones. 2008;40(4):201–210.

Amin B, Hosseinzadeh H. Black Cumin (Nigella sativa) and Its Active Constituent, Thymoquinone: An Overview on the Analgesic and Anti-inflammatory Effects. Planta Med. 2016;82(1-2):8-16. doi:10.1055/s-0035-1557838

Amin B, Taheri Heravi MM, Hosseinzadeh H. Effects of intraperitoneal thymoquinone on chronic neuropathic pain in rats. Planta Med 2014; 80: 1269-1277

Amin B, Hosseinzadeh H. Black Cumin (Nigella sativa) and Its Active Constituent, Thymoquinone: An Overview on the Analgesic and Anti-inflammatory Effects. Planta Med. 2016;82(1-2):8-16. doi:10.1055/s-0035-1557838

Appendino G, Belcaro G, Cornelli U, Luzzi R, Togni S, Dugall M, et al. Potential role of curcumin phytosome (Meriva) in controlling the evolution of diabetic microangiopathy. A pilot study. Panminerva Med. 2011;53(3 Suppl 1):43–49.

Araújo, J.R.; Gonçalves, P.; Martel, F. Chemopreventive effect of dietary polyphenols in colorectal cancer cell lines. Nutr. Res. 2011, 31, 77–87.

Asdaq S.M., Inamdar M.N. Potential of garlic and its active constituent, S-allyl cysteine, as antihypertensive and cardioprotective in presence of captopril. Phytomedicine. 2010;17:1016–1026. doi: 10.1016/j.phymed.2010.07.012.

Astrup A., Kristensen M., Gregersen N.T., Belza A., Lorenzen J.K., Due A., Larsen T.M. Can bioactive foods affect obesity? Ann. N. Y. Acad. Sci. 2010;1190:25–41. doi: 10.1111/j.1749-6632.2009.05272.x.

Azimi P, Ghiasvand R, Feizi A, Hariri M, Abbasi B. Effects of Cinnamon, Cardamom, Saffron, and Ginger Consumption on Markers of Glycemic Control, Lipid Profile, Oxidative Stress, and Inflammation in Type 2 Diabetes Patients. Rev Diabet Stud. 2014;11(3-4):258-266. doi:10.1900/RDS.2014.11.258

Bai N., He K., Roller M., Lai C., Shao X., Pan M., Ho C. Flavonoids and phenolic compounds from Rosmarinus officinalis. J. Agric. Food Chem. 2010;58:5363–5367.

Bag A, Chattopadhyay RR. Evaluation of Synergistic Antibacterial and Antioxidant Efficacy of Essential Oils of Spices and Herbs in Combination. PLoS One. 2015;10(7):e0131321. Published 2015 Jul 1. doi:10.1371/journal.pone.0131321

Bagul M., Kakumanu S., Wilson T.A. Crude garlic extract inhibits cell proliferation and induces cell cycle arrest and apoptosis of cancer cells in vitro. J. Med. Food. 2015;18:731–737. doi: 10.1089/jmf.2014.0064.

Baker, I.; Chohan, M.; Opara, E.I. Impact of cooking and digestion, in vitro, on the antioxidant capacity and anti-inflammatory activity of cinnamon, clove and nutmeg. Plant Foods Hum. Nutr.2013, 68, 364–369.

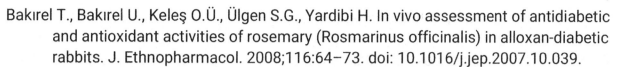
Bakırel T., Bakırel U., Keleş O.Ü., Ülgen S.G., Yardibi H. In vivo assessment of antidiabetic and antioxidant activities of rosemary (Rosmarinus officinalis) in alloxan-diabetic rabbits. J. Ethnopharmacol. 2008;116:64–73. doi: 10.1016/j.jep.2007.10.039.

Balasubramanian S, Roselin P, Singh KK, Zachariah J, Saxena SN. Postharvest Processing and Benefits of Black Pepper, Coriander, Cinnamon, Fenugreek, and Turmeric Spices. Crit Rev Food Sci Nutr. 2016;56(10):1585-1607.

Bashir MU, Qureshi HJ. Analgesic effect of Nigella sativa seeds extract on experimentally induced pain in albino mice. J Coll Physicians Surg Pak 2010; 20: 464-467

Baum L, Lam CW, Cheung SK, Kwok T, Lui V, Tsoh J, et al. Six-month randomized, placebo-controlled, double-blind, pilot clinical trial of curcumin in patients with Alzheimer disease. J Clin Psychopharmacol. 2008;28(1):110–113. doi: 10.1097/jcp.0b013e318160862c

Baydar, H.; Saˇgdiç, O.; Özkan, G.; Karadoˇgan, T. Antibacterial activity and composition of essential oilsfromOriganum,ThymbraandSaturejaspecies with commercial importance in Turkey.Food Control2004,15,169–172

Bayet-Robert M, Kwiatkowski F, Leheurteur M, Gachon F, Planchat E, Abrial C, et al. Phase I dose escalation trial of docetaxel plus curcumin in patients with advanced and metastatic breast cancer. Cancer Biol Ther. 2010;9(1):8–14. doi: 10.4161/cbt.9.1.10392.

Bayet-Robert M, Kwiatkowski F, Leheurteur M, Gachon F, Planchat E, Abrial C, et al. Phase I dose escalation trial of docetaxel plus curcumin in patients with advanced and metastatic breast cancer. Cancer Biol Ther. 2010;9(1):8–14. doi: 10.4161/cbt.9.1.10392.

Belcaro G, Cesarone MR, Dugall M, Pellegrini L, Ledda A, Grossi MG, et al. Product-evaluation registry of Meriva(R), a curcumin-phosphatidylcholine complex, for the complementary management of osteoarthritis. Panminerva Med. 2010;52(2 Suppl 1):55–62.

Belcaro G, Cesarone MR, Dugall M, Pellegrini L, Ledda A, Grossi MG, et al. Efficacy and safety of Meriva(R), a curcumin-phosphatidylcholine complex, during extended administration in osteoarthritis patients. Altern Med Rev. 2010;15(4):337–344.

Bell, Maguelonne Toussaint-Samat; translated by Anthea (2009). A history of food(New expanded ed.). Chichester, West Sussex: Wiley-Blackwell. ISBN 978-1405181198. Cassia, also known as cinnamon or Chinese cinnamon is a tree that has bark similar to that of cinnamon but with a rather pungent odour

Belkaid Y, Segre JA. Dialogue between skin microbiota and immunity. Science. 2014;346(6212):954-959. doi:10.1126/science.1260144

Benhaddouandaloussi A, Martineau CL, Vallerand D, Haddad Y, Haddad SP. Antidiabetic effects of Nigella sativa are mediated by activation of insulin and AMPK pathways, and by mitochondrial uncoupling. 2008; January 1. Volume 32, ISSUE 4, P333.DOI:https://doi.org/10.1016/S1499-2671(08)24136-5

Bermúdez-Soto, M.J.; Larrosa, M.; García-Cantalejo, J.; Espín, J.C. Tomás-Barberan, F.A.; García-Conesa, M.T. Transcriptional changes in human Caco-2 colon cancer cells following exposure to a recurrent non-toxic dose of polyphenol-rich chokeberry juice. Genes Nutr. 2007, 2, 111–113.

Bermúdez-Soto, M.J.; Larrosa, M.; Garcia-Cantalejo, J.M.; Espín, J.C.; Tomás-Barberan, F.A.; García-Conesa, M.T. Up-regulation of tumor suppressor carcinoembryonic antigen-related cell adhesion molecule 1 in human colon cancer Caco-2 cells following repetitive exposure to dietary levels of a polyphenol-rich chokeberry juice. J. Nutr. Biochem. 2007, 18, 259–271.

Bernardo MA, Silva ML, Santos E, et al. Effect of Cinnamon Tea on Postprandial Glucose Concentration. J Diabetes Res. 2015;2015:913651. doi:10.1155/2015/913651

Bettaieb I, Bourgou S, Sriti J, Msaada K, Limam F, Marzouk B. (2011). Essential oils and fatty acids composition of Tunisian and Indian cumin (Cuminum cyminum L.) seeds: a comparative study. Journal of the Science of Food and Agriculture, 91: 2100–2107.

Blasa, M.; Angelino, D.; Gennari, L.; Ninfali, P. The cellular antioxidant activity in red blood cells (CAA-RBC): A new approach to bioavailability and synergy of phytochemicals and botanical extracts. Food Chem. **2011**, 125, 685–691.

Bojić M, Maleš Ž, Antolić A, Babić I, Tomičić M. Antithrombotic activity of flavonoids and polyphenols rich plant species. Acta Pharm. 2019;69(4):483-495. doi:10.2478/acph-2019-0050

Bom J., Gunutzmann P., Hurtado E.C.P., Maragno-Correa J.M.R., Kleeb S.R., Lallo M.A. Long-term treatment with aqueous garlic and/or tomato suspensions decreases Ehrlich ascites tumors. Evid. Based Complement. Altern. Med. 2014;2014:381649. doi: 10.1155/2014/381649.

Bonaccio M, Di Castelnuovo A, Costanzo S, et al. Chili Pepper Consumption and Mortality in Italian Adults. J Am Coll Cardiol. 2019;74(25):3139-3149. doi:10.1016/j.jacc.2019.09.068

Borrás-Linares I, Stojanović Z, Quirantes-Piné R, et al. Rosmarinus officinalis leaves as a natural source of bioactive compounds. Int J Mol Sci. 2014;15(11):20585-20606. Published 2014 Nov 10. doi:10.3390/ijms151120585

Bose S., Laha B., Banerjee S. Quantification of allicin by high performance liquid chromatography-ultraviolet analysis with effect of post-ultrasonic sound and microwave radiation on fresh garlic cloves. Pharmacogn. Mag. 2014;10:288–293. doi: 10.4103/0973-1296.133279.

Boskabady M. H, Shirmohammadi B. (2002). Effect of Nigella sativa on isolated guinea pig trachea. Archives of Iranian Medicine, 5: 103–107.

Bozin B., Mimica-Dukic N., Samojlik I., Jovin E. Antimicrobial and antioxidant properties of rosemary and sage (Rosmarinus officinalis L. and Salvia officinalis L., Lamiaceae) essential oils. J. Agric. Food Chem. 2007;55:7879–7885.

Bozin B, Mimica-Dukic N, Simin N, Anackov G. Characterization of the volatile composition of essential oils of some lamiaceae spices and the antimicrobial and antioxidant activities of the entire oils. Journal of agricultural and food chemistry. 2006;54(5):1822–8. doi: 10.1021/jf051922u.

Bradley J.M., Organ C.L., Lefer D.J. Garlic-derived organic polysulfides and myocardial protection. J. Nutr. 2016;146:403S–409S. doi: 10.3945/jn.114.208066.

Bukovska A, Cikos S, Juhas S, Il'kova G, Rehak P, Koppel J. Effects of a combination of thyme and oregano essential oils on TNBS-induced colitis in mice. Mediators Inflamm. 2007;2007:23296. doi: 10.1155/2007/23296.

Bundy R, Walker AF, Middleton RW, Booth J. Turmeric extract may improve irritable bowel syndrome symptomology in otherwise healthy adults: a pilot study. J Altern Complement Med. 2004;10(6):1015–1018. doi: 10.1089/acm.2004.10.1015.

Burlando, B.; Verotta, L.; Cornara, L.; Bottini-Massa, E. (2010). Herbal principles in cosmetics: properties and mechanisms of action. Boca Raton: CRC Press. p. 121. ISBN 978-1-4398-1214-3.

Burns J, Joseph PD, Rose KJ, Ryan MM, Ouvrier RA. Effect of oral curcumin on Dejerine-Sottas disease. Pediatr Neurol. 2009;41(4):305–308. doi: 10.1016/j.pediatrneurol.2009.04.030.

Burokas A, Moloney RD, Dinan TG, Cryan JF. Microbiota regulation of the Mammalian gut-brain axis. Adv Appl Microbiol. 2015;91:1-62. doi:10.1016/bs.aambs.2015.02.001

Butt MS, Pasha I, Sultan MT, Randhawa MA, Saeed F, Ahmed W. Black pepper and health claims: a comprehensive treatise. Crit Rev Food Sci Nutr. 2013;53(9):875-886. doi:10.1080/10408398.2011.571799

Camandola S, Plick N, Mattson MP. Impact of Coffee and Cacao Purine Metabolites on Neuroplasticity and Neurodegenerative Disease. Neurochem Res. 2019;44(1):214-227. doi:10.1007/s11064-018-2492-0

Cao H.X., Zhu K.X., Fan J.G., Qiao L. Garlic-derived allyl sulfides in cancer therapy. Anticancer Agents Med. Chem. 2014;14:793–799. doi: 10.2174/1871520614666140521120811.

Carlsen, M.H.; Halvorsen, B.L.; Holte, K.; Bohn, S.K.; Dragland, S.; Sampson, L.; Willey, C.; Senoo, H.; Umezono, Y.; Sanada, C.; et al. The total antioxidant content of more than 3100 foods, beverages, spices, herbs and supplements used worldwide. Nutr. J. 2010, 9, 3.

Carroll RE, Benya RV, Turgeon DK, Vareed S, Neuman M, Rodriguez L, et al. Phase IIa clinical trial of curcumin for the prevention of colorectal neoplasia. Cancer Prev Res (Phila) 2011;4(3):354–364. doi: 10.1158/1940-6207.CAPR-10-0098.

Casado FJ, Sanchez AH, Montano A. Reduction of acrylamide content of ripe olives by selected additives. Food Chem. 2010;119:161–166. doi: 10.1016/j.foodchem.2009.06.009.

Chandran B, Goel A. A randomized, pilot study to assess the efficacy and safety of curcumin in patients with active rheumatoid arthritis. Phytother Res. 2012;26(11):1719–25. doi:10.1002/ptr.4639.

Charron C.S., Dawson H.D., Albaugh G.P., Solverson P.M., Vinyard B.T., Solano-Aguilar G.I., Molokin A., Novotny J.A. A single meal containing raw, crushed garlic influences expression of immunity- and cancer-related genes in whole blood of humans. J. Nutr. 2015;145:2448–2455. doi: 10.3945/jn.115.215392.

Chattopadhyay RR. Hypoglycemic effect of Ocimum sanctum leaf extract in normal and streptozotocin diabetic rats. Indian J Exp Biol. 1993;31:891–3.

Cheng, C.; Zou, Y.; Peng, J. Oregano essential oil attenuates RAW264.7 cells from lipopolysaccharide-inducedinflammatory response through regulating NADPH Oxidase activation-driven oxidative stress.Molecules2018,23, 1857.

Cheung, S.; Tai, J. Anti-proliferative and antioxidant properties of rosemary Rosmarinus officinalis. Oncol. Rep.2007, 17, 1525–1531.

Int. J. Mol. Sci. 2014, 15 19198

Chichester, C. O., ed. (1986). Advances in Food Research. Advances in Food and Nutrition Research. 30. Boston: Academic Press. p. 79. ISBN 0-12-016430-2.

Choi, Y.; Lee, S.M.; Chun, J.; Lee, H.B.; Lee, J. Influence of heat treatment on the antioxidant activities and polyphenolic compounds of Shiitake (Lentinus edodes) mushroom. Food Chem.2006, 99, 381–387.

Chocolate. In: Drugs and Lactation Database (LactMed). Bethesda (MD): National Library of Medicine (US); 2006.

Chohan, M. The Impact of Digestion and Gut Bioavailability, in Vitro, on the Polyphenolic Associated Activity of Cooked Culinary Herbs. Ph.D. Thesis, Kingston University, Kingston upon Thames, UK, 2011.

Chohan, M.; Forster-Wilkins, G.; Opara, E.I. Determination of the antioxidant capacity of culinary herbs subjected to various cooking and storage processes using the ABTS*+ radical cation assay. Plant Foods Hum. Nutr.2008, 63, 47–52.

Chohan, M.; Naughton, D.P.; Jones, L.; Opara, E.I. An investigation of the relationship between the anti-inflammatory activity, polyphenolic content, and antioxidant activities of cooked and in vitro digested culinary herbs. Oxid. Med. Cell. Longev. 2012, 2012, 627843.

Chohan, M.; Naughton, D.P.; Opara, E.I. Determination of superoxide dismutase mimetic activity in common culinary herbs. SpringerPlus 2014, 3, 578.

Chou S-T, Chang W-L, Chang C-T, Hsu S-L, Lin Y-C, Shih Y. Cinnamomum cassia Essential Oil inhibits α-MSH-induced melanin production and oxidative stress in murine B16 melanoma cells. International Journal of Molecular Sciences. 2013;14(9):19186–19201.

Chopan M, Littenberg B. The Association of Hot Red Chili Pepper Consumption and Mortality: A Large Population-Based Cohort Study. PLoS One. 2017;12(1):e0169876. Published 2017 Jan 9. doi:10.1371/journal.pone.0169876

Chuang LT, Tsai TH, Lien TJ, Huang WC, Liu JJ, Chang H, et al. Ethanolic Extract of Origanum vulgare Suppresses Propionibacterium acnes-Induced Inflammatory Responses in Human Monocyte and Mouse Ear Edema Models. Molecules (Basel, Switzerland). 2018;23(8). doi: 10.3390/molecules23081987.

Chuang, L.; Tsai, T.; Lien, T.; Huang, W.; Liu, J.; Chang, H.; Chang, M.; Tsai, P.-J. Ethanolic extract of origanumvulgare suppresses propionibacterium acnes -induced inflammatory responses in human monocyte andmouse ear edema models.Molecules2018,23, 1987.

Chuengsamarn S, Rattanamongkolgul S, Luechapudiporn R, Phisalaphong C, Jirawatnotai S. Curcumin extract for prevention of type 2 diabetes. Diabetes Care. 2012;35(11):2121–7. doi:10.2337/dc12-0116.

Cilla, A.; González-Sarrías, A.; Tomás-Barberán, F.A.; Espín, J.C.; Barberá, R. Availability of polyphenols in fruit beverages subjected to in vitro gastrointestinal digestion and their effects on proliferation, cell-cycle and apoptosis in human colon cancer Caco-2 cells. Food Chem. 2009, 114, 813–820

Cocchiara, J.; Letizia, C.S.; Lalko, J.; Lapczynski, A.; Api, A.M. Fragrance material review on cinnamaldehyde. Food Chem. Toxicol. 2005, 43, 867–923.

Cohen MM. Tulsi - Ocimum sanctum: A herb for all reasons. J Ayurveda Integr Med. 2014;5(4):251-259. doi:10.4103/0975-9476.146554

Colica C, Di Renzo L, Aiello V, De Lorenzo A, Abenavoli L. Rosmarinic Acid as Potential Anti-Inflammatory Agent. Rev Recent Clin Trials. 2018;13(4):240-242. doi:10.2174/1574887113041809091095818

Corti R., Flammer A.J., Hollenberg N.K., Lüscher T.F. Cocoa and cardiovascular health. Circulation. 2009;119:1433–1441. doi: 10.1161/CIRCULATIONAHA.108.827022.

Costa J., Lunet N., Santos C., Santos J., Vaz-Carneiro A. Caffeine exposure and the risk of Parkinson's disease: A systematic review and meta-analysis of observational studies. J. Alzheimer's Dis. 2010;20:S221–S238.

Costello RB, Dwyer JT, Saldanha L, Bailey RL, Merkel J, Wambogo E (2016). "Do Cinnamon Supplements Have a Role in Glycemic Control in Type 2 Diabetes? A Narrative Review". J Acad Nutr Diet. 116 (11): 1794–1802. doi:10.1016/j.jand.2016.07.015. PMC 5085873. PMID 27618575.

Crespo YA, Bravo Sánchez LR, Quintana YG, Cabrera AST, Bermúdez Del Sol A, Mayancha DMG. Evaluation of the synergistic effects of antioxidant activity on mixtures of the essential oil from Apium graveolens L., Thymus vulgaris L. and Coriandrum sativum L. using simplex-lattice design. Heliyon. 2019;5(6):e01942. Published 2019 Jun 15. doi:10.1016/j.heliyon.2019.e01942

Cruz C., Correa-Rotter R., Sanchez-Gonzalez D.J., Hernandez-Pando R., Maldonado P.D., Martinez-Martinez C.M., Medina-Campos O.N., Tapia E., Aguilar D., Chirino Y.I., et al. Renoprotective and antihypertensive effects of S-allylcysteine in 5/6 nephrectomized rats. Am. J. Physiol. Renal Physiol. 2007;293:F1691–F1698. doi: 10.1152/ajprenal.00235.2007

Cruz-Correa M, Shoskes DA, Sanchez P, Zhao R, Hylind LM, Wexner SD, et al. Combination treatment with curcumin and quercetin of adenomas in familial adenomatous polyposis. Clin Gastroenterol Hepatol. 2006;4(8):1035–1038. doi: 10.1016/j.cgh.2006.03.020.

Daran AM, Rashid K, Ibrahim H, Jalil M, Yusof YM, et al. (2017) Toxic Trace Elements in Selected Edible Rhizomes of Medicinal Plants Using INAA and ICP-MS Techniques. Int J Complement Alt Med 6(4): 00195. DOI: 10.15406/ijcam.2017.06.00195

D'Archivio, M.; Filesi, C.; Varì, R.; Scazzocchio, B.; Masella, R. Bioavailability of the polyphenols: Status and controversies. Int. J. Mol. Sci. 2010, 11, 1321–1342

de Araújo Júnior JX, Julien C, Barrès C, et al. Cardiovascular effects of a novel synthetic analogue of naturally occurring piperamides. J Cardiovasc Pharmacol. 2010;56(3):293-299. doi:10.1097/FJC.0b013e3181ec061e

de J. Rostro-Alanis M, Báez-González J, Torres-Alvarez C, Parra-Saldívar R, Rodriguez-Rodriguez J, Castillo S. Chemical Composition and Biological Activities of Oregano Essential Oil and Its Fractions Obtained byVacuum Distillation 2019, May 17.

Del Baño M.J., Lorente J., Castillo J., Benavente-García O., Marín M.P., Del Río J.A., Ortuño A., Ibarra I. Flavonoid distribution during the development of leaves, flowers, stems and roots of Rosmarinus officinalis. Postulation of a biosynthetic pathway. J. Agric. Food Chem. 2004;52:4987–4992.

Del Campo J., Amiot M., Nguyen-The C. Antimicrobial effect of rosemary extracts. J. Food Prot. 2000;63:1359–1368.

De Martino, L.; De Feo, V.; Nazzaro, F. Chemical composition andin vitroantimicrobial and mutagenicactivities of seven Lamiaceae essential oils.Molecules2009,14, 4213–4230

de Mattos Duarte C, Verli H, de Araújo-Júnior JX, de Medeiros IA, Barreiro EJ, Fraga CA. New optimized piperamide analogues with potent in vivo hypotensive properties. Eur J Pharm Sci. 2004;23(4-5):363-369. doi:10.1016/j.ejps.2004.08.011

Dempe, J.S.; Scheerle, R.K.; Pfeiffer, E.; Metzler, M. Metabolism and permeability of curcumin in cultured Caco-2 cells. Mol. Nutr. Food Res. 2013, 57, 1543–1549.

Deodhar SD, Sethi R, Srimal RC. Preliminary study on antirheumatic activity of curcumin (diferuloyl methane) Indian J Med Res. 1980;71:632–634.

Derosa G, Maffioli P, Sahebkar A. Piperine and Its Role in Chronic Diseases. Adv Exp Med Biol. 2016;928:173-184. doi:10.1007/978-3-319-41334-1_8

De Sousa DP, Nóbrega FF, Santos CC, Benedito RB, Vieira YW, Uliana MP, Brocksom TJ, de Almeida RN. Antinociceptive activity of thymoquinone and its structural analogues: a structure-activity relationship study. Trop J Pharm Res 2012; 11: 605-610

de Souza Grinevicius VM, Kviecinski MR, Santos Mota NS, et al. Piper nigrum ethanolic extract rich in piperamides causes ROS overproduction, oxidative damage in DNA leading to cell cycle arrest and apoptosis in cancer cells. J Ethnopharmacol. 2016;189:139-147.

Deyno S, Eneyew K, Seyfe S, et al. Efficacy and safety of cinnamon in type 2 diabetes mellitus and pre-diabetes patients: A meta-analysis and meta-regression. Diabetes Res Clin Pract. 2019;156:107815. doi:10.1016/j.diabres.2019.107815

Dhandapani, K.M.; Mahesh, V.B.; Brann, D.W. Curcumin suppresses AP-1 and NF-κB transcription factors. J. Neurochem. 2007, 102, 522–538.

Dharmani P, Kuchibhotla VK, Maurya R, Srivastava S, Sharma S, Patil G. Evaluation of anti-ulcerogenic and ulcer-healing properties of Ocimum sanctum Linn. J Ethnophamacol. 2004;93:197–206.

Dhillon N, Aggarwal BB, Newman RA, Wolff RA, Kunnumakkara AB, Abbruzzese JL, et al. Phase II trial of curcumin in patients with advanced pancreatic cancer. Clin Cancer Res. 2008;14(14):4491–4499. doi: 10.1158/1078-0432.CCR-08-0024.

Di Mario F, Cavallaro LG, Nouvenne A, Stefani N, Cavestro GM, Iori V, et al. A curcumin-based 1-week triple therapy for eradication of Helicobacter pylori infection: something to learn from failure? Helicobacter. 2007;12(3):238–243. doi: 10.1111/j.1523-5378.2007.00497.x.

Diretto G., Rubio-Moraga A., Argandona J., Castillo P., Gomez-Gomez L., Ahrazem O. Tissue-specific accumulation of sulfur compounds and saponins in different parts of garlic cloves from purple and white ecotypes. Molecules. 2017;22:1359. doi: 10.3390/molecules22081359.

Dong J.Y., Kimura T., Ikehara S., Cui M., Kawanishi Y., Yamagishi K., Ueda K., Iso H., Japan Environment. Children's Study Group Chocolate consumption and risk of gestational diabetes mellitus: The Japan Environment and Children's Study. Br. J. Nutr. 2019;122:936–941. doi: 10.1017/S0007114519001806.

Dorrie J, Sapala K, Zunino SJ. Carnosol-induced apoptosis and downregulation of Bcl-2 in B-lineage leukemia cells. Cancer Lett. 2001;170:33–39.

Dragland, S.; Senoo, H.; Wake, K.; Holte, K.; Blomhoff, R. Several culinary and medicinal herbs are important sources of dietary antioxidants. J. Nutr.2003, 133, 1286–1290.

Durgaprasad S, Pai CG, Vasanthkumar, Alvres JF, Namitha S. A pilot study of the antioxidant effect of curcumin in tropical pancreatitis. Indian J Med Res. 2005;122(4):315–318.

Dutra, T.V.; Castro, J.C.; Menezes, J.; Ramos, R.; Nunes do Parado, I.; Machinski, M.; Graton, J.M.; de AbreuFilho, B.A. Bioactivity of oregano (Origanum vulgare) essential oil againstAlicyclobacillusspp.Ind. Crop. Prod.2019,129, 345–349.

Earley S, Gonzales AL, Garcia ZI. A dietary agonist of transient receptor potential cation channel V3 elicits endothelium-dependent vasodilation. Mol Pharmacol. 2010;77(4):612-620. doi:10.1124/mol.109.060715

Ebrahimi, A.; Schluesener, H. Natural polyphenols against neurodegenerative disorders: Potentials and pitfalls. Ageing Res. Rev.2012, 11, 329–345.

Elbarbry F, Ragheb A, Marfleet T, Shoker A. Modulation of hepatic drug metabolizing enzymes by dietary doses of thymoquinone in female New Zealand White rabbits. Phytother Res 2012; 26: 1726-1730

El Gazzar M, El Mezayen R, Marecki JC, Nicolls MR, Canastar A, Dreskin SC. Anti-inflammatory effect of thymoquinone in a mouse model of allergic lung inflammation. Int Immunopharmacol 2006; 6: 1135-1142

Ellam S., Williamson G. Cocoa and human health. Annu. Rev. Nutr. 2013;33:105–128. doi: 10.1146/annurev-nutr-071811-150642.

El-Mahmoudy A, Matsuyama H, Borgan MA, Shimizu Y, El-Sayed MG, Minamoto N, Takewaki T. Thymoquinone suppresses expression of inducible nitric oxide synthase in rat macrophages. Int Immunopharmacol 2002; 2: 1603-1611

Elshafie, H.S.; Armentano, M.F.; Carmosino, M.; Bufo, S.A.; De Feo, V.; Camele, I. Cytotoxic activity ofOriganum vulgare L. on hepatocellular carcinoma cell line HepG2 and evaluation of its biological activity.Molecules2017,22, 1435.

Epelbaum R, Schaffer M, Vizel B, Badmaev V, Bar-Sela G. Curcumin and gemcitabine in patients with advanced pancreatic cancer. Nutr Cancer. 2010;62(8):1137–1141. doi: 10.1080/01635581.2010.513802

Epps, C.T.; Stequist, B.P.; Lowder, K.T.; Blacker, B.C.; Low, R.M.; Egget, D.L.; Parker, T.L. Synergistic endo- and exo-interactions between blueberry phenolic compounds, grape variety fractions, chocolate covered strawberries, and fruit smoothies. J. Food Res. **2013**, 2, 33–47.

Erenmemisoglu A., Saraymen R., Ustun S. Effect of a Rosmarinus officinalis leave extract on plasma glucose levels in normoglycaemic and diabetic mice. Pharmazie. 1997;52:645–646.

Eskelinen M.H., Ngandu T., Tuomilehto J., Soininen H., Kivipelto M. Midlife coffee and tea drinking and the risk of late-life dementia: A population-based CAIDE study. J. Alzheimer'sDis. . 2009;16:85–91.

Etxeberria, U.; Fernández-Quintela, A.; Milagro, F.I.; Aguirre, L.; Martínez, J.A.; Portillo, M. Impact of polyphenols and polyphenol-rich dietary sources on gut microbiota composition. J. Agric. Food Chem.2013, 61, 9517–9533.

Fasolino I., Izzo A.A., Clavel T., Romano B., Haller D., Borrelli F. Orally administered allyl sulfides from garlic ameliorate murine colitis. Mol. Nutr. Food Res. 2015;59:434–442. doi: 10.1002/mnfr.201400347.

Fattori V, Hohmann MS, Rossaneis AC, Pinho-Ribeiro FA, Verri WA. Capsaicin: Current Understanding of Its Mechanisms and Therapy of Pain and Other Pre-Clinical and Clinical Uses. Molecules. 2016;21(7):844. Published 2016 Jun 28. doi:10.3390/molecules21070844

Ferlemi AV, Katsikoudi A, Kontogianni VG, et al. Rosemary tea consumption results to anxiolytic- and anti-depressant-like behavior of adult male mice and inhibits all cerebral area and liver cholinesterase activity; phytochemical investigation and in silico studies. Chem Biol Interact. 2015;237:47-57. doi:10.1016/j.cbi.2015.04.013

Fleenor, B.S.; Sindler, A.L.; Marvi, N.K.; Howell, K.L.; Zigler, M.L.; Yoshizawa, M.; Seals, D.R. Curcumin ameliorates arterial dysfunction and oxidative stress with aging. Exp. Gerontol.2013, 48, 269–276.

Friedman M, Levin CE, Lee SU, Lee JS, Ohnisi-Kameyama M, Kozukue N. Analysis by HPLC and LC/MS of pungent piperamides in commercial black, white, green, and red whole and ground peppercorns. J Agric Food Chem. 2008;56(9):3028-3036. doi:10.1021/jf703711z

Funk JL, Frye JB, Oyarzo JN, et al. Efficacy and mechanism of action of turmeric supplements in the treatment of experimental arthritis. Arth Rheum. 2006;54:3452–64.

Gammone MA, Efthymakis K, Pluchinotta FR, et al. Impact of chocolate on the cardiovascular health. Front Biosci (Landmark Ed). 2018;23:852-864. Published 2018 Jan 1. doi:10.2741/4620

Garcea G, Berry DP, Jones DJ, Singh R, Dennison AR, Farmer PB, et al. Consumption of the putative chemopreventive agent curcumin by cancer patients: assessment of curcumin levels in the colorectum and their pharmacodynamic consequences. Cancer Epidemiol Biomarkers Prev. 2005;14(1):120–125.

Garcia JP, Santana A, Baruqui DL, Suraci N. The Cardiovascular effects of chocolate. Rev Cardiovasc Med. 2018;19(4):123-127. doi:10.31083/j.rcm.2018.04.3187

García-Pérez, E.; Noratto, G.D.; García-Lara, S.; Gutiérrez-Uribe, J.A.; Mertens-Talcott, S.U. Micropropagation effect on the anti-carcinogenic activitiy of polyphenolics from Mexican oregano (Poliomintha glabrescens Gray) in human colon cancer cells HT-29. Plant Foods Hum. Nutr. 2013, 68, 155–162.

Garcia-Villalon A.L., Amor S., Monge L., Fernandez N., Prodanov M., Munoz M., Inarejos-Garcia A.M., Granado M. In vitro studies of an aged black garlic extract enriched in S-allylcysteine and polyphenols with cardioprotective effects. J. Funct. Foods. 2016;27:189–200. doi: 10.1016/j.jff.2016.08.062

Garlic. In: Drugs and Lactation Database (LactMed). Bethesda (MD): National Library of Medicine (US); 2006.

Genena A.K., Hense H., Smania Junior A., Machado de Souza S. Rosemary (Rosmarinus officinalis)—A study of the composition, antioxidant and antimicrobial activities of extracts obtained with supercritical carbon dioxide. Cienc. Tecnol. Aliment. 2008;28:463–469. doi: 10.1590/S0101-20612008000200030.

Ghannadi A, Hajhashemi V, Jafarabadi H. An investigation of the analgesic and anti-inflammatory effects of Nigella sativa seed polyphenols. J Med Food 2005; 8: 488-493

Gholap S, Kar A. Hypoglycemic effects of some plant extracts are possibly mediated through inhibition in corticosteroid concentration. Pharmazie. 2004;59:876–8

Gîrd, C.E.; Dutu, L.E.; Costea, T.; Nencu, I.; Popescu, M.L.; Tudorel, O.O. Preliminary research concerningthe obtaining of herbal extracts with potential neuroprotective activity note I. Obtaining and characterizationof a selectiveOriganum vulgareL. dry extract.Farmacia (Bucharest Rom.)2016,64, 680–687.

Godhwani S, Godhwani JL, Vyas DS. Ocimum sanctum: An experimental study evaluating its anti-inflammatory, analgesic and antipyretic activity in animals. J Ethnopharmacol. 1987;21:153–63.

Goel RK, Sairam K, Dorababu M, Prabha T, Rao ChV. Effect of standardized extract of Ocimum sanctum Linn.on gastric mucosal offensive and defensive factors. Indian J Exp Biol. 2005;43:715–21.

Golombick T, Diamond TH, Badmaev V, Manoharan A, Ramakrishna R. The potential role of curcumin in patients with monoclonal gammopathy of undefined significance–its effect on paraproteinemia and the urinary N-telopeptide of type I collagen bone turnover marker. Clin Cancer Res. 2009;15(18):5917–5922. doi: 10.1158/1078-0432.CCR-08-2217.

Gonceariuc, M.; Balmus, Z.; Benea, A.; Barsan, V.; Sandu, T. Biochemical diversity of theOriganum vulgaressp. vulgare L. andOriganum vulgare ssp. hirtum(Link) letswaart genotypes from Moldova.J. ASM Life Sci.2015,2, 92–100.

Grassi D, Ferri C, Desideri G. Brain Protection and Cognitive Function: Cocoa Flavonoids as Nutraceuticals. Curr Pharm Des. 2016;22(2):145-151. doi:10.2174/1381612822666151112145730

Gregersen NT, Belza A, Jensen MG, et al. Acute effects of mustard, horseradish, black pepper and ginger on energy expenditure, appetite, ad libitum energy intake and energy balance in human subjects. Br J Nutr. 2013;109(3):556-563. doi:10.1017/S0007114512001201

Grondona E, Gatti G, Lopez AG, Sanchez LR, Rivero V, Pessah O, et al. Bio-efficacy of the essential oil of oregano (Origanum vulgare Lamiaceae. Ssp. Hirtum). Plant foods for human nutrition (Dordrecht, Netherlands). 2014;69(4):351−7. doi: 10.1007/s11130-014-0441-x

Grover JK, Vats V, Yadav SS. Pterocarpus marsupium extract (Vijayasar) prevented the alteration in metabolic patterns induced in the normal rat by feeding an adequate diet containing fructose as sole carbohydrate. Diabetes Obes Metab. 2005;7:414−20.

Guarini G, Ohanyan VA, Kmetz JG, DelloStritto DJ, Thoppil RJ, Thodeti CK, et al. Disruption of TRPV1-mediated coupling of coronary blood flow to cardiac metabolism in diabetic mice: role of nitric oxide and BK channels. American journal of physiology Heart and circulatory physiology. 2012;303(2):H216−23. Epub 2012/05/23. 10.1152/ajpheart.00011.2012

Gupta S, Mediratta PK, Singh S, Sharma KK, Shukla R. Antidiabetic, antihypercholesterolaemic and antioxidant effect of Ocimum sanctum (Linn) seed oil. Indian J Exp Biol. 2006;44:300−4.

Gupta SC, Patchva S, Aggarwal BB. Therapeutic roles of curcumin: lessons learned from clinical trials. AAPS J. 2013;15(1):195-218. doi:10.1208/s12248-012-9432-8

Gutiérrez-Grijalva EP, Picos-Salas MA, Leyva-López N, Criollo-Mendoza MS, Vazquez-Olivo G, Heredia JB. Flavonoids and Phenolic Acids from Oregano: Occurrence, Biological Activity and Health Benefits. Plants (Basel). 2017;7(1):2. Published 2017 Dec 26. doi:10.3390/plants7010002

Gu Y., Yu S., Lambert J.D. Dietary cocoa ameliorates obesity-related inflammation in high fat-fed mice. Eur. J. Nutr. 2013 doi: 10.1007/s00394-013-0510-1

Guo Y.J. Experimental study on the optimization of extraction process of garlic oil and its antibacterial effects. Afr. J. Tradit. Complement. Altern. Med. 2014;11:411−414. doi: 10.4314/ajtcam.v11i2.27.

Ha A.W., Ying T., Kim W.K. The effects of black garlic (Allium satvium) extracts on lipid metabolism in rats fed a high fat diet. Nutr. Res. Pract. 2015;9:30−36. doi: 10.4162/nrp.2015.9.1.30

Hadad GM, Salam RA, Soliman RM, Mesbah MK. High-performance liquid chromatography quantification of principal antioxidants in black seed (Nigella sativa L.) phytopharmaceuticals. J AOAC Int 2012; 95: 1043-1047

Hadi A, Campbell MS, Hassani B, Pourmasoumi M, Salehi-Sahlabadi A, Hosseini SA. The effect of cinnamon supplementation on blood pressure in adults: A systematic review and meta-analysis of randomized controlled trials. Clin Nutr ESPEN. 2020;36:10-16. doi:10.1016/j.clnesp.2020.01.002

Hadi A, Mohammadi H, Hadi Z, Roshanravan N, Kafeshani M. Cumin (Cuminum cyminum L.) is a safe approach for management of lipid parameters: A systematic review and meta-analysis of randomized controlled trials. Phytother Res. 2018;32(11):2146-2154. doi:10.1002/ptr.6162

Hajhashemi V, Ghannadi A, Jafarabadi H. Black cumin seed essential oil, as a potent analgesic and antiinflammatory drug. Phytother Res 2004; 18: 195-199

Halvorsen, B.L.; Carlsen, M.H.; Phillipis, K.M.; Bøhn, S.K.; Jacobs, D.R.; Blomhoff, J.R. Content of redox-active compounds (i.e., antioxidants) in foods consumed in the United States. Am. J. Clin. Nutr. 2006, 84, 95–135.

Hamedi A, Pasdaran A, Zebarjad Z, Moein M. A Survey on Chemical Constituents and Indications of Aromatic Waters Soft Drinks (Hydrosols) Used in Persian Nutrition Culture and Folk Medicine for Neurological Disorders and Mental Health. J Evid Based Complementary Altern Med. 2017;22(4):744-752. doi:10.1177/2156587217714145

Hamdan A, Haji Idrus R, Mokhtar MH. Effects of Nigella Sativa on Type-2 Diabetes Mellitus: A Systematic Review. Int J Environ Res Public Health. 2019;16(24):4911. Published 2019 Dec 5. doi:10.3390/ijerph16244911

Hamzalıoğlu A, Mogol BA, Lumaga RB, Fogliano V, Gökmen V. Role of curcumin in the conversion of asparagine into acrylamide during heating. Amino Acids. 2013;44(6):1419-1426. doi:10.1007/s00726-011-1179-5

Han X, Beaumont C, Rodriguez D, Bahr T. Black pepper (Piper nigrum) essential oil demonstrates tissue remodeling and metabolism modulating potential in human cells. Phytother Res. 2018;32(9):1848-1852. doi:10.1002/ptr.6110

Han X, Parker TL. Antiinflammatory Activity of Cinnamon (Cinnamomum zeylanicum) Bark Essential Oil in a Human Skin Disease Model. Phytother Res. 2017;31(7):1034-1038. doi:10.1002/ptr.5822

Hanai H, Iida T, Takeuchi K, Watanabe F, Maruyama Y, Andoh A, et al. Curcumin maintenance therapy for ulcerative colitis: randomized, multicenter, double-blind, placebo-controlled trial. Clin Gastroenterol Hepatol. 2006;4(12):1502–1506. doi: 10.1016/j.cgh.2006.08.008.

Hannan JM, Marenah L, Ali L, Rokeya B, Flatt PR, Abdel-Wahab YH. Ocimum sanctum leaf extracts stimulate insulin secretion from perfusd pancreas, isolated islets and clonal pancreatic beta-cells. J Endocrinol. 2006;189:127–36

Haraguchi, T.; Kayashima, T.; Okazaki, Y.; Inoue, J.; Mineo, S.; Matsubara, K.; Sakaguchi, E.; Yanaka, N.; Kato, N. Cecal succinate elevated by some dietary polyphenols may inhibit colon cancer cell proliferation and angiogenesis. J. Agric. Food Chem. 2014, 62, 5589–5594.

Hassouna I., Ibrahim H., Gaffar F.A., El-Elaimy I., Latif H.A. Simultaneous administration of hesperidin or garlic oil modulates diazinon-induced hemato- and immunotoxicity in rats. Immunopharmacol. Immunotoxicol. 2015;37:442–449. doi: 10.3109/08923973.2015.1081932

Hayek N. Chocolate, gut microbiota, and human health. Front. Pharmacol. 2013;4 doi: 10.3389/fphar.2013.00011.

He, X.; Marco, M.L.; Slupsky, C.M. Emerging aspects of food and nutrition on gut microbiota. J. Agric. Food Chem.2013, 61, 9559–9574.

He ZY, Shi CB, Wen H, Li FL, Wang BL, Wang J. Upregulation of p53 expression in patients with colorectal cancer by administration of curcumin. Cancer Investig. 2011;29(3):208–213. doi: 10.3109/07357907.2010.550592

Heinrich U., Neukam K., Tronnier H., Sies H., Stahl W. Long-term ingestion of high flavanol cocoa provides photoprotection against UV-induced erythema and improves skin condition in women. J. Nutr. 2006;136:1565–1569.

Heng MC, Song MK, Harker J, Heng MK. Drug-induced suppression of phosphorylase kinase activity correlates with resolution of psoriasis as assessed by clinical, histological and immunohistochemical parameters. Br J Dermatol. 2000;143(5):937–949. doi: 10.1046/j.1365-2133.2000.03767.x.

Higginbotham E, Taub PR. Cardiovascular Benefits of Dark Chocolate?. Curr Treat Options Cardiovasc Med. 2015;17(12):54. doi:10.1007/s11936-015-0419-5

Ho SC, Chang KS, Chang PW. Inhibition of neuroinflammation by cinnamon and its main components. Food Chem. 2013;138(4):2275-2282. doi:10.1016/j.foodchem.2012.12.020

Hollman, P.C.; Cassidy, A.; Comte, B.; Heinonen, M.; Richelle, M.; Richling, E.; Serafini, M.; Scalbert, A.; Sies, H.; Vidry, S. The biological relevance of direct antioxidant effects of polyphenols for cardiovascular health in humans is not established. J. Nutr.2010, 141, 989S–1009S. Int. J. Mol. Sci. 2014, 15 19197

Holt PR, Katz S, Kirshoff R. Curcumin therapy in inflammatory bowel disease: a pilot study. Dig Dis Sci. 2005;50(11):2191–2193. doi: 10.1007/s10620-005-3032-8.

Hosseinzadeh H, Parvardeh S, Asl MN, Sadeghnia HR, Ziaee T. Effect of thymoquinone and Nigella sativa seeds oil on lipid peroxidation level during global cerebral ischemia-reperfusion injury in rat hippocampus. Phytomedicine 2007; 14: 621-627

Hou LQ, Liu YH, Zhang YY. Garlic intake lowers fasting blood glucose: meta-analysis of randomized controlled trials. Asia Pac J Clin Nutr. 2015;24(4):575-582. doi:10.6133/apjcn.2015.24.4.15

Hritcu L, Noumedem JA, Cioanca O, Hancianu M, Postu P, Mihasan M. Anxiolytic and antidepressant profile of the methanolic extract of Piper nigrum fruits in beta-amyloid (1-42) rat model of Alzheimer's disease. Behav Brain Funct. 2015;11:13. Published 2015 Mar 29.

Huang MT, Ho CT, Wang ZY, Ferraro T, Lou YR, Stauber K, Ma W, Georgiadis C, Laskin JD, Conney AH. Inhibition of skin tumorigenesis by rosemary and its constituents carnosol and ursolic acid. Cancer Res. 1994;54:701–708.

Huang SC, Ho CT, Lin-Shiau SY, Lin JK. Carnosol inhibits the invasion of B16/F10 mouse melanoma cells by suppressing metalloproteinase-9 through down-regulating nuclear factor-kappa B and c-Jun. Biochem Pharmacol. 2005;69:221–232

Hussein AA, Meyer JJ, Jimeno ML, Rodriguez B. Bioactive diterpenes from Orthosiphon labiatus and Salvia africana-lutea. J Nat Prod. 2007;70:293–295.

Ide H, Tokiwa S, Sakamaki K, Nishio K, Isotani S, Muto S, et al. Combined inhibitory effects of soy isoflavones and curcumin on the production of prostate-specific antigen. Prostate. 2010;70(10):1127–1133. doi: 10.1002/pros.21147.

Iqbal, Mohammed (1993). "International trade in non-wood forest products: An overview". FO: Misc/93/11 – Working Paper. Food and Agriculture Organization of the United Nations. Retrieved 12 November 2012.

Iranshahy M, Javadi B. Diet therapy for the treatment of Alzheimer's disease in view of traditional Persian medicine: A review. Iran J Basic Med Sci. 2019;22(10):1102-1117. doi:10.22038/ijbms.2019.36505.8694

Iriti, M.; Vitalini, S.; Fico, G.; Faoro, F. Neuroprotective herbs and foods from different traditional medicines and diets. Molecules2010, 15, 3517–3555.

Jaggi RK, Madaan R, Singh B. Anticonvulsant potential of holy basil, Ocimum sanctum Linn., and its cultures. Indian J Exp Biol. 2003;41:1329–33.

Jaggi RK, Madaan R, Singh B. Anticonvulsant potential of holy basil, Ocimum sanctum Linn., and its cultures. Indian J Exp Biol. 2003;41:1329–33

Jalil A.M., Ismail A. Polyphenols in cocoa and cocoa products: Is there a link between antioxidant properties and health? Molecules. 2008;13:2190–2219. doi: 10.3390/molecules13092190.

Jamali N, Jalali M, Saffari-Chaleshtori J, Samare-Najaf M, Samareh A. Effect of cinnamon supplementation on blood pressure and anthropometric parameters in patients with type 2 diabetes: A systematic review and meta-analysis of clinical trials. Diabetes Metab Syndr. 2020;14(2):119-125. doi:10.1016/j.dsx.2020.01.009

Jang H.J., Lee H.J., Yoon D.K., Ji D.S., Kim J.H., Lee C.H. Antioxidant and antimicrobial activities of fresh garlic and aged garlic by-products extracted with different solvents. Food Sci. Biotechnol. 2018;27:219–225. doi: 10.1007/s10068-017-0246-4.

Janssens P.L., Hursel R., Martens E.A., Westerterp-Plantenga M.S. Acute effects of capsaicin on energy expenditure and fat oxidation in negative energy balance. PLoS ONE. 2013;8:e67786. doi: 10.1371/journal.pone.0067786.

Janssens P.L., Hursel R., Westerterp-Plantenga M.S. Capsaicin increases sensation of fullness in energy balance, and decreases desire to eat after dinner in negative energy balance. Appetite. 2014;77:44–49. doi: 10.1016/j.appet.2014.02.018.

Jiang X.Y., Zhu X.S., Huang W.Z., Xu H.Y., Zhao Z.X., Li S.Y., Li S.Z., Cai J.H., Cao J.M. Garlic-derived organosulfur compound exerts antitumor efficacy via activation of

MAPK pathway and modulation of cytokines in SGC-7901 tumor-bearing mice. Int. Immunopharmacol. 2017;48:135–145. doi: 10.1016/j.intimp.2017.05.004.

Jin C, Wu X, Zhang Y. Relationship between antioxidants and acrylamide formation: a review. Food Res Int. 2013;51:611–620. doi: 10.1016/j.foodres.2012.12.047

Johnson JJ. Carnosol: a promising anti-cancer and anti-inflammatory agent. Cancer Lett. 2011;305(1):1-7. doi:10.1016/j.canlet.2011.02.005

Johnson JJ, Syed DN, Suh Y, Heren CR, Saleem M, Siddiqui IA, Mukhtar H. Disruption of androgen and estrogen receptor activity in prostate cancer by a novel dietary diterpene carnosol: implications for chemoprevention. Cancer Prev Res (Phila) 2010;3:1112–1123.

Joshi H, Parle M. Evaluation of nootropic potential of Ocimum sanctum Linn.in mice. Indian J Exp Biol. 2006;44:133–6

Judelson D.A., Preston A.G., Miller D.L., Muñoz C.X., Kellogg M.D., Lieberman H.R. Effects of theobromine and caffeine on mood and vigilance. J. Clin. Psychopharmacol. 2013;33:499–506. doi: 10.1097/JCP.0b013e3182905d24.

Julianti E, Rajah KK, Fidrianny I. Antibacterial Activity of Ethanolic Extract of Cinnamon Bark, Honey, and Their Combination Effects against Acne-Causing Bacteria. Sci Pharm. 2017;85(2):19. Published 2017 Apr 11. doi:10.3390/scipharm85020019

Jung Y., Park H., Zhao H.Y., Jeon R., Ryu J.H., Kim W.Y. Systemic approaches identify a garlic-derived chemical, Z-ajoene, as a glioblastoma multiforme cancer stem cell-specific targeting agent. Mol. Cells. 2014;37:547–553. doi: 10.14348/molcells.2014.0158.

Jungbauer, A.; Medjakovic, S. Anti-inflammatory properties of culinary herbs and spices that ameliorate the effects of metabolic syndrome. Maturitas2012, 71, 227–239.

Kaefer, C.M.; Milner, J.A. The role of herbs and spices in cancer prevention. J. Nutr. Biochem.2008, 19, 347–361.

Kahkeshani N, Saeidnia S, Abdollahi M. Role of antioxidants and phytochemicals on acrylamide mitigation from food and reducing its toxicity. J Food Sci Technol. 2015;52(6):3169-3186. doi:10.1007/s13197-014-1558-5

Kalaivani P, Saranya RB, Ramakrishnan G, et al. Cuminum cyminum, a dietary spice, attenuates hypertension via endothelial nitric oxide synthase and NO pathway in renovascular hypertensive rats. Clin Exp Hypertens. 2013;35(7):534-542. doi:10.3109/10641963.2013.764887

Kanai M, Yoshimura K, Asada M, Imaizumi A, Suzuki C, Matsumoto S, et al. A phase I/II study of gemcitabine-based chemotherapy plus curcumin for patients with gemcitabine-resistant pancreatic cancer. Cancer Chemother Pharmacol. 2011;68(1):157–164. doi: 10.1007/s00280-010-1470-2.

Kang N, Yuan R, Huang L, et al. Atypical Nitrogen-Containing Flavonoid in the Fruits of Cumin (Cuminum cyminum L.) with Anti-inflammatory Activity. J Agric Food Chem. 2019;67(30):8339-8347. doi:10.1021/acs.jafc.9b02879

Karna, P.; Chagani, S.; Gundala, S.R.; Rida, P.C.G.; Asif, G.; Sharma, V.; Gupta, M.V.; Aneja, R. Benefits of whole ginger extract in prostate cancer. Br. J. Nutr.2012, 107, 473–484.

Karthikeyan K, Ravichandran P, Govindasamy S. Chemopreventive effect of Ocimum sanctum on DMBA-induced hamster buccal pouch carcinogenesis. Oral Oncol. 1999;35:112–9.

Kaschula C.H., Hunter R., Cotton J., Tuveri R., Ngarande E., Dzobo K., Schafer G., Siyo V., Lang D., Kusza D.A., et al. The garlic compound ajoene targets protein folding in the endoplasmic reticulum of cancer cells. Mol. Carcinog. 2016;55:1213–1228. doi: 10.1002/mc.22364.

Katz D.L., Doughty K., Ali A. Cocoa and chocolate in human health and disease. Antioxid. Redox Signal. 2011;15:2779–2811. doi: 10.1089/ars.2010.3697.

Kaur G., Padiya R., Adela R., Putcha U.K., Reddy G.S., Reddy B.R., Kumar K.P., Chakravarty S., Banerjee S.K. Garlic and resveratrol attenuate diabetic complications, loss of β-cells, pancreatic and hepatic oxidative stress in streptozotocin-induced diabetic rats. Front. Pharmacol. 2016;7:360. doi: 10.3389/fphar.2016.00360.

Kaur G, Upadhyay N, Tharappel LJP, Invally M. Pharmacodynamic interaction of cumin seeds (Cuminum cyminum L.) with glyburide in diabetes. J Complement Integr Med. 2019;16(4):/j/jcim.2019.16.issue-4/jcim-2018-0080/jcim-2018-0080.xml. Published 2019 Jul 26. doi:10.1515/jcim-2018-0080

Kelly JR, Clarke G, Cryan JF, Dinan TG. Brain-gut-microbiota axis: challenges for translation in psychiatry. Ann Epidemiol. 2016;26(5):366-372. doi:10.1016/j.annepidem.2016.02.008

Kelm MA, Nair MG, Stasburg GM, DeWitt DL. Antioxidant and cyclooxygenase inhibitiory phenolic compounds from Ocimum sanctum Linn. Phytomedicine. 2000;7:7–13

Kensara O., ElSawy N., Altaf F., Header E. Hypoglycemic and hepato-protective effects of Rosmarinus officinalis in experimental diabetic Rats. UQU Med. J. 2010;1:98–113.

Kerimi A, Williamson G. The cardiovascular benefits of dark chocolate. Vascul Pharmacol. 2015;71:11-15. doi:10.1016/j.vph.2015.05.011

Keshavarz, M.; Bidmeshkipour, A.; Mostafaie, A.; Monsouri, K.; Mohammadi-Motlagh, H.-R. Anti-tumor activity of Salvia officinalis is due to its anti-proliferative effects. Cell J.2011, 12, 477–482.

Khalil O., Ramadan K., Danial E., Alnahdi H., Ayaz N. Antidiabetic activity of Rosmarinus officinalis and its relationship with the antioxidant property. Afr. J. Pharm. Pharmacol. 2012;6:1031–1036.

Khan A, Safdar M, Ali Khan MM, Khattak KN, Anderson RA. Cinnamon improves glucose and lipids of people with type 2 diabetes. Diabetes Care. 2003;26(12):3215-3218. doi:10.2337/diacare.26.12.3215

Khan N., Monagas M., Andres-Lacueva C., Casas R., Urpí-Sardà M., Lamuela-Raventós R.M., Estruch R. Regular consumption of cocoa powder with milk increases HDL cholesterol and reduces oxidized LDL levels in subjects at high-risk of cardiovascular disease. Nutr. Metab. Cardiovasc. Dis. 2012;22:1046–1053. doi: 10.1016/j.numecd.2011.02.001.

Khajehdehi P, Pakfetrat M, Javidnia K, Azad F, Malekmakan L, Nasab MH, et al. Oral supplementation of turmeric attenuates proteinuria, transforming growth factor-beta and interleukin-8 levels in patients with overt type 2 diabetic nephropathy: a randomized, double-blind and placebo-controlled study. Scand J Urol Nephrol. 2011;45(5):365–370. doi: 10.3109/00365599.2011.585622.

Khanum, H.; Ramalakshmi, K.; Srinivas, P.; Borse, B.B. Synergistic antioxidant action of oregano, ajowan and borage extracts. Food Nutr. Sci. **2011**, 2, 387–392.

Kim SG, Veena MS, Basak SK, Han E, Tajima T, Gjertson DW, et al. Curcumin treatment suppresses IKKbeta kinase activity of salivary cells of patients with head and neck cancer: a pilot study. Clin Cancer Res. 2011;17(18):5953–5961. doi: 10.1158/1078-0432.CCR-11-1272.

Kim MS , Kim JY . Cinnamon subcritical water extract attenuates intestinal inflammation and enhances intestinal tight junction in a Caco-2 and RAW264.7 co-culture model. Food Funct. 2019;10(7):4350-4360. doi:10.1039/c9fo00302a

Kim, S.; Jeong, S.; Park, W.; Nam, K.C.; Ahn, D.U.; Lee, S. Effect of heating conditions of grape seeds on the antioxidant activity of grape seed extracts. Food Chem.2006, 97, 472–479.

Kim S., Kim J., Cho H., Lee H.J., Kim S.Y., Kim S., Lee S., Chun H.S. Carnosol, a component of rosemary (Rosmarinus officinalis L.) protects nigral dopaminergic neuronal cells. Neuroreport. 2006;17:1729–1733.

Kim, S.S.; Oh, O.; Min, H.; Park, E.; Kim, Y.; Park, H.; Han, Y.N.; Lee, S.K. Eugenol suppresses cyclooxygenase-2 expression in liposaccharide-stimulated mouse macrophage RAW264.7 cells. Life Sci. 2003, 73, 337–348.

Kim S, Kim DB, Jin W, et al. Comparative studies of bioactive organosulphur compounds and antioxidant activities in garlic (Allium sativum L.), elephant garlic (Allium ampeloprasum L.) and onion (Allium cepa L.). Nat Prod Res. 2018;32(10):1193-1197. doi:10.1080/14786419.2017.1323211

Kim S., Kim Y., Park S.M. Body Mass Index and Decline of Cognitive Function. PLoS ONE. 2016;11:e0148908. doi: 10.1371/journal.pone.0148908.

Kim W.T., Seo S.P., Byun Y.J., Kang H.W., Kim Y.J., Lee S.C., Jeong P., Seo Y., Choe S.Y., Kim D.J., et al. Garlic extract in bladder cancer prevention: Evidence from T24 bladder cancer cell xenograft model, tissue microarray, and gene network analysis. Int. J. Oncol. 2017;51:204–212. doi: 10.3892/ijo.2017.3993.

Kocaadam B, Şanlier N. Curcumin, an active component of turmeric (Curcuma longa), and its effects on health. Crit Rev Food Sci Nutr. 2017;57(13):2889-2895. doi:10.1080/10408398.2015.1077195

Kodali R.T., Eslick G.D. Meta-analysis: Does garlic intake reduce risk of gastric cancer? Nutr. Cancer. 2015;67:1–11. doi: 10.1080/01635581.2015.967873.

Kodera Y., Ushijima M., Amano H., Suzuki J., Matsutomo T. Chemical and biological properties of S-1-propenyl-l-cysteine in aged garlic extract. Molecules. 2017;22:570. doi: 10.3390/molecules22040570

Kondratyuk, T.P.; Pezzuto, J.M. Natural product polyphenols of relevance to human health. Pharm. Biol.2004, 42, 46–63.

Kooti W, Hasanzadeh-Noohi Z, Sharafi-Ahvazi N, Asadi-Samani M, Ashtary-Larky D. Phytochemistry, pharmacology, and therapeutic uses of black seed (Nigella sativa). Chin J Nat Med. 2016;14(10):732-745. doi:10.1016/S1875-5364(16)30088-7

Kositchaiwat C, Kositchaiwat S, Havanondha J. Curcuma longa Linn. in the treatment of gastric ulcer comparison to liquid antacid: a controlled clinical trial. J Med Assoc Thail. 1993;76(11):601–605.

Kozlowska M, Laudy AE, Przybyl J, Ziarno M, Majewska E. CHEMICAL COMPOSITION AND ANTIBACTERIAL ACTIVITY OF SOME MEDICINAL PLANTS FROM LAMIACEAE FAMILY. Acta poloniae pharmaceutica. 2015;72(4):757–67. Epub 2015/12/10. PubMed PMID

Kunnumakkara AB, Sailo BL, Banik K, et al. Chronic diseases, inflammation, and spices: how are they linked?. J Transl Med. 2018;16(1):14. Published 2018 Jan 25. doi:10.1186/s12967-018-1381-2

Kunnumakkara AB, Bordoloi D, Padmavathi G, et al. Curcumin, the golden nutraceutical: multitargeting for multiple chronic diseases. Br J Pharmacol. 2017;174(11):1325-1348. doi:10.1111/bph.13621

Kurd SK, Smith N, VanVoorhees A, Troxel AB, Badmaev V, Seykora JT, et al. Oral curcumin in the treatment of moderate to severe psoriasis vulgaris: a prospective clinical trial. J Am Acad Dermatol. 2008;58(4):625–631. doi: 10.1016/j.jaad.2007.12.035.

Kwak J.S., Kim J.Y., Paek J.E., Lee Y.J., Kim H.R., Park D.S., Kwon O. Garlic powder intake and cardiovascular risk factors: A meta-analysis of randomized controlled clinical trials. Nutr. Res. Pract. 2014;8:644–654. doi: 10.4162/nrp.2014.8.6.644.

Kwon, H.K.; Hwang, J.S.; Therefore, J.S.; Lee, C.G.; Sahoo, A.; Ryu, J.H.; Jeon, W.K.; Ko, B.S.; Im, C.R.; Lee, S.H.; et al. Cinnamon extract induces tumor cell death through inhibition of NF-κB and AP1. BMC Cancer 2010, 10, 392–402.

Labban L., Mustafa U.E.-S., Ibrahim Y.M. The Effects of Rosemary (Rosmarinus officinalis) Leaves Powder on Glucose Level, Lipid Profile and Lipid Perodoxation. Int. J. Clin. Med. 2014;5:297–304. doi: 10.4236/ijcm.2014.56044.

Lahiff C, Moss AC. Curcumin for clinical and endoscopic remission in ulcerative colitis. Inflamm Bowel Dis. 2011;17(7):E66. doi: 10.1002/ibd.21710.

Lal B, Kapoor AK, Asthana OP, Agrawal PK, Prasad R, Kumar P, et al. Efficacy of curcumin in the management of chronic anterior uveitis. Phytother Res. 1999;13(4):318–322. doi: 10.1002/(SICI)1099-1573(199906)13:4<318::AID-PTR445>3.0.CO;2-7.

Laszczyk M.N. Pentacyclic triterpenes of the lupane, oleanane and ursane group as tools in cancer therapy. Planta Med. 2009;75:1549–1560.

Latiff LA, Parhizkar S, Dollah MA, Hassan ST. Alternative supplement for enhancement of reproductive health and metabolic profile among perimenopausal women: a novel role of Nigella sativa . Iran J Basic Med Sci 2014; 17: 980-985

Lavorgna M, Orlo E, Nugnes R, Piscitelli C, Russo C, Isidori M. Capsaicin in Hot Chili Peppers: In Vitro Evaluation of Its Antiradical, Antiproliferative and Apoptotic Activities. Plant Foods Hum Nutr. 2019;74(2):164-170. doi:10.1007/s11130-019-00722-0

Leach MJ, Kumar S (September 2012). "Cinnamon for diabetes mellitus". Cochrane Database Syst Rev (9): CD007170. doi:10.1002/14651858.CD007170.pub2. PMC 6486047. PMID 22972104.

Lee K.W., Kim Y.J., Lee H.J., Lee C.Y. Cocoa has more phenolic phytochemicals and a higher antioxidant capacity than teas and red wine. J. Agric. Food Chem. 2003;51:7292–7295. doi: 10.1021/jf0344385

Lee YC, Chen PP. A review of SSRIs and SNRIs in neuropathic pain. Expert Opin Pharmacother 2010; 11: 2813-2825

Lee MS, Kim CT, Kim IH, Kim Y. Effects of capsaicin on lipid catabolism in 3T3-L1 adipocytes. Phytotherapy research: PTR. 2011;25(6):935–9. Epub 2011/06/01. 10.1002/ptr.3339

Lei X, Liu M, Yang Z, Ji M, Guo X, Dong W. Thymoquinone prevents and ameliorates dextran sulfate sodium-induced colitis in mice. Dig Dis Sci 2012; 57: 2296-2303

Leyva-López N, Gutiérrez-Grijalva EP, Vazquez-Olivo G, Heredia JB. Essential Oils of Oregano: Biological Activity beyond Their Antimicrobial Properties. Molecules. 2017;22(6):989. Published 2017 Jun 14. doi:10.3390/molecules22060989

Li W.R., Shi Q.S., Liang Q., Huang X.M., Chen Y.B. Antifungal effect and mechanism of garlic oil on penicillium funiculosum. Appl. Microbiol. Biot. 2014;98:8337–8346. doi: 10.1007/s00253-014-5919-9.

Li X., Kim H.Y., Cui H.Z., Cho K.W., Kang D.G., Lee H.S. Water extract of zanthoxylum piperitum induces vascular relaxation via endothelium-dependent NO-cGMP signaling. J. Ethnopharmacol. 2010;129:197–202. doi: 10.1016/j.jep.2010.03.003.

Li M., Yan Y.X., Yu Q.T., Deng Y., Wu D.T., Wang Y., Ge Y.Z., Li S.P., Zhao J. Comparison of immunomodulatory effects of fresh garlic and black garlic polysaccharides on

RAW 264.7 macrophages. J. Food Sci. 2017;82:765–771. doi: 10.1111/1750-3841.13589.

Li R, Jiang Z. (2004). Chemical composition of the essential oil of Cuminum cyminum L. from China. Flavour and Fragrance Journal, 19: 311–313.

Li, Z.; Henning, S.M.; Zhang, Y.; Zerlin, A.; Li, L.; Gao, K.; Lee, R.-P.; Karp, H.; Thames, G.; Bowerman, S.; et al. Antioxidant-rich spice added to hamburger meat during cooking results in reduced meat, plasma, and urine malondialdehyde concentrations. Am. J. Clin. Nutr. **2010**, 91, 1180–1184.

Li Q., Cui Y., Jin R., Lang H., Yu H., Sun F., He C., Ma T., Li Y., Zhou X., et al. Enjoyment of Spicy Flavor Enhances Central Salty-Taste Perception and Reduces Salt Intake and Blood Pressure. Hypertension. 2017;70:1291–1299. doi: 10.1161/HYPERTENSIONAHA.117.09950.

Li L, Chen J, Ni Y, Feng X, Zhao Z, Wang P, et al. TRPV1 activation prevents nonalcoholic fatty liver through UCP2 upregulation in mice. Pflugers Archiv: European journal of physiology. 2012;463(5):727–32. Epub 2012/03/08. 10.1007/s00424-012-1078-y

Liang S, Ji HF. The pharmacology of curcumin: is it the degradation products? Trends Mol Med. 2012;18:138–43.

Link, A.; Balaguer, F.; Goel, A. Cancer chemoprevention by dietary polyphenols: Promising role for epigenetics. Biochem. Pharmacol.2010, 80, 1771–1792.

Liu Q., Meng X., Li Y., Zhao C.N., Tang G.Y., Li H.B. Antibacterial and antifungal activities of spices. Int. J. Mol. Sci. 2017;18:1283. doi: 10.3390/ijms18061283

Liu Q., Meng X., Li Y., Zhao C.N., Tang G.Y., Li S., Gan R.Y., Li H.B. Natural products for the prevention and management of Helicobacter pylori infection. Compr. Rev. Food Sci. F. 2018;17:937–952. doi: 10.1111/1541-4337.12355.

Liu C.H., Bu X.L., Wang J., Zhang T., Xiang Y., Shen L.L., Wang Q.H., Deng B., Wang X., Zhu C., et al. The Associations between a Capsaicin-Rich Diet and Blood Amyloid-beta Levels and Cognitive Function. J. Alzheimers Dis. 2016;52:1081–1088. doi: 10.3233/JAD-151079.

Liu J., Ji F., Chen F.M., Guo W., Yang M.L., Huang S.X., Zhang F., Liu Y.S. Determination of garlic phenolic compounds using supercritical fluid extraction coupled to supercritical fluid chromatography/tandem mass spectrometry. J. Pharm. Biomed. Anal. 2018;159:513–523. doi: 10.1016/j.jpba.2018.07.020.

Lo A., Liang Y., Lin-Shiau S., Ho C., Lin J. Carnosol, an antioxidant in rosemary, suppresses inducible nitric oxide synthase through down-regulating nuclear factor-κB in mouse macrophages. Carcinogenesis. 2002;23:983–991

Locatelli D.A., Nazareno M.A., Fusari C.M., Camargo A.B. Cooked garlic and antioxidant activity: Correlation with organosulfur compound composition. Food Chem. 2017;220:219–224. doi: 10.1016/j.foodchem.2016.10.001.

Ludy M.J., Moore G.E., Mattes R.D. The effects of capsaicin and capsiate on energy balance: Critical review and meta-analyses of studies in humans. Chem. Senses. 2012;37:103–121. doi: 10.1093/chemse/bjr100.

Lukaczer D., Darland G., Tripp M., Liska D., Lerman R.H., Schiltz B., Bland J.S. A pilot trial evaluating Meta050, a proprietary combination of reduced iso-alpha acids, rosemary extract and oleanolic acid in patients with arthritis and fibromyalgia. Phytother. Res. PTR. 2005;19:864–869. doi: 10.1002/ptr.1709.

Lv J., Qi L., Yu C., Yang L., Guo Y., Chen Y., Bian Z., Sun D., Du J., Ge P., et al. Consumption of spicy foods and total and cause specific mortality: Population based cohort study. BMJ. 2015;351:h3942. doi: 10.1136/bmj.h3942.

Lyczko J, Masztalerz K, Lipan L, Lech L, Carbonelle-Barrachina A, Szumny A. Chemical determinants of dried Thai basil (O. basilicum var. thyrsiflora) aroma quality. Industrial Crops and Products. 2020, November 1, Volume 155; 112769.

Määttä-Riihinen KR, Kähkönen MP, Törrönen AR, Heinonen IM. Catechins and procyanidins in berries of vaccinium species and their antioxidant activity. Journal of Agricultural and Food Chemistry. 2005;53(22):8485–8491.

Macdonald, R.S.; Wagner, K. Influence of dietary phytochemicals and microbiota on colon cancer risk. J. Agric. Food Chem. 2012, 60, 6728–6735.

Magdy MA, Hanan el-A, Nabila el-M. Thymoquinone: Novel gastroprotective mechanisms. Eur J Pharmacol 2012; 697: 126-131

Mahgoub AA. Thymoquinone protects against experimental colitis in rats. Toxicol Lett 2003; 143: 133-143

Maia L., de Mendonca A. Does caffeine intake protect from Alzheimer's disease? Eur. J. Neurol. 2002;9:377–382. doi: 10.1046/j.1468-1331.2002.00421.x.

Maierean SM, Serban MC, Sahebkar A, et al. The effects of cinnamon supplementation on blood lipid concentrations: A systematic review and meta-analysis. J Clin Lipidol. 2017;11(6):1393-1406. doi:10.1016/j.jacl.2017.08.004

Maiolo SA, Fan P, Bobrovskaya L. Bioactive constituents from cinnamon, hemp seed and polygonum cuspidatum protect against H_2O_2 but not rotenone toxicity in a cellular model of Parkinson's disease. J Tradit Complement Med. 2018;8(3):420-427. Published 2018 Apr 30. doi:10.1016/j.jtcme.2017.11.001

Maillard, L. C. (1912). "Action des acides amines sur les sucres; formation de melanoidines par voie méthodique" [Action of amino acids on sugars. Formation of melanoidins in a methodical way]. Comptes Rendus (in French). 154: 66–68.

Maity TK, Mandal SC, Saha BP, Pal M. Effect of Ocimum sanctum roots extract on swimming performance in mice. Phytother Res. 2000;14:120–1.

Majdalawieh AF, Fayyad MW. Immunomodulatory and anti-inflammatory action of Nigella sativa and thymoquinone: A comprehensive review. Int Immunopharmacol. 2015;28(1):295-304. doi:10.1016/j.intimp.2015.06.023

Majumdar, A.P.N.; Banerjee, S.; Nautiyal, J.; Patel, B.B.; Patel, V.; Du, J.; Yu, Y.; Elliot, A.A.; Levi, E.; Sarkar, F. Curcumin synergizes with resveratrol to inhibit colon cancer. Nutr. Cancer **2009**, 61, 544–553.

Manach C, Scalbert A, Morand C, Rémésy C, Jiménez L. Polyphenols: food sources and bioavailability. Am J Clin Nutr. 2004;79(5):727-747. doi:10.1093/ajcn/79.5.727

Mancini E, Camele I, Elshafie HS, De Martino L, Pellegrino C, Grulova D, et al. Chemical composition and biological activity of the essential oil of Origanum vulgare ssp. hirtum from different areas in the Southern Apennines (Italy). Chemistry & biodiversity. 2014;11(4):639–51. doi: 10.1002/cbdv.201300326.

Mancini-Filho J, van-Koiij A, Mancini DAP, Cozzolino FF, Torres RP. Antioxidant activity of cinnamon (Cinnamomum zeylanicum, breyne) extracts. Bollettino Chimico Farmaceutico. 1998;137(11):443–447.

Mandal S, Das DN, De K, Ray K, Roy G, Chaudhuri SB, et al. Ocimum sanctum Linn: A study on gastric ulceration and gastric secretion in rats. Indian J Physiol Pharmacol. 1993;37:91–2.

Mansour MA, Nagi MN, El-Khatib AS, Al-Bekairi AM. Effects of thymoquinone on antioxidant enzyme activities, lipid peroxidation and DT-diaphorase in different tissues of mice: a possible mechanism of action. Cell Biochem Funct 2002; 20: 143-151

Mao QQ, Xian YF, Ip SP, Che CT. Involvement of serotonergic system in the antidepressant-like effect of piperine. Prog Neuropsychopharmacol Biol Psychiatry. 2011;35(4):1144-1147. doi:10.1016/j.pnpbp.2011.03.017

Marks DM, Shah MJ, Patkar AA, Masand PS, Park GY, Pae CU. Serotonin-norepinephrine reuptake inhibitors for pain control: premise and promise. Curr Neuropharmacol 2009; 7: 331-336

Marongiu B, Piras A, Porcedda S, et al. Supercritical CO2 extract of Cinnamomum zeylanicum: chemical characterization and antityrosinase activity. Journal of Agricultural and Food Chemistry. 2007;55(24):10022–10027.

Marsik P, Kokoska L, Landa P, Nepovim A, Soudek P, Vanek T. In vitro inhibitory effects of thymol and quinones of Nigella sativa seeds on cyclooxygenase-1-and-2-catalyzed prostaglandin E2 biosyntheses. Planta Med 2005; 71: 739-742

Martín M.A., Goya L., Ramos S. Antidiabetic actions of cocoa flavanols. Mol. Nutr. Food Res. 2016;60:1756–1769. doi: 10.1002/mnfr.201500961

Martínez-Rodríguez JL, Gutiérrez-Hernández R, Reyes-Estrada CA, et al. Hepatoprotective, Antihyperlipidemic and Radical Scavenging Activity of Hawthorn (Crataegus oxyacantha) and Rosemary (Rosmarinus officinalis) on Alcoholic Liver Disease. Altern Ther Health Med. 2019;25(4):54-63.

Maskarinec G., Jacobs S., Shvetsov Y., Boushey C.J., Setiawan V.W., Kolonel L.N., Haiman C.A., Le Marchand L. Intake of cocoa products and risk of type-2 diabetes: The multiethnic cohort. Eur. J. Clin. Nutr. 2019;73:671–678. doi: 10.1038/s41430-018-0188-9

Matsumoto C., Petrone A.B., Sesso H.D., Gaziano J.M., Djousse L. Chocolate consumption and risk of diabetes mellitus in the Physicians' Health Study. Am. J. Clin. Nutr. 2015;101:362–367. doi: 10.3945/ajcn.114.092221

Matthews A, Haas DM, O'Mathúna DP, Dowswell T. Interventions for nausea and vomiting in early pregnancy. Cochrane Database Syst Rev. 2015;2015(9):CD007575. Published 2015 Sep 8. doi:10.1002/14651858.CD007575.pub4

Michel CG, El-Sayed NS, Moustafa SF, Ezzat SM, Nesseem DI, El-Alfy TS. Phytochemical and biological investigation of the extracts of Nigella sativa L. seed waste. Drug Test Anal 2011; 3: 245-254

Miglio, C.; Chiavaro, E.; Visconti, A.; Fogliano, V.; Pellegrini, N. Effects of different cooking methods on nutritional and physicochemical characteristics of selected vegetables. J. Agric. Food Chem. 2008, 56, 139–147.

Mnif S, Aifa S. Cumin (Cuminum cyminum L.) from traditional uses to potential biomedical applications. Chem Biodivers. 2015;12(5):733-742. doi:10.1002/cbdv.201400305

Mohamed E.H., Baiomy A.A.A., Ibrahim Z.S., Soliman M.M. Modulatory effects of levamisole and garlic oil on the immune response of wistar rats: Biochemical, immunohistochemical, molecular and immunological study. Mol. Med. Rep. 2016;14:2755–2763. doi: 10.3892/mmr.2016.5551

Mohamed A, Shoker A, Bendjelloul F, Mare A, Alzrigh M, Benghuzzi H, Desin T. Improvement of experimental allergic encephalomyelitis (EAE) by thymoquinone; an oxidative stress inhibitor. Biomed Sci Instrum 2003; 39: 440-445

Momtaz S, Hassani S, Khan F, Ziaee M, Abdollahi M. Cinnamon, a promising prospect towards Alzheimer's disease. Pharmacol Res. 2018;130:241-258. doi:10.1016/j.phrs.2017.12.011

Moore J, Yousef M, Tsiani E. Anticancer Effects of Rosemary (Rosmarinus officinalis L.) Extract and Rosemary Extract Polyphenols. Nutrients. 2016;8(11):731. Published 2016 Nov 17. doi:10.3390/nu8110731

Morales, F.J.; Jiménez-Pérez, S. Free radical scavenging capacity of Maillard reaction products as related to color and fluorescence. Food Chem. 2001, 72, 119–125.

Moran AE, Carothers AM, Weyant MJ, Redston M, Bertagnolli MM. Carnosol inhibits betacatenin tyrosine phosphorylation and prevents adenoma formation in the C57BL/6J/Min/+ (Min/+) mouse. Cancer Res. 2005;65:1097–1104

Moreno, S.; Scheyer, T.; Romano, C.; Vojnov, A. Antioxidant and antimicrobial activities of rosemary extracts linked to their polyphenol composition. Free Radic. Res.2006, 40, 223–231.

Morihara N., Hino A., Yamaguchi T., Suzuki J. Aged garlic extract suppresses the devegopment of atherosclerosis in apollipoprotein E-knockout mice. J. Nutr. 2016;146:460S–463S. doi: 10.3945/jn.114.206953.

Morihara N., Hino A., Miki S., Takashima M., Suzuki J. Aged garlic extract suppresses inflammation in apolipoprotein E-knockout mice. Mol. Nutr. Food Res. 2017;61:1700308. doi: 10.1002/mnfr.201700308.

Morovati A, Pourghassem Gargari B, Sarbakhsh P. Effects of cumin (Cuminum cyminum L.) essential oil supplementation on metabolic syndrome components: A randomized, triple-blind, placebo-controlled clinical trial. Phytother Res. 2019;33(12):3261-3269. doi:10.1002/ptr.6500

Morrison DJ, Preston T. Formation of short chain fatty acids by the gut microbiota and their impact on human metabolism. Gut Microbes. 2016;7(3):189-200. doi:10.1080/19490976.2015.1134082

Moss M, Smith E, Milner M, McCready J. Acute ingestion of rosemary water: Evidence of cognitive and cerebrovascular effects in healthy adults. J Psychopharmacol. 2018;32(12):1319-1329. doi:10.1177/0269881118798339

Moubarz G, Embaby MA, Doleib NM, Taha MM. Effect of dietary antioxidant supplementation (Cuminum cyminum) on bacterial susceptibility of diabetes-induced rats. Cent Eur J Immunol. 2016;41(2):132-137. doi:10.5114/ceji.2016.60985

Muangkote S, Vichitsoonthonkul T, Srilaong V, Wongs-Aree C, Photchanachai S. Influence of roasting on chemical profile, antioxidant and antibacterial activities of dried chili. Food Sci Biotechnol. 2018;28(2):303-310. Published 2018 Oct 1. doi:10.1007/s10068-018-0475-1

Mueller K, Blum NM, Mueller AS. Examination of the Anti-Inflammatory, Antioxidant, and Xenobiotic-Inducing Potential of Broccoli Extract and Various Essential Oils during a Mild DSS-Induced Colitis in Rats. ISRN gastroenterology. 2013;2013:710856. doi: 10.1155/2013/710856

Mueller, M.; Hobiger, S.; Jungbauer, A. Anti-inflammatory activity of extracts from fruits, herbs and spices. Food Chem.2010, 122, 987–996.

Muhammad TS. Characterization of black cumin seed oil and exploring its role as a functional food. Faisalabad: University of Agriculture; 2009

Mulinacci, N.; Ieri, F.; Giaccherini, C.; Innocenti, M.; Andrenelli, L.; Canova, G.; Saracchi, M.; Casiraghi, M.C. Effects of cooking on the anthocyanins, phenolic acids, glycoalkaloids, and resistant starch content in two pigmented cultivars of Solanum tuberrosum L. J. Agric. Food Chem. 2009, 56, 11830–11837.

Mustafa HN. Neuro-amelioration of cinnamaldehyde in aluminum-induced Alzheimer's disease rat model. J Histotechnol. 2020;43(1):11-20. doi:10.1080/01478885.2019.1652994

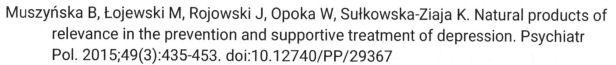

Muszyńska B, Łojewski M, Rojowski J, Opoka W, Sułkowska-Ziaja K. Natural products of relevance in the prevention and supportive treatment of depression. Psychiatr Pol. 2015;49(3):435-453. doi:10.12740/PP/29367

Mutabagani A, El-Mahdy SAM. A study of the anti-inflammatory activity of Nigella sativa L. and thymoquinone in rats. Saudi Pharm J 1997; 5: 110-113

Myneni A.A., Chang S.C., Niu R.G., Liu L., Swanson M.K., Li J.W., Su J., Giovino G.A., Yu S.Z., Zhang Z.F., et al. Raw garlic consumption and lung cancer in a chinese population. Cancer Epidemiol. Biomarkers Prev. 2016;25:624–633. doi: 10.1158/1055-9965.EPI-15-0760. [PMC free article]

Nagella P., Thiruvengadam M., Ahmad A., Yoon J.Y., Chung I.M. Composition of polyphenols and antioxidant activity of garlic bulbs collected from different locations of Korea. Asian J. Chem. 2014;26:897–902. doi: 10.14233/ajchem.2014.16143A.

Naimi M, Vlavcheski F, Shamshoum H, Tsiani E. Rosemary Extract as a Potential Anti-Hyperglycemic Agent: Current Evidence and Future Perspectives. Nutrients. 2017;9(9):968. Published 2017 Sep 1. doi:10.3390/nu9090968

Namazi N, Khodamoradi K, Khamechi SP, Heshmati J, Ayati MH, Larijani B (April 2019). "The impact of cinnamon on anthropometric indices and glycemic status in patients with type 2 diabetes: A systematic review and meta-analysis of clinical trials". Complement Ther Med. 43: 92–101. doi:10.1016/j.ctim.2019.01.002. PMID 30935562

Narendhirakannan RT, Subramanian S, Kandaswamy M. Biochemical evaluation of antidiabetogenic properties of some commonly used Indian plants on streptozotocin-induced diabetes in experimental rats. Clin Exp Pharmacol Physiol. 2006;33:1150–7.

Nehar S, Kumari M. Ameliorating effect of Nigella sativa oil in thioacetamide-induced liver cirrhosis in albino rats. Ind J Pharm Edu Res 2013; 47: 135-139

Nematolahi P, Mehrabani M, Karami-Mohajeri S, Dabaghzadeh F. Effects of Rosmarinus officinalis L. on memory performance, anxiety, depression, and sleep quality in university students: A randomized clinical trial. Complement Ther Clin Pract. 2018;30:24-28. doi:10.1016/j.ctcp.2017.11.004

Neufingerl N., Zebregs Y.E., Schuring E.A., Trautwein E.A. Effect of cocoa and theobromine consumption on serum HDL-cholesterol concentrations: A randomized controlled trial. Am. J. Clin. Nutr. 2013;97:1201–1209. doi: 10.3945/ajcn.112.047373.

Neukam K., Stahl W., Tronnier H., Sies H., Heinrich U. Consumption of flavanol-rich cocoa acutely increases microcirculation in human skin. Eur. J. Nutr. 2007;46:53–66. doi: 10.1007/s00394-006-0627-6.

Neveu, V.; Perez-Jiménez, J.; Vos, F.; Crespy, V.; du Chaffaut, L.; Mennen, L.; Knox, C.; Eisner, R.; Cruz, J.; Wishart, D.; Scalbert, A. Phenol-Explorer: An online comprehensive database on polyphenol contents in foods. Database2010, doi:10.1093/database/bap024 (accessed on 23 June 2014).

Nicastro HL, Ross SA, Milner JA. Garlic and onions: their cancer prevention properties. Cancer Prev Res (Phila). 2015;8(3):181-189. doi:10.1158/1940-6207.CAPR-14-0172

Nicastro H.L., Ross S.A., Milner J.A. Garlic and onions: Their cancer prevention properties. Cancer Prev. Res. 2015;8:181–189. doi: 10.1158/1940-6207.CAPR-14-0172.

Nicoli, M.C.; Anese, M.; Parpinel, M.T.; Franceschi, S.; Lericia, C.R. Loss and/or formation of antioxidants during food processing and storage. Cancer Lett. 1997, 114, 71–74.

Nonaka G-I, Morimoto S, Nishioka I. Tannins and related compounds. Part 13. Isolation and structures of trimeric, tetrameric, and pentameric proanthicyanidins from cinnamon. Journal of the Chemical Society, Perkin Transactions 1. 1983:2139–2145.

O'Donnell A, McParlin C, Robson SC, et al. Treatments for hyperemesis gravidarum and nausea and vomiting in pregnancy: a systematic review and economic assessment. Health Technol Assess. 2016;20(74):1-268. doi:10.3310/hta20740

Olmedo, R.; Nepote, V.; Grosso, N. Antioxidant activity of fractions from oregano essential oils obtained bymolecular distillation.Food Chem.2014,156, 212–219.

Oniga, I.; Puscas, C.; Silaghi-Dumitrescu, R.; Olah, N.; Sevastre, B.; Marica, R.; Marcus, I.;Sevastre-Berghian, A.C.; Benedec, D.; Pop, C.E.; et al.Origanum vulgaressp. vulgare: Chemical compositionand biological studies.Molecules2018,23, 2077.

Opara, E.I.; Chohan, M. Culinary Herbs and Spices: Their Bioactive Properties, the Contribution of Polyphenols and the Challenges in Deducing Their True Health Benefits. Int. J. Mol. Sci. 2014, 15, 19183-19202.

Osakabe, N.; Yasuda, A.; Natsume, M.; Yoshikama, T. Rosmarinic acid inhibits epidermal inflammatory responses: Anticarcenogenic effect of Perilla frutescens extracts in the murine two-stage skin model. Carcinogenesis 2004, 25, 549–557.

Oskouei Z, Akaberi M, Hosseinzadeh H. A glance at black cumin (Nigella sativa) and its active constituent, thymoquinone, in ischemia: a review. Iran J Basic Med Sci. 2018;21(12):1200-1209. doi:10.22038/ijbms.2018.31703.7630

Ozdemir B, Ekbul A, Topal NB, et al. Effects of Origanum onites on endothelial function and serum biochemical markers in hyperlipidaemic patients. J Int Med Res. 2008;36(6):1326-1334. doi:10.1177/147323000803600621

Pal M., Angaru S., Kodimuthali A., Dhingra N. Vanilloid receptor antagonists: Emerging class of novel anti-inflammatory agents for pain management. Curr. Pharm. Des. 2009;15:1008–1026. doi: 10.2174/138161209787581995.

Pan, M.H.; Lai, C.S.; Ho, C.T. Anti-inflammatory activity of natural dietary flavonoids. Food Funct. 2010, 1, 15–31. 96

Pandey, K.B.; Risvi, S.I. Plant polyphenols as dietary antioxidants in human health and disease. Oxid. Med. Cell. Longev.2009, 2, 270–278.

Pattanayak P, Behera P, Das D, Panda SK. Ocimum sanctum Linn. A reservoir plant for therapeutic applications: An overview. Pharmacogn Rev. 2010;4(7):95-105. doi:10.4103/0973-7847.65323

Pellegrini, N.; Chiavaro, E.; Gardana, C.; Mazzeo, T.; Contino, D.; Gallo, M.; Riso, P.; Fogliano, V.; Porrini, M. Effect of different cooking methods on color, phytochemical concentration, and antioxidant capacity of raw and frozen brassica vegetables. J. Agric. Food Chem. 2010, 58, 4310–4321.

Peng X, Cheng K-W, Ma J, et al. Cinnamon bark proanthocyanidins as reactive carbonyl scavengers to prevent the formation of advanced glycation endproducts. Journal of Agricultural and Food Chemistry. 2008;56(6):1907–1911.

Percival S.S. Aged garlic extract modifies human immunity. J. Nutr. 2016;146:433S–436S. doi: 10.3945/jn.115.210427

Perez-Fons L., Garzon M.T., Micol V. Relationship between the antioxidant capacity and effect of rosemary (Rosmarinus officinalis L.) polyphenols on membrane phospholipid order. J. Agric. Food Chem. 2010;58:161–171.

Pérez-Jiménez, J.; Neveu, V.; Vos, F.; Scalbert, A. A systematic analysis of the content of 502 polyphenols in 452 foods and beverages—An application of the Phenol-Explorer database. J. Agric. Food Chem.2010, 58, 4959–4969.

Pérez-Jiménez, J.; Neveu, V.; Vos, F.; Scalbert, A. Identification of the 100 richest dietary sources of polyphenols—An application of the Phenol-Explorer database. Eur. J. Clin. Nutr.2010, 64, s112–s120.

Perez-Torres I., Torres-Narvaez J.C., Pedraza-Chaverri J., Rubio-Ruiz M.E., Diaz-Diaz E., Del Valle-Mondragon L., Martinez-Memije R., Lopez E.V., Guarner-Lans V. Effect of the aged garlic extract on cardiovascular function in metabolic syndrome rats. Molecules. 2016;21:1425. doi: 10.3390/molecules21111425

Perry NSL, Menzies R, Hodgson F, et al. A randomised double-blind placebo-controlled pilot trial of a combined extract of sage, rosemary and melissa, traditional herbal medicines, on the enhancement of memory in normal healthy subjects, including influence of age. Phytomedicine. 2018;39:42-48. doi:10.1016/j.phymed.2017.08.015

Perveen T, Haider S, Zuberi NA, Saleem S, Sadaf S, Batool Z. Increased 5-HT levels following repeated administration of Nigella sativa L. (black seed) oil produce antidepressant effects in rats. Sci Pharm 2014; 82: 161-170

Pesakhov, S.; Khanin, M.; Studzinski, G.P.; Danilenko, D. Distinct combinatorial effects of the plant polyphenols curcumin, carnosic acid and silibinin on proliferation and apoptosis in acute myeloid leukemia cells. Nutr. Cancer **2010**, 62, 811–824.

Petyaev I.M., Bashmakov Y.K. Dark chocolate: Opportunity for an alliance between medical science and the food industry? Front. Nutr. 2017;4:43. doi: 10.3389/fnut.2017.00043.

Poeckel D., Greiner C., Verhoff M., Rau O., Tausch L., Hörnig C., Steinhilber D., Schubert-Zsilavecz M., Werz O. Carnosic acid and carnosol potently inhibit human 5-lipoxygenase and suppress pro-inflammatory responses of stimulated human polymorphonuclear leukocytes. Biochem. Pharmacol. 2008;76:91−97

Polasa K, Raghuram TC, Krishna TP, Krishnaswamy K. Effect of turmeric on urinary mutagens in smokers. Mutagenesis. 1992;7(2):107−109. doi: 10.1093/mutage/7.2.107. Prakash J, Gupta SK. Chemopreventive activity of Ocimum sanctum seed oil. J Ethnopharmacol. 2000;72:29−34.

Prasad S, Tyagi AK, Aggarwal BB. Recent developments in delivery, bioavailability, absorption and metabolism of curcumin: the golden pigment from golden spice. Cancer Res Treat. 2014;46(1):2-18. doi:10.4143/crt.2014.46.1.2

Prasad NS, Raghavendra R, Lokesh BR, Naidu KA. Spice phenolics inhibit human PMNL 5-lipoxygenase. Prostaglandins Leukot Essent Fatty Acids. 2004;70(6):521-528. doi:10.1016/j.plefa.2003.11.006

Prashanth MK, Revanasiddappa HD, Lokanatha Rai KM, Veeresh B. Synthesis, characterization, antidepressant and antioxidant activity of novel piperamides bearing piperidine and piperazine analogues. Bioorg Med Chem Lett. 2012;22(23):7065-7070.

Prashar R, Kumar A, Hewer A, Cole KJ, Davis W, Phillips DH. Inhibition by an extract of Ocimum sanctum of DNA-binding activity of 7,12-dimethylbenz[a]anthracene in rat hepatocytes in vitro. Cancer Lett. 1998;128:155−60

Prucksunand C, Indrasukhsri B, Leethochawalit M, Hungspreugs K. Phase II clinical trial on effect of the long turmeric (Curcuma longa Linn) on healing of peptic ulcer. Southeast Asian J Trop Med Public Health. 2001;32(1):208−215.

Pulido-Moran M, Moreno-Fernandez J, Ramirez-Tortosa C, Ramirez-Tortosa M. Curcumin and Health. Molecules. 2016;21(3):264. Published 2016 Feb 25. doi:10.3390/molecules21030264

Qi J, Buzas K, Fan H, Cohen JI, Wang K, Mont E, Klinman D, Oppenheim JJ, Howard OM. Painful pathways induced by TLR stimulation of dorsal root ganglion neurons. J Immunol 2011; 186: 6417-6426

Qin J, Li Y, Cai Z, Li S, Zhu J, Zhang F, et al. A metagenome-wide association study of gut microbiota in type 2 diabetes. Nature. 2012;490(7418):55−60. Epub 2012/10/02. 10.1038/nature11450

Qin N, Yang F, Li A, Prifti E, Chen Y, Shao L, et al. Alterations of the human gut microbiome in liver cirrhosis. Nature. 2014;513(7516):59−64. Epub 2014/08/01. 10.1038/nature13568

Qiu S.L., Chen J., Qin T., Hu Y.L., Wang D.Y., Fan Q., Zhang C.S., Chen X.Y., Chen X.L., Liu C., et al. Effects of selenylation modification on immune-enhancing activity of garlic polysaccharide. PLoS ONE. 2014;9:e86377. doi: 10.1371/journal.pone.0086377.

Qizilbash N., Gregson J., Johnson M.E., Pearce N., Douglas I., Wing K., Evans S.J.W., Pocock S.J. BMI and risk of dementia in two million people over two decades: A retrospective cohort study. Lancet Diabetes Endocrinol. 2015;3:431–436. doi: 10.1016/S2213-8587(15)00033-9.

Queipo-Ortuño, M.I.; Boto-Ordóñez, M.; Murri, M.; Gomez-Zumaquero, J.M.; Clemente-Postigo, M.; Estruch, R.; Cardona-Diaz, F.; Andrés-Lacueva, C.; Tinahones, F.J. Influence of red wine polyphenols and ethanol on the gut microbiota ecology and biochemical biomarkers. Am. J. Clin. Nutr.2012, 95, 1323–1334.

Radad K, Hassanein K, Al-Shraim M, Moldzio R, Rausch WD. Thymoquinone ameliorates lead-induced brain damage in Sprague Dawley rats. Exp Toxicol Pathol 2014; 66: 13-17

Rai V, Iyer U, Mani UV. Effect of Tulasi (Ocimum sanctum) leaf power supplementation on blood sugar levels, serum lipids and tissue lipids in diabetic rats. Plant Foods Hum Nutr. 1997;50:9–16.

Raghavan S. Handbook of Spices, Seasoning and Flavorings, Vol. 53, CRC Press, Boca Raton. Journal of Chemical Information and Modeling. (2007), 10.1017/CBO9781107415324.004

Raghavendra, R.H.; Naidu, A.K. Spice active principles as the inhibitors of human platelet aggregation and thromboxane biosynthesis. Prostaglandins, Leukot. Essent. Fat. Acids2009, 81, 73–78.

Ramiro-Puig E., Castell M. Cocoa: Antioxidant and immunomodulator. Br. J. Nutr. 2009;101:931–940. doi: 10.1017/S0007114508169896.

Ramos S., Martín M.A., Goya L. Effects of cocoa antioxidants in type 2 diabetes mellitus. Antioxidants. 2017;6:84. doi: 10.3390/antiox6040084.

Ramos, S. Cancer chemoprevention and chemotherapy: Dietary polyphenols and signaling pathways. Mol. Nutr. Food Res. 2008, 52, 507–526.

Redovniković I.R., Delonga K., Mazor S., Dragović-Uzelac V., Caric M., Vorkapic- Furac J. Polyphenolic content and composition, and antioxidative activity of different cocoa liquors. Czech J. Food Sci. 2009;27:330–337

Richart SM, Li YL, Mizushina Y, et al. Synergic effect of curcumin and its structural analogue (Monoacetylcurcumin) on anti-influenza virus infection. J Food Drug Anal. 2018;26(3):1015-1023. doi:10.1016/j.jfda.2017.12.006

Ringman JM, Frautschy SA, Cole GM, Masterman DL, Cummings JL. A potential role of the curry spice curcumin in Alzheimer's disease. Curr Alzheimer Res. 2005;2(2):131–136. doi: 10.2174/1567205053585882.

Rios-Silva M., Santos-Alvarez R., Trujillo X., Cardenas-Maria R.Y., Lopez-Zamudio M., Bricio-Barrios J.A., Leal C., Saavedra-Molina A., Huerta-Trujillo M., Espinoza-Mejia K., et al. Effects of Chronic Administration of Capsaicin on Biomarkers of Kidney Injury in Male Wistar Rats with Experimental Diabetes. Molecules. 2018;24:36. doi: 10.3390/molecules24010036.

Romier, B.; van de Walle, J.; During, A.; Larondelle, Y.; Schneider, Y. Modulation of signaling nuclear factor-κB activation pathway by polyphenols in human intestinal Caco-2 cells. Br. J. Nutr.2008, 100, 542–551.

Romier-Crouzet, B.; van de Walle, J.; During, A.; Joly, A.; Rousseau, C.; Henry, O.; Larondelle, Y.; Schneider, Y. Inhibition of inflammatory mediators by polyphenolic plants extracts in human intestinal Caco-2 cells. Food Chem. Toxicol.2009, 47, 1221–1230.

Rozin P., Schiller D. The nature and acquisition of a preference for chili pepper by humans. Motiv. Emot. 1980;4:77–101. doi: 10.1007/BF00995932.

Sakina MR, Dandiya PC, Hamdard ME, Hameed A. Prelimnary psychopharmacological evaluation of Ocimum sanctum leaf extract. J Ethnopharmacol. 1990;28:143–50.

Sakkas H, Papadopoulou C. Antimicrobial Activity of Basil, Oregano, and Thyme Essential Oils. J Microbiol Biotechnol. 2017;27(3):429-438. doi:10.4014/jmb.1608.08024

Sampath S, Mahapatra SC, Padhi MM, Sharma R, Talwar A. Holy basil (Ocimum sanctum Linn.) leaf extract enhances specific cognitive parameters in healthy adult volunteers: A placebo controlled study. Indian J Physiol Pharmacol. 2015;59(1):69-77.

Sancho E, Batlle E, Clevers H. Signaling pathways in intestinal development and cancer. Annu Rev Cell Dev Biol. 2004;20:695–723.

Sankaranarayanan C, Pari L. Thymoquinone ameliorates chemical induced oxidative stress and beta-cell damage in experimental hyperglycemic rats. Chem Biol Interact 2011; 190: 148-154

Santos HO, Macedo RCO. Cocoa-induced (Theobroma cacao) effects on cardiovascular system: HDL modulation pathways. Clin Nutr ESPEN. 2018;27:10-15. doi:10.1016/j.clnesp.2018.06.001

Sarer E, Scheffer JJ, Baerheim Svendsen A. (1982) Monoterpenes in the essential oil of Origanum majorana. Planta Medica 46:236–239

Sarkar A, Lavania SC, Pandey DN, Pant C. Changes in the blood lipid profile after administration of Ocimum sanctum (Tulsi) leaves in the normal albino rabbits. Indian J Physiol Pharmacol. 1994;38:311–2.

Sarpras M S, Chhapekar SS, Ahmad I, Abraham SK, Ramchiary N. Analysis of bioactive components in Ghost chili (Capsicum chinense) for antioxidant, genotoxic, and apoptotic effects in mice. Drug Chem Toxicol. 2020;43(2):182-191. doi:10.1080/01480545.2018.1483945

Satoh T., Izumi M., Inukai Y., Tsutsumi Y., Nakayama N., Kosaka K., Shimojo Y., Kitajima C., Itoh K., Yokoi T., et al. Carnosic acid protects neuronal HT22 cells through activation of the antioxidant-responsive element in free carboxylic acid- and catechol hydroxyl moieties-dependent manners. Neurosci. Lett. 2008;434:260– 265.

Sausbier M., Schubert R., Voigt V., Hirneiss C., Pfeifer A., Korth M., Kleppisch T., Ruth P., Hofmann F. Mechanisms of NO/cGMP-dependent vasorelaxation. Circ. Res. 2000;87:825–830. doi: 10.1161/01.RES.87.9.825

Senanayake UM, Lee TH, Wills RBH. Volatile constituents of cinnamon (Cinnamomum zeylanicum) oils. Journal of Agricultural and Food Chemistry. 1978;26(4):822– 824.

Scapagnini G., Davinelli S., Drago F., de Lorenzo A., Oriani G. Antioxidants as antidepressants: Fact or fiction? CNS Drugs. 2012;26:477–490. doi: 10.2165/11633190-000000000-00000.

Scalbert, A.; Johnson, I.T.; Salmarch, M. Polyphenols: Antioxidants and beyond. Am. J. Clin. Nutr. 2005, 81, 215s–217s.

Scalbert, A.; Williamson, G. Dietary intake and bioavailability of polyphenols. J. Nutr.2000, 130, 2073S–2085S.

Scapagnini G, Davinelli S, Di Renzo L, et al. Cocoa bioactive compounds: significance and potential for the maintenance of skin health. Nutrients. 2014;6(8):3202-3213. Published 2014 Aug 11. doi:10.3390/nu6083202

Schink A , Naumoska K , Kitanovski Z , et al. Anti-inflammatory effects of cinnamon extract and identification of active compounds influencing the TLR2 and TLR4 signaling pathways. Food Funct. 2018;9(11):5950-5964. doi:10.1039/c8fo01286e

Scholey A., Owen L. Effects of chocolate on cognitive function and mood: A systematic review. Nutr. Rev. 2013;71:665–681. doi: 10.1111/nure.12065.

Sedaghat R, Roghani M, Khalili M. Neuroprotective effect of thymoquinone, the Nigella sativa bioactive compound, in 6-hydroxydopamine-induced hemi-parkinsonian rat model. Iran J Pharm Res 2014; 13: 227-234

Shan, B.; Cai, Y.; Brooks, J.; Corke, H. The in vitro antibacterial activity of dietary spice and medicinal herb extracts. Int. J. Food. Microbiol.2007, 117, 112–119.

Shang A, Cao SY, Xu XY, et al. Bioactive Compounds and Biological Functions of Garlic (Allium sativum L.). Foods. 2019;8(7):246. Published 2019 Jul 5. doi:10.3390/foods8070246

Sharm M, Kishore K, Gupta SK, Joshi S, Arya DS. Cardiaprotective potential of Ocimum sanctum Linn in isoproterenol induced myocardial infraction in rats. Mol Cell Biochem. 2001;498:39–46.

Sharma RA, Steward WP, Gescher AJ. Pharmacokinetics and pharmacodynamics of curcumin. Adv Exp Med Biol. 2007;4:453–70.

Sharma RA, McLelland HR, Hill KA, Ireson CR, Euden SA, Manson MM, et al. Pharmacodynamic and pharmacokinetic study of oral Curcuma extract in patients with colorectal cancer. Clin Cancer Res. 2001;7(7):1894–1900

Sharma RA, Euden SA, Platton SL, Cooke DN, Shafayat A, Hewitt HR, et al. Phase I clinical trial of oral curcumin: biomarkers of systemic activity and compliance. Clin Cancer Res. 2004;10(20):6847–6854. doi: 10.1158/1078-0432.CCR-04-0744

Shaterzadeh-Yazdi H, Noorbakhsh MF, Hayati F, Samarghandian S, Farkhondeh T. Immunomodulatory and Anti-inflammatory Effects of Thymoquinone. Cardiovasc Hematol Disord Drug Targets. 2018;18(1):52-60. doi:10.2174/1871529X18666180212114816

Sherman PW, Billing J. Darwinian Gastronomy: Why We Use Spices: Spices taste good because they are good for us. BioScience. 1999;49(6):453–63.

Shi Z., Riley M., Brown A., Page A. Chilli intake is inversely associated with hypertension among adults. Clin. Nutr. ESPEN. 2018;23:67–72. doi: 10.1016/j.clnesp.2017.12.007.

Shi Z, Zhang M, Liu J. Chili Intake Is Inversely Associated with Chronic Kidney Disease among Adults: A Population-Based Study. Nutrients. 2019;11(12):2949. Published 2019 Dec 4. doi:10.3390/nu11122949

Shi Z., Riley M., Taylor A.W., Page A. Chilli consumption and the incidence of overweight and obesity in a Chinese adult population. Int. J. Obes. 2017;41:1074–1079. doi: 10.1038/ijo.2017.88.

Shi Z., Riley M., Brown A., Page A. Chilli intake is inversely associated with hypertension among adults. Clin. Nutr. ESPEN. 2018;23:67–72. doi: 10.1016/j.clnesp.2017.12.007.

Shimouchi A, Nose K, Takaoka M, Hayashi H, Kondo T. Effect of dietary turmeric on breath hydrogen. Dig Dis Sci. 2009;54(8):1725–1729. doi: 10.1007/s10620-008-0550-1. [

Shin S.S., Song J.H., Hwang B., Noh D.H., Park S.L., Kim W.T., Park S.S., Kim W.J., Moon S.K. HSPA6 augments garlic extract-induced inhibition of proliferation, migration, and invasion of bladder cancer EJ cells; implication for cell cycle dysregulation, signaling pathway alteration, and transcription factor-associated mmp-9 regulation. PLoS ONE. 2017;12:e0171860. doi: 10.1371/journal.pone.0171860.

Shishodia S, Majumdar S, Banerjee S, Aggarwal BB. Urosolic acidinhibits nuclear factor-kappaB activation induced by carcinogenic agents through suppression of IkappaBalpha kinase and p65 phosphorylation: Correlation with down-regulation of cyclooxygenase 2, matrix metalloproteinase 9, and cyclin D1. Cancer Res. 2003;63:4375–83.

Shishehbor F, Rezaeyan Safar M, Rajaei E, Haghighizadeh MH. Cinnamon Consumption Improves Clinical Symptoms and Inflammatory Markers in Women With

Rheumatoid Arthritis [published online ahead of print, 2018 May 3]. J Am Coll Nutr. 2018;1-6. doi:10.1080/07315724.2018.1460733

Shoba G, Joy D, Joseph T, Majeed M, Rajendran R, Srinivas PS. Influence of piperine on the pharmacokinetics of curcumin in animals and human volunteers. Planta Med. 1998;64(4):353-356. doi:10.1055/s-2006-957450

Shukla, Y.; Singh, M. Cancer preventive properties of ginger: A brief review. Food Chem. Toxicol.2007, 45, 683–690.

Siddiqui N.A., Haider S., Misbah-ur-Rehman M., Perveen T. Role of herbal formulation of garlic on lipid profile in patients with type 2 diabetes related dyslipidemia. Pak. Heart J. 2016;49:146–150.

Simonne, A.H, Archer, D.L. Acrylamide in foods: a review and update. University of Florida. IFAS Extention. FCS8759. http://edis.ifas.ufl.edu/fy578. (Last access: Feb1, 2014)

Singh S. Comparative evalution of antiinflammatory potential of fixed oil of different species of Ocimum and its possible mechanism of action. Indian J Exp Biol. 1998;36:1028–31.

Singh S, Das SS, Singh G, Schuff C, de Lampasona MP, Catalan CA. Composition, in vitro antioxidant and antimicrobial activities of essential oil and oleoresins obtained from black cumin seeds (Nigella sativa L.). Biomed Res Int 2014; 2014: 10

Singh, M.; Arseneault, M.; Sanderson, T.; Murthy, V.; Ramassamy, C. Challenges for research on polyphenols from foods in Alzheimer's disease: Bioavailability, metabolism, and cellular and molecular mechanisms. J. Agric. Food Chem.2008, 56, 4855–4873.

Singletary K, MacDonald C, Wallig M. Inhibition by rosemary and carnosol of 7,12-dimethylbenz[a]anthracene (DMBA)-induced rat mammary tumorigenesis and in vivo DMBA-DNA adduct formation. Cancer Lett. 1996;104:43–48.

Singletary K., MacDonald C., Wallig M. Inhibition by rosemary and carnosol of 7,12-dimethylbenz[a] anthracene (DMBA)-induced rat mammary tumorigenesis and in vivo DMBA–DNA adduct formation. Cancer Lett. 1996;104:43–48

Singletary KW, Rokusek JT. Tissue-specific enhancement of xenobiotic detoxification enzymes in mice by dietary rosemary extract. Plant Foods Hum Nutr. 1997;50:47–53.

Sinkovic A., Suran D., Lokar L., Fliser E., Skerget M., Novak Z., Knez Z. Rosemary extracts improve flow-mediated dilatation of the brachial artery and plasma PAI-1 activity in healthy young volunteers. Phytother. Res. PTR. 2011;25:402–407. doi: 10.1002/ptr.3276.

Sivarajan M, Lalithapriya U, Mariajenita P, et al. Synergistic effect of spice extracts and modified atmospheric packaging towards non-thermal preservation of chicken meat under refrigerated storage. Poult Sci. 2017;96(8):2839-2844. doi:10.3382/ps/pex057

Sohn C.W., Kim H., You B.R., Kim M.J., Kim H.J., Lee J.Y., Sok D.E., Kim J.H., Lee K.J., Kim M.R. High temperature- and high pressure-processed garlic improves lipid profiles in rats fed high cholesterol diets. J. Med. Food. 2012;15:435–440. doi: 10.1089/jmf.2011.1922

Solà R., Valls R.M., Godàs G., Perez-Busquets G., Ribalta J., Girona J., Heras M., Cabré A., Castro A., Domenech G., et al. Cocoa, hazelnuts, sterols and soluble fiber cream reduces lipids and inflammation biomarkers in hypertensive patients: A randomized controlled trial. PLoS One. 2012;7:e31103. doi: 10.1371/journal.pone.0031103

Soliman G.Z.A. Effect of Rosmarinus officinalis on lipid profile of streptozotocin-induced diabetic rats. Egypt. J. Hosp. Med. 2013;53:809–815. doi: 10.12816/0001643.

Somers-Edgar, T.J.; Scandlyn, M.J.; Stuart, E.C.; le Nedelec, M.J.; Valentine, S.P.;

Rosengren, R.J. The combination of epigallocatechin gallate and curcumin suppresses ERα-breast cancer cell growth in vitro and in vivo. Int. J. Cancer **2008**, 122, 1966–1971

Soni KB, Kuttan R. Effect of oral curcumin administration on serum peroxides and cholesterol levels in human volunteers. Indian J Physiol Pharmacol. 1992;36(4):273–275.

Sood S, Narang D, Thomas MK, Gupta YK, Maulik SK. Effect of Ocimum sanctum Linn.on cardiac changes in rats subjected to chronic restraint stress. J Ethnopharmacol. 2006;108:423–7.

Sood S, Narang D, Dinda AK, Maulik SK. Chronic oral administration of Ocimum sanctum Linn.augments cardiac endogenous antioxidants and prevents isoproterenol-induced myocardial necrosis in rats. J Pharm Pharmacol. 2005;57:127–33.

Sotelo-Félix J.I., Martinez-Fong D., Muriel P., Santillán R.L., Castillo D., Yahuaca P. Evaluation of the effectiveness of Rosmarinus Officinalis (Lamiaceae) in the alleviation of carbon tetrachloride-induced acute hepatotoxicity in the rat. J. Ethnopharmacol. 2002;81:145–154.

Sowbhagya HB. Chemistry, technology, and nutraceutical functions of cumin (Cuminum cyminum L): an overview. Crit Rev Food Sci Nutr. 2013;53(1):1-10. doi:10.1080/10408398.2010.500223

Srinivasan M. Effect of curcumin on blood sugar as seen in a diabetic subject. Indian J Med Sci. 1972;26(4):269–270.

Strasser B, Gostner JM, Fuchs D. Mood, food, and cognition: role of tryptophan and serotonin. Curr Opin Clin Nutr Metab Care. 2016;19(1):55-61. doi:10.1097/MCO.0000000000000237

Stahl L, Miller KB, Apgar J, et al. Preservation of cocoa antioxidant activity, total polyphenols, flavan-3-ols, and procyanidin content in foods prepared with cocoa powder. J Food Sci. 2009;74(6):C456-C461. doi:10.1111/j.1750-3841.2009.01226.x

Suguna P, Geetha A, Aruna R, Siva GV. Effect of thymoquinone on ethanol and high fat diet induced chronic pancreatitis-a dose response study in rats. Indian J Exp Biol 2013; 51: 292-302

Sun F., Xiong S., Zhu Z. Dietary Capsaicin Protects Cardiometabolic Organs from Dysfunction. Nutrients. 2016;8:174. doi: 10.3390/nu8050174.

Sun YE, Wang W, Qin J. Anti-hyperlipidemia of garlic by reducing the level of total cholesterol and low-density lipoprotein: A meta-analysis. Medicine (Baltimore). 2018;97(18):e0255. doi:10.1097/MD.0000000000010255

Szychowski K.A., Rybczynska-Tkaczyk K., Gawel-Beben K., Swieca M., Karas M., Jakubczyk A., Matysiak M., Binduga U.E., Gminski J. Characterization of active compounds of different garlic (Allium sativum L.) cultivars. Pol. J. Food Nutr. Sci. 2018;68:73–81. doi: 10.1515/pjfns-2017-0005

Taghizadeh M, Memarzadeh MR, Abedi F, et al. The Effect of Cumin cyminum L. Plus Lime Administration on Weight Loss and Metabolic Status in Overweight Subjects: A Randomized Double-Blind Placebo-Controlled Clinical Trial. Iran Red Crescent Med J. 2016;18(8):e34212. Published 2016 May 23. doi:10.5812/ircmj.34212

Takashima M., Kanamori Y., Kodera Y., Morihara N., Tamura K. Aged garlic extract exerts endothelium-dependent vasorelaxant effect on rat aorta by increasing nitric oxide production. Phytomedicine. 2017;24:56–61. doi: 10.1016/j.phymed.2016.11.016.

Takooree H, Aumeeruddy MZ, Rengasamy KRR, et al. A systematic review on black pepper (Piper nigrum L.): from folk uses to pharmacological applications. Crit Rev Food Sci Nutr. 2019;59(sup1):S210-S243. doi:10.1080/10408398.2019.1565489

Tang WH, Wang Z, Levison BS, Koeth RA, Britt EB, Fu X, et al. Intestinal microbial metabolism of phosphatidylcholine and cardiovascular risk. The New England journal of medicine. 2013;368(17):1575–84. Epub 2013/04/26. 10.1056/NEJMoa1109400

Tangpao T, Chung H, Sommano SR. Aromatic profiles of essential oils from five commonly used Thai basils. Foods, 7 (2018), p. 175, 10.3390/foods7110175

Tapsell LC, Hemphill I, Cobiac L, et al. Health benefits of herbs and spices: the past, the present, the future. Med J Aust. 2006;185(S4):S1-S24.

Tareke, E.; Rydberg, P.; Karlsson, Patrik; Eriksson, Sune; Törnqvist, Margareta (2002). "Analysis of acrylamide, a carcinogen formed in heated foodstuffs". J. Agric. Food Chem. 50 (17): 4998–5006. doi:10.1021/jf020302f. PMID 12166997.

Teixeira B, Marques A, Ramos C, Serrano C, Matos O, Neng NR, Nogueira JMF, Saraiva JA, Nunes ML. Chemical composition and bioactivity of different oregano

(Origanum vulgare) extracts and essential oil. 2013 August 30. Volume93, Issue11. Pages 2707-2714.

Thomas, R.; Williams, M.H.; Sharma, H.; Chaudry, A.; Bellamy, P. A double-blind, placebo-controlled randomised trial evaluating the effect of a polyphenol-rich whole food supplement on PSA progression in men with prostate cancer—The UK NCRN Pomi-T study. Prostate Cancer Prostatic Dis.2014, 17, 180–186.

Thomas, R.H.; Bernards, M.A.; Drake, E.E.; Guglielmo, C.G. Changes in the antioxidant activities of seven herb and spice-based marinating sauces after cooking. J. Food Compos. Anal. **2010**, 23, 244–252.

Thomson M., Al-Qattan K.K., Divya J.S., Ali M. Anti-diabetic and anti-oxidant potential of aged garlic extract (AGE) in streptozotocin-induced diabetic rats. BMC Complement. Altern. Med. 2016;16:17. doi: 10.1186/s12906-016-0992-5.

Torres-Alvarez, C.; Núñez-González, A.; Rodríguez, J.; Castillo, S.; Leos-Rivas, C.; Báez-González, J.G.Chemical composition, antimicrobial, and antioxidant activities of orange essential oil and its concentratedoils.CyTA J. Food2017,15, 129–135.

Torres-Palazzolo C., Ramirez D., Locatelli D., Manucha W., Castro C., Camargo A. Bioaccessibility and permeability of bioactive compounds in raw and cooked garlic. J. Food Compos. Anal. 2018;70:49–53. doi: 10.1016/j.jfca.2018.03.008

Tremaroli V., Bäckhed F. Functional interactions between the gut microbiota and host metabolism. Nature. 2012;489:242–249. doi: 10.1038/nature11552.

Tremblay A., Arguin H., Panahi S. Capsaicinoids: A spicy solution to the management of obesity? Int. J. Obes. 2016;40:1198–1204. doi: 10.1038/ijo.2015.253.

Trevisan MT, Vasconcelos Silva MG, Pfundstein B, Spiegelhalder B, Owen RW. Characterization of the volatile pattern and antioxidant capacity of essential oils from different species of the genus Ocimum. J Agric Food Chem. 2006;54:4378–82.

Tsai, P.-J.; Tsai, T.-H.; Yu, C.-H.; Ho, S.-C. Evaluation of NO-suppressing activity of several Mediterranean culinary spices. Food Chem. Toxicol.2007, 45, 440–447.

Tung Y-T, Yen P-L, Lin C-Y, Chang S-T. Anti-inflammatory activities of essential oils and their constituents from different provenances of indigenous cinnamon (Cinnamomum osmophloeum) leaves. Pharmaceutical Biology. 2010;48(10):1130–1136.

Tuntipopipat S, Muangnoi C, Failla ML. Anti-inflammatory activities of extracts of Thai spices and herbs with lipopolysaccharide-activated RAW 264.7 murine macrophages. J Med Food. 2009;12(6):1213-1220. doi:10.1089/jmf.2009.1118

Tuohy, K.M.; Conterno, L.; Gasperotti, M.; Viola, R. Up-regulating the human intestinal microbiome using whole plant foods, polyphenols, and/or fiber. J. Agric. Food Chem.2012, 61, 8776–8782.

Turnbaugh PJ, Ley RE, Mahowald MA, Magrini V, Mardis ER, Gordon JI. An obesity-associated gut microbiome with increased capacity for energy harvest. Nature. 2006;444(7122):1027–31. Epub 2006/12/22. 10.1038/nature05414

Tuzcu Z, Orhan C, Sahin N, Juturu V, Sahin K. Cinnamon Polyphenol Extract Inhibits Hyperlipidemia and Inflammation by Modulation of Transcription Factors in High-Fat Diet-Fed Rats. Oxid Med Cell Longev. 2017;2017:1583098. doi:10.1155/2017/1583098

Tzounis X., Rodriguez-Mateos A., Vulevic J., Gibson G.R., Kwik-Uribe C., Spencer J.P. Prebiotic evaluation of cocoa-derived flavanols in healthy humans by using a randomized, controlled, double-blind, crossover intervention study. Am. J. Clin. Nutr. 2011;93:62–72. doi: 10.3945/ajcn.110.000075.

Usharani P, Mateen AA, Naidu MU, Raju YS, Chandra N. Effect of NCB-02, atorvastatin and placebo on endothelial function, oxidative stress and inflammatory markers in patients with type 2 diabetes mellitus: a randomized, parallel-group, placebo-controlled, 8-week study. Drugs R D. 2008;9(4):243–250. doi: 10.2165/00126839-200809040-00004.

Vadhan-Raj S, Weber D, Wang M, Giralt S, Alexanian R, Thomas S, et al. Curcumin downregulates NF-KB and related genes in patients with multiple myeloma: results of a phase 1/2 study. Blood. 2007;110(11):357a

Van Breemen, R.B.; Tao, Y.; Li, W. Cyclooxygenase-2 inhibitors in ginger (Zingiber officinale). Fitoterapia 2011, 82, 38–43.

Vaillancourt F, Silva P, Shi Q, Fahmi H, Fernandes JC, Benderdour M. Elucidation of molecular mechanisms underlying the protective effects of thymoquinone against rheumatoid arthritis. J Cell Biochem 2011; 112: 107-117

Vallverdú-Queralt A., Regueiro J., Martínez-Huélamo M., Rinaldi Alvarenga J.F., Leal L.N., Lamuela-Raventos R.M. A comprehensive study on the phenolic profile of widely used culinary herbs and spices: Rosemary, thyme, oregano, cinnamon, cumin and bay. Food Chem. 2014;154:299–307. doi: 10.1016/j.foodchem.2013.12.106.

Vanithadevi B., Anuradha C.V. Effect of rosmarinic acid on insulin sensitivity, glyoxalase system and oxidative events in liver of fructose-fed mice. Int. J. Diabetes Metab. 2008;16:35–44.

Varghese S, Kubatka P, Rodrigo L, et al. Chili pepper as a body weight-loss food. Int J Food Sci Nutr. 2017;68(4):392-401. doi:10.1080/09637486.2016.1258044

Patcharatrakul T, Gonlachanvit S. Chili Peppers, Curcumins, and Prebiotics in Gastrointestinal Health and Disease. Curr Gastroenterol Rep. 2016;18(4):19. doi:10.1007/s11894-016-0494-0

Vauzour, D.; Rodriguez-Mateos, A.; Corona, G.; Oruna-Concha, M.J.; Spencer, J.P. Polyphenols and human health: Prevention of disease and mechanisms of action. Nutrients2010, 2, 1106–1131.

Vats V, Yadav SP, Grover JK. Ethanolic extract of Ocimum sanctum leaves partially attenuates sterptozotocin-induced alterations in glycogen content and carbohydrate metabolism in rats. J Ethnopharmacol. 2004;90:155–60

Veenstra JP, Johnson JJ. Oregano (Origanum vulgare) extract for food preservation and improvement in gastrointestinal health. Int J Nutr. 2019;3(4):43-52. doi:10.14302/issn.2379-7835.ijn-19-2703

Visanji J.M., Thompson D.G., Padfield P.J. Induction of G2/M phase cell cycle arrest by carnosol and carnosic acid is associated with alteration of cyclin A and cyclin B1 levels. Cancer Lett. 2006;237:130–136.

Vlachojannis J, Erne P, Zimmermann B, Chrubasik-Hausmann S. The Impact of Cocoa Flavanols on Cardiovascular Health. Phytother Res. 2016;30(10):1641-1657. doi:10.1002/ptr.5665

Vujicic M, Nikolic I, Kontogianni VG, Saksida T, Charisiadis P, Vasic B, et al. Ethyl Acetate Extract of Origanum vulgare L. ssp. hirtum Prevents Streptozotocin-Induced Diabetes in C57BL/6 Mice. Journal of food science. 2016;81(7):H1846–53. doi: 10.1111/1750-3841.13333.

Wang J., Zhang X.M., Lan H.L., Wang W.J. Effect of garlic supplement in the management of type 2 diabetes mellitus (T2DM): A meta-analysis of randomized controlled trials. Food Nutr. Res. 2017;61:1377571. doi: 10.1080/16546628.2017.1377571.

Wang W., Cheng J.W., Zhu Y.Z. The JNK signaling pathway is a novel molecular target for S-propargyl-l-cysteine, a naturally-occurring garlic derivatives: Link to its anticancer activity in pancreatic cancer in vitro and in vivo. Curr. Cancer Drug Targets. 2015;15:613–623. doi: 10.2174/1568009615666150602143943.

Wang C, Cai Z, Wang W, et al. Piperine attenuates cognitive impairment in an experimental mouse model of sporadic Alzheimer's disease. J Nutr Biochem. 2019;70:147-155. doi:10.1016/j.jnutbio.2019.05.009

Wang, W.; Heideman, L.; Chung, C.S.; Pelling, J.C.; Koehler, K.J.; Birt, D.F. Cell-cycle arrest at G2/M and growth inhibition by apigenin in human colon carcinoma cell lines. Mol. Carcinog. 2000, 28, 102–110.

Wannissorn B, Jarikasem S, Siriwangchai T, Thubthimthed S. Antibacterial properties of essential oils from Thai medicinal plants. Fitoterapia. 2005;76(2):233-236. doi:10.1016/j.fitote.2004.12.009

Whiting S., Derbyshire E.J., Tiwari B. Could capsaicinoids help to support weight management? A systematic review and meta-analysis of energy intake data. Appetite. 2014;73:183–188. doi: 10.1016/j.appet.2013.11.005.

Wickenberg J, Ingemansson SL, Hlebowicz J. Effects of Curcuma longa (turmeric) on postprandial plasma glucose and insulin in healthy subjects. Nutr J. 2010;9:43. doi: 10.1186/1475-2891-9-43.

Wu Y., Wu Z.R., Chen P., Yang L., Deng W.R., Wang Y.Q., Li H.Y. Effect of the tyrosinase inhibitor (S)-N-trans-feruloyloctopamine from garlic skin on tyrosinase gene expression and melanine accumulation in melanoma cells. Bioorg. Med. Chem. Lett. 2015;25:1476–1478. doi: 10.1016/j.bmcl.2015.02.028

Xavier, C.P.; Lima, C.F.; Fernandes-Ferreira, M.; Pereira-Wilson, C. Salvia fruticosa, Salvia officinalis, and rosmarinic acid induce apoptosis and inhibit proliferation of human colorectal cell lines: The role in MAPK/ERK pathway. Nutr. Cancer 2009, 61, 564–571.

Int. J. Mol. Sci. 2014, 15 19201

Xiao J., Xing F.Y., Liu Y.X., Lv Y., Wang X.G., Ling M.T., Gao H., Ouyang S.Y., Yang M., Zhu J., et al. Garlic-derived compound S-allylmercaptocysteine inhibits hepatocarcinogenesis through targeting LRP6/Wnt pathway. Acta Pharm. Sin. B. 2018;8:575–586. doi: 10.1016/j.apsb.2017.10.003.

Xu Y.S., Feng J.G., Zhang D., Zhang B., Luo M., Su D., Lin N.M. S-allylcysteine, a garlic derivative, suppresses proliferation and induces apoptosis in human ovarian cancer cells in vitro. Acta. Pharmacol. Sin. 2014;35:267–274. doi: 10.1038/aps.2013.176. [PMC free article]

Yang Y, Zhang J, Weiss NS, et al. The consumption of chili peppers and the risk of colorectal cancer: a matched case-control study. World J Surg Oncol. 2019;17(1):71. Published 2019 Apr 17. doi:10.1186/s12957-019-1615-7

Yasui, K.; Baba, A. Therapeutic potential of superoxide dismutase for resolution of inflammation. Inflamm. Res. 2006, 55, 359–363.

Yesil-Celiktas O., Sevimli C., Bedir E., Vardar-Sukan F. Inhibitory effects of rosemary extracts, carnosic acid and rosmarinic acid on the growth of various human cancer cell lines. Plant Food Hum. Nutr. 2010;65:158–163.

Yi, W.; Wetzstein, H.Y. Anti-tumorigenic activity of five culinary and medicinal herbs grown under greenhouse conditions and their combination effects. J. Sci. Food Agric. **2011**, 91, 1849–1854.

Yoo, K.M.; Lee, C.H.; Lee, H.; Moon, B.; Lee, C.Y. Relative antioxidant and cryoprotective activities of common herbs. Food Chem. 2008, 106, 929–936.

Yoo D.Y., Kim W., Nam S.M., Yoo M., Lee S., Yoon Y.S., Won M.H., Hwang I.K., Choi J.H. Neuroprotective effects of Z-ajoene, an organosulfur compound derived from oil-macerated garlic, in the gerbil hippocampal CA1 region after transient forebrain ischemia. Food Chem. Toxicol. 2014;72:1–7. doi: 10.1016/j.fct.2014.06.023

Yoo M., Lee S., Kim S., Hwang J.B., Choe J., Shin D. Composition of organosulfur compounds from cool- and warm-type garlic (Allium sativum L.) in Korea. Food Sci. Biotechnol. 2014;23:337–344. doi: 10.1007/s10068-014-0047-y

Yoshioka M., St-Pierre S., Drapeau V., Dionne I., Doucet E., Suzuki M., Tremblay A. Effects of red pepper on appetite and energy intake. Br. J. Nutr. 1999;82:115–123. doi: 10.1017/S0007114599001269.

Yuan S., Li X., Jin Y., Lu J. Chocolate Consumption and Risk of Coronary Heart Disease, Stroke, and Diabetes: A Meta-Analysis of Prospective Studies. Nutrients. 2017;9:688. doi: 10.3390/nu9070688.

Yuan Y, Shu C, Zhou B, Qi X, Xiang J. Impact of selected additives on acrylamide formation in asparagine/sugar Maillard model systems. Food Res Int. 2011;44:449–455. doi: 10.1016/j.foodres.2010.09.025.

Yulug B, Kilic E, Altunay S, et al. Cinnamon Polyphenol Extract Exerts Neuroprotective Activity in Traumatic Brain Injury in Male Mice. CNS Neurol Disord Drug Targets. 2018;17(6):439-447. doi:10.2174/1871527317666180501110918

Zanzer YC , Plaza M , Dougkas A , Turner C , Östman E . Black pepper-based beverage induced appetite-suppressing effects without altering postprandial glycaemia, gut and thyroid hormones or gastrointestinal well-being: a randomized crossover study in healthy subjects. Food Funct. 2018;9(5):2774-2786. doi:10.1039/c7fo01715d

Zaoui A, Cherrah Y, Mahassini N, Alaoui K, Amarouch H, Hassar M. Acute and chronic toxicity of Nigella sativa fixed oil. Phytomedicine 2002; 9: 69-74

Zardast M., Namakin K., Kaho J.E., Hashemi S.S. Assessment of antibacterial effect of garlic in patients infected with Helicobacter pylori using urease breath test. Avicenna J. Phytomed. 2016;6:495–501.

Zhang, X.L.; Guo, Y.S.; Wang, C.H.; Li, G.Q.; Xu, J.J.; Chung, H.Y.; Ye, W.C.; Li, Y.L.; Wang, G.C. Phenoliccompounds fromOriganum vulgareand their antioxidant and antiviral activities.Food Chem.2014,152,300–306.

Zhang Y., Li H.Y., Zhang Z.H., Bian H.L., Lin G. Garlic-derived compound S-allylmercaptocysteine inhibits cell growth and induces apoptosis via the JNK and p38 pathways in human colorectal carcinoma cells. Oncol. Lett. 2014;8:2591–2596. doi: 10.3892/ol.2014.2579

Zhao Y, Chen ZY. Roles of Spicy Foods and Their Bioactive Compounds in Management of Hypercholesterolemia. J Agric Food Chem. 2018;66(33):8662-8671. doi:10.1021/acs.jafc.8b02975

Zheng J, Zhou Y, Li Y, Xu DP, Li S, Li HB. Spices for Prevention and Treatment of Cancers. Nutrients. 2016;8(8):495. Published 2016 Aug 12. doi:10.3390/nu8080495

Zheng, W.; Wang, S.Y. Antioxidant activity and phenolic compounds in selected herbs. J. Agric. Food Chem.2001, 49, 5165–5170.

Int. J. Mol. Sci. 2014, 15 19195

Zhu BT, Loder DP, Cai MX, Ho CT, Huang MT, Conney AH. Dietary administration of an extract from rosemary leaves enhances the liver microsomal metabolism of endogenous estrogens and decreases their uterotropic action in CD-1 mice. Carcinogenesis. 1998;19:1821–1827.

Zhu Z, Luo Z, Ma S, Liu D. TRP channels and their implications in metabolic diseases. Pflugers Archiv: European journal of physiology. 2011;461(2):211–23. Epub 2010/11/27. 10.1007/s00424-010-0902-5

Zhu F, Cai YZ, Keb J, Corke H. Dietary plant materials reduce acrylamide formation in cookie and starch-based model systems. J Sci Food Agric. 2011;9:2477–2483. doi: 10.1002/jsfa.4491.

Zhu F, Cai YZ, Keb J, Corkea H. Evaluation of the effect of plant extracts and phenolic compounds on reduction of acrylamide in an asparagine/glucose model system by RP-HPLC-DAD. J Sci Food Agric. 2009;89:1674–1681. doi: 10.1002/jsfa.3640.

Zuccotti GV, Trabattoni D, Morelli M, Borgonovo S, Schneider L, Clerici M. Immune modulation by lactoferrin and curcumin in children with recurrent respiratory infections. J Biol Regul Homeost Agents. 2009;23(2):119–123

Zunino SJ, Storms DH. Carnosol delays chemotherapy-induced DNA fragmentation and morphological changes associated with apoptosis in leukemic cells. Nutr Cancer. 2009;61:94–102.

OTHER BOOKS IN THE SERIES

The Culinary Medicine Textbook: A Modular Approach to Culinary Literacy

Part 1: The Basics

Part 2: The Food: Fruit, Vegetables, Grains, Protein and Fats/Oils

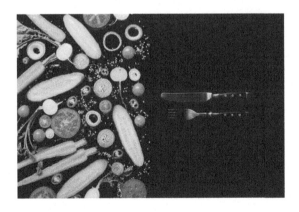

Part 3: The Diets

Part 3: The Kitchens

Part 5: The Specialties – Pregnancy, Lactation, Brain Health, Obesity, Heart Health, Seniors, Pediatrics, Athlete, Allergies/Intolerances, Diabetes, Intestinal Health, Immunity, Psychiatry, Cancer, and more

Made in the USA
Monee, IL
06 December 2024